THE
CHRISTIAN THEOLOGICAL
TRADITION

GENERAL EDITORS:
Catherine A. Cory
David T. Landry

CONTRIBUTORS:
Catherine A. Cory

David S. Cunningham

Michael J. Hollerich

David G. Hunter

Rev. J. Michael Joncas

Shirley Jordan

Anne King-Lenzmeier

Carol J. Lahurd

David T. Landry

Terence L. Nichols

David Penchansky

Rev. Thaddeus J. Posey

Rev. David W. Smith

SIMON & SCHUSTER CUSTOM PUBLISHING

"The Magdalen Reading," by Rogier van der Weyden.
Reproduced courtesy of the Trustees, National Gallery, London.

Cover design: Sam Pitino

Printed in the United States of America

10 9 8 7 6 5 4 3

ISBN 0-536-59579-8
BA 97668

SIMON & SCHUSTER CUSTOM PUBLISHING
160 Gould Street/Needham Heights, MA 02194
Simon & Schuster Education Group

Copyright Acknowledgments

Maps

The following are reprinted from *Reading the Old Testament: An Introduction*, by Lawrence Boadt, 1984, by permission of Paulist Press: **Figure 3.1:** The Journey of Abraham from Ur to Canaan; **Figure 3.3:** Map Indicating the Traditional Route of the Exodus; **Figure 4.2:** The Divided Kingdom, Judah and Israel, During the Reign of Solomon's Son, Rehoboam.

Figure 4.3: Map of the Ancient Near East, reprinted from *Understanding the Bible*, by Stephen L. Harris, by permission of Mayfield Publishing Company.

Figure 6.1: Palestine in New Testament Times, reprinted from *Reading the New Testament: An Introduction*, by Pheme Perkins, 1978, by permission of Paulist Press.

Figure 7.2: Map of Paul's Missionary Journeys, reprinted from "Early Christianity in the Roman Empire," by Richard L. Jeste, from *Patterns in Western Civilization*, edited by James Woelfel and Sarah Chappell Trulove, 1991, Ginn Press.

The following are reprinted from *The Christian Centuries, Vol I: The First Six Hundred Years*, by Jean Danielou and Henri Marrou, 1964, by permission of Paulist Press: **Figure 7.3:** Map of the Expansion of Christianity at the End of the 1st Century CE, and **Figure 8.1:** Extension of Christianity at the Middle of the 3rd Century.

Figure 12.3: The Carolingian Empire at the Treaty of Verdun, reprinted from *The Western Heritage*, Fifth Edition, by Kagan, Ozment, and Turner, 1995, Prentice-Hall, Inc.

The following are reprinted from *Religions on File*, by Randal Gray and Dinah Hanlon, 1990: **Figure 13.1:** Map of Trade Routes at the Time of Muhammad; **Figure 13.2:** Map of Islamic Expansion to 750; and **Figure 13.3:** World Islamic Populations Today.

Figure 14.5: Boundaries Between Christianity and Islam About 1100, reprinted from *Europe and the Middle Ages*, Second Edition, by Edward Peters, 1989, Prentice-Hall, Inc.

Figure 19.2: Map of the Swiss Confederation at the time of Ulrich Zwingli, reprinted from *The Age of Reform: 1250-1550*, by Steven Ozmert, by permission of Yale University Press.

Figure 19.7: Map of the Division of Christendom by the Reformation (mid-16th century), reprinted from "The Reformation and Its Impact," by Scott H. Hendrix, from *Patterns in Western Civilization*, edited by James Woelfel and Sarah Chappell Trulove, 1991, Ginn Press.

Figure 21.1: European Voyages of Discovery During the 15th and 16th Centuries and the Colonial Claims of Spain and Portugal, reprinted from *The Western Heritage*, Fifth Edition, by Kagan, Ozment, and Turner, 1995, Prentice-Hall, Inc.

Figure 23.1: Map of U.S. Territories, 1810, reprinted from *Historical Atlas of Relgion in America*, Edwin S. Gaustad, editor, 1976.

Photo Credits

26 Figure 2.1: Creation of the Heavenly Bodies, Mosaic from the Cupola of San Marco, Venice, Italy/Alinari - Art Resource, NY; **27 Figure 2.2:** Expulsion of Adam and Eve, Mosaic from the Cupola of San Marco, Venice Italy/Alinari - Art Resource, NY; **37 Figure 3.2:** Mosaic in San Vitale, Ravenna. Abraham and the Three Angels and the Near-Sacrifice of Isaac/Alinari - Art Resource, NY; **54 Figure 4.1:** A 13th-century Miniature Illustrating the Festivities that Took Place When David Brought the Ark of the Covenant to Jerusalem/The Pierpont Morgan Library - Art Resource, NY; **67 Figure 5.1:** Model of the Jerusalem Temple (after the renovations of Herod the Great)/Courtesy of The Department of Theology, University of St. Thomas; **84 Figure 6.2:** The Tombs of the Kings in Jerusalem/Courtesy of The Department of Theology, University of St. Thomas; **92 Figure 6.3:** The Samaritan Woman Meeting Jesus at the Well/Erich Lessing - Art Resource, NY; **99 Figure 7.1:** Saint Paul on the Road to Damascus, Miniature from the Hours of Etienne Chevalier, Musee Conde, Chantilly, France/Giraudon - Art Resource, NY; **118 Figure 8.2:** Christ as a Seated Philosopher/Alinari - Art Resource, NY; **118 Figure 8.3:** Christ as the Good Shepherd/Alinari - Art Resource, NY; **118 Figure 8.4:** Christ Sitting on the Orb of the World, Enthroned with Angels and St. Vitale the Ecclesiasticus/Alinari - Art Resource, NY; **119 Figure 8.5:** Grafitto of a Christian Worshipping a Crucified Ass, Museo Nazionale Romano delle Terme, Rome, Italy/Alinari - Art Resource, NY; **139 Figure 9.1:** Sarcophagus of Christ Handing Peter the Law/Alinari - Art Resource, NY; **142 Figure 9.2:** Church of Santa Sabina in Rome, View Towards Apse/Alinari - Art Resource, NY; **143 Figure 9.3:** Sanctuary of the Church of Santa Sabina in Rome/Alinari - Art Resource, NY; **144 Figure 9.4:** Baptistery of the Orthodox in Ravenna/Alinari - Art Resource, NY; **153 Figure 10.1:** St. Augustine in the Garden, Museo di San Marco, Florence, Italy/Alinari - Art Resource, NY; **165 Figure 11.1:** Interior of Hagia Sophia in Constantinople/Giraudon - Art Resource, NY; **167 Figure 11.2:** Icon of "The Holy Trinity"/Used by permission of St. Vladimir's Seminary Press, Crestwood, NY 10707; **167 Figure 11.3:** Icon of "Christ the Divine Wisdom"/Used by permission of St. Vladimir's Seminary Press, Crestwood, NY 10707; **167 Figure 11.4:** Icon of "Virgin of Tenderness"/Used by permisson of St. Vladimir's Seminary Press, Crestwood, NY 10707; **180 Figure 12.1:** Model of an Ideal Medieval Monastry/Photo by Fotowerkstätte Schmölz & Ulrich KG, Cologne, used by permission of Weidenfeld & Nicholson, Ltd., England; **181 Figure 12.2:** Floor Plan of an Ideal Medieval Monastry, St. Gall, Chapter Library/Foto Marburg - Art Resource, NY; **185 Figure 12.4:** Christ Enthroned, Bibliotheque Sainte-Genevieve, Paris, France/Giraudon - Art Resource, NY; **186 Figure 12.5:** Exterior of Charlemagne's Palace Chapel at Aix-la-Chapelle/Foto Marburg - Art Resource, NY; **187 Figure 12.6:** Interior of Charlemagne's Palace Chapel, Throne in Royal Loge/Foto Marburg - Art Resource, NY; **205 Figure 13.4:** Marble Mosaic Detail from Courtyard Wall of Umayyad Mosque, Damascus, Syria/Courtesy of The Department of Theology, University of St. Thomas; **205 Figure 13.5:** Ibn Tulun Mosque, Cairo, Egypt/Courtesy of The Department of Theology, University of St. Thomas; **205 Figure 13.6:** Calligraphic Rendering of the Islamic Statement of Faith/Institute of Islamic Research, Islamabad, Pakistan; **205 Figure 13.7:** Calligraphic Quotation from the Qur'an in the Shape of a Boat/Commission for Racial Equality, London; **215 Figure 14.1:** The Dream of Pope Innocent, by Giotto di Bondone, Upper Chruch, S. Francesco, Assisi, Italy/Alinari - Art Resource, NY; **218 Figure 14.2:** Bronze Crucifix from the Church of St. Francis of Assisi/Alinari - Art Resource, NY; **219 Figure 14.3:** Mary Seated with Child, Tympanum of West Right Hand Door of Chartres Cathedral/Giraudon - Art Resource, NY; **221 Figure 14.4:** Interior of Chartres Cathedral/Foto Marburg - Art Resource, NY; **236 Figure 15.1:** An Illuminated Manuscript Page of St. Thomas Dictating to a Scribe, Bibliotheque Municipale, Laon,

Color Plates

Table of Contents

Preface

The textbook you are about to read is a very unusual one, for it is not the work of one or even two people, but a collaborative work involving thirteen separate authors, five or more reviewers, and two editors. What follows is the rather remarkable story of how this textbook came into being.

In the fall of 1990, the Theology department at the University of St. Thomas (a comprehensive, Catholic, liberal arts university) created a new first course in Theology, a course that all undergraduate students would take as part of the three-course requirement in the curricular area "Faith and the Catholic Tradition." The new first course was entitled "The Christian Theological Tradition," and it was designed to give students a one-semester introduction to the whole of Christian history, from Genesis to Vatican II. The reasons that this course was created were manifold. However, a major factor was the realization that students who came to St. Thomas were increasingly less prepared to handle what were previously classified as "introductory" courses in theology. Through no fault of their own, fewer and fewer students were coming to St. Thomas with any real knowledge about the Catholic tradition, the contents of the Bible, the major doctrines of the Christian faith, or the meaning of the various parts of Christian liturgy. "The Christian Theological Tradition" was created, in part, to provide the basic knowledge necessary for further study in theology, the foundation on which advanced learning could be built.

The backbone of the new course was to be a long list of primary texts that would be taught in all sections. Included on this list were seminal biblical texts from the Pentateuch, the prophets, the gospels, and Paul's letters; the decrees of important church councils like Nicaea, Constantinople, Chalcedon, Trent, and Vatican II; Christian spiritual writings such as the those of Julian of Norwich; and works by the greatest theologians in Christian history, such as Augustine, Aquinas, and Luther. Although the course was built around the primary texts, it needed a textbook to "fill in the gaps" between these readings and to provide a context for the readings themselves.

The theology faculty considered numerous possible textbooks, but found none that met all of its needs. Eventually the theology department decided on a textbook, but we were cognizant of the book's flaws, and the prospect was raised at that time of eventually writing our own textbook. After a few years of teaching "The Christian Theological Tradition," the drawbacks of the textbook we were using became increasingly apparent. In the spring of 1994 the theology department created a committee to explore the possibility of writing a textbook specifically for "The Christian Theological Tradition." The committee met in the summer of 1994, and made first efforts at both a table of contents and sample chapters. The results were sufficiently encouraging that the committee made a recommendation to the whole department that it proceed with the textbook project, and the recommendation was approved.

The first task of the committee was to find authors for each of the proposed 24 chapters. This was not as difficult as it might appear, since when it comes to covering the length and breadth of the Christian theological tradition, the Theology department at the University of St. Thomas possesses an embarassment of riches. Due to the large size of the undergraduate student body at St. Thomas (approximately 5000 students) and the three-course requirement, the theology department is unusually large, with 28 or so full-time members. Because of this, the committee was able to find authors for each of the chapters who are truly experts in the areas to be covered, many of them scholars with a national reputation. Eventually 13 people volunteered to write one or more chapters. The two people who were chosen to be the general editors of the textbook then wrote various grant proposals in search of funds to finance the project. When the proposals were accepted by the Bush Foundation and the Aquinas Foundation, the final hurdle had been cleared and serious work on the project could begin.

The writing of the chapters took place between the fall of 1994 and the winter of 1996. As a first draft of each chapter was completed, it was submitted to the textbook committee, which met together with the author to suggest improvements, additions, and deletions. The author then revised the chapter and, in some cases, resubmitted it to the committee for final approval.

By the beginning of the fall semester of 1995, more than half of the chapters had been completed, and the decision was made to pilot those chapters that were ready in sections of "The Christian Theological Tradition" that were being taught that semester. Students from about a dozen sections of the course read different chapters and provided feedback to their instructors, who then passed it on to the authors. Further revisions were made in several chapters, and the final products were then submitted to the general editors so that they could begin to prepare them for publication.

The two general editors completed their work in the winter and spring of 1996. Each chapter was read and then revised for consistency of style, clarity of expression, coherence with the other chapters, brevity (whenever possible), and simplicity. The general editors also prepared the glossary and the index, coordinated the use of prints, photos, and diagrams, worked with the publisher on copyright permissions, read the galley proofs, and negotiated the terms of the publishing agreement. The completion of that agreement was the final step in the long journey which has led to the appearance of this textbook.

The preceding history reveals several points that deserve to be highlighted. The first is the degree to which this was a collaborative effort. In the table of contents, the name of the author(s) of each chapter is listed. These people are primarily responsible for the contents of these chapters, and deserve the lion's share of whatever credit accrues to them. However, significant contributions to these chapters were also made by the five members of the textbook committee and by the two general editors. Moreover, the *textbook* is a direct result of the creation of the *course* "The Christian Theological Tradition," and this course is the result of the work of the entire Theology department. Although individual chapters are often primarily the work of a single person, the textbook as a whole is the creation of a much larger group of people working together toward a common goal. It should be noted that when we first mentioned to one publisher that our "collective" plans for this textbook, he shook his head at us, skeptical that a project involving the collaboration of thirteen different people would ever be completed. The fact that we were able to complete it demonstrates the extraordinary spirit of cooperation that has characterized this project from beginning to end. Criticism was given constructively and received in the same spirit. Decisions about what to include or exclude were always made in the spirit of compromise. The greater good of the final product was always foremost in the minds of the participants, rather than self-interest or personal gain. All these factors have contributed to making the textbook what it is.

A second point to be made is that there are a number of people within the department and outside of the department who made special contributions and deserve to be singled out for thanks.

The members of the textbook committee put in countless hours reading successive drafts of manuscripts, suggesting improvements, and debating among themselves which points were essential and how best to express them to a student audience. Cathy Cory, Michael Hollerich, David Landry, Terence Nichols, and Rev. David Smith were full-time members of the committee, while Rev. Jan Michael Joncas and Rev. Thaddeus Posey OFM Cap. also served on the committee. The chair of the Theology department, Don Briel, guided the textbook project from beginning to end, and provided crucial assistance and leadership in several "administrative" aspects of the project, such as the solicitation of funds and the negotiation of the contract to publish the textbook.

The textbook would not have been possible without the financial support of the Bush Foundation, through the auspices of the Curriculum Review Task Force of the University of St. Thomas, and the Aquinas Institute. Special thanks in this regard must go to Nancy Zingale, chair of the Curriculum Review Task Force, and Msgr. Terrence J. Murphy, Chancellor of the University of St. Thomas and director of the Aquinas Foundation. We would also like to thank Mark Stansbury-O'Donnell, of the Art History Department at the University of St. Thomas, for his help in selecting and identifying prints and photographs to be included in the textbook. We thank Phyllis Karasov, the university's legal counsel, and Dean Noreen Carrocci for helping us negotiate the contract with Simon & Schuster. The administration at St. Thomas, especially Rev. Dennis Dease, President, and Academic Vice President Ralph Pearson, have been supportive of the project from the beginning. We are grateful to Barbara Sherry and and William Kay at Simon & Schuster for helping us to navigate the always unexpectedly tricky path from writing to publication. Finally, we would like to thank the hundreds of students who read parts of the textbook prior to its publication and helped us gear it better for their eyes. This textbook was written for them, and it is our fervent hope that it will help them better understand and appreciate the Christian religion and the discipline of theology. If we succeed in this goal, all the work and effort will have been worth it.

David Landry
Cathy Cory
St. Paul, Minnesota
April 1, 1996

Chapter 1

Introduction

Introduction

Who are we? Why are we here? How should we act? How should we understand and relate to the world in which we live? Is there a Power or personal Being that exists beyond ourselves? How do we relate to this Power or personal Being?

Everybody, in one way or another, faces questions about the meaning of human existence. The responses people propose to these questions are sometimes organized into a worldview or a religion. A worldview or **religion** provides an overall way of seeing and relating to ourselves, other people, the world in which we live, and possible realities beyond this world. Starting from experience, it asks what experience means and how as a result we should respond to the people, forces, and things that surround us. More specifically, religion is a worldview that believes in something beyond the "ordinary"—in God or gods, some unseen Power or powers, something beyond human existence. Religion is a way to relate to ultimate reality.

Social scientists have offered a variety of definitions of religion. Some have sought to identify the "substance" or "essence" of religion. For example, the French sociologist, Émile Durkheim, proposed the following definition in 1915: "A religion is a unified system of beliefs and practices relative to sacred things, that is to say, things set apart and forbidden—beliefs and practices which unite into a single moral community called a Church, all those who adhere to them" (Durkheim, 59). Others have sought to identify what religion does in society. For example, Milton Yinger writes: "Religion…can be defined as a system of beliefs and practices by means of which a group of people struggles with the ultimate problems of human life" (Yinger, 7). Finally, the anthropologist Clifford Geertz has developed a symbolic definition that has proved remarkably fruitful in interdisciplinary discussions of religion. He writes: "Religion is (1) a system of symbols which acts to (2) establish powerful, pervasive, and long-lasting moods and motivations in [people] by (3) formulating conceptions of a general order of existence and (4) clothing these conceptions with such an aura of factuality that the moods and motivations seem uniquely realistic" (Geertz, 4). It should be clear that religion is a complex human reality with multiple characteristics that can be investigated from a variety of perspectives.

There are, of course, many religions in the world. The most prominent are Christianity, Islam, Hinduism, Buddhism, tribal religions (of Africa, Asia, North America, Australia, etc.), Confucianism, Taoism, Shinto, and Judaism. Of these Judaism, Christianity, and Islam are **monotheistic** religions, based on a belief in "one God" (*monos* "one" + *theos* "god"). Hinduism, Shintoism, and most tribal religions are usually considered **polytheistic** religions, based on a belief in "many gods" (*polus* "many" + *theoi* "gods"). Perhaps surprisingly, there are forms of Buddhist religion that are **agnostic** (unsure about the existence of God or gods) or **atheistic** (denying that God or gods exist at all). The Jewish, Christian, and Muslim traditions, which are most influential in the Western world, believe God to be personal, all knowing, all powerful, just, loving, and the creator of everything that exists.

Religion is more than just a collection of statements or "beliefs." It includes emotions, rituals, institutions, stories, habits, attitudes, and norms of behavior. In this book we will consider several "dimensions" that are widely, if not universally, shared by religions.

I. Seven "Dimensions" of Religion

In his book *The World's Religions*, Ninian Smart proposes seven dimensions that are helpful in understanding this complex human reality that we call "religion". These dimensions are not "pieces" of a religion, so much as "facets" or "aspects." They cannot be treated separately from one another, because they are interrelated and they interact with one another. Smart's seven "dimensions" of religion include the following:

1. *Experiential/Emotional*—People gain experience of life. There are some experiences in particular that seem to give rise to religion: encountering natural or supernatural forces that produce a sense of fear or awe, contemplating one's own death, having an "otherworldly" vision, encountering a person who seems to possess the key to salvation or personal happiness, feeling united with all of reality, or experiencing very strong emotions (such as at the birth of a child, or the death of a loved one).

2. *Social/Institutional*—People who have these experiences seek out others with similar experiences and form groups for support. Gradually these groups grow in size and complexity and, as a consequence, require organizational structures to keep them functioning effectively.

3. *Narrative/Mythic*—In the group, people pass on their experience in stories. In many cases these stories are eventually collected in written form and become the sacred texts of the religion, their scriptures.

4. *Doctrinal/Philosophical*—As people ask questions about the experiences and the stories, they explain them rationally as best they can. Some meanings cannot be expressed rationally, but must remain as expressed in the stories themselves.

5. *Practical/Ritual*—If the group understands their experiences to relate to powers or beings beyond visible, everyday experience, they work out concrete ways of relating to those powers or beings (for example, liturgy or worship). They also work out formalized ways of relating to normal people and things (for example, court etiquette).

6. *Ethical/Legal*—The group decides what actions and way of life are appropriate to their experiences and their understanding of those experiences. They also develop laws to govern the community they have formed.

7. *Material/Artistic*—In living out these six dimensions, they produce material things (buildings, songs, art objects) in a way that is expressive of and appropriate to their experiences and their understandings.

In brief, people have experiences (dimension #1); come together with others (dimension #2); try to share and understand the experiences in story (dimension #3) and reasoned discourse (dimension #4); and seek to live them out in solemn or sacred acts (dimension #5), everyday behavior (dimension #6), and the material facilities they use (dimension #7).

The order of the seven dimensions of religion as they are outlined here has a certain logical attractiveness, and was probably the order in which the founders of the religion (and later converts to the religion) experienced them, but it is not the order in which most of us first encountered religion. Most people do not convert to a religion, but are socialized into their family's religion or worldview. Perhaps the first dimension they experience is the ethical/legal dimension, when they are told as children not to do something. When they ask why not, they are often told a story (the narrative dimension) rather than being given a reasoned explanation (the doctrinal dimension); they are too young for doctrine. They also experience the social, ritual, and material dimensions before they understand the reasons for them. Children attend worship services, learn songs and prayers, and experience artistic images without fully comprehending them. They may encounter the doctrinal dimension of religion in religious education classes or parochial school, but only later, as they get older, do they finally (if ever) share the core experiences that are the basis for all the rest. When people do finally share the core experiences at the base of their inherited worldview, they find that everything else has deeper meaning than they realized. Typically, they say the rest "comes to life." Often they have to re-think it all. This process is called "adult conversion"—not conversion from one worldview to another, but conversion of a person from a merely theoretical knowledge of a worldview to a deeply personal relationship with it.

Students may wish to keep in mind the seven dimensions of religion as they try to distinguish the different religions they will study and the different forms of Christianity that have existed over the centuries.

II. Forms of Christianity

Although all Christians find common ground in faith in Jesus Christ, there are considerable differences among the various forms of the Christian religion, just as there are considerable differences between Christianity and the other world religions. Differences can be seen within each of the seven dimensions of a worldview.

At the *experiential/emotional* level, some Christians are "world-embracing," seeing in the dominant culture manifestations of the Christian worldview. Others, like contemplative monks, are "world-rejecting," and so they abandon the dominant culture to seek God in solitude. Still others, like social activists, are "world-transforming," seeking to change the dominant culture to conform to Christian values. At the *social/institutional* level, some Christians, like Catholics and the Orthodox, tend to be hierarchically structured with "bishops," "priests," "deacons," etc. in positions of leadership. Others, like the Society of Friends or "Quakers," consider everyone in the group to be equal.

With respect to the *narrative/mythic* dimension, all Christians would claim the Bible as sacred scripture. However, certain groups of Christians disagree over the status of some books of the Bible. They would also vary in their judgments concerning other productions of Christian literature. At the *doctrinal/philosophical* level, the disagreements among Christian churches can be especially fierce. There are intense arguments about what God has or has not revealed, disputes about how to interpret the Bible, debates about how Christianity ought to relate to other world religions, and questions about whether a certain course of action is faithful to the vision of Jesus, to name only a few of the differences over doctrine.

The most visible differences may be observed at the *practical/ritual* level: the use of incense at an Orthodox liturgy, extensive preaching in a Presbyterian worship service, and speaking in tongues in a charismatic revival. At the *ethical/legal* level Christian churches differ on such concrete issues as the morality of the death penalty, how a society is to spend its taxes, whether Christians can serve in the military, or whether abortion is permissible under any circumstances. Finally, Christians differ in terms of the *material/artistic* dimension of religion. Some Christians will build Gothic cathedrals while others will erect Congregational meeting halls. Some Christians will vocalize Gregorian chants, others vigorously sing Lutheran chorales, while others will sway to the sound of spirituals.

Differences in these dimensions of the Christian religion can sometimes result in different forms of Christianity called **denominations**. While a Missouri synod Lutheran, a member of the Serbian Orthodox church, a Baptist, and a Roman Catholic are all members of the Christian religion, their denominations exhibit distinctive characteristics, distinctive "family" traits within the "tribe" of Christians. One goal of this book will be to explain how the major Christian denominations arose and how they are different from one another.

III. The Christian Theological Tradition

The overarching purpose of this textbook is to introduce students to the academic discipline responsible for the study of religion, namely theology, and to help students use the tools and methods of theology to study one religion in particular, namely Christianity. **Theology** is the reflective element of religion—it is thinking about religion. In the famous words of St. Anselm [d. 1109], theology is "faith seeking understanding." This reflection is not limited to our own thoughts or to our own experiences. Rather, it is enriched by the experiences and reflections of many humans over many centuries, and it is this tradition that forms the subject matter of the following textbook.

One particularly important element of the Christian theological tradition is the development and articulation of Christian doctrine. A fast and fairly accurate way to describe or understand a religion at any particular point in time is simply to list the major beliefs held by its leaders and practitioners. Later in the textbook, we will refer to some doctrinal statements and arguments that illustrate the distinctiveness of various forms of Christianity, but there is more to the Christian religion than just doctrine. In fact, we will begin with a series of stories: the biblical narratives on which the Christian religion is based. We will also pay attention to rules governing Christian social interaction, to directions for ritual, and to ethical guidelines. With the help of the photographs and drawings in this book, we will study the material and artistic responses of Christian churches at various eras.

However, before we begin our examination of the Christian theological tradition, certain foundational terms must be explained. Two concepts central to Christianity and theology are revelation and faith.

A. Revelation

Most of the monotheistic and polytheistic world religions claim not only that God (or the gods) exist, but that our knowledge of God (or the gods) depends, not just on human reason, but on **revelation**, i.e., the deliberate contact and self-disclosure between God (or the gods) and humanity. More specifically, from the perspective of the monotheistic world religions, revelation is a term that refers both to God's act of disclosing Godself to believers and to what has been so revealed (i.e., the true nature of God, humanity, the created order and God's will for humanity and the created order). The focus here is on the Christian understanding of revelation, as that understanding develops through history and is systematically explored and presented in theology.

Christian theologians distinguish between general and special revelation. General revelation is given to all human beings. The usual media by which general revelation takes place include nature and conscience. From a Christian perspective, nature is said to reveal God in a general sense because it seems to point beyond itself to a creator. At the same time, this revelation given in nature is partial and imperfect: we cannot tell from nature that the creator is a personal being or that the creator cares for us as individuals. The human conscience—a kind of intuitive, inner sense of what is right and wrong, or a recognition of a fundamental moral law—is also said to reveal God. However, the revelation given through conscience is also, from a Christian perspective, partial and imperfect: it can be severely distorted by social pressures in cultures where, for example, theft or killing is honored or human sacrifice is practiced.

Special revelation is given to particular (groups of) human beings. The media by which special revelation takes place include mystical experience, history, and personal encounter. Mystical experience refers to the direct and individual human experience of contact with and by a transcendent power; it may be expressed in visions (things seen), locutions (things heard), dreams, etc. For Jews, Christians, and Muslims human history is also the site for God's contact with and intervention on behalf of humanity. For example, Jews point to God's actions in rescuing slaves from bondage in Egypt, Christians point to the life of Jesus, and Muslims point to an angel's dictation to Muhammad as instances of special revelation in history. For Christians, personal encounter with Jesus Christ in the power of the Holy Spirit is viewed as the premiere form of special revelation.

Many of the mystical experiences, historical interventions and personal encounters perceived as special revelation have been handed down to later generations both by word-of-mouth and in written forms. The handing on of this special revelation is known in theology as oral and written tradition (from the Latin word *tradere* "to hand on"). For Jews, Tanakh (later called the Old Testament by Christians) is the record of oral and literary traditions comprising the special revelation granted to this people. Christians, recognizing the revelatory character of this material, incorporated it into their Bible, which also includes records of oral and literary traditions about Jesus of Nazareth and his earliest followers (later called the New Testament). Although Muslims recognize that Jews and Christians have their sacred books, for the followers of Islam the Qur'an holds pride of place as the written record of special revelation.

Revelation is enshrined in the practices of communal worship. Thus, people learn about aspects of revelation from hymns, from the prayers and readings that are recited during worship, from the biblical stories that are recalled and retold in the worship services. Revelation may also be confirmed in the lives of those who are held to be exemplars of the way of life founded in God's contact. These persons are called saints. Thus we can see how special revelation is handed on in tradition in a variety of ways: oral teaching, written scriptures, worship and devotional practices, the lives of those the community holds up as role models, and in the on-going life of the community itself.

B. Faith

Many people think that faith refers only to the set of beliefs that one holds. Like revelation, faith has many aspects. We can talk about **faith** as trust, as personal insight or knowledge-in-action, and as a set of beliefs.

Christian faith involves trust in God as revealed in and by Jesus. Through faith one commits oneself wholeheartedly to the vision of reality and promise of fulfillment manifest in Christian revelation. As persons entrust themselves to God, they gradually develop a personal insight or knowledge-in-action about God. They come to a conviction that trust in God leads to action to further God's cause in the world, and they make their conviction concrete in works of justice and charity. Finally, arising from a life of trust and knowledge-in-action, persons may come to formulate beliefs, i.e., propositions about God, humanity, and the created order which carry a claim to be true, not only on the basis of reason but as a consequence of revelation. Religious beliefs more or less adequately express one's knowledge-in-action about God, founded in a trusting relationship between God and the person holding the beliefs. Theology as "faith seeking understanding" will be concerned with all of these aspects of faith: the trusting commitment of the Christian to God, the knowledge-in-action gained by a Christian through participation in a particular faith tradition, and the beliefs the Christian formulates and examines.

IV. Theology

Intellectual disciplines explore reality from particular perspectives. They employ distinct methods to arrive at their conclusions and a specialized vocabulary to report their conclusions. For example, geology is an intellectual discipline that explores the earth from the perspective of its material composition and transformation using the methods of natural science; it employs a specialized vocabulary including terms such as "igneus rock," "plate tectonics," etc. Similarly, psychology is an intellectual discipline that explores human beings from the perspective of their conscious and unconscious activity using the methods of social science; it employs a specialized vocabulary using terms such as "ego," "id," "libido," and so on.

One must be careful not to confuse the methods and vocabulary of the different disciplines. While statistical analysis of human group interaction might be very useful in sociology, it has less value in art history. Musicians, sea captains, and baseball fans all use the term "pitch" but in widely varying ways. Moreover, one should recognize that each of the disciplines has definite limits. One would not ask a geologist about stock market fluctuations, even though Wall Street is located at a particular site on the globe.

Theology is an intellectual discipline that explores (religious) reality from a particular perspective, namely God as ultimate ground and goal of all reality. It employs particular methods in its exploration of God and the rest of reality in the light of God. Over the centuries it has developed a specialized vocabulary to clarify its questions and enshrine its conclusions. Theology also has its limits. The following sections will present theology as an intellectual discipline, sketch some of the sources used in theological thinking, and explain some of the specialized vocabulary used by this discipline.

A. Theology as an Intellectual Discipline

The term theology comes from two Greek words: *theos*, meaning "God" or "the divine," and *logos*, meaning "discourse," "story," or "word." Thus "theology" is "the study of God" or "discourse concerning the divine." Defining theology as "the word of God" poses somewhat of a problem, because the phrase "word of God" is ambiguous. It might mean "God's address to human beings" or "human beings' discourse about God." Both senses of the phrase have been associated with theology at different times in its history. As God's address to human beings, theology was identified with interpreting the Bible, liturgy (public group worship), and spiritual experience.

Today, and especially in the Western world since about the 13th century, theology is also understood as organized and coherent discourse about God, usually in an academic or church setting. There is one potential problem with defining theology as organized and coherent discourse about God. A significant number of people living today, especially in the wealthier, developed nations, deny the existence of God and therefore would claim that theology has no subject matter.

For them, "theology" would make as much sense as "unicornology," since neither God nor unicorns exist (although certain people might have believed and still do believe in either or in both).

Some theologians have responded to this claim by saying that theology is a "confessional" discipline, adequate and coherent for those who have a faith experience of God. Just because people blind from birth cannot personally vouch for the existence of art (nor become experts in art history), one cannot deny that paintings exist or that humans can systematically study them. Similarly, just because some people do not recognize the existence of God (or the status of theology), this does not necessarily mean that God does not exist or that human beings cannot systematically study God. Other theologians have claimed that those who deny the existence of God simply misunderstand the term; if they had more adequate understanding, they would both affirm God's existence and the legitimacy of theology.

Still other investigators claim that the proper subject of theology is not God as such, but human beings' understandings of God through history and in contemporary society. These people would probably use the term "Religious Studies" rather than "Theology." They study humans' practice of religion, but set aside the question of whether or not these practices are true (much as one can investigate the behaviors of the Ku Klux Klan without determining whether the ideology of white supremacy is true).

The major difficulty for theology as an intellectual discipline comes from the fact that God is not available for human investigation in the same way that the earth is available for a geologist, reports of dreams and neurotic behavior are available for a psychologist, or musical scores or field recordings are available for a musicologist. Theology's prime subject matter will always remain elusive and mysterious. But this does not mean that theology is impossible as an intellectual discipline. "The past" is elusive and mysterious, but it can be explored by historians; "love", "courage", and "justice" are also elusive and mysterious, but they can be explored by philosophers and poets. Theologians claim that God and reality understood in the light of God can be investigated, but that the sources and methods appropriate for this investigation will be different from those used in other disciplines.

B. The Value of Studying Theology

The fact that it is so difficult to find agreement among theologians and the fact that its subject matter is so mysterious leads some students to wonder whether they would be better served not to study theology at all. What reasons are there for studying theology?

First, most people throughout history have been religious. In all ages except our own (the late 20th century), the predominant shapers of beliefs and values have been religious systems, which have usually taught that the supreme good of human beings lies not simply in material prosperity or in unbounded pleasure, but in a proper and harmonious relationship with the unseen spiritual world or ultimate Reality to which religion is a bridge. Even today, a devout Hindu, Christian, Jew, Muslim, or a Lakota Sioux would probably agree in this basic belief. Thus, one reason for studying religion seriously and critically is that perhaps the religious claim is true—perhaps a right relationship with the unseen world of God is as important, or even more important, than material prosperity or pleasure, even though these latter are the goals stressed by 20th-century United States culture.

Second, many of the students taking this course will probably identify themselves as Christians. However, because we live in a more secular (non-religious) world, educated people today probably know and understand less about their own faith than at almost any other period in Christian history. Understanding the sources, history, and development of Christianity should deepen their understanding of their own faith and their own heritage.

Third, much of what is identified as "Western civilization" has been formed and shaped by the Christian theological tradition. Without knowledge of the Bible and Christian history much of Western architecture, art, music, poetry, and literature is simply unintelligible.

Fourth, even if one were to decide that God does not exist and that all religious worldviews are false, one would come in contact with other people who believe in the existence of God and who commit themselves to particular religions. If one expects to interact peacefully and productively with such people in society, it would be helpful, if not necessary, to understand their worldviews.

Students may well not be sure what they believe at the beginning of this study. Such a state of mind is common for people in late adolescence and early adulthood (and in some people throughout their lives). The struggle to understand unfamiliar traditions and worldviews should help to clarify one's own.

C. Sub-divisions of Christian Theology

Intellectual disciplines normally divide their investigations among a variety of specializations. Some sociologists study family interactions, others criminal behavior, still others trends in urban, suburban and rural populations. In the discipline of business one could specialize in a variety of fields, such as accounting, marketing, finance or management. Similarly, the investigations of theology are divided among various specializations. Traditionally, theology has been divided into four major categories.

Biblical theology studies the written documents found in the Bible. Biblical theologians usually specialize in either the Old Testament or the New Testament. Biblical theology investigates how these documents were formed, how they were selected to be part of the Bible, what they meant to the original "authors" and "audience," what they might mean for contemporary belief and practice, and how they reflect God's address to humanity. Since Christians claim the Bible as a privileged source for coming to know God and God's relation to the world and humanity, all Christian theologians must take the Bible into account in their investigations.

Historical theology studies how Christian faith developed in the various periods of history after the biblical era. It tries to determine what movements are permanent, authentic manifestations of what God intends for humanity, which are limited to a particular era, and which are deformations of God's intent. Historical theologians usually specialize in a particular period, for example, ancient Christianity (the "patristic era"), medieval Christianity, the Reformation, or the modern period.

Systematic theology studies the basic formulations of Christian belief (called "dogmas" or "doctrines") and how they relate to one another. Employing the information gained in biblical and historical theology, systematic theologians try to understand the realities affirmed in Christian teaching and attempt to express them in language understood by contemporary believers. Systematic theologians may treat such subjects as the Trinity (the foundational Christian understanding of God), christology (Jesus as the messiah of God), theological anthropology (human beings in relation to God), or ecclesiology (the meaning and mission of the church).

Moral theology focuses on the values arising from Christian beliefs and attempts to identify the behaviors that are congruent and incongruent with these values. Moral theology has both individual and social dimensions, discussing character formation, growth in holiness, and virtues and vices, as well as international relations, human rights, and social justice. Moral theologians attempt to determine what ought to be done in the light of the vision of reality found in biblical, historical and systematic theology.

More recent conceptualizations of theology as a discipline have added new categories, such as world religions or comparative religion, as well as more specialized areas of study within the traditional categories, such as spirituality, liturgy, and peace and justice.

V. Key Questions and Themes

In this book, we will pay special attention to two over-arching sets of questions, questions that every religion must address. In addition, we will focus on five themes that are keys to the way that Christianity in particular answers these questions.

The first set of questions involves **anthropology**, or the "study of human beings." The nature of human beings is of crucial importance to religion. Is there something about human nature that explains things like the persistence of war, oppression, torture, criminal activity, quarrels and broken relationships? If so, what is it about humanity that has these effects, and what is the cause of this situation? Are some humans "good" and others "evil?" If so, how do we distinguish one from the other? What should we do about those people who are evil?

The second set of questions involves **soteriology**, or the "study of salvation." If, as most people throughout history have agreed, there is something very wrong with human beings and their world, what might be done to respond to this situation? Can we be saved, rescued, or enlightened? What form does the rescue take? Should it be conceived in terms of the development of an authentic humanity in this life, survival of a spiritual soul in heaven, resurrection of the body in a new life, or entry into a mysterious state that is not "existence" and not "non-existence?" How do we obtain salvation? Can we do it for ourselves, or do we need outside help? What role do success and comfort play in the good human life? What is success? What brings happiness?

The five themes that are keys to the way in which Christianity answers these questions are God, creation, revelation, Jesus, and the church. For each theme there are certain questions that we will address.

1. *God*—Does a God or do gods exist? If so, what is God or what are the gods like? Is God personal and conscious, or some sort of impersonal force? Are the gods good or evil? Can the gods be trusted? If there are several gods, how do they relate to each other? How much does God know, and how much can God do? Does God interrelate with the world of our experience, and, if so, how? Does God know us personally? Does God care about us? Are we called by God to act justly toward other humans?

2. *Creation*—Was the world we live in created, had it always existed, or did it just happen by the chance play of physical forces? Is it even real, or just some sort of illusion? Does God interact with the world of our experience in a continuing way? If God or the gods created it, can they do what they want with it, make changes in it, or work "miracles"? If the gods care about humans, do they have the power to "make things turn out well" for the humans they favor? Or are God's powers limited?

3. *Revelation*—Has God made an effort to communicate with humans? Has God asked humans to respond in some way? If so, does this "revelation" take a public form ("public revelation") which those who received it then pass on to others in an authoritative way? In other words, do other humans have some obligation to believe what certain humans say about what God has revealed to them? Can an individual have

visions or other psychic or spiritual experiences, and if so, what authority do these "private revelations" have? Does God answer prayers? How should humans pray?

4. *Jesus*—Who is Jesus? Did he even exist? Is he a human "just like us," or was (is) there something special about him? What significance, if any, does his life, so long ago, have for humans today? Is his significance limited to his wise sayings and the upright moral example he provides? Does he have some role to play in the "salvation" of human beings? Is he consciously alive somewhere, does he know who we are, and does he want to have a personal relationship with us?

5. *Church*—Is it important for humans to relate to each other and form cooperative associations (churches) as they pursue these questions and seek "salvation"? Or can we do what needs to be done on our own? Do humans form churches on their own initiative, or is there some sense in which God "calls" us together? How does God relate to the churches that exist? Are the churches the way they are because God wants them to be like that, or have the churches developed in response to human cultures in a way that might change in the future? How do, or should, different churches relate to each other?

Throughout the textbook, all of these questions will be addressed with a view to the religious and socio-political situations of the historical period being studied. As you read, try to imagine what experiences lie behind the different ways that people at various times and in various places have attempted to answer these questions. Pay special attention to the experiences on which these answers have been based. Then ask whether your worldview has been influenced by similar experiences. Such an exercise can keep the Christian tradition and other traditions you study from being just words. We believe that you will find your own curiosity being activated, you will begin to notice new connections between old ideas and experiences, you will understand better why other people think the way they do, and you will find your own view of the world around you changing.

Key Terms:

religion	scriptures
theology	denomination
monotheistic	biblical theology
polytheistic	historical theology
agnostic	systematic theology
atheistc	moral theology

Questions for Reading:

1. Learn and be able to explain the seven dimensions of religion proposed by Ninian Smart.

2. What is a denomination? Give examples of the ways in which Christian denominations have different understandings of the various dimensions of the Christian religion.

3. What is the distinction between general and special revelation? What are some of the various ways in which special revelation is thought to occur?

4. What are the three aspects of faith?

5. What is the major problem with defining theology as an intellectual discipline? What are some of the possible solutions to this problem?

6. What reasons are there for studying theology?

7. Define the four sub-divisions of theology.

Works Consulted/Recommended Reading:

Durkheim, Émile. *The Elementary Forms of the Religious Life*. Trans. Joseph Ward Swain. London: George Allen and Unwin, 1915.

Geertz, Clifford. "Religion as a Cultural System." In *Anthropological Approaches to the Study of Religion*. Ed. Michael Banton. London: Tavistock, 1966.

Rausch, Thomas P. *The College Student's Introduction to Theology*. Collegeville, MN: Liturgical Press/ Michael Glazier, 1993.

Smart, Ninian. *The World's Religions*. Englewood Cliffs, NJ: Prentice-Hall, 1989.

Yinger, J. Milton. *The Scientific Study of Religion*. New York: Macmillan, 1970.

Part I: The Old Testament

An examination of the Christian theological tradition must begin with the Bible, for the Bible comprises the sacred texts (or **scriptures**) of Christianity and hence is the foundation upon which Christianity and all of its theology is built. The Bible refers to a group of books that all Christians regard as "revealed" or "inspired" by God. The word **canon** is used to refer to the list of books regarded as "inspired" or authoritative for a given religious community. All Christians refer to their canon as the Bible, although for some Christians (e.g. Protestants) the canon consists of 66 books and for others (e.g. Catholics and Orthodox) it consists of 73 (or more) books.

Christians divide the Bible into two major sections: the Old Testament and the New Testament. The Old Testament is the earlier collection of books, which was written by Jews or Israelites prior to the coming of Jesus Christ. The New Testament is the later collection of books. The word "**testament**" is a synonym for the word "**covenant**," which we can define provisionally as a sacred or formal agreement between two parties (in this case between God and human beings). Use of the terms "Old Testament" and "New Testament" refers then to the Christian belief that God made an "old" covenant with the Jews which is described in the Old Testament and a "new" covenant with the followers of Jesus Christ that is described in the New Testament. This section of the book deals with the Old Testament, and the following section discusses the New Testament.

I. The Nature of the Old Testament

The collection of books in the Bible known to Christians as the Old Testament consists of 39 books written in Hebrew (with some Aramaic) and an additional 7 books written in Greek. The Greek books are accepted as part of the canon by some but not all Christian groups. The books of the Old Testament were written over the course of at least a thousand years by many different individuals. Most of the books underwent a long editing process in which different portions of writings were combined with other works, and editors felt free to make additions, corrections and deletions. The books called the Old Testament all originated from the people known as Israelites or Jews, although they came to be regarded as sacred by both Jews and Christians.

The Old Testament was the scripture of the Jews before it became part of the scripture of the Christians. Christianity is an outgrowth of Judaism, and when Christians parted ways with Judaism, one of the things that they retained was their acceptance of the books of the Old Testament. Of course, the Jews do not call it the Old Testament, because for the Jews there is no New Testament to supplement or perhaps supplant it. The Jewish name for these texts is **Tanakh** which is an acronym for the three parts of the Jewish Scriptures, the Torah (the Law, the first five books), the Nevi'im (the Prophets) and the Khetubim (the Writings). Another name often applied to these books is the Hebrew Bible. Jews do not recognize the Greek portions of the Old Testament as Scripture, nor do Protestant Christians. Only Catholic and Orthodox Christians accept these seven books (which are usually grouped together and called the **Apocrypha**) as part of the Bible.

The canon of the Old Testament/Tanakh/Hebrew Bible, as it is accepted by Jews and different groups of Christians, can be summarized as follows:

Canon of the Old Testament

Roman Catholic and Orthodox	Protestant	Jewish Bible (Tanakh)
1. Genesis	1. Genesis	1. Bereshith ("In the beginning")
2. Exodus	2. Exodus	2. Shemoth ("Names")
3. Leviticus	3. Leviticus	3. Wayiqra ("And he called")
4. Numbers	4. Numbers	4. Bemidbar ("In the wilderness")
5. Deuteronomy	5. Deuteronomy	5. Debarim ("Words")
6. Joshua	6. Joshua	6. Yehoshua
7. Judges	7. Judges	7. Shofetim ("Judges")
8. Ruth	8. Ruth	17. Ruth
9-10. I and II Samuel	9-10. I and II Samuel	8. Shemuel
11-12. I and II Kings	11-12. I and II Kings	9. Melakim ("Kings")
13-14. I and II Chronicles	13-14. I and II Chronicles	24. Dibre Hayamim ("Chronicles")
15-16. Ezra and Nehemiah	15-16. Ezra and Nehemiah	23. Ezrah-Nehemyah
17. Tobit	Apocryphal	Noncanonical
18. Judith	Apocryphal	Noncanonical
19. Esther	17. Esther	21. Ester
20. Job	18. Job	15. Iyyob
21. Psalms	19. Psalms	14. Tehillim ("Praises")
22. Proverbs	20. Proverbs	16. Mishle ("Proverbs of")
23. Ecclesiastes	21. Ecclesiastes	19. Qoheleth ("Preacher")
24. Song of Solomon	22. Song of Solomon	18. Shir Hashirim ("Song of songs")
25. Wisdom of Solomon	Apocryphal	Noncanonical
26. Sirach (Ecclesiasticus)	Apocryphal	Noncanonical
27. Isaiah	23. Isaiah	10. Yeshayahu
28. Jeremiah	24. Jeremiah	11. Yirmeyahu
29. Lamentations	25. Lamentations	20. Ekah ("How")
30. Baruch	Apocryphal	Noncanonical
31. Ezekiel	26. Ezekiel	12. Yehezqel
32. Daniel	27. Daniel	22. Daniel
33. Hosea	28. Hosea	13. Tere Asar ("Twelve")
34. Joel	29. Joel	" "
35. Amos	30. Amos	" "
36. Obadiah	31. Obadiah	" "
37. Jonah	32. Jonah	" "
38. Micah	33. Micah	" "
39. Nahum	34. Nahum	" "
40. Habakkuk	35. Habakkuk	" "
41. Zephaniah	36. Zephaniah	" "
42. Haggai	37. Haggai	" "
43. Zechariah	38. Zechariah	" "
44. Malachi	39. Malachi	" "
45. I Maccabees	Apocryphal	Noncanonical
46. II Maccabees	Apocryphal	Noncanonical

II. The People: Hebrews, Israelites and Jews

The people who wrote and collected the books of the Old Testament are known alternately as **Hebrews, Israelites**, and **Jews**. This people began as an identifiable group around 1200 BCE. They described themselves both as a religious and a national entity. They inhabited the land now known as Israel, they worshipped a God they named Yahweh, and they told stories about their distant origin from a family of Mesopotamian semi-nomads (Abraham and his descendants). The word "Hebrew" refers to the ethnic group to which Abraham belonged. The descendants of Abraham who adhered to this religion eventually came to be called Israel (after Abraham's grandson), or the Israelites. The term "Hebrews" continued to be commonly used as the designation for this group when outsiders referred to them, but they usually referred to themselves as Israel or Israelites.

The abbreviations "BCE" and "CE" are part of a system of dating frequently used by biblical scholars. For the period "before Christ" for which the traditional abbreviation has been BC, we substitute "BCE," meaning "before the Common Era." For the period "after Christ" for which the traditional abbreviation has been AD (from the Latin "Anno Domini," meaning "Year of the Lord"), we substitute "CE," meaning "the Common Era." The new system of dating is an attempt to be sensitive to Jews, Muslims and other non-Christians who do not believe in Jesus Christ and naturally would not want to have such belief inscribed in their dating system. On the other hand, some theologians argue that since they are doing Christian theology a specifically Christian system of dating is more appropriate. To honor both concerns, this textbook will use BCE and CE in the chapters devoted to biblical literature, and BC and AD for the remainder of the chapters.

The terms "Jew" and "Jewish" had a later development. When the kingdom of Israel divided in 920 BCE, the Northern Kingdom was called Israel and the Southern Kingdom was called Judah, after the tribe that dominated that region. Two centuries later the Northern Kingdom was destroyed, and all that was left was the Southern Kingdom, Judah, which in turn was destroyed in 587 BCE. The members of the nation of Judah taken captive into Babylon had to establish a religious identity apart from the land of their ancestors. At that point, the religion of Israel evolved into a new form. This new expression of the Israelite religion came to be called "Judaism" from the original name of its nation of origin, Judah. From this origin also came the words "Jew" and "Jewish," which refer to followers of Judaism and or/members of the ethnic group from which Judaism originated.

III. The Issue of Inspiration

Jews and Christians read the biblical books in classes and in churches and synagogues, trying to understand and follow their teachings, because they believe that the Bible contains God's "revelation." The belief that the Bible is revealed by God leads them to refer to the Bible as "the word of God." The Judeo-Christian tradition asserts that the Bible is "inspired" by God. What exactly does all this mean? One thing that it does *not* mean is that God wrote the Bible. Jews and Christians believe in the Bible because they think that somehow God speaks through the Bible, that somehow the Bible contains the word of God. However, God does not speak directly in the Bible. God did not take pen in hand and write the book of Genesis. God employed *human* authors to communicate the truths that the Bible contains. For believers, the Bible is "inspired" by God, but it was *written* by human beings.

Where believers disagree is in regard to the *balance* of divine and human input into the Bible. While there are a great many views about the nature of the inspiration of the Bible, at the risk of oversimplification we can divide these into three main views.

First, there is the conservative or fundamentalist position, which argues that the Bible consists of mostly divine input and very little human input. This view suggests that the human authors of the Bible were merely vessels through which God or the Holy Spirit worked. The image suggested here is that of the Holy Spirit literally guiding the hand of the biblical writers, so that the books contain nothing of the ideas or personality of the writers themselves. They wrote down only what God told them to write, or even forced them to write. This view is called "**verbal inspiration**" and is held by the Orthodox Jews and fundamentalist Christians, both Catholic and Protestant. This view holds that God, in essence, dictated the Bible to its human authors. Since the Bible contains only divine input and no human input, since it contains only the word of God and not the words of humans, everything the Bible says must be true in every respect. Therefore fundamentalists typically deny that there are any errors in the Bible. This view is called "**biblical inerrancy**." Thus these people are forced either to deny many of the findings of modern science (e.g. the theory of evolution, the belief that the earth is several billion years old, etc.) or to produce alternate scientific theories that do not disagree with the biblical evidence. These believers are also usually more inclined to insist that the teachings of the Bible be taken literally.

On the other extreme, some people argue that the Bible contains *only* human input and no divine input. One might call this the "secular" (or non-religious) view of the Bible. Some people do not believe in God, or they believe in God but do not believe that God reveals himself to human beings, or they believe that God reveals himself, but that God did not reveal himself in these particular books. These people believe that what we have in the Bible is what the biblical authors think about God. Therefore, the opinions of the biblical authors may or may not be the truth. Since God did not have anything to do with the writing of the Bible, there is no guarantee that the Bible contains the truth. We can only judge this on a case-by-case basis.

There is also a middle position, which states that the Bible contains *both* human input and divine input, that the Bible is the "word of God" in the words of human authors. This is the official position of the Roman Catholic church as well as the position of most "mainline" Protestant churches. This position holds that God inspired the authors of the Bible to reveal the truth about God. However, advocates of this position do not mean this in the same way the fundamentalists do. Three important points separate this position from fundamentalism.

First, this middle position has a different view of the *authorship* of the Bible than the fundamentalist view. While maintaining that the Bible is the word of God, it also holds that the human authors retained a great deal of control over the final contents of biblical texts. The biblical authors used the language, images, understanding, and literary forms that were familiar to them. God did not dictate the Bible to these authors. God inspired them to write the truth, but the way that they expressed these truths and the language and concepts that they used remain their own.

Second, this middle position has a specific understanding of the *subject matter* of the Bible. According to this view, the Bible does not attempt to express scientific or historical truths, but theological ones. The Bible tries to express the truth about God and about humanity's proper relation to God. In essence, then, the Bible is concerned with *human beings and their salvation*, not with science or with history. God sees to it that the Bible contains the truths necessary for our salvation. However, the human authors express these truths in ways of their own choosing, and they do so by using the means that are available to them at the time. Therefore, if they speak of science or history, it is possible that they will make mistakes (or at least what appear to be mistakes to later generations). Another way to put this would be to say that God meets us where we are. God did not reveal modern physics and astronomy to the authors of Genesis because no one in their own time would have believed or understood them. In this view the Bible *can* contain mistakes, due to popular misconceptions during the time in which these texts were written, but these mistakes are secondary to the truth that the Bible reveals.

A third point that separates this position from fundamentalism is the conviction that very often the Bible speaks *symbolically*, and not always literally. This also helps to deal with the problem of seeming contradictions and mistakes in the Bible. When we say that the Bible speaks symbolically we mean that when the biblical authors try to express a truth they sometimes do so by telling a story or using a metaphor. The point can be valid or true, regardless of an ability to determine whether the events actually took place as described. For example, the story of Adam and Eve tries to express a truth about humanity: that humans are rebellious by nature and try to deny their dependence upon their Creator, and that humans are ultimately responsible for the evil in the world. This point is expressed in a story form. But even if Adam and Eve never existed, the point of the story may still be valid.

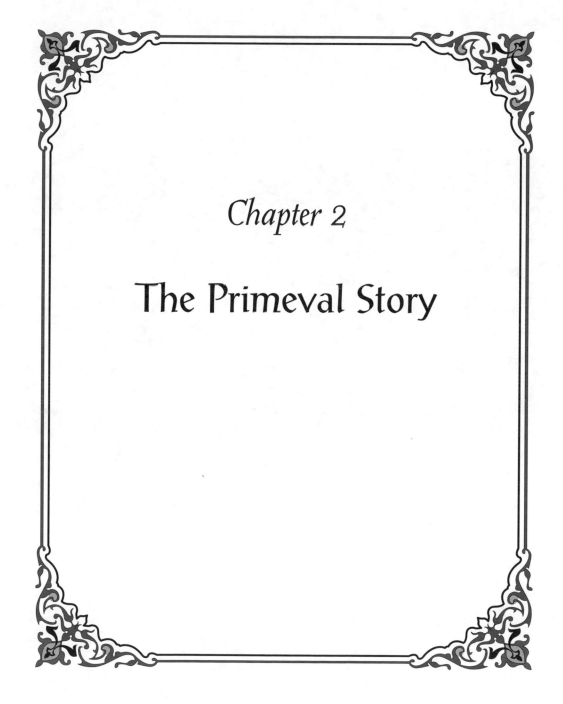

Chapter 2

The Primeval Story

The Primeval Story

Our examination of the books of the Old Testament begins with Genesis 1-11. These chapters are located at the beginning of the Old Testament, although they were generally not among the first parts of the Old Testament to have been written. Part of the process by which the various parts of the Old Testament were composed, edited, added to, and combined with other parts involved re-arranging the order of the books and their parts such that the books are not in any kind of chronological order. Nonetheless, the final placement of Genesis at the beginning of the canon and the placement of these eleven chapters at the beginning of Genesis probably reflects the view that these chapters serve as a proper introduction to Judaism as a whole, and hence serve as a proper introduction to Judaism's younger sibling Christianity as well.

I. The Creation Stories

The Bible offers two accounts of creation, quite different from each other. The first is found in Genesis 1:1-2:3; the second in Genesis 2:4-24. The two stories have different styles and vocabulary. For instance, the first story uses the word *Elohim* to describe God, whereas the second uses the word YHWH (usually pronounced "Yahweh"). They also differ significantly with respect to the order in which the creation takes place. Further, they differ in their portrayal of God. These traditions probably had independent oral existence—people told the stories from memory and passed them down to their descendants. Subsequently, they were written down, and then some time afterwards were combined into the form that we have them today.

Within the first five books of the Bible one may note four different sources or documents which were combined to make up the whole. They are the Yahwist (9th century BCE), the Elohist (8th century BCE), the Deuteronomist (7th-6th century BCE) and the Priestly writer (6th century BCE). Two of the four—the Yahwist and the Priestly writer—are represented here in the two different creation accounts. The division of the **Pentateuch** (first five books of the Bible, called in the Jewish canon the **Torah** or Law) into these different sources is called the **Documentary Hypothesis**.

Genesis 1:1-2:3 comes from the source that scholars call the **Priestly Tradition**. Although this story is placed first in the Bible, it was in fact written very late, probably sometime around the 6th century BCE or even later. One view of why it was placed first in the Bible is that it deals with ultimate beginnings. Genesis 1 offers the culmination of almost a thousand years of theological reflection. It was written as an attack on the prevailing religious sensibilities of the time, ancient Near Eastern nature religions.

Nature religions are characterized by belief in multiple gods, and by the understanding that the gods are understood as sexual beings. Sexual means two things: that there are gods and goddesses, male and female divinities; and that these gods and goddesses engage in sexual activity that brings about the fertility of the land. Further, these gods are located in the forces and cycles of nature, those places where nature manifests its power—(1) astronomical—sun, moon, stars; (2) meteorological—

rain, wind, storms, clouds; (3) geographical—mountains, bodies of water, trees. Cycles of nature refer to the turnings of the year, equinoxes and solstices, and the important times of planting and harvest.

In contrast to these nature religions' view of the world, the Priestly writer portrayed a single god, completely above nature and more powerful than any force in nature. In the text, the Israelite God has no corresponding "consort" or goddess. Yahweh does not produce the world through sexual generation, but rather through "fiat," that is, by speaking. For example: "Then God said, 'Let there be light'; and there was light" (Gen 1:3).

The biblical writer's attack on the prevailing religious sensibilities of the nature religions can also be seen in his description of the creation of the heavenly luminaries in Gen 1:14-15.

> And God said, "Let there be lights in the dome of the sky to separate the day from the night; and let them be for signs and for seasons and for days and years, and let them be lights in the dome of the sky to give light upon the earth.

It appears that the writer deliberately avoided using the terms "sun" and "moon" in the description, preferring rather "greater light" and "lesser light." The reason for this unusual reference is that the Hebrew terms for sun and moon are also the names for the gods embodied in those objects. For the Priestly writer, the sun and moon are merely "lamps," and glorified calendars and alarm clocks—decidedly not divine beings. God is the only one responsible for creation.

Another question raised by biblical scholars concerns the manner in which God created the universe. There are two possible translations of the first verse in Genesis 1: either "In the beginning God created the heaven and the earth, and the earth was…" or "In the beginning *when* God created the heaven and the earth, the earth was…" The question underlying these two different translations might be framed in this way: Did God create the world from previously existing stuff or did God create the world "out of nothing?" Although subsequent Christian tradition (and some Jewish traditions) affirmed that God created the world using no raw materials, for the Priestly writer, it was more important to affirm that God imposed order on the watery chaos. Order and structure are pleasing to God. Perhaps the Priestly writer was thereby suggesting that order and structure must also be present in the Israelite religious activities of animal sacrifice and prayer.

In summary, the priestly account of creation emphasizes the following four points:

(1) The creation is regarded as good. The Priestly writer indicates at the conclusion of each act of creation that "God saw that it was good" (Gen 1:10).

(2) The creation must be distinguished from God. Nature religions identify divine beings with the creation. The Priestly writer insists that God is completely different and more powerful than the creation.

(3) God created the world by fiat, that is, by the divine spoken word.

(4) God did not create the world through sexual activity.

Many biblical fundamentalists regard the creation story as a scientifically accurate account of the origin of the universe. Such assertions represent a misunderstanding of the function of this biblical material. Rather, the creation accounts might better be regarded as **myth**. When theologians use the term "myth," they do not mean stories that are fictional or untrue. By myth is meant those stories that a people tell about themselves and their origins that teach the most profound truths that the culture holds. These stories are the medium by which the ancient peoples addressed issues that could not be addressed in any other manner. As was stated earlier, Genesis 1 argues for a particular understanding of God and God's relationship to the created order. There was no intention on the part of this or any other biblical writer to provide a scientific or historical description of the origin of the universe. That is a scientific question best left to the scientists to determine. Therefore, any discussion of a "literal" seven days of creation, or arguments against the theory of evolution are not addressed by the biblical material. Rather, the writer made the theological affirmation that God created the world with no help and no competitors.

The second account of creation (Gen 2:4-24), which answers profound questions regarding the nature of the human person, does not as directly address the issues of God's relation to the created order. It is thought to have been written much earlier than the Priestly account. In strong contrast to the very abstract and remote God of the Priestly writer, the **Yahwist** (Genesis 2:5-3:24 and beyond) portrays God as very human-like, a concept that is called "anthropomorphism." God comes down at the pleasant time of the day to commune with the humans and enjoy the garden that he has made. The Yahwist writer describes God as fashioning the first humans out of clay, like a potter or a sculptor. The second account is much more human-centered, focused on the placement of humans within the world.

II. Sin and Humanity

A major theme of Genesis 1-11 involves the portrayal of human beings, or what might be called the **anthropology** of this particular biblical text. There are at least four features to this presentation that should be noted.

First, Genesis 1-3 claims that human beings are created by God, and are dependent upon God for their existence. Both creation stories make this point very clearly, and it is a crucial one in both the Jewish and Christian religions. Because human beings are created by God, a certain relationship exists between them that implies particular responsibilities on the part of humans. God is the creator and human beings are the creatures, or the created beings. This creator-creature relationship suggests that human beings by their nature are not independent, autonomous beings who can exist without God, but are dependent beings who are reliant upon God for everything. As a result, it appears that human beings should give God thanks and praise for this gift of life.

Second, Genesis 1 suggests that human beings are created in the image of God (see Gen 1:27). There is some kind of resemblance between God and human beings that does not exist between God and the other animals. Whether this resemblance is understood in terms of intelligence, power, physical likeness, the ability to reason, or the ability to distinguish right from wrong is not entirely clear. However, it is clear that human beings have a special status in God's eyes, and with this special status come certain responsibilities. God gives human beings "dominion" over the earth and all the other creatures in it. While some have interpreted this to mean that the earth and its resources are given by God to human beings to use and exploit as they see fit, it is probably more accurate to say that because humans resemble God, God entrusts the earth and its resources to the stewardship of human beings, to care for them as God would. God does not give the earth and its creatures to humans to exploit; rather God entrusts human beings as his representatives to be caretakers of the earth.

Third, Genesis asserts the intrinsic goodness of human beings. While Genesis 3-11 shows abundantly how human beings are capable of evil acts and wicked behavior, Genesis 1 makes it clear that this is not because human beings are created evil or are created by God in a flawed way. After God creates human beings, the text notes that "God saw everything that he had made, and indeed, it was very good" (Gen 1:31). This goodness certainly includes human beings. God created human beings for perfection, to live in harmony with himself and the other creatures in the world.

Finally, Genesis teaches that in spite of the fact that human beings are created good, distressingly often they decide to sin against God and disobey his commands, bringing disastrous consequences upon themselves. Although God created human beings to do good and be perfect, God gave human beings **free will**, that is, the capacity to decide whether to do good or evil. Of course God wants humans to decide to do good only, but humans all too often use their free will to do evil. This point is made most clearly in the mythical story of Adam and Eve. God gives Adam and Eve everything they need, and gives them only one command: not to eat of the tree of the knowledge of good and evil. After being tempted by the serpent (who, contrary to popular opinion, is not identified as Satan or the devil), Adam and Eve decide for themselves to disobey God and eat the fruit. They are told by the serpent that they will become "like God," and this provides their motivation for disobedience.

According to this story, Adam and Eve do not seem to be satisfied being creatures, being dependent upon God for everything. They wish to usurp God and put themselves in God's place. Their sin is an act of rebellion against God. According to Christian interpretation, this act destroys the proper relationship between God and human beings, between the creator and the creatures. The result is that human beings "fall" from the state of perfection intended for them by God into a state of misery and evil. Adam and Eve are banished from the Garden of Eden, and they each are cursed. Eve's curse involves painful childbirth and domination by her husband, while Adam's curse involves difficulty in tilling the earth as a farmer. Christian theologians refer to this story as the story of "**the Fall**," since it tells of how human beings lost the state of perfection intended for them before they sinned against the Lord.

Figure 2.1: Creation of The Heavenly Bodies, mosaic from the cupola of San Marco.

Figure 2.2: Expulsion of Adam and Eve, mosaic from the cupola of San Marco.

The story of the Fall does not end with Adam and Eve, however. The rest of Genesis 1-11 continues the story of the Fall, as it tells of how human beings continue to sin more and more seriously, with more and greater curses and punishments being the result. Adam and Eve commit a sin of disobedience, and they are cursed and banished from Eden. Following this, their son Cain murders his brother Abel, a far more serious offense. Cain is exiled from his home and cursed as well. In the stories following Cain's exile there is even more murder. In Genesis 4, a man named Lamech sings about murdering a man merely for striking him, and he indicates that blood revenge has increased from sevenfold to seventy-sevenfold. By Noah's generation there is all manner of sexual immorality and violence being committed by virtually every human being on earth. Once sin enters the world, the state of human beings declines rapidly, and human beings seem to be helpless to pull themselves out of their miserable condition without God's help. The rest of Genesis will tell the story of how God offers this help, and how human beings respond to God's offer.

III. God

One of the major functions of Genesis 1-11 is to introduce the reader to the Israelite God, who is known in the Old Testament by several names: Yahweh (or Jehovah), Elohim, El Shaddai, etc. In the original Hebrew language text, God's name is often simply indicated by four consonants, YHWH, and this is how the name of God will be indicated in this textbook. The Israelites considered the name YHWH to be too holy to pronounce or say out loud, and even to this day Jews do not pronounce the name of God, instead substituting an expression which means "the LORD."

There was a rich variety of beliefs about the gods in the ancient world, and it is important to understand the beliefs of the Israelites about their God in the context of this variety. Ancient people disagreed about how many gods there were, whether the gods were good or evil, and the degree to which the gods cared about human beings and interacted with them. Some people believed in male gods and female goddesses, while others saw their gods in more impersonal terms, as spiritual or natural "forces" to be reckoned with. Some religions even proclaimed human leaders such as emperors and kings to be gods. The emotions spawned by ancient peoples' experience of the gods ranged from love to terror, and their activity in relation to the gods varied accordingly. Animal sacrifice, human sacrifice, sacrifice of grains and cereals, prayer, and other forms of worship were all common in the religions of the ancient world. Where did the Israelites fit on this spectrum? How did their beliefs about YHWH compare to the beliefs of other religions about their gods?

One of the most important issues to consider is the question of how many gods exist. The belief that most clearly set the Israelites apart from the vast majority of their neighbors and contemporaries was their belief in only one God. Belief in only one god is known as **monotheism**, and to many observers this is the defining characteristic of the Israelite religion.

Other ancient people had a variety of beliefs about the number of gods. For example, some ancient people worshiped the forces of nature. They believed that "inanimate" things like rivers and trees were alive, and they prayed and offered sacrifices to the spirits that dwelled in nature. Among the most popular kinds of gods were sun-gods and moon-gods, rain (or thunder) gods and earth-goddesses. Worship of the forces of nature is called **animism**. Others believed that different gods oversaw different spheres of human activity, so that there might have been a goddess of love or a god of hunting. Believers offered prayers and sacrifices to these gods depending on the activity that they were engaged in. Any religion which involves belief in many gods is called **polytheistic**, although there are many different varieties of polytheism. Some ancient people believed that there were many national or territorial gods, with each god having his or her own unchallenged area or sphere of influence. In this view, the Babylonians would worship the territorial gods of Mesopotamia, while the Egyptians worshipped the gods who oversaw Egypt. Which gods a person worshiped would depend upon where one was or what group one belonged to, since gods would only help "their own" people, or could only help people within certain geographical bounds. Still another possibility is the belief that there are many gods that exist, but only one god who is best and most powerful.

Although the Israelites became known for their belief in only one god, they were not always monotheistic. Various parts of the Old Testament suggest that in the early stages one or another of the forms of polytheism mentioned above flourished among the Israelites. Nonetheless, Genesis 1 represents one of the later stages in the development of the Old Testament, and this text insists upon a strict monotheism. It is clear throughout the creation story that only one god is doing the creating. Moreover, it is clear that the sun and the moon and the other forces of nature are *not* gods, since YHWH creates them.

Another major characteristic that emerges in Genesis 1-11 is YHWH's power. YHWH's power is shown primarily through the creation of the world. All that YHWH needs to do in order to create is to speak. "Then God said, 'Let there be light'; and there was light" (Gen 1:3). YHWH creates all of the world and not just some portion of it. YHWH creates all of the forces of nature and all living creatures. Nothing that exists is created except by YHWH. YHWH's power is shown not only through creation, however, but also through destruction. Later in Genesis, when YHWH becomes angry at the evil and wickedness that have pervaded creation, he decides to destroy the world and its inhabitants through a catastrophic flood. The ability to cause this great flood also shows God's power. So great are YHWH's powers that it may be concluded that the Israelite God is in fact all-powerful. Theologians refer to this as God's **omnipotence**.

Another crucial point is that the Israelites believed that YHWH was a good God. Many ancient people saw their gods as evil beings whose anger needed constantly to be appeased, or as jealous and petty beings who were rather indifferent to human beings and their problems. By contrast, Genesis 1 emphasizes YHWH's goodness. Yahweh's goodness is reflected most of all in the goodness of creation itself. After each of the six "days" of creation, the text emphasizes that God looked upon what had been created, and "God saw that it was good" (Gen 1:12, 18, 21, 25). When YHWH was finished with creation, "God saw everything that he had made, and indeed, it was very good" (Gen 1:31). Hence YHWH must be a good god, since he created such a good world.

YHWH's goodness is also reflected in other aspects of Genesis 1-11, although it must be acknowledged that the Israelites did not always see YHWH as an exclusively good God. Their belief in God's goodness developed, as did their belief in God's oneness. Still, YHWH's goodness is reflected in the fact that YHWH loves and cares about the creatures in the world, providing them with the things they need to survive and flourish (like food), looking after them, and assisting them when they are in difficulty. YHWH is not indifferent to the plight of human beings, and although he does become angry with human beings at times, he is slow to anger. Theologians refer to the great goodness of YHWH as God's **benevolence**.

Another question that must be addressed in order to understand the Israelite God is the issue of YHWH's gender. Most other ancient religions believed in male gods and female goddesses. Often these religions even told stories in which these gods and goddesses created the world and its inhabitants through sexual activity. There is certainly no sexual activity on God's part in Genesis. God is complete and whole within Godself, and does not need a "partner" to create the world. Does this mean that God is "beyond" gender? The text is not entirely clear on this point. On the one hand, it is true that the Israelites used exclusively male pronouns for God. YHWH is frequently referred to as "he" or "him," and never as "she" or "her." This could lead one to the conclusion that YHWH is a male god. On the other hand, there is a poem in Genesis 1:26 which reads:

> So God created humankind in his image
> in the image of God he created them
> male and female he created them.

The parallelism of the poetry in this passage strongly suggests that when God creates humankind *in his image*, he creates humankind *male and female*. This implies that the "image of God" is not male only, but is male *and* female. God is not "beyond" gender, but neither is God one gender or the other. God has *both* male and female qualities. In this sense, it is probably most appropriate to refer to God sometimes as "he" and sometimes as "she," but not as "it."

Language about God

The Judeo-Christian tradition uses various names and descriptions for God. Some of the more popular names are God as "Father" or God as "King." Descriptions such as loving, merciful, and all-powerful are commonly applied to God. Theologians are careful to point out, however, that these are not literal descriptions or proper names. Our language about God is necessarily metaphorical or analogical.

An analogy is a comparison between two things which are similar in one respect, but dissimilar in others. For example, if we say that "John is a lion," then we mean that John is similar to a lion in some respects (perhaps he is brave or ferocious) but dissimilar in others (John does not have a long mane or a tail).

The same is true when we say that "God is our father." We are saying that God is like a human father in some respects—God cares for us like a (good) father would, God is the source of life, etc. But in other respects, God is not like a human father; God is not ignorant, or limited, or mortal, or confined to a body, like a human being.

Every positive quality that we ascribe to God comes from the human realm, and is drawn from human experience. Therefore when we apply these terms to God we are speaking analogically. The medieval theologian Thomas Aquinas argued that every positive quality that we ascribe to God—such as goodness, being, life, wisdom, or power—applies in a limited way to creatures, but in an unlimited way to God. God is the perfection of goodness, being, life, wisdom, and power.

It takes many analogies to describe God. No one name or description is adequate for God. But even many analogies fall short of a comprehensive description of God. The fullness and mystery of God will always be beyond the reach of human language, because God is infinite, and human language and concepts are finite.

Why is it important to recognize that our language for God is analogous? If we do not, then we mistake God for our images of him, and end by making God a larger version of ourselves, complete with our prejudices. God is "the Big Man upstairs" (as John Wayne is reputed to have said). The problem with this is that we can end in idolatry—worshiping an idol, or image, rather than the living God. Then we will tend to think that God is like we are, and is perhaps opposed to other people who are not like we are. The biggest mistakes in Christian history—i.e. wars of religion, inquisitions against heretics, and persecution of non-Christians—have come from the failure to realize that God is greater than our images of him, and loves those we do not love. Thus, though we cannot avoid using language or images of God, it is important to be aware that God is beyond our language and images.

A final issue raised by Genesis 1-11 involves God's relationship with human beings. As was mentioned earlier, God is portrayed as a loving god who cares about and provides for her creatures. However, the relationship between God and human beings changes somewhat when sin enters the picture. From the point of view of the text, God becomes angry in the face of human sin, and this anger results in punishment. This is clear from the way that God reacts to the disobedience of Adam and Eve, the murder of Abel by Cain, and the wickedness of Noah's generation. God punishes Adam and Eve by banishing them from the garden and pronouncing various curses upon them. God punishes Cain by exiling him and cursing the ground that he farms. God punishes the evildoers in Noah's generation by sending the flood to destroy them all.

Many who read the stories of Genesis 1-11 see all this as evidence that YHWH is a wrathful, vindictive god. However, two points must be made about YHWH's behavior in these instances. First, YHWH is portrayed as a *just* god in these stories. Justice here refers to treating each person according to what they merit or deserve. The stories leave no doubt that each of the persons who receive God's punishment deserve it. For example, God sends the flood because "the LORD saw that the wickedness of humankind was great in the earth, and that every inclination of the thoughts of their hearts was only evil continually" (Gen 6:5). Moreover, "the earth was corrupt in God's sight, and the earth was filled with violence" (Gen 6:11). Those who are innocent of any wrongdoing are protected by God, as God arranges for them to be rescued from the flood through the building of the ark. In every case in Genesis 1-11, the text emphasizes that those who are punished by God are punished justly.

Second, although YHWH is a just god, he is also a *merciful* God. Adam and Eve had been told that they would die if they ate of the fruit of the forbidden tree, but God did not kill them. YHWH reduced their punishment to banishment from Eden and even provided them with clothing for protection as they depart. Likewise, God did not kill Cain for murdering Abel, but exiled him, and even as he was pronouncing punishment, YHWH made arrangements for Cain to be protected from anyone who sought to kill him in revenge for Abel's murder. After the flood, God promised never again to destroy the earth and its creatures, no matter how wicked human beings might become. Thus is God's mercy shown alongside her justice.

Key Terms:

YHWH (Yahweh)	"the Fall"
Documentary Hypothesis	monotheism
Priestly writer	animism
Priestly tradition	polytheism
Yahwist tradition	omnipotence
myth	benevolence
anthropology	image of God
free will	

Questions for Reading:

1. What are the sources for the books of the Pentateuch? Why are there two creation stories in Genesis?
2. What are the differences between the Israelite idea of God and the ideas of the other ancient Near Eastern peoples?
3. What is meant by myth?
4. How does this portion of the Bible view the nature of humans?
5. What are the characteristics of the Israelite God?
6. What is meant by "the image of God" in Genesis 1?

Works Consulted/Recommended Reading:

Anderson, Bernhard. *Understanding the Old Testament*. 2nd ed. Englewood Cliffs, NJ: Prentice-Hall, 1966.

Brown, Raymond E., Fitzmyer, Joseph A., and Murphy, Roland E., eds. *The New Jerome Biblical Commentary*. Englewood Cliffs, NJ: Prentice Hall, 1990.

Dei Verbum (Dogmatic Constitution on Divine Revelation). In *The Documents of Vatican II*. New York: Crossroad, 1989.

McFague, Sallie. *Models of God: Theology for an Ecological, Nuclear Age*. Philadelphia: Fortress Press, 1987.

Metzger, Bruce and Murphy, Roland, eds. *The New Oxford Annotated Bible with Apocrypha*, New Revised Standard Version. New York: Oxford University Press, 1991.

Trible, Phyllis. *God and the Rhetoric of Sexuality*. Philadelphia: Fortress Press, 1978.

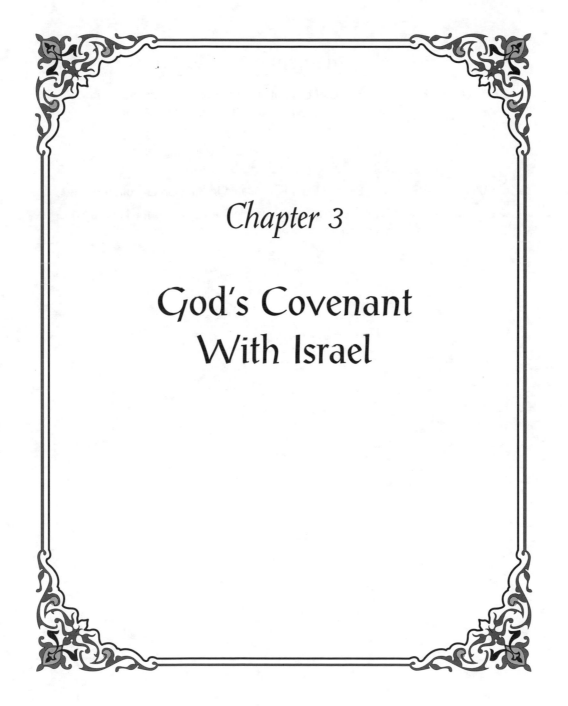

Chapter 3

God's Covenant
With Israel

Timeline

3000-2000 BCE	Beginnings of civilization in Mesopotamia (Sumer, Babylonia, Assyria) and in the areas of Syria and Canaan.
c. 1850	Abraham migrates to Canaan. Beginnings of the patriarchal period.
c. 1700	The **Enuma Elish** is circulated in Babylonian culture.
c. 1300-1250	Moses delivers God's people from Egypt in the Exodus. God's covenant people journey to the promised land.

God's Covenant With Israel

The book of Genesis begins with Israel's stories about the creation of the world and the origins of sin. These stories are followed by narratives about the earliest identifiable ancestors of the Israelite people: Abraham and Sarah; Isaac and Rebekah; Jacob, his wives and his twelve sons (especially Joseph). These stories probably carry more concrete historical recollections than the earlier ones. However, the primary purpose of the stories is not to relate historically accurate details of ancient events, but to explain how it was that YHWH came to claim this people as his own.

Genesis tells about Abraham's and Sarah's first encounters with God, about the promises that YHWH made to Abraham, and about how Abraham's descendants were eventually transplanted to Egypt. The book of Exodus picks up the story with Moses whom YHWH called to lead the Israelites out of slavery in Egypt. He is the one who received the Law from YHWH on Mount Sinai. Through these human persons, YHWH intervened in history on behalf of one particular people, the Israelites. Later inheritors of these stories, Christians, in particular, will understand that God's intervention had a wider purpose than that of Israel alone.

I. Abraham

Genesis 12-25 tells the story of Abram, the son of Terah, from the land of the Chaldeans, who lived sometime during the 18th century BCE. Abram, whose name YHWH would eventually change to **Abraham**, first encountered YHWH at Haran in northern Mesopotamia. YHWH spoke to Abram with authority and made a promise to him.

> Now the LORD said to Abram, "Go from your country and your kindred and your father's house to the land that I will show you. I will make of you a great nation, and I will bless you, and make your name great, so that you will be a blessing. I will bless those who bless you, and the one who curses you I will curse; and in you all the families of the earth shall be blessed" (12:1-3).

This passage introduces several important theological themes: revelation, promise and response, and covenant.

A. Revelation

The stories contained in the book of Genesis were already ancient at the time of their writing. The authors who put these oral traditions into writing understood that God had revealed himself to Abraham, the first **patriarch** (father or founder) of their people, and that God had also revealed his intentions for Abraham and his descendants. In Genesis 12, the reader is given no information about what the experience of revelation was like for Abraham. We are simply to understand that it was *God's initiative* to establish a relationship with Abraham, to begin a new nation with Abraham and eventually to bring this nation into the land then called Canaan, later called Israel.

In a later account of Abram's encounter with YHWH, Genesis 15, Abram's *experience* of revelation is described in some detail. Abram falls into a deep sleep, and YHWH speaks to him concerning the future destiny of his descendants. Finally, a deep and terrifying darkness surrounds him and Abram has a vision of a smoking fire pot and flaming torch. The story implies that it was YHWH who appeared to Abram in the smoking fire pot and flaming torch. Genesis 17 provides yet another account of YHWH's revelation to Abram. In this account, YHWH changes Abram's name to Abraham, because he will make Abraham "the father of a host of nations" (Gen 17:5).

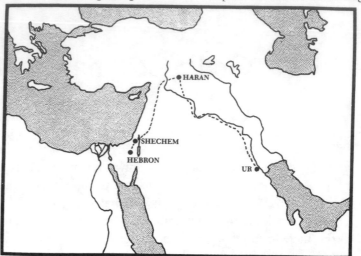

Figure 3.1: The journey of Abraham from Ur to Canaan

B. Promise and Response

According to the book of Genesis, YHWH offered Abram a vision of a new future. This new future is described as a *promise* that YHWH gave to Abram. The promise has several aspects: (1) he will have many *descendants*; (2) God will make him a *great nation*; (3) through him *all nations of the earth would be blessed* (Gen 12:1-3); and (4) he will be given a *land* for his descendants to live in (Gen 15:7). These ancient traditions are the basis of the Israelite and Jewish convictions that they are a "chosen people" living in a "promised land."

YHWH tells Abram to trust the promise, to leave his own land and his own people, and to follow the directions that he is given. In this encounter, Abram is challenged to believe what YHWH is saying and to trust that YHWH can bring it about. The narratives in Genesis describe just how Abram responded.

According to the book of Genesis, when Abram received YHWH's call, his initial response was to trust YHWH enough to leave his country and his kindred and, with his wife Sarai, his nephew Lot and their followers, go to the land of Canaan. Once he arrived there, his trust was tested and he did not always respond well. He and his kin moved about through the land of Canaan, which was already populated by other peoples, until a famine drove them to Egypt. Because his wife Sarai was very beautiful, Abram feared that the Egyptians would kill him so that the Pharaoh could take Sarai into his harem. In order to protect himself, Abram told them that Sarai was his sister. Believing that she was unmarried, the Pharaoh took her as his wife, but YHWH rescued her by afflicting Pharaoh and his house with plagues. Later virtually the same story is repeated with a different king. In both cases, Abram risks losing Sarai, the one through whom God's promise to Abram would be fulfilled.

YHWH seemed slow to fulfill his promise of a son for Abram. At the suggestion of Sarai, Abram tried to have a son by having sexual relations with his slave girl, Hagar. Hagar gave birth to a son named **Ishmael**. Under the customs of the time such a child would still be considered the child of Abram and Sarai. Abram tried to fulfill God's promise by his own means, but YHWH let Abram know that this was not the descendant through whom the mighty nation would be established. Instead, YHWH promised Sarai, already an old woman, that she would have a son, and God delivered on the promise with the birth of **Isaac**. Then, just as everything seemed to be falling into place,

YHWH asked Abraham to take Isaac his son, the only one through whom God's promises could be met, and to offer him as a sacrifice. Abraham proved his faith and stood ready to sacrifice his son, but the angel of YHWH intervened and provided an animal for Abraham to sacrifice instead. The promise that God made to Abraham would indeed be fulfilled.

Although this story raises many troubling questions about God and God's intentions toward Abraham, it describes well the character of Abraham as a person of faith. Whatever his earlier doubts about God's ability to fulfill his promise, finally Abraham demonstrates his total trust in YHWH through his willingness to give up his only beloved son. In a sense, everything in Abraham's life had been leading to this point. The writers of the New Testament will later refer to Abraham as a model of faith, because he believed in God's promise even before he could see it being fulfilled.

Figure 3.2: Mosaic in San Vitale, Ravenna. The illustration on the left describes the scene in which three visitors come to Abraham at the Oak of Mamre to announce Isaac's birth. The illustration on the right describes the scene of Abraham's near-sacrifice of Isaac.

C. Covenant

In the book of Genesis, YHWH is described as confirming his promise to Abram/Abraham and his descendants by "making a **covenant**" with Abraham. Genesis describes several acts of covenant between YHWH and Abraham, and it is interesting to compare their details. Here is one of the descriptions.

[YHWH] said to [Abram], "Bring me a heifer three years old, a female goat three years old, a ram three years old, a turtledove, and a young pigeon." He brought him all these and cut them in two, laying each half over against the other, but he did not cut the birds in two. And when birds of prey came down on the carcasses, Abram drove them away.

As the sun was going down, a deep sleep fell upon Abram, and a deep and terrifying darkness descended upon him.

When the sun had gone down and it was dark, a smoking fire pot and a flaming torch passed between these pieces. On that day the LORD made a covenant with Abram (Gen 15:9-13; 17-18).

Covenants were used for a variety of purposes, among them those for which we would use treaties and contracts today. Briefly, a covenant is a solemn agreement between two parties (individuals or groups) listing their respective rights and responsibilities in the relationship. Because it was sealed with an oath, ancient covenants carried a religious sense—a sense of being guaranteed by God. Modern people also sometimes seal solemn promises and statements with an oath. For example, witnesses in court promise to tell the truth "so help me God." The sense of the phrase "so help me God" is that God will punish the one who does not tell the truth. In the passage above, the animals are split in two and the participants in the covenant pass between them. The implication is that the covenant partners submit to the curse of becoming like the divided animals if they do not adhere to the terms of the covenant.

D. Children of Abraham

Genesis 24-50 continues with stories about Abraham's descendants, especially Isaac, **Jacob**, and Jacob's twelve sons—founders of the twelve tribes of Israel. As the authors tell the stories, they make a point of establishing just which people are, in fact, "descendants" and heirs of the promises to Abraham, including the "promised land." Thus, the stories describe how some of Abraham's descendants are chosen to inherit the promise, but others are not. The reader learns how God chose Isaac, not Ishmael, even though both were Abraham's sons and Ishmael was the first-born. In another story, Isaac's wife Rebekah gives birth to twins: Jacob and Esau. Esau is the first-born, but by deceit Jacob steals the "birthright" of primary inheritance and his dying father's special blessing. Thus, against all human standards of justice, Jacob becomes the inheritor of Abraham's promise. The stories go on to say that Jacob later becomes the victim of deceit. Jacob is exiled from the land of the promise and tricked shamelessly by his uncle Laban as he had tricked Esau. Only after years in exile and a wrestling match with a mysterious heavenly being is he able to inherit the promise in fact. It is during the wrestling match that Jacob is given the new name Israel, from which the Israelites take their name.

Just who was a legitimate descendant of Abraham was an important question in biblical times, since the promises of God are made to Abraham and his descendants. The importance of descent from Abraham partially explains the frequency with which biblical passages record the genealogies of the characters involved in the story. However, it should be recognized that one did not necessarily need to be from the bloodline of Abraham to claim him as an ancestor and to be considered part of the covenant people. The genealogies did not always reflect biological reality, but were often more of a political statement used to indicate inclusion and exclusion within a particular group or tribe. Indeed, the stories of the patriarchs in general are motivated more by political and theological concerns than by the desire to describe history with perfect accuracy.

This is not to say that the stories about the patriarchs have no historical base. While the exact historical value of these stories is disputed, studies have shown that customs presupposed in the patriarchal stories fit accurately the period in which the patriarchs are thought to have lived. Most importantly, the writers and readers of the Old Testament understood the *meaning* of these stories differently than modern readers often do. For the original writers and readers, the genealogies and stories about the ancestors of tribes and nations described present relationships among these tribes and nations more than they did relationships among historical individuals. This difference reflects deep cultural differences between the original readers of the Old Testament and modern Western readers.

A Cultural Difference: Genealogies

Among Arabian tribes today, whatever might be the biological reality, all members of a given tribe consider themselves to be descended from the tribe's common ancestors. If strangers join the tribe, they do so "in name and in blood," in a way similar to Western practices of adoption. That is, they take the tribe's ancestors as their own and promise to marry and raise their families within the tribe. The Arabs say that the newcomers have been "genealogized."

When two or more tribes enter into close relationship, for example a confederation of several tribes or the absorption of a weak tribe by a stronger one, a similar process occurs. If the two tribes are of relatively equal power, they may begin to speak of their common ancestors as brothers and sisters, much as they have now become brothers and sisters by the confederation. If one tribe is dominant over the other, the ancestors' relationship will be spoken of in a similar dominant way—for example as uncle and nephew, or father and son.

It is likely that the tribes of the Bible had similar practices. In fact, we can see an example of "genealogizing" in the Bible itself. In the stories of the conquest of Canaan, Caleb was a member of a tribe foreign to Israel, but he chose to ally himself with Israel and cooperated significantly with the Israelite tribes in the process of spying out and conquering the land. As a result, he and his family were "genealogized" into the tribe of Judah: they were given a share in the tribe's land, and Caleb, despite his actual foreign birth, was from that time on spoken of as a member of the tribe of Judah and as a descendant of Judah, the founder of the tribe.

E. Joseph and the Twelve Tribes of Israel

Jacob (Israel) had twelve sons by his two wives and two of their maids. These twelve sons founded the twelve tribes of Israel. **Joseph** and Benjamin were the two sons by Jacob's favorite wife Rachel, and Jacob favored them (especially Joseph). Joseph's brothers resented the favor Jacob showed him, so they sold Joseph as a slave to some traders going to Egypt. They told Jacob he had been eaten by wild animals. Joseph had various adventures in Egypt, all showing that no matter what humans try to do YHWH can rescue his favored people. Joseph was imprisoned on a false charge of attempted rape, but was rescued from prison and became a high Egyptian official. Then a famine in Canaan forced his brothers to come to Egypt seeking food, and they ended up begging Joseph for help without recognizing who he was. Joseph tested his brothers in various ways to see whether they had changed, and finally revealed himself to them, forgave them, and invited the whole family to settle in Egypt. Jacob died in Egypt and his descendants, later known as the Israelites, lived several generations there. Finally, an Egyptian Pharaoh came into power who was not favorably disposed toward the Israelite peoples and who enslaved them in various work projects. This is the setting for the book of Exodus, in which Moses leads the Israelites out of slavery in Egypt.

II. Moses

Exodus 1-20 introduces the reader to **Moses** and to the central, formative experience of the Israelite people—the Exodus, an experience which above all created their community and their religion. Moses is thought to have lived sometime during the middle part of the 13th century BCE. According to the book of Exodus, YHWH again took the initiative by calling Moses. YHWH directed and empowered Moses to rescue YHWH's people—the descendants of Abraham—from slavery in Egypt. He led them through the wilderness, established another covenant with them, and settled them successfully in the "promised land." This new covenant which they received at Mount Sinai shaped their religious and community life and acted as their "constitution." (It still serves today as the constitution of the State of Israel.) Thus, YHWH fulfilled the promises to Abraham expressed in the earlier covenant: many descendants and a land for them to live in. The best known feature of this "Mosaic" covenant is the Ten Commandments.

A. Moses the Prophet

Moses is called a **prophet**, the first and most important of the great Israelite prophets. The central point of prophecy is that prophets are *spokespersons for God*. The great Israelite prophets, like Moses in the book of Exodus, were called and chosen by God, were given messages from God to deliver to others, and experienced a powerful compulsion to convey those messages despite their own fears.

Moses experienced his prophetic call while in exile in Midian. YHWH attracted his attention with a bush that was burning but not being consumed by the fire. The initial message YHWH gave Moses was that Moses was to lead YHWH's people out of slavery in Egypt. Moses was commanded to announce this message to Pharaoh and to the Israelite people. Moses tried to avoid the responsibility, finally asking YHWH to "send someone else," but YHWH would not accept Moses' refusal.

In the course of trying to avoid his assignment Moses asked God what his name was, and received that famous and mysterious answer, "I am who am," which has been variously understood as "I am who exists without being caused by another," "I am who causes to be," or "I am who I am"—among numerous other explanations. In Hebrew the name is YHWH (Hebrew was written without vowels), but Jews considered the name too sacred to pronounce, substituting instead the word "Lord" (in Hebrew, "*Adonai*") wherever the name of YHWH was written. In the Exodus stories about Moses, the writers consistently refer to God as YHWH.

Assisted by his brother **Aaron** the Levite, Moses finally accepted his assignment and returned to Egypt with his message for the ruling **Pharaoh**, who was brutally oppressing the enslaved Israelites. The message was this: YHWH says, "Let my people go." Thus began a confrontation between Moses and Pharaoh which the book of Exodus, and ancient peoples in general, saw as a confrontation between YHWH and the gods of the Egyptians. At the time, and probably for centuries afterwards, neither the Israelites nor their neighbors thought of YHWH as being the *only* real God. The Israelites thought he was the only God *for them* (and often enough failed to be faithful even to this conviction). Much later they were to become convinced that their God was the only true God of all.

In order to get the Egyptian Pharaoh to release the Israelite people, YHWH gave Moses several magic tricks and a series of plagues to use against the Egyptians. Later, when Pharaoh finally released the people, God continued to protect and guide them in the desert by providing them with safe passage across the Red (reed) Sea, by giving them food and water in the desert, and finally safe passage into the "promised land." This confrontation between Moses and the Pharaoh, and the events which followed, revealed a number of characteristics of YHWH:

(1) YHWH was much more powerful than the Egyptian gods and the gods of the Canaanites.

(2) YHWH cared about earthly oppression and material needs: YHWH rescued the Israelites from slavery and settled them in a land which had the resources to support them.

(3) YHWH supported the Israelites in desert places where food and water could not otherwise be found.

(4) YHWH was a strong warrior who led Israel in battle against hostile neighbors.

Some modern theologians have drawn attention to these same characteristics of God to challenge churches to work for justice and to counteract the attitude that religion is concerned only with life after death.

The same Exodus narratives also reveal some characteristics of the Israelites:

(1) While they did not enjoy being slaves in Egypt, they were not inclined to try to escape. YHWH and Moses had to push them to cooperate.

(2) They did not have much confidence in YHWH's power. They were "slow learners" who kept forgetting how YHWH had just saved them and who failed to trust YHWH's protection.

(3) They were constantly grumbling about the hardships they were experiencing and blaming YHWH and Moses for their suffering.

(4) In general, it was YHWH who took all the initiative. Left to themselves, the Israelites probably would have remained where they were, or returned to Egypt after having left there.

YHWH "chose" the Israelite people not because of their good qualities, but in spite of their "stiff necks" (stubbornness). *Why* YHWH chose them remained a mystery even to the Israelites themselves. In the New Testament, Paul will remark that other peoples, including Christians, should not feel superior in this respect, since no one is *worthy* of God's call, and no one has lived up to God's call very well.

The following box summarizes YHWH's conflict with the gods of Egypt. Note how the story is told to show that YHWH is more powerful than the Egyptian gods. At first the Egyptian magicians could duplicate the plagues Moses was producing (but in an inferior way). But by the third plague they not only failed to duplicate the plague, they publicly admitted that YHWH had won the contest. As the plagues went on, other members of Pharaoh's court became convinced that YHWH had won, and tried to convince Pharaoh to give up. They also took steps to protect themselves, but Pharaoh held out, making insincere and inadequate promises, only to go back on them again and again.

The Ten Plagues

1. Water into blood—After Moses turned the water of the Nile river into blood, Pharaoh refused to release the Israelites because his magicians could duplicate the plague.

2. Frogs—After Moses brought swarms of frogs down upon the Egyptians, another plague which the Egyptian magicians could duplicate, Pharaoh promised Moses that if he took away the frogs he would release the Israelites, but he later broke his promise.

3. Gnats—With the third plague, the Egyptian magicians were unable to keep up, and told Pharaoh, "This is the finger of God." But Pharaoh continued to refuse to release the Israelites.

4. Flies—The swarms of flies did not affect the land of Goshen, where the Israelites dwelled. YHWH said, "Thus I will make a distinction between my people and your people." Once again Pharaoh broke a promise to release the Israelites long enough to sacrifice to YHWH.

5. Pestilence—When this plague brought disease upon all the livestock of the Egyptians, YHWH again showed his preference for Israel by sparing their flocks. Pharaoh was not moved.

6. Boils—The festering boils affected both animals and humans, even including the Egyptian magicians, but Pharaoh still refused to release the Israelites.

7. Hail and thunder—The hail and thunder that affected every region except the land of Goshen was so terrible that Pharaoh immediately summoned Moses and promised to release the Israelites, but he reneged on his promise as soon as the storms ceased.

8. Locusts—When Moses threatened the Egyptians with clouds of locusts that would devour their crops, Pharaoh agreed to let the men go, but he insisted the they leave the women and children behind. This was not acceptable to Moses, and he struck the Egyptians with the plague. Pharaoh beseeched Moses to end the plague with another promise that he failed to fulfill.

9. Darkness—After three days of darkness, Pharaoh agreed to let the Israelites go, as long as they left behind all of their livestock, but this was not acceptable to Moses.

10. Death of the firstborn—YHWH came and struck dead the firstborn of all the Egyptians and their livestock. The Israelites were told to sacrifice a lamb and mark their doors with the blood, so that YHWH would "pass over" their houses. After the plague, all the Egyptians, mourning their dead, urged the Israelites to go and gave them their valuables. Pharaoh told Moses and Israelites to go. The next day he would change his mind and pursue them.

One of the most curious features of the story about the confrontation between Moses and the Egyptian Pharaoh is the way YHWH "hardens Pharaoh's heart" thus delaying YHWH's victory and keeping the conflict going. The result of this hardening is to demonstrate YHWH's power more strikingly than would have been the case had Pharaoh been more reasonable. It becomes clear that YHWH has the power to overcome any resistance no matter how strong it is. At the same time, this feature of the story has raised many questions for later theologians, especially questions about what causes evil and whether humans truly have free will. The problematic character of this story is also reflected in later Jewish traditions: the Passover ritual (Seder), for example, includes the admonition, "Do not celebrate. Egyptians are dying." However, the authors and the original readers of these stories probably were not concerned with these questions and problems. They were just enjoying the story, watching YHWH play with an arrogant Pharaoh as a cat might play with a mouse.

B. Passover

The climax of YHWH's contest with Pharaoh is the tenth plague, the death of the firstborn. Before carrying out this plague, YHWH directed the Israelites to sacrifice a lamb and mark their doorways with the lamb's blood. When the angel came to kill the firstborn and saw the blood-marked doorways, the angel "passed over" those houses without causing any harm. The annual feast which later commemorated this event took the name "**Passover**" from this "passing over." Historically, the Passover marked the beginning of the Israelites' exodus from Egypt and their journey to the promised land.

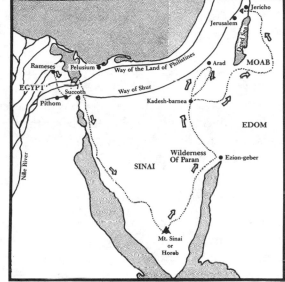

Figure 3.3: Map indicating the traditional route of the Exodus.

C. Passage through the Red Sea

Once they had escaped from Egypt, the Israelites found themselves in a new crisis. Pharaoh had changed his mind again and was pursuing them with his whole army and they were trapped on the shore of the Red Sea. But YHWH directed Moses to hold up his staff over the waters of the sea, and when he did, YHWH parted the waters so that the Israelites could pass through on dry land. When the Egyptians tried to follow, YHWH let the waters flow back and thus drowned their army.

What kind of miracle had the Israelites witnessed? There are two accounts of this event: a prose account in Exodus 14 and a poetic one in Exodus 15. Exodus 14:21 suggests a physical mechanism which YHWH used to divide the waters—a strong east wind that blew all night. The next verse gives an epic heightening of the same event that sounds more directly and flamboyantly miraculous: "the water like a wall to their left and their right" (Exod 14:22). Many scholars suggest that verse 21 is historically more likely, because they can point to another historical occasion when one of the shallow bodies of water in the Northern Sinai was divided by a strong wind, allowing an endangered group to escape. Still, it is likely that those who found themselves in this critical situation would have considered it a miracle that this event happened just when they needed it. They would *not* have considered it to be "just a coincidence," even if someone told them that it happened once before only a century earlier.

The poetic description of the passage through the Red Sea in chapter 15, especially the short form in verse 21, is considered by biblical scholars to be one of the oldest traditions preserved in the Bible:

> *The prophetess Miriam, Aaron's sister, took a tambourine in her hand, while all the women went out after her with tambourines, dancing, and she led them in the refrain: "Sing to the Lord, for he is gloriously triumphant; horse and chariot he has cast into the sea"* (Exod 15:20-21).

D. Wandering in the Desert

Once in the desert the Israelites faced new problems. They had no experience living in such a desolate area. They responded to these challenges by *grumbling*, blaming YHWH and Moses for their problems. YHWH responded by meeting their needs, but showed displeasure at their grumbling and allowed them to suffer for their lack of faith. They grumbled that there was no food: YHWH gave them "manna." They grumbled that they wanted meat: YHWH gave them quail. They grumbled that there was no water: YHWH gave them water from a rock. At one point, after Moses was absent for a prolonged period, they despaired and turned to the worship of false gods. Finally, they grumbled that the inhabitants of Canaan were too strong for them to enter the promised land. As punishment, YHWH sent them back into the desert to wander for another forty years until all those who had failed to trust his power died. YHWH would lead their descendants into the promised land, but not those who had refused to believe in YHWH's power.

It was during the period in the desert that YHWH revealed to the Israelites how they should live and how they should relate to YHWH. YHWH formed a new *covenant* with the Israelites through Moses at Mount Sinai.

E. Covenant at Sinai

YHWH's covenant with *Abraham*, expressed several different ways in different stories of Genesis, took a fairly simple form. However, YHWH's covenant with the Israelites through *Moses* is described in a more complex form, influenced by political covenants of the Ancient Near East. The covenant form began with a description of what the "Lord" (God or a political "superpower") had done for the person or community with whom the covenant was being made, then described the *response* to be expected, and finally listed the "blessings and curses" one might expect from God or the gods if the "oath" which sealed the covenant was kept or broken.

In historical terms, this combination of benefit freely given followed by expected response was characteristic of political covenants among Israel's neighbors. Some good examples are the Hittite covenants which began with the benefits the Great King had made for a neighboring people (or for their prince, who may in fact have been a puppet king who had been placed on the throne by the Great King) and then outlined the treaty obligations between this vassal state and the Hittite overlord. Secular political covenants involved quite a bit of self-interest on the part of the Great King. The "response" generally involved coming to the king's defense in time of need, sending in tribute money, and informing the king of any rebellions being planned.

In contrast to the secular political covenants of the time, YHWH did not get selfish advantage from this covenant with Israel. In this covenant YHWH reminded the Israelite people that he had rescued them from slavery in Egypt and had led them through the desert to freedom. YHWH asked them, for their part and as a response to this gift, to "keep the Ten Commandments."

Exodus 20 provides us with one of two descriptions of the Ten Commandments in the Bible. The other is located in Deuteronomy 5:6-21. Like the political covenants among Israel's neighbors, Exodus 20 begins with a description of what YHWH has done for the Israelite people (20:1-2). It is followed by a description of how the Israelites should respond to YHWH (20:3-20). As they are listed in Exodus 20, the commandments are not numbered. In fact, it is not even clear that there are ten. Protestant Christian traditions tend to number them differently than Catholic Christian traditions do. Both include all the verses and add up to ten, but they organize them differently within those ten numbers. Below is the traditionally Protestant enumeration of the Ten Commandments. Catholics would combine the first and second commandments on this list and divide the tenth into two separate commandments.

The Ten Commandments

1. I am the Lord your God, who brought you out of the land of Egypt, out of the house of slavery; you shall have no other gods before me.
2. You shall not make for yourself an idol, whether in the form of anything that is in heaven above, or that is on the earth beneath, or that is in the water under the earth.
3. You shall not make wrongful use of the name of the Lord your God.
4. Remember the sabbath day, and keep it holy.
5. Honor your mother and father.
6. You shall not murder.
7. You shall not commit adultery.
8. You shall not steal.
9. You shall not bear false witness against your neighbor.
10. You shall not covet your neighbor's house; you shall not covet your neighbor's wife, or male or female slave, or ox, or donkey, or anything that belongs to your neighbor.

Ancient Israelites and modern religious Jews do not consider the "Ten Commandments" to be arbitrary rules handed down by YHWH. Rather, the commandments are the desire of the God who has chosen, rescued, and blessed the community. The people of the covenant keep the laws not primarily to avoid God's anger, but rather to show gratitude for what God has done for them. The Law is not a burden but a gift from God. God has initiated a special relationship with their community: their faithfulness to the Law of Moses is their grateful response.

Unfortunately, the Israelites did not always keep the Law or obey YHWH's commandments, and the results were that they were punished by God and oppressed by their enemies. Indeed, the entire history of the Israelite people can be seen as a series of blessings and curses brought on by their success or failure in upholding the terms of their covenant with YHWH.

F. Ritual Enactment of the Covenant

Covenants were often sealed or renewed with a **sacrifice.** Animal and vegetable sacrifice was widespread among ancient people. Sacrifice was considered to be a gift given to God or other spiritual beings. The primitive sense is that valuable things can be transferred over from this world to the spirit world in a variety of ways. Fire seemed a divine medium for such exchange, since it is capable of turning solid, material things into spiritual substance. For example, in Judges 13:20, an angel "ascended in the flame of the altar." The death of an animal is another way to transfer value into the spiritual world since the soul, considered to be the most valuable part of the animal, can be freed from matter by death.

Worshipers transfer gifts to the spiritual world in order to develop and maintain a relationship with God and spiritual beings. While to some, such a sacrifice or gift may take on the appearance of bribery, at its best this giving is an attempt to build and maintain a relationship of caring and trust. People show their good dispositions to God by offering things of value in the confidence that God, who is good by nature and is now well disposed to them, will meet their needs. They might also offer sacrifice in order to show their appreciation for God's free gifts to them by giving God gifts in return.

If one is to create or confirm such a relationship, one must not be cheap or deceitful in one's gifts. The offerings must be "spotless," of good quality, such as one might offer to people of influence in human affairs. "First things" are especially valuable (firstborn animals, the first armful of harvested grain) because the "first" symbolizes and stands for the whole. When one offers the "first things," one is symbolically offering everything to God. An extreme example of the importance of offering something of value is Abraham's near-sacrifice of Isaac in Genesis 22. Although YHWH is the one who commanded this sacrifice, Abraham's compliance with the command showed his willingness to risk everything for God, since if this sacrifice were carried out everything Abraham had been living for would be destroyed. Fortunately, once Abraham showed YHWH that he was willing to carry it out, YHWH proposed an alternative sacrifice.

Exodus 24 describes the ritual sealing of the Mosaic covenant. Animals were sacrificed and their blood collected. Half of the blood was thrown on the altar. Then the Law was read and the people answered "All that YHWH has said, we will heed and do." Finally the other half of the blood was sprinkled on the people while Moses said:

> *This is the* blood of the covenant *which YHWH has made with you in accordance with all these words of his* (Exod 24:8).

The New Testament refers back to this covenant and its ritual enactment when it describes Jesus at the Last Supper—a meal closely connected with the Jewish Passover—taking bread and wine, sharing them with the disciples, and saying

> *This is my body, which will be given for you; do this in memory of me. This cup is the* new covenant in my blood, *which will be shed for you* (Luke 22:19-20).

Christians believe that Jesus, in his sacrifice on the cross, offered his life on behalf of humans. He asked humans to offer their lives to God in the act of faith by which they are justified.

Key Terms:

Abraham	Joseph
patriarch	Moses
Ishmael	Exodus
Isaac	sacrifice
Jacob	covenant
Israel	

Questions for Reading:

1. Identify and describe or explain YHWH's promises to Abraham.
2. What does it mean for individuals or tribes to "genealogize" new family or tribal members?
3. What is a "covenant"? Describe the covenant with Abraham and the covenant with Moses.

4. Describe the significance of the Ten Commandments, especially their relationship to the covenant with Moses.

5. Describe the contest between YHWH and the Egyptian gods represented by the plagues. What role was played by Moses and Aaron, the Egyptian magicians, and Pharaoh?

6. Why did ancient peoples offer sacrifices to the gods? Why are sacrifices killed or burned up?

Works Consulted/Recommended Reading:

Alt, A. "The God of the Fathers." In *Essays on Old Testament History and Religion*, pp: 1-100. Garden City: Doubleday, 1967.

Childs, B. *The Book of Exodus*. Philadelphia: Westminster Press, 1974.

Metzger, Bruce and Murphy, Roland, eds. *The New Oxford Annotated Bible with Apocrypha*, New Revised Standard Version. New York: Oxford University Press, 1991

Teubal, S. *Hagar and the Egyptian: The Lost Tradition of Matriarchs*. San Francisco: Harper & Row, 1990.

Thompson, T. L. *The Historicity of the Patriarchal Narratives*. Berlin, New York: de Gruyter, 1974.

van Seters, J. *Abraham in History and Tradition*. New Haven: Yale University Press, 1975.

Westermann, C. *The Promises to the Fathers: Studies on the Patriarchal Narratives*. Trans. D. E. Green. Philadelphia: Fortress Press, 1980.

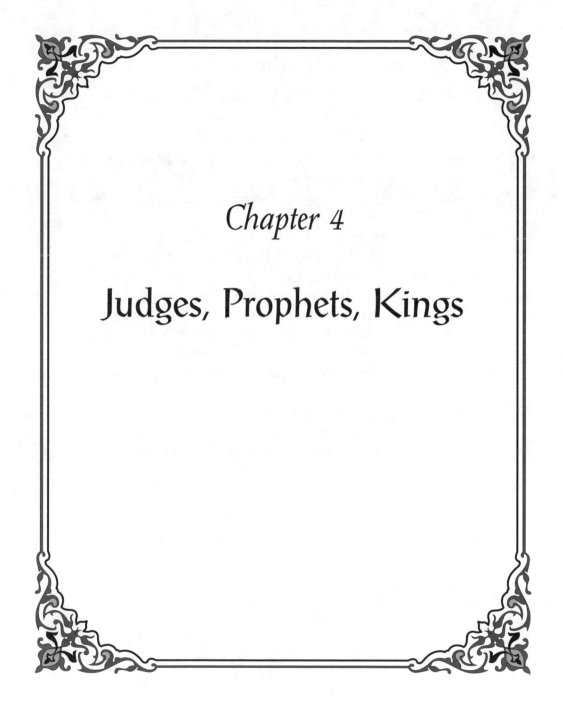

Chapter 4

Judges, Prophets, Kings

Timeline

c. 1250-1020 BCE	Joshua and the Israelites enter Canaan. The period of the Judges.
c. 1020-1000	Saul reigns as king of the Israelite people.
c. 1000-961	David is king of Israel and establishes Jerusalem as its capital.
c. 961-922	Solomon reigns as king of united Israel and builds the Temple in Jerusalem.
922	Solomon's kingdom is divided in two: the northern kingdom (Israel) and the southern kingdom (Judah).
c. 750-745	The prophets Amos and Hosea preach in the northern kingdom of Israel. Assyria becomes a world power.
c. 742-700	The prophet Isaiah preaches in the southern kingdom of Judah.
721	The northern kingdom of Israel is defeated by the Assyrians.
626-587	The prophet Jeremiah preaches in the southern kingdom of Judah. Babylon becomes a world power.
597	Judah is defeated by Babylon. The Babylonian Exile begins.
597-573	The prophet Ezekiel preaches in exile in Babylon.
587	The Jerusalem Temple is destroyed.
c. 540	The prophet known as Second Isaiah preaches during the exile.
c. 540	Persia becomes a world power.
538	King Cyrus of Persia issues a decree allowing the people of Judah to return to their homes.
458-420	Ezra and Nehemiah begin a religious reform of Judaism. The Temple in Jerusalem is rebuilt.

Judges, Prophets, Kings

The Pentateuch ends with an account of the death of Moses and the elevation of **Joshua** to be his successor. The story of Israel's covenant relationship with YHWH does not end here, however, for many of the promises that God made to Abraham and Moses have not yet been fulfilled: the promise of possession of the land of Canaan and of Israel becoming a "great nation."

This chapter covers the period from the beginnings of the rise of the nation of Israel following the Exodus (13th century BCE) to its fall as a nation (6th century BCE) when it was conquered by the Babylonians and the people were exiled in Babylon. During this time we note the establishment of the monarchy, the rise of the institution of prophecy, and the establishment of the centralized temple in Jerusalem. The books which record the history of this period are classified as the books of the Prophets, and are distinguished from the books of the Law (also called the Pentateuch or the Torah). Further, the books of the Prophets are divided into the **Former Prophets**, which are historical narratives, and the **Latter Prophets**, which are books that bear the names of actual Israelite prophets and contain their prophecies.

LAW (TORAH)	PROPHETS (NEVI'IM)
Genesis	Former Prophets:
Exodus	Joshua
Leviticus	Judges
Numbers	I-II Samuel
Deuteronomy	I-II Kings
	Latter Prophets:
	Isaiah
	Jeremiah
	Ezekiel
	The Twelve (Hosea, Joel, Amos, Jonah, Micah, Nahum, Habakkuk, Zephaniah, Haggai, Zechariah, Malachi)

The books of the Former Prophets are all part of a single, complex, collected work known as the **Deuteronomistic History**, so named because the author(s) were followers of the Deuteronomists, the ones who wrote the book of Deuteronomy in the Law. These books were actually written centuries later than most of the historical period they cover. Although the Deuteronomistic Historian (collector and editor of the Deuteronomistic material) provides a great deal of accurate historical information, getting his information from various oral and written stories from Israel's early tribal period and from the period of the kings, the main concern of the author was to provide a *theological* interpretation of Israel's history.

At the time the author was writing, Jerusalem had just been conquered and the Temple destroyed by the Babylonians (597-587 BCE). In many ways these experiences were too painful for the Israelites to comprehend. They created doubt in the minds of some Israelites as to whether the covenant was working, and whether YHWH was indeed faithful to the covenant. The Deuteronomistic Historian re-told the history of Israel from the beginning to show that the problem with the covenant was not with YHWH but with Israel. The books continually show how Israel's fortunes were directly correlated to her obedience to the covenant. When the Israelites followed the covenant and kept God's commandments, God was with them and they prospered. When the Israelites abandoned the covenant, breaking the commandments and worshiping other gods, YHWH withheld his protection from them and they were conquered and oppressed by their enemies.

The books of the Deuteronomistic Historian provided a way for Israel to try to make sense out of their experience of loss and abandonment by assuring the readers that God had always remained faithful to his covenant. The author sought to explain that even though life for the Israelite people would never again be the same, the Israelite God still cared for them and would restore Israel to their land. Thus the Deuteronomistic Historian, along with the prophets, crafted a distinctive understanding of God, a god who remained faithful to the covenant, sometimes to punish those who broke the covenant, but ultimately to reward those who faithfully followed its precepts, particularly by worshiping only YHWH, and not any of the other gods.

I. Judges: Conquest and Settlement

After the death of Moses, Joshua led the Israelites into the land of Canaan (late 13th century BCE). With the help of YHWH, the Israelites were able to conquer the people who occupied this land (although they did not gain complete and total control of the entire region), and the Israelites settled in the land of Canaan. A major factor in the Israelite victories was the **Ark of the Covenant.** The ark was Israel's most sacred object. On the one hand, the ark served as a *container* for various objects that were sacred to the Israelites, such as the two tablets of the law given to Moses. On the other hand, the ark was viewed as a *throne*, on which YHWH sat invisibly overlooking the people of Israel. The most important feature of the ark was that it was a direct manifestation of God's presence. Wherever the ark went, so went YHWH, and so went YHWH's power. For this reason the Israelites sometimes carried the ark into battle in the period of the conquest of Canaan, and the presence of Yahweh then ensured an Israelite victory. Eventually the ark was housed at the national shrine located at Shiloh, before it was moved some centuries later to its final resting place in the Jerusalem Temple.

After the conquest of Canaan, the nation of Israel was established. However, Israel had no single leader or any centralized government. Rather, Israel was a **tribal confederacy**. The twelve tribes of Israel separated themselves and each settled in a different portion of the land. Each tribe governed itself, ruled by elders. The tribes were united only in some matters of religion and in times of war. At times of national crisis, when the tribes had to act together, a different (but temporary) kind of leader emerged, the **judge** (*shofet* in Hebrew).

The judges were *charismatic* leaders. This meant that they were chosen by God and endowed with certain gifts that enabled them to lead. One could not "decide" to become a judge (or *shofet*), nor could one be "elected" as a judge. The main purpose of the judges was not to oversee legal disputes. They were primarily political and military leaders, who also had some religious functions.

According to the book of Judges, a certain pattern established itself in Israelite history. The pattern began with the Israelites failing to observe the terms of the covenant, worshiping other gods and behaving immorally. YHWH would become angry and withhold his protection from the Israelites, causing them to be afflicted and oppressed by their enemies. The Israelites would then repent of their sins and cry out to God for deliverance. God would heed their call by sending a judge, who would unite the people, call them to a renewed awareness of their covenant relationship with God, and lead them to military victories over their enemies. Once the judge died, however, the Israelites would fall back into a life of sin.

As the book of Judges progresses, the quality of the judges gradually declines, so that by the end of the book the Israelite society begins to deteriorate. The editor concludes: "In those days there was no king in Israel; all the people did what was right in their own eyes" (Judges 21:25). The Israelite tribal system had degenerated into anarchy.

II. Kings: The Demand for a Monarchy

In addition to this internal decline of tribal Israel, an external threat also presented the small nation with its most serious crisis. The **Philistines**, a people who lived on the coast of the Mediterranean sea near Israel, developed weapons made of iron, and their iron monopoly enabled them to defeat tribal Israel profoundly. This defeat led the Israelites to demand a king from the prophet and last of the judges, Samuel. Directed by YHWH, Samuel appointed **Saul**, a young man from the Israelite tribe of Benjamin. Saul began to assert his authority over the country, and reigned from approximately 1020-1000 BCE. However, Saul eventually proved unworthy to be king, and he lost the favor of YHWH. Acting as the agent of YHWH, Samuel opposed him, and vowed to find a new candidate for the monarchy.

A. Saul and David

Again under the guidance of YHWH, Samuel immediately found a new candidate for kingship and secretly anointed **David**, a young man from the tribe of Judah, to be king of Israel. Subsequently, David attached himself to Saul's royal court, distinguishing himself by defeating the Philistine champion Goliath, and leading the Israelite army to one of its few victories against their enemies. Saul became jealous of David, and sought to kill him. David was forced to flee.

After a period of instability caused by the conflict between Saul and David, and the steady decline of Saul's ability to rule effectively, the Philistines defeated Saul, and killed the king and most of his sons. David was quickly made king in the power vacuum that was left by Saul's death, and David reigned as king beginning in approximately 1000 BCE, until his death in 961.

David's first recorded royal act was to establish his new capital in **Jerusalem**, which had previously been unconquered by the Israelites. It became known as "the city of David." He moved the Ark of the Covenant to Jerusalem, and established his own control over the religious apparatus of Israel. From this point on, from the perspective of the Deuteronomistic Historian, most religiously important events took place in Jerusalem. Although people continued to practice religion in their own towns and villages, the Deuteronomistic Historian regarded such activity as suspect and even disloyal to YHWH. The reason for this was probably that the religious practice in rural areas tended to blend aspects of other religions and the worship of other gods into authentic YHWH worship, while the Deuteronomistic Historian believed that a "pure" form of YHWH worship was maintained in Jerusalem.

The Deuteronomistic Historian describes the period of David's rule as a sort of "golden age" of Israelite power, a time of unique divine approval and divine blessing. David's prophet, **Nathan**, declared that David would establish a dynasty which would never end. Speaking for YHWH, Nathan said, "Your house and your kingdom shall be made sure forever before me; your throne shall be established forever" (2 Samuel 7:16). There were many signs of God's approval of David, especially in the military arena. David's forces became dominant in the region. He expanded the outer borders of Israel in every direction (see 2 Samuel 8-10 for accounts of some of David's military victories).

David's personal fortunes declined in the latter half of his reign. He committed adultery with Bathsheba, the wife of one of his military commanders, named Uriah. She became pregnant, and after trying to cover up his deed with deception, the king had her husband Uriah murdered, so he could marry her (2 Samuel 11). God was displeased at this immoral behavior, and pronounced a severe punishment on David through the prophet Nathan (2 Samuel 12). This punishment included the death of the child he conceived with Bathsheba, a curse of continual warfare, and the creation of trouble within David's own house, that is, trouble with his children. One of his sons, Amnon, raped his half sister, Tamar, and was in turn killed by her full brother Absalom (2 Samuel 13). Absalom then organized a full-scale rebellion against his father, the king. During David's attempt to retake the throne, Absalom, his son, was killed. David, his authority regained, could not recover from the grief he felt at the loss of his son. "O my son Absalom, my son, my son Absalom! Would I had died instead of you, O Absalom, my son, my son!" (2 Samuel 18:33). In spite of all these difficulties, the king was still able to pass his kingdom on to his son **Solomon** relatively intact.

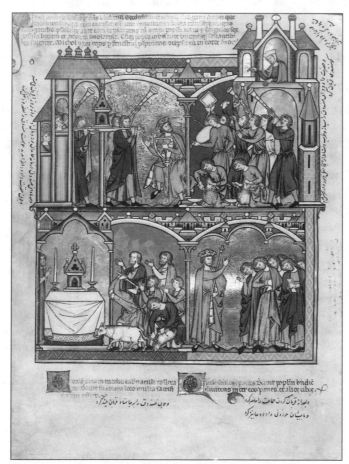

Figure 4.1: A 13th-century French miniature illustrating the festivities that took place when David brought the Ark of the Covenant to Jerusalem.

Many have noticed the troubling ambiguity of the portrayal of King David in I and II Samuel. On the one hand, he is portrayed as God's chosen servant, the king appointed by God. Many Israelites knew the story of YHWH's promise to David to always sustain his dynasty. Why then is the close of David's life so sordid? Certainly, there were anti-David factions within Israel who told unpleasant stories about him, and some of these were woven into the Deuteronomistic story. But why? Perhaps the biblical authors sought to teach their readers some moral lessons by recounting the failures of King David. For one thing, it was important for

Israelites to understand that even their kings were subject to the law of YHWH. In many cultures, the kings made the laws, and hence were considered above the law. In Israel, the laws did not come from the king, but from God. The story of David and Bathsheba reinforces the point that no one is above the law.

Another point that is made here is that the way in which David tries and fails to cover up his sins shows that it is impossible to hide things from God. God sees everything (God is all-knowing, or **omniscient**) and God will *punish* people for their sins. For Jews at this time, God's rewards and punishments were meted out in this life, not in the afterlife. The idea of life after death and eternal punishment or reward were concepts not yet known to the Israelites. This is why David is punished not by being sent to hell, but by having his son die and his other children rise up against him. Finally, the story of David's fall from grace also provides a warning to all Israelites about how one sin leads to another. David begins with a series of relatively minor indiscretions, but these lead him eventually to the serious sins of adultery and murder.

B. Solomon and the Division of the Kingdom

Solomon received the kingdom from his father David, and reigned from 961-922 BCE. Solomon was known for his great wisdom, his large harem (he is said to have had 700 wives and 300 concubines), and for his building projects. Most notably, Solomon built the **Temple** in Jerusalem, which became the center of Israelite religious life. Although he consolidated his father's power, Solomon's abuse of that power (excessive taxation, extensive use of slave labor, neglect of the concerns of the northern tribes) resulted in the division of the kingdom during the rule of his son Rehoboam. The Deuteronomistic Historian claimed that the division of the kingdom was God's punishment for Solomon's sins of idolatry, as Solomon was led in his old age by some of his foreign wives to worship their gods. The northern section of the kingdom split away and established its own government. From this point the northern kingdom is known as **Israel**, and the southern kingdom as **Judah** (from which we eventually get the term "Jew" and "Jewish").

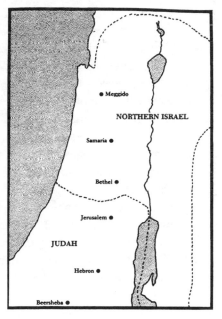

Figure 4.2: The divided kingdom, Judah and Israel, during the reign of Solomon's son, Rehoboam.

The Temple of Solomon in Jerusalem became the central focus of Israelite worship of YHWH, particularly in the south. Although northern shrines were built by the northern kings, the shrine in Jerusalem remained of vital importance for defining the character of the Israelite faith. A complex order of priests was organized to serve the needs of this massive and ornate construction, and the people from throughout the nation made pilgrimages to Jerusalem on important holidays to worship YHWH in the Temple. The Temple came to occupy an enormous place in the national religious consciousness, and it was a source of great pride and security to most Israelites. Many Judeans felt that as long as they had the Temple in Jerusalem and a son of David sitting on the throne, nothing really bad could ever happen to them.

The primary function of the Temple was to offer animal sacrifices to YHWH. People would bring their livestock offerings to the Temple to be slaughtered by the priests on specially designated altars. Depending upon the nature of the sacrifice, it would either be burned completely, shared with the priests, or eaten by the worshiper's family in a sacrificial meal. Although sacrifices continued in other locations, animal offerings in Solomon's Temple were more important, and ultimately for the Deuteronomistic Historian, the only valid sacrifices.

III. Prophets

Following David's establishment of a dynasty, the kingship in both Israel and Judah became a hereditary position, passed on from father to son. No longer were kings chosen by God, as Saul and David were. However, another kind of charismatic leader emerged in Israel following the establishment of the monarchy, a leader called and chosen by God specifically to express God's will and give God's view of the state of the covenant relationship with Israel. These leaders were called the **prophets**. There were prophets in Israel prior to the monarchy; Moses was certainly a prophet, indeed the greatest of the prophets, and Samuel and Nathan were prophets as well. However, the office of the prophets took on a renewed importance in the period of the monarchy. The prophets served as God's representatives in Israel, and their presence was increasingly necessary to provide a counterbalance to the absolute power of the king. For instance, when King David saw a woman who attracted him, what was there to stop him from taking her? What could she do? What could her husband do? After all, he was the king. In Israel, the prophets were there to challenge the power of the king.

The prophets usually had no delegated power within the royal courts of Israel and Judah, but spoke with a moral authority because their words were the very words of God. They were not primarily seers who foretold the future (although they did sometimes make such predictions). Prophets are more accurately understood as YHWH's spokespersons who addressed the events of their societies and acted as God's emissaries, sent to the people with a particular message for the present moment in history. Like the judges, prophets were *charismatic* leaders. One needed to be called by God and endowed with special gifts in order to be a prophet.

A crucial focus of the prophets' message was the state of Israel's covenant relationship with God, which determined Israel's political and economic fortunes. Knowing God's "state of mind" allowed the prophets to give advice on political matters, such as whether to go to war or not. If YHWH was looking with favor on Israel, then the prophets assured the Israelites that they could anticipate success. If Israel had violated the covenant, then the prophets foretold that a military defeat would be the result. The prophets also spoke out on social and ethical issues, condemning the social injustice of their own societies, even at great personal cost to themselves. It was the role of the prophets to speak up for the poor, the oppressed, and the powerless in Israelite society. Finally, the prophets also spoke of religious matters. The prophets became the primary proponents of monotheism to people who frequently were attracted to the polytheistic religious beliefs of their cultural neighbors.

The message of the prophets was often a negative, critical one, as they pronounced God's judgment on a sinful nation, group, or individual. Because of this, prophets were often in conflict with the other centers of power in Israel, particularly the power of the king. The political clout of the prophets led some kings to attempt to corrupt the office of prophet. These kings would appoint their own prophets whose job it was to create the illusion of divine approval for whatever policies the king was pursuing. Because of abuses such as these and the fact that some people were simply deluded into believing that God was speaking through them, a distinction must be made between true prophets and false prophets.

Although it was sometimes difficult for Israelites to tell the difference between true and false prophets until after the fact, there were some hallmarks of a true prophet. One sign of a true prophet was a willingness to stand up to the king. Of course the prophets did not *always* disagree with the king, but a prophet who never challenged the king might have been looked upon with suspicion. Some prophets (especially Elijah and Elisha) were said to have the ability to perform miracles, and this would have been a sure sign, as would the ability to predict the future correctly. Being on the king's payroll may have been taken by some as a bad sign for a prophet, although not all "court prophets" were false prophets.

A. The Assyrian Period (8th century BCE)

In the Old Testament period, major world powers always struggled for dominance of the region of the ancient Near East. Egypt and the two great Mesopotamian powers, Assyria and Babylon, all dominated the region at one time or another, and their power struggles usually involved the land of Israel. In the 8th century BCE, Assyria began to assert its dominance in the region. From their capital Nineveh on the banks of the Tigris river in what is modern-day Iraq, the Assyrians expanded their influence and began to threaten the smaller powers that lay between them and Egypt—nations that included Syria, Israel and Judah. In 721 BCE the northern kingdom of Israel was conquered by the Assyrians.

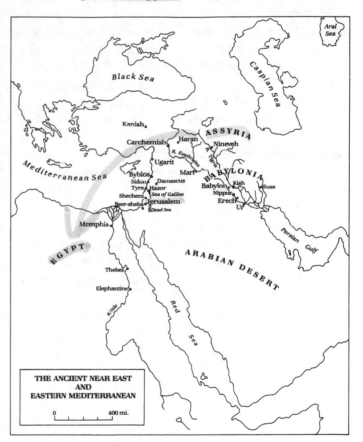

Figure 4.3: Map of the ancient Near East.

The period prior to the conquest was one of unprecedented prosperity for both the northern and southern kingdoms. However, this prosperity brought certain problems with it, and the prophets were quick to identify them. In this time, the cities of the two kingdoms began to take on increasing importance, at the expense of smaller towns and villages. High taxes were imposed on the rural poor to support the lifestyle of urban elites. Previously, under tribal Israel, the difference between the richest and poorest members of the community was relatively small. In the 8th century, however, large groups of nobility began to attach themselves to the royal family. These nobles were wealthy rulers and princes who gained and maintained their wealth through their abuse of the rights of the poor, especially rights to ancestral property and rights to redress in the legal system.

The earliest of the books of "Latter Prophets" was written at this time. The Latter Prophets are books that bear the names of the prophets of the 8th-5th centuries BCE. These books consist of various oracles (divine pronouncements) by these prophets and biographical stories about these prophets. Most of the prophets (but not all) stood in opposition to the royal administrations under which they lived. They frequently saw their warnings ignored and their admonitions unheeded. Sometimes the kings threw them in jail and threatened to execute them.

Two prophets emerged during the period of prosperity just before the Assyrian conquest and spoke particularly to the northern kingdom regarding the terrible moral illness that threatened to completely overwhelm the nation: the oppression of the poor by the rich. One might imagine how odd such a message would appear to Israel's ruling class—telling people who feel secure and complacent that they are in desperate danger. Of course these prophets were not taken seriously.

The first of the prophets, **Amos** (c. 750 BCE), was not a native of the northern kingdom, but rather came up from the south to prophesy in Bethel, the site of one of the royal chapels of the northern king, Jeroboam II. He was commanded by the priests of the temple in Bethel to go back where he came from, and prophesy to Judah (Amos 7). But Amos, in the tradition of Israelite prophecy, boldly condemned the social practices of the wealthy in the north, who luxuriated in their wealth and creature comforts, and mercilessly oppressed the poor (Amos 6). Amos threatened the north with horrible destruction because of their violation of covenant law. In fact, he regarded their mistreatment of the powerless no less a violation of YHWH's laws than if they had worshiped other gods.

The second prophet, **Hosea** (c. 745 BCE), was a northerner who spoke to his own people. He believed that YHWH had commanded him to marry a promiscuous wife, which he did (Hosea 1). His wife's unfaithfulness to him, and the children that she bore (which may or may not have been his), helped Hosea to portray how God felt at the people's religious unfaithfulness to him. As Gomer, Hosea's wife, treated Hosea, so Israel treated her husband YHWH. Hosea's broken heart paralleled YHWH's pain at Israel's abandonment of him for other gods. Hosea pled with Israel to return to YHWH. First using the image of a marriage relationship, and then the relationship of a parent to a child (Hosea 11), Hosea sought to remind Israel of their old memories in an effort to get them to change their ways.

Both prophets were unsuccessful in truly changing the nature of Israelite society, and in a short twenty-five years, the entire northern kingdom was destroyed by the Assyrians. From the prophetic point of view, this destruction was the judgment of YHWH upon a disobedient nation.

The southern kingdom of Judah, although not conquered, was utterly dominated both religiously and politically by Assyria for the next century. However, the Judean people, under the influence of the message of the prophet **Isaiah**, believed that Jerusalem was divinely protected from conquest because of the presence of the Solomonic temple and the Davidic dynasty—a descendant of David still ruled on the throne in Israel.

B. The Babylonian Period (7th-6th centuries BCE)

The final years of the 7th century saw the rise to power of the Neo-Babylonian Empire. At first the Babylonians struggled against the Assyrian empire which had been seriously weakened through internal dissension. Although the Egyptian monarch took his troops north to help the Assyrians, the combined efforts of Egypt and Assyria failed to slow the Babylonian juggernaut. Babylon defeated and destroyed Assyrian power, and the Pharaoh took his Egyptian army back home in disgrace. The failure of the Assyrians and Egyptians to stop the Babylonians left Judah wide open for conquest.

Jeremiah served as prophet in Jerusalem during this time. As the Babylonians advanced upon them, the people felt nervous, and flocked to the Temple, chanting over and over, "The Temple of YHWH. The Temple of YHWH. The Temple of YHWH" (Jeremiah 7:4). They believed that the presence of the Temple in Jerusalem made them invulnerable to Babylonian attack. Jeremiah threatened them with destruction, telling them that their invocation of the Temple would offer them no help but rather constituted "deceptive words" (Jeremiah 7, 26). Jeremiah admonished the people to depend less on their possession of a Davidic monarch and Solomonic temple and more on their own adherence to the sacred covenant with YHWH, a covenant that enjoined them to worship YHWH exclusively and to treat their fellow Israelites with justice. Jeremiah counseled the king to surrender to the Babylonian emperor Nebuchadnezzar, but instead King Zedekiah tried to flee with his family. The Babylonians apprehended him, murdered his sons in his sight and then poked out his eyes (2 Kings 25), so that the last sight he saw was that of his dead children. Finally, they destroyed Jerusalem and the Temple, and carried the king and most of the citizens in chains to Babylon.

C. The Exile (6th century BCE)

The destruction of the Temple and the deportation of many citizens to Babylon (an event known as the **Babylonian Exile**, or simply the Exile) was an unparalleled disaster for the Jewish people. The Exile took its place alongside the Exodus from Egypt as the defining moments in Israel's history, the events which loomed largest in the national consciousness. The Exile is such a watershed moment that historians and theologians often refer to events and people in Israel's history as being "pre-exilic" or "post-exilic." The Exile came to be understood (through the writings of the prophets and the Deuteronomistic Historian) as the ultimate punishment from God for Israel's failure to uphold the covenant. However, the Exile also represented hope to future generations of Jews, because Israel renewed its commitment to God and was eventually forgiven and allowed to return to the land. The covenant had not been broken.

The period in which the Judeans were in captivity in Babylon was the first time that they were compelled to maintain their identity while separated from the land. The northern kingdom, taken captive by the Assyrians, had not maintained its identity and ceased to exist as a separate entity. As far as we know, the exiled northern kingdom population turned away from the worship of YHWH and blended in with the religion and culture of their captors.

The Judeans fared better. The prophets taken into captivity with the other citizens of Judah, most notably **Ezekiel**, told the people that God had not failed them when they were defeated by the Babylonians. Rather, YHWH was using the Babylonians to punish them because of their unfaithfulness to the covenant. They remained in Babylon, hopeful that their renewed dedication to the exclusive worship of YHWH and loyalty to the covenant would persuade YHWH to return them to the land of promise. **Second Isaiah** (not the actual prophet Isaiah, but a later author of Isaiah 40-55), speaking to the Babylonian exiles, encouraged them that YHWH was no longer angry with them and would soon bring them back to Israel in a saving event as miraculous as the Exodus. It was during this period that the Israelites began to place more emphasis on codifying the Law of Moses in written form, rather than relying on oral traditions.

D. The Persian Period (6th-5th centuries BCE)

The Babylonian empire was short-lived, crumbling in the late 6th century BCE. The Persians (based in what is modern-day Iran) moved in to pick up the pieces. The Persian emperor Cyrus encouraged the various conquered peoples to return to the land of their birth and restore worship of their local gods. The biblical writers attribute Cyrus' edicts to the Spirit of Yahweh, and Second Isaiah actually calls Cyrus "messiah." Perhaps Cyrus felt that getting on the good side of all the local gods would ensure the length and stability of his own reign. In any case, the Judeans who were taken captive by Babylon were given permission to return to Palestine.

Most Judeans, who had been living in Babylonian colonies for upwards of forty years, saw no reason to return. However, a small group of Judean exiles did return, many under the leadership of Ezra and Nehemiah. The returning exiles tried to establish a new society, but could only maintain a small area around the rebuilt Jerusalem. The account of this rebuilding effort is found primarily in the biblical books of Ezra and Nehemiah. The returnees rebuilt the walls of the city, and after a while rebuilt the Temple. They were especially concerned with freeing the community of foreign elements and establishing religious practice in stricter conformity to their understanding of the covenant, which was laid out in the written scriptures that they brought back with them from Babylon.

Although those who returned from the Exile tried to restablish the close connection between the land of Israel and the religion practiced by its inhabitants, there were now so many Israelites settled in various places around the eastern Mediterranean that the *nation* and the *religion* could no longer be completely identified. New religious institutions, interpretations of tradition, and scriptures were developed in order to meet the needs of the new situation. These new religious phenomena combined with ancient traditions produced a new era in the Israelite faith, called Second Temple Judaism (so called because of the importance of the new, "second" Temple in its functioning). Although the Jews never returned to the splendor and autonomy they enjoyed during the monarchic period, the institutions (Temple, prophecy, monarchy) that had developed during this period were of crucial importance in the subsequent history of Judaism.

Key Terms:

Former Prophets	Jerusalem
Latter Prophets	prophet
Deuteronomistic Historian	Hosea
Assyria	Amos
Babylon	Jeremiah
Persia	Ezekiel
Ark of the Covenant	Isaiah
judge/*shofet*	Second Isaiah
Samuel	Ezra
Saul	Nehemiah
David	Exile
Solomon	

Questions for Reading:

1. Describe the Deuteronomistic Historian. Why did he write? When?

2. Describe leadership in tribal Israel. What was the role of the judge/*shofet*?

3. How did the Philistines affect the Israelite tribal system?

4. Describe the development of the monarchy in Israel, including an account of the reigns of Saul, David and Solomon.

5. What is the nature of the relationship between prophet and king?

6. Describe the message of the prophets Amos and Hosea. What were the social conditions in Israel during their time of ministry?

7. Describe the message of the prophet Jeremiah. What was the historical situation of Israel at the time he proclaimed God's word? Why did Jeremiah attack the Israelites' faith in the Temple?

8. How did the Exile affect the Israelites' faith? How did the return from the Exile affect the Israelites' faith?

Works Consulted/Recommended Reading:

Brown, Raymond E., Fitzmyer, Joseph A., and Murphy, Roland E., eds. *The New Jerome Biblical Commentary*. Englewood Cliffs, NJ: Prentice Hall, 1990.

McCarter, P. K. *1 Samuel*. New York: Doubleday, 1984.

McKenzie, Steven L. "Deuteronomic History." In *The Anchor Bible Dictionary*, Vol.2. New York: Doubleday, 1992.

Metzger, Bruce and Murphy, Roland, eds. *The New Oxford Annotated Bible with Apocrypha*, New Revised Standard Version. New York: Oxford University Press, 1991.

Polzin, R. *Moses and the Deuteronomist*. San Francisco: Harper & Row, 1980.

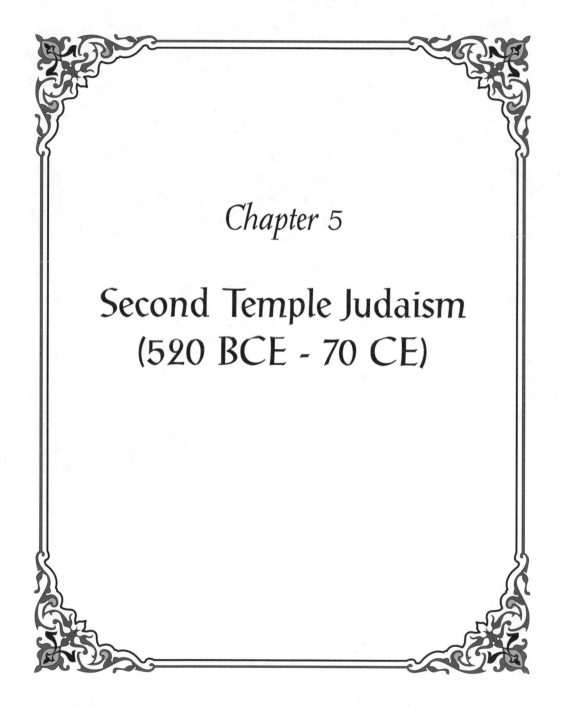

Chapter 5

Second Temple Judaism
(520 BCE - 70 CE)

Timeline

332 BCE	Alexander the Great conquers the Near East and begins the process of Hellenization.
168	The Maccabeans revolt against the Greek king Antiochus IV.
166	Palestine has its own independent monarchy.
c. 145	Beginnings of the Qumran community (?).
63	The Romans conquer Palestine.

Second Temple Judaism (520 BCE- 70 CE)

After the Persians under Cyrus defeated the Babylonians, the Jews who were exiled to Babylon were allowed to return to Palestine (as the biblical land of "Israel" would come to be called). Some Jews remained in Babylon, however, and a distinction is made then between Jews who lived in Palestine and Jews who lived outside of Palestine in the **Diaspora** (the word means "dispersion" and it refers to those Jews who were "dispersed" through historical circumstances outside the traditional Jewish homeland). The religion of these Palestinian Jews and Diaspora Jews developed in somewhat different ways. Diaspora Judaism centered more on the Torah and the **synagogue** than on the Temple and its sacrifices. Since these Jews now lived outside of Palestine, fewer and fewer of them spoke the traditional language of Hebrew. More and more of them spoke Greek, which became the universal language for most of the Mediterranean world after the conquests of Alexander the Great and the establishment of the Greek empire in the 4th century BCE. The importance of reading the Jewish Scriptures in the synagogue eventually led those outside of Palestine to translate the Scriptures from Hebrew into Greek. This translation is called the **Septuagint**.

I. Major Elements of Jewish Faith in the Second Temple Period

Those Jews who did return from exile in Babylon to Palestine shortly set about rebuilding the Temple in Jerusalem, which had been destroyed in 587 BCE by the Babylonians. This version of the Temple is distinguished from Solomon's Temple and is called the **Second Temple**. Although Judaism in Palestine after the Exile continued to be practiced in many ways that are similar to the pre-exilic period, there are distinctive elements as well, and so the Judaism of this period is referred to as "Second Temple Judaism." Temple sacrifice continued to be a major element of this religion, but in the Second Temple period obedience to the written Law (or Torah) takes on increased importance, and one begins to see traces of Jewish belief in a figure called the "**messiah**." We will begin this chapter with a closer look at the Temple, the Torah, and the messiah.

A. Temple

The major way of relating to God in the Jewish religion was through sacrifice. In fact, sacrifice was an important part of almost every ancient religion. Some of these religions offered sacrifices of animals and grain because they felt that they needed to "feed" their hungry gods. It was considered the priest's job to provide this service to the gods to appease them and prevent disaster from befalling the people. However, there is little evidence that the Jews understood their sacrifice as food for Yahweh.

The Hebrew Bible gives several reasons for sacrifice—gift (in petition or thanksgiving), purification (to remove the stain of some sin that had been committed), and fellowship (not all of the animal was sacrificed, and the portion that remained was eaten in a sort of communal meal with God). Thus farmers or shepherds would give a portion of their crops and livestock back to God in recognition of the fact that God had given them all that they had. A person who desired some favor from God could also offer a sacrifice. Finally, people who had sinned against God or their neighbor could "atone" for their sin through a sacrifice.

The sacrifices that were done by Jews involved grain, incense, and animals. These sacrifices were sometimes burned on an altar. In the case of animal sacrifices, more often the animal would be killed and the blood would be poured out on the foot of the altar. This was particularly the case in sacrifices offered to atone for sins, since the blood was thought to "wash away" the defilement caused by the sin.

There were many elaborate rules for how sacrifices were to be done. These can be reduced to four essential requirements. First, sacrifices could not be done by just anybody. Sacrifices had to be done by the right people, namely the **priests**. The Jews believed that God had set aside a portion of the people of Israel to specialize in making proper sacrifices. Thus the primary responsibility of the priesthood in Judaism did not involve conducting weekly worship services, but making sacrifices. The priesthood in Judaism was hereditary, traced through the male line. One could not "choose" to become a priest; one could only be born into the priesthood. There was one priest who exercised leadership over the other priests and was, in fact, the religious leader of the Israelite nation as a whole: the high priest.

Second, sacrifices had to be done at the right time. Although it was true that sacrifices went on almost continually in the Temple, certain times and seasons required sacrifices. For example, special sacrifices were always offered on the Sabbath, since this was a day set aside for God. In addition, there were three "pilgrimage" festivals, three times during the year in which Jewish men were supposed to journey to Jerusalem to make sacrifices. One of these festivals was **Passover**, which commemorated God's rescue of the Israelites from slavery in Egypt, when the angel of death "passed over" the homes of the Israelites which had been marked with lamb's blood and killed the first-born sons of the Egyptians. At Passover (which corresponded to the spring barley harvest) the people of Israel would sacrifice a lamb in commemoration of this event. Other pilgrimage festivals corresponded with the spring wheat harvest (Pentecost) and the autumn olive and fruit harvest (Booths). Another day set aside for sacrifice, but not requiring the attendance of all male Jews, was the Day of Atonement or **Yom Kippur**, the one day each year on which the high priest would offer a sacrifice for the sins of the nation as a whole.

Third, sacrifices had to be done with the correct offering. There were certain animals that one could sacrifice (bulls, lambs, pigeons, turtledoves—animals that were considered "clean") and other animals that one could not sacrifice (pigs, snakes—animals that were considered "unclean"). A general rule as well was that the *firstborn* belonged to God, so that one could not sacrifice just any bull or lamb, but only the firstborn and only an unblemished animal.

Finally, sacrifices had to be done at the right place. In Israel's early history, there were a number of altars and shrines at which sacrifices were done. After the building of the Temple in Jerusalem during the reign of Solomon, however, a king named Josiah eventually centralized all sacrifice in this one location. After Solomon's Temple was destroyed, the Jews set about the long, gradual process of re-building the Temple. At first the Second Temple was a modest building, not approaching the magnificent structure erected by Solomon. However, in the 1st century BCE a Jewish king named Herod the Great began a major renovation of the Temple, which (when completed around 66 CE) re-established the Temple in Jerusalem as one of the greatest structures in the ancient world.

The site of the Temple was considered the most sacred ground in the world to Jews. It was here that the divine realm and the human realm intersected. The innermost part of the Temple contained the **Holy of Holies**, where the Ark of the Covenant had been kept and God's presence dwelled. No

Figure 5.1: Model of the Jerusalem Temple (after the renovations of Herod the Great). The model is located at the Holyland Motel in Jerusalem.

one ever entered the Holy of Holies except once each year, when the high priest would enter to offer a sacrifice on the Day of Atonement. On the outside of the Temple was a court where Israel could assemble. The space between the outer court and the Holy of Holies housed the altar where all other sacrifices were conducted. This was a place of intersection between God and Israel where the priests gave God his animal sacrifices, grain, and incense.

B. Torah

When Israel was exiled to Babylon and the Temple was destroyed (587 BCE), the Jewish leaders struggled to explain to themselves why YHWH had allowed these terrible disasters to occur. Their explanation, given to them by God through the prophets, was that they had sinned gravely and thus violated the terms of the covenant. Israel had always believed that God made certain ethical and ritual demands on them as part of the covenant, and the reason for the Exile was their failure to live up to those demands. The answer to the problems of the Jewish people, then, was obvious: a renewed commitment to the terms of the covenant. The Jews in exile re-dedicated themselves to obedience to God's commands. Part of this effort involved a new emphasis on putting God's laws *in writing*.

This emphasis continued after the Exile was over. It was during the beginning of the Second Temple period, when the Jews were allowed to return to Palestine and to restore Jerusalem and the Temple, that the last of the four sources that make up the Pentateuch was written. The Priestly writer and the Deuteronomist are believed to have written in the 6th century BCE. Sometime thereafter these sources were combined with the other two documents (the writings of the Yahwist and the Elohist) to form the five scrolls of the Law, what Christians now call the first five books of the Old Testament.

Thus it is during the Second Temple period that Israel truly established its scriptures, or sacred books. At first these consisted only of the five scrolls of the Law, or the **Pentateuch**. The Jewish word for "law" is *Torah*, and this word can refer to these five books alone. Eventually some other books were accepted, at least by some Jews, as sacred scripture as well, and thus the word Torah can also refer in a more general sense to all of the books accepted as scripture by Israel. The books of the Prophets were gradually included in the canon of most Jews as a second major "section" of the Torah, although subordinate in importance to the Law. A third major section, called the Writings, was the last to be written and included in the Jewish canon. This section includes books of prayers and wisdom such as Psalms and Proverbs, and stories with theological themes such as the book of Job.

For the most part, the writing and editing of all these books took place over very long periods of time, and their inclusion into the Jewish scriptures was a gradual process that inspired a considerable amount of disagreement among the Jews. However, in its final Jewish form the canon consisted of three parts: Law, Prophets, and Writings. This threefold division is often referred to today by the acronym **Tanakh**, which combines the first letters of the Hebrew words for Law ("Torah"), Prophets ("Nevi'im"), and Writings ("Khetubim").

Regardless of how the scriptures were constituted at one historical moment or among one or another Jewish group, all Jews felt themselves to be bound by God's demands as they are expressed in the Torah. Thus obedience to the Torah took its place alongside Temple sacrifice as the main ways that Jews expressed themselves religiously. In order to be a Jew one needed to be circumcised (if you were male), sacrifice in the Temple at the prescribed times, and follow the Torah in one's daily life (which included following both the ethical guidelines and the special Jewish dietary restrictions called "keeping **kosher**").

C. Messiah

The Jews believed that they had a covenant relationship with God whereby if they followed the Torah and performed their sacrifices, God would fulfill certain promises to them. These promises included numerous descendants, possession of the land of Canaan (or Palestine), and the promise that the Jews would form a "great nation." For most of their history, it appears that these promises did not come true for the Jews. There is only one period in Israelite history in which the covenant appeared to be working as it really should: the kingdom of David. During David's rule the Israelites enjoyed unparalleled military success, economic prosperity, and religious unity. However, after David the kingdom was eventually split in two, and following the split the Jews were conquered successively by the Assyrians, the Babylonians, the Persians, the Greeks, and finally the Romans. The Jews suffered terribly under the rule of these foreign powers.

The Jewish explanation for these disasters was always the same. They believed that they must have sinned against the Lord and broken the covenant, which caused God to withdraw his protection and thus to expose the Jews to oppression by foreign powers. The Jews always blamed themselves, not God, for breakdowns in the proper functioning of the covenant. In this way of thinking, the solution was equally clear. The way to re-gain God's favor and release themselves from bondage to their enemies was to repent of their sins and begin adhering more precisely to the terms of the covenant.

During these times of oppression the Jewish prophets began to predict that God would send someone to rescue the Jews from their affliction, just as God had sent Moses to deliver them from slavery in Egypt, the judges to rescue them from the Philistines, and the prophets themselves to deliver God's messages. The most common and recent of these manifestations of God's will were the prophets, but there seems to have been a decline in prophecy starting in the 4th century BCE. Thus Israel began to hope for a different sort of divine agent. The figure around whom the Jewish hopes coalesced came to be called the **messiah**. The word "messiah" means "anointed one." The great leaders of Israel's past succeeded, they believed, because they had been *chosen* by God, and God's election of them was symbolized by the process of anointing with oil. Thus by using the term "messiah" the Jews simply expressed their belief that God would raise up a chosen leader from among the people to "save" them.

Exactly how this was going to happen was a matter of some disagreement, however. Some Jews believed in a political sort of messiah. They interpreted 2 Samuel 7 to mean that God would raise up a descendant of David and re-establish him on the throne of Israel. Other Jews anticipated an **apocalyptic** sort of messiah. Various Jewish "apocalyptic" groups believed that God would soon bring an end to this evil world, destroying the wicked and establishing a new Paradise for the righteous. Some thought that the messiah would bring all this about. The book of Daniel offers some support for the idea that God would send a heavenly emissary to purge the world of evildoers and rescue the righteous in a battle of cosmic proportions.

> As I watched in the night visions
> I saw one like a son of man coming with the clouds of heaven
> And he came to the Ancient One and was presented before him.
> To him was given dominion and glory and kingship,
> that all peoples, nations, and languages should serve him
> His dominion is an everlasting dominion that shall not pass away,
> and his kingship is one that shall never be destroyed (Daniel 7:13-14).

There are other passages in the Torah which seem to speak of yet another kind of messiah, although these passages are highly controversial. Isaiah 52-53, for example, speaks of a "**suffering servant**," one who takes the sins of the people onto himself and wins forgiveness for them through his suffering. Christians, of course, pointed to the Isaiah text (among others) to support their belief in Jesus as the messiah, while Jews disputed their interpretation of Isaiah 52-53, arguing that it is not about the messiah at all, and pointed to other biblical texts to support their conviction that Jesus was not the messiah. Still other passages (2 Samuel 7; Psalm 2) suggest that the messiah will be the "son of God." In spite of all these (alleged) references to the messiah in the Bible, it must be noted that some Jews did not believe in a messiah at all. Later Christians have a tendency to overemphasize the importance of the messiah in the Jewish faith, when in fact the level of belief in the messiah varied widely from one Jewish group to another.

II. Judaism in the Hellenistic Age

In 336 BCE a young Greek named Alexander took over the throne of Macedonia and immediately set about an ambitious program of conquest. Ten years later, Alexander the Great had conquered a substantial part of the known world, including Asia Minor, Syria, Israel, Egypt and Persia. Alexander's armies reached India before finally refusing to follow him any further. Alexander's plans for the people he conquered included what was called "**Hellenization**." The Greeks' word for their own country was "Hellas," and to "Hellenize" meant to spread Greek culture, or to attempt to turn people into "Greeks." Alexander saw Greek culture as superior to that of other peoples, and his goal was to impose Greek culture on his entire empire, such that people would speak Greek, dress like the Greeks, attend Greek schools, read Greek literature, and worship the Greek gods.

This program of Hellenization created a dilemma for the Jews. On the one hand, some Jews were enthusiastic about the Greek culture, and saw this as a way to "blend into" the new empire and avoid further suffering. On the other hand, many Jews were proud of their culture and religion, and felt that adopting Greek ways would force them to abandon the true path of Judaism, which would bring God's wrath down upon them even more harshly.

Alexander did not *force* people to adopt Greek culture, however, and so it was possible for these two groups of Jews to co-exist for a time under Greek rule. This changed in 175 BCE, when a new king named Antiochus IV ascended to power and began an effort to force the Jews to become Hellenized by stamping out Judaism. Antiochus prohibited the observance of the Torah and ordered that sacrifices in the Temple be made to the Greek god Zeus instead of YHWH. These actions enraged the Jews, and they revolted under the leadership of a family called the **Maccabees**. The Maccabean Revolt began in 167 BCE, and by 164 BCE the Jews had re-taken Jerusalem and re-dedicated the Temple to YHWH. Eventually the Maccabees were able to establish an independent Jewish state once again. The holiday that celebrates the consecration of the Temple following this victory is called **Hanukkah**, or the Festival of Lights. Some Jews did not think that the Maccabees should be controlling the Temple and the Jewish state, and they went off into the desert to await God's wrath. They were convinced that the world had become so corrupt that God would surely bring an end to it. This is the beginning of a strain of thought, called **apocalypticism**, that would become more and more popular in Judaism in the next few centuries.

III. Judaism in New Testament Times

By the middle of the 1st century BCE, the Jews had been conquered again, this time by the Romans. The Jews would continue under Roman domination for several centuries. Judaism at the turn of the millenium was a relatively diverse phenomenon. There were a number of different groups calling themselves "Jewish" that had rather different beliefs. Although all Jews agreed on the basic points of Judaism, for example that the way to please God was through Temple sacrifice and obedience to the Torah, different groups of Jews during the 1st century disagreed on points of emphasis involving Temple, Torah, and messiah.

A. Sadducees

The **Sadducees** were the party of the upper classes: the priests, the landed nobility, and the major property owners. The Sadducees occupied whatever roles of leadership were allowed by the Romans. As the priests of the Temple, they were the religious leaders of Judaism. In many ways they also functioned as political leaders. For example, the Sadducees dominated the highest Jewish court (the Sanhedrin) as well. According to the gospels, Jesus was put on trial before this body.

As the ruling aristocracy, the Sadducees were conservative in outlook. They wanted to preserve their power, to maintain the status quo, and so they tried as hard as they could to avoid change or reform. Many Jews resented the presence of the Romans in their homeland and actively sought to overthrow the Romans through violent revolution. One such group is called the "Zealots." However, to preserve their property and influence the Sadducees pursued close and cordial ties with the Romans. The Sadducees negotiated certain special privileges for the Jewish people, such as exemption from making sacrifices to the emperor as a god, or military service in the Roman legions, privileges which enabled them (in the Sadducees' view) to continue practicing authentic Judaism.

Temple: For the Sadducees, Temple sacrifice was the most important aspect of Judaism. This is not surprising, since the Temple is the source of both wealth and power for the priests who run it. However, the Sadducees did not support the Temple for purely selfish reasons. All Jews believed that sacrifice was a primary means of relating to God. The Sadducees simply emphasized Temple sacrifice more than any other group.

Torah: The Torah was essential to all Jewish groups, and the Sadducees were no exception. It was in the Torah, after all, that God's demands for sacrifices were set forth. Nonetheless, the Sadducees seemed to see obedience to the Torah as a rival in some ways to the dominance of Temple sacrifice, and they took steps to *limit* the influence of Torah. First, they accepted only the Law or Pentateuch, the first five books of the Old Testament, as scripture. The Law was most important to them since it is in the Law that the rules for sacrifice are laid out. They did not accept the Prophets or the Writings as part of the canon. Second, they insisted that the Law could only be interpreted literally. One could not add anything to what was in the written text. For this reason the Sadducees did not accept some of the more "recent" ideas in Judaism, such as resurrection, angels, or spirits.

Messiah: There is no evidence that the Sadducees believed in a messiah. Although there are no clear reasons for this, it is true that belief in a messiah tends to be more popular among the disenfranchised lower classes than among the ruling upper classes.

B. Pharisees

The **Pharisees** were also religious leaders, but they were not priests but scholars. They believed that the most important part of Judaism was not Temple sacrifice but obedience to the Torah in daily life. They were experts on the written Law and its interpretation. Their practice was rooted not in the Temple but in the synagogue, where the teachers (or "rabbis") read from the Torah and presided over subsequent arguments about its meaning and application to present problems and situations. The Pharisees believed strongly that the Torah affected the entirety of human existence, and they sought to develop rules for every area of human life based on the Torah.

Because of their emphasis on behaving in very strict accordance with the rules of the Torah, the Pharisees were known for pious living (alms, tithing, prayer, and fasting). The Pharisees also believed that the rules for ritual purity that operated in the Temple should be applied to everyday existence, and so they tried to avoid contact with anything that would make them "unclean." This is why Pharisees did not eat with or associate with tax collectors, prostitutes, or sinners. The word Pharisees (which means "separated ones") derives from the desire of this group not to be contaminated by the uncleanness of others.

Temple: The Pharisees still believed in Temple sacrifice, since it is prescribed in the Torah which they revered, but it was not as important to them as following the Torah in one's daily life.

Torah: The Torah was the most important part of Judaism for the Pharisees. They accepted all three parts (Law, Prophets, and Writings), which meant that they accepted some ideas mentioned only in the later books, such as the resurrection of the body on the last day. Their mode of interpretation was much more loose and innovative than the Sadducees. The Pharisees tried to apply the Torah to all aspects of daily life, but occasionally a situation or problem would come up for which there was no answer in the written Torah. In these cases the teachers of the Pharisees (the **rabbis**) would attempt to determine what the law should be, on the basis of what was written in the Torah. The teachings of the great rabbis on such matters were circulated in oral form from one community to another, and from one generation to another. These teachings eventually acquired much the same status as the written Torah, and (after some centuries) these teachings of the great rabbis were written down. The Mishnah and the Talmud, which are still read, studied and followed by Jews today, are examples of the practice of preserving the teachings of the great rabbis.

Messiah: The evidence suggests that the Pharisees believed in a messiah, and that the kind of messiah they were expecting was a royal messiah. Some passages in the Torah suggest that God will send a leader like King David to rescue the Jewish people. This leader would unite the Jewish people, lead them to victory over their oppressors, establish Israel as an independent nation, and assume the role of the nation's king. For the Pharisees, and indeed for most Jews, the common expectation was of a military/political messiah.

C. Essenes

The **Essenes** were a group of Jews who withdrew into the desert to wait for the end of the world. Many Jews throughout history believed that the world had become so evil that God would want to destroy it, just as he did in Noah's time with the Flood. This belief in the nearness of the end of the world is characteristic of **apocalyptic** groups. The Essenes believed that God was angry about the corruption of the Temple, and that this would cause him to destroy the present order and its evil inhabitants, and start over with only the righteous people. The Essenes were apparently founded by a priest of the Temple who was ousted from his position (along with other priests) by a rival Jewish group. This priest and his followers thought that the Temple had been corrupted by the new priests who were installed in their place.

Temple: The Temple was crucially important to the Essenes, but they thought that the sacrifice currently being done in Jerusalem was illegitimate and not acceptable to God because the wrong priests were making the sacrifices. The Essenes believed that they were the right priests, and that only if they were restored to the Temple would the sacrifices become effective once again.

Torah: The Essenes were similar to the Pharisees in that they accepted all three parts of the Hebrew Bible (Law, Prophets, Writings) as scripture and they wanted to adhere to the demands of the Torah as strictly as possible in their daily lives. However, if it is possible to imagine, they were even more rigorous about obedience to the Torah than the Pharisees. They believed that in order to survive the coming apocalypse, they needed to be as pure and holy as possible. This is why they followed the law so strictly, and also why they withdrew into the desert. The Pharisees tried to keep themselves pure by avoiding contact with sinners. This was not good enough for the Essenes. In order to prevent themselves from falling into temptation or coming into contact with uncleanness, they withdrew from normal society altogether.

Messiah: Because of the corruption of the Temple, this became the most important part of Judaism for the Essenes. The Essenes believed in *two* messiahs. The first was a royal messiah who would lead the children of light into battle with the children of darkness and then establish himself as king after the forces of good had vanquished the forces of evil. The second was a priestly messiah who would cleanse the Temple of the illegitimate priests, re-establish the Essenes as the correct priests, and install himself as the new high priest.

D. Scribes

The word "scribe" denotes an occupation based upon the knowledge of reading and writing. Since most people could not read or write, they relied upon the **scribes** to do these things for them. Scribes performed functions that made use of their literacy, such as writing out contracts for people, advising rulers, keeping official records, and taking care of correspondence. Scribes are often associated with the Jewish Law, and it is clear that scribes often served as copyists of the Jewish legal traditions, and some scribes were legal experts. Scribes did not constitute a coherent, organized group with a consistent point of view, and so were not a group like the Essenes, Pharisees, or Sadducees. However, there were scribes within most of these Jewish groups. Pharisees who interpreted the Torah, for example, must have been scribes.

E. "People of the Land"

It should be noted that the majority of Jews did not belong to any religious "party" such as the Pharisees, Sadducees, or Essenes. Most members of these groups belonged to the upper-classes, only perhaps ten percent of the population. Of the remaining ninety percent, the vast majority were peasant farmers or "**people of the land**." A small number of Jews were artisans, while many others belonged to the unclean class (those who performed distasteful tasks such as mining and tanning), and the "expendable" class (the "homeless" of Jewish society, who survived through begging or stealing).

These people usually did not have the time or the means to concern themselves with the specifics of the interpretation of the Torah or the composition of the priesthood. Very little is known about them, except that the other groups often avoided them or treated them with disdain because they could not or would not adhere to the "rules" of Judaism as strictly as these groups felt they should. A notable exception to this principle is the Jesus Movement, which was known for welcoming all sorts of "undesirable" people into its ranks.

F. Christians

Although much more will be said about the development of Christianity in the next chapter, it is important to realize that the first followers of Jesus can easily be understood as members of another group within Judaism, like the Sadducees, Pharisees, and Essenes. In its early decades, Christianity was not a religion separate from Judaism. Early "Christians" (they were not actually called by this name until several years after the death of Jesus) still considered themselves Jews, and they continued to believe in all of the major elements of Judaism: sacrificing in the Temple, obeying the rules of the Torah, being circumcised, and keeping kosher. Christians did have some distinctive attitudes, however, about the Temple, the Torah, and especially the messiah.

Temple: There is evidence in the gospels to suggest that (like the Essenes) Jesus and his followers were upset about how the Temple was being run. The scene in which Jesus enters the Temple and overturns the tables of the moneychangers and scatters those who are selling animals or grain is evidence that the Christians thought that the Temple had become corrupt. However, this did not mean that the Christians abandoned Temple sacrifice. The gospels show Jesus travelling to Jerusalem for the festivals as Jewish men were required to do, and Jesus' disciples continued to teach and preach at the Temple after his death. It seems that what these first Christians wanted was for the Temple to be *reformed*, not removed from their religion altogether.

Torah: Like other Jews, the earliest Christians believed that the Torah was a gift from God. They did not abandon observance of the rules and regulations of the Torah. In one gospel Jesus proclaims that he did not come to abolish the Law but to fulfill it. However, Jesus and his followers did have a different perspective on the Torah than some of their Jewish colleagues. Like the Essenes and the Pharisees, Christians accepted all three parts of the Torah (Law, Prophets, and Writings). In some cases the Christians were more strict about ethical matters than other Jews. For example, divorce and some forms of violence or retribution, which were allowed according to the Jewish law, were strongly frowned upon in early Christianity. Thus like the Pharisees, the Christians believed that the written law must be supplemented or reinterpreted. Their "supplements" came not from the Pharisaic rabbis, however, but from Jesus. In some cases, Jesus' teachings on the law were not designed to make them more strict, but more flexible. Several passages seem to suggest that Jesus and his followers believed that it was permissible to break the rule about working on the Sabbath if it was for a good cause (such as healing someone, or satisfying extreme hunger).

Messiah: Where Christians disagreed most with their counterparts in the other Jewish groups was in their belief that the messiah had already come, and that this messiah was Jesus of Nazareth. This is the single most important distinguishing feature of early Christianity: the Christians thought that the messiah had already come, while (most) other Jewish groups were still waiting for the messiah. Christians supported their claims that Jesus was the messiah by pointing out how the events of his life fulfilled prophecies in the Torah about the messiah, how he spoke with great wisdom and could perform miracles, and most important of all, how he rose from the dead after being crucified and appeared to his disciples.

Just *what kind* of a messiah Jesus was became a matter of some disagreement among various groups of Christians, but it is clear at least that Jesus did not fit the mold of a political/military messiah that the Pharisees and many other ordinary Jews were expecting. There are other ideas about the messiah expressed in the Torah, and the Christians began to explore them to try to discover who Jesus was and to find evidence to convince their fellow Jews that Jesus was in fact the messiah.

While the understanding of Jesus underwent some significant changes during the first decades of Christianity, one view that was popular among the earliest Christians was that Jesus was an apocalyptic messiah. They believed that Jesus had come once to warn them that the end of the world was near and to instruct them on how to survive the coming apocalypse, and that Jesus would come again soon (the "second coming") to inaugurate the end and to judge the living and the dead. As time went on and Jesus did not return, Christians modified their beliefs about the nearness of the end of the world.

IV. The Jewish War (66-70 CE)

The various Jewish groups co-existed more or less peacefully in Palestine until 66 CE, when war broke out between the Jews and the Romans. Almost all Jews strongly resented the Roman presence in Palestine, and some Jews advocated violent revolt. Minor rebellions had broken out several times prior to 66 CE. However, a series of events led to the development of a full-blown revolution in 66 CE, a revolution that was to prove disastrous for the Jewish people.

The revolt was led by the **Zealots**, a group of radical Jews who believed that once the war was started, Yahweh would enter it on the side of the Jews and help them defeat the vastly more powerful Romans. Their hopes were not realized, however, and the Romans quickly and easily defeated the Jews. Thousands of Jews were killed and their leaders crucified. The worst disaster, however, came in 70 CE, when Jerusalem was destroyed and the Temple burned to the ground. This time the Temple was never rebuilt.

This war proved fateful for all of the various groups within Judaism. Without the Temple, the Sadducees had lost the source of their wealth and power, and for all practical purposes, they ceased to exist. A large group of Essenes were accidentally discovered by the Romans in the desert and massacred. However, these Essenes did manage to hide their sacred texts in a cave before they were slaughtered. These texts were discovered in 1947 at Qumran, and are called the **Dead Sea Scrolls**.

The only group to survive the Jewish War relatively intact was the Pharisees. With the Temple gone, however, the Pharisees needed to undertake some major renovations in the Jewish religion. By the end of the 1st century, the Pharisees had invented a brand of Judaism that relied solely on the Torah, and eliminated the practice of sacrifice. This came to be called "**rabbinic Judaism**," and it is the brand of Judaism that survives in various forms today. The Christians too struggled with the destruction of the Temple, and the gospels are in many ways a theological response to this tragic event.

Key Terms:

diaspora	apocalyptic
synagogue	rabbis
Septuagint	Suffering Servant
messiah	Hellenization
priests	Maccabees
Passover	Hanukkah
Yom Kippur	Sadducees
Second Temple	Pharisees
Holy of Holies	Zealots
Pentateuch	Essenes
Tanakh	scribes
kosher	People of the Land

Questions for Reading:

1. What was the purpose of sacrifice? What kinds of rules did the Jews have about the sacrifices that they conducted?

2. What did the Jewish scriptures consist of? How did these scriptures develop?

3. Explain the development of the concept of the messiah in Jewish thinking, and distinguish between the different kinds of messiahs that Jews believed in.

4. What was "Hellenization" and how did Jews of the time react to it?

5. Compare and contrast the Sadducees, Pharisees, Essenes, and Christians in terms of their beliefs about the Temple, Torah, and Messiah.

6. What happened to each of the Jewish groups following the Jewish War of 66-70 CE?

Works Consulted/Recommended Reading:

Murphy, Frederick J. *The Religious World of Jesus: An Introduction to Second Temple Palestinian Judaism.* Nashville: Abingdon Press, 1991.

Perrin, Norman and Duling, Dennis C. *The New Testament: An Introduction.* 2nd ed. San Diego: Harcourt Brace Jovanovich, 1982.

Part II: The New Testament

The second major section of the Bible is the New Testament. The New Testament has continued to be a very important document for Christians throughout the centuries, because it provides the basis for articulating the Christian community's identity and for formulating much of its theology and moral principles. Christians call this section the "New Testament," because it outlines the new covenant between God and human beings made possible by the coming of Jesus Christ.

Like the Old Testament or Hebrew Bible, the New Testament is not always an easy document to read and interpret because it is an ancient piece of literature from a culture and historical time period vastly different from our own. At the same time, Christians treat it as a timeless document that has authority to direct and guide their lives. We will begin our study of the New Testament by describing it in general terms. What kinds of books are contained in the New Testament? How were these books collected into this larger document we call the New Testament?

I. Divisions of the New Testament

The first sub-division in the New Testament consists of the gospels. They are listed here with their most commonly accepted dates of composition.

Mark (c. 70 CE)   John (c. 90-100 CE)
Matthew (c. 80-85 CE)
Luke (c. 80-85 CE)

The gospels are the books which tell the story of the life of Jesus. Although they contain history, the gospels are more appropriately understood to be proclamation. Our English term "**gospel**" comes from the Anglo-Saxon "god-spell" which means "good tidings." The Greek word for "gospel" is *euan-gelion*, which means "good message" (of Jesus Christ). The writers of the gospels are called **evangelists**, that is, "preachers of the good news." The gospels proclaim early Christian communities' faith experience of Jesus as the messiah of God.

The gospels of Matthew, Mark, and Luke are called **synoptic** gospels, from the Greek "*synoptikos*" which means "seeing the whole together." These gospels tell the same general story about Jesus in the same kind of way and with more or less the same chronology. The gospel of John is quite different in terms of style, content, and theological perspective, and therefore must be read with different expectations. Although the gospels are included first among the books of the New Testament, they were not the first books to be written. In fact, Paul's letters were the first to be written.

The second sub-division of the New Testament is the Acts of the Apostles. This book is a continuation of Luke's gospel. It tells the story of the origins of Christianity after the death and resurrection of Jesus through the time of Paul's preaching in Rome—the period covering approximately 30 CE - 64 CE. It is thought to be written in the last quarter of the 1st century, after the destruction of Jerusalem and the Temple (70 CE). Although it reads like a history book, the Acts of the Apostles is not an objective re-telling of the story of the beginnings of Christianity. Rather, it gives us a *theological interpretation* of the events that led to Christianity's identification as a religion separate from Judaism.

The third sub-division of the New Testament consists of 21 letters addressed to a variety of Christian churches and individual Christians of the 1st and 2nd century CE. Thirteen of these letters are attributed to the missionary Paul, some of them written as early as 50-60 CE. This means that they are among the first books written in the New Testament, even though they are not listed first. Other letters bear the names of the apostles John, Peter, James, and Jude.

The book Revelation (c. 90-100 CE) makes up the fourth sub-division of the New Testament. This book is an apocalyptic account of a divine revelation to a Christian prophet named John. Apocalypticism involves a type of prophetic literature in which a writer critiques the situation in which he is living by writing symbolically about the disasters that bring about the end of the world.

II. The Question of Canon

Another question to be considered concerns how the New Testament itself was compiled. In addition to the books currently found in the New Testament, there existed a number of other Christian documents written and used by Christian communities in the 1st and 2nd century CE. Why did some sacred writings get into the New Testament, while others did not? Which books were admitted into the canon first? When and how did the "New Testament" come into existence?

The term "canon" means "rule" or "standard"—like a measuring stick. This term was first used in early Christian literature to refer to the "rule of faith," that is, the norm or measure of religious truth in the Christian tradition. Most often today, it is used to refer to the collection of authoritative writings of a particular religious group. For example, the canon for Islam is the Qur'an, while the canon for Judaism is the Hebrew Scriptures (roughly what we call the Old Testament), the Mishnah and the Talmud.

A. Theory About the Formation of the New Testament Canon

At the earliest stages of Christianity, there was no New Testament at all. Early Christians appropriated the scriptures of Judaism as their own, though sometimes selectively and certainly with different interpretations. For Paul and for the apostles of Jesus, "scriptures" meant *Jewish* scriptures. As Christians began to put together their own distinctive scriptures, they did so not all at once, but in stages.

First Stage: It is surprising to most Christians that the earliest collections of Christian texts did not include the gospels. In fact, these early collections probably consisted of some of the letters of Paul. In the second letter of Peter (c. 100-125 CE), the author says: "Paul, our beloved brother wrote you this in the spirit of wisdom that is his, dealing with these matters as he does in all his letters. There are certain passages in them hard to understand. The ignorant and unstable distort them (*just as they do the rest of scripture*) to their own ruin" (2 Pet 3:16). This is our earliest clue that Christians were beginning to collect Christian literature in order to create their own canon and that the letters of Paul had earned the same status as the Old Testament in these Christian communities.

Second Stage: There were many so-called gospels (stories of the life of Jesus or collections of his teachings) in the early years of the church, but the first reference to the four gospels as "scripture" comes from Justin and Clement in the middle of the 2nd century CE. Although he does not call them gospels, Justin mentions the "memoirs of the apostles" being read at liturgy (*Apol.* 1.67). Irenaeus (c. 180 CE) indicates that there was, already in his day, talk about the reliability and appropriateness of individual documents for use by Christians. For example, the gospel of Peter was banned from some communities because it was considered to contain false teaching about Jesus.

Third stage: Marcion (c. 140 CE), a Christian preacher in Rome, was responsible for the first canon of the New Testament. He was deeply troubled by the Jewish scripture's presentation of a violent and vengeful God, and therefore rejected all of the Old Testament scriptures. He even rejected much of Christian literature except the edited gospel of Luke and ten of the letters attributed to Paul. In effect, any text with Jewish overtones was excluded.

Marcion's action prompted other church leaders to form their own canons or lists of approved books. The most famous of these was the Muratorian canon, an official list of books probably developed in Rome in the latter part of the 2nd century CE. It included the four gospels, the Acts of the Apostles, thirteen letters attributed to Paul (excluding Hebrews), Jude, 1 John, 2 John, the Wisdom of Solomon (from the Old Testament Apocrypha), Revelation, and the Apocalypse of Peter.

The consistent elements in all of the lists that had been compiled in response to Marcion's canon were the four gospels, Acts of the Apostles and Paul's letters. Bishop Athanasius of Alexandria, in his *Festal Letter* of 367 CE, was the first to name the 27 books of the New Testament, as we have it today, as canonical. However, it was not until the Council of Trent in 1546 that the Catholic Church made an official statement concerning the canon of the Bible, listing the books it considered to be sacred and canonical. In other words, the canon of the New Testament was created over an extended period of time and from among a wide variety of Christian literature.

B. The Criteria for Canonicity

Why did some sacred Christian writings get into the New Testament, while others did not? Modern biblical scholars cannot fully reconstruct the history of the development of the canon, especially as it relates to the criteria used in this "sorting out" process. Yet, the writings of early church historians and theologians can provide some clues concerning the complexity of the early church's task of identifying a canon of Christian literature.

One criterion that appears to have been used among the early Christian churches was "apostolic origin," meaning that the book could be attributed to an apostle or to a disciple of an apostle. For example, some early church historians and theologians questioned whether the letter to the Hebrews and the book of Revelation ought to have been included in the canon because it could not be verified that Paul and John, the son of Zebedee and an apostle of Jesus, were their respective authors. Today, we understand the notion of apostolic authorship in the broadest sense, meaning that the book has some connection to the traditions associated with a particular apostle.

Other criteria are suggested by early church writers' discussions of *The Gospel of Peter*. The fragment still available to modern readers tells the story of the trial, death and resurrection of Jesus. It is a strange gospel, complete with enormous angels and a cross that talks. However, the early church historian Eusebius recounts that bishop Serapion of Antioch (c. 190 CE) forbade Christians to read it not because it was historically inaccurate, but because some of those who held it as sacred were led into heresy (wrong teaching) by its words.

The wrong teaching or **heresy** to which Serapion referred was **docetism**, which held that Jesus did not really suffer and die, but merely seemed to have done these things. Thus, the exclusion of the *Gospel of Peter* from the canon of the New Testament appears to have been a question of **orthodoxy** or right doctrine. However, Serapion's comments suggest two other factors that contributed to the formation of the New Testament canon: the authority of Christian church leaders to determine what was appropriate reading for their Christian communities, and the value of a tradition that can trace itself back to the apostles.

Thus it appears that the authority to decide which books contained sound teaching and which books had an apostolic origin was claimed by the bishops of the Christian church. However, the bishops did not simply impose their own preferences on an unwilling church. Some of the bishops resolved the question of canon by asking churches in various regions what books were being read in their services. So another criterion for inclusion appears to have been widespread acceptance in the churches. The decisions of the bishops about the canon were not simply their own but appear to have reflected the sentiments of the church as a whole.

Another factor to be considered in the history of the development of canon is the role of chance. In some cases, individual churches like the churches of Greece and Asia Minor were responsible for collecting sacred documents and distributing them to other churches, thereby insuring their preservation. Paul's letters are a good example. Still other early Christian literature that might otherwise have been included in the canon of the New Testament simply disappeared for reasons that are unknown to us. Today we have only brief quotations from them or references to them in other early Christian writings.

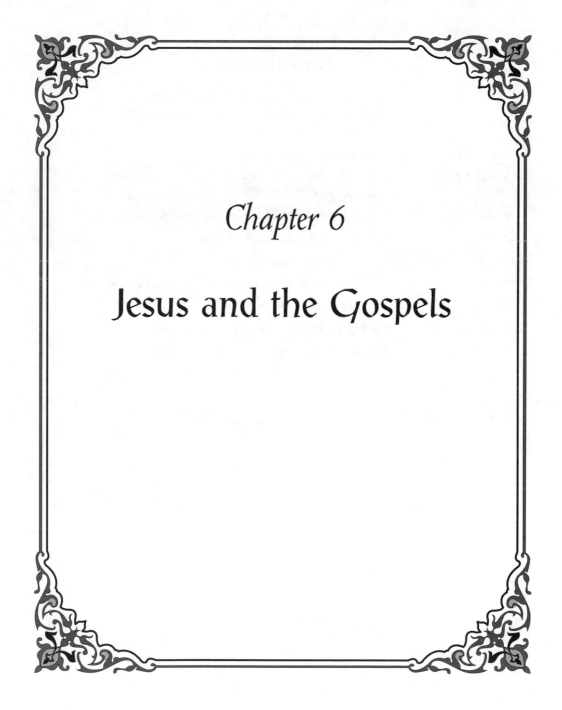

Chapter 6

Jesus and the Gospels

Timeline

37-4 BCE	Herod the Great is king of Palestine. During his kingship, Herod initiates a major renovation of the Jerusalem Temple.
6-4 BCE	Jesus of Nazareth is born.
4 BCE-39 CE	Herod Antipas is king of Galilee and the area to the east of Jordan.
26-36 CE	Pontius Pilate is procurator in Judea and Samaria.
c. 30	The death and resurrection of Jesus.
66-70	The Jewish war against Rome.
70	The Romans capture Jerusalem and destroy the Temple.
70?	The gospel of Mark is written.
80-85?	The gospels of Matthew and Luke are written.
90-100?	The gospel of John is written.

Jesus and the Gospels

Emerging from an obscure little town in Galilee in the early part of the 1st century CE, Jesus of Nazareth began his ministry of proclaiming the nearness of God's kingdom to his Jewish brothers and sisters. He was a teacher and a miracle worker, and many were drawn to follow him. At the same time, others were offended by the radicalness of his teaching and his critique of Jewish law. However, those who followed Jesus understood him to be the long-awaited messiah. As Jesus' disciples continued to proclaim the message of Jesus Christ, a reform movement was born within Judaism which later spread outward into the Gentile or non-Jewish world. This Jesus Movement came to be known as Christianity.

The gospels of the New Testament tell the story of Jesus of Nazareth. According to the gospels, his parents were Joseph and Mary. Tradition places his birth in Bethlehem of Judea, as foretold by the prophet Isaiah. Although the Christian calendar was designed to take as its pivotal moment Jesus' birth in the year 1 CE, an error in calculation makes 6-4 BCE a more accurate date. The gospels tell stories about his teaching and miracle working activity in Galilee and Jerusalem. They make reference to his attendance at synagogue and his participation in Jewish festivals. They also tell the story of his journey to Jerusalem which ended in his execution by crucifixion in approximately 30 CE, after which his followers declared him raised from the dead.

It is extremely difficult to say with certainty much more about the historical events in Jesus' life. Because the gospels were written after the death of Jesus by people who believed that he had been raised from the dead and that his death was part of God's plan, they were selective in the stories they told and the way in which they told them. In other words, the gospels are not primarily concerned with telling the history of Jesus, but rather the story of the Christ of faith, the one whom Christians proclaim as the Messiah of God.

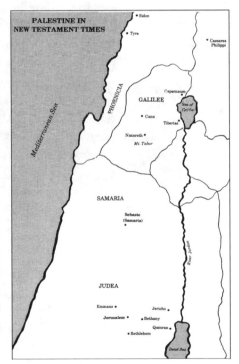

Figure 6.1: Palestine in New Testament times.

I. The Death and Resurrection of Jesus

Among all of the events recorded in the gospels, it is the death and resurrection of Jesus which continues to be the touchstone of the Christian faith. Each of the four canonical gospels tell of how Jesus was crucified and was raised from the dead three days later. The evidence for Jesus' resurrection varies from one gospel to another, but all include the fact that Jesus' tomb was found empty. They also tell of testimony from a messenger or messengers sent by God that Jesus has been raised. Three of the gospels contain stories about Jesus appearing to his followers after his death.

Within 1st-century Judaism, before the death of Jesus, there was already a debate going on about resurrection from the dead. Pharisees believed in the possibility of resurrection from the dead, but Sadducees did not. For those who did believe in resurrection from the dead, it was understood to be one of God's ways of rewarding the righteous ones who had suffered unjustly at the hands of their enemies. The book of Daniel provides a description of this expected resurrection:

> There shall be a time of anguish, such as has never occurred since nations first came into existence. But at that time your people shall be delivered, everyone who is found written in the book. Many of those who sleep in the dust of the earth shall awake, some to everlasting life, and some to shame and everlasting contempt. Those who are wise shall shine like the brightness of the sky, and those who lead many to righteousness, like the stars forever and ever (Dan 12:1-3).

The earliest Christians saw Jesus' resurrection from the dead as God's act of vindicating Jesus, after his shameful death by crucifixion. However, resurrection of the dead was also thought to happen only in the end time. Therefore, when Jesus was raised from the dead, his resurrection was seen as one of the first signs of the end time. Jesus was resurrected as God's Righteous One, and so his followers believed that God would soon rescue the rest of God's righteous ones. Now, the Christian believer would only need to wait for the glorious return of the Messiah, at which time the "Kingdom of God" would be fully established for the righteous and the wicked would be consigned to eternal damnation. Belief in the "second coming" of Jesus became an important feature of early Christianity. Indeed, most early Christians believed that Jesus would return within their lifetime.

Figure 6.2: The Tombs of the Kings in Jerusalem. The entrance to the interior of the tombs was once sealed by a round stone which can still be seen. The tomb in which Jesus was buried might have looked something like this one. Photo by Catherine Cory, 1985.

II. How the Gospels Came to Be

Most Christians are familiar with a variety of gospel stories, since excerpts from the gospels are incorporated into the worship services of most Christian traditions. However, Christians are less accustomed to asking the question, "How should we read the gospels?" The gospels are not history, strictly speaking. Neither are they biographies exactly. Two things must be considered when thinking about how the gospels ought to be interpreted: the process by which the gospels were written and the reason why the gospel story was written.

The stages of composition of the gospels can be described briefly as follows. (1) Shortly after the death and resurrection of Jesus, those who had once traveled with him and others who had become preachers of the "good news" began to hand on by word of mouth and in writing stories and sayings concerning Jesus' ministry and teachings. (2) Early Christian communities used these stories and sayings in worship and teaching, in preparation for Baptism, to encourage, to console, to resolve controversies, and to admonish the wrongdoers. Gradually they began to write down these stories and sayings of Jesus. However, as yet there were no written gospels as we know them. (3) Eventually, the gospel writers began to collect these oral and written traditions, arranging them into a coherent narrative or story of the life, death, and resurrection of Jesus Christ. The authors of the gospels selected and arranged these stories and sayings, with special attention to the particular situation of the communities for which they were writing.

Christians profess that the gospels tell us the truth about Jesus Christ. However, the written gospels are the end product of a complex process of development which, although it has its roots in the historical ministry of Jesus, got its impetus from Christian communities' *faith reflection* on the death and resurrection of Jesus. As inspired, the gospels are the Word of God, but they are written in the words of their human authors. Therefore, when Christians today read the gospels, they will want to read them with an awareness of the world in which they were written. They will also want to read them as we imagine that the authors wrote them—from the perspective of ending of the story, namely, the death and resurrection of Jesus.

A. The Synoptic Gospels

The gospels of Matthew, Mark, and Luke are called **synoptic** gospels, from the Greek word *synoptikos*, which means "seeing the whole together." These gospels tell the same general story of the life and teachings of Jesus Christ and they tell it in the same kind of way. Sometimes the similarities among the three gospels are so striking that one begins to ask, "Who copied whom?" This is called the **synoptic problem**. Stated briefly, the synoptic problem is concerned with the literary relationship between the gospels of Matthew, Mark, and Luke.

The three gospel versions of the parable of the mustard seed provide an excellent example of the synoptic problem:

Matt 13:31-32	Mark 4:30-32	Luke 13:18-19
He put before them another parable: "The kingdom of God is like a mustard seed that someone took and sowed in his field; it is the smallest of all the seeds, but when it has grown it is the greatest of shrubs and becomes a tree, so that the birds of the air come and make nests in its branches."	He also said, "With what can we compare the kingdom of God, or what parable will we use for it? It is like a mustard seed which, when sown upon the ground, is the smallest of all the seeds on earth; yet when it is sown it grows up and becomes the greatest of all shrubs, and puts forth large branches, so that the birds of the air can make nests in its shade."	He said therefore, "What is the kingdom of God like? and to what should I compare it? It is like a mustard seed that someone took and sowed in the garden; it grew and became a tree, and the birds of the air made nests in its branches."

The literary similarities among the three versions of the parable of the mustard seed are obvious. All three compare the kingdom to a mustard seed which, when it grows, becomes something very large so that the birds of the air can find shelter because of it. In fact, the wording is similar enough to suggest that two, or perhaps all three authors copied their parable from another written source.

At the same time, the literary differences among the versions also suggest that the individual authors, having a written source in front of them, deliberately altered that source for some reason. Matthew's gospel, for example, refers to the kingdom of heaven, rather than the kingdom of God. Luke's gospel describes the product of the growth of the mustard seed as a tree, while Mark's gospel calls it a shrub. Matthew's gospel calls it both a shrub and a tree. The question then is, "Who copied whom?" Which is the earliest of the gospels?

B. The Two Source Hypothesis

Biblical scholars have investigated a number of solutions to the synoptic problem. Although no one solution accounts for all of the variations in every segment of the synoptic gospels, the most commonly accepted solution is the **Two Source Hypothesis**. According to this hypothesis, Mark's gospel is the earliest of the three gospels to have been written, perhaps as early as 65-70 CE. The writers of the gospels of Matthew and Luke had access to Mark's gospel, selecting from it a variety of stories and teachings and following its time line without much alteration. However, the writers of the gospels of Matthew and Luke also had access to another source, a written document or documents, mostly containing parables and sayings of Jesus. Biblical scholars have named this hypothetical source **Q**, for the German word Quelle ("source").

The Two Source Hypothesis solves the synoptic problem by proposing that the writers of the gospels of Matthew and Luke composed their gospels by drawing from the gospel of Mark and Q, as their primary sources, and incorporating other traditional materials known only to their own communities.

Matthew's famous Sermon on the Mount (Matt 5:1-7:29) and its parallel Sermon on the Plain from Luke's gospel (Luke 6:17-49) are representative of the material that supposedly belonged to Q.

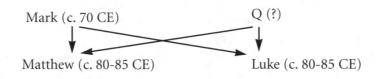

Matthew's stories about the birth of Jesus (Matt 1:1-2:23) represent some of the traditional materials known only to the community of Matthew's gospel. Likewise, stories like "the Prodigal Son" (Luke 15:11-32) and "the Good Samaritan" (Luke 10:25-37) belong to the traditional materials known only to the community of Luke's gospel.

C. The Authors of the Synoptic Gospels

Who wrote the synoptic gospels and to whom were they written? Although they now bear the titles "Matthew," "Mark," and "Luke," the original authors of the synoptic gospels are mostly unknown to us. Early Christian writers commented that the gospel we now know as the gospel of Mark was written by John Mark, a companion of Peter in Rome. However, since the gospel originally circulated anonymously, without an author's name attached to it, the later attribution of the gospel to John Mark is highly disputed. The most we can say about the author of the gospel of Mark is that he was a 1st-century Gentile (non-Jewish) Christian. The strong apocalyptic mood of the gospel suggests that the community was enduring some kind of persecution.

As with Mark, most scholars believe that the gospel of Matthew was not actually written by Matthew, the apostle of Jesus, but was written anonymously about 85-90 CE. The name of Matthew was attached to it sometime after the mid-2nd century when a church writer by the name of Papias was said to have written, "Then Matthew put together the sayings [of Jesus] in the Hebrew dialect and each one translated them as he was able" (Eusebius, *Eccl. Hist.* 3.39.16). Because of the large number of references to important Jewish figures and to symbols of the Jewish faith, the author and his community appear to have been Jewish-Christians, that is, Jews who became Christians.

The New Testament mentions three times a man named Luke who was a follower of Paul. From these three references we can conclude that Luke was a physician and a Gentile Christian (Phlm 24; Col 4:11-14; 2 Tim 4:11). However, like the gospels of Matthew and Luke, the gospel of Luke does not give many clues about the identity of its author. From his introduction, we know only that the author was not an eye-witness to Jesus' life. In other words, he was not one of the apostles. At the same time, he did have access to traditions, oral or written, from eye-witnesses and he was aware that others had attempted to write the gospel story of Jesus before him. This gospel was written for someone named Theophilus, which means "lover of God." He was Christian and, because Luke addresses him as "your excellency," he may have been a wealthy patron or a member of the Roman ruling class.

D. The Gospel of John

In addition to the synoptic gospels, the New Testament contains a fourth gospel called the gospel of John. This gospel is distinctively different from the synoptic gospels in a number of ways. Instead of parables and individual sayings or collections of sayings of Jesus, the gospel of John contains long discourses or speeches delivered by Jesus in a style akin to poetry. The gospel of John contains miracle stories similar in kind to those of the synoptic gospels, but the writer of John's gospel appears not to have known any of the same stories as those contained in the synoptic gospels. For example, the story about Jesus turning the water to wine at Cana (John 2:1-10) is found only in John's gospel. In addition, some of the important characters in John's gospel—most notably Nicodemus and the Samaritan woman—are absent from among the synoptic gospels. It also presents a somewhat different portrait of Jesus and his mission.

Early church tradition from the 2nd century CE identified the writer of this gospel as John, the son of Zebedee (one of the twelve in Mark's gospel). Also circulating in the 2nd century CE was another tradition about the authorship of the gospel of John—that his name was John, but that he was not an apostle of Jesus, and he lived a long life in Ephesus and wrote the gospel there. Whoever the author was, he appears to have been a Jewish Christian, writing for a community suffering from persecution at the hands of its Jewish brothers and sisters, toward the end of the 1st century CE.

III. The Gospels and their Christologies

An important feature and distinguishing mark of each gospel is its christology. The word **christology** derives from two Greek words: *Christos* meaning "the anointed" and *logos* meaning "word," or in this case "teaching." Thus, christology concerns teaching about Jesus who is the Christ. What do the gospels tell us about who Jesus is—as the Christ—and about what he does? An in-depth study of the gospels will reveal that each gospel has a distinctive christology, that is, a distinctive response to the question, "Who is Jesus as the Christ?"

A. Mark's Christology

In Mark's gospel, the reader is alerted to the question of christology even in its opening line: "The beginning of the gospel of Jesus *Christ*, the Son of God" (Mark 1:1). However, the reader is soon troubled by the narrator's repeated references to Jesus' demand that people not tell anyone about him (Mark 1:44), even when he is about to send his disciples out to preach the "good news" (Mark 3:13-19) or when he performs a great miracle (Mark 5:21-43). Biblical scholars call this phenomenon the **Messianic Secret**. Does Jesus not want people to know that he is the Messiah or the Christ (the title means "anointed")? If not, why not? The answer to these questions is to be found in the way that the writer of this gospel tells the story of Jesus' life.

There is no simple answer to the Messianic Secret. Perhaps the writer of Mark's gospel wanted to explain in retrospect why it was that some people, namely the Jews, did not accept Jesus and the message that he came to preach. By giving a backward look into the life and teachings of Jesus. Mark explains that Jesus deliberately kept some people from hearing and understanding his message. To the disciples, Jesus says, "To you has been given the secret of the kingdom of God, but for those outside, everything comes in parables; in order that they may indeed look, but not perceive, and may indeed listen, but not understand; so that they may not turn again and be forgiven" (Mark 4:11-12). Another possible explanation for the Messianic secret is that the writer of Mark's gospel wanted to illustrate in a literary way the forcefulness of the message of Jesus Christ. On one occasion, when Jesus healed a leper, he told the person not to tell anyone about it. Immediately, the person went out and did just the opposite—he went out to proclaim the word about Jesus (Mark 1:40-45). Likewise, at the conclusion of other miracle stories, Mark comments that Jesus' fame continued to spread. It was as if the message of God's kingdom simply could not be silenced.

There is another possible explanation for Mark's Messianic Secret that focuses on the suffering and death of Jesus. Many people expected the messiah to be a political leader who would lead great armies against their enemies. Therefore, when Jesus asked the disciples what people were saying about who he was, and Peter responded, "You are the Messiah," Jesus ordered them not to tell anyone about him (Mark 8:27-30). However, in answer to Peter's declaration, Jesus said, "The Son of Man must undergo great suffering, and be rejected by the elders, the chief priests, and the scribes, and be killed, and after three days rise again" (Mark 8:31). This he tells them openly (Mark 8:34). Jesus did not want people to identify him as the messiah, because people had the wrong idea of what that meant. Instead of the glorious and powerful messiah they had long awaited, he would be a messiah who must suffer.

Certainly the most important part of Mark's gospel is the **passion narrative**, the story contained in the final chapters which describes the arrest, trials, and crucifixion of Jesus (Mark 14:1-15:47). Mark stresses that Jesus knew beforehand that he would be killed and that it was part of God's plan that Jesus' death should bring about the forgiveness of sins for all who believe in him. Mark describes Jesus' words in this way: "For the Son of Man also came not to be served but to serve, and to give his life as a ransom for many" (Mark 10:45).

Much of Mark's gospel is also devoted to presenting the miracles of Jesus. Although part of the function of these miracle stories is to present further proof that Jesus is the messiah, and to demonstrate God's power over evil, they are also designed to show the faithful disposition of the recipients of these miracles and to offer these characters as good examples to the reader. It was their faith that made them well (see Mark 5:34). In contrast, the disciples of Mark's gospel are characterized by their fear (see Mark 4:35-41).

Mark's gospel contains fewer parables than the other synoptic gospels, but the two long parables that are found in the gospel are both crucial to its meaning and its understanding of Jesus. The Parable of the Sower (Mark 4:1-20) tells of a farmer who sows seed and finds that the seed grows in some kinds of ground, but not in others. Jesus explains that he is the farmer who sows "the word" which some people accept and others reject. Some produce good fruit, that is, go out to proclaim the gospel, and others do not. The Parable of the Wicked Tenants (Mark 12:1-12) tells of a man who rented out a vineyard to some tenants, who then refused to pay the rent and killed all of the owner's representatives, even his son. In this case, Jesus does not need to explain that God is the owner and he is the son who is rejected and killed. The parable ends with the owner destroying those evil tenants and giving the vineyard to others. The implication is that those who reject Jesus will be destroyed in the end, and the kingdom of God will be inherited by others.

B. Matthew's Christology

Matthew's gospel contains a somewhat different portrait of Jesus as the Christ: he is the new lawgiver who makes perfect the Law and provides ethical teachings to guide the Christian life. This point is demonstrated most clearly in the Sermon on the Mount (Matt 5:1-7:29).

The Sermon on the Mount is the first of five long discourses recorded in Matthew's gospel, perhaps corresponding to the five books of the Torah. It is also Jesus' first major teaching after his baptism in the Jordan and his testing in the wilderness. The testing in the wilderness should remind the gospel's readers of the Israelites' testing in the desert during the time of the Exodus. Matthew's gospel describes Jesus as going through events that are similar to the Exodus, but responding in a way that was quite different from the Israelites' response. The Israelites failed their test in the desert and grumbled against God. In contrast, Jesus is described as triumphing over the forces of evil, as he returns from the desert to preach God's kingdom.

The setting for Jesus' sermon is a mountain. Jesus takes the "sitting" position, the position of teacher who delivers God's Law. This mountain is the mountain of revelation, also recalling Mount Sinai from the Exodus story. Beginning with the Beatitudes ("Blessed are they...") Matthew describes Jesus as teaching a new and more perfect way of keeping the commandments and fulfilling the covenant relationship which existed between God and the people. Thus, in Matthew's gospel, Jesus is presented as the new Moses giving God's new Law to the people.

C. Luke's Christology

Luke's gospel has a keen interest in God's plan of salvation for all people, especially the poor and dispossessed. Throughout Luke's gospel the essential continuity between Judaism and Christianity is stressed. Luke presents Jesus as the fulfillment of all the promises that God made to Abraham and the Jews in the Old Testament. He makes numerous references to Jerusalem, because it is the place of the Temple and the place in which God's plan of salvation will be fulfilled in the death and resurrection of Jesus. He explains the difficulty of a *crucified* messiah by arguing that the Old Testament prophecies testify to the fact that this Messiah was destined to suffer.

Luke's special concern for the lowest segments of society is shown in his incorporation of several stories from the life of Jesus which highlight Jesus' compassion for those whom society has rejected. Jesus goes out of his way to associate with tax collectors and sinners. He allows women to take an active part in his ministry (Luke 8:1-3) and to serve in roles traditionally reserved for men (Luke 10:38-42). Luke's version of Matthew's Sermon on the Mount, called the Sermon on the Plain (Luke 6:20-49), not only shows Jesus blessing the poor and the hungry, but cursing those who are rich and comfortable. Throughout his gospel, Luke suggests that those who suffer injustice now will one day receive the good things of life, while those who have much now will suffer a reversal of fortunes (see Luke 1:51-53). Thus, Jesus is portrayed as the compassionate messiah who stands on the side of the poor.

D. John's Christology

The gospel of John contains a most distinctive portrait of Jesus as "the Word" who came down from the Father to dwell among humanity. The reader of John's gospel encounters this portrait of Jesus already in the prologue (introduction) of the gospel (John 1:1-18). Like most introductions, this prologue was probably written after the main part of the gospel, serving to highlight and foreshadow the main themes of the gospel as a whole. Its imagery recalls the literature of the Old Testament and the history of the Jewish people, especially the creation story in Genesis and the covenant imagery of the Pentateuch.

Why does John describe Jesus as the Word? The Greek term is **logos**, which can be translated as "word" or "reason." In addition to its many ordinary and popular usages, the word *logos* is a technical term in Greek (Stoic) philosophy, describing the unifying principle of all creation, the power that underlies all of creation, and the principle of order in the universe. For the Stoics, the *logos* represented the mind of God; they also believed that the human soul contained a spark of the divine *logos*. Humans can be in harmony with the deity and with creation, because they possessed a spark of the same divine *logos*, which was the mind of God.

Hellenistic Judaism had adopted some of this language about the *logos* to speak about God and God's relationship to creation. Philo of Alexandria, a 1st-century Jewish philosopher, combined the philosophical notion of the *logos* with the biblical notion of Wisdom, one of the powers of God. In the Old Testament, Wisdom (known as Sophia) is personified as God's partner in creation, who was with God from the beginning, and who came to dwell with Israel, God's chosen people. She is the one who teaches those who answer her invitation to be wise in God's ways. Thus, Philo understood the *logos* to be an intermediary between God and creation, a kind of second god who acted as God's instrument in creation. John uses similar imagery to describe how Jesus is God's Wisdom who came from the Father to dwell with humanity. He is the one who makes the Father known to us (cf. John 1:18). The event in which the divine "Word" came down from God and took on flesh is called, in theological terms, the **incarnation** (meaning "enfleshment").

This kind of christology that describes Jesus as the Logos who comes down from heaven to dwell with humankind is sometimes called **high christology**, because it focuses primarily on the divinity of Christ, in contrast to low christologies that focus first on the humanity of Jesus. John's gospel is also called a three stage christology, as the diagram below illustrates.

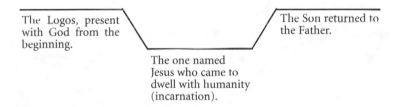

The Logos, present with God from the beginning.

The Son returned to the Father.

The one named Jesus who came to dwell with humanity (incarnation).

IV. Discipleship and the Kingdom of God

All four of the gospels of the New Testament mention the kingdom of God. In the gospels of Matthew and Mark, Jesus' first words of preaching are about the kingdom: "This is the time of fulfillment. The kingdom of God is at hand" (Mark 1:15; cf. Matt 3:2). Where or what is this kingdom of God? Certainly, it is not located in an earthly place, as we might speak of the British empire or the kingdom of Morocco. However, it is not to be equated with heaven, either. Perhaps we get a clearer understanding of the concept "kingdom of God," if we think of it in terms of the reign of God. The reign of God on earth is manifested in the coming of the Son, in the Spirit's presence among us, and in the conviction that God's grace is greater than all the powers of evil in the world. Thus, the gospel concept "kingdom of God" has apocalyptic overtones. It presupposes a situation in which, by the power of God, good has triumphed over evil.

The notion of "kingdom of God" also points to Christians' belief in God's presence among us. Luke's gospel contains the following passage, which illustrates well this aspect of the kingdom of God:

> *Asked by the Pharisees when the kingdom of God would come, [Jesus] said in reply, "The coming of the kingdom of God cannot be observed, and no one will announce, 'Look, here it is,' or, 'There it is.' For behold, the kingdom of God is among you"* (Luke 17:20-21).

Closely related to the gospels' teaching about the kingdom of God is the notion of discipleship. What does it mean to be a follower of Jesus? One answer to the question is to be found in Jesus' teaching on the demands of discipleship at the conclusion of the scene in which Peter confesses that Jesus is the Messiah. Jesus tells Peter that the Son of Man, as messiah, must suffer. Moreover, as a disciple of

Jesus, the believer must suffer as he suffered (Mark 8:34-38; Matt 16:24-27; Luke 14:26-27). Likewise, the parable of the Sower and the Seed (Mark 4:1-9) teaches about discipleship. The interpretation attached to the parable (Mark 4:13-20) explains the meaning of the four types of soil and how they correspond to four possible responses to the gospel. It also warns about those things that keep a person from responding to the gospel: an excessive concern for riches, approval, or power; an inability to withstand adversity; and a refusal to listen. The message of the parable is about hearing the "good news," accepting it, and preaching it to others. The one who does this is a true disciple.

In John's gospel, the stories and dialogues associated with Nicodemus and the Samaritan woman also teach about discipleship. One of these characters is a positive model of discipleship and the other is a negative model. Both misunderstand Jesus' words and fail to understand the significance of his message, at least at first. However, Nicodemus, a leader of the Jews and a teacher of Israel, eventually fades from the scene, unable to understand what Jesus was about and unable to become his disciple (John 3:10). In contrast, the Samaritan woman leaves her encounter with Jesus and returns to her village saying, "Come and see a man who told me everything I have done. Could he possibly be the Messiah?" (John 4:28-29). The narrator adds, "Many of the Samaritans of that town began to believe in him because of the word of the woman" (John 4:39). One need not wonder further which is the disciple of Jesus.

Figure 6.3: The Samaritan woman meeting Jesus at the well. Sixth-century mosaic from San Apollinare in Classe, Ravenna, Italy.

V. Baptism and Eucharist in the New Testament Traditions

Baptism and Eucharist are important for most Christian traditions of today's world. They were also important for Christians of the New Testament period. Unfortunately, the writings of the New Testament tell us little about how Baptism and Eucharist were actually celebrated in the first century of Christianity, but they do tell us something about their meaning or significance for early Christian communities. An early Christian missionary by the name of Paul wrote about the significance of Christian Baptism, describing it in terms of participation in the death and resurrection of Jesus.

> *Through baptism into [Christ's] death we were buried with him, so that, just as Christ was raised from the dead by the glory of the Father, we too might live an new life...in Christ Jesus* (Rom 6:4).

The author of the first letter of Peter describes Baptism as the means by which Christians are saved from sin (1 Pet 3:21) and born anew (1 Peter 1:23) to become "a chosen race, a royal priesthood, a holy nation, God's own people" (1 Peter 2:9).

Where did Christians get the idea for Baptism? According to the gospels, John the Baptist, a 1st-century CE Jewish prophet, preached a baptism of repentance (Mark 1:4-8; parallels). Therefore, Christian Baptism may have its roots in Jewish practice. However, the gospels also make a distinction between the baptism of John and the Baptism of the Holy Spirit which Jesus came to bring (Mark 1:7-8; parallels). Thus, Baptism became for the Christian not only a ritual of repentance, but also an initiation into the community of believers and an experience of the conferral of the Holy Spirit. Matthew's gospel describes a scene in which the risen Christ commissions his disciples to go out and make disciples of all nations, *baptizing* them in the name of the Father, of the Son, and of the Holy Spirit (Matt 28:19). Christians today use a similar phrase in their ritual of Baptism.

The word "Eucharist" comes from a Greek word meaning "to give thanks." According to the gospels, this is what Jesus did when he shared the last meal with his disciples. This is also what he commanded his disciples to do in memory of him. Although Christians in different communities attach different meanings to the Eucharistic celebration, many such interpretations are related to the event of Jesus' death and the last supper which he shared with his disciples (Mark 14:22-25). Paul gives us perhaps the earliest recorded tradition related the Eucharist:

> *I received from the Lord what I handed on to you, namely, that the Lord Jesus on the night in which he was betrayed took bread, and after he had given thanks, broke it and said, "This is my body, which is for you. Do this in remembrance of me." In the same way, after the supper, he took the cup, saying, "This cup is the new covenant in my blood. Do this, whenever you drink it, in remembrance of me." Every time, then, you eat this bread and drink this cup, you proclaim the death of the Lord until he comes!* (1 Cor 11:23-27).

On the one hand, Eucharist is a celebration of expectation concerning the return of the Messiah and the coming of God's kingdom. It is also a celebration of Christ's presence in the Christian community. Luke's gospel tells the story of two of Jesus' disciples walking to the town of Emmaus shortly after Jesus had been put to death in Jerusalem. While they were walking they were discussing what had happened in Jerusalem. The risen Jesus came up behind them, but in their sadness they failed to recognize him, until he sat down to dinner with them and "took bread, blessed and broke it, and gave it to them" (Luke 24:30). The risen Jesus made himself known to them in the celebration of Eucharist.

Equally important is the fact that the Eucharist has its roots in the celebration of Passover, the Jewish feast commemorating the Exodus event. It is a festival of remembrance concerning the loving kindness of God toward his people during their stay in the desert, but it is also a celebration of anticipation when all God's people will enjoy liberty. According to the synoptic gospels, Jesus' last supper with his disciples was the Jewish Passover meal. With that meal, Jesus established a new covenant in his blood: "This cup that is poured out for you is the new covenant in my blood" (Luke 22:20).

Baptism and Eucharist continue to hold a significant place in Christian traditions today, because both experiences are outward signs of that which Christians understand to be a new covenant through Jesus Christ. Through Baptism, Christians give public expression to their identity as people of the new covenant. Through Eucharist, Christians, in community, celebrate their covenant relationship with God as they await the experience of the fullness of that covenant in God's kingdom.

Key Terms:

passion narratives	christology
synoptic gospels	beatitudes
Two Source Hypothesis	Logos
Q	kingdom of God

Questions for Reading:

1. Explain some of the reasons why the death and resurrection of Jesus was an important event for early Christians and why they made it a central part of their theological reflection on the Christian faith.

2. Briefly describe what scholars have concluded about the stages of composition whereby the gospels came to be written.

3. What is the synoptic problem and how does the Two Source Hypothesis provide a possible answer to this problem?

4. Although all four gospels tell the story of Jesus' life, each provides a somewhat different portrait of Jesus. For each gospel, select one key idea that might answer the question "Who is Jesus?" or "What was Jesus sent to do?"

5. Although the New Testament tells us little about how early Christians celebrated Baptism and Eucharist, it does tell us something about the meaning they attached to these rituals. Explain.

Works Consulted/Recommended Reading:

Duling, Dennis C. and Perrin, Norman. *The New Testament: Proclamation and Parenesis, Myth and History*. 3rd ed. Fort Worth: Harcourt Brace, 1994.

Harris, Stephen L. *The New Testament. A Student's Introduction*. Mountain View, CA: Mayfield Publishing, 1995.

Metzger, Bruce and Murphy, Roland, eds. *The New Oxford Annotated Bible with Apocrypha*, New Revised Standard Version. New York: Oxford University Press, 1991.

Perkins, Pheme. *Reading the New Testament*. New York: Paulist, 1988.

Raisanen, Heikki. *The "Messianic Secret" in Mark*. Edinburgh: T & T Clark, 1990.

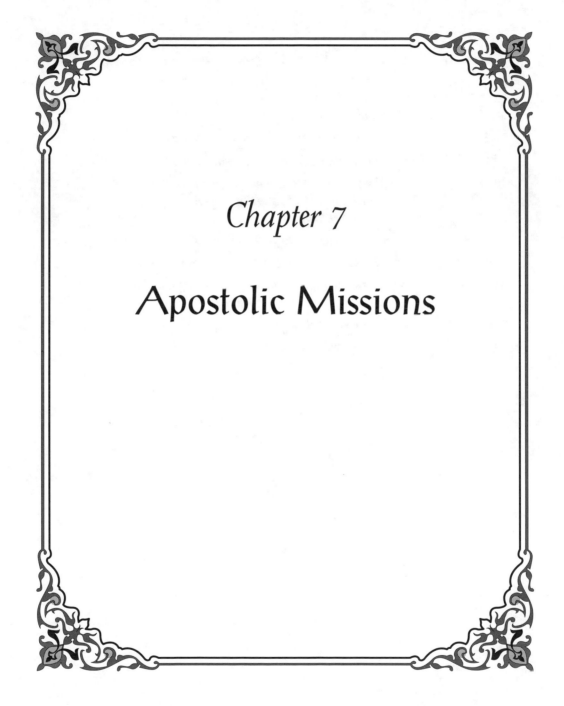

Chapter 7

Apostolic Missions

Timeline

c. 4-6 CE	Birth of Paul.
30?	Death of Jesus.
32-33?	Paul's conversion on the road to Damascus.
37-40	A Christian church is established at Antioch.
48	The Jerusalem Conference meets to decide whether Gentile converts must observe Jewish Torah regulations.
49	A Christian church is already in existence in Rome.
49-50	Paul establishes the church at Corinth.
50-55	Paul writes his letters to the churches he founded during his missionary journeys.
56?	Paul is arrested in Jerusalem.
58?	Paul is tried and sent to Rome.
60?	Paul is killed by the Roman Emperor Nero.

Apostolic Missions

After the death and resurrection of Jesus, the message about him spread rapidly throughout the ancient world. Although Christians were still a tiny minority in the Roman Empire in 100 CE, the seeds of Christianity's emergence as the dominant religion in the Mediterranean world were sown by the success of the 1st-century missionaries. By the end of the 1st century, Christian churches thrived in most of the major cities of the Roman Empire. However, Christianity grew so rapidly in its first decades, and with so little institutional control, that the religion quickly began to mean different things to different people. The result was that Christianity in the 1st century was an extremely diverse religious phenomenon, with all sorts of people calling themselves "Christians" but having some very different beliefs and practices.

In spite of the diversity of beliefs and practices in 1st-century Christian churches, it is also possible to see traces of what will later become their unifying force. Already, from the beginning, the apostles and first followers of Jesus held a place of status within the churches as teachers and spiritual guides for the Christian communities. Some Christian communities gave to Peter a special status as the first of the apostles. Later, the **bishops** and leaders of the church would trace the source of their teaching authority back to Peter and the apostles. The early churches also proclaimed the same basic message, namely that Jesus was the messiah and Son of God, the one who was crucified, but also raised from the dead by God's power, so that all who believe might have eternal life. Later, the leaders of these churches used this basic message to formulate and refine **doctrine** (teaching) concerning the nature of God, the relationship between God and Jesus, and a variety of other issues that divided the churches. In addition, Christian communities had an intense belief in the power of the Holy Spirit acting in their midst as comforter, inspiration, and guide in the Christian life. Finally, it was during this early period that the books which will later be known as the New Testament were being written. In the centuries that follow, they will become known as the **canon** or list of religious documents which are authoritative for defining the Christian faith and governing its way of life.

I. The Apostle Paul

The most prolific of the first generation of Christian missionaries was **Paul**. His importance for the spread of early Christianity is attested by the amount of space in the New Testament that is devoted to him: fourteen of the twenty-seven books in the New Testament were included because they were believed to have been written by Paul. Another New Testament book, The Acts of the Apostles, devotes a majority of its pages to describing Paul's missionary activities. These books are the main sources for our understanding of Paul's life and message.

A. An Overview of Paul's Life

Paul was reportedly born in the city of Tarsus, in Asia Minor (modern-day Turkey), into a Jewish family who belonged to the party of the Pharisees. Paul's membership in this group meant that he was known for pious behavior and spent a great deal of time studying the Torah. In fact, it seems that Paul surpassed even the other Pharisees in his devotion to the Law, as he says in one of his letters: "I advanced in Judaism beyond many among my people of the same age, for I was far more zealous for the traditions of my ancestors" (Gal 1:14). Although Paul clearly received an outstanding education in the ways of Judaism, his letters also show that he gained a broad knowledge of the Greek language and culture. It is this combination of Judaism and Hellenism in his background that enabled Paul to assume the leadership of Christianity when it was beginning to make the transition from a small Jewish sect to a major world religion.

Little is known of Paul's life prior to his becoming a Christian, although many scholars theorize that he was a Jewish missionary. In Paul's time Judaism actively sought to make converts, and there were many Gentiles who were interested in Judaism, which was attractive to them in large part because of its monotheism and strict ethical code. People who were attracted to Judaism but uncertain whether to become fully Jewish (perhaps because of other Jewish requirements such as circumcision and the kosher dietary restrictions) were called "God-fearers," and they would often attend the synagogue and listen to the readings of the Torah and debates over the Jewish Law. Jewish missionaries like Paul would attend these services and attempt to persuade these "God-fearers" to become full Jews.

It is probably in this capacity that Paul first encountered the Christian message, since the synagogues would also have been the first place that Jewish-Christian missionaries would have gone to spread their belief that the messiah had come. The Christian message apparently outraged Paul, as it did many other Jews. The reasons for this are unclear. Perhaps Paul simply rejected the idea that Jesus was the messiah and thought that the Christian missionaries were heretics for claiming that he was; perhaps some specific parts of Jesus' teaching (for example his apparent disagreement with some parts of the Pharisaic interpretation of the Law) offended Paul. At any rate, Paul felt strongly enough about the dangers of this new teaching that he sought and received permission from the Jewish authorities to persecute Christians. Jewish persecution of Christians was not uncommon in the 1st century CE, and could involve beatings, imprisonment, and even execution. Paul is said to have imprisoned Christians and also to have attended and approved of the killing of a great Christian leader named Stephen (see Acts 7-8).

It was while he was involved in the persecution of Christians that Paul became a follower of Jesus Christ. Paul himself never describes the conversion experience in any detail, but the Acts of the Apostles (9:1-22) tells us that Paul was on the road to Damascus (to arrest Christians) when he was blinded by a bright light and he heard a voice from heaven which said, "Saul, Saul, [Paul's Jewish name] why do you persecute me?" Paul answered, "Who are you, Lord?" The voice replied, "I am Jesus, whom you are persecuting" (Acts 9:4-5). This experience convinced Paul that Jesus was in fact the messiah. He was led into Damascus, where his blindness was cured and he was baptized as a Christian by a man named Ananias.

Our evidence for certain events in Paul's life, such as the details of Paul's conversion, Paul's participation in the martyrdom of Stephen, and his final arrest and trials, is found only in the Acts of the Apostles. It must be said that the interests of the author of the Acts of the Apostles (also the author of the gospel of Luke) were more theological than historical. What this means is that Acts is not universally regarded as being a completely reliable source for historical information about Paul, or other figures and events in early Christian history. Paul's letters themselves are usually regarded by historians as a more reliable source. Hence in this overview of Paul's life we rely more on Paul's letters than on Acts, and we attempt to acknowledge those places where evidence is used from the less reliable Acts of the Apostles.

After this revelation, Paul immediately re-directed his missionary zeal toward the Christian message. His first journeys were to his home region of Cilicia and Arabia. There is no record of any great successes in these areas. At some point Paul was brought to Antioch in Syria, where for the first time the message about Jesus as the Christ was preached to Gentiles rather than exclusively to Jews. When this happened, the question arose as to whether these Gentiles must become "Jewish" in order to convert to Christianity. Up to this point, the Christian movement had retained all of the requirements of Judaism. Did these Gentiles then also need to become circumcised, follow the Torah, sacrifice in the Temple, and keep kosher? Or was it enough that they believed in Jesus Christ, without taking on the other requirements of the Jewish faith? The answer given in Antioch was that faith in Jesus Christ was enough, and that Gentiles were not required to do such things as becoming circumcised and following the Jewish Law. This "innovation" in Christianity—a **gospel** without the Law and circumcision—was immediately successful. Large numbers of Gentiles began converting to this new "version" of Christianity.

This new gospel created a storm of controversy among Christian Jews who believed strongly that there could be no compromise about the retention of all the elements of Judaism. In 48 or 49 CE a conference was called to discuss the question of whether Gentiles needed to become Jews in order to convert to Christianity. This meeting is called

Figure 7.1: Saint Paul on the road to Damascus.

the **Jerusalem Conference**. Paul and Barnabas, the leaders of the church in Antioch, attended the conference and defended the position that the Gentiles did not need to follow the Law and become circumcised. Opposed to them was a group of conservative Jewish-Christians who supported requiring all Christians to keep the requirements of Judaism. The leaders who were to decide the question were the Jerusalem apostles, led by Peter, John, and James "the brother of the Lord."

Exactly what happened at the Jerusalem Conference is a matter of some dispute. Paul records that the conference ended with the Jerusalem apostles completely vindicating his gospel and approving unconditionally of his preaching of this new version of Christianity to the Gentiles (Gal 2:1-10). The Acts of the Apostles records more of a compromise, where Gentiles are released from some of the requirements of Judaism, but not all (Acts 15:19-21). Apparently, the issue was not decided once and for all at the conference, as Paul continued to have difficulty with conservative Jewish-Christians who often tried to undermine his subsequent missionary efforts. Sometimes Paul was even forced to confront the same Jerusalem apostles who had given approval for his activities (see Galatians 2).

Whatever the precise outcome of the Jerusalem Conference, Paul felt that he had been given a mandate by God to preach a gospel without the Law and circumcision to the Gentiles. After the conference he began a series of ambitious missionary journeys which included travels to Cyprus, Asia Minor, Macedonia, and Greece. These journeys were a stunning success. Paul founded numerous churches and made thousands of converts, becoming probably the greatest missionary Christianity has ever seen.

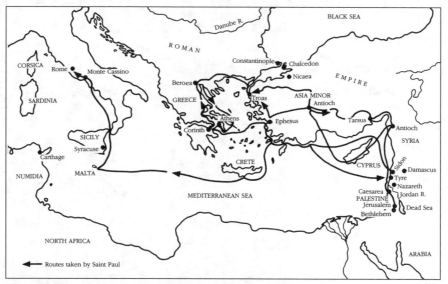

Figure 7.2: Map of Paul's missionary journeys.

The letters of Paul found in the New Testament are all written to churches that he himself founded (with one exception, the letter to the Romans), and they all contain Paul's specific responses to the questions, needs and problems of that particular church. After Paul left a community—either because he wanted to continue his missionary work elsewhere or because he was forced by persecution to leave—he would communicate with the church he left behind through the mail, especially if he heard that there was some problem or crisis facing the community. Some of these letters survived and were eventually included in the canon of the New Testament.

It must be acknowledged that not all of the letters traditionally ascribed to Paul were actually written by him. One of them (the letter to the Hebrews) does not actually have Paul's name attached to it. Only seven of the other thirteen letters are universally believed by scholars to have been written by Paul (1 Thessalonians, 1 & 2 Corinthians, Galatians, Philippians, Philemon, and Romans). Authorship of the other six letters (2 Thessalonians, Colossians, Ephesians, 1 & 2 Timothy, and Titus) is disputed to varying degrees. Many scholars believe that these letters were written by disciples of Paul in their master's name. The practice of writing a document with a false name attached—called "**pseudonymity**"— was quite common in the ancient world.

Paul's career came to an end when he journeyed to Jerusalem, apparently to deliver a collection he had been taking to relieve the victims of a famine there. Paul was hated by many Jews (and Jewish-Christians) for having abandoned the Jewish elements in his gospel. Paul's appearance in a city or town often caused a riot, and because of this he spent a good deal of time in jail for disturbing the peace. According to Acts, Paul's final return to Jerusalem caused such a riot (Acts 21:27-36). Paul was arrested and eventually taken to Rome, where church tradition has it that he was executed by the Roman emperor Nero.

B. The Authority of Paul as an Apostle

In almost every one of Paul's letters he identifies himself as an **apostle**. The word "apostle" comes from the Greek word "*apostello*," which means "to send out." An "apostle," then, is "one who is sent out." Christians meant by the term "one who is sent out by Jesus to preach the word about him." Thus, an apostle is distinct from a **disciple**. The word "disciple" refers simply to a learner or a follower. One could be both a disciple and an apostle (like Peter and John, who both followed Jesus during his lifetime and were sent out by him to preach the word to others), but one could be a disciple without being an apostle. It was quite possible to have been a follower of Jesus, but not specifically sent out by him to preach the word. It was presumed by many early Christians that in order to be an apostle, one must have known Jesus and been sent out by him to preach during his lifetime.

By this definition, it would be impossible for Paul to be an apostle, because he never knew Jesus during his lifetime. However, Paul claimed that he was an apostle, because he had been sent out by Jesus to preach the word. This mission simply had not been given to him during Jesus' lifetime, but in a revelation that took place after Jesus' death and resurrection.

Paul's revelation-based claim to be an apostle is eventually accepted by the church as a whole, as is attested by the inclusion of Paul's letters in the canon of the New Testament. However, the fact is that Paul often struggled to be accepted as an apostle during his lifetime. In fact, much of the controversy that dogged Paul throughout his career can be attributed to the question of whether or not he was a "real" apostle like Peter and John. Many people were skeptical about his claim to have had a revelation, and felt more comfortable with the leadership of people like Peter and John, who had been among Jesus' original twelve disciples and whose apostleship was not in dispute.

C. An Overview of Paul's Message

It is no easy matter to summarize Paul's message. Paul's writing is often difficult to understand, and his letters were not written to satisfy the curiosity of future generations, but to meet the concrete needs of particular 1st-century communities. Nonetheless, Paul's letters are important for describing a number of important themes in Christian theology.

Many scholars and church leaders have located the "center" of Paul's theology in the principle of **justification** by faith alone, which is prominent in the letter to the Galatians and in the letter to the Romans. In both of these letters, Paul argues strongly that one cannot find justification by the works of the Law, but only through faith in Jesus Christ. What does Paul mean by this? One of the meanings of the word "justification" has to do with alignment. If the right hand margin on a printed page has been made perfectly straight, then it is a "justified" right margin. If the margin is crooked or ragged, then it is not justified. Hence justification in general can refer to making straight something that is crooked, or even more generally to fixing or repairing something that is broken. In a religious context, justification refers to one's relationship with God. If this relationship is good (or "straight"), then a person is "justified." If this relationship is broken (or "crooked"), then a person is not justified. Hence, "justification" refers to the state of being in a right relationship with God, and a person who is "justified" is one who is in a right relationship with God.

Both the Jewish and Christian faiths assume that human beings in their present state are not in a right relationship with God. This poor relationship is caused by sin. Human beings sin against God, and this sin creates distance between ourselves and God. We are estranged from God by sin. The question is how to overcome this distance. How can we "repair" this broken relationship with God? When Paul refers to "justification by works" and "justification by faith," he is speaking of two different and opposing theories about how our broken relationship with God can be repaired.

1. Justification by Works

Justification by works, which many people feel is characteristic of traditional Judaism, involves two responses to the question about how humanity can repair its broken relationship with God. First, if our bad relationship with God is caused by sin, then the solution is to avoid sin as much as possible. Judaism held that God assists in the process of avoiding sin by giving people the Law of Moses to follow. The Law helps people to know what counts as a sin and what does not, what is pleasing to God and what is not. Second, when people do sin, they must try to "make up" or atone for that sin by doing some good deed. In Judaism, for example, one could atone for sin by doing such things as performing sacrifices, fasting, praying, or giving alms (donating money to the poor). These are the works or good deeds prescribed by the Law.

2. Justification by Faith

Justification by faith is the theory that Paul supports. He begins by arguing that justification *by works* simply does not work, for two reasons. On the one hand, it is impossible for human beings to successfully avoid sin. On the other hand, it is impossible for human beings to "make up" for sins with good deeds. As Paul understands the problem, our sins are an affront to God. They cannot be atoned for with a prayer or a donation. In fact, no good deed can ever really atone for sin.

Perhaps the two meanings of the Greek verb *dikaioun* ("to justify") can help us understand why Paul argues that a person can only be justified by faith. One meaning of the word *dikaioun* is "to acquit," as in a court of law. When Paul says that we cannot be justified by our works, he means that if human beings were judged on the merits of their case, according to what we really deserved, no one would be justified. Because of our sinful nature, no one would ever be able to stand as acquitted before God. It is impossible for human beings to use good works to "earn" acquittal. The only way we can be acquitted is if God simply gives it to us as a free gift, in spite of the fact that we do not deserve it. This idea of God's bestowal of a free gift is what theologians mean by the term "**grace**."

The other meaning of *dikaioun* is "to make upright." According to this meaning of the word, someone must act in our behalf to *make us* upright or to *put us* in right relationship with God. Paul describes justification as God's free gift, not as something we have earned or deserve. God has given this gift by sending his son Jesus Christ. For Paul, Jesus' death on the cross functions as a sacrifice that makes us upright, that makes us able to stand before God in right relationship. This understanding of the purpose of Jesus' death—that Jesus died for our sins—is called "**sacrificial atonement**." The death of Jesus constitutes, for Paul, God's offer of salvation to human beings. We cannot bridge the gulf between God and ourselves through our own efforts, but we can allow God to bridge this gulf for us. On account of Jesus' death we have **salvation** (that is, we have been rescued from harm) and **redemption** (we have been bought back for God). He is our **expiation** (sacrificial offering for the removal of sin). Through him, the Christian experiences freedom and **sanctification** (we have been made holy).

What, then, does Paul mean when he talks about justification *by faith alone*? God's offer of justification in Jesus Christ is a free gift. Therefore, all we need to do in response is accept it, and we do this simply by believing that it is true, that is, by having faith. We cannot bring about our justification by our works. Any good deeds that we could do would not be enough to earn us an acquittal in God's tribunal of justice. However, we can be made righteous, not by our own efforts but by accepting in faith the free gift offered by God. Faith, as Paul understands it, is not confined to a set of beliefs which one learns. Rather, it should be understood as trust. For Paul faith is active trust or trust that manifests itself in the way the believer lives his or her life. He describes it as "faith working through love" (Gal 5:6).

Paul's teaching on justification by faith appears, at first glance, to be fairly straightforward and unambiguous. However, depending what one understands Paul to be saying (or not saying), his message can have strikingly different ramifications. At the heart of the ambiguity are questions concerning what Paul thinks about sin and how he conceives of human nature. It is unclear from Paul's writings whether or not he thinks that human nature, of itself, is capable of any good. In his letter to the Romans, for example, he says that humans were made capable of knowing God, but they chose not to—implying their capacity to do good, in spite of their choice to do evil (Rom 1:19). If we assume that Paul had this view of human nature in mind, then we can also argue that Paul would allow for the possibility that, although God justifies, humans can do good deeds that aid in their salvation. However, later, Paul says that human beings, by themselves, are unable to win the inner war of the spirit (or inner will) over the flesh (Rom 7:14-24). In this way of thinking, humans are simply too sinful by nature to do good. Our sins are simply too serious for us to be saved.

Because of this ambiguity, there are very different interpretations of Paul's principle of justification by faith alone. Some Christians, especially Catholics, interpret Paul to be saying that human beings are still capable of goodness, and hence they believe that it is not simply one's faith but also one's deeds that determine whether the individual is saved. Other Christians, especially Lutherans, interpret Paul to be saying that the focus should be on the goodness of God, not humanity. In this view, God and God alone can save us from our sinful condition. These Christians have found in Paul's principle of justification by faith alone the essence of the Christian faith. The disagreement over this idea continues to divide Christians even to this day.

3. Life in Christ

Although in such letters as Galatians and Romans Paul's major focus is how persons are to be justi-fied, all of his letters together reveal an equal concern for how persons are to live as Christians. Thus, Paul's emphasis on "life in Christ" accompanies the theme of justification by faith. As Romans and 1 Corinthians demonstrate, for Paul God's grace-filled gift of Christ's death both reconciles sinners to God and unites all baptized Christians with Christ and with each other to form Christ's body. The source of this unity, Paul believes, is the fact that the Spirit of God dwells in them.

> For just as the body is one and has many members, and all the members of the body, though
> many, are one body, so it is with Christ. For in the one Spirit we were all baptized into one body—
> Jews or Greeks, slaves or free—and we were all made to drink of one Spirit (1 Cor 12:12-13).

In light of this spiritual union with Christ, Paul expresses serious concern for how Christians treat each other and their own bodies. For example, in 1 Corinthians 5-6 he counsels Corinthian Christians to practice strict sexual morality. In Galatians 5 he warns against self-indulgence, greed, and a combative spirit. Likewise, in 1 Corinthians 8-14, Paul discusses numerous issues relating to Christian worship, such as the proper use of the Lord's Supper or Eucharist. Living the good Christian life does not earn one salvation in Paul's view. Rather, a moral life is the expected response to God's grace in Christ Jesus. This is Paul's command: "You are in Christ, so live in Christ."

Life in Christ expresses itself ritually in Baptism and Eucharist. Paul taught that in Baptism the believer was incorporated into Christ. The baptized went down into the water in order to be bap-tized into his death and to be buried with him so that, just as he was raised from the death, they could walk in the new life of a Christian (Rom 6:1-4). Similarly, Paul saw Eucharist as a way in which Christians participated in the body of Christ (1 Cor 10:16). At the same time, it ought to be the source of their unity with other Christians. If the Eucharist is not the source of their unity, it will be their condemnation (1 Cor 11:17-34).

II. Other Apostolic Missions

The growth of Christianity during the 1st and 2nd centuries was not limited to the cities visited by Paul or to the churches which he founded. Rather, it is only the case that we have considerably more information about the Christian communities that Paul founded. This is due in large part to the fact that so many of his letters were preserved among the books of the New Testament. In contrast, there is relatively little information available with which to reconstruct a portrait of early non-Pauline Christian communities (Christian churches not founded by Paul). Yet, Christian literature of a cen-tury or two later and early traditions of individual churches suggest that these other churches also have a very long and colorful history, dating back to the 1st and 2nd centuries of the common era of Christianity and Judaism.

From the Acts of the Apostles and the writings of 2nd- and 3rd-century Christian historians and theologians, we can piece together bits of information about 1st- and 2nd-century non-Pauline Christianity to give us at least a glimpse of their community life. In particular, we will focus upon the Christian communities at Jerusalem, Rome, Alexandria, and Antioch, which, together with Constantinople, come to be identified as the **patriarchal sees** (meaning "head or leading seats") of the early Christian church. These churches become very important players in the history of Christianity in both the East and the West during the next centuries of its development. We will also comment briefly on the variety of Christian churches that emerge in places outside of these central churches.

A. The Jerusalem Church

The church in Jerusalem was among the more important Jewish-Christian communities of the 1st century CE. While no evidence exists concerning the point at which this Jewish community identified itself as Christian, it appears to have been firmly established by 48-49 CE, when Paul and Barnabas went there for a meeting with its leaders concerning the admission of Gentile converts to this new way (Acts 15; Gal 2). According to Paul's letter to the churches in Galatia and several references in Acts of the Apostles, the leader of the Christian church at Jerusalem was James, identified as the brother of the Lord (Gal 1:18; 2:9, 12; Acts 12:17; 15:13). Historians do not know what happened to this church after the Romans sacked Jerusalem in 70 CE.

Unfortunately, our sources tell us little more about how the Christian community at Jerusalem functioned or about the tasks assumed by its leaders. However, we do know that it gave special honor to its leader, James, and to the apostles and the presbyters or elders of the community (Acts 15:22). It appears that the Christian community at Jerusalem retained the practice of circumcision and other legal requirements of Judaism, along with their newly founded Christian beliefs and practices. Further, concerning worship and lifestyle, the Acts of the Apostles describes the Christians at Jerusalem as sharing all things in common, going to the Temple daily, and gathering to "break bread" in their homes (Acts 2:42-47). The breaking of bread is a reference to the celebration of Eucharist. Acts of the Apostles also tells us that these early Christians were sometimes called "followers of the Way" (Acts 9:2; 16:17; 19:9, 23; 24:14, 22).

B. The Church of Rome

Already in the 1st century BCE, there was a large, and perhaps influential Jewish community in Rome. Literature and archeological data of the time suggests that, by the 1st century CE, Rome had a population of approximately 40,000-50,000 Jews and ten to thirteen synagogues. Christianity in Rome probably emerged out of these Jewish communities and from among the Gentile "God-fearers" who had attached themselves to their synagogues. Like other Jewish-Christian communities, these Christians probably still saw themselves as part of a reform movement in Judaism.

By the time Paul wrote to the Christian communities in Rome, perhaps around 55 CE, they had undergone some rather significant changes. In Acts of the Apostles, Luke mentions Priscilla and Aquila, a husband and wife missionary team who had fled Rome when emperor Claudius expelled the Jews from Rome in 49 CE. Apparently there had been some fighting between Jews and Jewish-Christians over teachings about Jesus as the Christ, and Claudius decided to settle the problem by getting rid of the whole lot. Thus, the Christian communities at Rome were left for a time with only their Gentile membership, although some Jewish-Christians may have returned after Claudius' death in 54 CE. At the time of Paul's writing, it appears that Jews and Christians were still fighting, since Paul indicates that Christians in Rome ought to remember their roots and not think themselves better than their Jewish brothers and sisters (Rom 11:17-24).

Although we cannot say for certain when the Christian communities at Rome were founded, they appear already to have been strongly established by 49 CE. Likewise, we cannot say who brought Christianity to Rome, although Church historians and other writers of the 2nd, 3rd, and 4th centuries associate Peter with its early years, if not with its founding. According to Eusebius, a 4th-century church historian, Peter was martyred in Rome, in approximately 64 CE.

C. The Church at Antioch in Syria

From Paul's letter to the churches in Galatia and several references in Acts of the Apostles, we know that there was also a Christian community at Antioch in Syria rather early in the 1st century CE (Acts 11:19-20; Gal 2:12). Acts of the Apostles indicates that the Jerusalem church sent Barnabas to help shepherd the church at Antioch, approximately 37-40 CE (Acts 11:19-25). Like the Christian communities founded in Jerusalem and Rome, the initial thrust of Christian missionary activity in Antioch appears to have been among its Jewish communities. However, Gentiles were also joining their church. Acts of the Apostles notes that it was at Antioch that the name "Christian" was first used (Acts 11:27).

Syria is also the likely home of an early Christian writing called the *Didache* or "The Teaching of the Twelve Apostles," believed to have been written in the late 1st century or early 2nd century CE. Its catechetical section (teachings about the Christian way of life) has many parallels with the gospel of Matthew, which also may have originated in Syria. Its liturgical section (teachings about the right ways to worship) highlights the importance of Baptism and the Eucharist for its Christian communities. It also reflects a church organization which held the Christian prophet in a place of honor and authority within its Christian communities. Acts of the Apostles also mentions the presence of Christian prophets in Antioch (Acts 13:1).

D. Christianity in Alexandria and Egypt

In addition to the churches of Jerusalem, Rome, and Antioch, Acts of the Apostles offers a few other very tentative clues about the spread of Christianity elsewhere during the 1st century CE. For example, Acts of the Apostles mentions a certain Apollo from Alexandria in Egypt who was "both an authority on scripture and instructed in the new way of the Lord" (Acts 18:24-25). Himself a Jew, he became a Christian and embarked on his own missionary ventures. Paul mentions him in relation to his preaching in Corinth (1 Cor 1:12; 3:5-9). Along with Athens and Antioch, Alexandria was one of the primary centers of Hellenistic culture prior to the beginnings of Christianity in the 1st century CE. In particular, it was noted for its philosophers and students of Plato's writings.

Although no written evidence exists concerning the origins of the Christian church at Alexandria and the Nile valley, it must have been established fairly early, since Christian writers of the 2nd century were arguing against certain other teachers from this place, whom they labeled as Christian heretics (teachers of false doctrine). Among some of Alexandria's famous Christian writers are Clement of Alexandria, Origen, Cyprian, and Athanasius. All four figure predominantly in the articulation of Christian teaching as it develops through the 4th century.

E. Christianity in Ethiopia, Edessa, Adiabene and Beyond

Acts of the Apostles tells of the conversion of another early Christian, an official from the court of the queen of Ethiopia who, while on his return trip from pilgrimage to Jerusalem, was baptized by Philip (Acts 8:26-40). Again, written history is mostly silent about early beginnings of the Christian church in Ethiopia, although Rufinus, another 4th-century church historian, notes that king Ezana converted to Christianity in the mid-4th century, making his kingdom of Aksum a Christian nation. He also tells about Frumentius, a Syrian by birth and a one-time slave in Ethiopia who was ordained by Athanasius of Alexandria to serve the church in Ethiopia (*H. E.* I, 9-10). This ordination created a special bond between these two churches which endured through much of their history into the modern period.

The Ethiopian Christian church preserves among its early traditions some interesting answers to questions for which written history is otherwise silent. For example, the Ethiopian church holds within its traditions the name of the eunuch baptized by Philip on the road to Gaza, identifying him as Juda, also called "Djan Daraba." They also claim within their tradition the identity of one of the three wise men who, according to Matthew's gospel, went to Bethlehem to worship the child Jesus, namely, King Bazan (Balthazar) who ruled Ethiopia for seventeen years at the turn of the era.

There are numerous other traditions concerning the apostles and the expanse of their missionary activity in the first centuries of Christianity. In his *History of the Church*, Eusebius indicated that the apostles were scattered over the whole world and that their influence could be felt in different areas: Thomas in the region of the Parthians, John in Asia, Peter in Pontus, Galatia, Cappadocia, Bithynia, and Rome, and Andrew in Scythia (*Hist. Eccl.* III.I.1). Concerning Thomas, Gregory of Nazianzus wrote further that he preached the gospel in India and was martyred there (*Or.* 25).

Two other locations are worthy of brief mention in the early history of Christianity: Edessa in Eastern Syria and Adiabene in Persia. Again, our information is sparse. However, Christianity is believed to have come to Adiabene at the end of the 1st century through the preaching of Addai. His Christian missionary activity supposedly followed upon an earlier Jewish mission in which Izates, the king of Adiabene, and his mother, Queen Helena, were converted to Judaism. Tradition has it that both were buried in Jerusalem.

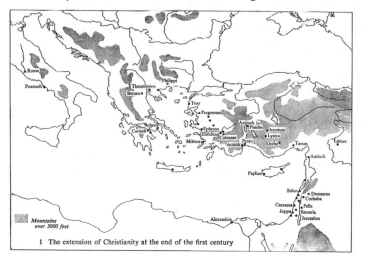

1 The extension of Christianity at the end of the first century

Figure 7.3: Map of the expansion of Christianity at the end of the 1st century CE.

The Christian church at Edessa also claimed Addai as its founder. Eusebius tells of a tradition in which King Abgar, who had been very ill and who had heard about Jesus' miracles, received a letter from Jesus delivered by one of Jesus' disciples who also healed him of his illness. Later, Thomas sent Thaddeus to his city to teach about Christ (*Hist. Eccl.* I.13). This tradition is especially important to the Armenian church who claims its origin through the apostle Thomas.

In sum, although reliable information about the first hundred years of Christianity is very sketchy, we can see several important trends developing in its history. We can see that early Christianity spread very rapidly, especially among the larger centers of culture and trade. It grew and developed in a rather charismatic fashion, without much institutional control, and it gave birth to diverse and distinctive communities, all of whom called themselves "Christian." Thus, for each of these communities, their Christian identity meant something quite different from other Christian communities. This early history helps us to understand why the major thrust of the next period in early Christian history must be, of necessity, the articulation and clarification of Christian doctrine or teaching.

Key Terms:

Paul   justification
gospel   justification by works
Jerusalem Conference   justification by faith
pseudonymity   sacrificial atonement
apostle   grace
disciple   patriarchal see

Questions for Reading:

1. Why was there so much diversity of belief in early Christianity? What elements of early Christianity would later be used to unify the church?

2. Give an account of Paul's activities prior to his becoming a follower of Jesus Christ, and explain how he eventually came to follow Jesus.

3. What happened at the Jerusalem Conference?

4. Define the term "apostle" (distinguishing it from the term "disciple") and explain why Paul had difficulty being accepted as an apostle in his lifetime. Is he ever recognized as an apostle by the Church?

5. Explain the difference between justification by works and justification by faith. Which does Paul prefer? Why?

6. Name the four major non-Pauline Christian churches of the 1st and 2nd centuries CE and the New Testament apostles or preachers associated with them. Which, if any, originated as Jewish-Christian communities?

Works Consulted/Recommended Reading:

Bornkamm, Gunther. *Paul*. New York: Harper & Row, 1971.

Daniélou, Jean and Marrou, Henri. *The First Six Hundred Years. The Christian Centuries*, Vol. 1. New York: Paulist Press, 1964.

Di Berardino, Angelo, ed. *Encyclopedia of Early Christianity*. Trans. Adrian Walford. New York: Oxford University Press, 1992.

Metzger, Bruce and Murphy, Roland, eds. *The New Oxford Annotated Bible with Apocrypha*, New Revised Standard Version. New York: Oxford University Press, 1991.

Perrin, Norman and Duling, Dennis C. *The New Testament: An Introduction*. 2nd ed. San Diego: Harcourt Brace Jovanovich, 1982.

Part III: The History of Christianity

I. Scripture and Tradition

Christianity, like Judaism and Islam, is a "religion of the book." Parts I and II of this textbook have explored the character of the Christian sacred book, the Bible. All Christian churches accept the Bible as the revealed word of God, even if they do not agree fully on the precise list of books to be included in the Old Testament. During the 2nd and 3rd centuries, Christians gradually came to agree that God's public revelation in Christ ended with the death of the apostolic generation. The canon was therefore "closed," and no new books were considered for inclusion in the New Testament. The biblical canon of Old and New Testaments has remained *the only universally accepted standard* for defining the character of Christianity.

With the passage of time, however, a religion of the book faces a problem. In different historical circumstances, there are a host of *new* problems and issues that surface, problems and issues that are not addressed at all (at least directly) in the sacred texts. These new experiences will require new insights into the fixed revelation. The canonical texts will need to be *interpreted* so that they speak to the challenges of the contemporary world and address the needs and problems of contemporary Christians. But even here potential problems surface, because there is always conflict over how the scriptures should be interpreted. Disagreements about the meaning of the canonical text may require invoking another standard or authority outside of scripture, if the disagreement is to be resolved.

Moreover, even if there were no "gaps" in the answers provided by the Bible to the questions of Christian life, there would still be a role in Christianity for ideas, writings, and thoughts that are not biblical in their origins. The canonical text needs to be brought alive if it is to energize the faithful. The endless fertility of the human imagination continues to create new symbols, literary forms, prayers and ceremonies, role models for Christian life, ways of organizing the community, and innovations of many other kinds, to nurture and refresh the religion.

For all of these reasons, Christianity (like Judaism and Islam) has found it necessary to *supplement* the original revelation with a concept of **tradition** which effectively mediates or communicates the written revelation to later generations. "Tradition" here refers to the accumulated wisdom of the church's teachers, whereby the faith derived from the scriptures, contained in the creeds, and expressed in the liturgy is *interpreted* for contemporary believers. All Christian churches employ tradition at least in some sense. However, the Christian churches are divided on just how important and just how reliable "tradition" is. The most serious division is between the Catholic and Orthodox churches, on the one hand, and the Protestant churches on the other. The Catholics and the Orthodox hold that scripture and tradition are in *continuity* with one another, and hence that tradition is a reliable source for Christians asking questions about behavior and belief. Catholics and Orthodox also agree that tradition is equal or nearly equal in importance to the Bible. Protestant forms of Christianity are more skeptical about the reliability of tradition, and attempt to place much less emphasis on it. Protestants prefer to rely on *the Bible alone*, although in practice the different Protestant churches have all developed some form of "tradition," creating a wide variety of solutions for dealing with historical change and development.

The rest of this book is devoted to telling the story of the *history* of Christianity from the time of Christ up to the present. This historical approach has been chosen for three reasons. First, narrative (the telling of stories) is typical of the Bible's own approach to revelation, probably because it is such an effective and entertaining way of communicating truth. Second, especially since the conversion of the Roman Empire, Christianity has been an inseparable element of the history of Western civilization, understood in the broadest sense (though we will see that Christianity also has a history *outside* Western civilization). Since the history of the church is so much a part of the history of the Western world (and vice versa), it is valuable for students to know this history. Finally, a historical approach seems the fairest and most efficient way to illustrate both the continuity and the diversity of Christianity. In order to explain best how groups of Christians came to differ from one another—and how Christians continue to agree on some fundamental things—it is necessary to show the *origins* of the disagreements and the *process* by which agreements were reached.

II. The Divisions of Christian History

It is customary to divide the history of Christianity into three different periods, each of which has been marked by the differentiation of new types of Christianity:

(1) The early Christian or "patristic" period (2nd - 5th centuries).

During its early years Christianity grew away from its Jewish roots and spread throughout the Roman Empire. Christianity developed the institutions, doctrines, and practices which gave it its classic shape. During the 4th century, the church underwent a momentous change from a persecuted minority to the established religion of the state. Theological disagreements and cultural divisions with their roots in the councils of the 4th and 5th centuries would eventually lead to the separation of several Christian churches in the Middle East. The history of this period is covered in chapters 8-10.

(2) The medieval period (6th - 15th centuries).

This period is marked by major geographical shifts in the Christian world. In the 5th century the Roman Empire in the West succumbed to "barbarian" invaders and the Western Christian church, led by the pope of Rome, shouldered the burden of rebuilding civilization on a Christian foundation. After the 7th century, the spread of Islam, the third great monotheistic faith in addition to Judaism and Christianity, led to the loss of most of North Africa, the Middle East, and even parts of Europe. During this period the Christianity which had existed in the Eastern (Greek) and Western (Latin) halves of the Roman Empire permanently split into Eastern Orthodoxy and Western Roman Catholic Christianity. The medieval period came to a close with Catholic Christianity locked in crisis and seeking to reform itself. At the same time the cultural movement of the Renaissance was renewing European culture and moving it towards a new stage of human self-awareness. The history of this period is found in chapters 11-17.

(3) The modern period (16th - 20th centuries).

The modern period is usually further divided into the Reformation and post-Reformation periods.

a. The Reformation (16th-17th centuries). Frustrated tensions for reform finally split Western Christianity into Roman Catholicism and the various types of Protestant Christianity. The result was the destruction of the old internationalist ideal of Christianty ("Christendom") and its replacement by nationalized state churches. The reforming vanguard was led by Martin Luther in Germany and Ulrich Zwingli and John Calvin in Switzerland. They became the architects of the Lutheran and the Reformed types of Protestantism, respectively. In England King Henry VIII withdrew the English ("Anglican") church from communion with the pope; this began a turbulent century and a half during which the attempts of English monarchs to impose a modified Protestantism led to the revolt of a small number of dissatisfied English Protestants, "Puritans" as they were called, who wanted an English national church along Calvinist lines. Smaller numbers of Christians sought a more radical reform by abandoning the notion of infant baptism, withdrawing from participation in the state, and returning to the voluntary principle of Christianity in the days before Constantine. Their enemies called them "Anabaptists" or "re-baptizers" because of their commitment to adult or "believer's" baptism. Catholicism itself engaged in a renewal movement known as the Catholic Reformation, partly in response to the challenges posed by the Protestant reform movements. The Reformation period is discussed in chapters 18-20.

b. Post-Reformation (18th-20th centuries). The dawning of the age of world exploration and of European colonialism saw the spread of Christianity, by force and by persuasion, to the newly discovered continents in the Western hemisphere, and also eastward to India and the Far East. The globalization of Christianity had begun. This is also the period of the scientific revolution, beginning with the astronomical discoveries of Copernicus and Galileo, which was to force a searching re-examination of the Christian revelation. Separation of church and state, cultural secularization, modern movements of emancipation, the spread of democratic political systems, urbanization and industrialization, the rollback of European colonialism around the globe, continual intellectual challenges from modern science, philosophy and history: these fundamental trends of the past two hundred and fifty years have been the context for Christianity's engagement with the modern world. This has perhaps been more true of Christianity in America than anywhere else. At the Second Vatican Council (1962-65), Catholicism made its most sustained effort to engage the modern world in a constructive but critical way. The history of Christianity in the post-Reformation period is dealt with in chapters 21-24.

III. The Genealogy of Christianity

Since one reason for studying Christian history is to understand the reasons why there are different groups of Christians today, and since so much of this history is precisely concerned with conflicts and schisms between different groups of Christians, it might be useful to have a "preview" of this aspect of Christian history before we begin. The following chart is a sketch of the Christian family tree up to the modern period. It is intended to highlight the major "forks in the road" and to indicate, in a rough sort of way, the genetic affiliation of the main branches of the Christian family. The chart ends with the 18th century, when the secularization of the state got underway, beginning in post-revolutionary America. The separation of church and state was, in effect, a deregulation of religion. It led to intense religious competition and the rise of many new churches, especially in America, which has been a spiritual greenhouse for the production of new strains of Christianity. These American churches are explored in chapter 23.

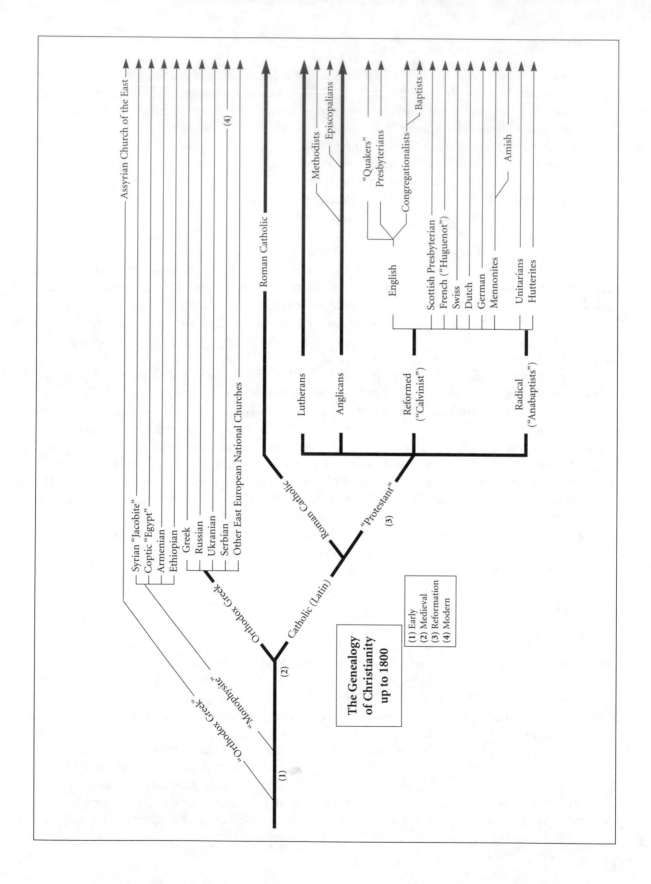

Assyrian Church of the East

Syrian "Jacobite"
Coptic "Egypt"
Armenian
Ethiopian

Greek
Russian
Ukranian
Serbian
Other East European National Churches

Roman Catholic

Methodists
Episcopalians

"Quakers"
Presbyterians
Congregationalists
Baptists

Amish

Lutherans

Anglicans

English

Scottish Presbyterian
French ("Huguenot")
Swiss
Dutch
German
Mennonites
Unitarians
Hutterites

Reformed
("Calvinist")

Radical
("Anabaptists")

Orthodox Greek

Catholic (Latin)

Roman Catholic

"Protestant"

(3)

"Orthodox Greek"

"Monophysite"

(2)

(4)

**The Genealogy
of Christianity
up to 1800**

(1) Early
(2) Medieval
(3) Reformation
(4) Modern

(1)

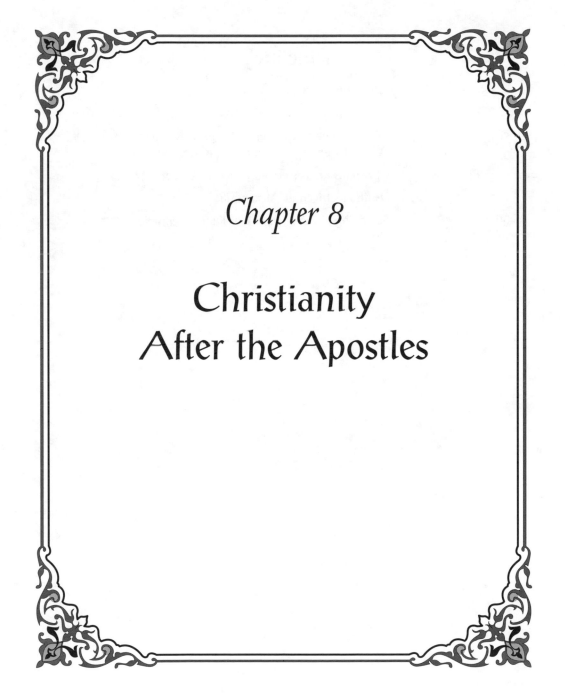

Chapter 8

Christianity
After the Apostles

Timeline

c. 165 AD	Justin is martyred in Rome.
c. 190	Clement is teaching at Alexandria.
c. 178	Irenaeus is elected bishop of Lyons. His chief work is **Against Heresies**, an attack against gnosticism.
c. 250	Christians are persecuted under the emperor Decius.
251	Death of Origen of Alexandria.
306	Beginning of the reign of Constantine, emperor of Rome.

Christianity After the Apostles

The term "early Christianity" refers to the period between the 2nd century and the 5th century, approximately the time between the writing of the last books which came to be known as the New Testament and the Council of Chalcedon (451 AD). This period is traditionally called the **patristic** era, because the major writers of the time are known as the "fathers" (*patres* in Latin) of the church. In several branches of the Christian tradition (mainly Catholic, Orthodox, and Anglican), the patristic writings have a special prestige because of their role in shaping the Christian tradition.

The patristic period is important because it was the time when Christianity assumed many of the classical features which mark it as a distinct religion separate from Judaism. It was during this period that Christians resolved, first, to retain the Jewish scriptures, and second, to define the **canon** (the authoritative list of inspired books) which would constitute the New Testament. Thus they created a distinctly *Christian* Bible composed of an "Old" and a "New" Testament. The fundamental Christian doctrines of the Trinity and the incarnation were also defined at this time. Another patristic legacy is the three-fold ordained ministry of bishop, priest, and deacon, which still exists in Catholic, Orthodox, and Anglican churches today.

The patristic era is usually subdivided into two periods: the first being the time between the writing of the last books of the New Testament and the beginning of the reign of Constantine (306-337) and the Council of Nicaea (325); the second being the time between the Council of Nicaea and the Council of Chalcedon (451). This chapter covers the earlier period and the next chapter will treat the latter period.

I. The Spread of Christianity in the Patristic Era

The main development of early Christianity after the apostolic period (the time of the apostles) was the formation of a distinctive Christian identity. The factors that contributed to early Christianity's identity formation were its gradual break with Judaism, the delay in Christ's return, and Christianity's encounter with the Greco-Roman world.

A. Christianity's Break With Judaism

The earliest followers of Jesus did not see Christianity as a separate religion, but as a sect or reform movement within Judaism. Judaism in the 1st century AD was able to accomodate a fair amount of diversity within itself. Christians saw themselves as one group within Judaism, distinct from other Jews in the fact that they believed that Jesus was their long awaited Messiah. However, when the Romans destroyed Jerusalem and the Jewish Temple in 70 AD, the "tolerated" status of Christians within Judaism began to change. Judaism lost one of its central institutions, and as a consequence had to find a new way to define itself. Groups like the Sadducees and the Essenes gradually disappeared from Jewish life: the Sadducees because of their link with the Temple and its priesthood, the Essenes because the Romans destroyed their major community at Qumran. The role of the Pharisees gradually was taken over by rabbis who set in motion a redefinition of Judaism that eventually produced the Mishnah (interpretations of Jewish scripture) and the Talmud (discussions of the Mishnah and case law related to intepretations of the Torah), both of which are currently part of the Jewish canon.

This redefinition of Judaism resulted in a tightening of its boundaries. As a consequence, sometime after the fall of Jerusalem, it appears that Christian Jews were banned from Jewish community life. This meant that they lost the protection that had been granted to Judaism as a tolerated religion in the Roman Empire. With the loss of this legal protection Christianity became vulnerable to persecution. However, another factor also contributed to Christianity's gradual separation from Judaism, namely, the large number of Gentiles who were converting to Christianity, making it no longer an exclusively Jewish sect.

B. The Delay of Christ's Return

The earliest Christians believed that Christ's resurrection was a sign of the beginning of the end time, which would be completed very soon when Christ returned in glory. However, when the first generation of Christians began to die, those who were waiting for Christ's return had to deal with the unexpected delay. Christians began to realize that Christ might not return for quite some time. Thus the delay of the end made Christians aware that it was important to preserve the movement for the future. Moreover, some Christians thought that the second coming was delayed because the church had not completed the task that Christ had given to it: to spread the gospel to the whole world. Therefore the delay of Christ's return led Christians to pursue their missionary activities with great zeal. They took the risen Christ's commission to preach the gospel to all nations (Matt 28:19) and turned the movement outwards to the larger **pagan** (non-Christian, non-Jewish) world of the Roman Empire.

There Christians encountered a number of challenges such as the intellectual tradition of Greek philosophy, the opposition of the Roman state, and the intense diversity of the empire's many religions. Endowed with the keen sense of religious integrity which it had inherited from Judaism, Christianity met these challenges successfully. Evidence of its ability to adapt can be found in the fact that, of all the empire's religions, only Judaism and Christianity have survived as living traditions.

C. The Move into the Greco-Roman World

The risk of persecution did not keep Christians from spreading their message and winning converts. By the end of the 3rd century Christian communities existed from Spain in the West to Mesopotamia in the East, and even as far as Persia, beyond the Roman Empire's eastern frontier. This geographic spread covered three main linguistic environments: Latin in the Western Roman world; Greek in most of the eastern Roman world; and Syriac in scattered parts of the East. Although Greek was the dominant language, each of these geographic areas eventually produced their own Christian literature, beginning with biblical translations and commentaries on scripture.

The Christian message circulated by word of mouth and through household connections, street corner preaching, and public lectures. The cities in particular were highly competitive religious "free markets," in which many cults and religions contended for the attention and loyalty of followers. There were the traditional official cults of the cities and the various ethnic groups of the empire. There were shrines and oracles where people sought more personal forms of religious experience, such as healing and divine guidance for life's problems. Religions imported from Egypt, Syria, and Persia including the religion of the Persian god Mithras (later to be called Sol Invictus or the Unconquered Sun), which spread especially in the army, and devotion to the Egyptian goddess Isis also won large followings in the cities. Particularly popular were the **mystery religions**, so-called because they relied on initiating converts into secret rituals and mysteries about a particular god or goddess. Part of the reason that these religions proved so popular was the satisfaction of being part of a select group or for the fellowship and the occasional feasting. Sometimes the mystery religions

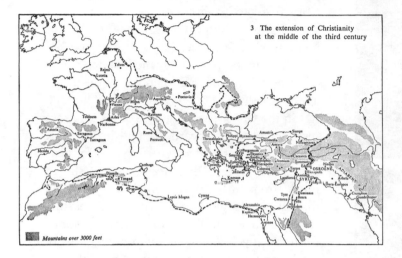

Figure 8.1: Extension of Christianity at the middle of the 3rd century.

disclosed the prospect of an afterlife, but in general the pagan world was skeptical about any meaningful existence beyond the grave. The popularity of magic and astrology during this period also reflects a widespread and fatalistic fear of looming cosmic forces which dictated human destiny.

Christian converts seem to have been seeking the same kinds of things that drew people to other religions and cults: desire for healing, the need for practical and spiritual counsel, the promise of fellowship and mutual support, a sense of personal meaning in one's life, and the like. Christianity provided these same things, but in a uniquely powerful form. Christians were widely known and admired for helping and supporting each other in their community life. Christians were also known for their complete devotion to Jesus as savior and Son of God. A sign of Christians' confidence in their religion was the fact that persecuted believers showed such a supreme certainty and hopefulness in the face of death, based on their belief in the resurrection of Jesus. Against the cosmic determinism that plagued the people of this time, early Christianity stressed human free will and responsibility. There was nothing in paganism to match this.

Portrayals of Christ in Christian Art

Despite the focus of Christian faith on the person of Jesus, it is interesting to note that no actual likeness of him survives. Christians at first were reluctant to use paintings or statues of any kind, for fear of committing the sin of idolatry. This reluctance began to disappear in the 4th and 5th centuries, as more and more people became Christians. However, even before that time Christians used paintings to decorate walls of tombs and house churches. Likenesses of Jesus were first adopted from generic pagan models that were compatible with Christian ideas about Jesus: the Good Shepherd and the philosopher-teacher being favorite types.

Figure 8.2 shows a statue of Christ as a seated philosopher, dated mid-fourth century. He is often represented in Christian art as a philosopher teaching the true philosophy of Christianity to his disciples

Figure 8.3 shows Christ as the good shepherd, from a late 3rd century sarcophagus.

Late in the 4th century the first depictions of Jesus with long hair and beard begin to appear [see Figure 9.1 of chapter 9]. After 500 AD in the Greek-speaking East, Jesus is always represented with a beard, though in the West the youthful unbearded type survived for centuries. Also in the 4th century, Jesus is shown more frequently as reigning in heavenly majesty, either giving the Law to his earthly representative, St. Peter, or receiving honor from the angels and saints. Representations of Christ on the cross are not found until the 5th century. Before that time Christians tended to use a bare cross.

Figure 8.4, sixth-century San Vitale in Ravenna, shows Jesus sitting on the orb of the world, attended by angels, and receiving the martyr's crown from St. Vitalis. The figure on the right is the bishop who built the church.

8.4

II. Roman Attitudes Toward Christianity

As a rule the Roman Empire did not persecute people for their religious beliefs, so long as they did not seem to threaten Roman peace and prosperity. Because Judaism was a very ancient religion, the empire exempted it from having to participate in the **imperial cult**, a partly political and partly religious ceremony in honor of the emperor who was recognized as a divinity. Christians, however, did not share this exemption. Once Christians were no longer accepted as a sect within Judaism, they became suspect as something that was new and unfamiliar. Until the 3rd century persecutions were sporadic and local affairs. However, in 250 AD the Emperor Decius targeted the Christian church for the first truly universal persecution. His motive is uncertain, but he probably wanted to return the empire to traditional beliefs and customs, as a way of unifying the empire and pleasing the gods.

Under the emperor Decius' orders, travelling commissioners issued certificates to all Roman citizens to verify that they had offered sacrifice to the emperor's image. Christians who died for their faith, rather than offer sacrifice to the emperor's image, were called **martyrs** (Greek for "witnesses"). Their bodily remains were venerated as holy **relics** and the anniversaries of their deaths were celebrated as religious feasts. Those who were arrested and stood firm but were not put to death were called **confessors**; they enjoyed great prestige in the churches, and sometimes claimed the right to forgive sins. Those Christians who did offer sacrifice to the emperor created a crisis afterwards when they regretted their sin of **apostasy** (falling away from the faith) and pleaded to be re-admitted to communion with their Christian brothers and sisters.

According to early Christian sources, the most frequent charge that pagans made against Christians was atheism. "Atheism" in this sense did not mean the absolute denial of the existence of a divine being or beings. Rather, it described the Christians' stubborn and intolerant refusal to agree with a broad pagan consensus concerning patriotism, the gods, and classical civilization. A good Roman citizen was one who served in the military, supported and worshiped the emperor, sacrificed to the Roman system of gods, and upheld Roman cultural values. The Romans agreed that the proper maintainance of society depended upon everyone doing their part in all of these areas. Christians dissented from this consensus. Christians said publicly that the gods were demonic deceptions and that worshiping them was idolatry. They refused to offer sacrifice to the emperor because this amounted to idolatry. Thus pagans viewed them as unpatriotic and even actively seeking the downfall of Rome. Pagans also found Christianity difficult to accept,

Figure 8.5: A 2nd-century pagan graffito of a Christian worshiping a crucified ass. The inscription reads, "Alexamenos worships god."

because the God of the Bible seemed to be unfair, revealing himself to Israel alone. Furthermore, Christianity claimed that this special relationship with one people culminated in God's appearance in human form, as a man who had been subjected to a shameful death as a criminal.

While some pagan critics admired Jesus personally, they were offended by the belief that he was divine. Enlightened pagans believed in a single highest divinity existing beyond the many gods of polytheism. Belief in the divinity of Jesus implied that there could be *two* supreme gods. Furthermore, the very idea of a divine incarnation (God taking on human flesh) was thought to be unworthy of God. Pagan thinkers influenced by the philosophy of Plato believed that the spiritual was inherently superior to the material, so they found the doctrines of incarnation and resurrection unbelievable and even offensive. Christians were regarded as gullible because they emphasized "faith" more than "knowledge." They were also accused of political irresponsibility for preaching a morality of non-violence (see Matthew 5-7), which seemed dangerous and foolish to an empire with enemies on its borders.

III. The Apologists and the Defense of Christianity

Christian **apologists** (the word means "defender") tried to respond to Roman criticisms of Christianity. They insisted that Christians were loyal citizens who prayed for the emperor when he engaged in just wars, even though they themselves refused to fight in them. They also attempted to explain, in imagery and terminology that made sense to pagans, what it was that Christians believed and how they lived their lives.

The most important accomplishment of the apologists of the 2nd and 3rd centuries was the development of the **Logos** theology. Logos theology was important for the apologists because it established a link between pagan philosophy and Christian theology. The Greek word *logos* can mean two things: (1) the spoken or written word; (2) internal reason or mind. Therefore, as spoken or written Word, the Logos could stand for the scriptures and their proclamation. As reason or mind, the Logos of God could also be identified as the divine Mind which some philosophers saw as a secondary divine principle after God himself. However, Christians identified the Logos as Jesus. Following the opening chapter of the gospel of John, they believed that this "secondary divine principle," the Logos, had became human and dwelt among us. The apologists claimed that the pagan acceptance of the Logos principle was the first step toward a full acceptance of the Gospel, with the realization that Jesus was the Logos in human form. Since their Savior was divine Reason (Logos) incarnate, the apologists could argue that the Christian life was based on reason, and all who lived according to reason therefore already had some kind of knowledge of God.

IV. The Development of Christian Doctrine

To a degree that is unique among the world's religions, the history of Christianity has been preoccupied with debates about **orthodoxy** (correct doctrine). The factors that helped determine orthodox Christian doctrine were many: the church's preaching, its biblical interpretation, its notions of discipleship, its communal life and ministry, its central rituals of Baptism and the Eucharist, and its prayers and hymns. These different aspects of Christian life were "carriers" of the faith in Jesus as Savior and Son of God. They made up a tradition which was understood in its details and its totality as the work and witness of the Spirit of God, poured out upon believers through Jesus' death and resurrection. The early Christian period was especially concerned with establishing the orthodox doctrines of the Trinity and the incarnation.

A look at the development of the doctrine of the **Trinity** (the relationship of the three "persons" of Father, Son, and Holy Spirit in one Godhead) shows how orthodox doctrine was determined by factors such as evidence from the Bible and the assumptions inherent in Christian rituals. In terms of evidence from scripture, Christians saw that the idea of the Trinity is found throughout the New Testament. The New Testament describes the God of Israel, whom Jesus called "Father;" Jesus who is the Word made flesh (John 1:14) and the Son who died as a ransom for many (Mark 10:45); and the Spirit who is God's presence among believers after Jesus' ascension (Acts 2). In terms of Christian rituals, the baptismal formula also revealed the threefold character of God, because the Christian was initiated in the name of the Father, the Son, and the Holy Spirit (Matt 28:19). Baptized Christians were understood to be sealed with the Spirit, which was the cause of holiness in the church. Likewise, the structure of early Christian **creeds** (short summaries of belief), which originated as baptismal instructions, reflected this trinitarian focus: they are usually divided into three sets of clauses dealing with the Father, the Son, and the Spirit, respectively. The 4th-century church would formally define the Trinity as three persons sharing one divine nature.

The doctrine of the incarnation was also present in its early stages of formation in the first centuries of the early Church. The doctrine of the **incarnation**, meaning "enfleshment," is concerned with the belief that Jesus Christ is the eternal Son of God who took on flesh, and was therefore fully human and fully divine. Christians believed that Jesus became present to them through the Eucharist. Early descriptions of the Eucharist can be startlingly realistic in the way they equate the elements of bread and wine with the flesh of Christ, the Son of God. In the mid-2nd century Justin wrote:

> For we do not receive these things as common bread or common drink; but as Jesus Christ our Savior being incarnate by God's word took flesh and blood for our salvation, so also we have been taught that the food consecrated by the word of prayer which comes from him, from which our flesh and blood are nourished by transformation, is the flesh and blood of that incarnate Jesus (First Apology 66).

Even earlier, Ignatius of Antioch (c. 110) had called the Eucharistic bread "the medicine of immortality."

Despite basic agreement on issues like the divinity of Jesus Christ, there was at first a considerable diversity in the early Christian movement. There were various approaches as to how communities should be organized, how Christians ought to live, what biblical books they should accept, and what they ought to believe. The diversity perhaps reflected the speed with which Christianity spread, the new challenges awaiting the movement once it grew out of its Jewish matrix, and the adjustment to the delay in Christ's return. In such unsettled conditions it was natural for there to be a degree of trial and error.

By the end of the 2nd century this diversity was fading, as the main standards of **catholic** (the word simply means "universal") Christianity became recognized: 1) agreement on the core books of the New Testament and on the necessity of retaining the Jewish scriptures; 2) the development of short summaries of beliefs called creeds, which were used to instruct candidates for baptism; and 3) the universal acceptance of the office of the **bishop** as the leader of the local Christian community. These three elements—canon, creed, and **episcopacy** (government by bishops)—consolidated Christian identity in a compact and durable form which would enable it to survive the eventual collapse of the whole ancient world in which it had come into being.

A. The Gnostic Challenge

In the history of early Christianity's efforts at establishing a consolidated Christian identity, a number of exotic flowers bloomed and withered. Some movements within Christianity were dangerous enough (from the point of view of church authorities) that the falsehood of their teachings needed to be exposed and faithful Christians needed to be warned not to follow them. Such movements are called heretical. **Heresy** means "false teaching," or teaching that is opposed to **orthodoxy** (correct teaching). In this sense of the word, "heresy" can only exist if there is an "orthodoxy" by which it is measured.

The most celebrated of these heretical movements was **gnosticism** (from the Greek word *gnosis*, meaning "knowledge"). Gnosticism was a type of religious **dualism**, which means that it saw reality as divided between two hostile principles, one representing good and the other evil. The gnostics claimed to have access to a special kind of knowledge available to them alone. To quote an ancient gnostic formulation, this was the knowledge of "who we were, and what we have become, where we were, where we were placed, whither we hasten, from what we are redeemed, what birth is, what rebirth" (Clement of Alexandria, *Excerpts from Theodotus*).

Gnosticism proposed that human beings, at least those who are capable of being saved, are essentially fragments of divinity which have become trapped in this evil world of matter and suffering. Their true home is in a spiritual realm which existed before the creation of this cosmos. In that spiritual realm the godhead dwells, along with a host of subsidiary divine principles, usually expressed in gendered pairs of male and female, which come forth or emanate from the divine source. Gnostic texts call these beings "aeons." The gnostics account for the creation of this physical universe by describing a myth about the fall or sin of one of the aeons and the imprisonment of some of the divine substance in the flesh of human beings. This fallen aeon governs the universe very badly, unaware of the higher realm and foolishly thinking that he alone is God. In some gnostic myths, this incompetent being is equated with the God of the Old Testament. Sometimes he is called the *Demiurge*.

According to the gnostics, Christians who possess this secret knowledge are rescued from their earthly exile by Christ, who was sent from heaven to bring them knowledge of their true nature. He did not really become flesh but only *seemed* to have a body; in reality he was a spiritual being who could not suffer or die. Gnostic Christology was thus a form of **docetism**, from a Greek word meaning "to seem or appear to be." The gnostic Christ delivered the *gnosis* privately to one of his disciples, who then passed on the revelation orally or in writing to his followers, the gnostics themselves. Gnosticism appealed to people because of its sense of disgust with the world as it was. Also, because it was an elite group, it created in its members a powerful sense of belonging. Because salvation was based on a heightened consciousness within the soul, gnosticism was less likely to demand dramatic actions that could attract the attention of state authorities who might be opposed to it.

A late 2nd-century Christian named **Irenaeus**, bishop of the church in Lyons, in southern Gaul (modern day France), wrote a lengthy work traditionally known as *Against Heresies*, primarily in response to gnosticism. Besides being a significant opponent of gnosticism, Irenaeus is our most detailed witness to mainstream Christianity in the 2nd century, when pluralism and diversity were greatest. His defense of orthodox teaching of that time focused on the threefold criteria of canon, creed, and episcopate mentioned above. Irenaeus was the first early Christian writer to mention all four canonical gospels together as a group. Besides written scriptures, he also stressed the oral tradition of apostolic teaching, a type of creed which he calls "the rule of faith." Irenaeus understood this creed to be a measure by which orthodoxy is determined. Thus Irenaeus makes an explicit contrast between the rule of faith, which is public and everywhere the same, and the teachings of the gnostics, which are esoteric and contradictory.

Irenaeus pointed to the bishops as the authorized preservers of the **apostolic tradition**, because they stand in a living chain that goes back to Jesus' first followers. This claim, he says, is open to verification by anyone who wishes to examine it. All they need do is trace the succession of the bishops of a given church back to the apostles. Interestingly, he singles out the church in Rome as a special reference point for the apostolic tradition. In a passage whose exact meaning has been hotly debated, he appears to say that what is taught in Rome can be assumed to be taught everywhere.

Against the gnostics, Irenaeus taught the goodness of the created though fallen world, including our bodies, which will be restored to life by God at the end of the world. The Son of God entered our world not just to deliver a saving knowledge but to *change* us: "The Son of God became Son of Man so that the sons of men might become sons of God." Thus Irenaeus described the redemption effected by Jesus Christ as a **recapitulation**, a doing over again of all that had gone wrong in human history. In his view, God's revelation was not a matter of acquiring knowledge; it had to be accepted in faith and trust in order to be understood.

V. The Birth of Theology

We have thus far spoken about doctrine or teaching more than theology as such. The word **theology** literally means "discourse or talk about God." Early Christian authors adopted the word from Greek philosophy, which contained a rich literature dealing with divinity. The Greeks treated "theology" as a branch of philosophy and therefore as a subject of rational and systemic reflection, like all branches of philosophy. For Christians, on the other hand, theology meant a reflective faith response to a reality revealed to them in Jesus Christ. The revelation of God-in-Christ was the primary thing, the "given" or the "data," and it was only "known" in the sense that it was passed on to believers by tradition and accepted in faith. It was not available for study in the sense that an object in the world of nature was available for study; it was a reality which evoked a response of belief, and theology was simply the reflective element in that response.

Theological literature understood in the broad sense of "reflection on Christianity" was produced in abundance in the early Christian period: biblical commentaries, sermons, apologetic works, polemical treatises (books attacking false versions of Christian life and doctrine), acts of martyrs (stories about the deaths of various martyrs), church orders (documents governing the life of the church, such as the *Didache* or the *Teaching of the Twelve Apostles*), lives of saints, and other spiritual literature. However, theology as an academic subject for teaching and research hardly existed before the emergence of universities in the middle ages. The closest ancient parallel to medieval university theology was found in the Christian community in Alexandria in Egypt.

Alexandria was one of the greatest centers of scholarship in the ancient world. It was the home of the Library, with its enormous book collection, and the Museum, a center for study and lecturing. If Christians in Alexandria were to compete with pagans on an equal footing, they, like the Jewish community which preceded them, could not afford to ignore the role of study and learning in theology. It is probably not an accident that many of the Christian gnostics of whom we have knowledge came from Alexandria.

The focus of Christian scholarship in Alexandria was the **Catechetical School**, an academy for advanced studies in Christianity. Two of the most important early Christian theologians, Clement of Alexandria (150-c. 215) and **Origen of Alexandria** (c. 185-c. 251), served as directors of the school. Origen in particular was renowned among both Christians and pagans for his exceptional learning and scholarly productivity. As a beloved teacher he inspired a generation of students who went on to become missionaries, bishops, and theologians in their own right. Wealthy lay people generously supported his scholarly labors. He taught and wrote in Alexandria for years until he had a serious falling out with Demetrius, the rather arrogant bishop of Alexandria, because the bishop of Caesarea in Palestine had ordained Origen a priest without Demetrius' permission. As a result, Origen spent the last two decades of his life in Palestine, where he left the great library he had accumulated and his own invaluable writings.

Origen believed that the theologian had a calling from the Holy Spirit. Though the theologian was compelled to accept what apostolic tradition taught, he had a right to investigate subjects which apostolic tradition had not already defined. In this way, members of the church who were endowed with intellectual talent and had advanced in personal holiness were called to a deeper understanding of the church's faith beyond that held by simple believers. Origen left the Christian tradition with a massive intellectual and spiritual legacy. In the area of biblical interpretation, Origen's use of the **allegorical** method (looking for a hidden spiritual meaning beneath the bare literal meaning of the text) was especially influential. Likewise, his homilies were copied and circulated everywhere. In addition, works of spirituality such as *On Prayer* have exerted a permanent influence on Christianity.

Two of his works deserve special mention. His *Against Celsus*, written quite late in life, is a lengthy response to the first serious non-Christian critique of Christianity of which we have record. Along with Augustine's *On the City of God*, it is one of the most important apologies from the early Christian period. The other book is a product of Origen's youth, the treatise called *On First Principles*, a bold exposition of Christian doctrine which could be called the first Christian systematic theology. The book is partially lost because of later condemnations of some of Origen's ideas (such as the pre-existence of souls, the idea that human souls existed in heaven before they were born into bodies), but enough survives in translation and in the original Greek to give a good idea of its contents. It was a highly creative statement of Christian teaching with the help of Platonic philosophy, all in the name of defending scripture and apostolic tradition.

VI. Christian Life and Community

Standards of membership in the early Christian churches were, at first, very high because the church was thought of as an ark of the saved, the only refuge in a drowning world. The *Didache*, for example, is an excellent witness to the Christian commitment to rigorous standards of behavior and the expectation that the church would be a community of saints. A prospective convert underwent years of preparation before being judged fit for baptism. Certain occupations were forbidden, especially if they involved bloodshed (such as being a gladiator), illicit sexual activity, and pagan religious ceremonies. There was also a prohibition against teaching because the myths about the gods were taught in school. Military service was severely frowned upon because of the profound Christian rejection of bloodshed, although by the late 2nd century there is evidence of Christians who were soldiers. Early Christian sources said that a soldier who was baptized should refuse to kill or to take the military oath.

By the 3rd century the growth in numbers of Christians seems to have caused a decline in standards. This led to heated debates over what to do with those who failed to live up to the promises of their Baptism. Churches in large cities like Rome developed more lenient disciplinary codes which allowed repentant sinners to regain admission to the sacraments. By the 4th century, after the conversion of the Roman emperor Constantine, the problem of diluted standards would become even greater. Despite these problems, however, the convert to Christianity joined a strong and energetic local community which was aware of being linked, horizontally, to other such communities around the Roman world and beyond, and "vertically" to the angels and martyred saints who praised God in heaven. The heavenly chain of communication was experienced in the liturgy and in prayer, with the angels thought of as individual protectors and co-worshipers with the earthly church.

The fellowship of the bishops was the chief institutional expression of the churches' catholicity or universality. At the same time, the bishop was the overseer of a local church or group of churches. The blend of local and universal was symbolized by the fact that the bishop was elected locally by the board of presbyters ("elders"), with the consent of the laity, but could not be consecrated as a bishop without the cooperation of several other bishops. Bishops were regarded in principle as equal, all being successors of the apostles, but bishops in larger cities naturally carried more weight than those in small towns. A few bishops, chiefly Rome, Alexandria, and Antioch, enjoyed exceptional influence and prestige, with the "primacy" of the Roman bishop seen as unique.

The bishops exercised primary control over the teaching and governing aspects of the church. They also presided at Eucharist. However, they did not enjoy a complete monopoly of authority. All Christians were thought to enjoy the gifts of the Spirit (such as prophecy) through Baptism. Although prophecy gradually waned as a force in community life, it probably lasted longest in North Africa. The *Didache* shows a very early state of affairs when travelling prophets, teachers, and "apostles" outranked local bishops and deacons. Likewise, the charismatic authority of martyrs and confessors was a powerful force in church life, as monks and nuns would be in the 4th century after the end of persecution. According to Origen, Christian teachers also possessed a charismatic authority based on the gifts of wisdom and holiness, though they were still bound to respect the apostolic tradition.

Christian churches kept in touch through official letters called *letters of peace*, through the travels of business people and other folk, and through formal meetings with neighboring churches on matters of common interest. As the church's organization grew, it took on the character of a state within the state, so to speak. When persecution failed to crush this alternative society, the way was open in the 4th century for the Roman Empire to win over Christianity by merging with it rather than by destroying it.

Key Terms:

patristic era	catholic
canon	creeds
pagan	bishops
mystery religions	episcopacy
imperial cult	gnosticism
martyrs	dualism
confessors	docetism
apostasy	Irenaeus of Lyons
polytheism	apostolic tradition
apologists	recapitulation
Logos	*Didache*
orthodoxy	Catechetical School of Alexandria
heresy	Origen of Alexandria
Trinity	allegorical interpretation
incarnation	

Questions for Reading:

1. The early Christian period is important because that is when Christianity assumed many of its most characteristic features. Give some examples of these characteristic features.

2. What effect did the fall of Jerusalem in 70 A.D. have on the Christian movement?

3. What sorts of motives seem to have attracted converts to Christianity during the 2nd and 3rd centuries?

4. Why were Christians persecuted? (Pay special attention to the charge of atheism.)

5. What role did the Logos theology play in the writings of the Apologists?

6. What were the most important factors in the formation of orthodox Christian doctrine? (Illustrate with reference to Baptism and the Eucharist.)

7. By the end of the 2nd century, a universal ("catholic") Christian consensus was beginning to take shape. What were the main standards which helped to consolidate Christianity's identity?

8. Gnosticism was a type of religious dualism. How was its dualism reflected in its view of the creator God of the Old Testament?

9. How did Irenaeus of Lyons emphasize the theme of *unity* in contrast to gnostic dualism?

10. How did Origen of Alexandria see the calling of the theologian, in relation to the apostolic tradition of the church?

11. The bishop played the key role in the life of the local Christian community and also served as the main link to Christian communities elsewhere. What were his local responsibilities? What competing local authority did he still have to deal with?

Works Consulted/Recommended Reading:

Baur, Walter. *Orthodoxy and Heresy in Earliest Christianity*. 2nd ed. Trans. Georg Strecker. Philadelphia: Fortress Press, 1971.

Chadwick, Henry. *The Early Church*. Pelican History of the Church, vol. 1. Baltimore, Md.: Penguin Books, 1967.

Crouzel, Henri. *Origen: The Life and Thought of the First Great Theologian*. Trans. A. S. Worrall. San Francisco: Harper & Row, 1989.

Daniélou, Jean and Marrou, Henri. *The First Six Hundred Years. The Christian Centuries: A New History of the Catholic Church*, vol. 1. Trans. Vincent Cronin. New York: McGraw-Hill Book Co., 1964.

_____ . *From Shadows to Reality: Studies in the Biblical Typology of the Fathers*. Trans. Dom Wulstan Hibberd. Westminster, MD: Newman Press, 1960.

_____ . *A History of Early Christian Doctrine before the Council of Nicaea*. 3 vols. Trans. John A. Baker. London: Darton, Longman, & Todd, 1964-77.

Dodd, E. R. *Pagan and Christian in an Age of Anxiety*. New York: W. W. Norton & Co., 1970.

Grant, Robert M. *Augustus to Constantine: The Thrust of the Christian Movement into the Roman World*. New York, Evanston, London: Harper & Row, 1970.

Kelly, J. N. D. *Early Christian Creeds*. New York, Evanston, & London: Harper & Row, 1960.

Kugel, James L. and Greer, Rowan A. *Early Biblical Interpretation*. Library of Early Christianity. Philadelphia: Westminster Press, 1986.

Lane Fox, Robin. *Pagans and Christians*. New York: Alfred A. Knopf, 1987.

Origen. *Contra Celsum*. Intro., notes, and trans. Henry Chadwick. Cambridge, New York, Melbourne: Cambridge University Press, 1986.

Pelikan, Jaroslav. *The Emergence of the Catholic Tradition (100-600)*. *The Christian Tradition: A History of the Development of Doctrine*, vol. 1. Chicago & London: University of Chicago Press, 1971.

Robinson, James, ed. *The Nag Hammadi Library*. Rev. ed. San Francisco: Harper & Row, 1988.

Rudolph, Kurt. *Gnosis: The Nature and History of Gnosticism*. Trans. R. McL. Wilson. San Francisco: Harper & Row, 1987.

Sanders, E. P., ed. *The Shaping of Christianity in the Second and Third Centuries*. *Jewish and Christian Self-Definition*, vol. 1. Philadelphia: Fortress Press, 1980.

Snyder, Graydon F. *Ante Pacem: Archaeological Evidence of Church Life before Constantine*. Mercer University Press, 1985.

Trigg, Joseph Wilson. *Origen: The Bible and Philosophy in the Third-Century Church*. Atlanta: John Knox Press, 1983.

Wilken, Robert L. *The Christians As the Romans Saw Them*. New Haven & London: Yale University Press, 1984.

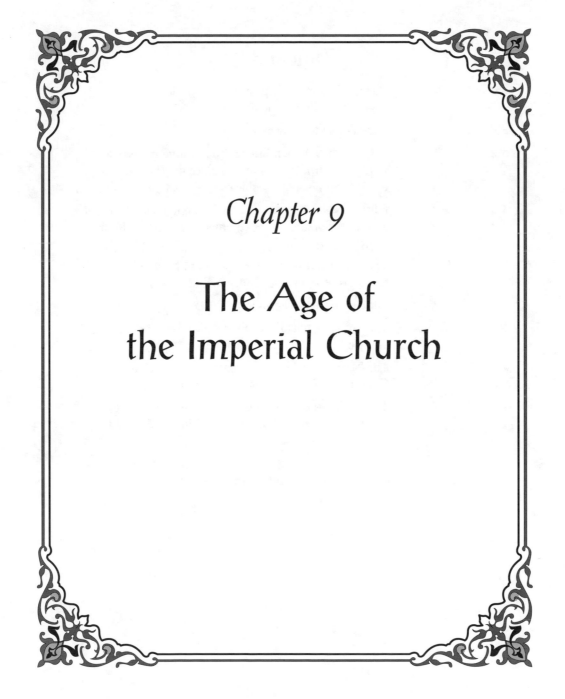

Chapter 9

The Age of
the Imperial Church

Timeline

251-356 AD	Antony becomes a hermit in the Egyptian desert. Beginnings of monasticism in the East.
306	Constantine is emperor of Rome.
312	Battle of the Milvian Bridge. Constantine receives a vision in which he was told to place the "heavenly sign of God" on his soldiers' shields.
313	Edict of Milan announces universal religious toleration and the restoration of seized property to the Christian churches.
325	The first ecumenical council is held at Nicaea, and the teachings of Arius are condemned as heresy.
328	Athanasius becomes bishop of Alexandria.
380-381	The Roman emperor Theodosius I makes Christianity the sole legal religion of the empire.
381	The Nicene creed is confirmed and expanded at the Council of Constantinople.
431	The teachings of Nestorius are condemned as heresy and Mary is declared to be the Mother of God at the Council of Ephesus.
451	The Council of Chalcedon issues a definition of faith concerning the doctrine of the incarnation.

The Age of the Imperial Church

During the course of the 4th century Christianity underwent a great reversal in its relationship with the Roman Empire. At the start of the 4th century it endured the last and most serious of the persecutions. But shortly after this the conversion of the Emperor **Constantine** (reigned 306-337) inaugurated a new era in which Christianity first won legal toleration and then was established as the empire's official religion. Christianity had begun as a tiny Jewish splinter group looking forward to Jesus' second coming and the establishment of the kingdom of God. Now it embarked on its long career as an established religion, indeed the only religion approved and promoted by the government. The union of church and state profoundly influenced Christianity. This chapter discusses Constantine's conversion and the transformation of Christianity into an "imperial church" (the church of the Roman Empire), the church councils and doctrinal developments of the period, and important trends in Christian life.

I. Constantine and His Legacy

A. Rise to Power and Religious Policies

Constantine came to power at a time when the Roman Empire was divided into sections ruled by an imperial board or college. This system had been invented by the Emperor Diocletian (reigned 284-305), who had restored the empire to stability after it almost collapsed in the 3rd century CE. In 303, in an attempt to force the empire's peoples to return to traditional Roman values, Diocletian had inflicted a brutal persecution on Christianity. Although the persecution failed, it left the churches bitterly divided over what to do with those who had lapsed in their faith during the persecution. Schisms broke out in Egypt and in North Africa; in the latter area Christians in the **Donatist** movement refused to accept sacraments from Catholic clergy who were accused of being associated with those who had handed over copies of the Bible to Roman police to be destroyed.

Constantine's father had been a co-ruler with Diocletian. When his father died in 306, Constantine succeeded him. For the next six years he fought for control of the western half of the empire. The crucial battle came in 312, when he defeated his last Western rival at the Battle of the Milvian Bridge outside of the city of Rome. Before the battle he became convinced that he would achieve victory with the help of the Christian God. According to one account, he had a dream in which he was told to place the "heavenly sign of God," probably the first two letters of Christ's name (Greek chi and rho, or "Chi-Rho," letters which resemble *x* and *p*, superimposed on one another), on the shields of the soldiers. A later account by his biographer, Bishop Eusebius of Caesarea, says that he had a daytime vision of a cross of light above the sun, with the words "By this sign, conquer." The following year he and his Eastern counterpart, the emperor Licinius, met in Milan and agreed to announce universal religious toleration and the restoration of seized property to the Christian churches, a decision traditionally known as the **Edict of Milan** (313). Constantine later went to war with Licinius and defeated him in 324, thus uniting the whole empire under his single rule until his death in 337.

Modern historians have argued about whether Constantine was really a Christian. During the decade after 312, the evidence of his official coins (a traditional way for emperors to advertise their allegiances) is ambiguous. Some coins represent him under the sponsorship of the Unconquered Sun, a pagan form of monotheism especially popular in the army—but also a religion less offensive to Christianity than polytheism. Nevertheless, after 312 Constantine produced a constant flow of letters and decrees which demonstrate his deep involvement in the Christian church, even though he was not baptized until just before he died. He called councils and enforced their decisions by exiling dissenters and burning condemned books. He subsidized the construction of new churches, especially in Palestine, which was a Christian "holy land" from this time forward. He made his new eastern capital of Constantinople, founded on the site of the ancient city of Byzantium, into an explicitly Christian city.

Christianity represented for him above all a divine guarantee of victory over evil. That is why he adopted the Chi-Rho and the cross as imperial symbols. He believed that God had chosen him for a special mission to bring the Roman Empire to Christianity, in return for which God would bless his reign and give the empire peace and prosperity.

> Upon the triumphal arch of the magnificent church he built over the grave of St. Peter, Constantine inscribed the following grateful dedication to Christ: "Since under you leadership the Empire rose once again triumphant to the stars, Constantine the victor has founded this audience hall in your honor."

He saw the Christian church as providing heavenly support—through the prayers of its clergy—and a common religion to hold the empire's diverse peoples together, even though Christians were still just a small proportion of the population. To realize these goals, he gave the clergy benefits such as tax exemption and the power to act as judges in civil lawsuits. Christian values influenced his laws. He confiscated the wealth of pagan temples, ended their state subsidies, and imposed certain restrictions on Jews. Nonetheless, he never revoked the Edict of Milan. It was his successors, especially **Theodosius I** (reigned 379-95), who made Christianity the sole legal religion of the empire.

B. Constantine's Impact on the Development of Christianity

There are several ways in which the reign of Constantine left a lasting impression on Christianity. First, Constantine established the practice of calling an **ecumenical** or **general council** (a universal gathering of Christian bishops) to resolve urgent issues affecting the whole church. These councils and their decrees are absolutely crucial to the development of Christianity from the 4th century forward. Second, his conversion and his policies as emperor greatly increased the rate of conversion to Christianity, although contemporary observers like Eusebius admitted that many of these conversions were less than sincere. Third, Constantine founded the city of Constantinople, which can be seen as a symbolic beginning of the Byzantine Empire, the name which historians give to the continuation of the Roman Empire in the east. The Byzantine Empire lasted for over a thousand years and served as a bulwark of Christianity against Muslim expansion until the Ottoman Turks (Muslims) finally captured Constantinople in 1453. This Christianized Eastern Roman Empire became the center of what we now call Eastern Orthodox Christianity.

Moreover, Constantine inaugurated a model of Christian kingship in which the king receives his authority to rule directly from God, not from an institution such as the church. In the words of Constantine to Eusebius of Caesarea, he was a kind of "universal bishop," entrusted by God with the oversight of the empire as a whole, including the church. He was not supposed to take over the spiritual work proper to the church, but to ensure that the church performs its tasks rightly. This type of Christian kingship was imitated by Byzantine emperors and also by kings and emperors in the medieval period and even (in some cases) into the modern period.

Finally, he inspired the growth of a Christian devotion to the Roman state as an institution willed by God. Henceforth Christians eagerly demonstrated their patriotism by holding public office and serving in the army. This Christian patriotism had both positive and negative aspects. In a positive sense it reflected a deepened awareness of civic responsibility. To Christians like Eusebius, it seemed logical that Christians should not flee from the world, but rather should seek to exercise power in the world whenever possible, exercising that power on behalf of the gospel. This new patriotism and civic involvement provided an answer to pagan critics who had accused Christians of shirking their public duties while enjoying the benefits of the peaceful, stable, and prosperous Roman Empire.

On the other hand, access to power exposed Christianity to great risks. For example, when Christianity became associated with the Roman Empire, Christians began serving in the military in greater numbers, although others questioned whether military service was really compatible with the teachings of Jesus. Many early Christians believed that Christ's teachings (in the Sermon on the Mount, for example) required them to be pacifists, and hence they refused to fight in war. Modern churches such as the Mennonites and the Quakers continue to hold this view. Another issue was the possible corruption of the church. Wealth and political influence threatened the integrity of the church's government. Bishops were tempted to switch from one city to another in the hope of increasing their power and influence, and church laws against this practice were not entirely successful. There was also a growing tendency to equate Christianity with the civilization of the Roman Empire, when in fact many Christians lived outside of the empire's jurisdiction. Constantine's conversion, for instance, exposed Persian Christians across the eastern border to persecution as suspected traitors. Finally, there was the ominous beginning of religious coercion: the institutional church using its privileged position within the state to persecute unbelievers and heretics.

II. Dogmatic Development: Trinity and Incarnation

The most significant theological achievement of the 4th and 5th centuries is the defining of the dogmas of the Trinity and the incarnation, the complementary doctrines about God which distinguish Christianity from all other religions. A **dogma** is a religious teaching based on divine revelation and defined by the church. Why were these important dogmas not defined until centuries after Jesus' death? Although the basic shape of the Christian doctrine of God had been in place from the beginning, precise definitions were still lacking and numerous important issues were unresolved, including some which were as yet hardly recognized as problems (such as the humanity of Christ). A good deal of theological trial and error was necessary before consensus was possible.

We should also remember that until the 4th century there was no church structure that really spoke for everybody. The solution to this problem was the development of ecumenical councils. However, even the councils were not a perfect institution. The emperors often influenced church councils, since they now had a big stake in the outcome. Church rivalries also played a role. As a result, not all the councils held during these years are recognized as "ecumenical" (or "worldwide"). The "validity" of some councils was questioned because not all bishops were included, or because undue outside influence was brought to bear on the council's participants. Of the many councils that were held in the early centuries of the Christian church, those which are accepted as true councils (by Catholics, Orthodox, and most mainstream Protestant churches) are the ones which met at Nicaea (325), Constantinople (381), Ephesus (431), and Chalcedon (451).

A. Nicaea (325)

We noted earlier that ecumenical councils are called to address urgent issues affecting the whole church. The issue that provoked the Council of Nicaea was the teaching of **Arius**, a priest from Alexandria in Egypt, about the relation between God and his Son. The Prologue of John's Gospel (Jn 1:1-18) and the Logos theologians of the 2nd and 3rd centuries had recognized a distinction between God and his Word, between the Father and the Son. Arius argued that only God the Father could be called "God" in the full sense of the word. Only the Father could be said to be *without beginning*; all else had a beginning, including the Son or the Word. The Son was a "second-class" god who was necessary in order to be the link between the truly transcendent God and the rest of the universe, both in creating the world and in redeeming it, since the philosophical axiom of God's *impassibility* denied that divinity could suffer or change. Since the transcendent God could not interact with the world in order to redeem it, redemption would be the mission of a subordinate god, the Son or the Word.

Arius' critics objected to his teaching because *it turned the Son of God into a being so much less than God as to be virtually a creature himself.* Both sides could quote the gospel of John to support their positions. Jn 14:28 has Jesus say, "The Father is greater than I," a text beloved of Arius and his supporters, called Arians. However, John's gospel also has Jesus say in 10:30, "The Father and I are one," and in 14:9, "Whoever has seen me has seen the Father." **Athanasius of Alexandria** (d. 373) made the anti-Arian case most forcefully. According to Athanasius, the heart of the Bible's teaching is that in Christ humans could see the true God, not a subordinate or underling: "For in him [Christ] all the fullness of God was pleased to dwell, and through him God was pleased to reconcile to himself all things, whether on earth or in heaven, by making peace through the blood of his cross" (Col 1:19-20). No subordinate god was necessary to protect true divinity from contact with the world. Only the one true God could save us; anything less put our salvation in doubt. There was never a time when the Son did not exist.

At Nicaea the bishops indicated their opposition to Arianism by approving a creed or statement of beliefs. This statement of beliefs comes to be called the **Nicene Creed**. In it the bishops adapted an already existing creed by inserting a few phrases designed to *link* Father and Son as closely as possible and hence to express their opposition to the position of Arius, who *separated* the Father and the Son by denying the true divinity of the Son. Most importantly, they asserted that the Son is "one in being with the Father," in contrast to the Arians, who claimed that the Son did not share the same substance as the Father. Unfortunately, the Greek word which the bishops used for "one in being"—*homoousios* (literally, "of the same substance")—created problems. It could be misunderstood in a materialist sense, as if God were "stuff" which could be divided, or even taken to mean that Father and Son were simply the *same* being. Besides being philosophically suspect to many educated bishops, the word was also not from the Bible, whereas earlier creeds consisted of biblical language and images. As a result, rather than settling things, Nicaea provoked decades of controversy, made all the worse by the shifting opinions and policies of the emperors themselves.

B. Constantinople (381)

After a half century of strife, the decision of the Council of Nicaea was affirmed once and for all when the new emperor, Theodosius I, recognized it as the law of the empire. The celebrated edict of 380 known as *Cunctos Populos* not only mandated the creed of Nicaea but also named the bishops of Rome and Alexandria as the judges of orthodox doctrine. *Cunctos Populos* was followed in 391 by a sweeping edict against paganism. The reign of Theodosius was thus the time when Christianity really became the sole legal religion of the empire.

> From Theodosius the Great's decree Cunctos Populos: "We command that all the peoples whom the moderation of our mercy rules, should practice the religion which . . . the divine Peter the Apostle brought to the Romans, and which is plainly the one followed by the pontiff [pope] Damasus and Bishop Peter of Alexandria, a man of apostolic sanctity. Following apostolic discipline and gospel teaching, we are to believe in the single deity of Father and Son and Holy Spirit, under equal majesty and revered trinity. We order that the name of 'Catholic Christians' is to belong to those who follow this law. But the rest we judge are mad and insane for sustaining the dishonor of heretical teaching, and their assemblies do not have the name of 'churches.'"

At Theodosius' instigation a council of bishops met in the eastern capital of Constantinople in 381. At this time the Nicene Creed was confirmed and expanded. The expansions were designed to clarify the Council of Nicaea on a point that had only recently become a disputed issue, the divinity of the Holy Spirit. Nicaea had ended its creed rather abruptly by saying only "And we believe in the Holy Spirit." The article on the Holy Spirit was now expanded with new clauses which recognized the Spirit's traditional functions of inspiration ("spoke through the prophets") and sanctification ("giver of life" in the sense of being the redeeming presence of God's grace within believers). The new clauses also asserted that the Father is the source of the Spirit and that the Spirit is accorded *worth and dignity equal to that of the Father and the Son.*

This form of the Nicene Creed has become the most universally accepted benchmark of the Christian faith outside of the Bible itself. Although different churches recite slightly different versions of the Nicene creed, this is the creed that is recited in churches today.

> *We believe in one God, the Father, almighty, maker of heaven and earth, and of all things visible and invisible.*
>
> *And in one Lord Jesus Christ, the only-begotten Son of God, begotten from the Father before all ages, light from light, true God from true God, begotten not made, one in being with the Father [or: of the same substance as the Father], through whom all things were made, who for us and for our salvation came down from heaven, and was incarnate from the Holy Spirit and the Virgin Mary and was made man, and was crucified for us under Pontius Pilate, and suffered and was buried, and rose the third day according to the scriptures, and ascended into heaven and sits on the right hand of the Father, and is coming again with glory to judge both living and dead, whose kingdom shall have no end.*
>
> *And in the Holy Spirit, the Lord and giver of life, who proceeds from the Father, who with the Father and the Son is jointly worshipped and jointly glorified, who spoke through the prophets; in one holy catholic and apostolic church. We acknowledge one baptism for the forgiveness of sins; we look for the resurrection of the dead and the life of the world to come. Amen.*

This clarification of the original creed of Nicaea reflects important theological advances made by Basil of Caesarea (330-79), his brother Gregory of Nyssa (331/40-c. 395), and Basil's friend Gregory of Nazianzus (c. 329-90). These three are often referred to as the **Cappadocian Fathers**, because they came from the central region of Asia Minor known as Cappadocia. They represent the highest point of advance in the long process by which ancient Christianity gradually appropriated Greek philosophical ideas and incorporated them into Christianity.

Where development of the doctrine of the Trinity is concerned, the Cappadocians were responsible for several accomplishments. First, they distinguished the meaning of abstract terms such as "person" and "substance" as applied to the Trinity. Henceforth everyone agreed to say that the divine "substance" was the nature which Father, Son, and Spirit have as God, no one of them more so than the others. But this divine substance, the Godhead, exists in three aspects or modes called "persons," each marked by its distinctive qualities. Though these qualities do make for an ordering of the three, this is simply in respect of the particular qualities (e.g., the Father begetting the Son, or the Spirit being sent by the Father) and not in respect of their divinity. One person of the Trinity is not "more God" than another. Second, the Cappadocians clearly recognized that all language about God could only be an *analogy*, not a literal description of what God really was. God in his own nature, they insisted, was unknowable; we know him only from his effects recorded in the Bible and seen in the world. In the same way we cannot "see" the wind, but we can see its effects on the trees. Finally, they admitted that the Bible alone might not be a sufficient standard for defining the full divinity of the Spirit. The Bible needed to be supplemented by the evidence of the church's tradition, such as the trinitarian character of the baptismal ritual (where people are baptized "in the name of the Father and of the Son and of the Holy Spirit"). In other words, the Cappadocians recognized that what Christians believed had to be consistent with the way they worshiped. Gregory of Nazianzus even suggested there had been a gradual revelation of the reality of the Trinity, with the process beginning in the Old Testament and extending beyond the New Testament itself into the life and experience of the church. In each period God had disclosed as much as, but not more than, people were prepared to receive.

C. Ephesus (431) and Chalcedon (451)

Christians had always confessed Jesus to be both human and divine. However, the divine aspect tended to receive greater emphasis. Once the Council of Nicaea had firmly established that his divinity was the same as that of God the Father's, Christians were forced to think more carefully about the **incarnation** (John 1:14: "And the Word became flesh.") of this fully divine Son. What did it mean to say that the one true God had taken on flesh and suffered and died for human beings? Did this mean, for example, that God *as God* had really suffered and died? How could God be said to die?

The problem was even more complex, however. It seems that many theologians, including Athanasius, understood the incarnation to consist of the union of the Logos or Son of God *with a human body but not with a human soul*. In other words, the Logos took the place of Christ's human soul. Athanasius, for instance, often described the flesh of Christ—and the Gospel of John had explicitly mentioned *only* the flesh in the incarnation—as an *instrument* which the Logos had assumed in order to reveal himself to human beings and to renew our nature. This view of the incarnation made it easier to see how divine and human were joined in one being, but it seems a very deficient view of the humanity with which God was united, as though human flesh had been adopted by divinity for purposes of travel to our dimension. After a theologian named **Apollinaris of Laodicaea** taught explicitly that Christ had no human soul, other Christians repudiated his model of the incarnation, because they believed that Christ had redeemed *all* of human nature. As Gregory of Nazianzus put it, "What was not assumed [by the Word in the Incarnation] was not saved." If Jesus did not have a human soul, then the souls of humans were not saved by him. Henceforth everyone recognized that it must have been a complete human nature, body and soul, with which the Son of God was united.

Gregory saw that Christ needed to have had a complete human nature for human beings to have been saved by him, but it remained difficult to see how divinity and humanity could co-exist in a single person. Two broadly different approaches to the problem emerged in the 5th century. The **School of Antioch** was concerned to protect the integrity of each aspect of the incarnation, the divine and the human: on the one hand, the Logos' full divinity had to be protected from having inappropriate contact with the reality of time and space; and on the other hand, the gospel testimonies to Jesus' full humanity (his birth from Mary, his growth in knowledge, his temptations, his suffering and death, etc.) had to be respected. Therefore Antiochene theologians preferred to talk about the Word's assumption of a complete human being, or of the "indwelling" of Christ's human nature.

However, their opponents, the **School of Alexandria**, thought that the Antiochenes risked dividing the incarnation into two separate realities, indeed into two persons. Alexandrian theologians took the divine-human fact of the incarnation as their starting point. From the instant of his conception Jesus had been both God and man. Divinity and humanity were so indissolubly joined that it was no longer appropriate to see them in any way as separate realities in the incarnation. The real subject of all the actions reported of Jesus in the gospels was the Word of God, but the Word *incarnate*, i.e., personally united with a human nature in a single reality. This human nature was indeed complete so far as soul and body were concerned. But it lacked personal "identity," to use modern language; its identity was that of the Word. Alexandrian views were deeply rooted in the faith of ordinary Christians, above all in their experience of union with Christ in the Eucharist. The great Alexandrian spokesman Cyril of Alexandria (c. 375-444) wrote to a leader of the School of Antioch:

> *Proclaiming the death according to the flesh of the Only-begotten Son of God, that is, Jesus Christ, confessing his resurrection from the dead, and his ascension into heaven, we celebrate the unbloody sacrifice in the churches, and so proceed to the mystical consecrated gifts, and are sanctified, having become partakers of the holy flesh and precious blood of Christ, the Savior of us all. And not as common flesh do we receive it, not at all, nor as a man sanctified and associated with the Word according to the unity of dignity, or as having had a divine indwelling, but as truly the life-giving and very flesh of the Word himself.*

The "christological" controversy between the School of Antioch and the School of Alexandria began to come to a head when an Antiochene theologian named **Nestorius** became Patriarch of Constantinople in 428. Nestorius began to preach that it was inappropriate to call Mary the Mother of God (in Greek, *Theotokos*, "the Godbearer"), on the grounds that God could not be said to have been born. Nestorius held that at best Mary was only the Mother of Christ, the man. At the **Council of Ephesus** in 431, Mary was declared to be the Mother of God and Nestorius' doctrines were condemned. It is widely doubted today that he actually held the views which the council condemned, but the turbulence and bitterness of the council's proceedings, inflamed by church rivalries, did not make for a charitable discussion of views.

The Council of Ephesus did not bring an end to the debate about Jesus' humanity and divinity. Twenty years later a new emperor was persuaded to convene another assembly. The canons and definition of the **Council of Chalcedon** (451) represent the decisive stage in the development of the early Christian doctrine of Christ. Here is the central portion of the council's definition of the incarnation:

> *Wherefore, following the holy fathers [of Nicaea, Constantinople, and Ephesus], we all with one voice confess our Lord Jesus Christ one and the same Son, the same perfect in Godhead, the same perfect in manhood, truly God and truly man, the same consisting of a reasonable soul and a body, of one substance with the Father as touching the Godhead, the same of one substance with us touching the manhood, "like us in all things apart from sin" (Heb 4:15); begotten from the Father before the ages as touching the Godhead, the same in the last days, for us and for our salvation, born from the Virgin Mary, the Theotokos, as touching the manhood, one and the same Christ, Son, Lord, Only-begotten, to be acknowledged in two natures, without confusion, without change, without division, without separation; the distinction of natures being in no way abolished because of the union, but rather the characteristic property of each nature being preserved, and concurring into one person and one subsistence, not as if Christ were parted or divided into two persons, but one and the same Son.*

The bishops tried to pacify the warring factions by a balanced statement which drew on both Antiochene and Alexandrian traditions and phrasing. The key contribution came in the form of a long letter, called a *Tome*, from Pope Leo of Rome. From Leo's letter the fathers took the formula that *in* the incarnation there were two distinct *natures*, the divine and the human, united without separation and without confusion in a single *person*, Jesus Christ, the Son of God. Dissenters from this view believed that it sold out the teaching of Cyril of Alexandria. The most they would concede was that Christ was *from* two natures, but *after* his incarnation it was right only to speak of one, in the sense of a single reality. As a result, the dissenters from Chalcedon were labelled **monophysites** (from Greek *monos*, "one," and *physis*, "nature," hence "believers in a single nature").

The Councils of Nicaea, Constantinople, Ephesus and Chalcedon marked the greatest institutional and doctrinal unity which the Christian tradition has ever achieved. Ironically, the latter two councils also led to the first permanent splits (or "schisms") in the church. Those whose views were condemned at Ephesus as "Nestorian" were eventually forced to move across the eastern border into Persian territory, from where they spread as far east as China. The Council of Chalcedon caused even greater damage to Christian unity. Several modern Christian churches in the Middle East originated as protests against Chalcedon's definition of the two natures in Christ.

III. The Life of the Church

The 4th and 5th centuries saw important developments in other areas besides politics and theology. We will discuss three: the consolidation of the church's universal government; the rise of monasticism; and trends in liturgy and church design.

A. Church Government

Until the 4th century Christianity had consisted of a confederation of local churches linked by a common faith and the fellowship of the bishops. In theory all bishops were equal successors of the apostles, but in reality the bishops of the larger cities dominated. The Council of Nicaea recognized regional spheres of interest centered in Rome, Alexandria, and Antioch (the largest cities in the empire) as well as Jerusalem (which always had a special status as a "holy" city). To these four was soon added Constantinople, the new eastern capital. Four of these cities were located in the eastern part of the Roman Empire (Antioch, Alexandria, Jerusalem, and Constantinople), with only one in the west (Rome). The bishops of these cities eventually gained the honorary title of **patriarch**. The idea later developed in the Eastern churches that the five patriarchs should share spiritual jurisdiction as a committee or college. Such a system never got much beyond the level of theory, however, mainly because of rivalry among the patriarchs.

The church of Rome represented a special case in that it was the only church with a convincing claim to *primacy* (literally, being first). The Roman church and its bishop had always shown a sense of responsibility for the Christian churches as a whole. Rome's unique prestige was based mainly on its possession of the tombs of both Peter and Paul, and its location in the capital of the empire. In the 4th century Eastern bishops and theologians looking for support abroad often went to Rome as a refuge and a court of appeal, although the Easterners never accepted that the bishop of Rome had the right to intervene in their affairs without being asked first. The bishop of Rome eventually came to be called the **pope**. (The word comes from the Latin *papa*, which means "father." At first all bishops were called "popes," but eventually the title was restricted to the bishop of Rome.) A major concern for the bishop of Rome was the growing ambition of the church of Constantinople, which according to several conciliar canons (statements issued by church councils) possessed an authority second only to that of Rome's. This claim to authority was made on the ground that it was the "new Rome."

The sermons, letters, and decrees of Pope Leo I (reigned 440-461) expressed many of the ideas which have remained basic to the **papacy** (the government of the pope) ever since: that Peter was the chief of the apostles; that he was divinely commissioned to rule the church at the center of the empire; that the pope is the direct successor of Peter, "the doorkeeper of the kingdom of heaven," as Leo called him (see Matt 16:15-19); and that the pope's authority is grounded not in his personal merit but in the merits of Peter.

Figure 9.1: A relief on a sarcophagus, i.e., a stone casket dating from about 380, which has the very common artistic theme of Christ handing Peter the Law in the form of a scroll; Peter is holding a cross, broken at the top, in token of Christ's prediction in Jn 21:18-19 that Peter would die a martyr's death.

Peter's confession according to Matt 16:15-19.

"[Jesus] said to them, 'But who do you say that I am?' Simon Peter answered, 'You are the Messiah, the Son of the living God.' And Jesus answered him, 'Blessed are you, Simon son of Jonah! For flesh and blood has not revealed this to you, but my Father in heaven. And I tell you, you are Peter, and on this rock I will build my church, and the gates of Hades will not prevail against it. I will give you the keys of the kingdom of heaven, and whatever you bind on earth will be bound in heaven, and whatever you loose on earth will be loosed in heaven.'"

These ideas concerning papal primacy would not be fully applied even in the West until the Germanic invasions and the conquests of Islam radically reshaped the Christian map and left the papacy largely in a world of its own, and they were never fully accepted in the East. Although Eastern Christians did not view the primacy of Rome the same way that Westerners did, the acceptance of Leo's *Tome* at the Council of Chalcedon testifies to the regard in which the Eastern bishops held the Roman church: "Peter has spoken through Leo," they cried. They meant not that Leo's teaching was true just because it was Leo who had said it, but that in their judgment Leo had correctly expressed the faith which they held. In the Christian East, the most common interpretation of Peter's confession of faith in Mt 16:16-19 was that the "rock" on which Jesus founds the church was not the *person* of Peter but his faith in Christ, which was professed by all. Eastern Christianity has traditionally seen the Roman bishop as, at most, "the first among equals," meaning that he has a unique spiritual prestige, a primacy of honor, but not a right of command over other patriarchs.

B. Monasticism and the Ascetical Movement

The 4th century also saw the rise of monasticism and of the ascetical movement in the Eastern Roman Empire. **Asceticism** refers to the training or discipline of the passions and the appetites. Monasticism refers to the practice of monks. The word **monk** comes from the Greek word *monachos*, meaning a single or a solitary person. It was coined in the 4th century as a name for the many men and women who had begun to withdraw to secluded desert regions to lead lives of prayer and spiritual discipline. It is not a coincidence that this happened just about the time when Christianity was winning acceptance by the Roman Empire. The monastic life replaced martyrdom as the model of Christian perfection.

Tradition credits **Antony of Egypt** (251-356) with being the father of Christian monasticism. According to the *Life of Antony* written by Athanasius of Alexandria, Antony chose to change his life when, as a young soldier on leave from the Roman army, he heard the gospel story of Christ's counsel to the rich young man: "If you would be perfect, go and sell what you have and give the money to the poor, and come follow me" (Matt 19:21). His basic motive was thus the full discipleship of Christ and his command to be perfect (Matt 5:48). The monk struggled to subdue human appetites and passions of all kinds (for food, for possessions, for comfort, for freedom, for sexual union, and so on), for the sake of restoring the original innocence of humanity before the Fall. In the eyes of these early monks, the struggle for perfection required a departure from the normal life of the world, either through enclosure (hence the term *cloister*) or through actual withdrawal into the desert. In fact, devout groups of Christian men and women were already practicing asceticism within church communities long before Antony; his main innovation was physical seclusion.

Despite the desire for separation from the world, monks aspired to support themselves and to work for the good of others. They did not coldly leave the rest of humanity to its fate. Monks often remained close enough to towns and villages to serve as advocates for those in need, to proclaim Christ's message to the high and the mighty, to heal the sick and counsel the troubled, and above all to serve as an example to others. Ordinary Christians saw them as living links to heaven. Even the pillar saints of Syria, who mounted columns in order to withdraw from society, were pursued into the desert by pilgrims and by communities of monks who settled around them. Christian asceticism was not a condemnation of the world as such but a personal struggle against the reign of sin and of the demons in the soul. Therefore the movement did not condemn Christians who continued to live in the world, nor did it protest against the conversion of the empire to Christianity. Although monasticism had a generally positive impact on both the monks and those whom they served and prayed for, examples of destructive fanaticism were not unknown. Monks occasionally inspired mob violence against pagans and pagan shrines, or pursued ascetical self-denial in extreme forms such as the wearing of chains.

The primary model for the monastic life was Jesus himself, who was unmarried, had no permanent home, and said no human obligation should stand in the way of the kingdom of God. Other important New Testament models included the ascetical prophet John the Baptist and Paul, who pursued a celibate lifestyle and recommended virginity over marriage to his followers (1 Cor 7:8). Another biblical inspiration was the communal sharing of property in the Jerusalem church (Acts 2:44-45). There were also antecedents in Judaism, such as the Essene monasticism of Qumran and the communities of Jewish contemplatives in Egypt described by Philo of Alexandria. There were pagan ascetics, too, influenced by philosophical ideas of the superiority of the spiritual realm over the material. The ascetical life appealed to many high-minded pagans as well as to Christians.

Alongside the hermit or solitary type of monasticism, there were also communities of monks. This kind of monasticism is called **cenobitic** monasticism, from the Greek words for "common life." Organized communities were governed by a spiritual leader called an **abbot** (from the Aramaic word for "father"). They usually followed a written rule and a routine of manual labor and public and private prayer. The rules and routines—along with the separation from society—were designed (in part) to help monks avoid sin.

The monk Evagrius (345-399) was Egyptian monasticism's most important teacher. From him stems the traditional list of the seven deadly sins, although his list actually analyzed eight of them: gluttony, lust, love of money, sadness, anger, boredom, vanity, and pride. Basil of Caesarea, one of the Cappadocians, formulated a rule for cenobitic monasticism which stressed mutual service and works of charity. If you live alone, he asked, whose feet will you wash? (The reference is to Jesus' washing of his disciples' feet at the Last Supper in the Gospel of John.) Basil's rule has dominated monasticism in Orthodox Christianity. Monasticism also flourished in Syria, independent of developments in Egypt. Syrian monasticism was notable for its extreme forms of self-denial, such as that of the pillar saints.

Gradually, written and oral accounts, including Athanasius' *Life of Antony*, spread monastic theory and practice throughout the Christian world. Monasticism and ascetical ideals began to become popular in the West starting in the 4th century. Books about the sayings and lives of the desert fathers and mothers (monasticism was open to women as well as men) became central texts in the spiritual literature of the Christian tradition, and monasticism would come to play a crucial role in the development of Christianity in the West.

C. Religious Life and Church Architecture

The newly-won support of the Roman emperors and the rapid growth of the church affected the worship life of Christians. This is shown most visibly in the development of church architecture. For the first three centuries, Christians met for the weekly Eucharist and for other activities in private homes adapted for worship. Of these "house churches" the best example is a mid-3rd century house church discovered in the Syrian town of Dura-Europas, on the Roman frontier with Persia. The town was abandoned by the Romans when the Persians attacked it in 256. As a result, it was not built over by later churches the way other house churches must have been. Only a short distance away archaeologists found a Jewish synagogue. An assembly hall, with a raised podium (presumably for the bishop), had room for about 65 to 75 people. A smaller room had been altered into a baptistery (a place for baptism), with a step-up basin covered by a canopy and arches. The baptistery's walls were decorated with frescoes (wall paintings) of subjects such as Adam and Eve, the Good Shepherd, the Samaritan Woman at the Well, David and Goliath, and Peter and Jesus walking on the water.

Publicly identifiable Christian churches began to appear even during the reign of Diocletian, a notorious enemy of Christianity who instituted the Great Persecution in 303. One report indicates that there was a Christian church directly across the street from Diocletian's palace, an indication of the security the Christian community enjoyed prior to the unexpected trauma of the Great Persecution. After the rise of Constantine, church construction mushroomed, with the help of imperial subsidies, in order to accommodate the crowds of new converts and to celebrate the church's new status.

These new buildings were of three types. The most common is called a **basilica** (from the Greek word for "royal") because it was an adaptation of the standard rectangular layout of royal audience halls and public buildings in Roman cities. The Christian version of a basilica was an audience hall for Christ, the heavenly king.

Figure 9. 2: Church of Santa Sabina in Rome, early 5th century, showing the basilica plan.

It consisted of a long rectangular building, often with two or even four side aisles along the central hall, which was called the *nave*. In larger churches a shorter crossing section called a *transept* was often built at the end or partway down the nave. A rounded extension called an *apse* was usually found at the east end of the nave, in the direction of Jerusalem. The bishop's chair, his *cathedra* (a bishop's church is therefore known as a **cathedral**), was on the back wall of the apse, where he sat with his priests in a semi-circle around him. Sermons were given from this chair, the symbol of his teaching authority.

Figure 9.3: Sanctuary of the Church of Santa Sabina in Rome.

This end of the church was called the *sanctuary* ("holy place") and was set off from the rest of the church by a screen or a rail, reflecting the distinction between the clergy and the laity. The *altar* was a removable table placed in the nave. The only other furniture was a raised pulpit for reading the scriptures. There were no pews or kneelers; the congregation stood for the service. The interiors of large churches were richly decorated with hanging curtains, marble, lamps, gold inlay and *mosaics* (pictures made of small fragments of colored glass) on the walls of apse and sanctuary. Scholars have often noted the contrast between the plain exterior of the buildings, usually unadorned brick, and the rich ornamentation of the interior: believers entered a place where the worship service or *liturgy* (literally, "the people's work") was a participation in the worship of the angels in the heavenly Jerusalem. The basilica served the weekly liturgy of the Eucharist.

A quite different design from the long axis of the basilica was the centered focus of the church type called a **memoria**, built to honor the tomb of a saint or martyr, or a holy site such as the cave in Bethlehem where Christ was believed to have been born. A memoria could be octagonal or cruciform in shape, or even circular, in which case it was called a *rotunda*. The lines of vision oriented the visitor to the middle of the building, where the shrine or tomb lay. The *memoriae* are important witnesses to the growing Christian devotion to the physical remains of the dead and to the belief in the spiritual power of the saints, both in heaven and on earth. In the case of pilgrimage sites in Palestine, memorial churches testify to the growing desire to experience salvation in connection with the physical *location* of the saving events of Jesus' life.

A third type of Christian structure was the **baptistery**, where at Easter new Christians were initiated into the faith. A baptistery, like a memoria, had a centered design. Instead of a tomb, the focus was on the baptismal font into which the candidate stepped.

The association with a tomb was intentional, since Christian Baptism was understood as an identification with Christ's death, burial, and resurrection. Baptisteries could be either free-standing or attached to churches.

Figure 9.4: Baptistery of the Orthodox in Ravenna, late 4th-5th centuries.

The religious life of ordinary Christians was oriented around the sacraments of Baptism and the Eucharist. In the 4th century Baptism for adults was still common, with many people intentionally deferring their Baptism until adulthood. Infant Baptism did not become the norm, apparently, until the 5th century. Most laypeople received the Eucharist each week, unless they were **catechumens** (candidates for Baptism who were undergoing instruction in the Christian religion) or **penitents** (people who were denied communion because of serious sin such as murder, adultery, or apostasy), both of whom had to leave the liturgy after the biblical readings and the sermon. Penitents for serious sin usually performed a lengthy public **penance** (a penalty) before they could be re-admitted to communion. Post-baptismal forgiveness for serious sin was extended only once, after public confession to the bishop and his clergy. Otherwise, fasting, works of charity, and prayers such as the Our Father (Matt 6:9-13) were recommended as the normal means of forgiveness for less serious sins.

The familiar year-long cycle of religious feasts began to take shape during the 4th century, anchored by Easter and its season of penitential preparation called **Lent**. Following Easter came the season of **Pentecost** (commemorating the day on which the Holy Spirit descended upon the apostles), a time of joy and also of further instruction for the newly baptized. Christ's birth (Christmas) was celebrated in the West on December 25, previously the pagan feast of the Unconquered Sun. The feast days of the martyrs' deaths were also becoming more prominent points in the calendar, and sometimes the occasion of riotous celebration—to the consternation of the bishops, who realized that some of the enthusiasm was a carryover of pagan habits of feasting at the graveside of deceased family members.

Key Terms:

Constantine	patriarch
Theodosius I	papacy
ecumenical council	Pope Leo I
dogma	asceticism
Arius	monk
Athanasius	Antony of Egypt
Nicene Creed	cenobitic monasticism
Cappadocian Fathers	abbot
incarnation	Basil of Caesarea
Theotokos	cathedral
Council of Nicaea	basilica
Council of Constantinople	memoria
Council of Ephesus	baptistery
Council of Chalcedon	catechumen
Apollinaris of Laodicaea	penitent
School of Antioch	penance
School of Alexandria	Pentecost
Nestorius	Lent
monophysite	

Questions for Reading:

1. What was the great change which Christianity in the 4th century experienced in its relationship with the Roman Empire?

2. What two things did Constantine expect from the Christian church?

3. Part of Constantine's influence on the Christian tradition consisted of fostering a Christian devotion to the Roman Empire. Assess both the positive and the negative aspects of this identification with the state.

4. In rejecting Arius' teachings, the Council of Nicaea ruled that the Son was "one in being" with the Father. What did Arius teach, and why did Christians like Athanasius oppose his teaching?

5. How did the Cappadocians contribute towards the definition of the Trinity as this doctrine was declared at the Council of Constantinople?

6. Explain the basic approaches to understanding the union of divine and human in the incarnation taken by the School of Antioch and the School of Alexandria.

7. What was the teaching of the Council of Chalcedon on the union of divine and human in the incarnation (answer in terms of "nature" and "person"), and why did many Eastern Christians refuse to accept the council's definition?

8. Christianity never had a written "constitution" to define its government. During the period of the 4th-5th centuries, what was the status of the Roman pope in the universal church? (Describe this both from the point of view of the popes, as seen in the writings of Pope Leo I, and from the point of view of eastern bishops.)

9. What was the historical circumstance in which monasticism arose, and what was its main inspiration?

10. How did the floor plan of the church design called the basilica reflect the distinction between laity and clergy in the church?

Works Consulted/Recommended Reading:

Barnes, T. D. *Constantine and Eusebius*. Cambridge, Mass., & London: Harvard University Press, 1981.

Baynes, Norman H. "Eusebius and the Christian Empire." In *Byzantine Studies and Other Essays*, pp. 168-72. London: Athalone Press, 1955.

Beskow, Per. *Rex Gloriae: The Kingship of Christ in the Early Church*. Stockholm: Almquist & Wiksell, 1964.

Brown, Peter. *Society and the Holy in Late Antiquity*. London: Faber & Faber, 1982.

Chitty, Derwas. *The Desert a City: An Introduction to the Study of Egyptian and Palestinian Monasticism under the Christian Empire*. Crestwood, N.Y.: St. Vladimir's Seminary Press, 1966.

Frend, W. H. C. *The Donatist Church: A Movement of Protest in Roman North Africa*. Oxford: Clarendon Press, 1952.

_____ . *Martyrdom and Persecution in the Early Church*. Garden City, N.Y.: Doubleday & Co., 1967.

Hanson, R. P. C. *The Search for the Christian Doctrine of God: The Arian Controversy 318-381*. Edinburgh: T & T Clark, 1988.

Kelly, J. N. D. *Early Christian Creeds*. 3rd ed. New York: Longman, 1972.

King, N. Q. *The Emperor Theodosius and the Establishment of Christianity*. London: SCM Press, 1961.

MacMullen, Ramsay. *Christianizing the Roman Empire (A.D. 100-400)*. New Haven & London: Yale University Press, 1984.

_____ . *Constantine*. New York, Evanston, San Francisco, London: Harper & Row, 1969.

Mathews, Thomas. *The Clash of the Gods: A Reinterpretation of Early Christian Art*. Princeton: Princeton University Press, 1993.

Meer, F. van der and Mohrmann, Christine. *Atlas of the Early Christian World*. Trans. and ed. Mary F. Nelson and H. H. Rowley. London & Edinburgh: Nelson, 1958.

Metzger, Bruce and Murphy, Roland, eds. *The New Oxford Annotated Bible with Apocrypha*, New Revised Standard Version. New York: Oxford University Press, 1991.

Murray, Robert. *Symbols of Church and Kingdom: A Study in Early Syriac Tradition*. London & New York: Cambridge University Press, 1975.

Tsafrir, Yoram, ed. *Ancient Churches Revealed*. Washington, D.C.: Israel Exploration Society & Biblical Archaeological Society, 1993.

Weitzmann, Kurt, ed. *Age of Spirituality: Late Antique and Early Christian Art, Third to Seventh Century*. New York: Metropolitan Museum of Art, 1979.

Chapter 10

Augustine of Hippo

Timeline

311 AD	Beginnings of the Donatist schism.
354	Augustine is born in Thagaste in North Africa.
c. 374	Augustine joins the quasi-Christian cult known as the Manichees.
384	Augustine arrives in Milan and meets Ambrose.
387	Augustine is baptized by bishop Ambrose.
388	Pelagius comes to Rome to teach.
391	Augustine is ordained a presbyter.
396	Augustine becomes bishop of Hippo in North Africa.
397-401?	Augustine writes the **Confessions**.
c. 410	Caelestius, one of Pelagius' disciples, begins to teach Pelagian doctrines in North Africa.
418	The teachings of Pelagius are condemned by the bishop of Rome, and Pelagius and Caelestius are banished by the emperor.
430	Augustine's death.

Augustine of Hippo

Of all the thinkers of the early Christian period, Augustine of Hippo was surely the greatest and the most influential, at least among Western Christians. The sheer extent of his work is staggering, including hundreds of treatises and sermons, ranging from philosophical discussions of the nature of good and evil, to moral essays on marriage and celibacy, to commentaries on the books of the Old and New Testaments, to speculative theological treatises on the Trinity, and much else besides. Western Christian notions of original sin and grace received their distinctive character from Augustine's teaching. Catholic understandings of the sacraments and the nature of the church were also definitively shaped by his work. Augustine's thinking even affected Christian views on the relation between the church and the wider political and social world.

One of the remarkable things about Augustine in contrast to most ancient people is that we actually do know a lot about his life. Not only has he been blessed with graceful biographers (ancient and modern), but Augustine himself in his *Confessions* narrated in some detail the course of his first thirty-three years. Although the *Confessions* is carefully constructed to convey Augustine's later theological understanding and interpretation of his life, nonetheless the basic accuracy of the events that he describes is not disputed.

I. Historical Situation

Augustine was born in the year 354 in the small backwater town of Thagaste in the Roman province of North Africa (modern day Algeria). Barely thirty years had passed since the first Roman emperor had embraced the Christian faith, and it would take some time before Christianity became the official religion of the Roman Empire. The first fifty years of Augustine's life saw a dramatic change in the character of the church and society, which in many ways mirrored his own life and concerns.

The rise of Constantine marked the end of nearly three hundred years of intermittent persecution by the Roman authorities; the "age of the martyrs" had come to an end. The Christian church could now look forward to an unparalleled period of growth and development. Large numbers flocked to the Christian communities, encouraged by the imperial favor now bestowed on the Christian religion. Needless to say, these converts did not always reflect high standards of morality, and Christian preachers in the later 4th century AD often expressed their frustration at those who did not cease to be "pagan" when they entered the church doors. Some Christian teachers even looked back with nostalgia to the age of persecutions, when (so they claimed) the threat of death had produced more authentic Christians.

The question of how to be an authentic Christian was one that troubled many Christians in the later 4th century, and it hovers persistently over Augustine's *Confessions*. The monastic movement, whose origins were discussed in the previous chapter, had posed the question in the starkest possible way: is it necessary to abandon the city, to leave all that bound one to "the world" (sex, marriage, career, family) in order to follow Christ faithfully? The words of Jesus from Matthew's Gospel were echoed again and again in the stories of the lives and deeds of the holy men and women who had given up the glamour and risks of secular society for monastic seclusion: "If you wish to be perfect, go, sell your possessions, and give the money to the poor…then come, follow me" (Mt 19:21, cited in Athanasius, *Life of Antony* 2).

The ascetic rejection of sex, marriage, property, and career became associated in the minds of many Christians with the path of perfection. The story of Augustine's own life, as he narrated it in the first nine books of his *Confessions*, presupposes this understanding of Christian holiness. Augustine's decision to accept the Christian faith and to be baptized at the age of thirty-three was intimately connected with his decision to renounce marriage and a successful career. Judging from his account in the *Confessions*, the prospect of being a married Christian simply did not interest him.

If the conversion of the emperor Constantine and a widespread optimism about the new possibilities of a Christian Roman Empire characterized Christian hopes in the first half of Augustine's life, the opening decades of the 5th century brought profound disillusionment. In the year 410 the city of Rome was attacked and sacked by the Gothic chief **Alaric** (an Arian Christian). Twenty years later, as Augustine lay dying at Hippo, another northern people, the Vandals, were consolidating their control over Roman North Africa. The fall of Rome provoked one of Augustine's greatest works, **On the City of God**. Pagan critics had suggested that the rise of Christianity and the abandonment of the traditional worship had led to the decline and fall of the empire. To them Augustine responded with a vast apologetic work, arguing that pagan religion was both morally and spiritually bankrupt. As for the fall of the empire, Augustine noted that it had largely been built on the lust for domination, and that Christians had to look elsewhere for the "city of God."

II. Early Life and Conversion of Augustine

Augustine came from a family of modest means, not impoverished, but not excessively wealthy. His father does not seem to have had any serious religious affiliation, until he became a Christian late in life. Augustine's mother, **Monica**, on the other hand, was a devout Christian who prayed eagerly for her son to embrace the faith and who, as time went on, exerted a great influence upon him. At a young age Augustine was enrolled as a catechumen (literally "a person undergoing instruction") in the church. But for someone of Augustine's depth and complexity, there was to be no easy entrance into the Christian religion.

Part of the difficulty stemmed from Augustine's own acute and restless intellect. He excelled in school, especially in the study of Latin rhetoric or public speaking. After studying in his hometown of Thagaste, in nearby Madaurus, and later in the capital Carthage, Augustine became a teacher of Latin rhetoric. In an effort to escape horrendous teaching conditions and rowdy students, Augustine travelled from Carthage to Rome to Milan, where he received a distinguished post as professor of rhetoric.

But Augustine's love of ancient Latin literature drew him further and further from the Christianity of his mother. At the age of nineteen Augustine read a philosophical work of Cicero, called the **Hortensius**, which included a review and critique of the various schools of ancient philosophy. The treatise filled him with a desire to "love and see and pursue and hold fast and strongly embrace wisdom itself, wherever found" (*Conf.* III.iv.8). When he dipped into the scriptures to see how they compared with the wisdom of Cicero, Augustine found them "unworthy in comparison," that is, inferior in literary style. More than ten years were to pass before Augustine could read the Bible and take it seriously again.

The other significant aspect of Augustine's life at this time was his discovery of the pleasures of sex. As he described it in the *Confessions*, the "bubbling impulses of puberty befogged and obscured my heart so that it could not see the difference between love's serenity and lust's darkness" (II.ii.2). After what may have been an initial period of promiscuity, Augustine settled down into a monogamous relationship, known to the Romans as "concubinage" (literally, "sleeping together"). Such liaisons were common, especially between upwardly mobile young men and women of servile or lower-class backgrounds. Augustine always seems to have regarded the relationship as a temporary one, a sexual convenience until it was time to contract a marriage with a woman of wealth and proper standing. Nonetheless, he loved the woman deeply and with her had a son, whom they named **Adeodatus** (literally, "gift of God"). One of the most poignant passages in the *Confessions* is Augustine's description of the pain he felt when he and his concubine finally parted after thirteen years together: "My heart which was deeply attached was cut and wounded, and left a trail of blood. She had returned to Africa vowing that she would never go with another man" (VI.xv.25). Nowhere, however, in all his voluminous works, does Augustine ever tell us her name.

Around this time (c. 374), when Augustine was about twenty years old, he became involved with a quasi-Christian cult known as the "**Manichees**." The sect derives its name from Mani, a prophet and visionary who lived in the 3rd century AD in Mesopotamia. At the heart of Mani's teaching was the notion that from the beginning of time there have existed two fundamental realities: a principle or power of good (the kingdom of Light) and a power of evil (the kingdom of Darkness). The kingdom of Light basically consisted of spirit, and the kingdom of Darkness consisted of matter and the dark elements, such as smoke. These two powers, according to the Manichees, were co-eternal and co-equal.

Because of its inherent restlessness and desire for conquest, the kingdom of Darkness invaded the kingdom of Light and succeeded in swallowing up a large chunk of it. By generating an elaborate series of spiritual beings, the kingdom of Light defended itself and managed to produce a created world, though part of that world (the material part) was considered to be evil. The aim of this creation was to liberate the elements of spiritual light which are still trapped in evil matter. The waxing and waning of the moon for the Manichees signaled special times when light was being returned to its source. One special place for the liberation of spirit from matter was the bodies of the Manichean leaders (the **Elect**). When these special persons, who were celibate and vegetarian, ate selected fruits and vegetables, their digestive organs were thought to facilitate the escape of the light from darkness. To engage in sex or to partake of meat, the Manichees believed, was to perpetuate the enslavement of spirit in matter. Although both of these activities were allowed to those on the fringes of the sect (the **Hearers**), they were forbidden to the Elect.

Augustine remained a Hearer in the Manichean sect for nine years. He was attracted by their clear answer to a question that would long exercise his mind: where does evil come from? Since the Manichees believed (like some of the 2nd century gnostics) that the God of the Old Testament was a vicious demon, their criticisms of the Hebrew scriptures appealed to Augustine's sense that the Bible was a document unworthy of a philosopher. For example, the Manichees mocked the polygamy (multiple wives) of the patriarchs in Genesis as sexual degeneracy.

Most of all, Augustine was persuaded by the Manichees' dualistic conception of the human person. The Manichees could explain why it was that Augustine felt himself torn between his intellectual desire for truth and wisdom, on the one hand, and his craving for sexual delight and worldly success, on the other hand. Their answer was that Augustine's spirit belonged to the kingdom of Light, but his body belonged to the kingdom of Darkness. In other words, Manichean dualism helped explain

Augustine to himself and, significantly, absolved him of responsibility for the actions of his "wicked" half. When Augustine finally does come to reject the views of the Manichees, an important aspect of his conversion away from Manicheism and toward orthodox Christianity came through a recognition that the human person is a unity and that this unity implies moral accountability.

During most of his twenties Augustine remained attached to the Manichees. However, as he tells the story in the *Confessions*, he was growing increasingly skeptical and critical of Manichean theology. In these years Augustine became interested in astrology and discovered the disconcerting fact that astrologers generally had more reliable scientific data (e.g., for predicting eclipses of the sun and moon) than did the Manichees. This rational failure of the Manichees' "science" was troubling, and Augustine soon realized that even the most authoritative Manichean teachers were unable to answer his questions. Even more dissatisfying to someone as philosophically minded as Augustine was the Manichees' view of God (the kingdom of Light) as fundamentally weak and vulnerable to invasion by evil. Augustine came to see that even though the Manichees believed in a so-called "spiritual" world (light, goodness) in conflict with a "material" world (darkness, evil), their idea of God was really modelled on a kind of material substance. Such a God, Augustine came to hold, was not worth believing in (see *Conf.*, book VII).

By the time that Augustine arrived in Milan, in the autumn of 384, he had virtually abandoned the Manichees, but had not yet found a persuasive alternative. Augustine now encountered certain ideas and individuals who were to lead him back to the Christianity of his youth. He began to attend the sermons of **Ambrose** of Milan, a learned Christian bishop and former provincial governor. Ambrose was just the sort of eloquent, educated Christian that the young Augustine could admire. Furthermore, Ambrose was skilled in the allegorical method of biblical interpretation, which he had learned from Greek Christian writers such as Origen of Alexandria. Ambrose taught Augustine that the embarrassing aspects of the Old Testament, which the Manichees had held up to ridicule, could be interpreted non-literally, that is, as symbols of moral or spiritual truths.

Even more significant, at the urging of Simplicianus, a priest of Milan who had taken an interest in the young professor, Augustine began to read certain "books of the Platonists," namely the writings of the 3rd-century AD philosopher **Plotinus**, as recorded by his disciple **Porphyry**. In these writings Augustine found a philosophy, now called "Neoplatonism," which gave him a new way to think about God, the world, and evil that enabled him finally to break with the harsh dualism of the Manichees. Neoplatonism also was to serve as a sort of intellectual bridge which would lead Augustine ultimately to Christianity.

In the teaching of Plotinus, God was a reality that surpassed all human categories of knowing or describing. In fact, rather than use the name "God," Plotinus preferred to speak of the supreme Being as "the One," to characterize its primary quality of pure simplicity or oneness. While the One could not be comprehended or grasped in its essence or entirety by the human mind (whose knowledge is always partial and fragmentary), nonetheless the Neoplatonists taught that this One produced a succession of other realities or substances from itself: Intellect, Soul, and, finally, Matter. Each level of being proceeds from the higher one and depends on the higher level for its life and order, just as in a human being one might say that the life or soul serves to organize the physical functions of the body. Even Matter, Plotinus taught, was capable of being formed and directed towards the good, although left on its own it tended to disorder, corruption, and non-being. It is this character of Matter which is "evil" in the primary, though non-moral, sense.

Augustine found Neoplatonism an exhilarating alternative to the views of the Manichees. Here was a vision of God as truly supreme, the source of all being, goodness, and beauty; God was *Being* itself, the "I am who I am" of Exodus 3:14. If God and all that came from God was truly good, Augustine reasoned, then evil itself cannot be a substance in the sense that the Manichees taught. Evil (in the non-moral sense) must be the tendency in the lowest level of creation towards disorder, corruption, and non-being, and this is the very opposite of the order, life, and being that come from God. But Plotinus also taught that there is evil in the moral sense, when rational creatures freely choose to turn towards the lower goods rather than towards the One who is their source. As Augustine describes it in the *Confessions*: "I inquired what wickedness is; and I did not find a substance but a perversity of will twisted away from the highest substance, you O God, towards inferior things, rejecting its own inner life and swelling with external matter" (VII.xvi.22).

Neoplatonism, Augustine tells us, seemed to be profoundly compatible with what he knew of Christianity, especially as it was being preached by bishop Ambrose. The views of God, creation, and evil could easily be assimilated; the Christian elements that were missing from Neoplatonism (Augustine tells us in hindsight) were the doctrine of divine incarnation and the notion of divine grace. The *Confessions* says little about what led Augustine at this time to move towards an intellectual acceptance of Christian teachings, but we are well informed about the moral dimensions of his struggle to embrace Christianity fully. In the eighth book of the *Confessions* Augustine describes in vivid detail the emotional turmoil he experienced as he tried to bring himself to the point of making a decision to be baptized.

The basic problem was that Augustine saw his conversion to Christianity as entailing a conversion to the monastic or ascetic way of life; to be a serious Christian meant that Augustine would have to abandon his career and his desire for sex, marriage, and family. After more than fifteen years of sexual activity, Augustine found himself subject to a habit which he had no longer had the power to break: "I...was bound not by an iron imposed by anyone else but by the iron of my own choice. ...The consequence of a distorted will is passion. By servitude to passion, habit is formed, and habit to which there is no resistance becomes necessity" (VIII.v.10). Augustine felt himself torn between two "wills," between two competing desires, neither of which was strong enough to overcome the other; and he found the internal division devastating.

In the famous garden scene in book eight of the *Confessions*, Augustine describes the moment when he finally decided to entrust himself into the hands of God. Looking back on his decision ten years later as he wrote the *Confessions*, Augustine saw the key to his conversion as his allowing God to produce in him the work of "continence" (i.e., abstention from sex) which he was unable to will on his own. As the figure of **Lady Continence** says in the paragraph preceding the garden scene: "Why are you relying on yourself, only to find yourself unreliable? Cast yourself upon him, do not be afraid. He will not withdraw himself so that you fall. Make the leap without anxiety; he will catch you and heal you" (VIII.xi.27). Only after experiencing himself as powerless and after reading the passage from Paul (Rom 13:14: "...put on the Lord Jesus Christ and make no

Figure 10.1: Saint Augustine in the garden.

provision for the flesh in its lusts") did Augustine find the division within himself healed: "…it was as if a light of relief from all anxiety flooded into my heart. All the shadows of doubt were dispelled" (VIII.xii.29).

Augustine's experience of his own conversion and his subsequent reflection on it were to prove foundational for the development of his theological vision. Central to this vision was Augustine's notion that human beings are impelled to their actions by their own deepest desires, by their "love." "A body by its weight tends to move towards its proper place…My weight is my love. Wherever I am carried, my love is carrying me." After the first sin of Adam and Eve, Augustine believed, all human beings are born with an inherent tendency to a pernicious form of self-love, a tendency to love the lower goods of the world rather than the God who is their source. Only the grace of God, the power of the Holy Spirit, can heal the damaged human will and transform it into a will that loves God and self properly: "By your gift we are set on fire and carried upwards: we grow red hot and ascend… Lit by your fire, your good fire, we grow red-hot and ascend, as we move upwards to the peace of Jerusalem'" (*Conf.* XIII.ix.10).

III. Augustine the Bishop

In the spring of 387 Augustine was baptized by bishop Ambrose at the Easter vigil. He returned to Africa the following year, shortly after the death of his mother in Italy. Augustine had originally hoped to live quietly in a monastic community with some devoted friends, but a man of his talents was much needed in the North African church. By the year 391 he had been ordained presbyter (literally "elder" or priest) of the seaport town of Hippo Regius, and by 396 he had become bishop. Though he was now tossed into an active life, he remained supportive of the monastic movement and even formulated guidelines for the communal living of monks and nuns (*The Rule of St. Augustine*) which became very influential in the middle ages.

From this point onward, during the final three decades of his life, Augustine was to be preoccupied with preaching, pastoral concerns and the writing of numerous theological and polemical treatises against the pagans, Manichees, and other Christian heretics. Among the controversies that absorbed his attention, the debates with the Donatists and the Pelagians were the most bitter and the most consequential for later Christian theology.

A. The Donatist Schism

The North Africa to which Augustine returned in 388 was deeply divided in a schism that had already lasted for nearly a century. During the last persecution (c. 303) the emperor Diocletian had issued an edict directing Christian clergy to hand over all copies of the scriptures to be burned. Some bishops had cooperated with the authorities, and others had pretended to do so by handing over copies of heretical writings instead. In North Africa, where the spirit of the martyrs had long been strong, opposition to any collaboration with the persecutors was especially fierce. Those who handed over the scriptures were dubbed ***traditores*** ("traitors") and were judged guilty of **apostasy** (renunciation of one's religious faith); many Christians refused to acknowledge that these bishops or priests had any authority in the church.

In 311 when Caecilian, a new bishop of Carthage, was elected, great opposition arose. One of the bishops who had consecrated Caecilian, it was claimed, had been a *traditor*. Furthermore, Caecilian himself had had a dubious record during the recent persecution. A large number of bishops in North Africa refused to recognize the legitimacy of Caecilian, and soon a rival bishop of

Carthage was elected in his place. The opponents of Caecilian, soon to be called "**Donatists**" (from Donatus, the name of one of the early rival bishops of Carthage), appealed to the emperor Constantine. After consulting with the bishop of Rome and a Western council, the emperor decided against the Donatists. From this point onward, the Donatists regarded all non-Donatist Christians as illegitimate; Donatism in their view represented the true Christian church, and outside of that church there was no salvation.

Throughout the 4th century Donatism thrived in North Africa, especially in the countryside where hostility to Roman rule had always run high. In some places bands of roving brigands with clubs, known as the "**Circumcellions**," tried to enforce Donatism with violence. Some scholars have seen the movement as grounded in the social protest of the poor and disenfranchised against the power of wealthy landowners. But there was a serious theological side to Donatism as well. The Donatists saw themselves as the true continuation of the church of the martyrs. They emphasized that the church must be pure and holy and set apart from the world. As long as a bishop remained allied with the (false) church of Caecilian and his successors, the Donatists argued, he remained tainted by sin and unable to bestow the grace of God in any way. Donatists believed, therefore, that sacraments administered in the non-Donatist churches (e.g., Baptism) were invalid because those churches did not possess the power of the Holy Spirit.

In the 390s when Augustine began his priesthood and episcopacy, Donatist Christians probably outnumbered Catholics in North Africa. Augustine immediately began to engage the Donatists in debate and to write polemical treatises against the sect. He challenged them on a variety of grounds. First he questioned whether their historical facts were correct; he cited the evidence of investigations showing not only that Caecilian and his consecrators had not been *traditores*, but that certain Donatist bishops had been. But Augustine's most significant arguments were theological ones. Whatever holiness the Donatists might have possessed, he argued, was now destroyed by their schism. Unity is a primary characteristic of the church, and to violate that unity, Augustine taught, is to violate the essentials of Christian charity.

Furthermore, Augustine maintained, universality or **catholicity** was another distinguishing feature of the church. Both the promise made to Abraham (Gen 12:3), which St. Paul had recalled (Gal 3:8), and Jesus' own command to his disciples after the resurrection (Acts 1:8), were prophecies of the worldwide spread of Christianity. The Donatist claim to represent the faithful remnant, the only pure and holy church, was as arrogant as it was unfounded. The true church, Augustine argues, is the catholic church, that is, the church of Christians united throughout the world. The holiness of the church is the holiness of Christ, not the holiness of human beings. In this life good and bad persons are mixed together within the one body of the church. In fact, Augustine notes, in this life all people are stained by sin and that is why the church itself in all its members prays the words of the Lord's Prayer, "Forgive us our trespasses…"

In response to the Donatist notion that the sacraments administered by a sinful priest or bishop (i.e., a *traditor*) were invalid, Augustine answered that Jesus Christ is the source of any grace conveyed in sacramental actions. Therefore, even when a minister is guilty of the gravest sins, the effectiveness of the sacraments themselves remains unchanged. A guilty priest brings greater guilt upon himself by his actions, Augustine argued, but the sacraments themselves remain effective. Augustine could even recognize the validity of the baptisms conveyed by Donatist clergy, since they had been carried out in the proper form. Augustine's notion of the character of the sacraments, as well as his idea of the universality or catholicity of the church, were to become standard aspects of Catholic teaching from this point onward.

B. The Pelagian Controversy

It is ironic that Augustine's last and greatest opponents were to come from the very group that had so attracted him to orthodox Christianity: the monks and ascetics of Rome. Augustine's initial conversion to Christianity was very much a conversion to the life of ascetic renunciation and monastic seclusion. But in the decade or so after his conversion, leading up to his writing of the *Confessions* (c. 397), Augustine's thought had begun to turn in a fundamentally different direction than that of most of the leaders of the ascetic movement. By the time he wrote the *Confessions* Augustine had developed two distinctive notions that deeply troubled many of his contemporaries. One is his view that sin, in particular the "**original sin**" of Adam and Eve, has thoroughly damaged human nature. Even the newborn baby is not innocent of the tendency towards greed and envy that is the sign of a distorted will in the human person (*Conf.* I.vii.11). The other distinctively "Augustinian" idea is that God's grace, the gift of charity bestowed by the Holy Spirit, is absolutely necessary to change the orientation of the human will and to direct the human heart towards God.

Before the time of Augustine there had not been any extensive discussion among Christians about the effect of sin on the human will or the nature of the grace that saves humanity. If anything, in response to the fatalism and pessimism of gnostics and Manichees, most Christians, especially among the Greek fathers of the church, taught that human nature remained fundamentally sound. Original sin, however real and pernicious it may have been, did not deprive human beings of the two great gifts that represented the divine image in humans: freedom and reason. Especially in the monastic movement of the 4th century, we find Christian thinkers emphasizing that it is entirely within the power of human beings to free themselves from evil habits and to conform themselves to the precepts of Christ.

Pelagius was a monk from Britain who came to Rome probably about the same time as Augustine's last sojourn there (388). For more than twenty years Pelagius taught and gave spiritual advice to Christians at Rome who were interested in pursuing the ascetic way of life. Like Augustine, Pelagius was a bitter opponent of the Manichees, and he attempted to undermine their influence among Christians. However, he was also a Christian reformer, who sought to convince the wealthy and worldly Christians of Rome that they could be authentic Christians by turning away from sinful lives and living lives of simplicity and monastic rigor. In the process of developing this spiritual teaching Pelagius also expressed views about sin, grace, and human nature that led to a serious conflict with Augustine.

The core of Pelagius' teaching, which he may have derived from Eastern Christian theologians, was that God has given human beings the power to know right from wrong (reason) and the ability to choose to do either (free will). To deny either of these, Pelagius reasoned, was to question the goodness of God's creation and to make nonsense of the Christian belief concerning the justice of rewards and punishments in the afterlife. God would be unjust to punish us for sins that we could not avoid. True, there is sin in the world, especially in the social customs of the non-Christian world, and sin can sometimes create habits that become almost second nature. Nevertheless, Pelagius argued, with sufficient effort and help from the "grace" of God (i.e., the Jewish law, the teachings of Christ, and the forgiveness of sins), human beings are capable of overcoming the power of sin and living holy lives. The proof of the basic integrity of human nature, according to Pelagius, could be seen in the many examples of those who lived virtuously even before the coming of Christ.

Pelagius' teaching appears to have caused no complaints during the decades when he taught in Rome. However, in the wake of Alaric's sack of Rome in 410, Pelagius and some followers left the city and fled to North Africa and eventually to Jerusalem. While visiting Carthage one of Pelagius' less diplomatic disciples, Caelestius, began to teach "Pelagian" doctrines in an extreme form that shocked the North African bishops, Augustine among them. Caelestius denied that the sin of Adam and Eve caused harm to anyone but themselves. Newborn infants were born in exactly the same state in which Adam and Eve were originally created, that is, in innocence. The condemnation of Caelestius by a synod of African bishops (411) marks the beginning of the Pelagian controversy. For the next twenty years Augustine actively attacked traces of Pelagian views wherever he found them. Ultimately, the theology of Augustine and the North African bishops was to triumph, at least in the West. In the year 418 the teachings of Pelagius were condemned by the bishop of Rome, and Pelagius and Caelestius were banished by the emperor.

At stake in the Pelagian controversy, as Augustine saw it, was the very notion of Christian salvation. If, as Pelagius claimed, human nature had been left fundamentally undamaged by original sin, then there was no need for Christ's saving death or the action of God's grace. The test case was the Baptism of newborn children: if it is appropriate to baptize infants (both Pelagius and Augustine agreed on this point), then the infants must have inherited from their parents some sin which needed to be washed away in Baptism. But Augustine's view was also based on the notion that God's grace is necessary throughout human life in order to create in human beings the love that oriented them towards God. Whereas Pelagius had insisted on human freedom in order to urge people to take responsibility for their actions, Augustine saw this emphasis on human self-sufficiency as leading to pride. Human beings can take no credit for any good action, according to Augustine, since even the very will to do good has been created in them by the grace of God.

In the long run Western Christian tradition was to side with the teaching of Augustine. Pelagianism was ultimately seen as too naive and optimistic a view of human nature after the Fall. On the other hand, there were also elements in Augustine's theology that the church did not embrace in their totality. One of these is the idea that God has predestined some people to be saved and others to be damned ("**predestination**"). In the course of the Pelagian controversy, Augustine eventually argued that, since salvation depends entirely on the will of God, God's grace must be completely effective and even irresistible; in other words, by not giving some people the grace to be saved, God was effectively choosing to condemn them.

Throughout the 5th century, especially in the monasteries of southern Gaul (modern day France), some Christian monks and bishops questioned whether Augustine had gone too far in denying any role to the human will. While agreeing with Augustine on original sin and the absolute necessity of grace, these thinkers—who have come to be called, inaccurately, "semi-Pelagians"— argued that there must be cooperation between God and the person being saved, perhaps even a prior good disposition. If no human freedom was involved, they reasoned, there would be no point in preaching the gospel or offering correction to one's fellow monks. In a definition of faith issued at the **Synod of Orange** (529), the bishops of Gaul repeated the Augustinian teaching that God "first inspires in us both faith and love of himself, so that we will faithfully seek the sacrament of baptism and then with his help be able to fulfill the things which please him after baptism." Nonetheless the bishops also emphasized that once grace has been received, the individual Christian must labor faithfully and cooperate with God's grace. There is no divine predestination to evil.

The questions raised in the Pelagian controversy were to be opened once again in the 16th century. When the Protestant reformers challenged the Roman Catholic practice of linking salvation with the performance of certain "good works", they appealed to the authority of Augustine who had stressed the utter priority of God's grace before any human action. The Catholics responded by noting Augustine's teaching that God's grace creates in human beings a will transformed by love, which then desires to do good works. Both sides could appeal with some legitimacy to certain aspects of Augustine's teaching. Despite the divergences that developed between Protestant and Roman Catholic forms of Christianity, both sides still share Augustine's conviction that all human beings have lost their innocence in the sin of Adam and Eve and that the grace of the Holy Spirit must be given to move people towards God.

Key Terms:

On the City of God	Circumcellions
Elect	Plotinus
traditores	Pelagius
Hearers	Adeodatus
Donatists	Porphyry
catholicity	predestination
Monica	Manichees
Ambrose	Synod of Orange

Questions for Reading:

1. How did the rise of the monastic movement affect Augustine's thinking about marriage in his *Confessions*?

2. What were the conditions that led Augustine to compose *On the City of God*?

3. What were some of the main ideas of the Manichees? What made these ideas attractive to the young Augustine?

4. What were the main ideas of the Neoplatonists? How did Neoplatonism help to free Augustine from the Manichees?

5. What was the problem of the "two wills" (or the "divided will") that Augustine experienced prior to becoming Christian? How did the advice of Lady Continence help to resolve this problem?

6. How did the Donatist schism begin? What were the Donatists' main theological ideas?

7. What were Augustine's primary theological arguments against the Donastists?

8. What were the main ideas of the monk Pelagius? What were Augustine's primary theological arguments against Pelagianism?

9. How did Augustine's ideas about sin and grace lead to the notion of "predestination"? How did the Synod of Orange respond to this view of Augustine?

Works Consulted/Recommended Reading:

Bonner, G. *St Augustine of Hippo. Life and Controversies*. 2nd ed. Norwich: The Canterbury Press, 1986.

Brown, P. *Augustine of Hippo. A Biography*. Berkeley: University of California Press, 1969.

Chadwick, H. *Augustine*. Oxford and New York: Oxford University Press, 1986.

Markus, R. A. *Conversion and Disenchantment in Augustine's Spiritual Career*. Villanova: Villanova University Press, 1989.

O'Donnell, J. J. *Augustine. Confessions*. 3 vols. Oxford: Clarendon Press, 1992.

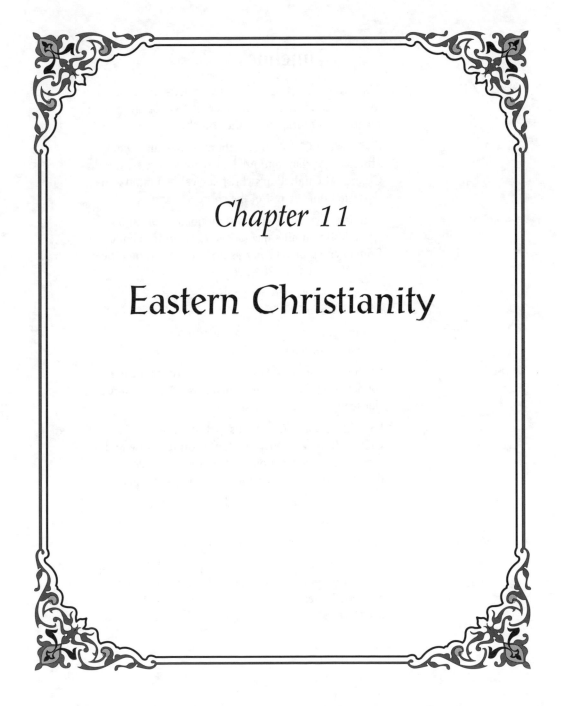

Chapter 11

Eastern Christianity

Timeline

431 AD	The Assyrian Church of the East rejects the decision of the Council of Ephesus to condemn Nestorianism and separates from the rest of the church.
451	Five Eastern Christian churches (Armenian, Coptic, Ethiopian, Syrian, and Malankar Syrian) reject the Council of Chalcedon's christological definition and separate from the rest of the church.
527-565	Justinian is emperor at Constantinople. During his reign, Justinian attempts (unsuccessfully) to reunite the Roman emperor which was first divided during the reign of Diocletian (284-305).
538	Justinian rebuilds Hagia Sophia ("Church of Holy Wisdom").
787	Second Council of Nicaea decides in favor of the veneration of icons.
867	Photius, patriarch of Constantinople, issues a letter condemning the Roman church's use of the **filioque** clause in the Nicene creed.
1054	Pope Leo IX and Cerularius, patriarch of Constantinople, argue over the **filioque** clause and excommunicate each other. The traditional date for the separation of Eastern and Western Christianity.
1204	Knights of the Fourth Crusade launch an attack against Constantinople.
1296-1359	Lifespan of Gregory Palamas. He defends the hesychasts in his work known as **The Triads.**
1439	Council of Florence attempts to heal the breach between Eastern and Western Christianity, but is unsuccessful.

Eastern Christianity

Many North Americans instinctively assume that the major forms in which Christianity has flourished are "Catholic" and "Protestant," since these are the forms that have dominated in the Western world, especially Europe and the Americas. This chapter will provide a brief overview of another major branch of worldwide Christianity, namely "Eastern Christianity." The sheer number and variety of the Eastern Christian churches can be daunting to a beginning student. After a brief introduction on how Christianity came to be divided into "East" and "West," we will consider four categories of Eastern Christian churches, determined by their acceptance or rejection of various ecumenical councils' teachings. We will first discuss the Eastern Orthodox churches, who accept the teachings of seven ecumenical councils. We will then sketch two other forms of Eastern Christianity: the five "non-Chalcedonian churches" and the "Ancient Assyrian Church of the East." We will conclude with a glance at the "Eastern Catholic churches."

I. The Byzantine Context

The development of Eastern churches, separate from their Western counterparts, was in part a consequence of the division of the Roman Empire into two halves: Eastern and Western. The separation of the eastern and western parts of the Roman Empire was a gradual process. In the latter part of the 3rd century, the emperor Diocletian (reigned 284-305) attempted to strengthen his empire, which had grown too large for a single person to govern, by dividing it between himself and a co-emperor, each with separate royal bureaucracies. When Diocletian went to live in the East, the balance of power and the empire's resources also shifted to the eastern part of the empire. Later, the emperor Constantine attempted to bring the empire back together again. In order to better position himself to lead the united Roman Empire, Constantine moved its capital from Rome in the western part of the empire to Constantinople (formerly Byzantium) in the East. After his death, however, his three sons redivided the empire.

The emperor Justinian (reigned 527-565) attempted one last time to reunite the eastern and western parts of the empire. His military expeditions into Italy and North Africa to reclaim Roman territory from the migrating barbarians were generally successful, but the fighting left these lands economically destitute. After a while, his armies were no longer able to control the onslaught of barbarian peoples into the empire. From this time forward, the eastern and western parts of the empire would have less and less in common. The western part of the empire had already been suffering from political struggles, but under the barbarian migrations of the 4th and 5th centuries, Rome and the Western empire lost their power and prestige. As a result, Constantinople became the sole capital of what was known as the Byzantine empire. It continued to function as the "New Rome" until 1453, when the Ottoman Turks (Muslims) captured it. Because of the distinctive historical and cultural circumstances of the two parts of the empire, Christianity in the East and the West would also develop quite differently.

II. The Eastern Orthodox Christian Churches

One kind of Christianity that emerged in the eastern part of the Roman Empire is Eastern Orthodox. The term "**orthodox**" is formed from two Greek words meaning "right praise" or "right opinion." Orthodox Christians consider themselves to be a single church in the sense that they share a single faith and the same Byzantine liturgical, canonical and spiritual heritage. However, at the level of church government, Orthodoxy is a communion of churches. The bishops of these churches gather together at a council or regional synod to resolve theological questions or questions related to worship. These churches were led by the four "**patriarchs**" of Constantinople, Alexandria, Antioch, and Jerusalem. The four patriarchs functioned collegially, although all Orthodox Christians recognize the patriarch of Constantinople as "first among equals." From the 9th century onward, Byzantine missionaries established national churches among various ethnic groups. Their initiatives produced Orthodox churches of Russia, Romania, Greece, Serbia, Bulgaria, Georgia, Cyprus, Poland, Albania and Czechoslovakia, among others. Members of nearly all of these Orthodox churches reside in North America, although the greatest number are representatives of Russian and Greek Orthodoxy.

Since Orthodoxy comprises such diversity, we will here consider only a few aspects of this form of Christianity. First, we will look at its theory of church-state relations, that is, its understanding of the relationship between the emperor and the patriarch of the Orthodox Christian Churches. Second, we will review the teachings of the [first] seven ecumenical councils in order to describe the distinctive doctrinal position of Orthodox Christian Churches. Third, we will examine some characteristics of the worship and spirituality of this kind of Christianity: veneration of icons, Byzantine liturgy, and hesychast spirituality. Finally, we will examine some of the reasons for the permanent split between the Eastern churches and the Western Roman Catholic Church.

A. Church and State in Byzantine Theory

During the reign of the Roman emperor Constantine I, one of his court clerics, **Eusebius** of Caesarea (c. 260-c.340), formulated the fundamental principle of Byzantine imperial theory: "as in heaven, so on earth." According to this theory, the Byzantine emperor serves as God's viceregent on earth, acting as the living representative of Christ. The emperor's rule on earth mirrors the rule of God in heaven. Byzantine social order, the harmonious activity of humankind in a Christian state under the emperor's absolute rule, parallels God's celestial order, the harmonious arrangement of all created things under divine sovereignty.

The fact that in the East (unlike the West) the emperor played a major role in religious as well as political affairs can be illustrated by two actions of the Emperor Justinian (527-565). First, Justinian produced a monumental compilation of Roman law entitled the **Codex Juris Civilis** ("Code of Civil Law") which combined the legal wisdom of Roman civilization, the moral principles of Christianity and the heritage of Greek philosophy. Second, in 538 Justinian rebuilt the great **Hagia Sophia** ("Church of Holy Wisdom") in Constantinople as the image of the harmonious working together (**symphonia**) of empire and church for the common good. When the emperor entered the sanctuary of Hagia Sophia to offer to the patriarch and clergy the bread and wine to be transformed during the divine liturgy, he stood as representative of an empire under God.

Because church and empire were seen as one, the patriarch of Constantinople worked in concert with the emperor. However, the emperor had considerable power both in choosing the patriarch and in setting the agenda for meetings of church leadership. The difference between the power of the patriarch and the emperor can be illustrated by the distinction between synods and councils.

Figure 11.1: Interior of Hagia Sophia in Constantinople. This great Christian church was converted into a mosque after the Muslim conquest of Constantinople in 1453.

Working in close cooperation with the "holy synod" (a gathering of local bishops), the patriarch tried to resolve doctrinal and jurisdictional disputes so that the truth of the gospel might be maintained and the peace of the empire preserved. However, when issues of the highest importance were at stake, the emperor convened a general or "ecumenical" (meaning "worldwide") council of bishops who, in theory, represented the entire Christian world. The emperor was then responsible for proclaiming the council's decisions to the people as imperial law.

Western writers have sometimes termed this Byzantine political theory **Caesaro-papism**, meaning that the civil ruler ("Caesar") also served as head of the church ("pope"). However, it would be more accurate to describe the emperor as the "supreme defender of the church" working in concert with the patriarch. The "head" of the Byzantine church was always considered to be Christ, while the emperor was only his representative. This Eusebian theory of church-state relations contrasts with that worked out by Augustine in his *City of God*. Eusebius thought in terms of continuity between heaven and earth, while Augustine thought in terms of discontinuity. Augustine saw the "city of God" as radically distinct from the "city of man" in this fallen world. Eusebius saw the emperor, ruler of the "city of man," as also the representative leader of God's empire on earth.

B. Teachings of the (First) Seven Ecumenical Councils

In order to understand the distinctive character of Orthodox Christian churches, it is necessary to examine some of their teachings. Orthodox Christians recognize as **dogma** (a set of doctrines authoritatively proclaimed by a church) the teachings of the seven ecumenical councils which were held between 325 and 787. Other Christian groups recognize fewer than these seven councils, while still others (e.g. the Roman Catholic Church) recognize the teachings of these seven as well as many other councils held subsequent to them. The topics treated by these seven councils that define the faith of Orthodox Christian churches fall into three categories: the nature of the Trinity, the proper understanding of Jesus, and the use of icons.

During the 4th century, the focus of attention was on the developing theology of the Trinity, articulated in central questions such as: "What is the relation of Christ to God the Father?" and "In what sense can God be Father, Son and Holy Spirit and still be one?" The **Council of Nicaea** (325 AD) responded to these questions by teaching that Christ was "of one being" **homoousios** with God the Father, not a creature as Arius taught. The **Council of Constantinople** (381) clarified that the Holy Spirit was equal to the other two persons of the Trinity.

From 431 to 681 the focus of attention shifted to consider the proper understanding of Jesus, articulated in such questions as: "If Christ is true God, in what sense is he also authentically human?" and "If he is at the same time God and man at once, how can he be one reality?" The **Council of Ephesus** (431) taught that Mary, the mother of Jesus, should be venerated as "*Theotokos*" ("Mother of God"). This safeguarded the unity of the person of Jesus: Mary, as mother of the person of Jesus, could properly be called "Mother of God," since Jesus is one human-divine person. The **Council of Chalcedon** (451) further clarified that Christ "perfect in Godhead and perfect in humanity is made known to us in two natures.... The difference of the natures is in no way destroyed because of the union, but rather the property of each nature is preserved, and both concur in one person and one *hypostasis*." Two additional councils were held in Constantinople, in 553 and 681, respectively, which further clarified the teaching of Chalcedon on the understanding of Christ as one person comprising two natures.

The third issue to receive attention during the era of the seven ecumenical councils was triggered by controversies over icons. An **icon** is a visual representation of Christ, Mary, angels or saints. Icons are most commonly painted on wood, but also appear as mosaics or frescoes affixed to church walls, as portraits in metal or (rarely) as statues. Those who venerated icons (the **iconodules**) saw them not merely as a form of artistic decoration but as fundamental to the authentic profession of Christian faith. Their opponents (the **iconoclasts**) considered the veneration of icons as superstitious at best and idolatry at worst. The second ecumenical **Council of Nicaea**s held in 787 decided in favor of the iconodules. The bishops saw this controversy as a continuation of the earlier christological debates of the 5th through 7th centuries. The teaching of the council was that since Christ did not simply "appear" on the earth but took a real human body enjoying a genuine human nature, it is not only possible but necessary to portray him visually: to refuse to portray Christ visually is in effect to deny the reality of his human nature.

Thus, the Council declared in promoting the veneration of icons:
This is the faith of the apostles,
This is the faith of the fathers,
This is the faith of the Orthodox,
This faith has made firm the whole world.

C. Veneration of Icons

In the light of what has been written above concerning icons, it is clear that they form a fundamental expression of Orthodox Christianity. Icons play a central role in all Orthodox worship: incense is burned before them, candles are lit to honor them, worshipers bear them in procession, prostrate before them and/or kiss them. An important feature of Orthodox churches is the **iconostasis** ("icon-screen"), a wall bearing icons arranged in a prescribed order, which divides sanctuary from nave. Icons also adorn private homes and are even carried by faithful individuals as devotional aids, much as a Roman Catholic might wear a crucifix.

The Orthodox believe that icons confer grace, mediating between the divine and human realms. Therefore, as a means of communion between heaven and earth, icons play a sacramental role in Orthodoxy. By contemplating an icon, an Orthodox believer passes into sacred space and sacred time, effectively encountering the person or mystery depicted. Unlike many Western visual representations of biblical scenes or church legends, an icon does not attempt to provide a snapshot of a historical event or a psychological portrait, but an encounter with a spiritual reality. This difference could be easily illustrated by the contrasting treatment of the light source in post-medieval Western religious painting and in Eastern iconography. In the Western pieces, the artist indicates "natural" light sources such as the sun, moon, candles, etc., by carefully depicting shadows. But in an icon there are no shadows; the light sources lies "behind" or "within" the art-piece, inviting the observer to enter into its

Figure 11.2: Andrei Rublev "The Holy Trinity" (1411).

Figure 11.3: "Christ the Divine Wisdom," School of Salonica (14th century).

Figure 11.4: "Virgin of Tenderness," School of Constantinople (14th century).

radiant world. Icons also employ a fixed color scheme and method of depicting subjects. The one who produces an icon does not seek to express his or her individual artistic vision so much as to provide a means of encounter with the divine. Thus each step of producing an icon—from the preparation of the colors and brushes to the crafting of precious metal containers—is marked by prescribed prayer. In other words, producing an icon is not so much an artistic act as an act of worship.

D. Byzantine Liturgy

If icons represent the most characteristic visual artifacts of Orthodoxy, the Byzantine liturgy represents its most characteristic ceremonial creativity. Produced by a fusion of the monastic practices of Syria, Cappadocia and Constantinople with the public worship of the imperial church, the Byzantine Eucharistic liturgy takes three characteristic forms: the "Liturgy of St. John Chrysostom" (the usual form), the "Liturgy of St. Basil," and the "Liturgy of the Presanctified Gifts."

The Liturgy of John Chrysostom begins with the *Enarxis* ("Opening") consisting of prayers, hymns, and responses. The "*Monogenes*" chant, a stirring and powerful expression of Orthodox faith in Christ as "one person in two natures," appears as part of the second hymn, sung by the assembled worshipers (or by the choir on their behalf):

> *Only begotten Son and Word of God, immortal One, who humbled Yourself for our salvation taking flesh by the Theotokos and ever-virgin Mary, You became man without change; and were crucified, O Christ our God, conquering death by death; being one of the Holy Trinity, together glorified with the Father and the Holy Spirit: save us!*

The liturgy continues with the part of the service devoted to readings from Scripture, begun with the Little Entrance (a procession of clergy and ministers through the body of the church bearing a highly decorated book of scriptural readings) and the "*Trisagion*" hymn (another powerful expression of Orthodox Trinitarian faith sung by the assembly or the choir):

> *Holy God, Holy Mighty One, Holy Immortal One, have mercy on us! (Three times)*
> *Glory to the Father and to the Son and to the Holy Spirit now and forevermore. Amen.*
> *Holy Immortal One, have mercy on us.*
> *Holy God, Holy Mighty One, Holy Immortal One,*
> *have mercy on us!*

This service of the Word continues with two readings: an Epistle (usually taken from one of the New Testament letters) and a Gospel. Preaching may follow at this point.

The ritual high point of the Orthodox Liturgy then takes place: the Great Entrance. This is another procession of clergy and ministers through the body of the church, but this time they carry liturgical fans, incense, and the bread and wine which will be consecrated later in the service. Popularly understood as a dramatic reenactment of either Jesus' triumphal entrance into Jerusalem or his funeral cortege, the congregation and/or choir accompanies the procession with the singing of the "Cherubic Hymn:"

> *We, who mystically represent the Cherubim [an order of angels] and sing the thrice-holy hymn to the life-giving Trinity, let us set aside the cares of life that we may receive the King of all invisibly escorted by the Angelic Hosts. Alleluia!*

After another prayer and the recitation of the Creed, the Eucharistic Prayer or "*Anaphora*" is prayed by the presiding priest with some sung interventions by the congregation and/or choir. The characteristic mode of Byzantine worship is wonderfully expressed in the opening of the *Anaphora* (the equivalent of the "Preface" in the Roman Catholic Mass). First, the priest and people exchange the dialogue: "The grace of our Lord Jesus Christ and the love of God the Father and the communion of the Holy Spirit be with you all"/"And with your spirit"/"Let us lift up our hearts"/"We lift them up to the Lord"/"Let us thank the Lord"/"It is proper and right." Then, the priest rhapsodically exults in the mystery of God's interaction with humanity:

> *It is right and proper to praise, bless, glorify, thank and worship You in all places of Your dominion; for You are God ineffable, beyond comprehension, invisible, beyond understanding, ever-existing and always the same, You and Your only-begotten Son, and Your Holy Spirit. You have brought us from non-being into being, and when we fell You raised us up again, and You have not ceased doing everything to lead us into heaven and grant us Your Kingdom to come. For all these we thank You, and Your only-begotten Son, and Your Holy Spirit; for blessings of which we know and of which we do not know; for benefits apparent and non apparent that have been bestowed upon us. We also thank you for this Liturgy which You have condescended to accept from our hands, even though You are surrounded by thousands of Archangels and myriads of Angels, by the Cherubim and Seraphim, six-winged, many-eyed, borne aloft and singing the victory song, proclaiming, heralding, and saying: (with congregation and/or choir) Holy, Holy, Holy, Lord of Angelic Hosts, heaven and earth are full of your glory. Hosanna in the highest! Blessed is He who comes in the name of the Lord! Hosanna in the highest!*

The consecration of the bread and wine is followed by another prayer and group recitation of the Lord's Prayer. After communion the priest blesses the assembly with the remaining consecrated bread and wine while the congregation and/or choir sings:

> *We have seen the true Light; we have received the heavenly Spirit; we have found the true faith, worshipping the undivided Trinity; for this has saved us.*

Further prayers and blessings conclude the service. Then all who have attended, whether or not they have received sacramental communion, are invited to come forward to the priest before the iconostasis to receive a portion of the *antidoron*, blessed bread to be consumed for the journey back "into the world."

While this description of the liturgy and these few texts may suggest something of the other-worldly character of Orthodox worship, it cannot convey the complexity of the ceremony, its impact on all the senses, and its profoundly popular yet theologically sophisticated character.

E. Hesychast Spirituality

A final characteristic of Orthodox Christianity is its hesychast spirituality, especially associated with the 14th-century theologian, Gregory Palamas. **Hesychia** means "inner stillness" or "silence of the heart." A **hesychast** is one who seeks *hesychia* through various ascetic disciplines, most notably the use of the **Jesus Prayer**. This is a very brief prayer (usually "Lord Jesus Christ, Son of the living God, have mercy on me, a sinner"), which the person repeats in rhythm, usually coordinated with his or her breathing and/or heartbeat. The goal of reciting the prayer in this manner is to have the prayer "descend from the mind into the heart," allowing the believer to enter into meditation, an experiential union with God. This Christian prayer technique might be compared to the *mantras* of certain non-Christian religions.

Barlaam the Calabrian, a South Italian monk and neo-Platonist philosopher living in Constantinople in the 14th century, attacked the hesychast movement as gross superstition. Did not scripture itself forbid "vain repetition" in prayer? Were not the physical techniques a form of self-hypnosis or an attempt to manipulate God through magic? Worst of all, was not the hesychasts' claim to experience God unmediated in the here-and-now a blasphemous denial of God's utter transcendence and unknowability? In response to Barlaam, **Gregory Palamas** (1296-1359), a monk of Mount Athos in Greece, defended the hesychasts' practice in his work commonly known as *The Triads*. Gregory here distinguished between God's essence (which remains unknowable to humans in the next life as well as in this) and God's energies (which are God himself in action encountering humanity). By means of the divine "energies" saints participate through grace in a union of love with the divine. Gregory's teaching on the energies of God was confirmed by three local councils held in Constantinople in 1341, 1347 and 1351: the hesychast movement was vindicated.

F. The Separation of Christian East and West

There were a number of issues that led to the division of Christianity into Eastern (Byzantine) and Western churches. We have already noted differences in the ways that each understood the relationship between church and state. There were also considerable cultural differences between East and West, evidenced in the fact that the West was Latin-speaking while the East was Greek-speaking. Because of these cultural differences, Eastern Christianity developed a spirituality and worship style that was more mystical in orientation than Western churches.

While these differences are significant, they need not have led to the separation of Christianity into Eastern Orthodoxy and Western Christianity. In fact, it is difficult to name one particular event that brought about their separation. Instead, we will consider several situations that gradually, over an extended period of time, led to the separation of these two churches. Perhaps one of the most decisive events was the Fourth Crusade in 1204. The crusades created considerable tension between East and West, as knights from the West marched through the Eastern empire conquering lands that had been taken over by Muslims and then declining to return control of them to their original Byzantine owners. However, Orthodox Christians have never been able to forget how the knights of the Fourth Crusade besieged and conquered the city of Constantinople itself. Even today Orthodox Christians have not forgiven the Latin or Roman church for this atrocity.

Another major issue that brought about the eventual separation of Eastern and Western Christians concerns the relationship of the Holy Spirit to the Father and the Son. Both Eastern and Western Christians believed that the Holy Spirit was personal, in the same way that the Father and Son are persons of the Trinity, and that the Spirit was fully divine. Orthodox Christians believed that the Father is the sole source of being in the Trinity. This belief was preserved in the original form of the Nicene-Constantinople creed: "We believe in the Holy Spirit who proceeds from the Father." However, perhaps as early as the 6th century, some Christian churches in the West began adding the phrase "and the Son" to the creed, declaring that the Holy Spirit proceeded from the Father *and the Son*. In Latin the phrase is ***filioque***. Orthodox Christians opposed this addition, because it implied a radically different understanding of the nature of God.

The addition of the *filioque* to the creed was not formally accepted by the church at Rome until the 11th century. When it was accepted, it was done without the consent of Eastern Christian leadership. Orthodox Christians consider the first seven ecumenical councils, from which the Nicene-Constantinople creed originated, to be one of the highest expressions of God's continued presence in the church. Therefore, no one has the right to tamper with the contents of this creed. Moreover, the Orthodox claimed, everyone had agreed at the second council of Nicaea (787), the last of the early ecumenical councils, that tradition ought to be preserved intact: "We take away nothing and we add nothing… We preserve without change or innovation all the ecclesiastical traditions that have been handed down to us, whether written or unwritten." The *filioque* clause continues to be a major issue of separation between Eastern Orthodox and Roman Catholics today.

The filioque controversy is related to another issue that gradually separated Orthodox and Roman Christians, namely, **papal primacy**. In Eastern Christianity, church leadership is understood to be conciliar (working together in council), rather than monarchial (having a single ruler over all). Orthodox Christians honor the pope as the first and elder brother among the bishops of the churches throughout the world. However, they do not give him any special power or jurisdiction over the churches of the East, nor do they attribute to him any spiritual gifts beyond those of other bishops. When it comes to speaking God's word to the world, neither the pope nor any other patriarch or bishop has highest authority. Rather, it is the ecumenical council where "the miracle of Pentecost is renewed; the Holy Spirit descends, the many become one in mind and heart, and the truth is revealed" (Ware, "Eastern Christendom," 129).

Two situations in the history of the relationship between Eastern Orthodoxy and the Roman Catholic church will help to illustrate the difficulties that arose over papal primacy. The first concerns Pope Nicholas I and Photius, patriarch of Constantinople in 861. Nicholas disagreed with Photius' appointment to the position of patriarch and reinstated his predecessor. Although the Eastern Orthodox church simply ignored Nicholas' order, they resented his interference. Later, in 867, Photius issued a letter condemning the Roman church's use of the *filioque* clause. In the same year, a council in Constantinople decided to excommunicate Pope Nicholas. The second situation is sometimes called the "Great Schism of 1054." The head of the Bulgarian church had written a document condemning a number of Roman practices that were not accepted in the Byzantine church. The primary issue, however, was the right of Eastern Orthodox churches to remain autonomous. In response, Pope Leo IX sent a delegate to Constantinople to resolve the problem. When the discussion got out of hand, the pope's delegate excommunicated the patriarch of Constantinople. In response, a synod of Constantinople excommunicated the pope's delegate. These excommunications were mutually withdrawn only recently, in 1965.

The churches of East and West differed on a number of other issues: rules about fasting, regulations concerning celibacy among clergy, the use of leavened or unleavened bread at Eucharist, circumstances in which divorce might be permitted, teachings about purgatory, and the proper way to celebrate the sacrament of Confirmation. Whatever brought about the separation of Orthodox and Roman Catholic Christians, perhaps the overall problem was that, because of cultural and political circumstances, they had become strangers to one another (see Ware, "Eastern Christendom," 147). Today, as Orthodox and Roman Catholic Christians gather together in dialogue, perhaps reconciliation will be possible.

III. The Non-Chalcedonian Eastern Christian Churches

Five ancient Eastern Christian churches (Armenian, Coptic, Ethiopian, Syrian and Malankar Syrian), completely independent of one another juridically, with different liturgical traditions and widely diverse histories, hold one doctrinal element in common: they all reject the christological definition of the Council of Chalcedon (451) which asserted that Christ is "one person in two natures, undivided and unconfused." Since the members of these churches believe that such a definition compromises the unity of Christ's person by focusing too much on distinctions concerning his humanity and divinity, they prefer the formula proposed by Cyril of Alexandria which refers to the "one nature of the incarnate son of God." These churches clearly reject the position of Eutyches, who held that the humanity of Christ had been absorbed into his single divine nature, yet they have often been erroneously called "**Monophysites**" (from the Greek words for "of one nature"). In the 5th century, these churches represented a very large segment of Eastern Christians, but today their numbers are greatly reduced. Most live in countries with a non-Christian majority population and/or until recently under hostile Marxist governments.

IV. The Ancient Assyrian Church of the East

No one is absolutely sure when Christianity spread beyond the confines of the Roman Empire, but Christian communities existed in the Persian Empire by early in the 3rd century. Never a majority of the Persian population, this Eastern church nonetheless grew to be quite large in the middle ages, but its numbers have been decreased in recent centuries because of conquests, massacres, and deportations. Today around 200,000 members of the church reside primarily in Iraq, Iran, Syria and Lebanon. The patriarch of the Ancient Assyrian Church of the East resides in Tehran, Iran.

An interesting social institution of this church was its **hereditary patriarchate**. From 1450 until the late 20th century, the patriarchs of this church were all drawn from one family bloodline, usually passing the leadership from uncle to nephew. This practice produced some patriarchs who assumed the office at a very early age (e.g., twelve) and whose older relatives governed for them as regents. This hereditary patriarchate came to an end in 1975 when Mar Shimoun XXIII was assassinated; his successor, Mar Denka IV, was freely elected from another bloodline.

Doctrinally, the Assyrian Church of the East accepts only the first two ecumenical councils as authoritative, rejecting the formulations of the Council of Ephesus in 431. Instead, the Assyrian church officially accepted the christology promoted by Nestorius, who maintained that Jesus held two separate natures (one the perfect man without sin who is son of Mary in the flesh, the other the divine word of God or *Logos* settled within him). For this reason, the Assyrian church had, in the past, been called "**Nestorian**." However, contemporary scholars avoid the term since the members of the church consider it insulting. Many contemporary scholars feel that this doctrine was embraced by the church more for political than for philosophical or theological reasons. The Christian faith as formulated at Ephesus was the official creed of the Roman Empire with whom the Persian Empire was often at war. The Assyrian Church of the East may have taken this doctrinal position to assert its independence from the Roman Empire and to prove its loyalty to the Persian Empire and its non-Christian fellow countrymen.

The Assyrian Church of the East recognizes seven sacraments, but their accounting varies. Universally accepted as sacraments are Baptism, Eucharist, Marriage and Holy Orders. Other rituals or religious objects that have sacramental status in various accounts are the blessing of monks, the office for the dead, the oil of anointing, absolution, holy leaven, the sign of the Cross and the consecration of a church or an altar. Baptism is usually performed in stages: at birth a child is washed with water blessed by a priest, and on the occasion of a great feast the child is immersed in water three times facing East and totally anointed with holy oil during the course of an elaborate community service.

Another interesting social institution of the Assyrian church is the marital status of its clergy. A 5th-century synod declared that celibacy should be obligatory for no one, including bishops and patriarchs, but from the 6th century on, the custom arose of only ordaining celibate monks as bishops. Those who take a monastic vow can return to secular life without disgrace or difficulty through a dispensation. Unlike other churches, the Assyrian Church of the East approves of the unlimited re-marriage of priests when their wives die. A priest is usually selected by his future parishioners, then ordained by his bishop with the laying on of hands.

The Assyrian Church of the East has virtually no art comparable to that of the Greek Orthodox churches or even the West Syrian churches. They rejected the use of icons and iconography, tolerating these holy images neither in their churches nor their homes. They use simple crosses at the entrance of their churches and over the altar, but they banned the crucifix (a cross upon which an artistic representation of the body of Jesus is placed) from all parts of their religious buildings. The church buildings themselves are unostentatious and simple, recognizable only by the shape of a simple cross on the outer wall above the church entrance, which is a narrow and low opening in the wall so that anyone entering has to stoop down to gain access.

Although the Assyrian Church of the East has traditionally had no official ties with other Christian churches, the present patriarch and the Roman Catholic pope John Paul II met in formal theological exchange in 1995. This conversation has opened the possibility of further "ecumenical" (referring here to the promotion of unity and cooperation) encounters between these two forms of Christianity.

V. The Eastern Catholic Christian Churches

The split between the Eastern and Western Christian churches, symbolized by the mutual excommunications of the bishops of Rome and Constantinople in 1054, became definitive in the minds of the common people of the East after the Crusades and the sacking of Constantinople by Western Christians in 1204. Both the Second Council of Lyons (1274) and the Council of Florence (1439) attempted to heal the breach between Eastern and Western Christianity, but neither was successful. Over time segments of the various Eastern churches re-established communion (formal ties) with Rome, although some Eastern churches such as the Maronites claim never to have been out of communion. These churches are sometimes called "**uniate**," because of their union with Roman Catholic churches, but the term is generally considered derogatory, and should be avoided.

Many non-Catholic Eastern Christians view the existence of these churches as an obstacle to Catholic-Orthodox reunion. They feel that the very existence of these Eastern Catholic churches is a denial of the reality of the Orthodox churches, that these unions were efforts to split local Eastern Christian communities, and that Eastern Catholics are really Orthodox who were taken away from their mother churches. *The Decree on Eastern Catholic Churches*, one of the documents of the Second Vatican Council (a gathering of Roman Catholic leaders held in the 1960's), presents present-day official Catholic teaching on these churches. It affirmed their equality with Western Roman Catholics. It also called Eastern Catholics to a rediscovery of their own traditions, and affirmed that they have a special vocation to foster ecumenical relations with non-Catholic Eastern Christians. Recent developments hold out hope that these and other ecumenical efforts may finally bear fruit, and that at least some non-Catholic Eastern Christians eventually may be re-united with their Catholic brothers and sisters in the East and the West.

Key Terms:

Orthodox

Constantinople

Justinian

Eusebius

Codex Juris Civilis

Hagia Sophia

symphonia

Caesaro-papism

dogma

icon

iconodule

patriarch

iconoclast

iconostasis

Hesychia

Jesus Prayer

Gregory Palamas

filioque

Monophysite

Nestorian

uniate

ecumenical

Questions for Reading:

1. Who governs the Eastern Orthodox Church? To what degree was the Byzantine emperor involved in the government of this church during the period in which the Byzantine empire existed? What principle justified the emperor's involvement in the church?

2. Compare and contrast the various Eastern Churches in terms of their acceptance or rejection of the teachings of the first seven ecumenical councils.

3. What is an icon? What arguments were made for and against the veneration of icons, and how was the dispute over icons finally resolved? What function do icons serve in the Eastern Orthodox church? Do all Eastern churches accept the veneration of icons?

4. What is hesychia? How does one achieve it? What arguments were made for and against hesychia, and how was the dispute over it finally resolved?

5. What events or circumstances led to the separation of Eastern Orthodox and Roman Catholic Christians?

6. What are the distinctive elements in the beliefs and practices of the Non-Chalcedonian Eastern Christian churches and the Ancient Assyrian Church of the East?

Works Consulted/Recommended Reading:

Atiya, A. *A History of Eastern Christianity*. London: Methuem and Company, 1968.

Attwater, D. *The Christian Churches of the East*. 2 vols. Milwaukee: Bruce, 1961.Constantelos, D. *Understanding the Greek Orthodox Church: Its Faith, History and Practice*. New York: Seabury, 1982.

Ellis, J. *The Russian Orthodox Church: A Contemporary History*. London-Sydney: Croom Helm, 1986.

Every, G. *Understanding Eastern Christianity*. Bangalore: Dharmaram Publications, 1978.

Hussey, J. M. *The Orthodox Church in the Byzantine Empire*. Oxford: Clarendon Press, 1986.

Lossky, V. *The Mystical Theology of the Eastern Church*. Cambridge: James Clarke and Company, 1957.

Meyendorff, J. *Byzantine Theology: Historical Trends and Doctrinal Themes*. New York: Fordham University Press, 1974.

Meyendorff, J. *The Orthodox Church*. Crestwood, NY: St. Vladimir's Seminary Press, 1981.

Pelikan, J. *The Christian Tradition: A History of the Development of Doctrine, Volume 2; The Spirit of Eastern Christendom (600-1700)*. Chicago: University of Chicago Press, 1974.

Podipara, P. J. *The Thomas Christians*. Bombay: St. Paul Publications, 1970.

Roberson, R. G. *The Eastern Christian Churches: A Brief Survey*. Rome: Pontifical Institute of Oriental Studies, 1988.

Schmemann, A. *The Historical Road of Eastern Orthodoxy*. Crestwood, NY: St. Vladimir's Seminary Press, 1977.

Schulz, H. *The Byzantine Liturgy: Symbolic Structure and Faith Expression*. New York: Pueblo, 1986.

Spidlik, T. *The Spirituality of the Christian East: A Systematic Handbook*. Cistercian Studies, 79. Kalamazoo, MI: Cistercian Publications, 1986.

Ware, K. "Eastern Christendom." In McManners, John, ed. *The Oxford Illustrated History of Christianity*, pp. 123-162. Oxford: Oxford University Press, 1992.

_____. *The Orthodox Church*. New York: Penguin Books, 1984.

_____. *The Orthodox Way*. London: Mowbray and Company, 1979.

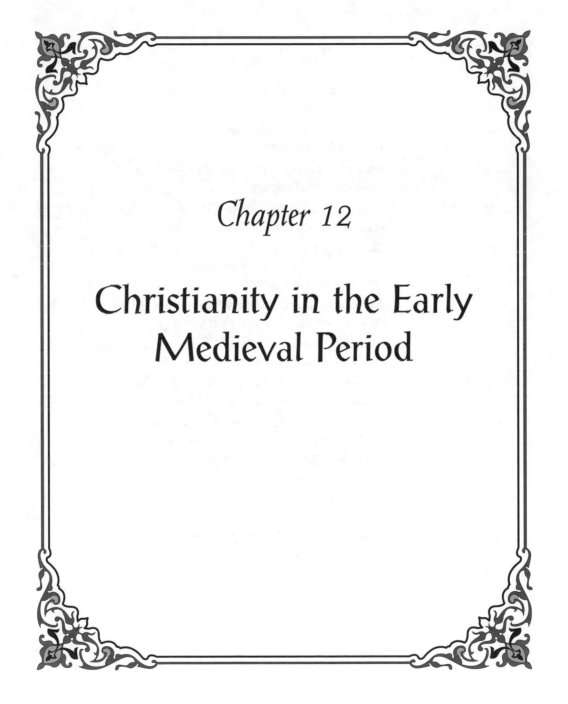

Chapter 12

Christianity in the Early Medieval Period

Timeline

330-379 AD	Lifespan of Basil of Caesarea, the "Father of Eastern Monasticism."
360-435	Lifespan of John Cassian, the "Father of Western Monasticism."
480-547	Lifespan of Benedict of Nursia, the founder of Benedictine monasticism.
590	Gregory I is elected pope. He is the first to style the pope as "servant of the servants of God."
768	Charlemagne is crowned "emperor of the Romans" by pope Leo III. His empire would come to be known as the Holy Roman Empire.
c. 785	The Roman Rite, the primary form of liturgy for the Roman Catholic Church, is established.
910	Louis the Pious founds a new Benedictine monstery at Cluny. Beginning of the Cluniac reform movement.
942-1022	Symeon the New Theologian. A noted monk, abbot, theologian, and mystic of Eastern Christianity.
1033-1109	Anselm of Canterbury. A theologian known for his "debt-satisfaction" theory of the atonement and his ontological argument for the existence of God.
1073	Pope Gregory VII is elected pope. Known as the "reform pope," he attempts to correct a number of abuses in the church.
1075	Gregory VII issues his **Dictatus Papae** asserting the primacy of the pope.

Christianity in the Early Medieval Period

he 6th through 11th centuries make up what is called the "Early Medieval Period" of Western Christianity. In the popular imagination this era is frequently termed "The Dark Ages." It was a time when civilization declined, classical Greek learning all but disappeared, superstition was rampant, and human life was "nasty, brutish and short." However, it might be more useful to think of this time as "The Middle Ages," a transitional period situated between the decline of the Roman Empire of the West and the rise of European nationalism. This chapter explores several features of early medieval Christianity: the development of monasticism; the evolution of the papacy, specifically the pope's authority; and the formulation of the "Holy Roman Empire." We will also explore some of the cultural contributions of this period and some of its major theological figures.

I. The Development of Monasticism

The term **monasticism** comes from the Greek word *monos*, meaning "one," "solitary," or "alone." Early forms of monasticism were primarily lay movements. While deacons, priests, and bishops might associate themselves with monastic ideals and practices, most monks and nuns were lay people passionately concerned with their own salvation and convinced that they needed to separate themselves from mainstream society in order to achieve salvation. In Eastern Christianity, the monastic movement had its roots in the 3rd and 4th centuries AD. Some monks lived as hermits in the desert. The most famous of these early hermits was Antony of Egypt (251-356). Some, like Antony's contemporary Pachomius (290-346) lived an organized communal life in monasteries located in the wilderness far from society. Still others, under the direction of Basil of Caesarea (330-379), developed a kind of monasticism that might be described as urban monasticism. Basil saw hospitality for society's marginalized as a special mark of the monastic vocation, and so his monks lived in buildings close to cities and villages where the monastic community could provide various forms of social service: caring for the sick, raising orphans, providing food and clothing for the poor, offering employment for the destitute. Basil's influence on the development of monasticism was so great that he is known as the "Father of Eastern monasticism."

The "Father of Western Monasticism" was **John Cassian** (360-435). After ascetic training in both Bethlehem and Egypt, John organized monasteries for monks and nuns near Marseilles and in the region of Provence (modern-day France). John wrote two famous works which took the ideals of Eastern monasticism and applied them to Western situations. His purpose was to establish a standardized form of monasticism for Christianity in the West. In *The Conferences*, he outlined the progressive stages of the spiritual life as he had come to understand them from personal experience and from conversation with famous Eastern spiritual guides. In *The Institutes* he described the pattern of living that was characteristic of a genuine monastic community and prescribed practical methods of overcoming spiritual failings.

Although John Cassian founded no monastic communities in the British Isles, his ideals were highly influential on the forms of monastic life that developed there. **Celtic monasticism** originated sometime toward the end of the 5th century or the beginning of the 6th century. Its two emphases were to have strong impact on the early medieval Western Roman Empire. The first was the love of scholarship. Although other monastic communities gave rudimentary education to their members, Irish monks developed more highly specialized monastic schools, placing high priority on literacy, preservation and transmission of knowledge and on the production of manuscripts. The second emphasis that was to have strong impact on the early medieval West was the penitential practice of self-imposed exile from the monastery. This Irish monastic practice sent monk-missionaries throughout vast stretches of northern Europe to preach the gospel message. The combination of scholarship and missionary activity made Irish monks important sources of social and cultural transformation in northern Europe.

The standardized form of Western monasticism so desired by John Cassian finally appeared in the *Rule for Monasteries* of **Benedict of Nursia** (480-547). Little is known of Benedict's life other than his Roman ancestry, his life as a hermit in a cave and his establishment of a monastic community at Monte Cassino. Monks who followed Benedict's *Rule* took vows of poverty, chastity, obedience and stability (permanent commitment to a particular community of monks). They gathered eight times a day for community prayer. Lauds (Morning Prayer at dawn), Vespers (Evening Prayer at sunset) and Matins (a lengthy vigil prayed in the dead of night) were the hinges of the *Opus Dei* ("work of God"). Shorter prayers interrupted the work day (Tierce, Sext, Nones). Other prayers were prescribed for the dormitory at rising (Prime) or before sleep (Compline). Each monk had particular work responsibilities assigned him by his monastic superiors. They ate their meals together in silence or accompanied by spiritual readings. Although the ascetic practices outlined in Benedict's *Rule* were quite moderate and balanced by comparison to other monastic rules, still the monks fasted for a significant proportion of the year. Thus the essence of Benedict's *Rule* can be summed up in a Latin motto: "Ora et labora" ("Pray and work").

This Benedictine form of monasticism eventually became the primary style of monastic life in the West. When a founder wanted to establish a monastery, he or she would either choose a rule to follow, like Basil's, Augustine's, or Benedict's *Rule for Monasteries*, or create one of his or her own. The rule described how the community should live its life together. A Benedictine monastery is a community of monks who follow the rule of Benedict and aspire to live out his special vision of Christian life.

By the 10th century, numerous monasteries had been built throughout the Roman Empire of the West. However, most of these monasteries were, in one way or another, under the influence of secular rulers and wealthy nobles. In some ways, this was beneficial for monasteries, because they depended upon these wealthy nobles and rulers to be their protectors and financial supporters in time of need. In other ways, monasteries suffered under this influence. When wealthy landlords deeded

Figure 12.1: Model of an ideal medieval monastry, based on the floor plan of the Monastery of St. Gall.

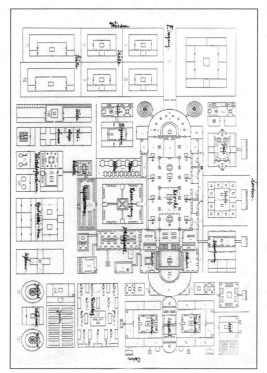

Figure 12.2: Floor plan of an ideal medieval monastry, based on the floor plan of the Monastery of St. Gall.

the monks land to build their monasteries, the monastery became, for all practical purposes, part of the **feudal system**. Their abbot was now a vassal of the lord, owing the lord certain services like military assistance against his enemies, and the monastery now needed serfs or peasants to help farm the land. The monastery, in turn, was responsible to provide the serfs with basic necessities of life. Monasteries lost even more independence through **lay investiture**. According to this practice, the emperor and secular leaders took upon themselves the right to appoint bishops, abbots, and other church officials. Their appointees were not necessarily holy men, nor were they necessarily trained in spiritual matters. Rather, they were given appointments because of their family connections. Sometimes they obtained their appointments through **simony** (the buying and selling of spiritual things, including church leadership positions). All of these factors contributed to the gradual decline of the spiritual focus of the monastery.

The spiritual decline of monasticism began to change when William the Pious founded a new Benedictine monastery at Cluny in 910 AD. This monastery committed itself to a reform of monasticism by demanding the strictest observance of Benedict's *Rule of Monasteries* and renewed dedication to the liturgical (worship) practices of monastic life. The **Cluniac reform movement**, under the direction of the monastery's abbots, was determined to maintain the spiritual character of the Church. The abbots spoke out against secular leaders who attempted to wield control over bishops and other clergy. They taught that the pope in Rome was the only one who ought to have authority over the clergy. They also spoke out against **concubinage**. Although celibacy was required of monks, it was not universally required of "secular" clergy, that is, priests who did not belong to a monastery and who lived in the cities and villages, ministering to the people there. As a result some of these "secular" clergy maintained concubines in a relationship something like marriage. The Cluny reformers denounced this practice, arguing that the clergy ought to be celibate so that the church might be their spouse. The position of the reformers eventually won the day, and Roman Catholicism has continued to require celibacy of its bishops and priests to the present day.

II. The Evolution of the Papacy

The relationship between the emperor and church leadership was expressed quite differently in the Roman Empire of the East and the West during the early medieval period. In the East, the emperor had authority over the patriarchs even to the point of calling councils and prescribing solutions to doctrinal issues in the church. In the West, the pope and other church leadership managed to keep this kind of interference to a minimum. The general decline of the Western Roman Empire in the 5th and 6th centuries further enhanced the supremacy of the pope, but the most significant development of the papacy came in the early medieval period. The histories of two popes from this era, one at the beginning and one at the end, namely, Pope Gregory I and Pope Gregory VII, demonstrate most clearly the evolution of the influence of the papacy during the early medieval period.

A. Pope Gregory I

Pope **Gregory** I (c. 540-604) is so notable a figure that tradition refers to him as "Gregory the Great." The son of a Roman nobleman, Gregory spent his young adulthood in civic service, so that eventually he occupied the office of prefect of the city of Rome. By around 574 Gregory retired from public life, sold his inherited possessions and used the proceeds to care for the poor. He established several monasteries and he lived the monastic life himself, following the *Rule* of Benedict with such intensity that he damaged his physical health. Eventually he was called out of the monastery to serve as a church leader, first as a regional deacon, charged with care for the physical and spiritual needs of the city's destitute, and later as an ambassador to Constantinople. After another interlude in the monastic life, Gregory was elected pope in 590.

The fourteen years that Gregory served as pope were notable for his missionary outreach. Gregory himself sought to evangelize the Lombards on the Italian continent and directed Augustine of Canterbury to undertake a missionary tour to Britain to preach the Christian message to the Anglo-Saxons. He supported this outreach while maintaining cordial relations with the Byzantine emperors, keeping up communication with the Christian communities in the surviving urban areas of the West, and overseeing the day-to-day functioning of the city of Rome. More than 850 of Gregory's letters are preserved, addressed to emperors, patriarchs, bishops, subdeacons and notables, revealing a man of prodigious energy, convinced that the future of Christianity lay with the Germanic peoples north of the Alps and not simply in the Christian East. He was the first to style the pope as *servus servorum Dei* ("servant of the servants of God").

B. Pope Gregory VII

Gregory VII (c.1020 -1085) was elected pope nearly 500 years after Gregory I's pontificate (reign as pope). The reign of pope Gregory VII demonstrates how the institution of the papacy developed into a European political power in addition to its role as a religious center. His given name was Hildebrand and he had committed himself at an early age to the life of a monk. For over twenty years he had served as secretary to five popes and was firmly convinced of the need for a strong church independent of lay political control if its spiritual life was to be reformed. Hildebrand was a person of passionate moral uprightness—a friend once described him as a "holy Satan."

Pope Gregory VII was a fierce supporter of the reforms advocated by the monastery at Cluny. From the time of his election as a "reform pope" in 1073, Gregory VII attacked three issues with particular vigor: **simony** (the buying and selling of ecclesiastical offices and/or spiritual goods), **alienation of property** (deeding church goods as the private inheritance of bishops' or priests' children) and **lay investiture** (secular powers controlling the appointment of church officials). As one might expect, the pope's position on these issues created conflict between himself and the political powers of the West. The German emperor Henry IV forced a confrontation when he appointed three bishops to sees (a bishop's official seat or center of authority) in Italy, all of which were under the pope's jurisdiction. Gregory VII responded by excommunicating Henry and calling on Henry's subjects to force him to recant.

In 1077, Henry IV did public penance outside of Gregory's castle retreat at Canossa, and was temporarily reconciled with the pope, but in 1080 the breach reopened. Gregory again excommunicated Henry, and, in response, Henry appointed and installed his own anti-pope Clement III. The **investiture controversy** was settled finally with the Concordat of Worms. The emperor renounced his claim to appoint bishops, but he retained control of many other imperial rights over the church in Germany. Rulers continued to bestow property and other expensive gifts on bishops and other church leaders in hopes of influencing them in their favor. However, politically, at least, clergy had obtained some measure of independence by Gregory's reform.

Gregory's intention in confronting these three issues was to free the church from political control and to establish the authority of the pope over the entire Christian world. In his *Dictatus Papae* issued in 1075, Gregory VII proclaimed that the pope, as supreme judge under God alone, held supreme power over all Christian souls; all bishops and abbots were subject to him and he alone held absolute powers of absolution (the power to forgive sins) and excommunication (the power to exclude someone from membership in the church). The history of the papacy in the high middle ages will witness the practical working out of these claims.

III. The Holy Roman Empire

Between the pontificates of Gregory I and Gregory VII, the social, political and religious configuration of Western Christianity was transformed. Two centuries before Gregory I, only southern Europe was thoroughly Christianized. Most northern Europeans worshiped one or more non-Christian gods. However, by the time of Pope Gregory VII's reign, Christianity was firmly established in western Europe, Scandinavia, and much of eastern Europe. Partly this was a consequence of the transformation of the old Western Roman Empire into the "Holy Roman Empire."

The end of the Western Roman Empire was marked by great movements of peoples. Historians term these movements as "migrations" or "invasions," depending on whether they are considered circumstantial accompaniments to the fall of the empire or its cause. After the last resident Western emperor, Romulus Augustulus, was deposed in 476, a Frankish warrior chieftain named Clovis, who converted to Christianity and was baptized in 498, collaborated with the remaining Romans to establish a Christian dynasty north of the Alps, in ancient Gaul (modern-day France). Clovis' dynasty is identified as the **Merovingian** kingdom named after his grandfather Merowig. The Frankish peoples controlled considerable territory in Europe at this time, but their organizational structure was mostly tribal, with local chieftains governing smaller autonomous regions. Although the Merovingian kings attempted to create a centralized government, they were never successful in doing so. Severely weakened during the 7th century in a series of internal power struggles, the Merovingian kings finally ceded power to a leader of the major landowners in the region, Charles Martel.

Charles Martel gave his name to the next dynasty—the **Carolingians**. Charles Martel is best known for his military victory in 732-733 over the Arabs of 'Abd ar-Rahman who were approaching Tours on a looting raid of the wealthy shrine of St. Martin there, but he also led a series of campaigns in Burgundy and Aquitaine extending Frankish dominion beyond northern Gaul. A significant feature of the Carolingian dynasty was its relationship with the Catholic Church. With the approval of Pope Zecharias, Charles Martel's son, Pippin III, forced the last of the Merovingian kings into a monastery and had himself anointed King Pippin I in 751. It was the first coronation ceremony in Francia to include anointing with oil and the act of crowning by a bishop. This action was important for church-state relations since it implicitly acknowledged the rights of the pope to arbitrate in political power struggles. The fact that the king was anointed with oil also implied the quasi-priestly character of the king and connoted divine approval of his coronation. Later, at the request of Zecharias' successor, Pope Stephen II, the Carolingian kings became the political protectors of the papacy as replacements for the ineffective Byzantine emperor.

It was Pippin's son, Karolus, who became the most famous of the Carolingian rulers, known by the name **Charlemagne** ("Karolus the Great"). During his long reign (768-814), he had significant impact on the development of Christian worship, by imposing the liturgical practices of Rome throughout his empire. He also made important contributions to the development of culture, by establishing a scholarly brain trust at his court and raising the educational standards of his clerics and courtiers. The so-called "Carolingian renaissance" produced a group of scholars whose work in poetry, history, textual criticism, theology and philosophy rivaled the great achievements of Greece and Rome and whose preservation projects transmitted much of the classical Greco-Roman heritage to the later middle ages. On Christmas Day 800 Pope Leo III crowned Charlemagne, who already styled himself "king of the Franks and of the Lombards," as "emperor of the Romans." By Charlemagne's death in 814, he had created a Christian empire stretching from the Spanish March (near the border between modern-day Spain and France) to the edge of Germany and from northern Italy to the straits of Dover (between modern-day England and France). His empire would come to be known as the "Holy Roman Empire."

Charlemagne's son and heir, Louis the Pious, sponsored continued church reform, most notably imposing the *Rule* of Benedict as the sole organizational document for all monks and nuns in the empire. However from the late 820s through Louis' death in 840, he was in continual conflict with one or more of his sons and a bitter civil war broke out at Louis' death. By the treaty of Verdun in 843, the Carolingian Empire was split into several different parts. It remained divided and weakened through the latter part of the 9th century and into the early part of the 10th century.

The "Holy Roman Empire" experienced a revival under the leadership of Henry I (919-936) and Otto I (936-973), the founders of the **Ottonian** dynasty. Otto I proved himself a strong supporter of the church, appointing clerics to positions of responsibility, sponsoring missionary encounters in eastern Europe and even responding to a papal request for military assistance. In gratitude for Otto's services, Pope John XII anointed and crowned him emperor, a title and position conferred in turn on Otto's son and grandsons. The yoking of papal and imperial power in the Ottonian dynasty eventually led to numerous conflicts over control of the church. These conflicts reached their climax in the stand-off between Pope Gregory VII and Emperor Henry IV mentioned above.

Figure 12.3: The Carolingian empire at the Treaty of Verdun, 843. At his death, Louis the Pious' empire was divided among his three children: Charles the Bald, Lothar, and Louis the German. Lothar retained the title "Holy Roman Emperor."

IV. Cultural Contributions of the Early Medieval Period

A number of remarkable and significant cultural developments took place in the Western Roman Empire during the early medieval period, especially during the so-called "Carolingian Renaissance." We will consider three expressions of this cultural creativity: the forging of the Romano-Frankish liturgy (the Roman Rite), the creation of Romano-Frankish (Gregorian) chant, and the development of Romanesque architecture.

Prior to the Carolingian period, Christian worship in the West was conducted in Latin, but otherwise there was no "standardized" form of service. Prestigious cities such as Milan, Braga, Lyons and Paris developed texts and ceremonies as well as calendars of feasts and occasions that were particular to their own location. In an attempt to unify his empire, Charlemagne directed that the Christian worship practices of the city of Rome should become the norm throughout his territories. To this end Charlemagne sent one of his scholar-courtiers to ask Pope Hadrian I for a "pure Gregorian" **sacramentary** (a book of the prayers needed by a priest to celebrate the Eucharist) popularly believed to have been composed by Pope Gregory I. Around 784-785, Hadrian sent such a book to the imperial court at Aachen, where it was deposited in the palace library to serve as the exemplar for all copies of sacramentaries to be used in Charlemagne's empire. However, the book was incomplete, and as a result it was supplemented with texts and ceremonies familiar to Frankish worshipers. This fusion of sober, classical Roman prayer with the dramatic, exuberant Frankish prayer forms the core of the **Roman Rite**, the primary form of liturgy for the Roman Catholic church.

This attempt to standardize worship throughout the Carolingian empire encouraged much artistic activity. The prayer texts themselves had to be copied into volumes intended for liturgical use. These manuscripts were often decorated with intricate designs or devotional pictures. The ceremonial clothing worn by the clergy during public worship demanded the skills of weavers, dyers and embroiderers. Workers in precious metals and stones produced covers for the liturgical books and vessels for housing saints' relics, burning incense and serving holy communion.

In conformity with his unification policy, Charlemagne's *General Admonition* of 780 mandated, among other reforms, the use of Roman music at worship services throughout the empire. In fact, the **Gregorian chant** that was created for Roman Rite worship, seems to be a fusion of chants used in the city of Rome together with the native chants of the Frankish churches. These chants were sung in unison and varied in complexity from simple recitation tones (that allowed biblical texts to be heard by worshiping assemblies prior to the invention of microphones) to melismatic melodies in which fifty or more notes

Figure 12.4: Christ Enthroned.

might decorate a single syllable. This chant repertoire is one of the richest expressions of the Christian spirituality in the early medieval period.

By the 9th century, some worship centers (bishops' churches and major monasteries) developed liturgical music in which more than one melody was sounded. Music of such complexity demanded the development of notational systems which grew up in the 9th century. By the 11th century, notation had become so accurate that one could learn a new chant directly from a written page without the guidance of a singer who already knew the piece. The development of notation in turn led to further advances in musical art.

Another important cultural development of this period was Romanesque architecture. Strictly speaking **Romanesque architecture** refers to the style of buildings constructed in western Europe between the end of the 11th century and the rise of the Gothic style in the middle part of the 12th century, but we will use it to refer to the buildings developed during the Carolingian and Ottonian dynasties. Romanesque was an adaptation of ancient Roman architectural practices to the changed circumstances of the early middle ages. The outstanding achievement of Romanesque architects was the development of stone vaulted buildings which would replace the highly flammable wooden roofs of pre-Romanesque buildings. Introducing vaulting (especially in "barrel" or "tunnel" form) led to the erection of heavy walls and piers in place of the light walls and columns that had been used to support wooden roofs. These thick-walled buildings usually had only small openings for light, creating a fortress-like impression. Churches built in this style probably symbolized safety and security in the turbulent society of the 10th and 11th centuries. A fascinating example of the transition into Romanesque architecture is Charlemagne's palace chapel at Aachen built between 792 and 805. One the one hand, its polygonal, domed shape is reminiscent of Byzantine architecture; on the other, its massive walls, narrow windows and vaulting all look forward to later developments.

Figure 12.5: Charlemagne's palace chapel at Aix-la-Chapelle, exterior.

Churches in the early medieval period underwent a number of artistic and architectural changes. Carolingian architects created what was termed "westworks," a multi-storied facade usually flanked by bell towers before the entrance of the church building. Monastic communities developed churches with multiple chapels and altars for the devotional practices of individuals or groups, thus transforming the earlier patristic principle of "one people gathered around one altar in one church building." Churches at major shrines developed special walkways called "ambulatories" that allowed visitors access to the saints' relics even when services were being held in the main body of the church. Facades, doors and windows of Romanesque churches were often decorated with carvings and sculptures that served to teach people the Bible stories and other elements of their faith through the medium of art.

Figure 12.6: Charlemagne's palace chapel at Aix-la-Chapelle. The interior shows Charlemagne's throne in the seating area set aside for the king.

V. Major Theological Figures in the Early Medieval Period

Some scholars of the early medieval period suggest that this era provided us with rather few great popes or theologians. While this may be generally correct, particular theologians of eminence still grace this epoch, indicating that critical reflection upon the reality of God and the beliefs and practices of the Christian religion occurred in the early medieval period. We will consider two representatives each from the Eastern and Western theological tradition.

Probably the most important early medieval Eastern theologian is **Pseudo-Dionysius the Areopagite**. The real identity of this author remains unknown. In some of his writings the author claims to be a young man who heard Paul the Apostle preach in Athens and was thus converted to the Christian faith (Acts 17:34). Because of this claim, many medieval theologians considered his writings to be "sub-apostolic," second only to sacred scripture itself. Thomas Aquinas, for example, ascribes great authority to the writings of "Denys." In fact, the author was probably a Syrian monk writing in the early 6th century since the texts reveal a strongly neo-Platonic philosophical foundation. Pseudo-Dionysius is perhaps most famous for his so-called ***via negativa*** ("negative approach") in which all affirmations concerning God must be denied since the divine reality so supersedes any earthly quality that might be used to describe it. Pseudo-Dionysius' characteristic theological method appears in this passage from *The Mystical Theology*:

> *The Cause of all is above all and is not inexistent, lifeless, speechless, mindless. It is not a material body, and hence has neither shape nor form, quality, quantity, or weight. It is not in any place and can neither be seen nor be touched. It is neither perceived nor is it perceptible. It*

suffers neither disorder nor disturbance and is overwhelmed by no earthly passion. It is not pow-erless and subject to the disturbances caused by sense perception. It endures no deprivation of light. It passes through no change, decay, division, loss, no ebb and flow, nothing of which the senses may be aware. None of all this can either be identified with it nor attributed to it (Pseudo-Dionysius: The Complete Works, *140-141*).

Another Eastern theologian who is representative of the early medieval period is **Symeon the New Theologian** (942-1022). Born into the Byzantine empire, Symeon was a monk, abbot, theologian, and poet—one of the most Spirit-centered of all Christian writers. Anticipating the claims of 20th century charismatic Christians, Symeon asserted that it was possible for every baptized Christian to attain direct, conscious experience of the Holy Spirit even in this life. The belief that it is possible to achieve direct communion with the divine is called "**mysticism**." His *Hymn 25* communicates both mystical insight and theological precision in a rapturous outpouring of language:

—But, Oh, what intoxication of light, Oh, what movements of fire!
Oh, what swirlings of the flame in me, miserable one that I am, coming from You and Your glory!
The glory I know it and I say it is Your Holy Spirit,
who has the same nature with You and the same honor, O Word;
He is of the same race, of the same glory,
of the same essence, He alone with Your Father
and with You, O Christ, O God of the universe!
I fall down in adoration before You.
I thank You that You have made me worthy to know, however little it may be,
the power of Your divinity.
I thank You that You, even when I was sitting in darkness,
revealed Yourself to me, You enlightened me,
You granted me to see the light of Your countenance
that is unbearable to all.
I remained seated in the middle of the darkness, I know,
but, while I was there surrounded by darkness,
You appeared as light, illuminating me completely from Your total light.
And I became light in the night, I who was found in the midst of darkness.
Neither the darkness extinguished Your light completely,
nor did the light dissipate the visible darkness,
but they were together, yet completely separate,
without confusion, far from each other, surely not at all mixed,
except in the same spot where they filled everything.
So I am in the light, yet I am found in the middle of the darkness.
So I am in the darkness, yet still I am in the middle of the light.
—How can darkness receive within itself a light and, without being dissipated by the light,
it still remains in the middle of the light?
O awesome wonder which I see doubly,
with my two sets of eyes, of the body and of the soul!

(Symeon the New Theologian: The Discourses, 24-25).

The first representative of Western early medieval theology has already appeared in our discussion on the evolution of the papacy. Pope **Gregory I** was not only a statesman and an important church leader, he was also a noted pastoral theologian. His *Homilies on Ezechiel* and his *Homilies on the Gospels* are filled with exegetical insights applied to the life-situation of his hearers. His *Dialogues* is a delightful collection of anecdotes about the saintly ascetics and wonder-workers of Italy. More importantly, in his *Pastoral Rule* and *Moral Teachings from Job* Gregory created the earliest manuals of moral and ascetic theology. In the following passage from the *Moral Teachings from Job*, Gregory discusses a core issue of **soteriology** (doctrine about salvation): why Jesus had to be sacrificed for humanity.

> *[T]he Devil himself, tripping us up radically in our first parents, held man bound in his captivity in a seemingly just way,—man, who, created with a free choice, consented, under his persuasion, to what was unjust. For man, created unto life in the freedom of his own will, was, of his own accord, made the debtor of death. This fault, therefore, had to be taken away; but it could not be taken away except through sacrifice. A sacrifice, then, was to be sought; but what kind of a sacrifice would be discovered that would suffice for the absolving of men? It would not be just that victims from among brute animals should be slain on behalf of rational man.... If the victim was to be rational, a man would have to be offered; and if it was to cleanse men of sin, the victim must be a man without sin. But how should a man be without sin, if he were the offspring of a sinful heritage? That is why the Son of God came, for man's sake, into the womb of the Virgin, where, on our behalf, He was made Man. From mankind He took its nature, but not its fault. He made a sacrifice on our behalf. For the sake of the sinner He delivered up His body as a Victim without sin, a Victim who would be able both to die in respect to His humanity and to cleanse us in respect to justice* (W. A. Jurgens, The Faith of the Early Fathers, 316).

Another Western theologian who is representative of the early medieval period is **Anselm of Canterbury** (1033-1109), who could equally well be considered a figure transitional to the high middle ages. Anselm was a Benedictine monk who eventually rose to the position of Archbishop of Canterbury. Anselm made several great contributions to the Christian understanding of God, two of which will be described here. First, in his *Cur Deus Homo* (*Why Did God Become Man?*), Anselm constructed a "debt-satisfaction" theory of the **atonement**, arguing that the sin of Adam could only be forgiven if sufficient satisfaction for that sin were offered to the Father. But only a divine person could adequately resolve the debt incurred by human sin. Therefore God had to become human if humanity was to be restored to God's friendship. However, Anselm's greatest theological contribution appears in his so-called **ontological argument** for the existence of God. In his *Proslogion*, Anselm argued that God, understood as "a being than which nothing greater can be thought," must necessarily exist, since if that being existed only in thought, one could conceive of that being also existing in reality, which would be greater.

To conclude this section, three things can be said about the theological developments of the early medieval period. First, in an era of great social and political turmoil, theologians took great pains to preserve the heritage of patristic thought (that is, the thought of the early Church Fathers). They did this by means of compilations of early Christian literature: collections of ancient Christian sermons, extracts from patristic writings, "chains" of patristic commentary on the Bible, systematized lists of citations on a particular topic, and canonical collections (in which patristic teaching on Christian living and church discipline appeared). Second, monasteries were primarily responsible for developing a theology aimed at helping Christians attain sanctification. The writers of these texts consciously employed images and symbols in an attempt to evoke an experience of God for their readers. These images and symbols dealt with archetypal human experiences of fear, anxiety, humiliation, sickness, hope, joy, confidence and friendship. Thus theology was never simply intellectual speculation but a response of the whole person to the divine mystery (e.g., Symeon the New Theologian's *Hymn* 25). Third, toward the end of the period, theologians evinced an ever-more confident trust in human reason and new forms of systematic inquiry developed (e.g., Anselm of Canterbury's *Proslogion*) that would bear fruit in the high medieval scholastic period.

Key Terms:

monasticism

John Cassian

Benedict of Nursia

feudal system

simony

lay investiture

alienation of property

concubinage

Cluniac Reform Movement

Gregory I

Gregory VII

Charlemagne

Holy Roman Empire

sacramentary

Roman Rite

Gregorian chant

Romanesque architecture

Pseudo-Dionysius the Areopagite

via negativa

Symeon the New Theologian

mysticism

Anselm of Canterbury

Anselm's theory of atonement

Questions for Reading:

1. Why is John Cassian known as the "Father of Western monasticism"? What contribution did he make to its development?

2. What were the two major contributions of Celtic monasticism to the development of the early medieval Western Roman empire?

3. What was the Cluniac Reform Movement? Where did it originate? What abuses was it addressing?

4. Who was Gregory I? What were his major accomplishments?

5. Who was Gregory VII? Describe the investiture controversy in which he was involved. What was the outcome of the controversy?

6. Identify and briefly describe the roles of the three dynasties involved in the formulation of the "Holy Roman Empire" during the early medieval period.

7. Describe one major theological contribution of two Eastern theologians of the early medieval period, Pseudo-Dionysius the Areopagite and Symeon the New Theologian.

8. Describe one major theological contribution of two Western theologians of the early medieval period, Pope Gregory I and Anselm of Canterbury.

Works Consulted/Recommended Reading:

Barraclough, Geoffrey. *The Medieval Papacy*. New York: Harcourt, Brace and World, 1968.

Bullough, Donald A. *The Age of Charlemagne*. 2nd ed. New York: Exeter Books, 1980.

Cowdrey, Herbert Edward John. *The Cluniacs and the Gregorian Reform*. Oxford: Clarendon Press, 1970.

Fichtenau, Heinrich. *The Carolingian Empire*. Trans. Peter Munz. New York: Harper, 1963/1965.

Hillgarth, J. N. *Christianity and Paganism, 350-750: The Conversion of Western Europe*. Rev. ed. Phildelphia, PA: University of Pennsylvania Press, 1986.

Hussey, Joan Mervyn. *The Orthodox Church in the Byzantine Empire*. Oxford: Clarendon Press, 1986.

Jurgens, W. A. *The Faith of the Early Fathers. Volume Three*. Collegeville, MN: The Liturgical Press, 1979.

Kantorowicz, Ernst Hartwig. *The King's Two Bodies: A Study in Mediaeval Political Theory*. Princeton, NJ: Princeton University Press, 1957.

Laistner, Max Ludwig Wolfram. *Thought and Letters in Western Europe, AD 500-900*. London: Methuen, 1931.

Lawrence, Clifford Hugh. *Medieval Monasticism: Forms of Religious Life in Western Europe in the Middle Ages*. 2nd ed. London: Longman, 1989.

Leyser, Karl J. *Rule and Conflict in an Early Medieval Society: Ottonian Saxony*. Bloomington, IN: Indiana University Press, 1979.

McKitterick, Rosamund. *The Frankish Church and the Carolingian Reform 789-895*. London: Longman, 1977.

Noble, Thomas F. X. *The Republic of Saint Peter: The Birth of the Papal State, 680-825*. Philadelphia, PA: University of Philadelphia Press, 1984.

Pseudo-Dionysius. *The Complete Works*. Trans. Colm Luibhead. Classics of Western Spirituality. New York: Paulist Press, 1987.

Riché, Pierre. *Education and Culture in the Barbarian West, Sixth through Eighth Centuries*. Trans. John J. Contreni. Columbia, SC: University of South Carolina Press, 1976.

Southern, Richard William. *Saint Anselm: A Portrait in a Landscape*. Cambridge-New York: Cambridge University Press, 1990.

Symeon the New Theologian. *The Discourses*. Trans. C. J. DeCatanzaro. Classics of Western Spirituality. New York: Paulist Press, 1980.

Tellenbach, Gerd. *The Church in Western Europe from the Tenth to the Early Twelfth Century*. Trans. Timothy Reuter. Cambridge Medieval Textbooks. Cambridge: Cambridge University Press, 1993.

Ullmann, Walter. *A Short History of the Papacy in the Middle Ages*. London: Methuen, 1972.

Wallace-Hadrill, John Michael. *The Frankish Church*. Oxford: Clarendon Press-Oxford University Press, 1983.

Chapter 13

Islam

Timeline

570 AD	Birth of Muhammad in Mecca.
610	Muhammad is called to be Allah's prophet and receives the first of a series of Qur'anic revelations.
622	Muhammad and his followers make **hijra** ("migration") to Medina and Muhammad founds the **umma** ("community") of Islam.
624	The Muslims defeat the Meccans at the Battle of Badr.
630	The Muslims conquer Mecca and Muhammad rededicates the **Ka'ba** to Allah.
632	Muhammad's death.
632-661	Period of the "Rightly Guided Caliphs:" Abu Bakr, Umar, Uthman, and Ali.
680	Battle of Karbala which results in the death of Husayn and defeat of Shi'a ("partisans of Ali").
732	Charles Martel stops Muslim expansion in Europe at the Battle of Tours.
1095-1291	Crusades are launched against the Muslims to recover the Holy Land.
1000-1492	Christian reconquest of Spain.
1453	Muslim Turks reconquest of Constantinople.

Islam

For many people in the West today the word "Islam" suggests images of brutal warriors in head scarves or silent women in cloaks and face veils. Such images represent a very limited view of Islam, one of the three great Western religious traditions. "**Islam**" means "submission" to the one God, and its followers who submit to God's will are called **Muslims**. As an organized religion, Islam arose on the Arabian peninsula in the early 7th century under the leadership of Muhammad. As do Judaism and Christianity, Islam traces its monotheistic origins to the spiritual father Abraham.

I. The Prophet Muhammad in Arabia

Just as Christianity developed during a time of religious pluralism and social change in the Roman Empire, Islam arose in a tumultuous time in Arabia's history. Before this time, most people lived a nomadic or *bedouin* life-style. Because tribal loyalty was essential to survival, the members of the tribe were tightly bound together by responsibilities to one another. They fostered a set of values that helped them survive the harsh life of the desert: "bravery in battle, patience in misfortune, protection of the weak, persistence in revenge, and defiance of the strong" (Fisher, 23). With the introduction of city life, people became more class conscious and less able to maintain the values and close-knit ties of nomadic life. **Mecca**, the major trade city in Arabia, was developing a strong and prosperous economy at this time, but the people living in the Arabian peninsula were experiencing extreme economic hardship. The peninsula of mountains, deserts, and dry steppes was populated by Arabic-speaking tribes who carved out their living by herding, trading, and some settled agriculture. While Mecca also had its poor, many in the city were thriving on the trade of spices and agricultural goods, on the traffic of caravans from other lands, and all the new ideas they brought with them. The tension between the prosperous rulers of Mecca and the impoverished peoples of the peninsula provided one of the contexts for the emergence of Islam, which attempted to establish a more just economic system.

Although there were some Arabian Christians and Jews living in the Arabian peninsula, most Arabians were pagan or polytheist. They recognized numerous tribal and nature deities, as well as a remote high god known by the name *Allah*. From a Muslim perspective, this time would later be called a "time of ignorance." The city of Mecca was the location of the *Ka`ba*, a pilgrimage site for polytheists and Christians and the shrine for Allah and at least 360 images of other deities. Also popular was animism, the belief that all elements of nature (trees, stones, water) are inhabited with sacred powers. People also believed in jinn, good spirits that were responsible for the

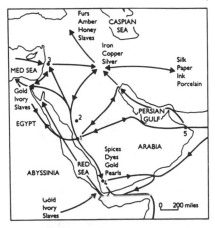

Figure 13.1: Map of trade routes at the time of Muhammad.

blessings people received and demonic spirits that brought curses upon people. Into this environment of religious pluralism, Muhammad would make the assertion that *Allah* was the only God, not simply a god who ranked above other gods.

Transliterating Arabic

The language of the Qur'an and of Islamic religious practice around the world is Arabic. As one of the Middle Eastern Semitic languages (which include Hebrew and Aramaic, two of the languages of the Bible), Arabic contains numerous consonantal sounds not found in English. Accent marks and specific letters are often used to signal their presence when an Arabic word is transliterated into English:

The symbol ` represents the letter `ain, a guttural sound, as in **Ka`ba**.

The symbol 'represents the letter **hamza**. The hamza is a glottal stop, pronounced like the middle of the expression, "uhoh," as in **Qur'an**.

The symbol **q** represents the letter **qaf**, an Arabic letter like **k**, but pronounced in the back of the throat. Thus, Qur'an is pronounced **qoor'AN**.

The prophet **Muhammad** (570-632 CE) was born into the Quraysh tribe, a prosperous and politically powerful group of families living in Mecca. Despite the status of his ancestral tribe, his own family was not wealthy. His father had died only months before Muhammad was born. Then, at age six, when his mother died, he was orphaned, to be adopted finally by an uncle. As a young man Muhammad was employed by an older wealthy widow, Khadija, whom he later married, to manage her trading business based in Mecca. Muhammad was very successful in business. However, his righteous nature and practice of making contemplative retreats to a nearby mountain signaled Muhammad's suitability for a different vocation. A favorite story recalls that when Muhammad, as a boy, accompanied his uncle on a trade caravan to Syria, a Christian monk recognized that the twelve-year-old was destined to become a prophet. At this time, many Arabians were hungry both for an alternative to paganism and for relief from the oppression of Qurayshi dominance.

When he was about forty, Muhammad was already known to be leaning toward the worship of only one god. However, at this time, he began receiving what he believed to be divine revelations during the month of Ramadan in 610 CE. According to Muslim tradition, the one god Allah sent the angel Gabriel to deliver messages to Muhammad to be recited aloud as guidance to the followers. Muhammad's biographers report that a Christian cousin of his wife helped persuade Muhammad that the messages were of divine origin and that he had been chosen as a prophet by the same God who had chosen Abraham and Moses before him. Indeed, the Muslim name for God, *Allah*, means "the God" in Arabic; and the generic root for "god," *al*, corresponds to the Hebrew *el* found in such biblical names as *Elohim* (translated "God," "gods," or "deity") and *Beth-el* ("house of God"). As Muhammad continued to receive revelations and gain followers, the words of his revelations were recorded by his associates. Shortly after the Prophet's death, the revelations were collected and arranged in an authoritative Arabic version of Islam's scripture known as the **Qur'an**. Early prophetic messages urged Arabians to embrace faith in the one God, to practice regular charity, and to prepare for final judgment.

Muhammad's condemnation of polytheism and economic oppression, as well as his popularity among the people, evoked the anger and opposition of the powerful Quraysh leaders in Mecca. Faced with death threats, Muhammad and the other new Muslims fled north to the city of **Medina** in 622 and founded the first Islamic community or *umma* with Muhammad as political and spiritual leader. This migration, called **hijra** in Arabic, begins the Muslim calendar. Muhammad's followers later raided Meccan caravans and in 624 defeated a much larger Meccan army at the Battle of Badr. This major victory was interpreted as a sign of God's intervention on behalf of true monotheists and against polytheists, much as Hebrew authors many years earlier had interpreted the Exodus from Egypt and the subsequent conquest of Canaan as signs of God's providence. The Muslims lost the 625 Battle of Uhud, but then in 627 withstood a massive siege of Medina, called the Battle of the Ditch (after the Muslims' trench to block Meccan cavalry). Again the victory was seen as a sign of God's favor.

By 630 support for Muhammad and Islam had grown sufficiently to permit Muhammad and his followers to march on Mecca and accept the surrender of the city and its Qurayshi rulers. The *umma* (community) was re-centered in Mecca, and polytheism was prohibited. Muhammad cleared the Ka`ba of deity images and rededicated the shrine to the worship of the one God Allah. According to Muslim belief, the Ka`ba had originally been dedicated by the Hebrew ancestor Abraham and his son Ishmael (*Ismail* in Arabic). Muhammad's teachings and exemplary rule also institutionalized justice toward the needy of Arabian society and significantly improved the conditions for Arabian women. In polytheist tribal society before the time of Islam, female infants could be buried at birth by families desiring only sons. Wives (and their children) could be discarded by husbands without provision for their livelihood, and women had virtually no civil rights. With Muhammad and the Qur'an, women received a number of rights previously not available to them, including inheritance, property ownership, and the right of refusal of a marriage contract.

II. Islamic Expansion

Muhammad ruled first from Medina and later from Mecca. He continued to receive revelations until his death in 632, after which his followers chose a succession of four "rightly-guided **caliphs**" (deputies) who governed until 661. Disagreement over whether the new leader should be selected by consensus or whether he must be a blood descendant of Muhammad through his cousin and son-in-law **Ali** caused the formation of a splinter group, the **Shi`a** ("Shi`ites," i.e., the partisans of Ali). The Shi`a disapproved of the first three caliphs after Muhammad. However, when Ali himself became the fourth caliph, he faced revolt from two opposition groups and was finally assassinated in 661. The governor of Syria then seized rule of the Islamic community, moved the center of government to Damascus, and established the Umayyad dynasty. Struggles between the main body of Muslims, the **Sunnis**, and the Shi`a culminated in the battle of Karbala in 680, at which time Ali's son Husayn was killed. The battle is remembered in the annual religious observance *Ashura* among Shi`a Muslims, who now comprise about 15% of Muslims worldwide, with Sunnis the remaining 85%.

This dissension over the question of leadership succession resulted in two significant developments for Islam. First, it shifted control of the expanding Arab Muslim population from Mecca in Arabia to Damascus in Syria. Second, it helped replace the practice of choosing caliphs by consensus with hereditary dynasties that ruled for long periods. These included the Umayyads (661-750), the Abbasids (750-1258) based in Baghdad (now the capital of Iraq), and the Shi`ite Fatimids based in Egypt (969-1171).

Although Islamic political control was often gained by force, religious conversion was generally voluntary. Polytheists within Arabia were required to convert, but monotheists, such as Jews and Christians (the "People of the Book") were given protected status as religious minorities in exchange for a head tax (since they were not required to pay the Muslim charity tax). Although Jews and

Christians were often treated as second-class citizens, in general Islamic rulers of religious minorities demonstrated much more tolerance than did Christian European powers. Through a combination of conversion, negotiation and military conquest, Arab Islamic control had spread by the year 1000 across North Africa to Spain in the West and to India in the East. During the Middle Ages there were major Muslim empires based in Turkey (the Ottoman), Iran (the Safavid), and India (the Mughal).

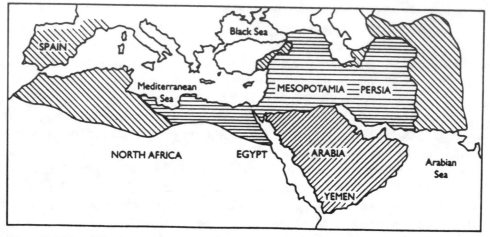

Figure 13.2: Map of Islamic expansion to 750.

During this long period of Islamic expansion it was primarily in the Mediterranean world that Muslims interacted, both peacefully and violently, with Jewish and Christian populations. In the 7th and 8th centuries, Muslims converted a cathedral in Syria into the Umayyad Mosque and built the Dome of the Rock on the former site of the Jewish Temple in Jerusalem, and those in Spain began constructing the Great Mosque at Cordova. For several centuries Jewish, Christian, and Muslim philosophers, theologians and scientists enriched each other's work in Europe and the Mediterranean, most notably at Alexandria in Egypt and Toledo in Spain. Cordova in Spain was the birthplace of two great non-Christian thinkers who were highly respected by Christian scholars: Muslim Ibn Rushd or "Averroes" (1136-1198) and Jewish philosopher Moses Maimonides (1135-1204). For a time it was the center of learning in Europe.

The cultural impact of the early Arab and Persian Muslims was experienced by many more people than those who are members of the worldwide *umma* (community) of Islam. Arab Muslim traders brought paper-making from China to Europe as early as 751. Islamic mathematicians, adapting Indian numerals, devised Arabic numerals, a much more efficient alternative to the Roman system. They also developed algebra and analytical geometry. During the "Dark Ages" in Europe, Muslims in cities like Baghdad, Cairo, and Toledo also made significant advances in astronomy, chemistry, medicine, and pharmacology. Another legacy of this era was the transmission of Greek philosophy to Europeans by the Arab Muslim translators of Plato and Aristotle.

III. The Crusades

Not all of the interaction between Muslims and non-Muslims was peaceful, however. Muslim military expansion north into Europe was halted in 732 when Charles Martel defeated the Muslims at the Battle of Tours in France. For nearly four hundred years Spanish Christians fought to restore Spain to Christian political rule, a reconquest culminating in 1492 with the defeat of the Muslim state of Granada in southern Spain and the 1492 Edict of Expulsion to remove first Jews and then Arab Muslims from Spain.

Most important among these armed encounters were the **Crusades**, a series of invasions from Christian Europe aimed at recapturing the Holy Land (Palestine and Syria) and protecting the Eastern Byzantine Empire from Turkish Muslim encroachment. Arab Muslims had originally occupied Jerusalem in 638, but had still permitted Christian (and later Jewish) access to religious sites in the holy city. During several centuries of relatively peaceful coexistence in Palestine many Christians continued in their faith, while others converted to Islam. The reasons for these conversions were varied. Sometimes political and economic incentives were involved. In addition, for some Christians, Islam presented a clear and unified alternative to the many contentious splinter groups of Christians, who were capable of violence over such issues as the doctrine of the Trinity.

The relative calm in places like Jerusalem was disturbed when, in 1009, the notoriously unstable Caliph Al-Hakim destroyed the Holy Sepulcher, the traditional location of Jesus' burial in Jerusalem. Although this vandalism was not typical of Muslim rule over the Holy Land, nevertheless it inflamed existing Christian resentment of Islamic presence and contributed to the religious motive of recapturing Christian holy sites.

Whatever the religious motives, the Crusades served Christians' political and economic motives as well. Byzantine Christians were already smarting from a 1071 defeat by the Muslim Seljuk Turks, which meant the loss of Asia Minor (now Turkey) to Islamic control. In Europe Pope Urban II sought to strengthen papal power over both Byzantine and Western Christians by calling for the defense of Jerusalem at a 1095 council in France, even though there was little evidence that the Arab-speaking Christians there wished to be liberated from the Muslims. Lastly, many nobles and knights who rallied to the call saw opportunities for military and economic gains. In fact, some Crusader knights remained in conquered territory such as Syria and set themselves up as feudal lords.

Between 1095 and 1291 Christians launched a series of military campaigns to remove Islamic rule or perceived military threats in Palestine, Syria, and Turkey. Militarily the Christians experienced only partial success, at a great cost to all involved. When Jerusalem was taken in 1099, Crusaders massacred thousands of Muslims, including women and children. In 1187 the Kurdish Muslim general **Salah al-Din (Saladin)** recaptured Jerusalem, and in 1192 he permitted Christian pilgrims back in the city. Christian Crusaders were finally expelled from Syria in 1291. In the East the era of the Crusades concluded in 1453 when the Ottoman Turks, aided by gunpowder artillery, stormed Constantinople, capital of the Byzantine Empire. The city, renamed Istanbul, became the seat of an extensive Ottoman Turkish Empire that remained in existence until the Turkish defeat in World War I.

Some Muslims viewed these Christian assaults as annoying border conflicts, but Arabs in the regions most affected by the attacks, such as Syria, have continued to pass down to succeeding generations often true accounts of Crusader brutality and perfidy. Few are unfamiliar with the story of Britain's Richard the Lion-Hearted, who at the surrender of Acre revoked his promise of amnesty and slaughtered civilian inhabitants. King Richard's betrayal is a startling contrast to the amnesty extended by Muslim leader Saladin when he recaptured Jerusalem. Ironically, although some Crusaders intermarried with Arab Muslim and Christian women, with the expectation of advancing European culture into the Muslim world, the resulting cultural exchange led to much more lasting Arab cultural influence on Europe than vice-versa.

A fascinating glimpse into Syrian Muslim reaction to Crusaders and their resistance of European culture is provided in the 12th century memoirs of a Syrian warrior and businessman, Usamah Ibn-Munqidh. Although he had many friends among the "Franks" (as the Arabs often called the Crusader knights), he complains that one tried to take his fourteen-year-old son back to France to "civilize" him and another tried to show him the correct way to face Mecca from Jerusalem, as if the direction would be the same as from Paris (see Ibn-Munqidh, 161-4).

Hundreds of years later the legacy of the Crusades continues to affect political and military relations, especially between Middle Eastern states and the West. For example, many Arabs (both Muslim and Christian) view Israel as a new "Crusader state" and fear intervention and persecution by Western nations.

IV. The Scripture of Islam

Most historians of religion agree that the Qur'an is the world's single most memorized and recited sacred text. Indeed, Qur'an means "recitation." This scripture is also decisive for law and daily life among many diverse populations worldwide. Revealed to the prophet Muhammad between 610 and 632 in Mecca and Medina, the Arabic text of the Qur'an is believed by Muslims to be the actual words of God. The Qur'an consists of 114 chapters or *surahs* arranged with the longer, later Medinan revelations first, followed by the shorter, earlier Meccan revelations. The Medinan chapters especially contain direct guidance about particular historical situations Muhammad and his followers were facing.

The tragic era of the Crusades is all the more unfortunate in view of the many similar teachings shared by the Bible and the Qur'an, the authoritative scripture of Islam. For Muslims the Qur'an is the last and most complete of God's revelations through human prophets, renewing the messages of the Jewish Torah and the Christian Gospel and correcting human distortions of those earlier revelations. Thus, Surah 3:84 urges Muslims to proclaim, "We believe in God, and what has been revealed to us and what was revealed to Abraham, Ismail [Ishmael], Isaac, Jacob, and the Tribes, and in the Books given to Moses, Jesus, and the Prophets, from their Lord: We make no distinction between one and another among them, and to God do we bow our will in Islam."

The Qur'an contains versions of many of the Bible's stories: creation, Noah and the flood, Abraham's near sacrifice of his son, Moses and the Exodus, and the birth of Jesus are a few. However, Christian readers will find it contains much less sustained narrative than do either of the two biblical testaments. Rather, the reiterative and poetic style of the Qur'an is more reminiscent of such wisdom-tradition writings as Psalms and Proverbs. For example, Surah 2:21-22 proclaims,

> *O ye people!*
> *Adore your Guardian-Lord,*
> *Who created you and those who came before you,*
> *That ye may have the chance to learn righteousness;*
> *Who has made the earth your couch,*
> *And the heavens your canopy;*
> *And sent down rain from the heavens;*
> *And brought forth therewith fruits for your sustenance;*
> *Then set not up rivals unto God when ye know the truth* (A. Yusuf Ali, trans. The Holy Qur'an.).

Despite many similarities in content, there exists an important difference between the Christian understanding of the Bible and the Muslim understanding of the Qur'an. While most Christians believe the Bible is the Word of God, they acknowledge that it is also the words of humans, although it is written with inspiration from God. For Christians the Word of God incarnate in Jesus Christ is God's most direct revelation to the world. Christianity teaches that the Bible *presents* God's truth but that Jesus Christ *is* God's truth. However, for devout Muslims, the Arabic words of the Qur'an are God's most direct revelation to humankind, and the Qur'an is believed to be eternal and uncreated.

These differing theologies of scripture present a challenge to Muslim-Christian dialogue. Because they have absolute confidence in the Qur'an as the direct words of God, most modern Muslims believe they must confine themselves to reinterpreting those exact words for their present circumstances, while respecting the original interpretation and the ways of the Prophet as the best exemplar of the Qur'an. Christians have slightly more latitude to apply modern critical methods of studying the Bible, because they accept the position that the Bible evolved gradually through the interplay of divine inspiration and human effort. Of course, from a Muslim perspective such latitude also suggests that Christians have comparatively less assurance in the accuracy of their scriptures.

For guidance in daily surrender to the will of God, Muslims turn primarily to the Qur'an. However, there are records of wise teachings of Muhammad and illustrative events in his life that are not found in the Qur'an. Therefore Muslims also consult the **sunna** (tradition and custom of Muhammad), as recorded in the **hadith** (reports of the sayings and deeds of Muhammad). The *sunna* is second in authority only to the Qur'an. Six major collections of *hadith* were compiled during the first 300 years of Islamic history, and an entire science was developed to analyze the authenticity of individual stories and sayings. Often the *hadith* provide a valuable supplement to material found in the Qur'an. For example, on the issue of how fathers are to treat their daughters, the prophet Muhammad reportedly said, "Whoever hath a daughter, and doth not bury her alive, or scold her, or prefer his male children to her, may God bring him into Paradise" (*The Sayings of Muhammad*, 117). A brief story illustrates the Prophet's insistence that deceased Jews and Christians, as well as Muslims, should be treated with respect: "And behold! a bier passed by Muhammad, and he stood up; and it was said to him, 'This is the bier of a Jew.' He said, 'Was it not the holder of a soul, from which we should take example and fear?'" (*The Sayings of Muhammad*, 66).

V. Major Islamic Beliefs

The notion of only one God sovereign over all the universe is shared by all three Abrahamic faiths—Christianity, Judaism, and Islam—although each religion has its own unique understanding of God's oneness and unity. The *She`ma*, the basic Jewish confession of this belief, is found in Deut 6:4:-5: "Hear, O Israel: The LORD is our God, the LORD alone. You shall love the LORD your God with all your heart, and with all your soul, and with all your might." When asked about the greatest commandment, Jesus answered in Mark 12:29 by quoting these same verses from Jewish scripture. The Muslim equivalent is the **Shahada**, the prime statement of belief: "I believe that there is no god but God and that Muhammad is the prophet of God." Also relevant is Surah 112 from the Qur'an, titled *Wahdeh* ("Oneness"): "Say, 'God is One, the Eternal God. He begot none, nor was He begotten. None is equal to Him.'"

For Islam the most dangerous human tendency is *shirk*, meaning "to associate something or someone with God." Thus, Islam is opposed to all forms of polytheism and idolatry, as well as to the Christian teaching that God is Father, Son and Holy Spirit. Islam's regard for God's holiness is evident in the strong prohibition against blasphemy, defined as "speaking against either God or Muhammad." In 1988, Salman Rushdie, a writer who had grown up as a Muslim in India, published the novel *The Satanic Verses*. Because the book satirizes Muslim belief in Muhammad and the Qur'an, Muslims around the world continue to be outraged by its publication and sale. This forceful reaction is akin to some Christians' opposition to the commercial film, "The Last Temptation of Christ," which depicted Jesus in dramatic scenes (offensive to some viewers) not found in the Bible. In both cases, these believers insist that avoiding blasphemy is a higher priority than free speech rights.

Muslims accept much of God's revelation to Jews and Christians and recognize Jesus as one of the three greatest prophets of God, along with Moses and Muhammad. Surah 19, entitled "Maryam" ("Mary"), retells Jesus' virginal conception through God's miraculous intervention, but makes clear that Jesus was in no way a divinity or son of God. Although the Qur'an refers to Jesus dozens of times, it contains virtually none of Jesus' teachings. The Qur'an also denies Jesus' crucifixion and resurrection. Rather, Muslim teaching suggests that God took Jesus alive to heaven, and another man was killed instead. In Muslim belief God would not allow an authentic prophet to die on a Roman cross. Besides, the Christian understanding of Christ's death as expiation for the sins of an alienated humankind clashes with the Muslim view that, through the Qur'an, God has provided humans with the guidance necessary to follow the "straight path" and thus receive eternal life in heaven.

A. The Five Pillars of the Faith

Judaism and Islam share an emphasis on continual obedience to God and God's laws. Islam's five "Pillars of the Faith" help define and direct daily living for Muslims:

1) *Bearing Witness.* Muslims are to demonstrate in their lives their commitment to this central belief: "There is no God but God and Muhammad is the messenger of God."

2) *Prayer.* At least five times each day Muslims conduct ritual washing, face Mecca, and recite ritualized prayers that are primarily passages from the Qur'an. This practice is very similar to the daily "Office" of Psalms, chanted by Christians dedicated to monastery and convent life. Muslims believe such frequent prayer helps maintain remembrance of God's presence and obedience to God's will in every aspect of life. On Fridays Muslims are encouraged to pray corporately in **mosques** (Muslim place of prayer), where they also hear preaching and commentary on the Qur'an.

3) *Fasting.* The holy month of Ramadan marks Muhammad's "Night of Power," when the prophet first received revelations from God. During this annual 28-day period Muslims (whose health permits) abstain from all food, liquid, tobacco, and sexual intercourse between sunrise and sunset. They also spend additional time in prayer, repentance, and recitation of the Qur'an.

4) *Almsgiving.* Many Islamic countries require a fixed percentage of one's net worth to be donated annually to the care of the poor, orphans, etc.. All Muslims are expected to share generously with those in need, especially during religious festivals, when families who can afford to slaughter and roast an animal must give a portion of the meal to others.

5) *Pilgrimage.* If financial and physical conditions permit, Muslims are to make one visit during their lifetime to the shrine of the Ka`ba at Mecca in Saudi Arabia. Annually a special time is dedicated to this pilgrimage, or *hajj*. Today, as many as two million peo-

ple gather for ten days to ritually commemorate many key events from the founding era of Islam and from the time of Abraham.

B. Jihad

Many Muslims also recognize a sixth pillar, that of **jihad**, inner striving to purify oneself of the forces of evil and to follow the way of God. *Jihad's* full range of meanings includes corporate striving to purify the Islamic community (or a given society) of anti-Islamic features. It also involves warfare to defend Islam and/or Islamic land and to spread Islamic territorial jurisdiction. An example of the former is the ongoing attempt by militants in Egypt to overthrow the Western-oriented government of Hosni Mubarak. As with the Christian "just war" tradition, the legitimacy of the second type, a military *jihad*, is often in the eye of the group or individual choosing to use force. Before undertaking a military *jihad*, Muslim rulers are to seek a *fatwa*, a judgment from Islamic law scholars, about whether warfare is justified in the particular circumstances. During the Gulf crisis of 1990-91 Iraq's Saddam Hussein claimed he was fighting a *jihad* against Kuwait and its Western allies. However, many Arab Islamic leaders opposed Hussein's aggression and obtained legal rulings so that they could join in the *jihad* to liberate Kuwait.

VI. Islam and the State

Because, for Muslims, all of earth and human society is subject to God's sovereignty, there can be no real separation of "church" and state. Theoretically, all Muslim rulers and governments are to submit to God's will. In practice Islamic political models range from intentionally Islamic states such as Iran to secularized military dictatorships such as Syria and Iraq to limited democracies with some Islamic character such as Jordan. However, militants in many Muslim countries are working both within the system and through violent means to replace secular, Western-oriented governments with more fully Islamicized rule.

Although much of Islamic law was codified during the first three centuries of Islam, the specifics vary considerably from country to country. In most Muslim countries there are two legal systems, one secular, and one religious, following **shari`a**, Islamic law. The *shari`a* is based upon the Qur'an and the *sunna*, or way of the prophet, together with human reason and community consensus. Today *shari`a* courts often deal primarily with such matters as inheritance and divorce.

VII. Islam in Today's World

Islam today is the world's second largest (and fastest-growing) religion, with about one billion adherents in comparison to Christianity's estimated 1.6 billion. There are still two major Islamic groups, Sunni comprising 85 percent and Shi`a comprising 15 percent. Shi`ites live primarily in Iran (the only country with a Shi`a majority), Iraq, and Afghanistan, although their numbers are increasing in such places as Lebanon and Palestine (the Occupied Territories of Israel). Although these two groups differ in their views of political governance, all Muslims share belief in the sovereignty and unity of God and in Muhammad as the final (human) prophet of God. Arabic continues to be the language of Islam and its holy book the Qur'an. Over 50 countries have Muslim majorities. The demographic center of the Islamic world is India/Pakistan, with the largest single Muslim population residing in Indonesia. Only one-sixth of Muslims live in the Arab Middle East. However, from both a religious and a cultural perspective, Arab Islam continues to exert influence greater than its relative size.

Islam is also the fastest-growing religion in the United States, with an estimated four to six million adherents. Many are immigrants and their descendants from Muslim countries. However, especially among African-Americans there are many new converts to Islam. Black Muslims in the United States consist both of orthodox Muslims and a much smaller group of followers of the political/religious movement known as the "Nation of Islam." Founded by Elijah Muhammad in the 1930s, today "the Nation" is led by Louis Farrakhan, who organized the 1995 "One Million Man March" in Washington, D.C. However, the vast majority of African-American Muslims align themselves with the rest of world-wide Islam. Ironically, a major spiritual leader is Warith Dean Muhammad, son of Elijah Muhammad. Like Malcolm X, Warith Dean Muhammad split off from the separatist Nation of Islam in favor of orthodox Islam.

Increasingly Muslims in all countries are drawing upon their scriptural traditions to help them meet the challenges of the modern world. Since many Muslims live in countries just recently liberated from Western colonialism, they are dealing with the same needs that face all in the developing world: stable government, economic development, education, health care, etc.. Many Muslims are also striving to achieve modernization without necessarily embracing such Western cultural features as materialism and secularism. Two particular challenges are creating political governments that are both Islamic and participatory, and enhancing women's rights and access to education and careers without weakening family structures. As Muslims meet such challenges in diverse ways, it becomes increasingly important for Western journalists and citizens to attempt to understand the complexity and variety within the worldwide Islamic community.

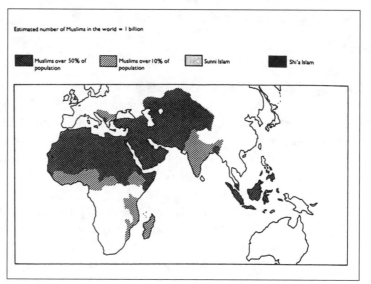

Figure 13.3: World Islamic populations today.

VIII. Islamic Art and Architecture

As the religion of Islam spread, Islamic art and architecture developed into important means for expression of faith. Muslim theologians maintained adherence to God's command against graven images first set out in the Ten Commandments. Therefore, except in Persia and India where miniature paintings did portray humans, artists avoided depicting God, Muhammad, and scenes of human life in their art. Instead, geometric designs, borders of vegetation, and calligraphy became standard in the decoration of stone, wood, metalware, and pottery. In Islam, elaborate geometric forms symbolize both the intricacy and the order and unity of God's creation.

Islamic architecture is especially prominent in the construction of mosques. Often the mosque style combines Islamic worship purposes with popular architectural features of a particular geographic area. Thus, the Umayyad mosque in Damascus incorporates the massive dome characteristic of Byzantine churches. In Persia mosque facades are covered with mosaic tiles, especially in blue. In eastern Yemen they are white-washed and accompanied by extremely tall minarets (towers for issuing the call to prayer fives times each day).

Calligraphy became another major artistic expression of Islamic faith. Because Muslims consider the Qur'an to be the actual words of God, it is no surprise that calligraphy is an important sacred art form. In flowing script, verses from the Qur'an and the sayings of Muhammad decorate walls, woven carpets, copper trays, etc.. Sometimes the script is arranged to suggest the shape of an object, such as a bird, boat, or mosque. Whether Islamic artists design mosques, weave carpets, engrave metal, or pen calligraphy, their activities are viewed as expressions of their religious devotion.

Figure 13.4: Marble mosaic detail from courtyard wall of Umayyad mosque, Damascus, Syria; built and remodeled between 7th and 14th centuries.

Figure 13.6: Calligraphic rendering of the Islamic statement of faith, in the shape of mosque towers or "minarets."

Figure 13.5: Ibn Tulun mosque (9th century), Cairo, Egypt.

Figure 13.7: Calligraphic quotation from the Qur'an in the shape of a boat.

Key Terms:

Islam	mosque
Muslim	caliph
Muhammad	Ali
Allah	Shi`ites
Ka`ba	Sunnis
Mecca	Crusades
Qur'an	*sunna*
Medina	*hadith*
umma	*shari`a*
hijra	*jihad*

Questions for Reading:

1. Explain the meaning of the terms "Islam" and "Muslim."

2. Describe the historical and religious conditions in 7th century Arabia when Islam began to develop as a formal religion.

3. What were the various roles of the prophet Muhammad in the rise of Islam?

4. Describe briefly how and where Islam spread between 622 and 1000.

5. List several causes and results of the Crusades.

6. Describe several key features of the Qur'an. As the holy book for Muslims, how does it compare with the Bible for Christians?

7. Explain the Islamic concept of God, including any important differences from Christian belief.

8. Why are politics and law religious issues for many Muslims?

9. Where is Islam a major presence in the world today?

10. What are some challenges facing Muslims at the end of the 20th century?

Works Consulted/Recommended Reading:

Ali, A. Yusuf. *The Holy Qur'an: Text, Translation, and Commentary*. Elmhurst, NY: Tahrike Tarsile Qur'an, Inc., 1988.

Cleary, Thomas, ed. *The Essential Koran: The Heart of Islam*. New York: Harper, 1993.

Cragg, Kenneth, and Speight, R. Marston. *Islam from Within: Anthology of a Religion*. Belmont, CA: Wadsworth, 1980.

Esposito, John L. *Islam the Straight Path*. New York: Oxford, 1991.

————————. *The Islamic Threat: Myth or Reality?* New York: Oxford, 1995.

Fisher, Sydney. *The Middle East: A History*. 2nd ed. New York: Alfred A. Knopf, 1989.

Glasse, Cyril. *The Concise Encyclopedia of Islam*. New York: Harper, 1989.

Holt, P. M. *The Age of the Crusades: The Near East from the Eleventh Century to 1517*. London and New York: Longman, 1986.

Ibn-Munqidh, Usamah. *An Arab-Syrian Gentleman and Warrior in the Period of the Crusades*. Trans. Philip K. Hitti. New York: Columbia University Press, 1929.

Lewis, Bernard. *The Arabs in History*. Rev. ed. New York: Harper, 1966.

Maalouf, Amin. *The Crusades through Arab Eyes*. Trans. Jon Rothschild. New York: Schoken, 1984 (a comprehensive assessment of the Crusader era from a modern Arab perspective).

Metzger, Bruce and Murphy, Roland, eds. *The New Oxford Annotated Bible with Apocrypha*, New Revised Standard Version. New York: Oxford University Press, 1991.

Rahman, Fazlur. *Major Themes of the Qur'an*. Minneapolis: Bibliotheca Islamica, 1980.

Speight, R. Marston. *God Is One: the Way of Islam*. New York: Friendship, 1989.

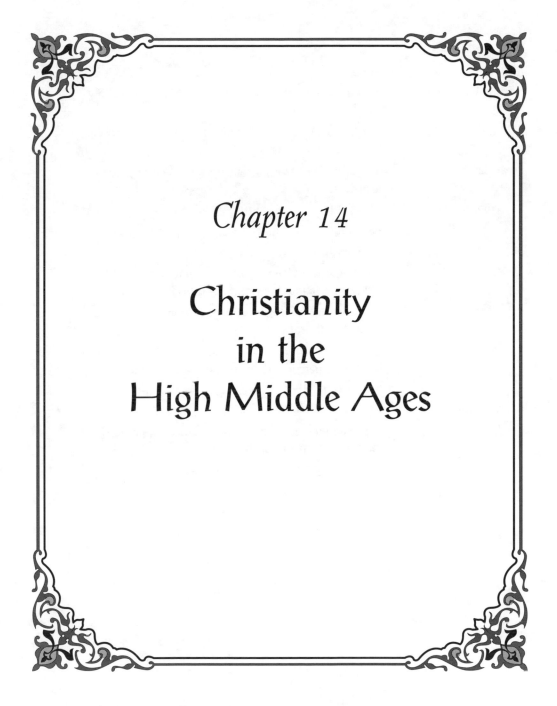

Chapter 14

Christianity
in the
High Middle Ages

Timeline

1095-1291 AD	A series of crusades are launched to reclaim the Holy Land from the Muslims.
1098	The Cistercian order is founded to restore Benedictine life to its original form.
1184	The Council of Verona condemns the Waldensians as heretics.
1198-1216	Reign of Pope Innocent III.
1209	Francis of Assisi founds the mendicant order known as the Franciscans.
1212	Fourth Lateran Council institutes some reforms of the clergy and defines the dogma of transubstantiation.
1220-1221	Dominic Guzman founds the mendicant order known as the Dominicans.
1232	Emperor Frederick II issues an edict permitting the hunting of heretics. The period of the inquisitions formally begins.
1294-1301	Reign of Pope Boniface VIII.
1302	Pope Boniface VIII issues **Unam Sanctam**, perhaps the most famous medieval statement on the relationship of church and state.

Christianity in the High Middle Ages

uring the 12th and 13th centuries, often called the "High Middle Ages," Christianity became thoroughly identified with European culture and society. The medieval church ran schools, licensed universities, owned and farmed land, tried to control fighting and violence and to discipline economic life, rebuked kings and emperors, engaged in its own diplomacy and politics, cared for the poor and the sick, and exercised legal control over issues relating to marriage, family, and inheritance. Modern historians have given the name of **Christendom** to this thorough merging of Christianity and its culture.

This chapter explains how the medieval period shaped the practices, doctrines, and institutions of Catholic Christianity. The following topics are examined: the spirit of creativity and innovation found in religious reform movements both within and outside of the church; the papacy and its emerging role as spiritual head of Christendom; devotional practice and religious life as a product of its society; the spread of the Gothic style in church architecture; and Christendom's relations with non-Christians. Theology and the medieval universities will be treated in the next chapter.

I. Reform Within the System: New Religious Orders

The story of medieval Christianity after the 11th century can be told as the institutional church's struggle to contain and absorb the religious zeal and creative energies unleashed by the Gregorian Reform and by the full recovery of civilization after the so-called "Dark Ages." Enthusiasm for reform at first stayed mainly within the bounds of the institutional church and produced a variety of new religious movements.

A. Monastic Renewal: The Cistercians

The *Rule* of St. Benedict inspired several new monastic orders, the most successful of which was the **Cistercians**. Named for their first house at Cîteaux in France, the Cistercians sought to restore the primitive Benedictine life in wilderness areas. They emphasized a highly austere life, manual labor, and self-support. They departed from the *Rule* in not accepting children into the monastery, in developing a strong governmental system which united all the houses of the order under a centralized authority (in contrast to the Benedictines' decentralized model), and in sponsoring a second order of lay brothers, the *conversi* (literally, "converts"), who took care of most of the day-to-day activities involved in running a monastery. The Cistercians developed marginal and unsettled areas, significantly expanding the amount of European land under cultivation. They grew rapidly, partly because of the prestige brought to the order by **Bernard of Clairvaux**, whose writing, preaching and fiery temperament made him a dominant figure in the 12th century. Ironically, their success eventually led to some of the same temptations of wealth and comfort which had plagued the Benedictine communities from which the Cistercians had split.

B. The Mendicant Orders: Franciscans and Dominicans

The most innovative orders were those of the **mendicants** (from a Latin word for "begging") or **friars** (from Latin *frater*, "brother"). The mendicants at first avoided priestly ordination. Their founders located them in towns and cities rather than in monastic isolation. The cities were home both to the uprooted poor and the newly prosperous middle class. Bringing the ideals of Christ and his apostles home to these people meant leaving the monastic cloister for the city street. The two most important founders of mendicant orders in the High Middle Ages were St. Francis of Assisi and St. Dominic.

St. Francis (c. 1182-1226) was born into a merchant family in Assisi (central Italy). As a young man he chose, rather like Antony of Egypt, to heed the gospel by abandoning his wealth and adopting a life of poverty. Unlike Antony, Francis gathered followers around him and commissioned them to preach the gospel and to witness to it in action. His new community became known as the Order of Friars Minor ("the lesser brothers") or **Franciscans**. Francis taught the renunciation of the goods of this world, for the sake of the gospel, but also the affirmation of the world's goodness. He sang nature's praises in poetry and popularized the use of the Christmas crèche (the stable setting of Jesus' birth) to show how God humbled himself for our sake and the world's. Francis sought to bring back to life the radicalism of Jesus' preaching in the Sermon on the Mount. For him that meant avoiding anything resembling an institutionalized religious life (income, property, books, houses, etc.), although he required his movement to be totally loyal to the church's clerical leadership.

The Franciscan movement became enormously popular. However, its popularity proved the undoing of its founder's vision. The institutional church, hungry for talented preachers, confessors, and teachers in the new universities, tried to shape the order along more conventional lines. Eventually a terrible conflict broke out between a minority party called the Spirituals, who were fanatically faithful to Francis' ideal of absolute poverty, and a majority party called the Conventuals, who were willing to make compromises for the sake of a broader mission. The radical minority known as the Spirituals wanted to withdraw for the sake of preserving Francis' vision in all its purity. However, Francis' vision also included the obligation to obey the church, which unfortunately took the Conventuals' side by endorsing compromises in the observance of poverty. When the pope at the Council of Viennes (1311-12) rejected both the Spirituals' insistence on real, practical poverty *and* their right to secede, they were forced into opposition, and became heretics in the eyes of the church.

St. Dominic (d. 1221) was a Spanish contemporary of Francis' who founded an order of a similar character, marked by a commitment to a life of communal poverty and public preaching. The mendicant orientation may have come from contact with Francis' movement. The **Dominican** order, unlike the Franciscans, at least allowed the acceptance of money. They also developed a strong organizational structure (again quite unlike the Franciscans) based on the principle of representative government. The Dominicans were further distinguished by the emphasis on preaching against heresy, which led them more quickly to the new universities and to a mission more directly identified with study. For this reason they are called the Order of Preachers.

C. The Beguines: Independent Lay Communities for Women

The enthusiasm for preaching and living the apostolic life also led to the formation of independent communities of laypeople, especially of women. Orders of friars and monks sponsored communities of sisters or nuns who kept the rule of their orders, but the greatest growth after the 12th century was among independent communities of laywomen known as **Beguines**. These groups had no rule or permanent religious vows, but followed some form of common life and were either engaged in contemplative prayer or in caring ministries for the sick and the poor. They were not obliged to renounce property, though many did, nor were they bound to a lifetime commitment. There was no centralized structure beyond the local community. Because of the flexibility and openness of the movement, the Beguines became vital sources of renewal and devotion, but also of dissent and heresy.

II. Dissent and Heresy

With rare exceptions, medieval heresy did not involve dissenting *beliefs and doctrines* so much as debate over *practical issues of worship, discipleship and ministry*. Lay reform movements which failed to gain institutional acceptance often became intensely *anti-clerical*, i.e., critical of the church's clergy for failing to live up to the ideals of the Gregorian reform. Hostility toward the clergy also led to opposition to the sacramental system which the clergy administered. People who held anti-sacramental views rejected the church's control of the forgiveness of sin, the doctrine of the real presence of Christ in the Eucharist, and the practice of praying for the dead, since private masses for the dead were an important source of clerical income.

The "Poor Men of Lyons" or **Waldensians**, named for their founder Valdes, are the best example of an apostolic life movement which was forced into dissent and anti-clerical and anti-sacramental heresy. Valdes studied the Bible and preached and practiced voluntary poverty, but he and his movement were denied official permission to preach. When they persisted, they were condemned at the Council of Verona in 1184. The condemnation hardened his group's resistance and turned them into an underground alternative church.

The **Cathars** (from the Greek word for "the pure ones"), who appeared in the mid-12th century, were rooted in the same soil of popular disenchantment with the clergy and the sacramental system. However, their critique was far more radical, for the Cathars taught a thorough-going dualism of a good god and an evil god. The world and the flesh were the work of the evil god. Marriage and reproduction were therefore rejected, as was eating any food which originated in animal intercourse, such as meat and dairy products. Killing and violence were also rejected. The Cathars were divided into a spiritual elite called the *perfect* and the rank and file laity called the *hearers*. Only the perfects adopted the full discipline and only they could administer the Cathar sacrament of the *consolamentum*, a laying on of hands which prepared the recipient on his deathbed for birth into eternal life. Part of Catharism's appeal lay in the spiritual superiority of the perfects as compared to many of the Catholic clergy. One reason the popes promoted the friars was to present a convincing Catholic alternative to the spirituality of the Cathars. Catharism was most widespread in southern France, where their location around the town of Albi gave rise to the name **Albigensians**. By the end of the 13th century papally sponsored crusades and inquisitions had virtually eliminated Catharism.

To deal with such heretical movements, the medieval church developed a two-pronged strategy: the preaching of the mendicants and the notorious machinery of religious repression known as the **inquisition**. In 1184 bishops were authorized to conduct investigations or *inquisitions* into accusations of heresy. At first the accused had the traditional protections of Roman law, which required accusations to be made in the form of sworn testimony. The accused were examined and if found guilty given a chance to repent. The unrepentant were excommunicated and surrendered to the secular authorities for imprisonment and, in rare cases, execution. However, after 1231 the papacy began to license teams of investigators who travelled around and collected testimony. It became customary to rely on anonymous accusations and to deny the accused the right to call witnesses. After

1252 torture was used to get confessions. Even worse excesses occurred in the 14th and 15th centuries, when secular governments tried to make the inquisition an instrument of political control.

III. The Primacy of the Papacy

In the early medieval period, Pope Gregory VII had envisioned the pope as the spiritual head of a single Christian society. His successors came close enough to realizing this vision that the High Middle Ages are sometimes called the period of the "papal monarchy." This does not mean that popes replaced kings and emperors as rulers of nations, but that kings and emperors were, for a time, subject to the moral and religious authority of the popes in ways that previous kings had never known.

The increasing power of the papacy was accompanied by a growing church bureaucracy in Rome. The 12th century saw the rise of the papal court or **curia**, staffed by the **college of cardinals**, a papal advisory team of Italian bishops and Roman clergy. Eventually the cardinals gained control of the right to elect the pope. The curia handled official correspondence, finances, record keeping, and legal business for the papacy. Training in canon law became a virtual requirement for the papal office, as the papacy became the last court of appeal for litigants from all over Europe. At the same time, friendly critics pleaded with the popes not to let their spiritual mission get swallowed up in bureaucratic routine. Below we consider two popes of the High Middle Ages whose reigns coincide with the height of papal power and the beginning of its decline.

A. Pope Innocent III and the Zenith of Papal Power

Innocent III (reigned 1198-1216) became pope at the age of thirty-seven, the youngest person ever to hold the office. He is perhaps best known for his political involvements. Besides being ruler of the Papal States, he had special feudal rights over Poland, Hungary, Aragon (in Spain), and Sicily. He believed he had an obligation to intervene politically whenever moral or religious issues were involved.

> Oath of Peter II, King of Aragon, made to Pope Innocent III: "I will defend the catholic faith; I will persecute heresy; I will respect the liberties and immunities of the churches and protect their rights. Throughout all of the territory submitted to my power I will strive to maintain peace and justice."

An example of Innocent III's power over kings is his disciplining of the king of England in a dispute over who would be appointed Archbishop of Canterbury. When the king objected to the canonically elected archbishop, Innocent III excommunicated the king and put all of England under **interdict** for five years. An interdict is a kind of "strike" in which the church shuts down the sacramental system (Eucharist, Baptism, Penance, etc.). Most English clergy seem to have honored the interdict. Eventually, the king of England surrendered, and even gave England to the papacy as a feudal holding.

Innocent never claimed that he intended to take over the legitimate rights of kings. His decrees and letters say plainly that he recognized the traditional distinction between the two powers, lay and clerical, of the one Christian society. However, he was capable of speaking in very bold terms about the pope's unique authority:

> *To me is said in the person of the prophet, "I have set thee over nations and over kingdoms, to root up and to pull down, and to waste and destroy, and to build and to plant" (Jer 1:10).... thus the others were called to a part of the care but Peter alone assumed the plenitude of power. You see then who is this servant set over the household, truly the vicar [= substitute] of Jesus Christ, successor of Peter, anointed of the Lord, a God of Pharaoh, set between God and man, lower than God but higher than man, who judges all, and is judged by no one...(Tierney, 131-132).*

Some of his policies failed badly. The crusade which he called against the Albigensian heretics in southern France (see below) backfired when nobility and clergy from northern France used the war as an opportunity for brutal conquest and exploitation. The **Fourth Crusade**, which he preached in 1202, never even got to the Holy Land. The crusaders hired out their services for attacks on Christian cities, first to Venetian merchant-princes and then to a discontented Byzantine prince who paid them to put him and his deposed father back on the imperial throne in Constantinople. The crusaders' sack of the city in 1204 and the establishment of a Latin patriarch in Constantinople embittered Orthodox Christians so much that reunion under any terms became unthinkable, even when the Muslim Turks finally destroyed the Byzantine Empire in 1453. So outraged were Orthodox Christians over this conquest by their supposed brethren that they now preferred to be ruled by Muslims than the pope: "Better the turban of the sultan than the tiara [crown] of the pope," they said.

Innocent's most fateful political maneuver may have been his sponsorship of the youthful Frederick II (reigned 1212-1250), heir of the Hohenstaufen dynasty of the Holy Roman Empire, as the rightful claimant to the imperial throne. In return for his support, Innocent made Frederick promise not to unite the empire, which controlled the north of Italy, with the kingdom of Sicily in the south. The medieval popes' greatest security fear was that the same ruler would control both the northern and southern borders of the Papal States. Unfortunately, Frederick reneged on the agreement after Innocent died. The papacy eventually triumphed in the fierce war which followed, but the struggle sapped its financial strength and its spiritual prestige. The war was an important turning point in the later medieval papacy's declining sense of spiritual mission.

The climax of Innocent's reign was the **Fourth Lateran Council** (1215). The council pressured the clergy to fulfill their pastoral duties of preaching, saying mass, and hearing confession, instead of attending to the financial aspects of the life of the church. It also instituted the "Easter duty," which required all laypeople to go to confession and to receive communion at least once a year. The council also defined the dogma of **transubstantiation**, concerning the reality of Christ's presence in the Eucharist. According to this teaching, the bread and wine are transformed by God's power in the action of a properly ordained priest, so that the body and blood of Jesus Christ are truly present in the Eucharist, albeit under the "species" (appearance) of bread and wine.

Figure 14.1: "The Dream of Pope Innocent," in which Francis shores up a collapsing church building, which happens to be the basilica of St. John Lateran, the home church of the pope as bishop of Rome.

Innocent's greatest service to the church may have been his endorsement of St. Francis of Assisi. Innocent prevented Francis' movement from suffering the fate of similar movements like the Waldensians because he recognized that it could provide the institutional church with desperately needed religious vitality and inspiration.

B. Pope Boniface VIII: The Papacy and National Kingdoms

The pontificate of **Boniface VIII** (reigned 1294-1303) exposed the real-world limits of papal power. By the beginning of the 14th century it was clear that the future lay with emerging national dynasties like those in England and France, not with the old ideal of an international Christian empire. The imperial ideal died with the papally-inspired execution in 1254 of the last of the Hohenstaufen rulers of the Holy Roman Empire. During the later middle ages, the church would find itself steadily subjected to the political needs of national kingdoms. Boniface VIII twice collided with the powerful French king Philip IV and twice he lost, first over the right of kings to tax the clergy of their realm, and then over the pope's right to pass judgment on the French bishops. In the latter struggle he failed to win the obedience of the French clergy, more than half of whom supported their king—an ominous forecast of the future trend towards the nationalization of Christianity. In retaliation, Boniface issued the bull **Unam Sanctam** (1302), probably the most famous medieval statement on church and state. Its teachings have often been cited as reasons for seeing Catholicism and the papacy as a threat to the stability of the political order. Boniface paid a price for his boldness: several months after *Unam Sanctam* appeared, Philip's agents arrested him, and he died soon afterwards.

Pope Boniface VIII in Unam Sanctam:

"We are taught by the words of the Gospel that in this church and in her power are two swords, a spiritual and a temporal one…. But the one is exercised for the church, the other by the church, the one by the hand of the priest, the other by the hand of kings and soldiers, though at the will and sufferance of the priest…if the earthly power errs it shall be judged by the spiritual power…. Therefore we declare, state, define, and pronounce that it is altogether necessary for salvation for every human creature to be subject to the Roman pontiff."

IV. Medieval Religious Life: The Mediation of Grace

Consistent with the medieval church's expansion throughout the social order, the sacramental system developed as a cradle to grave coverage of the whole of the human life span. Yet in another sense, medieval Christianity's sacramental practice had become a stunted version of the sacramental life of early Christianity. In the early church the sacraments were more *communal* in nature. By contrast, in the medieval church the sacraments took on a *more individualistic and private character*, symbolized, for example, by the universal adoption of private confession of sins to a priest, which has ever since remained Catholic practice. This "privatization" of the sacraments reflects the fact that church and society were now co-extensive and overlapped one another. The principle of "difference" between church and world was now maintained by the clergy rather than by the church as a whole.

As a result, the sacraments increasingly served to reinforce through ritual the separation between laity and clergy.

A. The Seven Sacraments

For a long time Christianity lacked a definite list of sacraments. For example, the ritual for anointing a king at his coronation was often considered a sacrament. In the 12th century the number of the sacraments was fixed at seven. Each **sacrament** was a symbolic ritual consisting of words and visible gestures or material substances (bread, wine, water, oil, etc.). When properly performed for a recipient disposed to its action, the sacrament became the means of transmitting an invisible reality, the grace or very presence of God. In the case of sacraments administered only once, an indelible mark was stamped on the soul, a mark that could never be erased. The sacrament caused God's grace in the soul *ex opere operato*, "by the very performance of the action." It is impossible to overstate how much this sacramental doctrine has shaped the life and character of Catholic Christianity. In the 16th century the Protestant reformers will seize on it as a central target of their protest.

Baptism brought the newborn Christian into the new life of grace. Extreme Unction (from Latin for "last anointing"), the sacrament today called the anointing of the sick, was given at life's end. *Confirmation*, the sealing in the Holy Spirit, was originally tied to Baptism but became a rite distinct from Baptism because it required the presence of a bishop, who would not have been available every time there were Baptisms. *Matrimony* (or Christian marriage) developed as a means of sanctifying the life of the laity. Its distinctive marks were its permanence, though both laity and clergy found creative ways to get around the church's prohibition against divorce, and its foundation in the *consent* of the married couple, in opposition to arranged marriages. *Holy Orders*, the rite of priestly ordination, set a priest apart from the laity and enrolled him in the international fraternity which governed the church. The Gregorian program of priestly celibacy was intended to detach the clergy from their local connections in family and property and to bind them to a higher calling as the ritually pure gatekeepers of the sacramental system.

The Eucharist—at which Christians ate bread and drank wine which had been transformed into the body and blood of Jesus—was the fundamental sacrament. Peoples' belief in the "real presence" of the body and blood of Jesus in the bread and wine could sometimes be crudely materialistic. Tales were told about "hosts" (pieces of Eucharistic bread) that bled and visions of the Holy Child in the priest's hands during the consecration. Some people engaged in the practice of kissing while the host was still in the mouth, because of its suspected power as a love potion. On the other hand, there were people who avoided communion altogether, thinking that they were unworthy recipients. In the churches, a lit candle signalled the presence of the host in the *tabernacle* or storage box on the altar, towards which respect was shown by *genuflection* (bending the knee, as would a vassal before his lord). The Eucharist even received its own feast, *Corpus Christi* ("Body of Christ"), established by the pope in 1264 in response to popular demand, especially from Beguine communities.

The three elements of the sacrament of Penance were defined as sorrow for sin, confession, and penance. The term "penance" comes from Latin *poena*, "punishment," and reflects the practice of the early church, when sinners who had been expelled from the community for their sins had to perform works of "satisfaction" before being re-admitted. The period of rehabilitation could last for years. In the early middle ages it became customary to accept substitutes such as giving alms or going on pilgrimage. At the same time it also became normal to grant absolution (forgiveness) for sin *before* the penance was completed. The feast of All Souls Day (November 2) was instituted in 998 specifically for saying Mass for those who died with unperformed penance. On special occasions the church granted cancellations called **indulgences** for penance not yet performed. A *plenary* indulgence (a kind of "blanket pardon," where punishment for all of an individual's sins was canceled) was first granted by the pope to those who pledged to go on the First Crusade (1095). By the late middle ages the bishops and the papacy, pressed for revenue, began licensing travelling preachers to sell indulgences. Although they were not supposed to claim that they could release the souls of the dead from purgatory, many did so anyway. This was the system that aroused the ire of Martin Luther and ignited the Reformation in 1517.

The idea that the recently departed were in need of prayers and indulgences reflects the development of the doctrine of **purgatory** (the destination of souls who are not condemned to hell but not deserving of immediate entrance into heaven). Various ancient ideas of a transitional state after death now crystallized as a definite belief in a middle state for dead souls. One rationale for the doctrine was the recognition that the days of the church as a community of the holy were long gone. The majority of Christians were now likely to die in a moral and spiritual condition of *venial sin* (minor sin) which, while it did not merit damnation, fell short of Christianity's high standards. Hence the appeal of a period of purification after death, in which the soul would be purged of its defects and made ready for the vision of God. Eastern Orthodox Christians saw this purging as a healing or therapy of the soul. Catholic Christians were more likely to see it in terms of punishment for sin.

B. Human Mediators: Christ, Mary, and the Saints

At the end of every Christian's life loomed the final judgment. From the beginning, Christianity had seen Jesus as "the judge of the living and the dead." In the Book of Revelation he is the King of Kings who will sit on the throne of judgment at the end of the world. The middle ages remained fascinated with this picture of Christ as king and judge. However, a powerful new devotion to

Figure 14.2: Bronze crucifix from the church of St. Francis in Assisi.

Christ's suffering humanity also came into being. Representations of him on the cross evolved from a stiff, heroic, victorious pose to that of a real human being who suffered a real death. By the end of the medieval period the crucified Christ was rendered so graphically as to border on the fantastic. Bernard of Clairvaux and other mystics fostered this devotion to Christ's human suffering. In general, Christians in the High Middle Ages were inspired by an enthusiasm for the "apostolic life," based on a desire to imitate Jesus' earthly life as fully as possible. The *stations of the cross* (a twelve-step pattern of prayer in remembrance of the events of Christ's passion and death) became a popular devotion, as did the veneration of the *Five Wounds* of Christ on the cross. No one preached and lived the imitation of Christ more convincingly than St. Francis. In an apparently spontaneous occurrence, he became the first person to manifest the mystical phenomenon of the *stigmata*, bleeding wounds in hands, feet, and side.

Mary also received enormous devotion from medieval Christians. Her popularity as Mother of God and as the Blessed Virgin goes back to the early church but the new attention to the humanity of Christ gave it a further boost. The connection with her son is evident in the traditional representation of her seated with the child in her lap. The representation of mother and son evolved towards more realistic poses in a way parallel to changed images of the crucifixion. Eventually these led to distinct artistic representations of mother and son such as the laughing child, the child playing with an apple or ball, the caressing child, the nursing child, etc. Pictures of Mary without the child also became popular, especially representations of her enthroned in heaven. Towards the end of the medieval period she appears frequently as the *mater dolorosa* (the mother of sorrows), holding the body of Christ after it was taken down from the cross, and as mother of mercy and pity.

The Cistercians, the Franciscans, and the Beguines were especially devoted to Mary. All Cistercian monasteries were under her protection and it was the Cistercians who popularized the use of the Hail Mary prayer. The *rosary* (the recitation of fifty "Hail Marys" along with other prayers, usually using a set of beads to help count the prayers) came into use at this time. Mary was also given a cycle of feasts in the worship year which commemorated events in her life. From the 12th century, collections of *Miracles of the Virgin* were gathered which celebrated her services to her followers. These stories typically show her as the dispenser of undeserved favors and mercies which soften or even subvert the normal workings of justice.

Figure 14.3: Mary Seated with Child, tympanum of west right hand door of Chartres cathedral. This pose became known as the Sedes Sapientiae, "Seat of Wisdom," because the Divine Wisdom of the Logos became incarnate in Mary. To symbolize the medieval conviction that classical and Christian learning could be harmonized because they came from the same divine source, the seven liberal arts and seven Greek and Roman masters are sculpted in the archivolts (the semicircular archway).

> A certain thief called Ebbo was devoted to the Virgin, and was in the habit of saluting her even on his marauding expeditions. He was caught and hanged, but the Virgin held him up for two days, and when his executioners tried to fix the rope more tightly, she put her hands on his throat and prevented them. Finally, he was released (**The Miracles of the Virgin**).

Another expression of the medieval desire for human mediators with God was the veneration of saints, a practice still observed in the Catholic and Orthodox Churches. It originated in the early church's belief in the *communion of saints*: the worship of the church on earth was a participation in the heavenly liturgy of the angels and the souls of the righteous. Since Christian martyrs were guaranteed a place in this company, it became customary to pray to them to intercede with God as go-betweens, and to recommend them as role models. These two functions of *intercession* and *imitation* became the foundation of the veneration of the saints. Neither intercession nor imitation were seen as a devaluing of Christ's status as mediator or as example. Rather, the saints were thought of as "grafted on" to Christ in a corporate identity in which all Christians were called to participate.

The medieval veneration of saints yielded a rich harvest of religious devotion, but also an abundance of commercialism, legend, and downright fraud. Saint devotion ranged from the sublime case of St. Francis to the ridiculous cult of St. Cunefort, venerated as the healer of children, who turns out to have been a dog that died while rescuing a child. The **canonization** (process of nomination and approval) of saints began at the grass roots level, though often orchestrated by interested church parties. By the 12th century final approval of saints was placed in the hands of the papacy. As canonization became more bureaucratically complex and more expensive, fewer saints were recognized officially. However, popular piety continued to nominate them at the local level.

C. *The Religion of Laypeople*

The nobility practiced their religion with the help of priests who lived on their estates, or through monasteries which they founded and supported financially. Elaborately illustrated prayer books called *books of hours* (so called because they adapted the monastic routine of daily prayer for lay use) helped their devotional life. By contrast, ordinary lay people depended on the parish system which had spread almost everywhere by now as a kind of "branch office" of the bishop's cathedral. Laypeople could not understand the Latin mass, but they heard the scriptures read in translation and were supposed to learn the commandments and central prayers like the Our Father, the Creed, and the Hail Mary. Pictures, statues, and plays were also used for instruction. Preaching was more the work of the friars than of parish priests, who often lacked education and sometimes could not themselves understand Latin, since seminaries (special schools for the education of the clergy) were not established until the 16th century.

Germanic and Slavic paganism left their mark on the religious practice of lay people. Folkloric religion merged with Christianity so thoroughly that the two are hard to distinguish, for instance the rural belief in holy wells and woodlands and widespread practice of blessing animals, crops, houses, weapons, etc. Blessed objects called *sacramentals* (a term coined by medieval theologians, who distinguished them from sacraments by saying that the former dealt with sanctifying *things* while the latter sanctified *people*) became and have remained popular features of Catholic life. Holy water is an excellent example. The blessed water used in baptisms was kept near the church door, and people signed themselves with it when entering church—and took some home for good luck.

Public processions were important expressions of religious life. Groups called *confraternities* or *guilds* offered laypeople an opportunity for fellowship and support. They were based on common interests such as a profession or trade. One function of such groups was to pay for prayers and private masses for deceased members. Pilgrimages to shrines near and far were another expression of lay piety. The most popular sites were Jerusalem and Rome, followed by Compostella in Spain, where St. James was believed to be buried. Compostella was so popular that medieval art always represents James in the travelling garb of a pilgrim. Other major destinations were the church of Mary Magdalene at Vézelay in France, and the tomb of Thomas Becket in the Cathedral of Canterbury in England.

The attraction of shrines was often their fund of **relics**, which were physical remains, articles of clothing, or possessions thought to have come from Christ, Mary, and the saints. Relics were prized for protection and healing. They were also a major source of revenue. Churches, towns and monasteries sought them eagerly because of their spiritual power and because they attracted travellers and donations. Their profit potential was so ironclad that they were used as collateral in loans. Theft of relics was common and expeditions were even mounted to seize them by force. In 1087 seafaring residents of Bari in southern Italy stopped in Myra in Asia Minor and liberated the relics of a 4th century bishop, St. Nicholas of Myra, thus inaugurating his long career in western European lore. However, the greatest heist of relics came when the Fourth Crusade hit the mother lode in Constantinople in 1204 and flooded the market with Byzantine booty.

V. Church Architecture: The Gothic Style

To a modern observer, the most dramatic testimony to the spirit of Christianity in the High Middle Ages is the Gothic cathedral, "the mind of the middle ages made visible," as a modern scholar has said of the cathedral of Chartres. From its homeland in central and northern France, Gothic architecture spread to neighboring countries and gradually displaced the previously dominant Romanesque style. The chief technical advance which led to the new style was the perfection of the groined or ribbed vault, in place of the older barrel or dome vaulting, and the replacement of the rounded arch by the pointed arch. This made it possible to raise the height of the building while at the same time reducing the amount of stone needed to bear the load. Buttresses were added outside the building to further distribute the weight. Walls became less massive and ponderous, allowing the rich use of glass windows and greatly increasing the amount of light which shone into the

Figure 14.4: The interior of Chartres cathedral, illustrating both the verticality of the design and the abundant light of the Gothic style of architecture.

nave of the church. As a result, the visual lines of a Gothic cathedral are strikingly vertical, the whole building seeming to soar and to direct the eye upwards. The windows were filled with stained glass arranged in geometrical patterns or as representational art. The use of light and of material decorations was meant to raise the minds of worshipers to the incorporeal light of God and to Christ, the true Light of the world. The careful geometrical calculations and balanced ratios which underlie Gothic architecture have led to the comparison of the style with the grand design and careful structure of medieval theology.

Gothic cathedrals served many purposes besides spiritual inspiration and aesthetic beauty. With their stained glass windows and abundant statuary—Chartres is said to contain as many as six thousand painted or sculpted personages—they became instruments of instruction for those who could not read. They were also powerful expressions of the social fabric: contemporary sources tell of entire populations, from the nobility to the peasantry, working voluntarily to build them. Financing such massive projects came from voluntary donations, from conquest, and from the profits of saints' shrines in the church precincts. Adjacent to the great churches, a host of related businesses flourished.

The size of the great cathedrals was not meant so much for large congregations at mass, as to accommodate public processions and crowds of pilgrims coming to see the collections of relics and to pray at shrines. One of the justifications for the first Gothic cathedral was the difficulty of displaying the relics amidst the crush of crowds on feast days. The liturgical de-emphasis is reflected in the displacement of the bishop's seat from its old central position in the apse, looking out to the congregation, to a side wing in the crossing, in order to make room for shrines for relics. Walkways called *ambulatories* were added behind the apse to ease the traffic flow. Side altars were built along the ambulatories for the saying of private masses. The building as a whole was actually more of a cluster of buildings, segmented for several distinct functions—symbolized above all by the wall or screen, called a *rood screen*, which separated the congregation of laity in the nave from the sanctuary where the clergy celebrated mass.

VI. The Foreign Policy of Christendom: Pagans, Jews, and Muslims

The Latin word *Christianitas*, meaning not "Christianity" as a religion but "**Christendom**," in the sense of a closed and totally Christian society, became widespread around the time of the First Crusade (1095). From this time European Christians began to think of their society as defined by its religious identity, in conscious opposition to groups which did not share that identity: pagans, Jews, and Muslims.

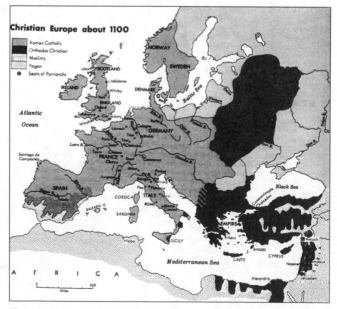

Figure 14.5: Boundaries between Christianity and Islam from about 1100.

A. Paganism on the Run

During the later middle ages, the last pagan holdouts in Europe yielded to Christianity. Denmark, Norway and central European nations like the Poles and Hungarians had already converted during the 11th century. By the 13th century the Livonians (Latvians), Prussians, and other Baltic peoples on Europe's northern shore had been added to the Christian fold. Only the Lithuanians remained pagan.

Until the 12th century conversion occurred in the manner traditional since the first Germanic tribes became Christian in the waning days of the Roman Empire: the royal or noble elite became Christian and brought their people along with them. A transition to conversion by conquest began with the Slavic people called the Wends in central and eastern Germany, whom a papally launched crusade in 1147 forcibly made into Christians. In the 13th century brutal warfare conducted especially by military orders such as the Teutonic Knights forced the Prussians and others to become Christian. The use of armed force, despite official Christian opposition to involuntary baptism, is part of a late medieval pattern of militarized expansion evident in the south and the east as well. In southern Europe the papacy had already in 1059 endorsed the Normans' seizure of Sicily from the Muslims, and by 1250 Spain had been regained as Christian territory. The East was the target of the most sustained military project of all, the Crusades.

B. Jews in Christian Society

The Jew was thus the only "outsider" who remained in Christendom. Medieval Jews suffered from numerous injustices. They were restricted to their own quarter of the city (the original *ghetto*) and made to wear identifying signs on their clothing. They could not appear in public at Eastertime. They were prohibited from owning Christian slaves, exercising dominance over Christians (which kept them out of local government), and acquiring land. In addition they were occasionally subjected to violent and bloody persecution and their goods were liable to seizure. Sometimes they were forced by law to attend Christian services, where attempts were made to convert them. Eventually they were expelled altogether from England and France.

Why were Jews treated so inhumanely? There appear to have been two major sources of medieval anti-Judaism: popular prejudice and bigotry against Jews, and the teachings of Christianity. Some of the popular prejudice was based on economic envy. Canon law forbade Christians to loan money at interest to other Christians. As a result, Jews naturally moved into trade and money-lending. They had a legal monopoly on money-lending until the 13th century. The Jews were also vulnerable targets for mass resentment in turbulent or troubling times. Rumors of ritual murder of Christians (the idea that Jews killed Christians and used their blood to make bread for their festivals) began to spread in the 12th century, as did stories about Jews desecrating the Eucharistic host. During the 14th century plague known as the Black Death, Jews were accused of causing the disease by poisoning wells. Persecutions of Jews also broke out in the wake of the crusading movement.

Another source of medieval anti-Judaism was the Christian *doctrinal* or *religious* teaching that the Christian church was the true Israel and the belief that the "stubborn" Jews who refused to accept Christianity inherited a collective punishment for the murder of Jesus ("His blood be on us and on our children," Matt 27:25). Such teaching was not the direct cause of medieval anti-Judaism, but it certainly contributed to powerful fears and prejudices once these began to appear. To their credit, the popes condemned persecutions and forced baptisms of Jews, and tried to discourage popular prejudices about ritual murder and well-poisoning. On the other hand, they firmly supported the legalized subordination of Jews to Christians.

One area in which constructive contacts between Jews and Christians occurred was among scholars and theologians interested in the Bible. Christian scholars gradually recognized they had much to learn from Jewish biblical interpretation, especially where the original Hebrew text was concerned. The great Jewish scholar Rashi wrote biblical commentaries which were also used by Christian scholars. At St. Victor's abbey in Paris, the 12th-century theologians known as the Victorines learned Hebrew and consulted Jewish biblical expertise.

C. Medieval Christianity and Islam: Holy Wars

Discussion of medieval Christianity and Islam is inseparable from the phenomenon of the **crusades**, which were Christian military expeditions against unbelievers (especially Muslims) and heretics. The medieval church made serious efforts to curb the violence that was endemic to feudal society. The Peace of God movement, for instance, was an attempt by the bishops in the 10th and 11th centuries to keep violent and sword-happy nobility from making war on fellow Christians. One purpose the crusades may have served was to divert knightly aggression and export it overseas against unbelievers.

The instigators of the crusades were usually popes. While the Gregorian reformers forbade the clergy themselves to shed blood, they were willing to recruit others to do it for them. The **First Crusade** (1095) is a case in point. The church had long encouraged the faithful to defend Christendom, and even promised eternal life to those who died in battle against unbelievers. However, Pope Urban II extended the church's promises to Christian soldiers in an attempt to move them from a defensive posture to an offensive one. According to later accounts of Pope Urban II's speech at a council at Clermont in southern France, the pope promised a plenary indulgence to all who took the crusading oath to go and free the holy places from their oppressors. Normally pilgrims were forbidden to carry arms, but Urban addressed these pilgrims as "soldiers of Christ."

The response was overwhelming. Within four years Western armies had re-conquered Jerusalem and established a network of Latin states in Syria and Palestine which lasted for almost a century. The invaders were no doubt motivated in part by greed and the lust for adventure, but historians now agree that a more potent force was the religious pull of Jerusalem, which for centuries had been a popular goal of Christian pilgrims. Jerusalem exercised a profound fascination on the religious imagination of medieval Christians. The growing popularity of the imitation of the earthly life of Jesus in the High Middle Ages spurred the appeal of pilgrimage to the land where he had actually lived. The papacy willingly granted to the crusader, as a new style of pilgrim, all of the traditional guarantees and benefits of the pilgrim, such as the protection of his land and family in his absence. The crusader was said "to take the cross," which was worn as his symbol. This was holy war in a literal sense: "God wills it" was said to be the slogan which Urban proclaimed at Clermont.

The ultimate expressions of warfare in the service of the gospel were the military orders, religious orders of knights who took monastic vows to defend pilgrims and the holy places. The most famous military orders were the Teutonic Knights, already mentioned, the Knights Templar, so called from their headquarters in Jerusalem, and the Knights of St. John or Hospitallers, so called because their original work was the maintenance of the Hospital of St. John in Jerusalem.

The crusades gave many Western Christians their first chance for direct contact with Islam. Although prejudice and hatred scarcely disappeared, Christians gave grudging respect to Muslim leaders like Saladin, who matched and exceeded Western ideals of chivalrous behavior. Frankish crusaders who settled in the new crusading states in Syria and Palestine sometimes learned Arabic and took wives from the native Christian communities in which they lived. Unfortunately, their standards of tolerance for Muslims rarely matched that which Muslims traditionally extended to Christians. Christians also attempted to convert Muslims to Christianity. A major purpose of the Franciscans and the Dominicans was to preach the gospel to unbelievers, chiefly Muslims. One of the most famous episodes in the life of St. Francis was his audience before the sultan of Egypt in 1219, in the middle of the Fifth Crusade. Granted a safe conduct during a truce, Francis was allowed to preach to the sultan and his court. The sultan was unimpressed with Christianity, and Francis was sent away.

Ultimately the crusades were not successful in regaining the Holy Land from Muslim control. Although the First Crusade did succeed in recapturing Jerusalem in 1097, it was lost again to the Muslims under the leadership of Saladin in 1187. Numerous subsequent crusades succeeded only in putting a stain on Christianity and increasing tension between Christians and Muslims. The Holy Land remained in Muslim hands.

Key Terms:

Christendom	college of cardinals
mendicants	Innocent III
Cistercians	interdict
Bernard of Clairvaux	Fourth Crusade
friars	Fourth Lateran Council
Franciscans	Boniface VIII
Dominicans	*Unam Sanctam*
St. Francis	transubstantiation
St. Dominic	indulgence
Beguines	purgatory
Waldensians	canonization
Cathars	relic
Albigensians	usury
inquisition	crusades
curia	First Crusade

Questions for Reading:

1. How did the mendicant religious orders differ from monastic orders? Explain the main issue in the struggle which broke out within the Franciscan order over the meaning of Francis' vision. Which party eventually triumphed, and why?

2. Medieval heresy more often involved disagreements about *practical* issues about Christian life and worship than disagreements about the interpretation of doctrines. Explain how typical themes in medieval heresy may be seen as an unintended by-product of the Gregorian reform, which had put so much emphasis on the role of the clergy.

3. The Gregorian reform gave the papacy the premier role in the structure of medieval Christian society: the pope was to be the supreme spiritual authority of the whole social order. Contrast the pontificates of Innocent III and Boniface VIII with specific reference to the success or failure which they enjoyed in their dealings with kings and other civil authorities.

4. In what sense does the sacramental system of the medieval church show a strong continuity with early Christianity?

5. Describe medieval laypeople's relationship to the sacrament of the Eucharist (answer in terms of what is said about their reception of the Eucharist and their attitude towards it).

6. How did the medieval sacrament of Penance differ from the way it was practiced in early Christianity?

7. What basic shifts occur in artistic representations of both Jesus and Mary during the High Middle Ages? Describe the main reasons for the medieval cult or veneration of the saints.

8. Describe how the Gothic style of church architecture differed from the previously dominant Romanesque style.

9. Why did Jews suffer from discrimination and occasional persecution in the high medieval period?

10. What were the reasons for the military campaigns called the crusades, and at whom were they directed? What were the effects of Innocent III's crusading policies?

Works Consulted/Recommended Reading:

Barraclough, Geoffrey. *The Medieval Papacy*. Harcourt, Brace, and World, 1968.

Bredero, Adrian H. *Christendom and Christianity in the Middle Ages*. Trans. Reinder Bruynsma. Grand Rapids, MI: Eerdmans, 1994.

Katzenellenbogen, Adolf. *The Sculptural Programs of Chartres Cathedral*. Baltimore: Johns Hopkins Press, 1959.

Knowles, David, and Obolensky, Dimitri. *The Middle Ages*. The Christian Centuries, vol. 2. New York, Paramus and Toronto: Paulist Press, 1969.

Lambert, Malcolm. *Medieval Heresy: Popular Movements from Bogomil to Huss*. New York: Holmes and Meier, 1977.

Le Goff, Jacques. *The Birth of Purgatory*. Trans. Arthur Goldhammer. Chicago: University of Chicago Press, 1981.

McGinn, Bernard. *Visions of the End: Apocalyptic Traditions in the Middle Ages*. New York: Columbia University Press, 1979.

Morris, Colin. *The Papal Monarchy: The Western Church from 1050 to 1250*. Oxford: Clarendon Press, 1989.

Reeves, Marjorie. *The Influence of Prophecy in the Later Middle Ages: A Study in Joachimism*. Oxford: Oxford University Press, 1969.

Riley-Smith, Jonathan. *The Crusades: A Short History*. New Haven & London: Yale University Press, 1987.

Rubin, Miri. *Corpus Christi: The Eucharist in Late Medieval Culture*. Cambridge: Cambridge University Press,1991.

Schimmelpfennig, Bernhard. *The Papacy*. Trans. James Sievert. New York & Oxford: Columbia University Press, 1992.

Simson, Otto von. *The Gothic Cathedral: Origins of Gothic Architecture and the Medieval Concept of Order*. 2nd ed., rev. Bollingen Series, 48. Princeton & London: Princeton University Press, 1962.

Smalley, Beryl. *The Study of the Bible in the Middle Ages*. Notre Dame, IN: University of Notre Dame Press, 1964.

Southern, R.W. *The Making of the Middle Ages*. New Haven & London: Yale University Press, 1953.

Southern, R. W. *Western Society and the Church in the Middle Ages*. Pelican History of the Church, vol. 2. Baltimore/Middlesex/Victoria: Penguin Books, 1970.

Tierney, Brian, ed. *The Crisis of Church and State 1050-1300*. Englewood Cliffs, NJ: Prentice-Hall, 1964.

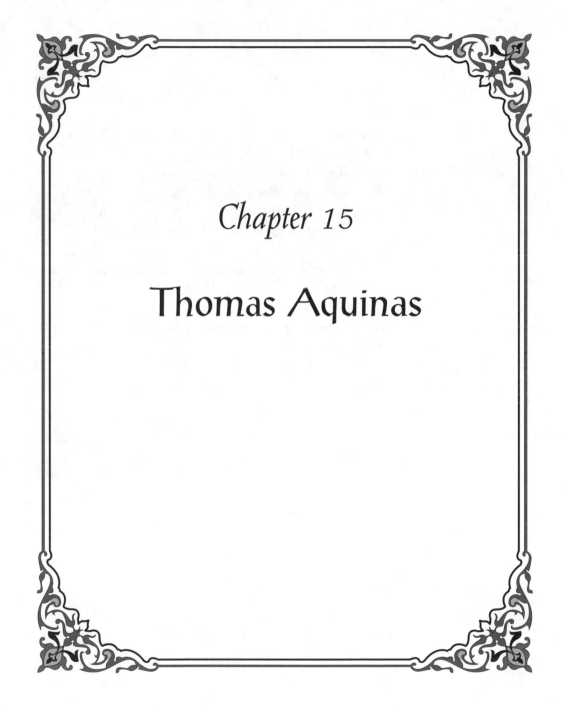

Chapter 15

Thomas Aquinas

Timeline

c. 1224 AD	Thomas Aquinas is born in Roccasecca in southern Italy.
1244	Thomas joins the Dominican order and resides at Paris under the instruction of Albertus Magnus.
1252	Thomas returns to Paris to teach after a brief stay at the Dominican **studium generale** in Cologne.
1272	Thomas moves to Naples to set up a Dominican school. There he begins work on his **Summa Theologiae**.
1273	Thomas has a profound spiritual experience of which he writes "All that I have written seems to me like so much straw compared to what I have seen and what has been revealed to me."
1274	Thomas dies, leaving his **Summa Theologiae** unfinished.
1323	Thomas is canonized as a saint.
1567	Thomas Aquinas is declared "Doctor of the Church."

Thomas Aquinas

The most famous and influential of the theologians of the medieval period was **St. Thomas Aquinas.** Aquinas was a 13th century Dominican friar and university professor who wrote literally dozens of works of theology and philosophy. The thinking embodied in these writings was to revolutionize Christianity in the same way that the writings of Augustine had done in the 5th century. Starting in the 13th century, a gradual but decisive shift takes place in the general theological orientation of Western Christianity from an "Augustinian" perspective to a "Thomistic" one.

I. The 13th Century

The writings of Thomas Aquinas can be very difficult for a modern person to understand. Part of the reason for this is that Aquinas is very much a man of his time. His writings were profoundly influenced by the cultural and intellectual climate of the 13th century. Therefore in order to understand Aquinas, one must understand something of the 13th century world, its history and culture.

A. The Christian World

In the time that had passed between Augustine and Aquinas the borders of the Western Christian world had shifted dramatically. In Augustine's time Christianity was the dominant religion throughout the Roman Empire, which included every region that bordered on the Mediterranean Sea: southern Europe, Asia Minor, the Middle East, and North Africa. However, the reach of Christianity had not yet fully extended to northern and eastern Europe, which were still largely controlled by non-Christian "barbarians." By Aquinas' time, many of the "Christian" territories that had been part of the Roman Empire had been lost to the Muslims (e.g. the Middle East, North Africa, and even part of Spain). Asia Minor was controlled by the Byzantine Empire, which was dominated by a Christian church—the Eastern Orthodox Church—that was no longer allied with the Western Roman Catholic Church. The sphere of influence of Western Christianity was now confined almost exclusively to Europe. However, in the intervening centuries the church did set itself to Christianize the barbarians of Europe, and they were largely successful in that process. By Aquinas' time northern and central Europe were firmly established as Christian regions, and they combined with southern Europe to define the reach of Western "Christendom."

B. Intellectual Climate

The 13th century saw a fortunate combination of positive circumstances. It was an unprecedented time of economic prosperity. This was the only time between the fall of Rome in the 5th century and the Enlightenment of the 18th century that Europe saw almost two centuries of good harvest and no major war or plague. By contrast, the 14th century that followed would be ravaged by the Black Death that killed about one-third of the population in some areas of Europe. The 13th century was also a time of outward curiosity and fascination. The Crusades flooded Europe with news of far away, exotic lands. Contact with Eastern Christians and Muslims brought classical texts such as the philosophical works of Aristotle to the attention of European scholars, who began to translate these texts into Latin. It was a time of higher education marked by the emergence of the university: *Naples, Paris, Oxford.*

The result of these circumstances was a flood of new learning pouring into Europe in four streams: Greek patristic (Eastern Christian), classical (pagan) Greek, Muslim, and Jewish. This flood was not accidental; European scholars sought it out. The problem they faced, in the presence of this new learning, was how to relate all of it to Christianity.

The *Greek patristic* stream—that is, the Greek writings of the early church fathers—came through contact with Eastern Orthodox Christianity. This contact had been renewed through the Crusades and through expanding trade, and the resulting interchange brought the writings of the early Greek church fathers to the attention of western European theologians. Much of this literature was being translated and studied by the Dominicans, which was the order to which Thomas Aquinas belonged. The biblical interpretations of the church fathers John Chrysostom and Origen were especially important to Aquinas.

The *classical (pagan) Greek stream*—that is, the writings of the great non-Christian philosophers of the Hellenistic period—was represented especially by **Aristotle**. His writings were translated both directly from Greek manuscripts and second-hand from Arabic copies that included Muslim commentary. Aristotle's ideas were a great challenge to the three "religions of the book" (Judaism, Christianity, and Islam), because scholars found themselves confronted by a non-Christian, non-Jewish, and non-Muslim account of reality that seemed more complete, more sophisticated, and more coherent than their own.

The *Muslim stream* was represented especially by **Avicenna** (980-1037) and **Averroes** (1126-98). Avicenna was noted for medical commentaries on the classical Greek physician-scholars Galen and Hippocrates, mathematical commentaries on the classical Greek mathematician Euclid, and philosophical commentaries on Aristotle. A century later, Averroes' commentaries on Aristotle were so esteemed in the West that he was called simply "the Commentator," as Aristotle was called simply "the Philosopher."

The *Jewish stream* was represented especially by **Moses Maimonides** (1135-1204), writing from Morocco where he had fled from Christian persecution in Spain. In his famous book *Guide of the Perplexed* he synthesized rabbinic Judaism and the Muslim form of Aristotelian philosophy. He also wrote very influential works on medicine and Jewish law.

These various streams of new learning challenged the Christian West. The issue these streams presented to Christian thinkers was not so much how to answer their challenge as how to *integrate* those positions—how to bring in the truths they expressed without being absorbed by them.

II. Scholasticism and the Rise of the University

Under the impact of these new ideas, both the setting and the method of Christian theology changed. The effect of these changes was to turn theology into something it had never been before: *an academic subject*, taught and written about by professors for students in school, and aimed at a deeper understanding of the truths of faith.

A. The Setting

In the early Christian church, theology was mainly the work of bishops and their advisors. Its goal was to defend and preserve the new faith and apply it to the various circumstances in which the new congregations found themselves. By contrast, theology in the early medieval period had mainly been the work of monks in monasteries. There the Bible and the writings of the church fathers were read, studied, and preserved, often in excerpts and condensed versions. An important effect of monastic theology was to preserve the heritage of early Christianity; monasteries became important centers for storing and copying *manuscripts* (literally, "handwritten books"). Monasteries also conducted schools for young monks and sometimes for children of the nobility.

Schools organized by bishops were called *cathedral schools* because they were connected to the bishop's church. The subjects taught at monastic and cathedral schools were the traditional seven liberal arts: grammar, rhetoric, logic, arithmetic, geometry, astronomy, and music. At some point new subjects were added to these arts: canon law (church law), civil law (based on rediscovered Roman legal codes), medicine, and theology.

At these schools, some "masters" (named from the Latin word *magister*, "teacher") became famous enough to attract students from abroad, who followed their masters from school to school. Masters such as Hugh, Richard, and Andrew, known collectively as the *Victorines*, gave the School of St. Victor its illustrious reputation. However, the most celebrated of the 12th century masters was **Peter Abelard** (1079-1142), who wrote numerous books and aroused constant controversy because he used the newly publicized logic of Aristotle to detect and resolve contradictions within traditional theological authorities such as the Bible and the church fathers. His career came to a sudden halt when he had an affair with a young woman named Heloise, whom he had been hired to tutor. That story and vivid accounts of his life first as a teacher and later as a monk (when the woman's family took action to guarantee that he would never sire children) are found in his autobiographical work *The History of My Calamities*.

By the 13th century, scholars had responded to the new challenges by transforming the cathedral schools at Paris, Oxford, and Bologna into the first **universities**. Medieval society often formed associations, or "guilds" as they were called, of tradesmen or craftsmen. A "university" originally meant the "guild" of teachers and students united in the "craft" of teaching and learning. The new universities developed permanent faculties, regular course offerings, examinations for formal degrees, a student body, and charters from the papacy or from royal authority which gave them some degree of self-government. Students flocked to them because of the opportunities which a degree made possible. The basic degree was the "baccalaureate" (from which we get our phrase "bachelor's" degree) in "arts," i.e., the liberal arts mentioned above. After studying the arts, a student might go on to specialize in canon law, civil law, medicine, or theology. Students became teachers themselves when they passed the "master's" exams and became "doctors" (from another Latin word which means "teacher"). Schools were often known for their academic specialization: Bologna for civil and canon law, Montpellier for medicine, and Paris for theology. The institution of the university was one of the medieval world's lasting legacies.

B. The Method

Medieval theology began as commentary on authoritative texts such as the Bible, written primarily by monks and for monks to aid them in their spiritual life. In the 11th and 12th centuries this began to change, in two main ways. First, scholars began to go beyond mere commentary on a *text* and started to investigate *topics* in their own right in focused studies called *questions*. Second, scholars began to contrast and compare traditional authorities as they became aware of contradictions in their sources. Abelard, who pioneered this approach, wrote a very influential work called *Yes and No* (*Sic et Non*). Aristotle's works on logic aided such analysis and even encouraged some writers to apply logic even to the truths of faith, such as the Trinity.

In the 13th century a third innovation occurred: the integration of Christian faith with a "naturalistic" view of the world, that is, with an understanding of the world as a purely natural system that can be understood by human reason without the aid of revelation. As more of Aristotle's works were translated into Latin, theologians found themselves confronted with a complete and rational worldview which seemed to have no need of divine revelation or even of a personal God who created the world. Aristotle's works were studied most eagerly by masters on the "arts" faculty—what today would be called the humanities *and* the sciences—some of whom held the radical view that Christian faith was incompatible with the new Aristotelian view of the world. Others, including Thomas Aquinas, believed that it was possible to integrate this new knowledge into the faith.

The theology that was written and studied in these new schools and universities has been given the name **scholasticism** from the Latin word for "school." In general, scholastic theology, the theology of the "Schoolmen," tried to harmonize faith with reason. Scholasticism tried to take the truths uncovered by philosophers like Aristotle and show how they were compatible with Christianity. It did this not by denying or revising elements of Christian faith, which depended on divine revelation, but by showing how reason could deepen one's understanding of what one believed on God's authority. This was how they interpreted the traditional definition of theology as "faith seeking understanding." In the 14th century many theologians would lose confidence that this harmonization was really possible. Yet in the end, scholasticism survived its successors, was revived by Pope Leo XIII in the late 19th century, and dominated Catholic theology in our century until very recently. The lasting influence of scholasticism, and that of its leading representative Thomas Aquinas, is reflected in the fact that so many Catholic colleges and universities are named after Aquinas, and in the fact that the works of Aquinas are still required reading in most Catholic schools and many non-Catholic ones as well.

III. Medieval Teaching and Learning

To understand the writing these new medieval scholars produced, one needs to recall that 13th century scholars and students taught and learned very differently from the way 20th-century scholars and students do. An understanding of how they learned is required before one can begin to understand why they wrote the way they did. Scholastic professors used two basic strategies for learning and teaching: they *commented on texts* and they *disputed questions*.

A. Texts

It was primarily through rediscovered texts that new learning was coming into Europe. So the task of the scholar was to read the texts, understand them, and then try to figure out what to do with the new ideas contained in them. One strategy for teaching and learning was the *lectura*, the Latin source of our modern word "lecture," in which a scholar publicly read a key text such as a book of the Bible or the famous philosophical book the *Sentences* of Peter Lombard, interspersing the reading with commentary. This strategy was only the beginning of the process, however. There remained the task of relating these ideas with other ideas into a larger whole, especially when there seemed to be conflicts between the various ideas.

B. Disputes

The process of relating the ideas found in texts from disparate worldviews into a new, larger whole was carried on in public disputes that were a sort of trial run for writing a book. As modern scholars write articles for journals to test out new ideas, medieval scholars held disputes for the same purpose. Anyone could show up at these public disputes.

A **disputed question** would be posed by the master, usually in the form "whether…or not," for example, "Whether God exists or not." The question was posed in an open way without presupposing which answer was correct. The *audience* began the discussion by proposing arguments for or against the question. One of the master's *graduate students* would try to respond to the arguments. In some cases the debate would become quite heated. It was not unusual to have noisy arguments and verbal fights on the floor of the meeting room.

The Master listened carefully to what was said, then had twenty-four hours to prepare an answer. In his answer the next day, the Master first would restate as clearly and effectively as possible every argument that had been offered the preceding day, then, in the light of that discussion, he would give his answer to the question he had proposed. Finally he would clarify any of the arguments that agreed with his position but may have been inexact, and answer *all* the objections on the other side. Effective Masters tried to reconcile as many of the seemingly conflicting points as possible.

C. Quodlibetal Debates

Sometimes professors held "**quodlibetal debates**" (loosely translated as "whatever you would like to debate") in which they did not announce a question beforehand. Rather they offered to respond to any question at all that anyone cared to ask. Only very good or very self-confident professors dared to hold one of these debates. From the standpoint of their colleagues, these provided an excellent opportunity to attack or embarrass the Master. If a Master argued poorly in the presence of his peers and attending students, he could lose his students, which could be financially and professionally disastrous. In medieval universities, professors did not have classrooms full of students delivered to them—students contracted individually with professors. Naturally, no student would want to contract with a professor who had been publicly humiliated or whose lack of intelligence had been demonstrated for all to see.

IV. Thomas Aquinas

Into this European university culture of the 13th century came a powerful new thinker: the Italian Thomas Aquinas, member of a new order of beggar preachers known as the Dominicans. Aquinas was born in 1224 or 1225, the son of a nobleman at Roccasecca in southern Italy. At a young age, Thomas was sent for school to the most famous Benedictine monastery of the day, Monte Cassino. His father hoped that some day Thomas might become the abbot of that prestigious monastery. Thomas did choose a religious life, but he did not choose to become a Benedictine.

Thomas was attracted to the new Order of Preachers (the "**Dominicans**")—an order that emphasized learning and poverty. Dominic, who died four years before Thomas was born, had founded his order to preach by word, deed, and a life of holiness. The Dominicans practiced radical

Gospel poverty. They were not allowed to own any possessions of their own, but instead relied on the charity of others, often by begging in the streets. When members of the order travelled from country to country, they walked. Dominicans were not allowed to ride. In addition to their vow of poverty, Dominicans vowed chastity and obedience as well. Unlike the older monastic orders, which usually set up their monasteries in rural areas, the Dominicans lived in the world of the medieval city, where their twin vocations of preaching and hearing confessions would be most useful. The Dominicans were also devoted to scholarship. Dominicans set up their own schools and programs of lifelong study to train their members. In addition, many Dominicans studied and taught in the most prestigious scholarly institutions of the day: the Universities of Paris, Naples, and Oxford.

Thomas' family strongly disapproved of his decision to join the Dominicans. This new order was not nearly as prestigious as the older Benedictine order, and the idea of Thomas joining an order of "beggars" probably did not appeal to his affluent family. When Thomas refused to yield to his family's wishes, his older brothers captured him and locked him up in a tower of the family castle while they attempted to change his mind. His brothers tried to expand his horizons and re-direct his interests by bringing him a prostitute, but Thomas seized a poker from the fireplace and convinced her to leave.

Thomas was an exemplary prisoner in a situation of friendly house arrest. He was allowed visits by Dominicans who brought him books to read. Eventually, after he had spent more than a year in the tower, he escaped. His family decided that they were not likely to change his mind, so they let him carry out his strange dream to live as a "beggar friar."

Now free, Thomas began his education as a Dominican. Thomas did not seem impressive to his fellow classmates, at least at first. Thomas was large and unusually quiet. He came from southern Italy, which was not considered the center of scholarship. His brother Dominicans called him the "Dumb [silent] Ox" because he seldom spoke in class. However, during the course of this education, Thomas impressed one of his teachers, Albert the Great ("Albertus Magnus" in Latin), the greatest scholar in the Dominican order in his day. Albert recognized and appreciated the promise of his young scholar. He commented to Thomas' classmates one day: "Gentlemen, you call Thomas the 'dumb ox.' But some day that ox will let out such a bellow that his noise will fill the earth."

Figure 15.1: An illuminated manuscript page of St. Thomas' writings, 13th C. The illustration is of St. Thomas dictating to a scribe.

Eventually Thomas settled down to teach at the University of Paris, the leading university of the day. He also taught in several Dominican schools in Italy. It was during these periods of teaching that Thomas wrote most of his theological works, of which there were a great many. His greatest work, the **Summa Theologiae** (literally a "summary or compendium of theology"), itself runs to three or four thousand pages in most editions. However, Thomas also wrote two other Summas, commentaries on all the writings of Aristotle, commentaries on most of the New Testament and parts of the Old Testament, collections of disputed questions, and small treatises on various other topics.

The incredible body of work produced by Aquinas in a relatively short amount of time can be attributed to his sheer genius and his extraordinary powers of concentration. He was accustomed to writing three or even four different books simultaneously. He would dictate part of the first book to one secretary (or "scribe"), and while he was writing he would dictate part of the second book to another scribe, and so on. So far as we can tell, Thomas worked out his most famous book, the **Summa Theologiae**, in his head before he put anything down on paper. There are no "rough drafts" of the book. In those cases where we do have work in Thomas' own handwriting, he wrote so rapidly and with so many abbreviations that only a few modern specialists are able to read it.

V. Major Themes of the Theology of Thomas Aquinas

Thomas' theology has had strong influence on Western theology since his time. Here are some of its major themes:

1. There is a natural order accessible to humans through their physical senses and human reason. This order of reality is called "nature." Beyond this, there is another order of reality not accessible to humans through their own powers. This order of reality is called "the supernatural" or "the transcendent." The idea of an invisible, transcendent order of reality would come under sharp critique by many thinkers during the Enlightenment, an 18th century intellectual movement.

2. Human beings would never understand the supernatural order or even know about most of it if God did not "reveal" to us both its existence and its meaning. We could not respond to it unless God freely gave us the power to do so. Theologians call this freely-given power "grace."

3. Although the supernatural order essentially transcends the natural order, the two orders are in harmony because the one God created both of them. The supernatural order is known by faith, and the natural order is known by reason. One cannot come to understand the supernatural order by reasoning from the natural order. Nonetheless, *faith properly understood cannot contradict reason properly understood*, and the power of grace perfects human nature and reason without destroying or replacing them. This insight is central to the idea of a "Catholic university" and justifies the role of theology in relation to secular disciplines. This part of Thomas' theology was rejected by the later medieval movement called "nominalism" (see chapter 16), a movement which was very influential in the time of Martin Luther.

4. Although reason can demonstrate a few facts about the invisible order, such as the existence of God, most truths of revelation, such as the Trinity, can be neither proven nor disproved by human reason.

5. God is the primary cause of everything in the universe; nevertheless humans act freely because God always moves things according to their natures and it is the nature of humans to act freely. Because God moves humans to act freely, humans are the secondary cause of their own acts. If a human does anything good, it is because God gave the grace to act that way. If a human does anything evil, it is the human's own fault.

6. Humans, exercising their freedom, have in fact sinned, breaking their relationship with God. This sin dates from the very beginning of human history. Because it goes back to the very beginning, and because all humans are affected by this reality of sin from the beginning of their lives, theologians speak of "original sin." God became human to rescue humans from the results of original sin. Thomas taught that if the first human had not sinned, God would not have become human. Other theologians of his day, especially Franciscan theologians, disagreed with this last point. They claimed that, while it was fitting for God to rescue humans from original sin by becoming human, nevertheless God would *still* have become human even if humans had never sinned.

7. In the sacraments we come into contact with the passion and death of Jesus. The sacraments are the instruments God uses to cause grace in humans. Because it is Jesus who acts in the sacraments, they are effective whether the human minister is "worthy" or not. This was the principle Augustine used to combat the Donatist claim that Catholic bishops who they saw as "traitors" could not give valid sacraments.

8. The church is the "mystical body of Christ," and it preserves and makes available revealed faith and the sacraments. Nevertheless, the church itself is in constant need of renewal and it must continually deepen its understanding of the faith and find better ways to express it.

9. It is the vision of God face-to-face in heaven that gives humans their highest happiness. To see God in this way, the human mind must be transformed and elevated by God's grace.

VI. The **Summa Theologiae**

The best known and most influential of Thomas' writings is the *Summa Theologiae*. A Summa is a summary or a comprehensive treatise on a particular subject. The *Summa Theologiae* is a "summary of theology." One of Thomas' greatest accomplishments is that he integrated Aristotle's philosophy into Christian theology, but Thomas would never have called himself a philosopher. Thus although there are quotations and insights drawn from philosophers in the *Summa*, it is a *theological* work. Unlike the philosophers of Thomas' time, who would argue that they work from reason alone, without using any knowledge that is "revealed" by God, in the *Summa* Thomas assumes revelation from God. Thomas quotes from the Bible and assumes that biblical teachings are true without "defending" them.

The preceding point shows that Thomas' goal in the *Summa* was not to prove that all the articles of the Catholic faith are true. Thomas knew that no one can prove articles of faith in themselves. However, Thomas did feel that one could offer real arguments for *theological positions about* those articles of faith or arguments *drawing out their implications*. For example, human reason cannot prove that God is a Trinity; but human reason can explain what the implications of that revelation are. Human reason cannot prove that God became incarnate in Jesus of Nazareth, but it can explain how it was "fitting" for God to do so. Thomas uses reason to connect the various truths of revelation to each other and to explain their meanings and implications in a world of ideas that seems in constant danger of falling apart.

Thomas indicates in the prologue to the *Summa* that he is writing for "beginners." However, this can be misleading. The "beginners" that Thomas speaks of were those who were beginning their study as Domincan friars. This means that they would already have earned a Baccalaureate degree, and hence would have already studied six years of philosophy, probably memorized one of the Gospels, and known Bible history fairly well.

A. The Form of the Summa

As mentioned above, Dominic founded his order to *preach* by word, deed, and a life of holiness. Pope Honorius III added a second mission to the order: to *hear confessions*. To help Dominicans carry out these two tasks, the order produced numerous guides for preachers and confessors. These guides were essentially practical treatises on the virtues (moral excellences, such as justice, charity, or fortitude) and vices (moral faults, such as hatred, gluttony, or pride).

This context helps explain why the largest part of Thomas' *Summa Theologiae* is the second part—a treatise on the virtues and vices. But the *Summa* differs from (most) other Dominican treatises by putting this section into a larger theological context. Thomas placed his ethical teaching in the following context: (1) where humans come from (God, whose image they are), (2) where they are going (to God) and how (by practicing virtues and avoiding vices), and (3) who and what gives them the *capacity* to go there—the *power* to practice virtue and avoid vice (Jesus Christ through the sacraments). These three topics form the three parts of the *Summa Theologiae*. The second part, the longest, is itself subdivided into two. Thomas himself wrote all of parts one and two, and a bit over half of part three; the rest of part three (called the "supplement") was completed by his assistant. Each part is divided into questions, each question into articles.

B. The Form of an Article

The fundamental building block of the *Summa*, the **article**, is based loosely on the disputed questions that were part of university life. As in the disputed question, in a written article (1) a question is proposed, arguments are listed both (2) against and (3) for the proposition, and then (4) the master/author gives his own view and (5) responds to the arguments with which he disagrees. However, the articles in the *Summa* did not "record" actual disputes that took place in Thomas' teaching career. They were written in the study, not taken from actual oral disputations.

Each article in the *Summa Theologiae* takes a standard five-part form as follows:

(1) Statement of the question, framed to expect the answer "yes" or "no." For example: "Whether God exists?"

This is the open question being posed by the article. Note that the form of the question itself does not suggest what its answer should be.

(2) Arguments on one side of the issue. Almost always Thomas begins by outlining the arguments that are opposite to the position that he will eventually take. For example: "*It seems that God does not exist....*"

Thomas will then outline the arguments, with their supporting reasons, in defense of this side of the issue, in this case the arguments in support of the claim that God does not exist. Usually these arguments are numbered in some way. Thomas will later raise objections to these arguments, but not until he reaches the part of the article that is devoted to such objections. Articles in the *Summa* tend to have a small number of arguments in comparison with the more difficult topics dealt with in disputed questions. In other words, Aquinas does not include every possible argument on each side of the issue in an article.

(3) An argument from an authority on the other side of the issue. Usually this involves a quotation from the Bible or from an early church father (usually a bishop) or theologian. The statement generally does not *argue for* its position, except insofar as the quotation from an authority qualifies as an argument. This part of the article is called the "Sed contra," and it indicates the position which Thomas will normally take as his own. However, Thomas has not yet indicated (for certain) his own position or his reasons for holding it. The "Sed contra" usually appears in the following form: "*But against this…*" or "*On the contrary….*"

The Article Form: An Example

Question 2 Article 3

Whether God exists?

It seems that God does not exist.

　　1. First argument against God's existence.
　　2. Second argument against God's existence.

But against this [a quotation from the Bible supporting God's existence].

I answer that [Thomas' own position and his reasons for holding it].

Replies to arguments with which Thomas disagrees.

To the first argument: [a reply to the first argument against God's existence].

To the second argument: [a reply to the second argument against God's existence].

---

(4) The body of the article or "response." In this part of the article Thomas gives his own view of the issue in question and his reasons for holding that view. Often Thomas will "divide the question," making distinctions to show that the proposal is true in one respect but false in another, or true in certain circumstances but false in others. This part of the article begins with:
"I answer that…" or "Response:…."

(5) Thomas concludes by giving replies to each of the arguments with which he wound up disagreeing, usually the arguments with which the article began. This part begins with: "*To the first argument…*" or "Reply to the first objection:…."

Thomas now applies the insights of his "response" to the first objection, agreeing with as much of it as he can while explaining why it is not true as it stands.

VII. Biblical Commentaries

The 12th and 13th centuries were a time of vigorous study of the Bible, and Thomas Aquinas was an avid and outstanding participant in this study. In the early medieval period many advances were made regarding the study of the Bible. It was during this period that the Bible was divided into chapters, and a start was made toward further subdivision into verses. Copies of the Bible were compared with ancient manuscripts to correct mistakes that had developed in the biblical text. Lists of such mistakes with their corrections were published, the "concordance" was developed (by which all the passages containing a particular word or idea are listed) to help scholars find particular passages in the Latin Bible and in the Church Fathers, and new dictionaries and other study aids were produced.

More important than these material aids was a new understanding, explained most clearly by Thomas Aquinas, of how literal meanings of scripture are related to symbolic or spiritual meanings. Earlier interpreters had appealed to the "spiritual sense" to find meaning in passages for which the "literal meaning" seemed absurd, false, or obscure. Thus, they sometimes read the words in a woodenly literal way and then denied that this "literal meaning" was true: the truth was a "spiritual meaning" that often was so loosely connected to the text that it would have meant nothing to the original human author or the author's original readers. For example, Exodus 23:19 gives the law "you shall not boil a kid in its mother's milk." Augustine claimed that it was impossible to read this passage literally, since this would be absurd as a law. Instead Augustine read the passage as a prophecy that Jesus would escape the slaughter of innocent children that King Herod undertook when he learned that the messiah had been born (Matt 2:13-18).

However, in the 13th century, scholars began to notice that Jews were indeed reading some "difficult" passages literally, such as the one just treated from Exodus. On its basis they refused to eat meat and milk or cheese at the same meal. This realization forced scholars to think again about their methods of interpretation.

For Thomas, the *literal sense* of a passage is "what the author means by the words." If the author uses metaphors and other figures of speech, the literal meaning is not the symbol used as a metaphor, but the normal human understanding of what the metaphor stands for or means. To know what this is, we have to know the historical/cultural situation of the time when the author wrote. So, for example, if the Bible says that God acted with his strong right arm, the literal meaning is not that God has a body with a right arm, but that God acted with power. Then, having decided what the author meant, we need to make sense of it. In the case of the passage about the kid, according to Thomas, although the kid being dead would not know what it was being boiled in, it seems especially cruel to boil it in the milk that its mother produced to feed it. The law made sense in its own time: it taught humans to be kind to each other by appealing to their pity for animals. Thomas also guessed that such a sacrifice might have been characteristic of pagan worship at that time, and so avoided for that reason.

The *spiritual sense* of scripture, for Thomas, is based not on the words as such but on the historical realities to which the words refer. *God* (and God alone) is able to create or influence things and events in such a way that the things and events themselves signify spiritual realities. Thus God led the Israelites out of Egypt to safety in such a way that the event could (1) rescue the Israelites in the time of Pharaoh and (2) signify the future rescue or salvation of all humans through the death and resurrection of Jesus. The Exodus was a real historical event, and that historical event prefigured a future historical and spiritual event.

Thus in brief, God creates, causes, or influences people, things, and events in such a way as to express spiritual realities. The human authors of the Bible describe these people, things, and events through a variety of literary forms: history, poetry, metaphor, and so forth. The literal meaning of their words involves the people, things, and events they are describing; the spiritual meaning of their words is the spiritual realities God intended to signify by those people, things, and events. Only the literal sense can be appealed to as a starting-point for reasoning to theological conclusions.

This new understanding of how to interpret scripture allowed theology to develop with new freedom. It also produced new commentaries that concentrated on the meaning the human author intended to convey. Unfortunately, although Thomas' commentaries on scripture were often very insightful, these positive results were sometimes obscured by the tendency to divide everything into parts and put them into categories: in places Thomas' commentaries look more like an outline of the text and dictionary of its terms than a commentary on it. Moreover, the spiritual senses that Thomas still attached to "people, things, and events" often looked suspiciously like holdovers from earlier interpreters.

VIII. Poetry and Mysticism

Modern students, confronted with Thomas' relentlessly logical and systematic theology, may be surprised to learn that Thomas also wrote poetry: the hymns for the celebration of *Corpus Christi* (a major Christian feast day). The translation by Gerard Manley Hopkins of the hymn "Adoro te devote, latens deitas" catches the union of theological insight and devotional depth. Here are stanzas one, two, and seven:

> Godhead, I adore thee fast in hiding; thou
> God in these bare shapes, poor shadows,
>   darkling now.
> See, Lord, at thy service low lies here a heart
> Lost, all lost in wonder at the God thou art.
>
> Seeing, touching, tasting are in thee deceived;
> How says trusty hearing? That shall be believed:
> What God's Son has told me, take for truth I do;
> Truth himself speaks truly or there's nothing true.
>
> Jesu whom I look at veilèd here below,
> I beseech thee send me what I thirst for so,
> Some day to gaze on thee face to face in light
> And be blest for ever with thy glory's sight.

Thomas' poetry and his theology were nourished by a deep and continuing experience of prayer. There is even evidence that he had periodic mystical experiences of conversations with certain of the saints over one or another aspect of his writing. This aspect of Thomas' scholarship reflects the Catholic teaching about the "communion of saints." Part of this teaching involves the idea that the dividing lines between this life and the next are not absolute, and that those on each side continue to care about their brothers and sisters on the other.

In one particular vision, as Thomas finished one section of what is today the "Third Part" of the Summa—specifically the part about Jesus Christ—an icon (painting) of Christ spoke to Thomas and said, "You have written well of me, Thomas. What would you like in return?" Thomas answered, "*Non aliam nisi Te*" (nothing but you). Near the end of his life Thomas had a vision of God so powerful that he quit writing altogether, although his assistants urged him to complete the *Summa*.

Thomas responded to their request, "After what I have seen, all that I have written seems to me like so much straw."

Shortly after his final vision, Thomas Aquinas died. Thomas was canonized as a saint in 1323, and in 1567 he was proclaimed a **Doctor of the Church**, an honor reserved for those whose teaching and scholarship have reflected Catholic Christian beliefs and have been important in the lives and faith of others. The church, by declaring him a saint, expresses its conviction that he received from God what he had seen in vision: he received that reality which made all his writing seem in comparison like "so much straw," the "what I thirst for so" of his hymn, the "nothing but you" that he had asked for earlier and had briefly glimpsed in his final vision.

Key Terms:

Thomas Aquinas
Aristotle
Avicenna
Averroes
Moses Maimonides
Peter Abelard
university

Dominicans
quodlibetal debates
scholasticism
article
Summa Theologiae
disputed question

Questions for Reading:

1. What positive factors contributed to 13th century scholarship?

2. What four streams of new ideas influenced medieval European scholarship?

3. What challenge faced European scholarship in the presence of this new knowledge? What did European scholars try to do in the face of this challenge?

4. What were the main activities of masters or professors in the medieval university?

5. Give an overview of the main features and major events in the life of Thomas Aquinas.

6. List and explain some of the main points of Thomas' theology. In particular:
   a. Explain the "natural" and "supernatural" orders. How can we come to understand and respond to the supernatural order?
   b. How do the "natural" and "supernatural" orders relate to each other? Can "faith" and "reason" contradict each other?

7. What two main tasks did the Dominican order, of which Thomas was a member, undertake? How do those tasks relate to the *Summa Theologiae*?

8. Explain the structure of an article in the *Summa Theologiae*.

9. What did Thomas contribute to biblical studies? What does he mean by the "literal sense" of a biblical passage? By the "spiritual sense"? Which can be used as a starting point for arguing to a theological conclusion?

Works Consulted/Recommended Reading:

Chenu, M. D. *Toward Understanding St. Thomas*. Trans. A. M. Landry and D. Hughes. Chicago: Regnery, 1964.

Davies, Brian. *The Thought of Thomas Aquinas*. Oxford: Oxford University Press, 1992.

McGonigle, Thomas D. and Quigley, James F. *A History of the Christian Tradition: From Its Jewish Origins to the Reformation*. New York: Paulist Press, 1988.

Metzger, Bruce and Murphy, Roland, eds. *The New Oxford Annotated Bible with Apocrypha*, New Revised Standard Version. New York: Oxford University Press, 1991.

Pegis, Anton C., ed. *Introduction to St. Thomas Aquinas*. New York: The Modern Library, 1948.

Weisheipl, James A. *Friar Thomas d'Aquino: His Life, Thought and Works*. 2nd ed. Washington, DC: The Catholic University of America, 1983.

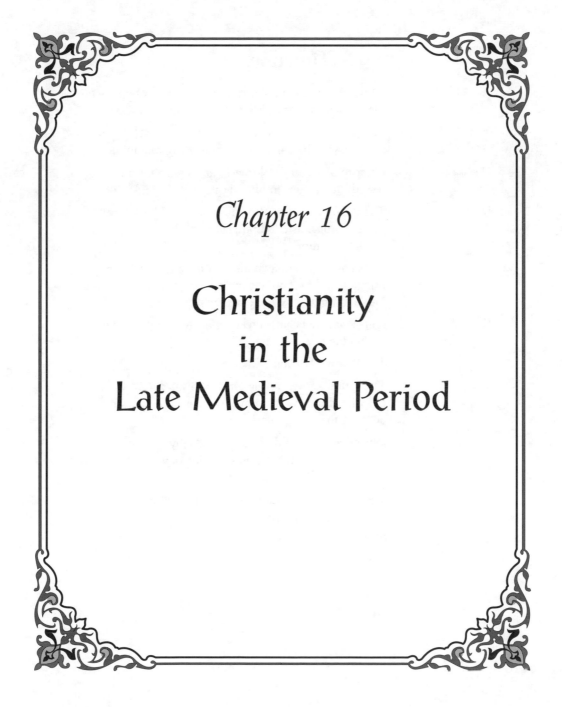

Chapter 16

Christianity
in the
Late Medieval Period

Timeline

1285-1347 AD	Lifespan of William of Ockham. William is famous for the nominalist principle known as Ockham's Razor.
1309-1377	The period known as the Avignon papacy when the pope moved the papal residence to Avignon, France.
c. 1342-1413	Lifespan of Julian of Norwich, an English mystic who records her visions in **Showings**.
1347-1351	The Bubonic plague, also known as the "Black Death," strikes Europe. Its effects are felt until the beginning of the 16th century.
c. 1347-1380	Lifespan of Catherine of Siena, a mystic who helped bring an end to the Avignon papacy, only to see it fall into the situation of the Great Schism.
c. 1375	John Wycliffe begins spreading his teachings of reform within the church.
1381	The Peasants' Revolt.
1378-1417	The period known as the Great Schism during which time the church would have two and sometimes three popes at the same time.
1414	John Hus is put to death as a heretic by the Council of Constance and the teachings of John Wycliffe are condemned.
1414-1417	The Council of Constance asserts the authority of conciliarism to end the Great Schism.
c. 1551	Catherine of Genoa writes her **Purgation and Purgatory**.

Christianity in the Late Medieval Period

The late medieval period (roughly 1300-1500) is seen often as a time of decline, disintegration, conflict and upheaval. Weather conditions in Europe were appalling, causing widespread drought and starvation. The Bubonic plague, or Black Death, was ravaging Europe, destroying nearly one-third of its population in some areas (1348-1350). The European economy was in shambles and its social institutions were crumbling, as well. The church hierarchy which people had come to depend on as a source of safety and security had now become a source of scandal. France and England were engaged in an extended conflict, a war that would come to be known as the Hundred Years' War (1337-1453). In spite of all these difficulties, this was also a time of great creativity which paved the way for later accomplishments in the Renaissance period.

The disintegration and the creativity of this period resulted in a number of very real challenges and opportunities for Christian faith and life. First, shifts in the intellectual climate of the late medieval period gave rise to nominalism, a development within scholasticism that would have a radical impact on theological inquiry. Second, there was the scandal of the Avignon papacy, the Great Schism, and the responses of reformers who sought to bring the church back to holiness. Third, the Black Death had a profound impact on the Christian imagination, specifically, its art and literature. Finally, the late medieval period saw the rise of mysticism, a spiritual phenomenon that provided people with direct experiences of humanity's deeply personal and intimate relationship with God.

I. Scholasticism and Nominalism

In the High Middle Ages, education was greatly influenced by the scholastic method. Its assumption was that truth was already available to the learner, whether in the writings of ancient authorities, in scripture, or in church teachings. One only needed to organize it properly, explain it clearly, and defend it appropriately. As a result, logic became an important part of the educational endeavor. Even in the area of medicine, students did no practical or laboratory work. Instead, they debated important texts in their field, and speculated about what conclusions they might draw from the texts. In the area of theology, the "Schoolmen" tried to take the truths uncovered by the philosophers and show how they were compatible with elements of Christian faith, which depended on divine revelation. They tried to show how reason could deepen one's understanding of what one believed on God's authority.

The impact of scholasticism on theology was profound, as we can see from Thomas Aquinas' *Summa Theologiae*. However, in the late medieval period, there was a gradual limiting of the subjects of speculation to those things that could be known through direct sensory experience. This development within scholasticism was called **nominalism**. It worked on the assumption that there was no common ground between the objects of rational knowledge and the objects of revealed knowledge. Knowledge of God was understood to be gained only through revelation. Therefore, one could not reason logically about God from one's experiences and say anything about God that was not already contained in revealed knowledge. Only particular, individual things were appropriate start-ing points for intellectual reflection. Thus, nominalism began the separation of philosophy from religious revelation. Faith and reason were no longer thought to belong together as earlier scholas-tics like Thomas Aquinas had assumed. God could be known only through revelation accepted in faith. God was understood to be absolutely free and sovereign. Therefore God's will was absolutely supreme. Humans ought to strive to know God's will. However, God's will could not be grasped by rational thinking. Rather, it is revealed in the promises and covenants of the scriptures, which had to be taken on trust.

The person most often associated with nominalism in the late medieval period is William of Ockham (c. 1285-1347). He argued that only individual things exist. Universal natures or essences such as "human nature" existed only as general concepts in the mind; they did not exist outside of the mind or in God. Universal or general terms like "human nature" were merely linguistic con-structions necessary for communication. A consequence of this view was that one could not know anything about God by reason. Aquinas had argued that we could understand something about the wisdom of God by using the analogy of human wisdom, or that we could know about the goodness of God by using the analogy of human goodness. God's wisdom or goodness was like human wis-dom or human goodness, but freed from every limitation and hence infinitely more perfect. For Ockham, on the other hand, "wisdom" and "goodness" were only concepts, not universal natures or qualities. Hence, according to Ockham, we can only know about God through revelation, accepted in faith, not through reason. Faith, not reason, is the basis for our relationship with God.

Philosophy, then, was about what could be deduced from our immediate experience, known through the five senses, and explained by logic. William upheld this idea with such rigor that it came to be called **Ockham's Razor**. The principle of Ockham's Razor states that our ideas about what we claim to know should be kept as simple as possible. The image of the razor cuts away useless ideas and explanations, accepting the simplest hypothesis that can explain the data. He was excommunicated by Pope John XXII in 1328 for his philosophical position and its suspected theological consequences. He responded by pointing out the pope's many heresies and his false claim to the papacy.

Some scholars suggest that nominalism was a particularly appropriate philosophy for this period because of its focus on the individual and its pessimism about one's ability to reason about God. It was an important movement because it would set the stage for several later developments. In particular, William of Ockham's nominalism, with its conviction that God could be known only through revelation, accepted by faith, would prepare the way for 16th century Reformation theology and its emphasis on justification by faith. Likewise, nominalism's concern about acquiring knowl-edge through the experience of particular occurrences would lay the foundation for the development of the natural sciences in the later 18th-century Age of Enlightenment.

II. The Avignon Papacy and the Great Schism

Throughout most of the middle ages, the Roman church was a dominant force for the preservation and development of the Western world. In the late medieval period, however, the church, or more accurately, the papacy, became a source of disunity and scandal. Once seen as the spiritual center of Europe, the role of Rome became increasingly confusing to the average Christian. Likewise, the pope, once seen as a bulwark of authority in both the religious and political spheres of influence, became little more than a pawn of the emerging nation-states.

A. The Avignon Papacy

The major crisis of the 14th century for the Western church was a scandal caused by the papacy. In 1309, the newly elected French Pope Clement V moved the papal court from Rome to Avignon in southeastern France. There were many circumstances that contributed to the move to Avignon. Rome had become a rather dangerous place to live, because of some disturbing political and religious fighting going on there, the consequence of a nasty fight between Clement's predecessor, Pope Boniface VIII (1294-1301), and the French king Philip. Philip may even have pressured Clement into the move, since this French archbishop had just recently been elected pope under Philip's influence. Some had suggested that the climate was more conducive to the health of the pope and his court. However, Clement himself, as pope, had the right to move the seat of the papacy anywhere he wished. This move, which appeared at first to be temporary, lasted well past Clement's lifetime, through six more popes, until 1377. This period would later be referred to derisively as "the Babylonian Captivity," taking its name from the original captivity of Jews in Babylon in the 6th century BC.

Since the reforms of Pope Gregory VII, the papacy had struggled to be free of secular control. In addition, the church centered in Rome had a particular status, because of the authority of tradition, of St. Peter, and the apostolic succession. By contrast, the papacy at Avignon was obviously under French influence, if not under France's complete control. This disturbed both the allies and enemies of France. It was feared that, with the "captivity" of the pope, the French could control all of European affairs from Avignon. To make matters worse, the pope lived richly in Avignon, and the luxuries of the papal court were paid for in part by shameful practices contrary to Christian faith and church law. These practices included the buying and selling of church offices (simony), the buying of **indulgences** (a pardon for punishment due as a result of a person's sin) to support the financial obligations of the Avignon papacy, **nepotism** (making exceptions to church laws for the advancement of one's relatives), and other unsuitable practices.

The problems of the Avignon papacy were made worse by the emergence of nation-states. While the late middle ages still had a feudal social structure, national identities and interests were beginning to develop, supported by developments in particular languages, a rising merchant class, and the acceleration of trade. The pope was supposed to be identified with the universality of the church and the Christian faith. Instead, with the Avignon papacy, the people had a pope seemingly under the control of one nation and one king. This would inevitably lead to a weakening of the authority and power of the papacy. These seeds of doubt about the pope's role as a temporal and then as a spiritual leader also eventually poisoned Christian thinking about the meaning and importance of a universal church.

B. The Great Schism

By the middle of the 14th century there was growing pressure from different circles for the pope to return to Rome. However, the Avignon controversy would not be settled quickly or easily. Pope Gregory XI moved the papal court back to Rome in 1377, only to die the following year. When the new pope, Urban VI, announced that he planned a reform of the curia (college of cardinals), a large faction of cardinals, most of them French, protested by calling for a return of the papacy to Avignon. Only a few months later, another group of protesting cardinals gathered to elect another pope, Clement VII. Urban VI stayed in Rome, and the other pope, Clement VII, returned to Avignon. This era in the history of the papacy is known as the "**Great Schism**." For a period of thirty-nine years the church would have two, and sometimes three reigning popes at the same time.

The problem of identifying the legitimate pope during the Great Schism became, in the end, a contest between the emerging nation-states and city-states of Europe for ultimate control of the papacy and the power thought to go with it. France and its allies (Scotland, Navarre, Castile, Naples) sided with the pope in Avignon, calling the pope in Rome the anti-pope. England and its allies (Scandinavia, northern Italy, Ireland, Portugal) declared for the pope in Rome, calling the pope in Avignon the anti-pope. Of course, it is also important to stress that not every nation or individual addressed the question along political lines. Many declared for one pope or the other because they authentically believed, on theological grounds, that the pope they supported was the proper successor of St. Peter.

After scandalizing the Christian world and being condemned by holy persons and saints, the schism was finally healed by a series of councils held in the early 15th century. The Council of Pisa (1409) elected a new pope, presumably to replace the two currently reigning popes, but certain factions refused to consider Pisa a valid council. Therefore, for a period six years, there were actually *three* popes. Finally, the Council of Constance (1414-1417) asserted the authority of conciliarism and deposed all three popes, choosing a rightful successor to replace them, namely, Martin V (reigned 1417-1431). According to the principle of **conciliarism**, the bishops of the church, in time of crisis and when gathered together in an official council, had a right to make binding decisions independent of the pope. Conciliarists held that the church consisted of the whole people of God. The pope was its head, but only one part of the church. In contrast, according to the the Council of Constance, a general council was a "lawful assembly which represented the universal church and had its power directly from Christ." Everyone, including the pope, must be obedient to this authority.

Thus the Council of Constance ended the schism, despite the fact that the council was never recognized as a legitimate council. The Council of Basel (1431-1449) also appealed to the principle of conciliarism in resolving some questions of church doctrine involving the Hussites of Bohemia (later known as the Czech Republic), and in attempting to further restrict some of powers of the pope. The council failed finally in 1449, after Pope Eugenius IV managed to regain some of the papacy's power and succeeded in briefly reuniting Western and Eastern Christianity at the Council of Florence in 1438.

A decade later, in 1460, Pope Pius II condemned conciliarism. However, considerable damage had been done to the authority of the papacy by this time. For more than a century the papacy had been mainly a divisive force, both politically and religiously. Instead of the steady reliance on Rome as the center of Christendom and on the faith passed on through the successors of St. Peter, there was rivalry, mutual accusation, and pettiness. The church would no longer be seen as a universal symbol that could overcome the boundaries of class and nation, of feudal obligation and responsibility. The movement toward national and territorial churches would not be stopped.

III. The "Black Death" and the Christian Imagination

It seemed to the population of Europe that the world was finally about to come to an end in 1347-51. Traveling from the Middle East, ships returning to Europe carried rats and fleas which spread two virulent forms of Bubonic plague: one spread by contact with the blood of its victims, the other by respiration as a form of pneumonia. We must bear in mind as the story unfolds that the ancient and medieval worlds were accustomed to periodic ravages by famine, plague, and illness. However, they had never experienced anything quite like this plague. It caused widespread panic and a belief that perhaps the biblical plagues of the scriptural book of Revelation had come upon them all.

Bubonic plague, which still exists in small pockets today, was especially devastating to late medieval Europe for a variety of reasons. One was the speed with which it killed. While the first form of plague could take up to five days for the victim to die, the second spread so quickly that the healthy could become ill and die in a night. Another was the horror of the disease itself. It was familiarly known as the "Black Death," because black growths and pustules appeared on the victim's body. These would burst, and gradually the entire body would swell, discolor and decay. Yet another reason for its devastation was the mystery of its transmission. Although doctors of the time did not know how many diseases were transmitted, they usually learned by process of elimination how to protect others from their spread. The fact that the plague was spread in two forms by two hosts made it virtually impossible to see how it was being transmitted, and, since both fleas and rats were a fact of life in the medieval world, they were not suspected. Perhaps the greatest consequence of the lack of knowledge about transmission was the havoc that Bubonic plague caused socially and culturally by seemingly striking at random. This pestilence, or "the pest" as it was called, knew and respected none of the trappings of wealth, influence, or status. It killed rich and poor, in cities and in the countryside, sinners and holy people. It simply did not discriminate.

Perhaps the greatest effects of the plague were on the Christian imagination. Panic increased as the disease spread and as others abandoned the suffering victims. Many could not receive the last rites (the sacrament of anointing of the sick), because a priest was not available or because one would not come. Special dispensations were given for lay persons to hear the last confessions of the dying to reassure them that God would not forget them but forgive them at the end. A new kind of religious piety (devotional practice) also began to emerge. Some Christians chose to identify with the suffering of victims and families by increasingly meditating on the sufferings of the crucified Christ. Processions of flagellants (people who beat themselves as an act of penance) began to appear in the streets, praying for God's intervention in ending the plague. Some Christians made the Jews the scapegoats for the plague, and in some cities pogroms (organized massacres) erupted against them.

The Black Death produced several indelible artistic images that reflect the sentiments of the times. The first is a gruesome representation of death as a grinning skeleton holding the traditional scythe (a tool for gathering in the harvest), hovering over the dead and decaying, and showing the healthy and prosperous where their futures lie. The second is the bloody portrayal of Christ on the cross, with discolored flesh and weeping wounds. These artistic representations of Christ's crucifixion were meant to warn people that this world was a passing one. However, they also gave hope to Christians, because they believed that, by Christ's redemptive death on the cross, better things awaited those who experienced great suffering as Christ had suffered. The third artistic representation that was typical of this time was the figure of the **pieta**, in which Mary mourns over her crucified son. It encouraged Christians to identify their suffering and death with that of Christ, and to wonder at the amazing love of God present even in life's most difficult moments.

While many Christians fled from the infected (contemporaries observed that "charity was dead"), others helped the ill and dying, ministering to them despite the great risk to themselves. Many were

Figure 16.1: The Crucifixion, from the Isenheim Alterpiece by Matthais Grüenwald (1510-1515).

Figure 16.2 A pieta from Germany c. 1300. The crucified Christ in the arms of his mother.

clergy and religious; others were devout lay persons. Among them were two saints named Catherine: Catherine of Siena, who will be discussed in a later section of this chapter, and Catherine of Genoa. Despite the fact that Catherine of Genoa lived after the worst period of plague, she remained amid the plague victims and people suffering from other diseases, establishing a hospital for all the needy. She was later joined by her husband, both of them pledging their lives to chastity and to the service of the poor. Her most lyrical and important work is the *Purgation and Purgatory*, which speaks of the cleansing given to us by God, a cleansing which will leave us shining brightly, as gold is refined in the fire. Her attitude is characteristic of many devout Christians of the late medieval period who decided that, in solidarity with those who suffer, they were made to be like Christ in the world, working and caring for others through God's strengthening spirit.

In this selection from her works, Catherine describes the process of God loving and cleansing the souls here and in purgatory:

> Not that those souls dwell on their suffering;
> they dwell rather on the resistance they feel in themselves
> against the will of God,
> against His intense and pure love bent on nothing
> but drawing them up to him.
> and I see rays of lightning
> darting from that divine love to the creature,
> so intense and fiery as to annihilate not the body alone,
> but, were it possible, the soul.
> These rays purify and then annihilate.
> The soul becomes like gold that becomes purer as it is fired,
> all dross being cast out
>
> (Catherine of Genoa, 79).

The importance of the Black Death cannot be underestimated. Its toll was devastating not only in the depletion of Europe's population, but also in the loss of a sense of certainty, in the breakdown of social organization, and in radical changes in Christian attitudes and lifestyle. The enormous number of clergy and religious who died during the great pestilence left a vacuum which needed desperately to be filled. It was filled sometimes by uneducated and unlettered priests, ordained as quickly as possible so as to have the sacraments available once more to the populace. Some of those ordained were probably not morally suited to priesthood. Abuses were on the rise, whether from ignorance, misinformation, or deliberate callousness. Thus, preachers arose who rallied the people against the abuses of a corrupt church, suggesting it was these which brought God's wrath upon the people. We now turn to these figures and the religious and social unrest caused in large part by the plague.

IV. Revolts Against Church and State

As the legitimacy of the Avignon papacy weakened, the monarchies of France, England, and Germany attempted to put controls on the church's leadership and on its ability to raise taxes to support its projects. Opposition was not limited to the political arena, however. Lay religious movements were beginning to emerge as critics of church corruption and religious superstition. Two reformers of the late medieval period, John Wycliffe and Jan Hus, are often mentioned together and seen as forerunners of the Protestant Reformation. In reality, Wycliffe and Hus lived in different places at different times, and left legacies which are distinct from one another.

A. John Wycliffe

John Wycliffe (1330-1384) was a highly controversial figure in the late middle ages. He was well educated, and an ordained priest. Indeed, Wycliffe even had a patron and a steady church post in England. He was a man of quick temper and incisive thought. In the early phase of his preaching, Wycliffe appealed not only to Christians scandalized by the Avignon papacy, but also to advocates of English nationalism. He believed that the clergy ought to live a life of poverty, without ownership of property, somewhat like the mendicant orders, and therefore he began to preach against the wealth and power of the clergy and the Avignon papacy. He also believed that the English kings ought to have the right to appoint candidates to key church positions and to collect taxes in their own land. Both practices currently belonged to the authority of the pope, but Wycliffe saw them as sources of corruption in the church.

Wycliffe also challenged or denied several widely held church doctrines. For example, he held that it was not the "visible" church represented by the church of Rome that counted, but the "invisible" church of the saved. The trappings of the external church and its claims to be the "source" of salvation for Christians were both wrong and dangerous. Those whom God had predestined for salvation were chosen by God alone. He also taught that personal holiness ought to be the basis of religious authority in the church, not one's ecclesiastical rank or ordination. Wycliffe also attacked the doctrine of transubstantiation and the notion of the real presence of Christ in the Eucharist. If the bread and wine became in substance Christ's body and blood, then bread and wine must be *destroyed* in order to become Christ's body and blood. This destruction seemed to Wycliffe to have no place in the image of the loving God who had created universal realities in the first place. He called his doctrine one of "remaining." Christ was present in the Eucharist in a spiritual way, but the bread remained bread.

Wycliffe advocated a translation of the Bible into English. In fact, two translations were made under his commission around 1380-81, although neither was completed. He also wanted to found a group of poor followers who would preach as he did and represent a contrast to the corrupt clergy and religious orders. His ideal of a group of the poor eventually materialized in a group known as the **Lollards,** who implemented his ideas in a more radical way than Wycliffe probably intended. They were preachers, but much more active politically than Wycliffe himself. They advocated clerical poverty and confiscation of church property. They also distributed vernacular translations (in the language of the people) of the Bible and preached a return to the simple scripture-based Christianity of the early church. Whether or not Wycliffe was actually involved in the founding of the Lollard movement in England is a matter of dispute. However, they certainly spread his ideas and kept his legacy alive. They were active in several social uprisings, and as a result many were put to death.

B. Jan Hus

Jan Hus (1372-1415) was born in Bohemia (later known as the Czech Republic) shortly before the death of John Wycliffe. Like Wycliffe, he was well-educated, and an ordained priest. The figure of Wycliffe was to be a powerful one in his life, because they shared a number of common concerns about church reform. In fact, many of his teachings were taken directly from the writings of Wycliffe. For example, Hus accepted Wycliffe's teaching about the authority of scripture as the source of doctrine. However, he did not accept Wycliffe's doctrine of "remaining" in the Eucharist. What prompted him to begin preaching reform was the Great Schism. Appalled by the Schism, yet part of it (since Bohemia held for one of the anti-popes), he refused to support any of the various popes' actions. He was completely scandalized by the intention of one of the anti-popes to send a crusading force against Christians in Naples for political reasons. He railed against this move and against the corrupt practice of selling indulgences. This put him in jeopardy with the king of Bohemia, who profited from these practices. He preached widely in Czech and wrote on the Ten Commandments and the Lord's Prayer. His most important work was *De ecclesia* (On the Church). In it, he described the church as "the body of Christ," with Christ as its only head.

Hus was finally ordered to the Council of Constance (1414-1417) by the pope. The king of Bohemia, who had been protecting Hus against his opponents, released him under safe conduct to attend. Although Hus denied the allegations brought against him, especially concerning the Eucharist, the council did not believe him. They claimed that, like Wycliffe, Hus taught the doctrine of "remaining." When asked to recant (take back his radical beliefs), he protested that he could not take back what he never had believed in the first place. In the end, the council decided that Hus was a dangerous heretic, spreading the ideas of Wycliffe. He was stripped of his priesthood, condemned, and turned over to the secular authorities who put him to death. Unlike Wycliffe, he left no immediate followers. His execution muted the protests of others who might have shared his ideas, at least in Bohemia and among its close neighbors. However, his death eventually resulted in the establishment of a Czech national church known as the Hussites a century before the Reformation.

C. The Peasants' Revolt

Although the Peasants' Revolt of 1381 was confined to England, it is a powerful symbol of the social and political unrest engendered by the plague. In large part, the revolt was caused by the farm labor shortage resulting from the plague. The shortage was made even worse by the fact that peasants who had been farmers were leaving the farms for more interesting jobs as artisans. The large landowners were not pleased about their loss of income, and the higher wages they had to pay the workers who remained in farming. In order to recoup their losses and stop the flow of peasants off the land, the landowners shifted to wool production and other more profitable, less labor-intensive crops. They also managed to get extremely repressive legislation passed to keep peasants on their farms. They froze farm wages at very low levels and exacted very high taxes from the peasants.

The Peasants' Revolt came about because of the mistreatment and overworking and overtaxing of the peasantry. The preaching of the Lollards also inflamed an increasingly discontented populace. While the unrest in England proved serious, it did not threaten the social fabric for long. Within a year the revolt was extinguished with deadly force. Yet, this revolt and others like it would mark the beginning of the end of a workable feudal economy.

V. Mysticism in the Late Middle Ages

Although mysticism had been part of Christianity from its beginnings, it burst forth again with particular force in the 14th century. **Mysticism** is a particular spiritual phenomenon, which expresses itself in direct, intense experiences of union and oneness with God. The mystical "journey" at its simplest, consisted of three phases: **purgation** (cleansing from sin), **illumination** (an attraction to all the things of God, especially scripture and the divine office, the official prayer of the church), and finally **union** (the state of oneness with God). The experience of union might have been momentary, but it had lasting effects on the person, leaving them with an assurance of God's constant presence. Perhaps the reason that mysticism flourished in the 14th century was that the passionate and prophetic character of the mystic was sorely needed in a time when the church and the Christian people were wondering if they had indeed been abandoned by God, or if they were victims of God's wrath. In these troubled times, when the world seemed to be falling to pieces, people needed the guidance of the mystics.

Although mystics throughout the ages share certain characteristics in common, they also differ from one another. Some mystics were primarily **visionaries**, whose union with God produced visions which taught them about faith and often called them to prophecy or to service. Others were so overcome by the presence of God that they would experience **ecstasies** (from *ex-stasis*, standing outside). While in ecstasy, they experienced supernatural phenomena of various sorts: raptures, trances, various types of transformation (levitation, changes in appearance, miraculous events). Still others did not see visions or have raptures, but felt drawn closer to God in an experience of the "divine darkness" where they realized the full extent of how little God can be understood or perceived. Yet, whatever the differences in their experiences of God, mystics maintained that the most important quality of their extraordinary gifts was the love and union with God that these experiences brought about.

The church in general has always been somewhat suspicious of mysticism for a variety of reasons. Some persons claimed to have revelations from God, but did not. These people simply used the claim for their own purposes (e.g., status, recognition, or special favors). Another factor that influenced the church's reluctance to endorse mystical experiences was the number of women who had such experiences. Their claims of authority from God were a threat to the medieval understanding of woman's traditional role. In fact, mystics came from all social classes and levels of education, from many walks of life (they were not always clergy or religious), and from the ranks of both men and women. Some, whether their mystical experiences were genuine or not, held strange or possibly heretical ideas about God, Christ, or salvation. Mystics were usually judged during and after their lifetimes by their fidelity to the doctrines of the church, their accurate expression of Christian faith, their service to others, and their conformity to some known pattern of mystical growth.

In looking at Catherine of Siena and Julian of Norwich, two important mystics of the 14th century, and in referring back to Catherine of Genoa (discussed above) we can see the similarities and the differences of mystical experience in its immediacy, and in the way it inspired those who experienced God in this way to participate in the world and to act on its behalf.

A. Catherine of Siena

Born Caterina Benincasa, Catherine of Siena (c. 1347-1380) was the daughter of a large family of lower rank in Siena. From an early age, she saw herself as dedicated to Christ alone. Her opposition to marriage infuriated her parents, who confined her to their home where she decided to serve them lovingly. Her parents reluctantly accepted her choice when Catherine began having powerful prayer experiences, visions and raptures. She continued to live at home, devoted to contemplation. Catherine's prayer life had led her into a vision of mystical marriage to Christ. Her visions often were of the nourishing and cleansing blood of the sacrifice of Christ on the cross. Her emphasis on the blood of Christ may be due both to her Eucharistic devotion and to the suffering caused by the presence of plague among the populace. Yet, she was destined for more than contemplation in her short lifetime. In 1363, she became a Dominican **tertiary** (member of the lay third order) dedicated to serving, and especially to feeding the poor. She would give up her own meals to feed others, convinced that she could live on the substance of the Eucharist alone. Many sought Catherine's help, advice, or counsel because of her closeness to God and her saintly reputation. Before long, she became a local celebrity of sorts.

Living during the time of the Avignon controversy, Catherine criticized and implored the church to heal itself of scandal and abuse. She wrote letters to influential church figures all over Europe, including the popes, calling them back to the ways of God and God's church. It was her greatest desire to see an end to the captivity of the papacy in Avignon, and she lived long enough to help bring it about, only to see it fall into the situation of the Great Schism. Catherine also wrote of her experiences of God, not as autobiography but as a way to inspire other Christians to be faithful to the church despite its abuses. Her most famous work is the *Dialogue*. God is speaking in this excerpt:

> So the memory, all imperfect past, is filled at this breast
> because it has remembered and held
> without itself my blessings. Understanding receives the light.
> Gazing into the memory,
> it comes to know the truth and shedding the blindness of selfish
> love, it remains in the
> sunlight of Christ crucified in whom it knows both God and
> humanity. Beyond this knowledge,
> because of the union [with me] that she has realized, the soul
> rises to a light
> acquired not by nature nor by her own practice of virtue but by
> the grace of my gentle Truth
> who does not scorn any eager longing or labors offered to me
>
> (*The Dialogue*, 178-179).

Because of her deep spirituality, her thoughtful theology, and her devotion to the church, despite its problems, Catherine was declared a saint in 1461. Later, in the 20th century, she was proclaimed a **Doctor of the Church**, an honor reserved for those whose teaching and scholarship have reflected Catholic Christian beliefs and been important in the lives and faith of others.

B. Julian of Norwich

We know very little about Julian of Norwich (c. 1342-after 1413), except from her own writings and from the writings of Margery Kempe, a contemporary. Like Catherine, Julian had mystical experiences. Unlike Catherine, her mystical experiences were limited to one overwhelming set of visions, during a brief period of illness. She spent the remainder of her life contemplating and interpreting these visions (*shewings* or *showings*) to achieve a greater theological understanding of their meaning. Her mystical experiences are recorded in both a *Short Text* and a *Long Text*. One hypothesis, generally accepted, is that the short text was written immediately after her experiences, and the long text provides the reflection, thought, prayer, and theological explanation of the original visions.

We do not know whether or not Julian had already chosen her vocation at the time of her "showings," but we do know that before or shortly after she chose to live the life of an **anchoress** (a recluse who lived in solitude). Anchorites, male or female, were common in this period. They pledged to spend their entire lives in prayer and contemplation, and when they entered the anchorhold (their rooms attached to a church), they were enclosed as if they were being buried. The symbolism was dying to the world outside and devoting one's life to God in silence and prayer. When enclosed, they took on the name of the church to which they were related. Thus, we do not know Julian's birth name or history. Julian was the anchoress of the church of St. Julian at Norwich, England. Julian would have had one or two rooms in which to live, she would have had a single servant who took care of the tasks in the outside world such as shopping for food, and she was permitted a pet for company. She would have had two windows: one looked into the church, so that she could hear the Mass said and participate in the Eucharist; the other looked out to a small room where those seeking her wisdom and advice could come during certain hours of the day. These hours were limited so as not to disturb prayer, but were considered essential as a way of being of service to God's people. In many ways, anchorites acted as the spiritual counselors of their time.

Although not entirely unique to her, Julian speaks in her *Showings* of the Motherhood of God, and the Motherhood of Christ. Her use of gender references are fluid, moving easily from masculine to feminine and back, when speaking of God. In this way, she both incorporates and transcends gender limitations when imaging God. Also in her visions, she is especially aware of the suffering Christ who redeems all. Her reflections on that mystical experience show that she spent her life dealing with the tumult of plague and disorder in Norwich. She speculates on the meaning of sin and struggles with the question of why God allows sin and evil to exist. Thus, her assertion that God says "all will be well" is not empty optimism, but thoughtful and prayerful conviction.

VI. Concluding Remarks

The combination of the problems of the papacy and the occurrence of the Black Death was devastating to people's beliefs about divine order in Christendom. Each alone would have produced major shifts in Christian thought and practice, and together they changed the landscape of the Christian imagination. This unrest led people to pay attention to charismatic figures who seemed to have answers, whether heretical preachers, orthodox mystics, or teachers and educators of the nominalist school. Later in the 15th century, the fall of Constantinople, the invention of the printing press, and the Spanish Reconquest, which drove the Muslims and Jews out of Spain, would lead to other new and dramatic changes. In the next chapter, we look at some of those dramatic changes in the movement that would come to be called "the Renaissance."

Key Terms:

nominalism

Avignon Papacy

Babylonian Captivity

Great Schism

simony

indulgences

nepotism

conciliarism

Black Death

pieta

John Wycliffe

transubstantiation

Jan Hus

mysticism

Catherine of Siena

tertiary

Doctor of the Church

Julian of Norwich

anchorite/anchoress

Questions for Reading:

1. Why do we speak of the 14th century as one of change and crisis?

2. What is nominalism? How does it differ from the scholasticism of the middle ages?

3. What is the "Babylonian Captivity?" Who was captive, where, and why? Why did the "Great Schism" first happen?

4. What was the "Black Death" and how did it come to Europe? What were the results? How did this plague get its name?

5. What was the impact of the Black Death on religious art and literature?

6. Who were John Wycliffe and Jan Hus? What were their concerns? What were the religious teachings that brought them into conflict with the authorities?

7. What exactly is mysticism and why was it considered an essential part of the spirituality of the late middle ages? What are the stages of mystical experience?

8. How does Julian of Norwich resemble Catherine in her mystical experience? How is she different?

Works Consulted/Recommended Reading:

Bynum, Caroline Walker. *Jesus as Mother*. Berkeley, CA: UCLA Press, 1982.

Catherine of Siena. *The Dialogue*. Trans. S. Noffke. New York: Paulist Press, 1980.

Catherine of Genoa. *Purgation and Purgatory & The Spiritual Dialogue*. Trans. S. Hughes. New York: Paulist Press, 1979.

Chadwick, Owen. *The Reformation*. Baltimore: Penguin, 1964.

Copelston, Frederick. *History of Philosophy*, vol. III. New York: Doubleday, 1963.

Egan, Harvey. *Christian Mysticism*. Collegeville, MN: Liturgical Press, 1992.

Huizinga, Johan. *The Waning of the Middle Ages*. New York: St. Martin's Press, 1985.

Jantzen, Grace. *Julian of Norwich, Mystic and Theologian*. London/New York: SPCK/Paulist Press, 1988.

Julian of Norwich. *Showings*. Eds. Colledge and Walsh. New York: Paulist Press, 1978.

Pelphrey, Brant. *Julian of Norwich: Christ our Mother*. Collegeville, MN: Liturgical Press, 1989.

Tuchman, Barbara. *A Distant Mirror: The Calamitous 14th Century*. New York: Ballantine, 1978.

Ullman, Walter. *The Short History of the Papacy in the Middle Ages*. London: Methuen, 1972.

Zeigler, Philip. *The Black Death*. New York: A. Knopf, 1969.

Part IV: The Modern Period

Western history has traditionally been divided into three periods: ancient, medieval, and modern. But there are problems with such a scheme. When, exactly, does the modern period begin? What are its characteristics? What makes it different from the medieval period? There is no universally accepted answer to these questions. In fact dividing history into periods is an artificial construct of historians. History itself, like an individual life, flows along from year to year without sharp breaks. Still, periodization is a useful device to organize the huge mass of historical information. In the same way, we find it convenient to divide an individual life into childhood, adolescence, maturity, and old age, though we know there are no sharp breaks between these episodes.

The modern period follows the medieval and is in many respects its opposite. Let us consider, first, the characteristics of the medieval period, then of the modern.

I. The Medieval Period

First, medieval social structure was strongly hierarchical. The late medieval French notion of the three estates of society was typical of late medieval social structure: the third or lower estate was made up of peasants, merchants, and tradesmen; the second estate was the clergy, the first estate was the nobility, made up of counts, dukes, princes, and headed by the king. This notion of hierarchy survived in France until the king and aristocracy were overthrown by the French revolution in 1789. In the medieval period, one's immediate loyalties were not to a state or nation, but to one's immediate feudal superior: a peasant was bound to his lord, that lord was bound to a higher vassal, and that vassal to a higher lord or the king. The church was also structured hierarchically, with laity subordinate to priests, priests subordinate to bishops, and bishops subordinate to the pope. Likewise, religious orders each had their own hierarchical chain, with each person subject to an immediate superior. Needless to say, women were in almost all cases subordinate to men.

The aim of this hierarchy was social unity. The idea was that if each person observed his or her place in the hierarchy, social order would be maintained. The medieval period was the last age in Western history which attempted to achieve a universal social unity, and this unity was built on the Christian religion. The goal was to produce a Christian society, identified by the term "Christendom," which was understood as an organic whole and included all members of society (except Jews, Muslims, and heretics), governed by the emperor and the pope.

Just as medieval people saw society as hierarchically structured, so they saw the cosmos and its inhabitants structured according to a great chain of being, stretching from simple, inanimate beings like rocks, through plants, animals, human beings, angels, and finally to God. Beings higher in the hierarchy were thought to have more life, consciousness, and freedom than lower beings. Humans were capable of sinking to the level of animals, or rising almost to the level of angels, depending on their participation in God's grace. Medieval people pictured the universe or cosmos with the earth at the center or lowest point, hell at the center of the earth, and the moon, planets, and stars circulating around the earth. Above the moon was the region of the planets, above that the region of the stars, each governed by its own angel, and above that the Empyrean, the region of God and heaven, where the Risen Christ and the blessed dwelt. Fellowship with God was seen as the end or goal of humanity and the angels. Generally, medieval thinkers like Aquinas were more interested in the place of creatures in this hierarchical scheme, and how creatures are directed to and return to God, than in individual creatures as such.

The most typical artistic expression of the medieval period was probably the cathedral. Cathedrals were vast towering buildings whose spires reached for the sky, symbolizing the medieval thrust towards the transcendent. Probably the greatest medieval theological work was Aquinas' *Summa Theologiae*, which analyzed the procession of all creatures from God and explained how they returned to God. The greatest work of medieval literature was Dante's *Divine Comedy*, an imaginative vision of Dante's descent into hell, ascent through purgatory and through paradise, to the vision of beatitude. In sum, the overriding medieval interest, as expressed in art, philosophy, and theology, was in the relation and the return of creatures to God.

II. The Modern Period

The modern period sharply contrasts with the medieval period, for its overriding interest is in exploring the secular world, human beings, and nature in *themselves*, rather than in their relation to God. Thus the modern attitude may be characterized as *secular* (non-religious), whereas the medieval attitude was more religious and transcendent. Six major movements characterize the modern period: globalization, pluralism, nationalism, individualism, democracy, and interest in nature, which led to the development of modern natural science, the dominant intellectual force of modernity. Let us consider these six in order.

Globalization and Pluralism: Medieval society was unaware of the enormous expanse of territory and the variety of races, languages, and religions which exist on the earth. Their principal experience of foreigners was of the Jews and the Muslims. But in 1492 Columbus discovered America, and in 1498 Vasco da Gama discovered a sea route around Africa to India. Within decades the West Indies and Americas were being colonized and missionaries were travelling to Asia. Suddenly the medieval church was confronted with whole new continents and races which had never heard of Christianity. This immense broadening of horizons is what scholars mean by "globalization"—the consciousness of living in a global world rather than just in one's immediate neighborhood, town, region, or country. Pluralism is the encounter with a diversity of non-Christian and foreign peoples, including civilizations like India and China which are much older than Christianity.

Nationalism: Characteristic of the early modern period was a development of national consciousness, national languages, and nation states. Nationalism, while incipient, was subdued in the middle ages, when the universal language of scholars and politics was Latin, and Christendom was (theoretically) united under one pope and one emperor. However, during the 15th and 16th centuries, modern nations began to develop. Thus in 1492 Ferdinand and Isabella joined their kingdoms to create modern Spain. In the early part of the 16th century, Henry VII and Henry VIII unified England into a national entity. Francis I and later kings did the same for France. During the 16th and 17th centuries, national languages began to replace Latin in religion (at least among Protestants), scholarship, and politics. Thus in 1521 Luther translated the New Testament into

German and thereby shaped the emerging German language. Shakespeare's plays and the King James translation of the Bible (1611) shaped the development of English. By the mid-16th century it was clear that the medieval ideal of one universal Christian empire sharing one language and consciousness was defunct.

Individualism: Medieval life was corporate. People thought of themselves not as individuals but as members of a social group, and the organic unity of society was strongly emphasized. But both the Renaissance and the Reformation stressed the importance of the individual. Renaissance art glorified individuals, usually noblemen; the individual portrait is virtually a creation of the Renaissance. The Reformation emphasized that persons are saved by their individual faith in Jesus Christ, more than by being members of the church. Before this time, medieval Catholics typically trusted in God's salvation because of their participation in the sacraments and membership in the church. Reformation Lutherans were confident of salvation because of their individual faith in Jesus as savior. Where medieval piety emphasized corporate and communal salvation, Reformation piety emphasized individual salvation.

Democracy: The Reformation and Renaissance emphasis on individualism led to more representative and democratic forms of government, in contrast to medieval hierarchical and monarchial models. Representative government began to develop in the free cities of Renaissance Italy and in other free European cities. Likewise, Reformation and Radical Reformation churches were organized in ways that were less hierarchical and more congregationally structured—individual congregations could elect their own ministers. This was the pattern of the Puritan churches of colonial New England, whose church government patterns influenced the development of American democracy. In most countries governments have become steadily less aristocratic and more democratic all through the modern period.

Nature and science: The new interest in individual things led to an interest in nature for its own sake. In the Renaissance, there was much interest in observing and drawing nature—landscape paintings appear for the first time since antiquity. Leonardo da Vinci and others dissected human corpses to study human anatomy. By the 17th century, this new interest in individual beings and in nature led to the development of modern science, the intellectual movement which has most shaped modern consciousness.

Each of these movements has continued to develop throughout the modern period. Each of them is more pronounced in the 20th century than in any previous century. Most of them have their roots, however, in the Renaissance and the Reformation. The Renaissance and the Reformation are the subjects of chapters 17-21. In turn, the Renaissance and the Reformation provide the context for the Enlightenment and its aftermath, more properly called the modern period. The issues and movements connected with the modern period will be treated in chapters 22-24.

Chapter 17

The Renaissance

Timeline

c. 1350 AD	Beginnings of the Renaissance movement.
c. 1450	The invention of moveable type makes modern printing possible.
1453	Constantinople falls to the Muslim Turks.
1461-1559	Feudal territories of France are consolidated into a single kingdom.
c. 1466-1536	Lifespan of Desiderus Erasmus. Erasmus' New Testament became the basis for many subsequent translations of the Bible into the vernacular.
1469	Ferdinand and Isabella unite their Spanish kingdoms in alliance.
1478	Ferdinand and Isabella persuade Pope Sixtus IV to set up an inquisition to investigate and punish heretics in Spain.
1485-1547	The Tudor kings, Henry VII and Henry VIII, strengthen and consolidate English monarchial powers.
1492	The Christian reconquest (**reconquista**) of Spain from the Moors. Columbus sets sail for the Americas. Jews are exiled from Spain.

The Renaissance

As the previous chapter indicated, the late medieval period was a time of chaos and suffering, affecting almost every aspect of peoples' lives. However, it was also an unprecedented time of growth and creativity. It was during this time that many of the characteristics which we associate with modernity began to appear. There was an expansion of trade, banking, and craft manufacturing, organized by a wealthy merchant class who patronized art and architecture. Under the rule of powerful kings and queens, the modern nation-states of France, Spain, and England gradually emerged. The invention of the printing press led to an enormous increase in the number of books available to people and an expansion of education. Navigators explored the coast of Africa, opened sea-routes to India and the East, and discovered the Americas.

During the late medieval period and into the early modern period, roughly 1350-1600, there was also a revival of interest in the Latin and Greek classics, a renewed interest in the natural world, in the individual person, in history and literature, and an astonishing burst of creativity in art and architecture. This cultural movement, this "rebirth" of learning and art is called the **Renaissance**. The word "renaissance" means rebirth; it began in Italy and subsequently spread to other European countries. Gradually it transformed the Christian European worldview from a medieval outlook, which emphasized community more than the individual, and the next life more than this life, to a more modern outlook, which emphasized the individual, the natural world, and the opportunities available to the human person in this life.

I. The Beginnings of the Renaissance Movement

Along with the rapid surge in population after the devastation of the Bubonic plague, there are a number of factors that set the stage for the cultural movement known as the Renaissance. These included the development of a new commerce that had its source in trade, the emergence of nation states, and the discovery of printing.

A. The New Commerce

From 900-1100 Europe's economy had been largely agricultural and its social structure was based on the principles of feudalism. Peasants worked on large estates owned by wealthy landlords, producing food and clothing for themselves and their lords. Trade was conducted largely by barter (exchange of goods using no money). Gradually during the 12th through 16th centuries, trade, towns, and a money economy began to increase. The merchants of Venice, Genoa, and Pisa (Italy) made fortunes shipping spices from the East to places like Flanders and England, and carrying back wool, cloth, and metal. In the 15th century, the Medici family of Florence (Italy) controlled an international banking system with outlets in eight European cities; their banks also sold wool, silk, and other merchandise. Some of their profits were paid to Florentine artists who beautified their city with buildings, sculptures, frescoes, and paintings. Over time, a wealthy urban business class emerged, a class which would eventually displace the landed aristocracy as the dominant class in society.

B. The Nation States

In theory, Christendom of the late medieval period was unified by the spiritual authority of the Catholic church and the political authority of the Holy Roman Emperor. In practice, Europe was a patchwork quilt of small kingdoms, principalities (territories ruled by princes), and duchies (territories ruled by dukes), with little centralized power. During the Renaissance, however, powerful kings and queens began to control larger regions, most notably Spain, France, and England. The feudal territories of France, originally governed by independent nobles, were consolidated into a single kingdom during the period from 1461 to 1559. Likewise, English monarchial power was strengthened and consolidated by the Tudor kings, Henry VII (1485-1509) and Henry VIII (1509-1547). The result of these consolidations was the emergence of national monarchies which were often at odds with the church. In 1534, Henry VIII declared himself head of the church in England, and thereby separated the Church of England from the Roman Catholic Church.

The situation in Spain was somewhat different from that of France and England. When Ferdinand of Castile and Isabella of Aragon married in 1469, they brought together two poorly ruled kingdoms and made of them an alliance with considerable political and economic power. Both Ferdinand and Isabella were Catholic, and together they set out to strengthen their borders and Christianize their domain. In 1492, after centuries of war between Spanish Christians and Spanish Muslims (Moors), Spain succeeded in capturing the last independent Muslim Spanish city, Grenada, in southern Spain, thus completing the 700 year reconquest (*Reconquista*) of Spain from the Moors. Finally, in 1502 Muslims who refused to convert to Christianity were forced to leave Grenada altogether.

Ferdinand and Isabella held firm control over the Spanish church, and in that way helped to ensure the unity of Spain. In 1478 Ferdinand and Isabella, persuaded Pope Sixtus IV to set up in Spain a legal body, called the *inquisition*, to investigate and punish heretics. This legal system, though nominally controlled by the church, was actually under the control of the Spanish crown. The inquisition was used to persecute and even kill those thought to be enemies of the state or the church—especially Spanish Jews who had converted to Christianity (usually under threat of force), and were suspected of secretly practicing Judaism. In 1492 Spanish Jews were forced into exile. On the very day that Columbus set sail from Seville, shiploads of dispossessed Sephardic Jews (i.e., Jews of Spanish descent) were leaving for ports in Egypt and Turkey.

C. Printing

The invention of moveable type and hence of modern printing was perfected in Mainz, Germany, about 1450. Before this time, books (known as manuscripts) were copied by hand. This was a very slow process. According to a contemporary observer, the invention of moveable type made it possible for one person to print as much in one day as many could copy in a year.

Printing led to two major changes. One was an enormous expansion in learning. Previously, books were so expensive that they were mostly owned by institutions such as universities or monasteries, or by noble families. Printing allowed the emerging middle class also to own books. It is estimated that 6,000,000 books were printed between 1450 and 1500, more than had been produced in the previous thousand years. Of course, this had consequences for theological history. Between

Plate 1: *The Crucifixion*, c. 1420-25, by Hubert and/or Jan van Eyck. The Metropolitan Museum of Art, Fletcher Fund, 1933.

This famous painting in the Metropolitan Museum of Art (New York City) depicts a traditional theme: the crucifixion of Jesus. This crucifixion scene is part of a pair of panels in the Ghent Altarpiece; the second panel depicts the last judgment (Matt 25:31-46). The artist(s) achieved a sense of perspective by gradually decreasing the intensity of colors and clarity of objects from the foreground to the background. The mountains and the city of Jerusalem are barely distinguishable as the background seems to fade in the distance. The casual observer might notice the overall sense of calm and peace conveyed by the painting. However, a closer look at the individual faces in the crowd reveals intense and violent emotion.

Plate 2: *The Adoration of the Shepherds*, 1476, by Hugo van der Goes. Center panel of the Portinari Altar piece. Uffizi, Florence, Italy.

This shows Mary, angels, and the shepherds adoring the infant Jesus (Luke 2:9-20). The flowers in the foreground symbolize Mary's purity. Realistic treatment of rustic scenes and people, made possible by oil paint, was to become characteristic of Northern European painting.

Plate 3: *St. Francis in the Desert*, c. 1485, by Giovanni Bellini. The Frick Collection, New York.

Here the Renaissance rediscovery of the beauty of landscape and nature is evident. The beauty of God, experienced by St. Francis, in mystical ecstasy, is mirrored in the landscape, radiant in its purity. The saint's sandals are in the hermitage behind him, and he stands barefoot before the holiness of God, as did Moses before the burning bush (Exod 3:5).

Plate 4: *Christ Delivering the Keys to Saint Peter,* 1482, by Pietro Perugino. Sistine Chapel, Vatican Palace, Vatican State.

This illustrates Matthew 16:19, in which Jesus says to Peter, "I will give you the keys of the kingdom of heaven." Popes had argued that this scriptural passage meant that Jesus has passed supreme apostolic authority to Peter, who had then passed the authority to the bishops of Rome. The scene is set in a Renaissance public square (piazza), and shows striking use of perspective; the tile lines converge to a central vanishing point.

Plate 5: *Annunciation,* c. 1490-95, by Lorenzo di Credi, Uffizi, Florence, Italy.

A beautiful rendering of a traditional theme: the angel's annunciation to Mary that she will bear a son who will be called "son of God" (Luke 1:26-38). The scenes below are from Genesis, showing Eve being born from Adam's side, the temptation by the serpent and the expulsion from Eden. Mary is here seen as the new Eve, who by her own obedience to God (see Luke 1:38) brings about reconciliation between God and humanity, even as Eve's disobedience brought about a divorce between God and humanity. Note the Renaissance architecture, the use of perspective, and the window opening out to nature—a favorite theme.

Plate 6: *The Last Supper,* c. 1495-98, by Leonardo da Vinci. Sta. Maria delle Grazie, Milan, Italy.

This badly damaged fresco in Milan shows Jesus at the last supper with his disciples. Note the use of perspective: the lines of the architecture converge on a vanishing point directly behind Jesus' head, while the light from the window functions as a natural halo. This fresco has become the archetype for thousands of pious imitations of the Last Supper scene, right down to our own time.

Plate 7: *Pieta,* c. 1500, by Michelangelo Buonarroti. St. Peter's Basilica, Vatican State.

This is one of the world's masterpieces of sculpture, completed by Michelangelo at age 24. Mary here holds the dead Jesus, resigned in her acceptance of God's will. Her face, too young for her age at this time of Jesus' death, was said by Michelangelo to express her purity. This is a very large sculpture (5'8" high), carved from one block of marble. It combines a medieval theme (Mary holding the dead Jesus), with a classical realistic treatment of the human body. In the judgment of Michelangelo's contemporary, the art historian Georgio Vasari, this sculpture, in its beauty and technical perfection, set a standard that would never be surpassed.

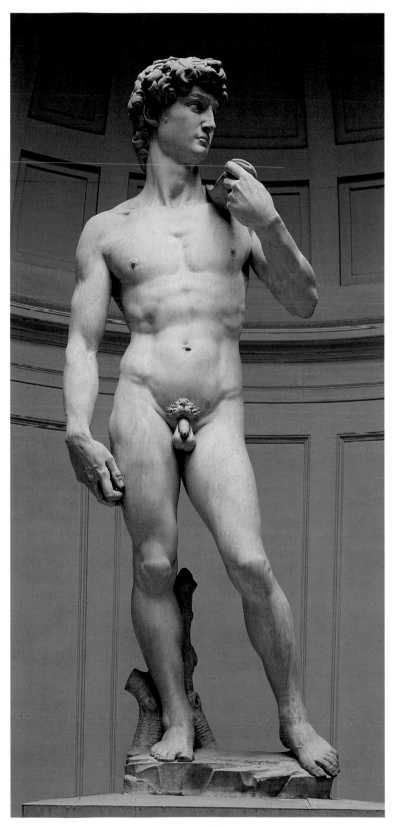

Plate 8: *David*, c. 1501-4, by Michelangelo Buonarroti. Frontal view. Accademia, Florence, Italy.

David is shown here in the style of Greek and Roman sculpture; one of the first free standing nude sculptures done since ancient times. Note the classical emphasis on the beauty of the human body, and on balance, proportion, and restraint. This gigantic statue (13' 8" high) was placed by the Florentines in their central piazza to symbolize their city's independence and resistance to tyranny. It is a portrait in marble on the Renaissance ideal: the self-sufficient man of action. Typical of the Renaissance, it combines a classical treatment with a biblical theme.

Plate 9: *Desiderius Erasmus*, c. 1523, by
Hans Holbein the Younger. The
Metropolitan Museum of Art, Robert
Lehman Collection, 1975.

An example of Renaissance por-
traiture, expressing their interest
in the individual, by a master
famous for the psychological
sensitivity of his portraits.

Plate 10: *Saint Peter's Basilica and
Piazza*, 1748, by Giovanni Battista
Piranesi. The Metropolitan Museum of
Art, Harris Brisbane Dick Fund, 1937.

This is a drawing of St. Peter's
basilica (largely designed by
Michelangelo) showing the huge
dome, piazza, and colonnade
(designed by Bernini, 1656). St.
Peter's basilica was until recently
the largest church in the world;
most churches would easily fit
inside it. It was erected on the
sight of old St. Peter's (a basilica
built by Constantine 324-25)
which in turn had been built over
the tomb of St. Peter, the apostle.
St. Peter's is the principal church
used by popes; from its front bal-
cony, the pope addresses crowds
assembled in the piazza. The
obelisk in the center had been
brought from Egypt by the Roman emperor Caligula in 41 AD.

1517 and 1520 about 300,000 copies of books and tracts by Martin Luther, who began the Protestant Reformation, were printed. This made the Reformation a mass movement, something that would have been impossible a century before.

A second change was that scholars could all work on identical printed texts, so that learning became a cooperative and cumulative endeavor, rather than an individual enterprise. Before printing, books that were copied by scribes each contained different errors and pagination, so that scholars could never be sure if they were working with an accurate text, or if they were working with the same text that other scholars were. Errors accumulated over the years, as they were passed on in successive copyings, so that by 1450 texts of the Bible (and other texts) contained many copyist's errors. Printing allowed scholars to begin to establish uniform, accurate texts, especially uniform texts of the Bible, which became more accurate with successive editions.

II. Renaissance Humanism

Renaissance **humanism** was an intellectual movement which sought to revive and teach Latin and Greek classics. It began in the cities of northern Italy, especially Florence, Rome, and Venice. Humanists sought out forgotten Latin texts in the libraries of old monasteries, studied Latin authors such as Cicero, and assimilated their values. The humanists also greatly expanded the study of Greek in the West. The interest in studying Greek was partly the result of an influx of Greek scholars from the Byzantine empire, who were fleeing from the advancing Muslim armies of the Ottoman Turks. In 1397 a Greek scholar came to Florence from Constantinople and began teaching Greek at the University in Florence. Later, after the fall of Constantinople to the Muslim Turks in 1453, many more Greek scholars fled to the West.

Greek studies were important especially because they allowed biblical scholars (such as Luther) to study the New Testament in its original Greek language, and hence to come closer to certain aspects of its original meaning. This was one of the driving forces behind the Reformation. However, the enthusiasm for Greek studies was not restricted to study of the Bible. It also led to the rediscovery of other elements of classical Greek knowledge and learning. When Plato's dialogues were translated into Latin in 1469, they became the basis for a recovery of a Christian neo-Platonic philosophy. Greek philosophy was widely influential during the Renaissance, but people were also interested in the recovery of Greek mathematics (especially Archimedes). The latter became crucial for the emergence of the scientific revolution in the 17th century.

It is hard today to imagine the excitement generated by Latin and Greek studies in the Renaissance. In 1488, when a visiting Italian humanist lectured on the second satire of Juvenal (a Roman poet) at the University of Salamanca, Spain, the throng of students was so thick that after two and one-half hours the lecturer had to be passed bodily over the heads of the audience in order to leave. A famous letter by the Florentine statesman, Niccolo Machiavelli, expresses a similar enchantment with the classics. Machiavelli had been exiled from Florence, and had been living at a country farm. His only companions during the day were uneducated country people, but in the evening he would read the the classics, and imagine himself conversing with the great writers of antiquity:

> *At the door I take off my muddy everyday clothes. I dress myself as though I were about to appear before a royal court as a Florentine envoy. Then decently attired I enter the antique courts of the great men of antiquity. They receive me with friendship; from them I derive the nourishment...for which I was born.... I talk with them and ask them the causes for their actions; and their humanity is so great they answer me. For four long and happy hours I lose*

myself in them. I forget all my troubles; I am not afraid of poverty or death. I transform myself entirely in their likeness (cited in Rice, 66).

Renaissance humanists were not the first ones to read classical authors. Works such as Virgil's epic poem, "The Aeneid," had been preserved in monasteries and read throughout the middle ages. However, the Renaissance brought a difference in interpretation and understanding. The earlier medievals read "The Aeneid" as though it were a Christian parable, with little sense of the difference between medieval and Roman culture. Similarly, medieval morality plays of Jesus' passion and death typically showed Jesus and his contemporaries as medieval people, not as ancient Jews. Renaissance humanists, on the other hand, were able to enter into the world of ancient Roman and Greek authors, recognize it as different, and absorb its values. In reappropriating ancient values while remaining Christian, they created a very different Christian culture from that of the middle ages. In particular, they forged a very different view of humanity and the world.

III. The Renaissance View of Humanity

Because the medieval world had been mostly rural and agricultural, people were very much aware of the communal nature of humanity. They were not much concerned about individuality or worldly accomplishment. As a result, we know the names of few medieval artists or architects. Medieval people tended to see life in this world as directed to eternity, therefore placing their hopes in the next life, rather than this life. It would make sense, then that the medieval period's most characteristic work of art was the cathedral, whose soaring spires and light-filled heights expressed the human desire for heaven and God. By contrast, the Renaissance strongly valued the individuality of the human person and emphasized individual accomplishment, fame, and glory (values which were Roman, but not medieval). Renaissance artists decorated their city squares with the statues of great men. Renaissance persons, as entrepreneurs, artists, soldiers, and explorers stressed human opportunities in this world. This attitude was summed up by the architect, Leon Battista Alberti, who proclaimed "Men can do anything with themselves if they will" (cited in *The Renaissance, Maker of Modern Man*, 19).

Humanists unashamedly placed humanity at the center of their world, and declared (following the ancient Greeks) that "Man was the measure of all things." Thus the typical work of Renaissance art was the individual portrait (a painting that seeks to create a realistic likeness of the person being portrayed), an art virtually unknown in the ancient world. The outlook of Renaissance writers, artists, and explorers was human-centered (**anthropocentric**), whereas that of the medieval period had been largely God-centered (**theocentric**). If the medieval ideal was the bishop, priest, pilgrim, or monk, the Renaissance ideal was the educated civic leader, soldier, nobleman, artist, or man of affairs, who could speak and reason eloquently, and serve the public good. Wealthy Renaissance merchants typically donated a large portion of their profits for art work to beautify the city.

In sum, the Renaissance ideal of humanity was more secular (non-religious), individualistic, and modern than the medieval ideal. To reconcile this more secular view of humanity with Christianity, Renaissance thinkers appealed to Genesis 1:26 ("And God said, 'Let us make humankind in our image, according to our likeness'") and Genesis 1:28 ("Have dominion over the fish of the sea and over the birds of the air and over every living thing that moves upon the earth"), thinking that God gave humanity a god-like status and authority over the earth (see Trinkaus, 344). As the image and likeness of God, persons were thought to be free, and endowed with an almost divine creativity. They believed that the possibilities of human persons were unlimited: they could sink to the level of the beasts, or become like an angel or a son of God, so great was their freedom.

IV. The Renaissance View of the World

The Renaissance was also marked by a new interest in and discovery of the natural world through art and the sciences. In art, the discovery of perspective (about 1420) brought about a revolutionary realism to painting, especially paintings of architecture. This realism also extended to paintings of the human body. The artist, Leonardo da Vinci, dissected over 30 cadavers, so as to discover from his own experience the structure of human anatomy. Landscape painting appeared shortly thereafter, a type of art that had disappeared during the middle ages. From the early 1500s, there developed an enthusiasm for cartography (mapmaking) all over Europe. In earlier medieval maps theology tended to dominate actual geography. For example, lands were shown radiating out from the center of the world at Jerusalem, the Holy City. In contrast, Renaissance maps were far more accurate, and reflected more realistically the world as it actually was. Thus geography became an independent science not subordinated to theology (Hale, 15-20).

Finally, the Renaissance coincided with the great age of exploration. Thus, the Renaissance movement's interest in and discovery of the natural world also involved travel to distant lands. Portuguese sailors explored the coast of Africa in the 1400s, and by 1498 they had sailed around the Cape of Good Hope to reach India. Columbus' "discovery" of the Americas opened up vast colonizing, commercial, and missionary possibilities. In earlier medieval times, although pilgrimages to holy places were common there had been relatively little interest in exploration for its own sake. For those people, the primary journey was vertical: the journey of the soul to God. However, the Renaissance, while still Christian, was far more interested in horizontal expansion, and in discovering the beauty, structure, and commercial opportunities of this world.

V. Humanist Education and Historical Criticism

The humanist ideal carried with it a new educational program as well, which was spread gradually over all of Europe. Humanists exalted human freedom and potential, and saw education as the way to develop that potential. In particular, they stressed a knowledge of literature and history, and the development of civic virtue, character, discipline, and eloquence. Their studies were centered on the *studia humanitatis* (humane studies) or liberal arts: Latin and Greek literature, history, and ethics. In studying Latin, students learned to read, write, reason, and speak well. These skills were especially necessary for civic leaders and scholars. The study of ethics taught the student duties to God, country, family, and oneself. The study of history taught ethics by example: in history one saw the concrete results of a life of virtue, or a life of vice, and learned noble examples on which one could pattern one's life. According to the Renaissance concept, these studies were liberal (from Latin, *libertas*, liberty) because they freed persons to develop their full human potential. The Renaissance educator Pietro Vergerio (1370-1444) wrote:

> We call those studies liberal which are worthy of a free man, those studies by which we attain and practice virtue and wisdom. That education which calls forth, trains, and develops those higher gifts of body and mind which ennoble men, and which are rightly judged to rank next in dignity to virtue alone (cited in Spitz, 157).

This education was mainly for nobility, but also for socially ambitious laymen (such as the sons of merchants), and, occasionally, for women. Isabella d'Este, a daughter of the ruling family of Ferrara (Italy), mastered Latin and some Greek, performed well on the lute, embroidered faultlessly, and could converse on equal terms with ambassadors (Plumb, 287). Proficiency in Latin was essential to the Renaissance experience, since it was the language of the church, diplomacy, scholarship, law, and medicine. However, humanist education also stressed training in virtue, physical excellence, and Christian religion. This notion of education remained the standard in Europe and America until the 20th century, where it is gradually being displaced by an emphasis on vocational and scientific training. Nonetheless, the ideal of a liberal education as necessary for the full development of human potential is still carried on in liberal arts schools, a legacy of the Renaissance.

The humanists, with their love of history and with more accurate printed texts, developed **historical criticism**, that is, the use of historical knowledge to evaluate existing traditions and institutions. An example of this is Lorenzo Valla's (1407-1457) efforts to expose the "Donation of Constantine" as a forgery. This document was allegedly a deed written by the emperor Constantine (c. 330), which granted the pope title to many of the imperial lands in Italy. These lands had since become the basis for the papal states. Valla, with his extensive knowledge of classical Latin, was able to show that the "Donation of Constantine" could not have been written in the 4th century, as claimed, because it used Latin words (such as the word used for the papal crown) which were not in use in the 4th century. Rather, he argued, it must have been written in the 8th century, and was therefore a forgery. This undercut the pope's claim to political authority in the papal states (though these states were not dissolved until the unification of Italy in 1870). This use of historical scholarship to criticize traditions, especially claims of the papacy and the church, was to become a major factor in the Reformation. Luther acknowledged Valla and John Wycliffe (1328-1384), author of the first English Bible, as important authorities in the area of historical criticism (Spitz, 168).

VI. Southern and Northern Renaissance

A distinction can be drawn between the Southern Renaissance, centered in Italy, and the Northern Renaissance, centered in northern Europe. The Southern Renaissance was primarily concerned with the recovery of Latin and Greek literature, art, and sculpture. In contrast, humanists of the Northern Renaissance used their knowledge of Greek and Latin to study the Bible and the church fathers in their original languages, and to urge a reform of the church based on the ideals of the Bible and the writers of the early church. The greatest of the northern humanists was **Desiderus Erasmus** (c. 1466-1536), a scholar learned in the writings of both the Latin and Greek early church writers, and the most famous writer of his age. In his *Handbook of the Christian Soldier*, Erasmus argued that true piety depends on the inner virtue of the spirit, rather than on conformity to external rites of the church. His popular satire, *In Praise of Folly*, lampooned the worldliness and vices of society and the church of his time. In 1516 he published a new edition of the Bible in Greek (the first since ancient times), accompanied by his own Latin translation. To arrive at the most accurate version, he had to compare many ancient Greek manuscripts of the New Testament. Erasmus' New Testament became the basis for many subsequent translations into the **vernacular** (language of the common people), including Luther's translation of the New Testament into German. Though he was later accused of undermining the institutional church by his satire and criticisms, Erasmus did not follow Luther in separating from the Roman church, but remained a devout yet critically minded Catholic.

VII. The Renaissance Popes

The popes of the Renaissance were humanists, patrons of art, and builders. Pope Nicholas V (1447-1455) collected over 5000 books to begin the Vatican library (one of the great libraries of the world). Julius II (1503-1513) commissioned art works from Michelangelo and Raphael, excavated the ruins of Rome to recover ancient statues, and began the rebuilding of St. Peter's Basilica, (which was continued under successive popes). In sum, the Renaissance popes rebuilt Rome, making it the center of the Italian Renaissance, and making the Vatican Museum one of the great art museums in the West. Unfortunately, they were less concerned about the spiritual reform of the universal church. For a century or more, earnest Catholics had been attempting to reform many abuses in the church: simony (the sale of religious objects and ecclesial offices), clerical worldliness and corruption, uneducated clergy and laity, absentee bishops, abuses of celibacy, the misuse of indulgences, and laxity in the practice of the faith. Instead of helping to address these concerns, the Renaissance popes were occupied with Italian affairs, and behaved more like Italian princes than shepherds of the universal church. For example, Julius II, the "warrior pope," donned armor and rode at the head of the papal troops in attacks on the Italian cities of Modena and Mirandola. As a result, though some individual churches and religious orders attempted reforms, the church as a whole was not reformed. When substantial reform did come, beginning in 1517 with Luther, it was met with papal opposition, not cooperation. This reform effort ended by fragmenting the church, a tragedy whose legacy is still with us today.

VIII. Renaissance Art

The Renaissance was one of the greatest periods of Christian and Western art. The discovery of perspective, of oil paints (by Flemish painters in the early 1400's), the rediscovery of portrait and landscape painting after almost a thousand years, and the return to classical and human-centered models of art and sculpture, all made Renaissance painting and sculpture brilliantly lifelike and realistic. Most Renaissance artists were Christians and therefore emphasized Christian themes in their art. However, unlike medieval artists, they also celebrated secular and pagan subjects, such as portraits of wealthy nobles or paintings of Greek or Roman gods. For more information, see Creighton Gilbert's *History of Renaissance Art* or the Metropolitan Museum of Art's *The Renaissance in the North*.

The color plates provide a glimpse of the magnificence of Renaissance art.

Key Terms:

Renaissance	theocentric
inquisition	*studia humanitatis*
humanism	historical criticism
anthropocentric	Desiderus Erasmus

Questions for Reading:

1. Discuss the factors that contributed to the birth of the Renaissance movement.
2. What was Renaissance humanism and why was it important?
3. Contrast the medieval and Renaissance view of humanity.
4. Contrast the medieval and Renaissance view of the world.
5. Explain the goal and practice of humanist education.
6. Why was the development of historical criticism important?
7. What were the strengths and weaknesses of the Renaissance popes?
8. What were the main characteristics of Renaissance art? Illustrate each of these by referring to one of the plates described in this chapter.

Works Consulted/Recommended Reading:

Gilbert, Creighton. *History of Renaissance Art.* Englewood Cliffs: Prentice Hall, 1973.

Hale, John. *The Civilization of Europe in the Renaissance.* New York: Atheneum, 1994.

National Geographic Society. *The Renaissance, Maker of Modern Man.* 1970.

Plumb, J. H. *The Italian Renaissance.* Boston: Houghton Mifflin, 1961, 1987.

Rice, Eugene F. Jr. *The Foundations of Early Modern Europe, 1460-1559.* New York: Norton, 1970.

Spitz, Lewis W. *The Renaissance and Reformation Movements.* Vol. I. Chicago, IL: Rand McNally College Publishing Company, 1971.

Trinkaus, Charles. *The Scope of Renaissance Humanism.* Ann Arbor, MI: University of Michigan Press, 1983.

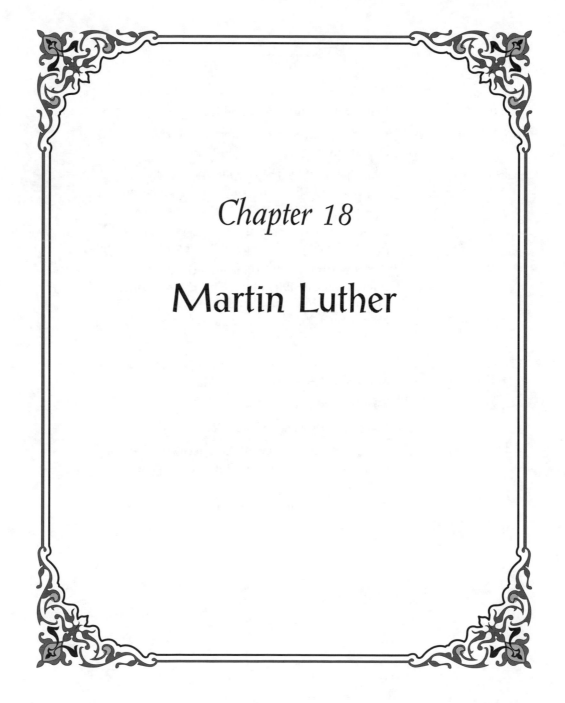

Chapter 18

Martin Luther

Timeline

1483 AD	Martin Luther is born in Eisleben, Germany.
1504-1505	Luther enters a monastery and is ordained a priest.
1512	Luther begins his career as professor of biblical studies at the University of Wittenberg.
1517	Luther posts his 95 Theses on the door of the Wittenberg Castle church calling for a debate on the issue of indulgences.
1519	Luther and John Eck debate at Leipzig and Luther publicly denies the authority of the pope.
1520	Luther writes several documents, including **On the Babylonian Captivity of the Church** and **Christian Liberty**, which summarize his theology and describe his call to reform.
1521	Luther is formally excommunicated by the pope.
1521	The Holy Roman Emperor, Charles V, issues the Edict of Worms, declaring Luther an outlaw.
1524-1525	The Peasants' Revolt.
1525	Luther marries Katherine von Bora.
1529	Six Lutheran princes protest the agreements made at the Second Diet of Speyer and thereby acquire the name "Protestant."
1530	The Augsburg Confession is signed.
1546	Luther dies in Eisleben, the place of his birth.

Martin Luther

hy are some Christians today known as Catholics and others identified as Protestants? To answer this question we need to look at the life of Martin Luther, a 16th century monk and university professor. Luther's life was shaped by his struggle with a central question: How are humans saved? He believed he found the answer to that question in his reading and study of the Bible. However, the answer to this question became explosive when it led him to criticize the theology and practices of the church.

The call for reform has been—and continues to be—a constant element in the history of the church. We have already seen the spirit of reform working in the medieval monastic communities and the friar movement. In the 16th century, however, efforts at reform led to the fragmentation of the Roman church and the establishment of the Lutheran church (among others). This was a consequence Luther himself had neither intended nor foreseen. Although Luther called for change and reform, he did not see himself as a religious innovator, introducing new ideas and practices into the Christian tradition. He understood his criticisms as an attempt to "re-form" the church in accordance with the beliefs and practices of the early church.

Who was this person? Why did he have such a powerful effect on the church and society at large? This chapter will focus on Martin Luther. The following chapters will examine other reform movements, both Catholic and Protestant, which occurred during and immediately following Luther's life.

I. Luther's Early Life

Luther was born on November 10, 1483 in the town of Eisleben, today located in northeastern Germany. At the time Luther was born, Germany did not yet exist and Eisleben was in Saxony, one of the many territorial states that formed the Holy Roman Empire. Luther's father, Hans, was from a family of peasants but he turned to the mining business and eventually owned his own mine shafts and copper smelters. Hans had high hopes for his son and was very pleased when Martin received his master's degree from the University of Erfurt. Hans assumed his son would now prepare for a career in law. However, Martin's plans suddenly and unexpectedly changed. Luther was returning to the University of Erfurt after a visit with his parents when he was caught in a violent thunderstorm. A bolt of lightning threw him to the ground and Luther cried out to the patron saint of miners: "Help me, St. Anne! I will become a monk!" A few weeks later, at the age of twenty-one, Luther entered an order of the Observant Augustinians.

This decision may not have been as sudden and unexpected as it appears. When Luther was caught in the thunderstorm, he was returning to the university from a leave of absence, taken just one month after beginning his law studies. He vowed to become a monk, a holy vocation that he believed would most nearly assure his salvation, at a significant crossroads in his life. When his father reacted with fury at his decision, Luther reminded him that he could do much more for his family with his prayers as a monk than he could ever do with his wealth and position as a lawyer. As with many others in his day and time, Luther had chosen the holiest life one could lead in order to secure salvation for himself and others.

Luther took his vow seriously, and appears to have been a very conscientious and dedicated monk. Only one year after entering the monastery Luther was ordained as a priest. Shortly thereafter the leader of his order, John von Staupitz, selected him for further education and a teaching career. Many years later, Luther declared, "If anyone could have gained heaven as a monk, then I would indeed have been among them" (WA 38,143). However, Luther's dedication to the holy life of a monk did not bring him the assurance of salvation he was seeking.

Some of Luther's doubts and questions can be traced to the **nominalist theology** he learned at the University of Erfurt. Nominalist theology saw salvation in terms of a contract between humans and God. If humans fulfilled their part of the contract by doing their best, then God would fulfill God's part by giving them grace. This was summed up in the phrase, "God will not refuse grace to those who do what is within them." Humans could not achieve salvation on their own, but if they did their best, God would graciously grant them the grace they needed to be saved. This understanding of salvation caused Luther incredible anguish and despair. He constantly wondered whether he had done his best. He saw himself as a poor, miserable sinner and God as a holy and righteous God. How could he ever do enough to earn the grace he needed to be saved?

The church offered grace and hope to sinners in the sacrament of Penance. As a monk, Luther confessed his sins daily but this did not bring him peace. Grace was offered in the sacrament, but had he done his best? Had he confessed all his sins? Was he truly sorry for his sins? Tormented by these questions, Luther came dangerously close to the unforgivable sin of despair. His confessor was finally driven to say, "God is not angry with you, but you are angry with God" (LW 54:15; WATr 1,47).

A. Justification By Grace Through Faith

Luther finally found peace with God through his study of the Bible. In 1512 Luther began his career as professor of biblical studies at the University of Wittenberg, a new school with only a few hundred students. His lectures during the next few years (on the Psalms, Romans, Galatians, and Hebrews) indicate that Luther experienced a gradual change in his understanding of God and God's relationship to humanity. This new view can be summed up in the phrase, *justification by grace through faith*. It may be helpful to look at each element of this phrase in detail.

Justification means "to be put right with God." This was Luther's central question: How can miserable, sinful humans "be put right with" a holy, righteous God? Years later, he said that he found the answer to that question through a new understanding of the *righteousness* of God. The "righteousness of God" originally terrified him because he understood it to refer to the holiness and perfection of God and he hated this righteous God who punishes unrighteous sinners. As he studied Paul's letter to the Romans, however, he came across the phrase, "The one who is righteous through faith will live" (Romans 1:17). Luther said that "righteousness" here does not refer to a quality that God possesses in order to judge people but to a gift God gives in order to save people. Luther later referred to this as **passive or alien righteousness** because it is *God's righteousness* (and not their own) which justifies people before God. Salvation does not depend on their own goodness or righteousness, but on God's righteousness, freely and lovingly given to sinners (LW 34:336-7; WA 54,185-6).

Justification is therefore *by grace*; it is a free gift from God. As sinners, humans do not deserve it and they can do absolutely nothing to earn it. Luther rejected nominalist theology with its call to "do what is within you," and he responded that justification is by grace *alone*. Humans do nothing to justify themselves before God. How, then, does God justify sinners? Through faith in Christ. Humans are saved by what God has done for them in Christ, not by what they do themselves. If people continue to bring their works before God, seeking to be saved by them, then they really do not have faith in what God has done for them in Christ. They need to depend completely and entirely on Christ, not on what they do.

Luther argued that even faith in Christ is not something people do. In other words, faith does not come because people try as hard as they can to believe. Luther described faith as a response to the Word of God, and that response is a gift from God. Luther understood the Word of God as preeminently Christ himself (John 1:1), but he also used this phrase to refer to preaching about Christ or to the Bible as a written testimony to Christ. However, Luther did *not* understand faith in Christ as assent to certain ideas or propositions about Jesus. It is much more than that. Thus, faith might be better translated as "trust," the willingness to risk anything and everything for Christ. For Luther, the central question was no longer, "Have I done what is within me?" Luther now asks: "Where do I place my ultimate faith and trust? In myself? Or in Christ?"

II. The Indulgence Controversy

Luther may have found the answer to his religious dilemma, but this does not explain how this brilliant but relatively obscure professor became a man known to popes and princes in his own day and acknowledged for his influence today, five hundred years later. His fame stems from his attack on the sale of indulgences, a practice associated with the sacrament of Penance. Penance was composed of several elements: **contrition** (sorrow for sin), confession of sin to a priest, **absolution** (forgiveness for the guilt associated with sin), and **works of satisfaction** (to remove the penalties or consequences of sin). These works might involve special prayers, fasting, pilgrimages, or giving alms (money) to the poor. They were called works of satisfaction because they were intended to provide satisfaction or compensation for sin. If these penalties were not paid in this life, then they would be in the next—in **purgatory**. Purgatory is a place or state following death in which sinners destined for heaven undergo the punishment still remaining for forgiven sins and thereby are "purged" or made ready for heaven.

According to the theology of the church, indulgences were only applied to the last stage in Penance, works of satisfaction. This meant that the sinner should still feel sorrow for sin, confess the sin, and receive forgiveness for the guilt associated with the sin. Indulgences released people from the penalties or works of satisfaction they still owed by drawing on the surplus good works of the saints and of Christ. These good works formed a **treasury of merit** under the control of the pope. When an indulgence was granted, the pope transferred these excess merits to the repentant sinner. Thus, for example, a sinner might receive an indulgence to offer prayers and alms instead of a pilgrimage as her work of satisfaction, and the merits of Christ and the saints would make up the deficiency.

Unfortunately, this practice of granting indulgences became vulnerable to abuse, especially as a means of raising funds. In 1517 Pope Leo X authorized Archbishop Albrecht of Mainz to sell a special indulgence throughout much of northern Germany. The proceeds for this indulgence were to be used to build St. Peter's Basilica in Rome and to pay the debts Albrecht had accumulated in acquiring the office of archbishop. In his instructions to the indulgence sellers, Albrecht claimed that the indulgences would remove guilt as well as punishment, persons already in purgatory could be released, and those who contributed money on their behalf need not be contrite or confessed.

A. The 95 Theses

Luther became involved in the issue of indulgences because a Dominican friar named Johann Tetzel was selling this special indulgence just across the border of Saxony and some of Luther's own parishioners were purchasing it. As a professor and priest, Luther decided to address this issue by calling for a discussion of indulgences in a public university debate. On October 31, 1517 Luther followed the usual practice for announcing public debates and posted his **95 Theses** on the door of the Wittenberg Castle church. These theses were written in Latin (the language of the educated class) and intended for an academic audience. The academic character of this debate changed when Luther's 95 Theses were translated into German (the language of the people) and rapidly disseminated by means of the printing press. Soon his 95 Theses were being discussed and debated by people throughout the Holy Roman Empire and beyond.

Why did the 95 Theses have such an impact? Luther clearly and powerfully expressed the reservations and questions that many others had regarding indulgences. He attacked the practice of selling indulgences on both theological and moral grounds, as indicated by the following examples:

> *Thesis 36. Any truly repentant Christian has a right to full remission of penalty and guilt, even without indulgence letters.*
>
> *Thesis 43. Christians are to be taught that the one who gives to the poor or lends to the needy does a better deed than the one who buys indulgences.*
>
> *Thesis 82. Why does not the pope empty purgatory for the sake of holy love and the dire need of the souls that are there if he redeems an infinite number of souls for the sake of miserable money with which to build a church?*
>
> *Thesis 86. Why does not the pope, whose wealth is today greater than the wealth of the richest king, build this one basilica of St. Peter with his own money rather than with the money of poor believers? (LW 31:25-33 [some changes in translation]; WA 1:233-238).*

Luther identified the last two questions as questions that were being asked by ordinary lay people. They certainly would have received hearty approval from those Germans who felt resentment and anger because the pope was taking money from them to build a church in Rome. Whereas strong central governments had developed in England, France and Spain, the Holy Roman Empire was an empire in name only. It was actually a loose union of many independent states, unable to resist the financial demands of the Renaissance popes who needed to raise money for their building projects and art collections. However, Luther's criticisms about the church went deeper than German complaints about the pope's financial demands. He began by raising theological and moral questions about the current practice of selling indulgences, but soon he would raise more challenging questions about the authority of the pope himself.

B. The Leipzig Debate

In the summer of 1519, Luther was engaged in a heated debate with John Eck, a fellow professor and theologian. Representatives of the church had already challenged Luther's criticism of indulgences by appealing to the authority of the pope. Luther therefore prepared for this debate by studying the decrees establishing the authority of the papacy. This research led him to question the preeminence and infallibility of the pope. In the course of the debate, Eck confronted Luther with the traditional arguments for the authority of the pope and then declared that anyone who denied this authority agreed with Jan Hus, the reformer who had been burned at the stake for heresy by the Council of Constance in 1415.

Luther initially denied that he was a "Hussite," but during a break in the proceedings he read Hus' statements on the church and was surprised to discover that he agreed with him. Luther returned to state that many of Hus' declarations were not heretical and that he should not have been condemned by the Council of Constance. Eck thus succeeded in having Luther publicly deny not only the authority of the pope but the authority of the councils of the church as well. The controversy over indulgences, a specific practice of the church, had become a controversy over church authority.

III. Luther's Excommunication

John Eck travelled to Rome with notes on the Leipzig Debate and condemnations of Luther by the universities of Cologne and Louvain. In June of 1520 a papal **bull** (a formal document issued by the pope) was published in Rome. This bull gave Luther sixty days to **recant** (formally deny his statements) or be excommunicated along with his followers. The bull, according to custom, called for the burning of Luther's books. Students and faculty at the University of Wittenberg responded by burning books of church law and scholastic theology. In an act of defiance, Luther also threw the papal bull that had condemned him into the flames. In January of 1521, Luther was formally excommunicated by the pope.

A. Writings of 1520

Throughout these events Luther continued to write, composing three very significant works in the year 1520. In his *Address to the Christian Nobility of the German Nation*, he called on the German princes and rulers to enact the reforms that church officials refused to undertake. He defended their right to do so by outlining his doctrine of the **priesthood of all believers**. In this doctrine Luther said that all Christians are made priests by Baptism, faith, and the gospel, but not all are called to exercise that office in the church. If church officials fail to reform the church, however, then Christian princes have the right to do so by virtue of their Baptism.

In his next treatise, *On the Babylonian Captivity of the Church*, Luther argued that the sacraments, especially the Eucharist, were being held "captive" by the church. Luther accepted the teaching about the **real presence** of Christ in the Eucharist (as opposed to a spiritual or figurative presence) because Jesus referred to the bread and wine as his body and blood. Luther, however, denied **transubstantiation**, the transformation of the bread and wine into the body and blood of Christ. This doctrine used concepts from the philosophy of Aristotle to describe how the bread and wine can continue to look, taste, and feel the same even after this change has occurred. According to the doctrine of transubstantiation, the **substance** (underlying reality) of the bread and wine changes into the substance of the body and blood of Christ, while the **accidents** (outer appearance) remain the same. Luther rejected this on the grounds that it is not biblical and that it relies on scholastic philosophy. Luther concluded that one should simply accept Jesus' words in faith and not attempt to use philosophy to describe or explain them. This agreed with Luther's general understanding of the sacraments in terms of the Word and faith; a Word of promise is offered in the sacrament and accepted by faith.

At first glance, Luther's understanding of sacraments appears to conflict with the practice of infant Baptism. How can an infant hear and accept the Word in faith? If faith is so important, would it not make more sense to baptize believing adults? Luther rejected this argument, in part because the church had been baptizing infants for centuries. He was a conservative reformer who believed that the tradition of the church should be preserved unless it was contradicted by the Bible. In Luther's view, infant Baptism not only did not contradict the Bible, it proclaimed the central message of justification by grace through faith. The infant is given faith by God, completely apart from its own efforts and abilities. Faith is a gift, and nowhere is this seen more clearly than in the Baptism of an infant.

Many of Luther's contemporaries, including Erasmus, saw *On the Babylonian Captivity* as his most radical work to date for in it Luther criticized the very heart of the church, its theology and practice of the sacraments. Of the seven sacraments of the church, Luther retained only two: Baptism and the Eucharist. At the beginning of his treatise, Luther still referred to Penance as a sacrament (because it was instituted by Christ and carries a Word of promise), but by the end of the treatise he concluded that it is not a sacrament because it lacks a "visible sign" (like the water of Baptism or the bread and wine of the Eucharist).

In Luther's third treatise, *Christian Liberty*, he described his theology of justification by grace through faith and outlined its consequences for living a Christian life. He posed the question: If justification is by faith alone, are Christians then free to live immoral lives? Luther answered this question by defining Christian freedom and describing the proper relationship between faith and works in the life of a Christian.

Figure 18.1 and 18.2: Title pages of Luther's Reformation writing: *To the Christian Nobility of the German Nation Concerning the Reform of the Christian Estate* (August, 1520); *The Freedom of a Christian* (November 1520). Woodcuts.

B. Diet of Worms

While Luther continued to write, his immediate political superior, Frederick the Wise of Saxony, was trying to negotiate a hearing for Luther before the princes and rulers of the Holy Roman Empire. Frederick had supported the election of the current emperor and persuaded him to promise that Luther would not be condemned without a hearing. Emperor Charles V therefore invited Luther to attend the next formal meeting, or **diet**, of the Holy Roman Empire of the German Nation. The emperor soon withdrew his invitation, however, when the pope's representative pointed out that Luther had already been condemned by the church and should not be granted a hearing by the laity. The tide changed yet again when the diet convened at Worms in 1521 and the rulers of various states and cities called on the emperor to bring Luther before them. They claimed that Luther's teaching had become so influential that condemnation without a hearing might lead to rebellion. The emperor once again invited Luther to attend the diet.

This political maneuvering would become commonplace in the years to come and was a significant factor in the success of the Lutheran Reformation. Although Charles V had inherited the right to rule over a substantial portion of western Europe (Spain, Austria-Hungary, parts of Italy, and the Netherlands), he was strongly opposed by the other European powers, especially the popes and the king of France. The Ottoman Turks also presented a significant military threat as they pressed up the Danube and into Charles' Austrian lands. Faced with the daunting task of ruling an extensive empire, without the benefit of modern communication or transportation, Charles was forced to compromise with the German princes again and again. His preoccupation with other threats meant that Charles could never fully devote himself to the religious and political divisions developing within the Holy Roman Empire.

These divisions would soon become apparent when Luther arrived at the Diet of Worms. Luther was hoping for an opportunity to present and defend his views, but those hopes were quickly dashed. As he stood before the assembly, a representative of the archbishop of Trier pointed to a pile of books and asked Luther two questions: Had he written these books? Was there a part of them he would now choose to recant? Momentarily taken aback, Luther asked for some time to consider his answer. He appeared before the imperial diet on the following day and this time his answer was clear and unequivocal:

> *Unless I am convinced by the testimony of the Scriptures or by clear reason (for I do not trust either in the pope or in councils alone, since it is well known that they have often erred and contradicted themselves), I am bound by the Scriptures I have quoted and my conscience is captive to the Word of God. I cannot and will not retract anything, since it is neither safe nor right to go against conscience. May God help me! Amen (LW 32:112-3; WA 7,838).*

Luther's declaration that he would not recant was followed by several days of unsuccessful meetings and negotiations. He finally left the city, and soon after the emperor issued the **Edict of Worms**, declaring Luther an outlaw and subject to capital punishment. Luther the monk and professor was now a heretic and outlaw. At the Leipzig Debate, Eck had compared Luther to Jan Hus, the reformer condemned and killed by the Council of Constance. How would Luther avoid meeting the same fate?

IV. Exile and Return

On his way home from the Diet of Worms, Luther's wagon travelled down an empty road in the woods. Suddenly armed horsemen attacked the wagon, his companions fled, and he was dragged away by his assailants. As word of his capture spread, many thought that they had heard the last of Luther. However, Luther's "kidnapping" had been arranged by his ally and ruler, Frederick the Wise of Saxony. To prevent discovery, Luther grew a beard, exchanged his monk's habit for the attire of a knight, and adopted the name Junker Jörg (Sir George). The protection Luther received from some of the German princes, especially Frederick of Saxony, ensured his continued survival. He would spend the next ten months hidden at Elector Frederick's castle, the Wartburg.

A. Wartburg Castle

Luther struggled with ill health and depression during his exile at Wartburg Castle and yet these were some of the most productive months of his life. In addition to publishing over a dozen books, Luther translated Erasmus' Greek text of the New Testament into German. This translation was so influential and widely read that it helped to create the modern German language. Luther translated the New Testament into German because he believed that Scripture was the sole authority in matters of faith and that all Christians should be able to read it in their own tongue.

In his preface to the New Testament Luther offered guidance on the proper way to read and interpret Scripture. He admonished Christians to properly distinguish between the *law* (the commandments of God) and the *gospel* (the promises of God). The law (which is found throughout the Bible, including the New Testament) condemns people, shows them their sin, and prepares them to receive the good news of the gospel. Keeping in mind that distinction between law and gospel, Luther emphasized once again that people are not saved by doing the works of the law but by trusting the promises of the gospel.

B. Return from Exile

As Luther continued to write and translate at Wartburg Castle, he heard disturbing reports of violence and upheaval at Wittenberg. Some of his friends and colleagues, in particular a fellow professor and priest named Carlstadt, had begun implementing Luther's reforms, and creating considerable unrest in the process. On Christmas Day 1521, Carlstadt celebrated the Mass without wearing the traditional robes and vestments, delivered parts of the liturgy in German, instead of Latin, and distributed both bread and wine to the assembled worshipers, instead of bread alone. Luther agreed with these reforms, at least in principle, but he was disturbed by the coercive manner in which they were carried out. He was especially troubled by episodes of **iconoclasm**, or "image-breaking," in which statues, stained glass and paintings were forcibly destroyed or removed from churches. He was also concerned that others were implementing reforms without consulting him and without regard for proper order and authority.

The town council of Wittenberg, seeking leadership and guidance, invited Luther to return. When he informed Frederick the Wise of the council's request, Frederick responded that he could not protect Luther if he came out of hiding. Luther returned to Wittenberg despite the warning and preached a series of sermons declaring that reform should be accomplished by persuasion and love, not by violence and force. He argued that faith must come freely, without compulsion, and that reform inevitably will follow when the Word of God is preached and believed. His call for moderation and patience was heeded and order was restored in Wittenberg.

C. The Peasants' War

A few years later, another group tried to push Luther's call for reform in a more radical direction. In 1524-1525 a group of peasants in southern Germany appealed to Luther's ideas in their call for economic and social justice. The princes had consolidated their power by imposing greater taxes and services on the peasants and displacing local law codes (which guaranteed common land) in favor of Roman law (which acknowledged only private property). In one of the most widely circulated lists of peasant demands, *The Twelve Articles*, the authors used Luther's language and ideas to prove the justice of their cause.

Luther responded with his own tract entitled *An Admonition to Peace*. In this tract, Luther condemned the princes and lords for their unjust treatment of the peasants and declared that they are bringing revolt on themselves. Luther then addressed the peasants, and although he acknowledged the justice of many of their demands, he rejected their call for rebellion and violence. Luther stated that even unjust and cruel rulers are ordained by God and Christians are required to obey them. Christians may only disobey the proper authorities when the gospel is in jeopardy. Luther did not believe that was the case here, and so he objected to the peasants' appeal to the gospel and Christian freedom to support their social and economic demands. He concluded that there was nothing specifically Christian at stake in this revolt and called on the princes and peasants to negotiate a peaceful resolution.

Luther travelled about the countryside, admonishing the peasants to maintain the peace, but he was met with jeers and threats. Luther responded to the peasants' continued rebellion with his infamous treatise *Against the Robbing and Murdering Hordes of Peasants*. In this work, he called on the princes to give the peasants one last chance to negotiate. If the peasants did not lay down their arms, Luther proposed the following measures:

> *Therefore let everyone who can, smite, slay, and stab, secretly or openly, remembering that nothing can be more poisonous, hurtful, or devilish than a rebel. It is just as when one must kill a mad dog; if you do not strike him, he will strike you, and a whole land with you* (LW 46:50; WA 18,358).

This tract was published just as the princes were killing the peasants by the thousands, even those who had surrendered or been taken prisoner. Luther was criticized for this treatise in his own day but he maintained his position against rebels, especially those who claim the Word of God to justify their rebellion. Luther's response to the Peasants' War clearly demonstrated that he did not equate social, political, or economic reform with his call for religious renewal.

V. Luther's Marriage

In 1525, at the peak of the Peasants' War, Luther took the sudden and unexpected step of marrying a former nun. Although Luther had taught for several years that celibacy and monastic asceticism were contrary to the Bible and that priests, monks, and nuns should be free to marry, he had not indicated any desire to do so himself. His change of heart was precipitated by the plight of Katherine von Bora, one of several nuns he had helped to smuggle out of a Cistercian convent two years earlier. By 1525 Luther had found homes or husbands for all of the women but Katherine. At the age of

26 Katherine's chances for marriage were slim, and after several potential suitors proved unacceptable, she offered to marry Luther himself. Luther accepted her offer in order to provide his father with grandchildren, to spite the pope who forbade clerical marriage, and to witness to his convictions before his martyrdom.

Luther's anticipated martyrdom never occurred, and the marriage he entered into at the age of 42 would last until his death two decades later. Although Luther declared that he felt neither "passionate love" nor the "burning" of desire when he married, genuine affection and love developed between husband and wife (LW 49:117; WABr 3,541). Luther and Katherine had six children, four of whom survived into adulthood. Katherine managed the household, which included several relatives,

Figure 18.3: Portrait of Martin Luther.

Figure 18.4 Portrait of Katharina von Bora.

student boarders, and frequent guests. Money was a constant concern, especially given Luther's reckless generosity. Katherine took charge of the family's finances and proved to be a shrewd businesswoman who supplemented the family's income by farming, brewing beer, breeding pigs, and taking in lodgers.

VI. The Protestants

In the years following Luther's marriage the division between those who accepted his reforms and those who did not continued to widen. In 1526 the First Diet of Speyer decided that until a council could be held to discuss recent religious developments, each German prince was free to act as he saw fit before God and the emperor. Some princes supported Luther while others remained loyal to the Roman church. This compromise was challenged three years later when the majority of princes at the Second Diet of Speyer declared that Lutheranism would be tolerated only in those areas where it could not be suppressed without violence. The diet further decided that religious liberty must be extended to Catholics in Lutheran lands, but the same liberty would not be given to Lutherans in Catholic lands. Six Lutheran princes protested this arrangement and thereby acquired the name **Protestant**. This attempt to re-establish Catholic faith and practice throughout Germany failed and Germany was divided into two camps, Catholic and Protestant.

Emperor Charles V came to Germany the following year (1530) to preside over the Diet of Augsburg, a meeting of German rulers summoned for the purpose of resolving the religious question. Luther was not permitted to attend this meeting since the Edict of Worms was in effect and he was still considered an outlaw. His friend and colleague, Philip Melanchthon, represented the Lutheran position and drafted a statement of faith known as the **Augsburg Confession**. Melanchthon hoped for a reconciliation between Catholics and Protestants and thus he stressed their common ground. The differences between the two parties were too deep to be resolved in this way, however, and the Augsburg Confession was rejected not only by Catholics but also by other Protestants. The Protestants of Switzerland and the south German cities submitted their own statements of faith while the Lutherans signed the Augsburg Confession. To this day the Augsburg Confession remains an important statement of Lutheran doctrine.

At the conclusion of the diet, Charles V ordered all Protestant territories to return to traditional religious practices by the following year or prepare for war. He was not able to act on his threat when the year ended but eventually he did engage the Protestant princes in battle. Neither side achieved a decisive victory and finally they were forced to reach a compromise.

In 1555, after twenty-five years of conflict, the **Peace of Augsburg** established the principle that each prince was free to choose either the Roman Catholic or the Lutheran faith. This was not religious freedom in the modern sense, however, for all the subjects of the prince were expected to follow the religion of their ruler. Those who did not share the religion of their prince were permitted, after selling their property, to migrate to another territory. As a result of this agreement, most of southern Germany remained Catholic while northern Germany adopted Lutheranism. The Lutheran faith eventually spread beyond Germany to Scandinavia, where it displaced Catholicism as the established church.

VII. The Lutheran Church

Although the most dramatic events of his life were behind him after 1525, Luther spent the next twenty years working with his supporters to form the Lutheran church. What structure or organization should this new church have? Luther was inclined to locate power in local, independent congregations but he concluded that they did not have the resources to deal with the problems facing the reform movement. He was unable to maintain the traditional episcopal structure in which bishops exercise authority, in part because the bishops had generally remained loyal to the Roman church. In addition, he was persuaded that the term "bishop" in the New Testament did not refer to a distinct office but to every pastor. Luther finally called on the princes to function as "emergency bishops" and assume responsibility for the work of re-organizing the church. However, Luther did not live to see the Peace of Augsburg and the establishment of the Lutheran church in Germany and Scandinavia.

Luther was not primarily concerned with the structure of the new church but with its preaching and worship life. He believed the true church was found where the Word was truly preached and the sacraments rightly administered. He did not think he was establishing this church for the first time or even re-establishing it after years of neglect. On the contrary, he believed that the true

Christian church had existed without interruption from the time of the apostles to his own day. Thus, despite his criticisms of the Roman church, Luther held that God had preserved the true church—through the preaching of the gospel and the administration of the sacraments—even under a church structure which had erred in many ways. Luther did not identify the church with a particular structure or organization but with a community of believers called by God. Those who responded to the Word in faith were the true but hidden church.

Luther believed, however, that the true preaching of the Word and the proper administration of the sacraments were being obscured by the current practices and structures of the Roman church. He concluded that the Lutheran church required a good translation of the Bible, a catechism to instruct the young, a reformed liturgy to correct abuses in worship, and a hymnbook to inspire and instruct the people. Luther himself would fulfill each of these requirements (Bainton, 254-255).

A. The Bible

Luther translated the New Testament into German during his exile at Wartburg Castle and started his translation of the Old Testament after his return to Wittenberg. A translation of the entire Bible was not printed until 1534 and he continued to revise this translation until his death. Luther believed the church must be founded on the Word of God and this Word should be accessible to all believers in their own language.

B. The Catechisms of 1529

Luther thought that Christians also required instruction in the doctrines and practices of the church. To determine the current state of Christian belief and practice, Luther asked his new prince, Elector John of Saxony, to organize a formal visitation of churches in his territory. Appalled by the results of the visitations, especially the lack of religious knowledge among the common people, Luther composed two **catechisms** (manuals of Christian doctrine) to instruct believers. Luther was following an ancient tradition in doing so, for catechisms can be traced to the earliest days of the Christian church. Luther organized his catechisms around five elements: the Ten Commandments, the Apostles' Creed, the Lord's Prayer, Baptism and the Eucharist. Luther wrote a *Large Catechism* for adults but his *Small Catechism*, written for children, had the greatest influence. Many Lutheran churches encouraged the practice of committing the *Small Catechism* to memory, a practice that still continues today.

C. Liturgy

Luther was a conservative reformer, inclined to maintain the status quo except where he felt it contradicted the gospel. This is evident in his reform of the liturgy. In the mass, the priest offers the body and blood of Christ as a sacrifice to God. Luther objected to this on the grounds that it makes the mass into a good work that humans perform for God. To emphasize the Word of promise that God offers in the sacrament, he changed the traditional Eucharistic prayer (with its reference to sacrifice) to a simple reading of the account of the Last Supper. However, since the prayers of the mass were still in Latin, Luther feared that most worshipers would not understand the significance of the change. As a consequence, he translated the liturgy of the mass into German. Luther maintained many of the traditional elements of the liturgy but he emphasized proclamation of the Word and religious instruction through the sermon.

D. Hymnbook

One of the most significant changes Luther made in the service was the active involvement of the congregation in the singing of hymns. The first German hymnal was published in 1524, containing four hymns written by Luther himself. Luther continued to write the words and occasionally the music for many other hymns, drawing on portions of scriptures (especially the Psalms) and Latin liturgical chants for inspiration. In his most famous hymn, "A Mighty Fortress Is Our God," Luther adapted Psalm 46 to express his faith in the midst of struggle:

> *God's Word forever shall abide,*
> *No thanks to foes, who fear it;*
> *For God himself fights by our side*
> *With weapons of the Spirit.*
> *Were they to take our house,*
> *Goods, honor, child, or spouse,*
> *Though life be wrenched away,*
> *They cannot win the day.*
> *The Kingdom's ours forever*
>
> (Lutheran Book of Worship, *Hymn 229*).

VIII. Luther's Death

In 1546, Luther travelled to Eisleben, the place of his birth, to settle a feud between the local rulers. Luther was 62 years old and had struggled with ill health throughout his life. He fell ill during this visit to his hometown and died of heart failure on February 18. A slip of paper found in his pocket summed up his central conviction that people are saved by grace alone: "We are beggars. That is true" (LW 54:476; WATr 5,318). Luther's influence is still felt today in his theological and biblical writings, his hymns, and the catechism he wrote to instruct children. His ideas and convictions have left their mark on the church which bears his name. His call for reform was one of many, however, and the impetus for reform did not end with his death. Other reform movements—both Catholic and Protestant—continued to address questions of authority, human nature, and salvation.

Key Terms:

nominalist theology	treasury of merit
penance	95 Theses
justification by grace through faith	Leipzig debate
passive or alien righteousness	bull
Word of God	recant
indulgences	priesthood of all believers
contrition	real presence
confession	transubstantiation
absolution	substance
works of satisfaction	accidents
purgatory	diet

Edict of Worms
law and gospel
iconoclasm
Peasants' War
Protestant

Augsburg Confession
Peace of Augsburg
episcopal
catechism

Questions for Reading:

1. Why did nominalist theology cause problems for Luther?

2. What did Luther mean by "justification by faith"? How did he come to this idea?

3. What were indulgences and how were they related to the sacrament of Penance? Why and how did Luther become involved in the indulgence controversy?

4. How did Luther's 95 Theses relate to the controversy over indulgences? How did this controversy become a controversy over church authority?

5. What was Luther's general understanding of a sacrament? How did this affect his views on Eucharist and Baptism?

6. Why did Luther refuse to recant at the Diet of Worms?

7. What did Luther do during his exile at Wartburg Castle? Why did he return to Wittenberg?

8. Why did Luther oppose the peasants' rebellion? What does this tell you about his understanding of reform?

9. What is the origin of the word "Protestant"?

10. How did Luther define the true church? When and where does it exist?

11. What innovations did Luther make with respect to the Bible, the catechism, the liturgy, and the hymnbook? Why did he consider these changes necessary?

Works Consulted/Recommended Reading:

Atkinson, James. *Martin Luther and the Birth of Protestantism*. Atlanta: John Knox Press, 1968.

Bainton, Roland H. *Here I Stand: A Life of Martin Luther*. Nashville: Abingdon Press, 1983.

Brecht, Martin. *Martin Luther: Shaping and Defining the Reformation 1521-1532*. Trans. James L. Schaaf. Minneapolis: Fortress Press, 1990.

Edwards, Mark and Tavard, George. *Luther: A Reformer for the Churches*. Philadelphia: Fortress, 1983.

Inter-Lutheran Commission on Worship. *Lutheran Book of Worship*. Minneapolis: Augsburg, 1978.

Kittelson, James M. *Luther the Reformer: The Story of the Man and His Career*. Minneapolis: Augsburg, 1986.

Metzger, Bruce and Murphy, Roland, eds. *The New Oxford Annotated Bible with Apocrypha*, New Revised Standard Version. New York: Oxford University Press, 1991.

Nestingen, James Arne. *Martin Luther: His Life and Teachings*. Philadelphia: Fortress, 1982.

Oberman, Heiko A. *Luther: Man between God and the Devil*. Trans. Eileen Walliser-Schwarzbart. New Haven: Yale University Press, 1989.

Ozment, Steven. *The Age of Reform 1250-1550: An Intellectual and Religious History of Late Medieval and Reformation Europe*. New Haven: Yale University Press, 1980.

Spitz, Lewis W. *The Protestant Reformation 1517-1559*. New York: Harper & Row, 1985.

von Loewenich, Walther. *Martin Luther: The Man and His Work*. Minneapolis: Augsburg, 1982.

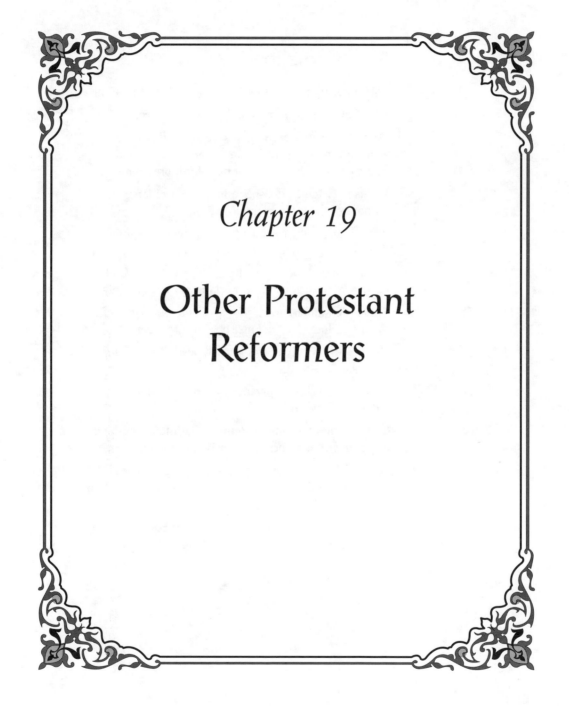

Chapter 19

Other Protestant Reformers

Timeline

1484 AD	Ulrich Zwingli is born in the Swiss canton of St. Gall.
1509	John Calvin is born in Pont-l'Evenque, France.
1519	After successful preaching in several small parishes, Zwingli comes to preach at a major church in Zurich. This marks the beginning of his reform preaching.
1527	William Tyndale publishes a translation of large portions of the Bible in English.
1529	Zwingli and Luther debate their differences regarding theology and church reform at Marburg.
1531	Zwingli dies at the battle of Kappel, a war that broke out when an incident of iconoclasm got out of hand.
1533-1553	Thomas Cranmer, archbishop of Canterbury, provides a stabilizing force for the English reform movement.
1534	King Henry VIII declares himself head of the church in England.
c. 1535	Calvin begins his involvement in the Reformation and moves to Geneva.
c. 1539	Calvin writes his famous **Reply to Sadoleto** in which he defended the principles of the Reformation.
1553	Queen Mary attempts to reverse England's reform movement and return the church to its pre-Reformation state.
1558	Queen Elizabeth I resumes the course of English reform and establishes the Church of England as it is known today.
1564	Death of John Calvin.

Other Protestant Reformers

The last chapter began with the question, "Why are some Christians today known as Catholics and others identified as Protestants?" It then went on to tell the story of Martin Luther, and of how his efforts to reform the church resulted in some new interpretations of traditional theological claims. At the end, the chapter described how the efforts of Luther and his followers led to the formation of the Lutheran Church.

Of course there are other Christians besides Lutherans and Roman Catholics. There are Methodists, Episcopalians, Presbyterians, and Baptists; there are members of the United Church of Christ, the Disciples of Christ, and the Assemblies of God. Indeed there are dozens of major Christian churches, and many more sub-divisions of those churches. Do the members of one of these denominations have very different beliefs from the members of another group? Why and how did Christians split into so many different groups?

The answers to these questions require an investigation of events in the 16th century—specifically, of reform movements that took place at the same time as, or immediately after, the work of Martin Luther and his followers. These movements will help explain the differing interpretations of the Christian message that characterize the various Christian denominations today. This chapter will examine a small but representative sample of four of these reform movements—two that center on a particular individual, and two others that draw on the contributions of a variety of thinkers.

Figure 19.1: Portrait of Ulrich Zwingli.

I. The Swiss Reformation

The country that we English-speakers know as "Switzerland" has an official Latin name: "Confederatio Helvitica," or the Confederation of Helvitica. Like the United States, Switzerland actually comprises a number of smaller states (called "cantons"). In the 16th century, these cantons were largely independent from one another, though they sometimes entered into federations as a means of maintaining their distance from the emperors of the Holy Roman Empire, who sometimes sought to control them. A religious leader who could form an alliance with the government of a canton would receive the same kind of military protection that Luther received from the Elector Frederick of Saxony. This is precisely what happened in the case of a bright and ambitious young priest by the name of **Ulrich Zwingli**.

Zwingli was born in 1484, making him just a few months younger than Martin Luther. His family were farmers, but because he showed some early intellectual gifts and an ear for music, more attention was given to his schooling. He attended university in Vienna (in modern-day Austria) and Basel (now on the French-Swiss border).

A. Another Erasmus

Basel was a city that had absorbed the "new learning" of the Renaissance with great enthusiasm. It had an active university, busy printing presses, and much scholarly discussion of the work of humanists such as Erasmus. Zwingli's education was a classical one, with a focus in philosophy. By 1506 he had finished the Master of Arts degree and was ready to pursue theology. At about the same time, a position came open for a parish priest in the town of Glarus, near his own hometown; as a well-educated local, he was the natural choice for the job. He became a priest and served the town for the next ten years. He continued to read and study the Greek and Latin classics, as well as the Bible and the writings of theologians such as Augustine and John Chrysostom.

In 1516 he also took on the responsibilities of priest at the nearby parish of Einsiedeln. There he became concerned about the same thing that had worried Luther: the tendency for Christians to forget that their salvation comes solely from God. Zwingli saw this occurring not only in the sale of indulgences (as had Luther) but also in the popular devotion to images. Zwingli's new parish had a shrine—a statue of the Virgin Mary—to which some people had attributed magical healing powers. Zwingli saw many people who visited the shrine, and worried that many of them had decided to worship a statue rather than God. His preaching at this popular shrine became well-known, and at the beginning of 1519 he came to Zurich—the biggest city in the region—to be the main preacher at the largest church in town.

In Zurich, Zwingli's extensive learning served him well; he read the Bible to large audiences in this powerful city. Practically no one owned a copy of the Bible, and the few who did would likely have been unable to read it. Zwingli's straightforward explanations of biblical stories must have shaken the people of Zurich out of their slumber. They started to ask questions, to think seriously about certain controversial questions (such as the morality of indulgences), and to ask themselves about the meaning of their beliefs. In short, they started to be interested in theology.

B. Agreements with Luther

Like Luther, Zwingli argued that the Bible alone should be the focal point for Christians. Human interpretations—no matter how authoritatively issued (for example, by the pope)—were not as reliable as the biblical text itself. Zwingli argued that if a traditional religious practice (such as fasting during Lent, the forty-day period leading up to Easter) was not required by Scripture, it should be considered optional. His view was not far from that expressed in Luther's treatise, *Christian Liberty*. Zwingli's position obviously put him into conflict with his immediate superior, the Bishop of Konstanz, who sent a deputy to give an address on the importance of adhering to the traditional teachings. However, Zurich was a sovereign canton, and the local council backed Zwingli; he was not punished for his dissenting views.

Zwingli reached similar conclusions to those of Luther on a number of other issues: that *faith* was the first Christian virtue, without which no one could be saved; that individual bishops, and even church councils, could make mistakes; and that clergy should be allowed to marry (Zwingli himself secretly married Anna Reinhart in 1522). However, also like Luther, he continued to uphold many of the traditional beliefs of the church—including beliefs that some later Protestant Christians would deny or deem irrelevant, such as the perpetual virginity of Mary and the importance of regular participation in communion. Nevertheless, on matters of difference, he was willing to take on the bishops and learned doctors in debate and discussion. His great learning and thorough knowledge of the original biblical languages made Zwingli an easy winner in these disputes.

C. Differences with Luther

Zwingli also went farther than Luther on some issues. He spoke loudly against "image-worship," which, he emphasized, is prohibited by the second commandment ("You shall not make for yourself an idol"). Drawing on his experiences at the shrine in his old parish at Einsiedeln, Zwingli concluded that if the people are surrounded by images, they will too easily forget that the image is meant simply to *remind* them to worship God alone, and will thus slip into the worship of the image instead. He thus argued that images should be removed from churches. This position, often known as **iconoclasm**, became one of the hallmarks of the Swiss Reformation. The removal of images was not always very peaceful and orderly. Rather than simply taking the statues from churches and placing them in museums, iconoclasts sometimes smashed windows and toppled statues. Within the city of Zurich itself, however, things were usually kept calm.

Zwingli also went farther than Luther on the question of the sacraments. Like Luther, he accepted only two sacraments, Baptism and the Eucharist. Concerning the Eucharist, he too rejected the idea of transubstantiation, and argued that there is no "sacrifice" in the mass (Christ having already been offered, once and for all, as the only necessary sacrifice). The distinctive element in Zwingli's doctrine of the Eucharist, however, was that he offered a purely *spiritual* interpretation of the description of Christ's body and blood. He based his claim on a quotation in the Gospel of John: "The spirit gives life; the flesh is useless" (John 6:63). Whatever value comes to believers during the Eucharist must come *spiritually*, not in any physical form. Thus Zwingli rejected the traditional doctrine of the "real presence." Instead, he argued for the "ubiquity of Christ" (ubiquity means "existing everywhere simultaneously"). His position was that the divinity of Christ is not confined to particular elements, but is everywhere at all times. Thus, for Zwingli, the Eucharistic service merely concentrates the mind and allows believers to remember the actions of Jesus in giving himself for their sake. The service is best understood as a "remembrance."

Zwingli's differences with Luther came to a head when they met at the city of Marburg in 1529 to debate their issues of disagreement. Both of them were stubborn, holding fast to their own interpretations. Neither one flinched, and both went away convinced that the other was simply wrong. Thus, on the one hand, the "Marburg Colloquy" (as it became known) was a failure: it showed that nothing could be settled merely by appealing to the Bible as "the final authority," since people would continue to disagree about the best interpretation of a biblical text. On the other hand, Zwingli helped Luther see just how far his own position was from that of the Roman Catholic Church, and just how difficult any kind of reconciliation between them would be.

D. Coming to a Bad End

The success of the Reformation in Zurich and other major Swiss cities led to considerable nervousness in those Swiss cantons that continued to accept all the teachings of the Roman Catholic Church. Zwingli was strongly opposed to any compulsion of religious belief; but many political leaders (on both sides) saw that differences in religious belief could provide an opportunity to gain new territory and additional income. To oppose the power of Zurich, five of the Catholic cantons formed a "defense league," allied to both the pope and the Holy Roman Empire. There were further outbreaks of dramatic and excessive iconoclasm, which had been easier to keep peaceable inside Zurich than in the general countryside. Eventually, full-scale war broke out, and Zwingli himself died in 1531 at the battle of Kappel, fighting on the side of Zurich—the city he had led through the Reformation.

Zwingli's influence is still strongly felt among many Protestants—especially those who are not Lutheran. His understanding of the Eucharist and his disapproval of images in worship have influenced many Protestant denominations in Switzerland, the Netherlands, England, and eventually, the United States. This influence is most clear in denominations that organize themselves around the "congregational" model (in which there are no bishops or regional synods, but in which the individual congregation makes most decisions). These denominations include the Christian Church (Disciples of Christ), United Church of Christ, and many Baptist churches.

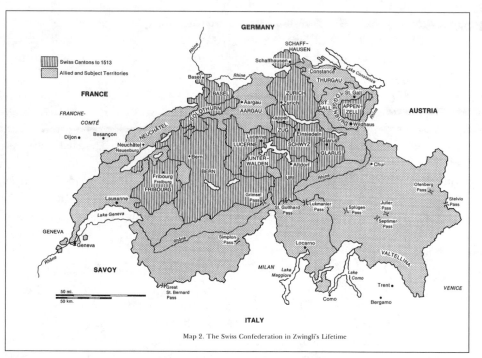

Figure 19.2: Map of the Swiss Confederation at the time of Ulrich Zwingli.

II. The Genevan Reformation

The city of Geneva (also in present-day Switzerland) was, at first glance, in much the same situation as Zurich. Fiercely independent, the city was situated on a border—with the Swiss cantons on one side and a major political power (in this case, France) on the other. The Genevan people relished their resistance to foreign powers, whether political or religious. In addition to the similarities of these two cities, the two men who led them through the Reformation had certain similarities as well.

A. The Lawyer-theologian

John Calvin was born in 1509 in Pont-l'Eveque, a city in northwestern France. His family was well-connected, and he and his brothers were prepared for the priesthood from an early age. He had many advantages, and showed himself to be something of a prodigy. He quickly mastered Latin and the whole range of classical texts, and learned the medieval method of disputation. By 1525, Calvin had received the Master of Arts degree and was fully prepared for a course of theological study. Suddenly, though, his father withdrew him from the University of Paris and sent him instead to Orléans, to begin a degree in law. Some historians have speculated that this change of mind may have been due to the outbreak of the Reformation and its increasing impact on the whole church after 1520. Perhaps Calvin's father wanted to keep his son out of the debates and division that seemed to be breaking out everywhere in the church. If so, he was ultimately unsuccessful; in 1531 Calvin abandoned his life as a lawyer and returned to theology.

By the mid-1530s, many of the ideas of the Reformation were beginning to reach France, and they caught Calvin's attention. He had made his views sufficiently well-known that when a series of anti-Catholic posters appeared overnight in Paris, Calvin was numbered among the suspects. He and a friend escaped to Basel, a free city that was thoroughly on the side of reform, where a number of the chief architects of the Reformation lived. Through conversations with them, and through his own diligence, Calvin began to produce the work for which he is most famous, and which he would continue to revise throughout his life. His *Institutes of the Christian Religion* is an attempt to provide a systematic statement of the beliefs of the Christian faith, written for the French rulers and others in France who wanted to learn about the new vision of Christianity that was being developed in the Reformation.

Figure 19.3: Portrait of John Calvin.

B. Calvin's Thought

Theology, Calvin says, is about our knowledge of God and our knowledge of ourselves. God has revealed to us what we should think and do by giving us the Law; but because it is impossible to obey this Law in its entirety, we are forced to confess our weaknesses and ask for God's mercy. Calvin, then, is very much of the same mind as Luther in his emphasis on the inability of human beings to save themselves by fulfilling the Law. They must rely on their faith alone, for only God can bring about their redemption.

One of Calvin's unique teachings concerns the doctrine of **election**—the idea that God chooses certain people with whom to enter into a special relationship or "covenant." Given our present-day emphasis on equal treatment for everyone, God's decision to "elect" certain persons may seem odd to us. Yet the Old Testament repeatedly describes God as calling out certain people and entering into a special relationship with them. Abraham and Sarah are chosen to be the founders of a new nation. The nation of Israel is chosen by God and is bound to God by the covenant between them. The prophets, too, are "appointed" or "chosen" by God. In the New Testament, God intervenes decisively by sending Jesus, who in turn chooses or calls particular followers. Later, the church is composed of those who are "called out" of their everyday lives into society and enter into a special relationship with God.

Calvin saw two reasons for God's election. First, it emphasizes God's sovereignty. God, being God, can make choices that we cannot comprehend. Second, election is meant to motivate and inspire those who are elected. It is not an act of favoritism, nor is it a reward for those who have done good deeds. In fact, being elected by God is something of a burden. It might even be dangerous: prophets were often exiled or killed, as were many of the early members of the church. Election is thus a forward-thinking idea; people are chosen not because they already *are* holy, but as a statement of God's plan to *make* them holy—to "set them apart" for a special task.

Calvin therefore argued for a logical extension of this idea: that God has already chosen some for salvation, and others for damnation. This concept is often called the doctrine of **double predestination**. Calvin reasoned that, if God is truly sovereign (supremely powerful and free from external control), the decision to save someone must be God's alone—it cannot depend on the decisions that human beings make during their lifetimes. Thus, we cannot know for certain, by looking at people's lives, whether or not they are among the "chosen," since predestination (like election) is not a reward for good deeds. On the other hand, however, the way we act can be a probable sign of the destiny that God has chosen for us.

At first glance, this view would appear to take away any motivation to do good. One might assume that "God has already decided my fate; nothing that I do will make any difference." But Calvin believed that double predestination was a *freeing* doctrine: it meant that people did not need to be anxious about the destiny of their souls, since that had already been determined. They could thus get on with the business of doing God's work in the world. Moreover, Calvin argued, God continues to act in the lives of the chosen, regenerating and sanctifying them. So people should not be fatalistic about their election, but they should allow God to use them to do good. Apparently, Calvin's views had precisely this effect on a great many people, given the enormous energy for social activism in those denominations that owe their beginnings to Calvin and his associates.

Calvin's understanding of the sacraments has many similarities to that of Luther and Zwingli. He too accepted only two sacraments—Baptism and the Eucharist. He understood Baptism as a symbol of forgiveness, an act of grace that welcomes people into the Christian faith and unites them with Christ. He believed that infants should be baptized, since all human beings are born in sin and are therefore in need of forgiveness. He also valued the Eucharist very highly, seeing it as the way in which God nourishes us (he often uses the phrase "The Lord's Supper" to refer to the act of communion). Like Luther and Zwingli, Calvin denied that Christ is "sacrificed" in the mass, and he was dubious about the language of transubstantiation. However, he attempted to transcend the question about the "real presence" (which divided Luther and Zwingli), arguing that we should dwell not so much on how the body of Christ is present *in the Eucharist*, but rather, how the body of Christ becomes present *in us*. In other words, how is it that, through the Eucharist, Christians become more perfectly united to Christ? He had three answers: first, it re-enacts Jesus' willingness to give himself to us, to sacrifice himself for our sake. Second, it is a thanksgiving and therefore a declaration of our faith, in which we accept what Christ has done for us. Finally, it is a communion, in which many Christians are united because they all partake of one body.

C. Calvin in Geneva

Calvin was passing through Geneva in 1536, shortly after the city had voted to become Protestant. One of the city's preachers pressed him into service to help educate the city about the Reformation. Thus began John Calvin's long and stormy relationship with this turbulent city.

In Geneva, Calvin was forced to face what had become, for the churches of the Reformation, their greatest problem: church authority. Under the Roman Catholic Church, the lines of authority had sometimes been abused, but at least they had been clear; everyone knew who had to be obeyed and who could be ignored. But such clear lines of authority were not available in Protestantism, given its claims about Christian liberty, the priesthood of all believers, and sole authority of the Bible (despite the different ways it was interpreted). One of Calvin's unique contributions is his attempt to supply an understanding of authority for the Reformation.

Calvin argued that, under the Protestant understanding, the church and its leaders still have authority; but this authority is based only on their willingness to preach the Word of God. In other words, the ministers only have authority as long as they express the will of Christ. How could this be assured? Calvin was worried that things would not go well if the task of exercising authority were entrusted *only* to government leaders or *only* to church leaders. He therefore established in Geneva a **Consistory**, something like a city council, which had twelve members: four from the government, four from the church leadership ("pastors"), and four church members who were not pastors ("elders"). Calvin also established other councils and committees to aid in the governance of the church and the city. The idea was to create a balance of power so that discipline would always be exercised in the spirit of Christ, and not for the interests of a particular person or group.

The idea of "balancing" power in this way is a noble one, but it does not always work. There were external pressures from powerful cities such as Bern and Zurich, concerning (for example) precisely what should be done at church services. There were conflicts within the Consistory itself, and there were disagreements with the government. Calvin, being a Frenchman, was at various times suspected of trying to undermine the Genevan government (which he certainly was not trying to do).

In the end, the delicate balance broke down, and Calvin and his colleagues were run out of town. They were replaced with weak, ineffective ministers, which led to such disorder that the Roman Catholic Church thought the city might be persuaded to return to the fold. The pope asked Cardinal Sadoleto to draft an appeal to the Genevan people, encouraging them to return to the traditions of Rome. The Genevans were unpersuaded, but they did want to write an effective reply to this well-constructed appeal. After asking several people and receiving several rejections, they turned reluctantly to Calvin.

He wrote a famous tract, now usually known as the *Reply to Sadoleto*, in which he turned the arguments of Cardinal Sadoleto back against the Roman Catholic Church. He argued that it was not the *Protestants* who had drifted away from the traditions of the church, but rather the *Catholics* who had done so—by not giving sufficient attention to the Bible. The following passage provides a taste of the polemical edge of Calvin's reply to Sadoleto:

> You teach that all that has been approved for fifteen hundred years or more by the uniform consent of the faithful is, by our rashness, torn up and destroyed.... [But] our agreement with antiquity is far closer than yours; all we have attempted has been to renew the ancient form of the Church which, at first distorted and stained by illiterate men of indifferent character, was afterwards criminally mangled and almost destroyed by the Roman pontiff and his faction.

Elsewhere in his reply, Calvin commented on his continuing paternal affection for the Genevan church. This comment was seen as an opening by some of the leaders of that city, who invited him to return; after considerable hesitation, he accepted.

Back in Geneva, Calvin helped the ministers draw up ordinances for the proper operation of religious services. He preached and taught, and in general he helped to shape the whole of the Protestant Reformation by making the city of Geneva into a grand religious experiment. Of course, Calvin's strong personality placed him in more-or-less constant conflict with some of the rulers of the city. Some of the religious laws of the city were quite strict by today's standards (for example, they forbade dancing, restricted public free speech rather severely, and regulated the names that could be used for newborn children). Some people chafed under these restrictions. Even so, the pious and serious Calvin probably did not expect to find the following unsigned note left in his pulpit one day:

> Big pot-belly, you and your fellows would do better to shut up.... We've had enough of blaming people. Why the devil have you renegade priests come here to ruin us? Those who have had enough take their revenge.... We don't want all these masters. Beware of what I say.

The investigations of this apparent death-threat turned up deeper levels of opposition in the city—not only religious, but political too (some government officials were accused of subversive discussions with France). Slowly, those who opposed Calvin's views gained power; but many also realized that his tough discipline and strong views had some value. He remained in the service of the Genevan church until the end of his life. He died in 1564 following a long illness, and was buried—as was his wish—in a common cemetery, without a tombstone.

Calvin's theological legacy is best exemplified today in the Christian Reformed Church, which continues to adhere fairly closely to his interpretation of the Bible. It has also followed Calvin in questioning and criticizing the (often anti-Christian) political and philosophical assumptions of the modern age. Calvin is also an important founding figure for the Presbyterian Church, even if it does not always place as much stress on the specifics of his theology. Following Calvin, the Presbyterian Church stresses the importance of learning biblical languages and of studying the Bible with care. In addition, Calvin's system of church government led to what is now called the "presbyterian" system, which uses a number of small representative bodies composed of laypeople rather than bishops ("presbyteries" and "synods") to govern the churches. In addition to providing a blueprint for the structure of the modern-day Presbyterian Church, this system has influenced a number of other denominations to develop a more representative system of church government. It also had a political influence, affecting the development of representative democracy in the United States and elsewhere.

III. The Radical Reformation

While the Reformation is dominated by the figures of Luther, Calvin, and Zwingli, it would not have had such significance and scope were it not for the hundreds of smaller, "fringe" movements that spread like wildfire through 16th-century Europe. These groups are many and various. Given their diversity, we should use caution when grouping them all under the single heading of "the Radical Reformation." The variations between them could be very great. There were "evangelical" radicals who usually objected to any form of violence, and hoped to invite others to join them through their example of a quiet witness. There were "revolutionary" radicals who believed that Christ was due to return to earth at any minute, and that the ungodly were to be converted as soon as possible—and by force if necessary. There were also "spiritual" radicals who emphasized the mystical elements of the faith, and minimized the importance of church services and political action. Given this diversity, this discussion will require a good deal of overgeneralization.

The Radical Reformers are so called because they sought to "radicalize" the thought of the better-known Protestant Reformers. The word "radicalize" attempts to suggest that these thinkers pushed certain Reformation claims to their logical conclusions; they went "one up" on Reformers such as Luther, Zwingli, and Calvin by taking one of their principles and emphasizing it more strongly. For example, some groups went further than did Luther in their sole reliance on the Bible. Others went further than did Zwingli in their rejection of traditional claims about the Eucharist and other sacraments. Still others went further than did Calvin in their claims about divine election and the need for a strict code of conduct. Whatever the specifics of each group's position, each sought to out-reform Luther, Calvin, and Zwingli, moving yet farther away from the practices which had dominated Christianity throughout the medieval period.

A. Four Distinctive Elements

What holds these diverse "radicals" together? Four factors unite *most* (though not all) of these groups. First and foremost was their agreement about the **voluntarist** principle—i.e., that becoming a Christian (and a member of a church) always requires an *active decision*. It never occurs simply because of where people live or because of their parents' beliefs. For the Radical Reformers, the church was always a "gathered" church, in which members actively sought out other like-minded individuals. It thus stood in opposition to the "parish" system (common in Roman Catholic, Lutheran, and some Reformed denominations) in which a person simply attended the church of one's own town or parish.

This "voluntarist" understanding of church membership had a special effect on the Radical Reformers' views about Baptism. Almost all of them had doubts about the appropriateness of infant Baptism, and some were explicitly hostile toward it. They agreed that Baptism was a cleansing from sin, and a dying and rising with Christ. However, they wondered in what sense Baptism brought the believer into a relationship with the community. While the Christian tradition generally claimed that it was certainly a welcoming of a person into the community, the Radical Reformers described it as an entry into a covenant with God. As such, it required a positive, active belief on the part of the person who would be baptized. Thus, they argued, only adults who were old enough to make such a decision could be baptized. This is usually referred to as **believer's baptism**. It continues to be practiced today in many Baptist denominations and in the Christian Church (Disciples of Christ).

Secondly, the Radical Reformers were not interested in making minor modifications in the church; instead, they advocated **restorationism**. They wanted a reconstitution of Christ's original church. Some groups thought this could be gained by returning to the church as described in the biblical book of the Acts of the Apostles; others looked forward to a future return of Christ that would restore the church with power. In either case, most groups were highly committed to basing their beliefs and actions upon a a literal interpretation of the Scripture. Some—the Hutterites, for example—argued against the ownership of private property, noting that the earliest Christians "would sell their possessions and goods and distribute the proceeds to all, as any had need" (Acts 2:45). Others turned to the teachings of the Sermon on the Mount, in which they were urged to strive toward perfection (Matt. 5:48).

Many Protestant denominations espouse some degree of restorationism, but very few are wholly committed to the idea. The culture of the ancient world was very different from ours today, and few are willing to adopt, without question, the attitudes toward (for example) women, slaves, and non-believers that seem to be promoted in the Bible. Nonetheless, some denominations practice restorationism by focusing on specific concerns that are present (or absent) in the Bible. For example, "Non-instrumentalist" denominations refuse to use or play any musical instrument that is not specifically mentioned in the Bible. This is a form of "restorationism," in that it seeks to "restore" the precise structures of the earliest Christian communities as they are described in the Bible.

Thirdly, the Radicals saw themselves as a chosen few, a righteous remnant to whom salvation had been granted. Some missionary work was carried out, but there was little interest in half-hearted believers. The Radical Reformers recognized that people cannot be coerced into true belief, and opted instead for a small but very devoted community. Most groups enforced fairly strict moral codes, but they never had the troubles that Calvin experienced in Geneva, because they did not believe that the civil authorities should be charged with enforcing religious rules. Instead, the religious community itself exercised authority, censuring or expelling those members who violated the codes of conduct. Closely related to this was their rejection of the idea of an "invisible church" where only God knows which persons are saved and which are damned. Salvation came through a conscious, free act of the believer; those who made this choice and stuck with it were the elect. One finds this emphasis today in a number of Protestant denominations, especially those that tend to see their own gathered community as distinct in some significant ways from the "normal" way of life in the outside world.

Finally, the Radical Reformers were very pessimistic about the rest of the world, that is, about those who stayed outside their own community. They often lived in separation from the rest of the society, sometimes in wholly isolated communities. Most would not hold public office or fight in wars. Their views were based on the Sermon on the Mount (Matt. 5-7), in which Jesus prohibits his followers from doing things that the civil government (or the culture) often encourages or requires—such as suing people, taking oaths, protecting one's property, judging others, and hating one's enemies. The Radical Reformers believed that the laws of the government should be obeyed, but only so long as they did not conflict with religious laws such as these.

While people were not expected to serve the government, they were expected to serve the Christian community. Congregations managed their own affairs, enforced their own rules of contact, and chose their own pastors. This required much more commitment to the Christian community than is commonly practiced today. Nevertheless, it can still be seen in some Amish communities, where longstanding Christian traditions take precedence over the changing practices of society. For example, Amish people still refuse to use electricity in their homes or travel in automobiles, using a horse and buggy instead. Other Christian groups also have adopted at least *some* aspects of this "separation from society." Many are pacifists, refusing to take part in war or in violence of any kind (as in some Mennonite groups, or in the Society of Friends, sometimes known as the "Quakers").

B. Isolation and Persecution

The distinctive practices of the Radical Reformers often put them at odds with more powerful forces in society. They were persecuted from all directions—not only by Catholics, but even by the mainstream Reformers. Luther was so distraught by many of their practices that he considered reincorporating many Catholic elements into his theology. Zwingli described the advocates of believer's baptism as heretics, and had them drowned. The Radicals were also persecuted by secular society, since many of their practices put them outside the mainstream of culture and sometimes even outside the civil law.

The unremitting persecution (which they experienced from all sides) created in the Radicals something of a siege mentality, and their own rhetoric sometimes became very fiery and dramatic— not an uncommon occurrence when a person or group feels cornered or surrounded. Here, for example, are the words of Melchior Hoffman, written in 1530:

> *Infant baptism is absolutely not from God but rather is practiced, out of willfullness, by Antichrists and the satanic crowd, in opposition to God and all his commandments, will, and desire. Verily, it is an eternal abomination to him. Woe, woe to all such blind leaders who willfully publish lies for the truth; their inheritance and portion is eternal damnation.*

These lines, worthy of the most fiery late-night television preacher, are the sort of thing that can inspire fanaticism. On the other hand, though, many of the Radical Reformers were quietly confident in the rightness of their cause and the injustice of their persecution. Consider these words by a Dutch woman who advocated believer's baptism, written just before her execution and addressed to her infant daughter:

> *There are many in this world who are enemies of the cross [of Christ], who seek to be free from it among the world, and to escape it. But, my dear child, if we could with Christ seek and inherit salvation, we must also help bear His cross; and this is the cross which He would have us bear: to follow His footsteps, and to help bear his reproach....He himself went before us in this way of reproach, and left us an example, that we should follow His steps; for, for His sake all must be forsaken, father, mother, sister, brother, husband, child, yea, one's own life.*

These two passages provide enough contrast to remind us that, even though we are here describing the Radical Reformers as one group, they also varied greatly from one another. But they were certainly united in the persecution they suffered.

Many Christian groups of the Radical Reformation eventually settled in the American colonies, primarily in an attempt to escape religious persecution in Europe. Their view that religious beliefs should not be enforced by the civil government had some impact on the principle of the separation of church and state found in the U.S. Constitution. Some of the groups that trace their roots to the Radicals—the Mennonites, the Amish, and the Moravian Brethren, for example—are often held up as communities which have come the closest to living out the teachings of Jesus.

IV. The English Reformation

In England, we witness the Reformation of an entire country, carried out by the will of its government. In this sense it is unlike the stories of those reformers who were working with either one particular city government (Zwingli in Zurich or Calvin in Geneva), or in direct opposition to all civil government (most of the Radical Reformers). The English Reformation was officially begun, driven, and completed at the behest of the British crown. Yet it was also the product of more than two centuries of serious theological reflection.

A. A Variety of Causes

The story behind the English Reformation, as it usually told, is a rather ugly one. The decision by **King Henry VIII** of England to break with the Roman Catholic Church was not due to any dispute over its teaching or doctrine. In fact, when the Reformation broke out, Henry remained on the Catholic side. Henry even authored (or at least, had signed his name to) a document upholding the validity of the seven traditional sacraments, thus receiving from the pope the title of "Defender of the Faith." However, Henry's first marriage (a typically arranged royal marriage to the daughter of the King of Spain, Katherine of Aragon) had not produced a male heir. This was considered a divine rejection of the union, which was irregular in any case. Katherine was the widow of Henry's brother, so the marriage had required a papal dispensation. After the union did not produce children, Henry wanted the marriage annulled. His request was refused, and despite much negotiation he was unable to change the pope's mind on this matter. He decided that it was easier to break with the Roman Catholic Church than to continue in his childless marriage.

Figure 19.4: Portrait of Henry VIII, king of England.

However, this is not quite the whole story. For one thing, there had been a gradual but consistent rise in the power of the English royalty throughout this era. These monarchs enjoyed increasing freedom in their dealings with the church, and especially with the pope. Even more importantly, Henry's break with Rome would never have been successful had not the stirrings of reform already begun in England. Back in the 14th century, John Wycliffe was already preaching many of the views that would later become central in the Reformation. He focused on the Bible alone, and believed that it should be available to the people. His view of predestination was almost as strong as Calvin's would be. He rejected transubstantiation and argued that the body and blood of Christ were present in the Eucharist not corporally, but "sacramentally, spiritually, and efficaciously." He doubted the supremacy of the pope, advocated married clergy, and believed that temporal rulers should work to reform the church. Thus many of the ideas of the Reformation had been first introduced to England more than two centuries before the birth of Martin Luther. Wycliffe's ideas were kept alive during the interim (in modified form) by a group called the Lollards. Although the Lollards themselves were beset by problems and viewed by many with suspicion, the reforms which they championed remained popular in many quarters of England. When the Reformation began to sweep through Europe, Wycliffe and the Lollards had seen to it that England was already prepared to go along.

The early 16th century also witnessed a flourishing intellectual rebirth in England. The great medieval universities of Oxford and Cambridge had been breeding grounds for all sorts of critical challenges to the traditional interpretations of the faith. Erasmus was professor of Greek at Cambridge for a while; a strong humanist tradition flourished. Thinkers such as Thomas More and John Colet were attracted by the rediscovery of ancient languages and classical modes of study, and this stimulated a fresh study of the scriptures. In 1527, an admirer of Luther named **William Tyndale** published a translation of significant parts of the Bible into English for the first time—a move which made it available to the common people, and which thereby threatened the monopoly which the church had enjoyed over its interpretation. In fact, Tyndale came under vicious attack from traditionalists in England, and he had to live in exile to continue his project of translation.

We will never know precisely what motives eventually led King Henry VIII to side with the forces of reform. He may have been acting primarily because of his divorce case, or his general suspicion of Catholic countries such as Italy and Spain. He may have had some appreciation for the new humanism that flourished in this period, or he may have just had a shrewd political instinct for recognizing which way the wind was blowing. In any case, he did three things in the early 1530s that changed the English Reformation from an intellectual and religious undercurrent into the official policy of the nation. First, he formally broke with the pope. Second, he placed the church under the control of the crown through Parliament. Finally, he dissolved the English monasteries and took control of their property holdings, thus creating a national church that was both politically and financially secure (and providing himself with considerable spoils with which he could win friends and influence people).

B. Opposition and Consolidation

Despite the tremendous power behind the reform, it also met with considerable opposition. For one thing, many families of the aristocracy had profited greatly from the systems of power and privilege that had accompanied their support of the traditional church structures. The translation of the Bible into English and the reduction in the power and influence of the clergy had made life more difficult for some of these families. Neither was the peasant class fully supportive of the reform. Popular piety was strong, and there was clearly some considerable resentment at the official effort to remove those elements of the faith upon which people had depended for centuries—including prayer for the dead, the belief in purgatory, and other elements of late medieval religion. England also saw its fair share of iconoclasm; most churches lost their images (including stained glass, sculpture, and other decoration). In Switzerland, the removal of images had enjoyed popular support, but in England it was often regarded as an excessive governmental intervention into the personal lives of believers.

When Henry died in 1547, he was succeeded by his only son, **Edward VI**. Since Edward was only nine years old at the time, the country went through a stormy period in which various nobles vied for power. These struggles were mostly won by advocates of reform; thus, during Edward's short reign, the country took a great leap away from traditional Catholicism. The strong-willed Protestant leaders swept away any traces of the former king's caution about the reform (and its revolutionary tendencies). All restrictions on reading, teaching, or preaching the scriptures were removed. Schools were reorganized, with their educational mission directed toward reform. However, the government was not strong enough to relax so many of the laws to which the public had become accustomed under Henry's comparatively heavy-handed reign. The reign of Edward thus witnessed a great deal of disruption, anarchism, and small-scale revolution—mirroring the power struggles that took place at the highest levels as to who would govern the country in the name of the child-king.

Under these circumstances, it may be surprising that the English Reformation stayed intact at all. One of its stabilizing forces was the Archbishop of Canterbury, **Thomas Cranmer**, who held that office throughout the entire period (1533-1553). He was politically astute and turned out to be an important figure: he argued successfully for the wider distribution of the Bible, and for further reductions in the social and financial privileges of priests. He helped to carve out the basic beliefs of the English Reformation, finalized in a document called the ***Thirty-Nine Articles***, which sets out the specific similarities and differences between the Church of England and the Roman Catholic Church. He also wrote much of the language of the ***Book of Common Prayer***—the first major liturgical document written in the English language, which set a standard for the language of worship in the English-speaking world that continues to the present day.

Cranmer's influence was interrupted in the mid-1550s. The last power-broker during Edward's reign, the Duke of Northumberland, was so extreme in carrying out measures of reform that he probably did more damage to the cause of the English Reformation than all of its Catholic opponents together. By enforcing all kinds of highly restrictive laws against the practice of traditional Christian piety, he offended just about everyone. King Edward's health failed in 1553, and the rightful heir to the throne was Mary, the eldest daughter of Henry VIII. Mary had remained a devout Roman Catholic throughout the English Reformation, and everyone knew that she would reverse the reform if she became queen. The Duke of Northumberland attempted to remove her from the line of succession, an act which outraged even the most loyal Protestants. Reform-minded British subjects did not want to tamper with the throne, despite their opposition to this particular monarch. Mary became queen in July 1553, and quickly reversed many of the reforms.

Queen Mary's changes might have been taken in stride, but her reign quickly became much too extreme. Queen Mary was a reactionary who believed that the English church easily could be restored to its pre-Reformation state. In 1555 a number of heresy trials began, and a significant number of the advocates of reform—bishops, clergy, teachers, and common people—were burned at the stake, including Thomas Cranmer himself. To this may be added that Mary presided over a disastrous war with France and a severe outbreak of disease in England. When Queen Mary died in 1558, all of England was ready for a reign more moderate than either hers or that of the Duke of Northumberland.

Figure 19.5: Portrait of Thomas Cranmer.

C. The Elizabethan Settlement

All of this helps to explain the significance of **Elizabeth I**, whose long reign established the Church of England as we know it today. She resumed the course of the reform, reversing much of the return to Catholicism that her sister had advocated during her short but dramatic reign. Elizabeth was successful because she avoided the excesses of earlier Protestant advocates, allowing for some degree of religious toleration and providing for the practice of popular piety. During her reign, England experienced an enormous flowering of intellectual and cultural life, for which it had had little leisure during the stormy first half of the 16th century.

Although Thomas Cranmer had been dead for three years when Elizabeth ascended the throne, her reign was very closely modelled on his philosophy and his spirit. Cranmer had always been very good at recognizing the positive value of the positions held by *both* the Catholic traditionalists *and* the Protestant reformers. The position that he developed for the English church therefore represented an attempt to hold together the best of both sides—an approach described by the Latin term *via media* ("middle way"). During the reign of Elizabeth I, this *via media* became more and more the norm.

A good example of this "middle way" can be found in the understanding of the Eucharist that developed in the Church of England. Cranmer accepted the idea of the "real presence" of Christ (as did Roman Catholics and Lutherans), but he also understood the bread and wine as a memorial of Christ's death (as Zwingli had taught). In the relatively final version of Cranmer's *Book of Common Prayer*, completed in 1559 under the reign of Elizabeth, *both* views are represented. Thus, Catholic and Protestant elements are fused together—a phenomenon that has become the hallmark of the English church.

Figure 19.6: Portrait of Elizabeth I.

D. Later Influence

At various times in its history, the Church of England (also known as the Anglican Church) has swung in a more "Protestant" or a more "Catholic" direction. In the 18th century, for example, a certain degree of routine and apathy in the church led **John Wesley** to advocate a much more lively form of religion, with considerably more attention to personal spirituality, Bible study, and evangelistic preaching. Although he wanted his movement to stay within the Church of England, it eventually became more and more independent, and is today know as the **Methodist Church**. In the 19th century, a group of teachers in Oxford sensed that the church was lacking some of the devotional and liturgical practices that had been part of its heritage. Their sermons, tracts, and books are collectively known as **The Oxford Movement**, and it led to a considerable revival of the "Catholic" elements of English Christianity. One of the leaders of the movement, **John Henry Newman**, converted to Roman Catholicism and was eventually named a cardinal.

With the expansion of the British colonial empire throughout the centuries following the English Reformation, the Church of England has had a considerable impact on Christianity throughout the world. In many countries, a slightly altered version of the Church of England has taken root—e.g., the Church of Australia, the Church of Ireland, and (in the United States) the **Episcopal Church**.

This chapter has provided a small sampling of the reform movements of the 16th century. While it has certainly not covered them all, it may help provide some sense of the origins of some of the Protestant denominations that are to be found in North America and Europe, among other places. It also gives us a better understanding of the different directions in which Christian theology developed during this period—especially in its understanding of authority, ministry, and the sacraments.

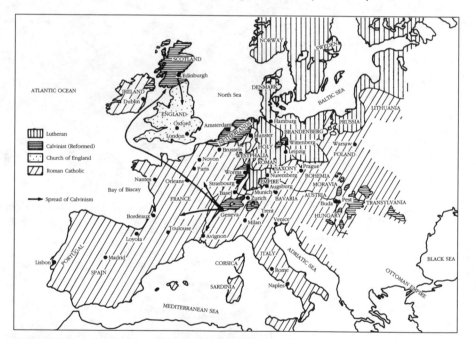

Figure 19.7: Map of the division of Christendom by the Reformation (mid-16th century).

Key Terms:

believer's baptism	Edward VI
Book of Common Prayer	election
John Calvin	Episcopal Church
Consistory	Henry VIII
Thomas Cranmer	*Institutes of the Christian Religion*
double predestination	Marburg Colloquy

Methodist Church

John Henry Newman

Oxford Movement

Reply to Sadoleto

restorationism

Thirty-Nine Articles

transubstantiation

William Tyndale

ubiquity of Christ

voluntarist principle

John Wesley

Ulrich Zwingli

Questions for Reading:

1. List at least two similarities and two differences between the teachings of Zwingli and Luther. Why was Zwingli so adamantly opposed to the use of images in worship?

2. Briefly describe Calvin's doctrine of election. Include a description of "double predestination."

3. How does Calvin's understanding of the Eucharist differ from that of Luther and that of Zwingli?

4. How did Calvin address questions about church authority? Include at least one specific example from his experience in Geneva.

5. Summarize the basic argument of Calvin's *Reply to Sadoleto*.

6. Why are the Radical Reformers called "radical"? List, and briefly describe, the "four distinctive elements" that characterize most of the Radical Reformers.

7. Why were the Radical Reformers especially subject to persecution?

8. List at least three events or movements that led to the English Reformation.

9. In what ways did the English Reformation meet resistance? Name at least two distinct sources of this resistance.

10. List the three monarchs who followed Henry VIII, and summarize the religious policy of each.

11. List the chief contributions of Thomas Cranmer and William Tyndale to the English Reformation.

12. List at least two movements or denominations that developed within the Church of England *after* the Reformation era.

13. Name at least one Christian denomination that has been significantly influenced by *each* of the four reformers or movements described in this chapter (Zwingli, Calvin, the Radical Reformation, and the English Reformation).

Works Consulted/Recommended Reading:

Dickens, A. G. *The English Reformation*. Glasgow: William Collins and Sons, Fontana Paperbacks, 1967.

Dickens, A. G. and Carr, Dorothy, eds. *The Reformation in England to the Accession of Elizabeth I*. Documents of Modern History. London: Edward Arnold, 1967.

Metzger, Bruce and Murphy, Roland, eds. *The New Oxford Annotated Bible with Apocrypha*, New Revised Standard Version. New York: Oxford University Press, 1991.

Parker, T. H. L. *John Calvin*. Icknield Way, England: Lion Publishing, 1975.

Potter, G. R. *Zwingli*. Cambridge: Cambridge University Press, 1976.

Potter, G. R. ed. *Huldrych Zwingli*. Documents of Modern History. London: Edward Arnold, 1978.

Potter, G. R. and Greengrass, M., eds. *John Calvin*. Documents of Modern History. London: Edward Arnold, 1983.

Williams, George H. *The Radical Reformation*. 3rd ed. Kirksville: Sixteenth Century Journal Publishers, 1992.

Williams, George H. and Mergal, Angel M., eds. *Spiritual and Anabaptist Writers*. Library of Christian Classics, vol. 25. Philadelphia: Westminster Press, 1957.

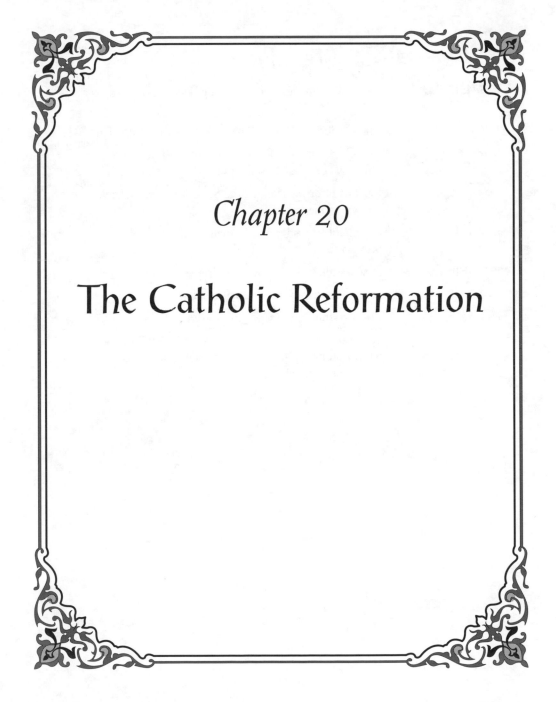

Chapter 20

The Catholic Reformation

Timeline

1495-1517 AD	Cardinal Ximenes leads Catholic reform activities in Spain.
1516	The Oratory of Divine Love is founded in Rome.
1528	The Capuchins, a reform branch of the Franciscans, is officially recognized by the pope.
1534	Ignatius of Loyola founds the Society of Jesus, also known as the Jesuits.
1534-1549	Pope Paul III institutes a limited number of reforms prior to the Council of Trent.
1545-1548	First session of the Council of Trent.
1551-1552	Second session of the Council of Trent.
1562-1563	Third session of the Council of Trent.
1581	Teresa of Avila and John of the Cross found a new reform branch of the Carmelite order known as the Discalced Carmelites.

The Catholic Reformation

The Roman Catholic Church responded to the Protestant Reformation with two overlapping yet distinct movements. One is called the **Counter-Reformation** and the other is called the **Catholic Reformation**. The Counter-Reformation, as its name implies, refers to the efforts of those who were loyal to the pope and supportive of the customary practices of the Roman Catholic Church to counter (go against) the teachings and practices of the Protestant reformers. Because it was a movement designed to aggressively stop Protestant teachings, ideas, and practices, it was polemical and negative in its form. In contrast, the Catholic Reformation refers to the efforts of those who wanted to bring about the internal rebirth of Catholic sensibility—in theology, spirituality, religious piety, and morality.

Although the Catholic Reformation is often studied in relationship to the Protestant Reformation, it is not a movement that simply reacts to the Protestant Reformation. In fact, it began before the initial crises of the Protestant Reformation, and continued even after the Reformation had resulted in the establishment of distinctive Protestant churches. Many of the figures belonging to the Catholic Reformation were as critical of the corrupt practices of the church as any of the Protestant reformers were. Rather then leaving the church, these Catholic reformers saw the abuses as an opportunity to challenge the church back to godly ways by reclaiming the traditions it had ignored or forgotten.

This chapter will focus upon the Catholic reform movements prior to, during, and immediately following the Council of Trent (1545-1563). The Council of Trent is an important event in Catholic reform because one of its functions was to respond to the Protestant Reformation. Another was to initiate an internal reform and spiritual reawakening based upon a re-evaluation of doctrinal issues that impacted the lives of 16th century Catholics. This chapter will look at the major movements of the Catholic Reformation, including the Council of Trent, the standardization of Catholic doctrine and practice, and the new spiritual awakening in Catholicism expressed both in the founding of religious orders and in the art of the period.

I. Pre-Tridentine Reform

Even before the Protestant reformers entered the scene, there were several early indications that Catholics were indeed ready for widespread reform and revival. The Catholic reform movements that took place immediately prior to the Council of Trent are sometimes called pre-Tridentine reforms. Foremost among these was the reform that took place in Spain under Cardinal Ximenes (1495-1517). After the Spanish *Reconquista* ("Reconquest"), Spain became an ardently Christian country. Monks and friars were required to make reforms consistent with their vow of poverty. Religious houses which did not comply with approved standards of behavior were dissolved, their revenues going to the education of children, to hospitals, and to the poor.

Cardinal Ximenes also created a university at Alcala which encouraged the study of Hebrew and Greek for the training of scholastic theologians and the encouragement of scholarly thought. A group of scholars under the Cardinal's direction produced a critical edition of the Bible in Hebrew, Greek and Latin with commentaries. The Spanish Inquisition would later destroy many of these "**Polyglot" Bibles** (containing several languages) along with the scriptures and numerous spiritual writings which had been translated into the native dialects, the vernacular (common speech) of the country. This was, in part, a Counter-Reformation movement directed against Protestant reformers who encouraged the common people to read the Bible and who spread their reform ideas through literature written in the vernacular. These Bibles appear also to have encouraged the Council of Trent's decision to declare that only one particular Latin translation of the Bible, the Vulgate, was the authoritative Bible of the Catholic Church.

During this time, many new religious orders were founded to revitalize the church, some coming out of this early Spanish reform. One of the most interesting developments of the pre-Tridentine period was a series of groups called "oratories." These oratories were groups of clergy who banded together for the purpose of prayer, meditation, and mutual support as they participated in discussions about how they might reform the church. The most famous of these was the Oratory of Divine Love which was founded in Rome in 1516. Likewise, a new religious order known as the Theatines was founded in 1524 by two members of the Oratory of Divine Love for the purpose of combatting the abuses and scandals that corrupted the church at that time by training reform-minded clergy for positions of leadership in the church.

Other religious orders dedicated to reform include the Congregation of the Mission founded by St. Vincent de Paul in 1625 and the Ursulines founded in 1535. The Congregation of the Mission (also known as the Lazarists or the Vincentians) contributed to the Catholic Reformation by preaching missions (renewal retreats for lay people) and by preparing young men for ordination to the priesthood. One of the reasons the Catholic Church suffered so much abuse and corruption was that many of its priests had little education and were poorly trained for the priesthood. The Ursulines were the first religious order of women to dedicate themselves to teaching. These new orders represent what we call the "active" life. They did not withdraw from the world, as monks and nuns had done for centuries before. Rather, their entire mission was directed outward in pastoral ministry to those in need. They lived an ascetic lifestyle and devoted themselves to serving others in hospitals, orphanages, and schools for children. They also placed great emphasis on living a life of charity, a life lived for others which was socially responsible and Christian in its inspiration.

Perhaps the most influential of these new orders was the **Society of Jesus** or the **Jesuits,** founded by **Ignatius of Loyola** in 1534. The small band who joined together with Ignatius was first called "the Company of Jesus." Like the mendicant orders, they lived a simple lifestyle, relying on alms for their livelihood. Ignatius intended for the Society to minister to the poor and to unbelievers, in particular, to work with children and those who could not read or write. His interest in converting unbelievers would anticipate one of the results of the Catholic Reformation, namely, a trend of missionary expansion into newly discovered lands. He was also committed to the reform of the church and to the education of its members. Thus the order became renowned for its achievements in education, especially higher education, including the education of members of the upper classes and the training of clergy. Their establishment as professors in the university system enabled the Jesuits to use their study of theology not only to serve the pastoral needs of the church but in disputes with the Protestant scholars of their times. The Jesuits viewed the Protestant reformers as disobedient to the church, whereas the Jesuits themselves took a vow of absolute obedience to the pope. They vowed to go without question and without delay wherever the pope might order them for the salvation of souls and the spreading of the true faith.

Ignatius of Loyola, the founder of the Jesuits, could not have seemed a more unlikely candidate for the religious life and sainthood. He was a Spaniard trained as a knight, shaped by a military background and way of thinking. His life before his conversion was not an exemplary one. He was even arrested once and accused of crimes in Pamplona, Spain, although we do not know the nature of the charges brought against him. His conversion came during a long convalescence after he was gravely injured during a battle. He had been reading devotional books, including a life of Christ and lives of the saints—the only books that were available to him. Inspired by these stories, he decided that he would become a soldier for Christ. Shortly afterward he went to a monastery and dedicated himself to prayer and meditation. He discovered—as did Luther—that he was tortured by his sins and by scruples. He was finally commanded by a confessor to stop punishing himself through excessive penance. He obeyed, and it is in this story of his life that we can see the great importance he would place on obedience in his new order.

During his stay at Manresa monastery, Ignatius also drafted the first sketch of his **Spiritual Exercises**, which would become the tool of spiritual formation for those who joined him in his quest. It is a month-long examination and participation of the individual in the drama of sin and salvation, leading to a turning over of everything, especially the will, to obedience to his religious superior, to the teachings of the church and its traditions, and for the spread of the faith. With his band of followers, Ignatius set off to offer himself to the pope for whatever service the church might need. Despite the papacy's resistance to the establishment of new religious orders, the Jesuits were officially recognized in 1539. Their motto sums up the Ignatian approach nicely: **Ad majorem Dei gloriam** ("To the greater glory of God").

In addition to these new orders, there were other pre-existing orders that underwent significant reforms and created new branches of their orders. These include the Capuchins, a reform branch of the Franciscan movement, and the Discalced ("without shoes") Carmelites, a reform branch of the Carmelite order. Both of these reforms met with great success but were at times in great peril. The **Capuchins**, whose influence and preaching would be vital to the Catholic reform movement, were almost condemned when their superior (and popular preacher) Bernardino Ochino converted to the Protestant cause. This scandal, plus the unwavering opposition of the Observant Franciscans to this new branch of the order almost led to their suppression. They weathered the crisis, however, and the Capuchins were recognized by the pope in 1528, getting their name from the unique four-pointed hood which they wore with their brown habit. They were perhaps the most successful of the movements to reconstruct the spirit of an older order, and much of the credit for this goes to their founder, Matteo da Bascio.

There were papal reforms, as well. Pope Paul III (reigned 1534-1549) was elected pope upon the recommendation of the previous pope who had attempted reform but was unable to carry it out. Although he was very much a Renaissance pope—enjoying the comforts of wealth and the power of his office—he was also intent on internal reform of the church. He appointed a number of reformers to the College of Cardinals (advisors to the pope and second in line of authority after the pope), all former members of the Oratory of Divine Love. He also appointed a reform commission to recommend changes in the way the church was run. Their report revealed some very serious problems: the papal office had become too secular; the cardinals needed to be less infatuated with the power and wealth of the world and more concerned about spiritual matters; abuses such as the selling of church offices and indulgences needed to be stopped. Pope Paul III instituted a few reforms immediately as the result of this commission, but many others would have to wait for the Council of Trent.

II. The Council of Trent and Catholic Reform

It is difficult to disentangle the threads of the Catholic Reformation neatly into those reforms that occurred before the important **Council of Trent** and those that took place afterwards. In general, Catholics agreed on the need for an official council to either reconcile with the reformers, especially Luther, or to refute them and inaugurate reform from within the church itself. Already in 1535, Pope Paul III announced his intention to call a council, but the council did not actually take place until 1545. There were a number of factors that led to this delay.

First, there was a problem about its location: the cardinals insisted it be in Rome, and the Holy Roman emperor, Charles V, insisted it be in Germany. Second, Charles V was pressuring Pope Paul III to call the council, but he wanted it to deal with the Lutherans who were causing political havoc in his territories. More specifically, he wanted some quick practical religious compromises to defuse the tension. The pope and the bishops, however, wanted to hold a doctrinal council rather than a practical one: they wanted to come to grips with the basic teachings of the church and then initiate an internal reform which would flow from this doctrinal clarification. Third, some church leaders wanted to avoid a council completely. Those with pure motives doubted whether it was possible to convene a general (ecumenical) council that would include all Christendom. Some opposed the council because of political motives. The French king was often at war with Germany, and a council held in Germany would offend French church leaders. Others opposed it out of fear. They doubted whether or not the pope would be able to maintain control of the council and its proceedings.

When the Council of Trent was finally convened in 1545, its location was somewhat of a compromise. The city of Trent, located in the Italian Alps, and situated between southern German regions and northern Italian ones, was barely inside Charles' domain, yet it offered easy access to Italy. The council was made up of three separate sessions, which spanned eighteen years and the reigns of four different popes. The first session (1545-48) was largely controlled by representatives of the pope and so dealt with doctrinal definitions; the second session (1551-52) dealt with a mixture of doctrinal and practical matters, and the third and final session (1562-63) concentrated mainly on disciplinary correction and means of regulating church activities in the future. Some meetings were poorly attended, the first session having only twenty-eight delegates. A number of Protestants were present at the second session, but discussions between the two sides broke down without coming to any mutual understandings. Italian church leaders attended in the greatest numbers; French church leaders were noticeably absent. Yet, despite all its difficulties, the Council of Trent was successful in initiating reform within the Catholic Church.

The council addressed a number of doctrinal issues that also had relevance for the Protestant Reformation. Whereas the Protestant reformers had said that a person was justified by faith alone, the delegates of the council asserted that faith alone was not sufficient for justification, but that it must be accompanied by hope and by love. They affirmed that grace indeed was the conduit of all good human actions, and that our nature, moved by God, could cooperate in good works. By contrast, the Protestant reformers had said that humans were incapable of any good work apart from grace. The Fathers of the council said that nothing could be done without God's grace, but that humans were capable of assent and cooperation with God's grace. In this they closely followed the arguments of Thomas Aquinas. They also said that faith could not be lost except through denying it utterly (apostasy), even though grace could be lost by turning away from God (mortal sin). With the Protestant reformers, they acknowledged that humans remain disordered after Baptism. However, against Luther and other reformers, the Fathers of the Council denied that our nature had been utterly destroyed by the Fall and made incapable of any good during this life.

Confronted by the Protestant reformers' appeal to the Bible as the sole authority, the council stated that the unwritten traditions of the church must also be received with reverence, since these were prayerfully stated by people acting in the power of the Holy Spirit. The sacraments were reasserted as essential to the Christian life. The number of sacraments was fixed at seven: Baptism, Confirmation, Eucharist, Matrimony, Holy Orders, Penance, and Extreme Unction (anointing of the sick). They also developed the notion of **sacramentals**, those religious objects or devotions which have tangible qualities, though they do not have the full efficacy and centrality of the seven official sacraments. An example would be holy water, blessed and tangible, used commonly, but used exceptionally in Baptism.

Attacked for the idea of the mass as a sacrifice, the Council of Trent reasserted that it was indeed a sacrifice to God for the sins of the world. They organized and defined the shape and order of the liturgy, which previously had had many variations. They identified Latin as the official language of worship. The **Vulgate** (a Latin translation of the Bible widely in use in the West at least from the 6th century and containing the books of the Apocrypha) was declared to be the only authoritative translation of the Bible. At the time of the Council of Trent, Latin was still the recognized, official language of the universities and the educated. However, it had already begun to fall into disuse among the common people. In response to this cultural change, Protestant reformers had been commissioning vernacular translations of the Bible, but they had also been using versions of the Bible that did not contain these apocryphal books in order to do their vernacular translations. Thus Catholics and Protestants emerged from the Reformation with two different canons of scripture.

Although the Council of Trent had addressed a number of doctrinal issues, it was also a pastoral council dedicated to eliminating abuses and inspiring holiness among the church's clergy. To correct abuses, the Fathers abolished the office of seller of indulgences. Bishops were given the power of supervision in their dioceses. Simony and nepotism were abolished; penalties were imposed for blasphemy and violations of celibacy. Luxurious dress and affluent lifestyles were discouraged among all Christians. Clerics who had previously worn the ordinary clothes of the time now had to wear special clerical garb. The **Breviary** (prayer book containing the liturgy of the hours, the official prayer of priests and monks) was reformed to make it clearer and simpler to use, giving primacy to scripture and removing other non-biblical readings.

The Council of Trent also exhorted the clergy to be devout shepherds of souls, and to that end, it established a means to educate them. It decreed that every bishop should either send candidates for orders to the university, or if there were no universities in the diocese, a **seminary** for their training should be founded and built. The training of the clergy was perhaps the most far-reaching results of the Council of Trent, and the Jesuit order was especially influential in implementing this aspect of the reforms. It greatly improved the clergy's ability to preach the Word, one of the principal reasons that many of the people had abandoned the Catholic Church for the preachers of the Protestant Reformation. Bishops and clergy were now to be preachers and teachers of their flock. A short summary of what had been upheld by Trent was put in the form of a brief summary teaching tool, intended for clergy, called the Catechism of Trent.

III. The Catechism of Trent

Pius V was responsible for commissioning a compressed and readable version of what had been out-lined at Trent as a way of regularizing what the church was teaching in terms of doctrine and practice. This **catechism** was intended primarily for the clergy, so that there might be uniform instruction of the people in the Catholic faith. The development of this official catechism was guided by Charles Borromeo, who had been an advisor to the bishops at the Council of Trent. Although his version of the catechism remained in wide use for nearly 150 years, the 16th century also produced another respected and widely read catechism written by Peter Canisius, a Jesuit. The latter catechism was admired by many for its clarity and persuasiveness even by Protestant preachers.

Both of these men lived and preached reform in their own lives, and their catechisms were merely an extension of their desire to see the spirituality of Catholicism restored to a more pure state. Both were named saints by the church they so ardently served: Charles Borromeo in 1610 and Peter Canisius in 1925. Borromeo was thought by many to be a model of how a bishop ought to behave: hardworking, pious, scholarly, and rigorous. However, his life also portrayed the irony of the era: he was made an archbishop at an early age by his uncle, the currently reigning pope, as an act of nepotism.

The Catechism of Trent and other Catholic Reformation catechisms like it were not altogether unique to the Council of Trent. Rather, the delegates of the council realized that Martin Luther's suc-cess in explaining the essence of his preaching and his doctrinal positions had been due in large part to the success of his *Small Catechism*, published in 1529 and widely circulated among the people in the vernacular. The catechisms emerging from the resolutions of the Council of Trent adopted a similar form, if not the vernacular language, in hopes of achieving the same results.

IV. The Revival of Mysticism in Spain

Although many new religious orders were founded and older orders reformed in the period imme-diately preceding the Council of Trent, others were being established or reformed during and immediately following the council. Some of these were vital to the conciliar process and its imple-mentation; all of them were important because of the spiritual fervor with which they led the people to a greater understanding of church doctrine and practice. In particular, Spain was experiencing a reform of the Carmelite order and the revival of mysticism in the persons of Teresa of Avila and John of the Cross.

Teresa of Avila had spent much of her life in a struggle between worldly comforts and the inte-rior life of prayer. At the age of 40 she experienced such a profound conversion, accompanied by ecstasies and visions, that she felt called to return to the simpler, harsher rule of the Carmelite founders. Thus Teresa and her protégé and follower, John of the Cross, established the **Discalced Carmelites**. The term "discalced" means "unshod," referring to the spiritual practice of going bare-foot in order to fulfill Jesus' mandate to provide themselves with nothing for the journey, not even sandals (Matt 10:9-10). Teresa's primary calling was to poverty and prayer. The "barefoot" Carmelites were to rely only on charity and the providence of God to support them. Teresa's first foundation was made in Avila in secret, for she knew the opposition her reforms would cause. She ultimately made seventeen separate foundations during her lifetime, traveling widely throughout Spain to do so. These foundations were made up of sisters who followed her example and teaching. However, there was no official recognition of these foundations or the Carmelite reform movement until 1581, when permission finally was granted for them to become a separate order along with the brothers organized by John of the Cross. Teresa's combination of common sense, political acumen, and profound spirituality enabled her to establish her foundations against opposition from other Carmelite branches and in spite of the suspicions of the Spanish Inquisition.

We have a great deal of Teresa's writings because the priests who served as her confidantes and advisors insisted that she write down her life and her method of prayer as a means of convincing the inquisitors that she was not a heretic. The most famous of these are her *Life*, an autobiographical account, and the *Interior Castle*, a description of her method of prayer. We also have a number of the writings of John of the Cross, including his exquisitely written poems in the *Ascent of Mount Carmel* and his *Dark Night of the Soul*. Teresa's and John's contemplation of God and their life lived from the center of that contemplation was one of the great contributions of the Carmelite reform movement. The simple beauty of their prayer of the heart and their focus on the love of God can be seen in these brief excerpts from their writings.

> *The important thing is not to think much but to love much;*
> *and so to do that which best stirs you to love*
> (Teresa of Avila, Interior Castle, 70).

> *To come to the knowledge of all desire,*
> *the knowledge of nothing . . .*
> *To come to the knowledge you have not*
> *you must go by a way you know not*
> (John of the Cross, Selected Writings, 137).

> *Let nothing upset you,*
> *Let nothing frighten you,*
> *Everything is changing;*
> *God alone is changeless.*
> *Patience alone attains the goal.*
> *Who has God lacks nothing;*
> *God alone fills all her needs*
> (Prayer of St. Teresa, written on the inside of her prayerbook).

> *How gently and lovingly*
> *You awake in my heart,*
> *Where in secret You dwell alone;*
> *And in your sweet breathing,*
> *Filled with good and glory,*
> *How tenderly You swell my heart with love*
> (John of the Cross, "The Living Flame of Love," in The Wisdom of the Saints, 203).

Both John of the Cross and Teresa of Avila are saints and Doctors of the Church. Teresa is one of only two women to have been awarded this title.

V. Art as a Reflection of the Reformation Period

The art of the Reformation period, both Catholic and Protestant, reflects a number of theological issues. When Protestant Reformation communities built new churches, they built them with a simplicity and austerity that did not exist in churches dating from the middle ages or before. Most often, however, older churches were merely taken over and the ornamentation removed. The walls were white-washed to cover paintings and elaborate decorations on the walls, and to bring a greater sensation of light and simplicity into the worship space. They stripped churches of their statues and ornamentation in order to concentrate on the centrality of the Word. On occasion these churches would even be stripped of their furniture so that only a pulpit (preaching stand) remained in a central place in the church.

Figure 20.1: A typical Protestant church of the period. This church formerly was a Gothic church with many statues, ornaments, and gilding (gold leaf decoration). In its "stripped down" version, it provides us with a good sense of contrast with Baroque Roman Catholic churches of the time.

The art of the Renaissance movement is recognizable for its realism. Among artists of the Protestant Reformation this realism was especially evident in their subject matter. Although some depicted actual scenes from the Bible, others focused on everyday life situations which could be used as visual metaphors for preaching and teaching about the moral life. In particular, the Dutch artists of the late 16th and early 17th centuries sought to depict in portraits, landscapes, and other types of art a variety of ordinary circumstances of life illustrating the beauty of creation, the positive and negative sides of human nature, the vanity of striving for power, and the human need for salvation. Although Germany did not produce any famous Protestant artists during the Reformation, Protestantism manifested itself in the creation of new kinds of music designed for the participation of large congregations of laypeople, rather than the highly trained choirs of the medieval church. The hymns were sung in the vernacular (rather than Latin), and the text of the hymns came from the Bible. Some of our most well-known Christian hymns, including several by Johann Sebastian Bach, date back to the time of the Reformation,

In contrast with their Protestant counterparts, Catholics not only preserved the architecture of the medieval churches whenever possible, but commissioned new ornamentation and art which would dramatically illustrate the truths of Catholic orthodoxy. The style begun in this period is termed the **Baroque**. While it had been influenced by the realism of the Renaissance, Baroque art and architecture added the dimension of light and darkness, suggesting that the division between this world and the heavenly realm is penetrable, at least through the mediation of the virgin Mary and the saints. In Figure 20.2, we have a scene in which Paul experiences his conversion on the road to Damascus. What is uniquely different is the perspective of the scene: the artist clearly is trying to personally involve the observer, who looks up at the horse at sky *as if* he or she was lying on the ground with St. Paul. There is an attempt to involve the worshipers, appealing to their feelings and engaging them in the movement of faith. Observers, as believers, were invited to put themselves into the story, to see the conversion as St. Paul experienced it. Note also the use of light to express the drama of the event.

Figure 20.2: This famous work of Paul's conversion on the way to Damascus is by Caravaggio, c. 1601, and typifies Baroque painting. Cerasi Chapel, Santa Maria del Popolo, Rome.

Baroque art also sought to impress its viewers with awesome displays of riches and to evoke in the viewer a sense of awe. Baroque churches were filled with rich and ornate illustrations of the great events of the Bible and church history. It would overwhelm the visitor with dramatic representations of the avenues of salvation available to the believer: Mary, the saints and relics, the crucified Christ, and symbols of the Eucharist.

In figure 20.3, the observer looks up at Bernini's famous statue of St. Teresa in ecstasy. This statue conveys to the observer complex devotional and erotic overtones as it portrays the saint caught up into the divine realm as her heart is pierced. The church is small and dark; the statue is a glance into the realms of heavenly light in which the human and the divine meet and are joined in bliss.

Figure 20.3: St. Teresa in Ecstasy, by Bernini, 1646. Santa Maria della Vittoria, Rome. Photo by Thomas King-Lenzmeier. This statue portrays the piercing of the heart that Teresa reports in the *Life*, 29:13-14.

Figure 20.4: A typical processional reflecting the Baroque Catholic sense of bringing the sacred out of the church and to the people. Photo by Susan Webster.

Figure 20.4 sums up many of the themes of this chapter and draws together the many strands of the Catholic Reformation. It shows a processional float, honoring the saint by bringing the presence of the art and ornamentation *out* of the church itself and *into* the everyday settings and lives of the people. As an art form, it was the intention of the Baroque to bring immediacy of experience, to appeal to the feelings and the emotional side of faith, to illustrate doctrine in a way that made pastoral sense and yet was compelling religiously and artistically.

VI. Concluding Reflections

The Reformation period was a turbulent time for both Catholics and Protestants. Yet from this age of turmoil emerged a clearer understanding of Christianity. Despite the scandal of disunity, Christians were now more apt to know what they believed and why. They were more informed participants in worship, and they had more powerful and inspiring preaching available to them. For Catholics, there was the additional result of the new spiritual awareness of the traditions of the church, their valuing of the sacraments, the desire to express their faith through charity and actions for the salvation of souls. Forced by crisis to define itself at the Council of Trent, Catholicism began to express in new ways what it held to be true. Through the council, the catechism, the new and reformed religious orders and the artistic and popular revivals of spiritual devotions, the Catholic Church found its way both to an inner reform and to a new place in the world.

Key Terms:

Counter-Reformation

Catholic Reformation

"polyglot" Bible

Ignatius of Loyola

Society of Jesus

Spiritual Exercises

Capuchins

Council of Trent

Catechism of Trent

Vulgate

breviary	John of the Cross
seminary	Discalced Carmelites
sacramentals	Baroque
Teresa of Avila	

Questions for Reading:

1. What is the difference between the Counter-Reformation and the Catholic Reformation? How are they related to one another?

2. What signs of reform were present in the Catholic Church even before the challenge of Luther and other Protestant reformers?

3. Who was Ignatius of Loyola and how did he shape the movement he founded? Why did the Society of Jesus become so important to the effort of Catholic reform?

4. For what purpose was the Council of Trent called? What difficulties did it encounter?

5. What were the doctrinal issues addressed by the Council of Trent, and what is their importance?

6. What were the disciplinary or practical reforms made by the Council of Trent?

7. What are the seven "official" sacraments? What is a sacramental?

8. Name three of the new orders founded during the Catholic Reformation. How are they different from previous religious orders?

9. Contrast the worship styles and decoration of churches in the Protestant and Catholic traditions during the Reformation period. What is the Baroque style of art, and how is it representative of the Catholic Reformation?

Works Consulted/Recommended Reading:

Adels, Jill Haak, ed. *The Wisdom of the Saints: An Anthology*. New York: Oxford, 1987.

Chadwick, Owen. *The Reformation*. Baltimore: Penguin Press, 1965.

Dupre, Louis and Wiseman, James, eds. *Light from Light: An Anthology of Christian Mysticism*. New York: Paulist Press, 1988.

Egan, Harvey. *An Anthology of Christian Mysticism*. Collegeville, MN: Liturgical Press, 1991.

_____. *Ignatius of Loyola the Mystic*. Collegeville, MN: Liturgical Press, 1991.

Hempel, Eberhard. *Baroque Art and Architecture in Central Europe*. Baltimore: Penguin, 1965.

John of the Cross. *Ascent of Mount Carmel & The Dark Night of the Soul*. Trans. Kiernan Kavanaugh. New York: Paulist Press, 1987.

_____. *Collected Works*. Trans. Kieran Kavanaugh and Otilio Rodriguez. Washington, DC: ICS Publications, 1976.

_____. *Selected Writings: John of the Cross*. Trans. Kieran Kavanaugh and Otilio Rodriguez. New York: Paulist Press, 1987.

McNally, Robert. *The Council of Trent, the Spiritual Exercises, and the Catholic Reform*. New York: Fortress Press, 1970.

Olin, John. *The Catholic Reform: From Cardinal Ximenes to the Council of Trent, 1495-1563*. New York: Fordham University Press, 1990.

Sheldrake, Philip. *Spirituality and History*. New York: Crossroad, 1992.

Short, William S. *The Franciscans*. Collegeville, MN: Liturgical Press/Michael Glazier, 1989.

Teresa of Avila. *Collected Works*, vol. I. Trans. Kieran Kavanaugh and Otilio Rodriguez. Washington, DC: ICS Publications, 1976.

_____. *The Interior Castle*. Trans. Kieran Kavanaugh and Otilio Rodriguez. New York: Paulist Press, 1979.

Wisch, Barbara and Munshower, Susan Scott, eds. *"All the World's a Stage—": Art and Pagentry in the Renaissance and Baroque*. University Park, PA: Penn State University Press, 1990.

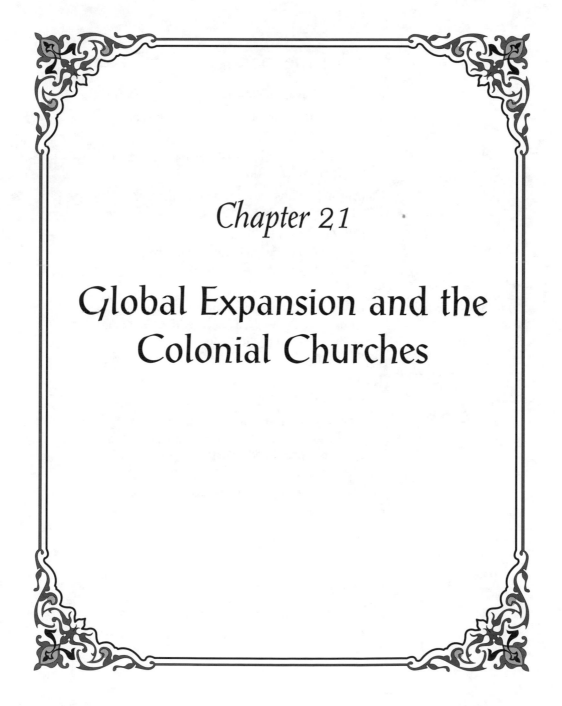

Chapter 21

Global Expansion and the Colonial Churches

Timeline

1271 AD	Marco Polo travels to the Orient.
1349	The Arab scholar Ibn Batuta travels to parts of Africa and the Orient.
1415	Henry the Navigator sends Portuguese ships south to explore the coast of Africa.
1482	Catholic missionary activity begins in the Congo with the conversion of King Afonso the Good and his family.
1492	Christopher Columbus sails west under the patronage of the Spanish government in order to find a new route to the Indies.
1493	Pope Alexander VI issues a series of bulls establishing a line of demarcation whereby newly discovered lands east of the line belonged to Portugal and lands west of the line belonged to Spain.
1498	The Portuguese explorer, Vasco da Gama, sails around the Cape of Good Hope.
1502	The Dominican friar Bartolomé de Las Casas is ordained a priest. He would later fight against the abuses of the **encomienda-doctrina** system in Spanish mission territories.
1542-1552	The Jesuit, Francis Xavier, is involved in missionary activity in India and Japan.
1582-1610	The Jesuit, Matteo Ricci, is involved in missionary activity in China.
1622	Pope Gregory XV establishes the Sacred Congregation for the Propagation of the Faith.
1633	French Catholic missionaries begin to arrive in the Americas.

Global Expansion and the Colonial Churches

One of the direct consequences of the Catholic Reformation was the expansion of Christianity into the New World. However, this expansion is actually the fourth stage in the growth of Christianity in the Western world. The first three stages involved the establishment of Christianity in the Roman Empire in the 1st through 4th centuries, the Christianization of "barbarian" Europe in the 5th through 9th centuries, and Christian missionary efforts in the Islamic world in the 11th through 15th centuries. In order to better appreciate the distinctive character of the fourth stage of the missionary effort, we will review briefly the circumstances of the three earlier missions.

In the first stage, during the first three centuries of Christianity's existence, the Christian community began to establish a solid footing in most parts of the Roman Empire, and even in outposts beyond the imperial borders. In the earliest years of Christianity's existence, Palestine—the place where the apostles began their preaching—was the heart of Christian territory; Asia Minor—where Paul had established a number of churches—was its backbone. However, by the latter part of the 4th century, Christianity had permeated the Roman Empire to such a degree that it had become the dominant religion in the empire. From Jerusalem across North Africa to Britain, wherever Rome governed, Christianity was well rooted. At the same time, during this stage, the most influential and firmly established early Christian communities were still to be found primarily along the Mediterranean coast.

The second stage of the expansion of Christianity corresponds with the period in the history of the Western Roman Empire sometimes known as the "Dark Ages." By this time, the Roman Empire's locus of power had shifted to Byzantium in the East. The western part of the empire suffered from weak leadership and from an influx of migrating peoples from the north and the east. The church at Rome, by default, was the only stable force in the Western empire. The Roman church's efforts to take the Christian message across the Alps to these "barbarian" peoples that had brought about the downfall of the Western Roman Empire had a two-fold purpose: to Christianize and to civilize. Although this missionary effort was carried out mostly by the Benedictine monks, it was not an organized effort. There was no planned "mission" program. Additionally, although sometimes individuals converted to Christianity, it was also common for entire regions or tribes to convert en masse.

These mass conversions of entire regions or tribes were not a question of a moral or intellectual decision or an experience of faith. They were mostly a question of loyalty to one's local chief. When the chief became a Christian so did the tribe. Thus mass conversions had more to do with political security and material needs than deep spiritual convictions. This was the most common pattern of conversion in western Europe during the second stage of the expansion of Christianity. Charlemagne's political conquests in Germany, for example, were followed by religious conversion of large numbers of people. As a result, although Christianity was a unifying cultural force, one could not assume that those who were baptized fully embraced the Christian faith.

Whatever can be said about the effectiveness of these first two stages of expansions, the early mission efforts were significant, because they began to set the standard for future mission policy. For example, in the feudal society of the early middle ages, when monasteries and dioceses were given lands and sovereign powers over all conquered peoples on that land, they also were able to institute the principle of **sanctuary**, which states that all who take refuge from civil authority in a church or on church land cannot be removed without the permission of the abbot or bishop. This principle helped establish the autonomy of ecclesiastical lands. Secondly, during these early stages of expansion the church at Rome had managed to establish itself as the central authority whereby people would be commissioned to go out and introduce the Christian faith into new areas. They were allowed a certain freedom in accommodating the teachings of Christianity to these "tribal" peoples, but the church at Rome retained its place as the symbol of catholicity (universality). Finally, the principle of **indigenization** (which states that the native people of the country take charge of the church in that country as soon as possible) was set forth as a basic ecclesiastical mission policy during these early stages. Thus the most promising young men among these new Christian communities were selected for training as priests and future bishops.

For the most part, the third stage of the mission effort of the church of Rome (11th-15th century) was initiated because of the failure of the Crusades. Although the Crusades were initiated to fight the Muslim armies who were advancing on the Western Roman Empire's borders and to win back the Holy Land from the Muslims, ultimately they did not succeed. Subsequently, Christians needed to negotiate with the Islamic rulers concerning travel, trade and other Western interests. The new mendicant orders of friars were largely responsible for the missionary effort during this third stage, and they brought to the church's mission endeavors a different theology. Persuasion, not conquering force, was their approach. Their emphasis was on the lived example of Christianity, and so they sought to show the world of Islam the moral and intellectual strengths of Christianity. The friars were also responsible for spreading Islamic language and culture to the Western Christian world. Educated Europeans were well aware of the scientific, medical and philosophical knowledge that the Islamic communities had shared with their Mediterranean neighbors. As a result the friars established "mission preparation" schools that taught Arabic and Islamic culture in order to prepare future missionaries for dialogue with the Muslims. Thus it was during this time that the missionary effort of Christianity began to take on a more formal structure.

This third stage of the expansion of Christianity corresponded with the beginnings of European exploration of new lands. Already in the 1290s, people living along the Mediterranean coast of Europe were beginning to hear fantastic tales of the Orient. An Italian named **Marco Polo** (1254-1324 AD) had visited these strange lands to the East and had found places of great wealth (spices, drugs, perfumes, and cloth) and great rulers. He lived there for seventeen years as a valued member of the court of the great Khan before returning to Italy. While in a Genoa prison, he dictated the memoirs of his sojourn to a fellow prisoner. This document and its subsequent oral renditions became the core of the European knowledge of the people and places of these unseen lands of the East. Thus for two centuries prior to the adventures of Christopher Columbus, news of these far off places and the riches of the people there had sparked the imaginations of many clerics and merchants of Italy and beyond.

Italians were not the only Europeans aware of places and peoples beyond their view. Portugal and Spain also were interested in exploring new lands. **Ibn Batuta** (1304-1368 AD), the Arab scholar who in 1349 traveled through parts of Africa and the Orient, recounted in his memoirs the splendor of other cultures, thereby confirming the tales of Marco Polo. He noted the extensive trading system that had developed across the Sahara and in the cities along the east coast of Africa. He also noted the key fact that caught the eyes of Europeans: these kingdoms of the interior of Africa based their trade on gold. By 1375 Spain had produced a pictorial map of the desert interior with the Lord of Mali holding "an orb of gold." In Spain this lord was rumored to be the wealthiest man on the face of the earth. Europeans were hungry for gold. It provided wealth and independence from the feudal system, and it assured them a place in the international trading system. The greed for gold was growing, and would fuel future European exploration efforts. Finally, in 1487, following a route similar to that of Ibn Batuta, some traders from Portugal reached the Mali capital of Timbuktu, a center of religion and learning, as well as trade. By 1500, the Spanish were visiting it as well.

Both the church leaders and the secular rulers of Europe wanted to control the wealth they saw in Africa, but they used separate avenues to accomplish their goals. The church of Rome made ecclesial overtures to those areas that it hoped to control. One such area was Ethiopia, which had had a Christian king since the earliest centuries of Christianity. At this point in history, Ethiopia was under the jurisdiction of the patriarch of Alexandria (an Eastern Orthodox bishop), but the pope invited the rulers of Ethiopia to enter into alliance with Rome instead. Independent of church leadership, the rulers of Spain and Portugal offered similar invitations designed to establish friendly relations with areas with which they hoped to trade. Although the efforts of the Roman church failed in Ethiopia, the rulers of Spain and Portugal had more success. The third stage of Christian expansion resulted in a widening of Europe's geographical and cultural horizons, but, as yet, church and state were not working together in the missionary effort. In the fourth stage, finally, church and state would be engaged in joint efforts of exploration and missionary work.

I. The Portugese Mission to Africa

The fourth stage of the expansion of Christianity, roughly 16th-17th century, represents the first unified church/state effort in encountering new peoples. Portugal's prince **Henry the Navigator** (1394-1460 AD) was primarily responsible for early efforts to expand the borders and influence of both the European culture and the Christian faith. After his conquest of Ceuta, Morocco, in 1415, Henry sent ships south to explore the coast of Africa. Thus he provided Portugal with information about the locations of the islands which they named Porto Santo, Madeira, Cape Verde, and the Azores. All of these islands were later colonized by Portugal. Cape Verde became Portugal's permanent base for trade with the nearby "Guinean coast." In every colonizing effort, Henry, a grand master of the Order of Christ (an order of Christian knights), faithfully saw to the spread of the Christian message. By Henry's death in 1460, his trading ships had reached 600 miles down the coast to Sierra Leone. Under Henry the Navigator, church and state were now working together. Thus, as they extended their routes along the African coast, each Portuguese expedition had both its religious component and its trading component.

Perhaps the best example of an early attempt at church and state cooperation in the Portuguese expansion was Portugal's attempt to gain control of the Congo in Africa. In 1482 Portuguese ships under the command of Diogo Cao reached the mouth of the Congo river (Angola), some 500 miles south of the equator. Here they encountered **Afonso the Good** (c. 1482-1543 AD), the eldest son of Nzinga of Nkouwou, king of the Congo. Nzinga, together with his household, readily accepted the Catholic faith. In turn, the Portuguese readily allied themselves with him. Given the superficiality of mass conversions, some, like Afonso, remained Catholic, while his brother and others maintained their traditional religion. A struggle ensued between the Christian and non-Christian factions at the time Afonso was to ascend to power. However, Afonso won his throne with the help of his Portuguese allies, and he ruled from 1506-1543 AD. As king, Afonso's major concern was maintaining a balance between acquiring European technology and holding back Portuguese greed. He wanted his people to convert to Catholicism. He also wanted to acquire the benefits of Portuguese technology for his people, but he saw clearly the need to control the Portuguese's insatiable appetite for riches and slaves. Though he failed in the end, Afonso labored religiously to establish this balance.

From the beginning, Portugal's missionary effort in the Congo was badly mismanaged. Letters between Afonso and both Manuel I (1495-1521 AD) and Joao III (1521-1557 AD), kings of Portugal, give witness to this tragedy. The record shows that these kings called each other "brother" and that friendly and mutually beneficial relations were within the realm of possibility. However, the church did not flourish in Africa, and the Africans hardly benefitted from their encounter with Europeans. Manuel I sent Augustinian canons (priests who lived a semi-monastic lifestyle, in this case, under the rule of Augustine) from Lisbon to the Congo. Within a short time, the canons, who were supposed to set an example of good Christian living for the native African Christians, gave up their common life, took women, and began trafficking in slaves. The same was true of the masons and artisans sent by Manuel. Later Afonso sent a group of his Congolese people to Portugal to learn Portuguese technology and to bring it back to their homeland. Some of them were enslaved upon arrival.

Despite the misbehavior of the missionaries in Africa and the mistreatment of Africans by Portugese both in Africa and in Portugal, the Congolese king continued to labor to bring his society into the corridors of church life. Henrique, Afonso's eldest son, was sent to study for the priesthood. He was ordained a priest by the age of 23. In 1518, Manuel I asked the Archbishop of Lisbon to ordain Henrique a bishop. In 1521 Henrique was ordained the auxiliary bishop of the Portuguese church of Funchal in the Madeira Islands. He returned home and worked in the Congo until his unexpected early death in 1531. With him died Afonso's hope for a church with an indigenous clergy directly connected to Rome.

Moreover, Afonso's hope for technological development also perished, this time because of the explosive growth of the slave trade. In fact, slavery became the major issue in the Congo encounter. Portuguese slavers kidnapped Afonso's own subjects. Though Afonso protested in letters to Manuel I and Joao III, it was to no avail. Both government officials and clergy were absorbed in the greed that marked the undoing of this missionary effort. With Afonso's death came the end of the first Christian era in the Congo. His brother, with the full support of the people, disbanded the church and began the fight against the Portuguese. The feudal system had produced church missionaries totally at the service of the state, but the possibilities of financial independence and the acquisition of a higher social rank led many European clerics to abandon their missionary commitment in favor of wealth and power. The church was faced with the fact that the faith which was preached in Portugal was not practiced in the Congo.

II. The Missions in the New World

Portugal and Spain continued to explore new worlds, and new lessons were learned with each venture. Christopher Columbus, an Italian who knew the stories of peoples of the East, sailed west under the patronage of the Spanish government in order to find a new route to the Indies in 1492.

The world he encountered became known as the West Indies, and later the Americas. In 1498, the Portuguese explorer, Vasco da Gama, sailed three ships around the Cape of Good Hope (on the southern tip of Africa) and into the Indian Ocean. Opero Cabal's voyage took him to Brazil, also on behalf of the Portuguese. Within twenty years Magellan had sailed through the straits on the southern tip of South America to reach the Pacific Ocean from the Atlantic. Eventually, Magellan would circle the globe, providing the westward route to India. Magellan, however, encountered the communities of the Pacific (especially the Philippines) in a spirit of conquest, rather than good will. He "explored" these new territories in order to claim them in the name of Christianity and the king of Spain. However, this spirit of conquest was not limited to Magellan or to the Spanish. Hans Meyer, a sailor, provided this account of the return of the Portuguese to the trading cities of east Africa in a 1505 expedition: "Admiral Dalmeda, with fourteen men of war and six caravelles, destroyed each of them [the trading cities] for all their goods and provisions."

The initial explorations launched by Portugal in the 1400s set off a chain of events on the European scene. First, Spain sought to create its own group of explorers in competition with the Portuguese, and it succeeded admirably. This competition created a great deal of tension between Spain and Portugal, which led the church in Rome (the arbitrator of all disputes between Christian countries) to "divide up" the New World between Spain and Portugal. In 1493, Pope Alexander VI issued a series of five bulls (the most solemn and weighty form of papal letters) that set the stage for mission and exploration policy for the next century. All peoples and lands encountered while going west of a line drawn through the Atlantic belonged to Spain. New lands disovered east of the line belonged to the Portuguese. The pope's decision created a new cooperative system between church and state in which the two kings not only became responsible for colonization of these new lands, but also for the ecclesiastical organizations within their jurisdictions.

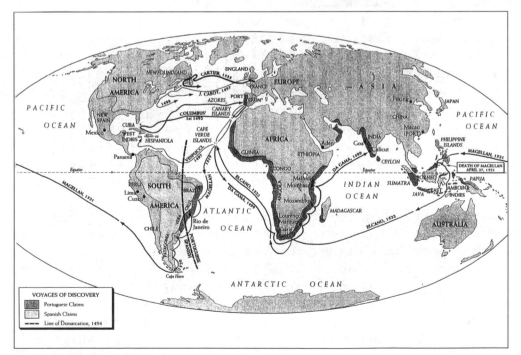

Figure 21.1: European voyages of discovery during the 15th and 16th centuries and the colonial claims of Spain and Portugal.

In the mission territories of both Spain and Portugal, the church was administered by the state in a system called **Royal Patronage**. The term "Royal Patronage" refers to the sum total of privileges that the church conceded, along with certain burdens, to Catholic founders of a church, or to those who acquire the right of patronage from the founders. These patrons were given the right to create dioceses in their newly colonized lands, to name bishops, abbots and priests in those dioceses, and, in general, to control the direction of missionary efforts in their colonies. Since patronage provided benefits but also made demands on the kings, it was an acceptable arrangement for the church. The crown was financially responsible for the missions and their personnel, but at the same time, the missions were a financial resource for the crown. Rome knew well that this would encourage Portugal and Spain to carry the Christian faith overseas. Over the years the popes added an extensive list of indulgences and privileges to this overseas Royal Patronage.

III. Royal Patronage and the Missionary Effort

The concept of Royal Patronage gave the kings of Spain and Portugal exclusive rights and responsibilities for the misssionary evangelizing work of the entire world. Neither the pope nor anyone else in Rome could interfere. Thus the fourth stage of the church's expansion marked the greatest and fastest growth of Christianity in its history. Because of the problems that arose with this type of Christianizing effort, the effects of which are still felt today, it also forced the Catholic Church to reexamine the way in which it had carried out its missionary work.

Efforts to evangelize new peoples under the Royal Patronage system were subject to all of the evils of conquest, greed, colonization and political manipulation. The kings were interested in trade and gold first. Thus colonization was primarily a process of military conquest. The native peoples who managed to survive, in particular, those who lived in the areas near the colony's base settlements, were totally subjugated. Agricultural production and mining for gold were the main concerns. The missionary effort was secondary. Anyone who wished to complain about this could not appeal directly to Rome, because all communication with Rome had to be sent via the crown. Thus patronage was protected.

In the Spanish territories of the western hemisphere, the conquistadors set up an organized system of "pueblos" called the ***Encomienda-Doctrina* System**. The system was a cooperative effort between the *encomendero* (the conquistador or his descendant) and the *doctrinero* (usually a mendicant friar) to build a sound economic and spiritual base in the new territories. The system was set up to integrate the Native Americans into the social and economic life of Spain, but also to establish Western Christian culture among the native peoples. Thus the Native Americans living in the pueblo learned Spanish economics. In the village workshop, skilled artisans wove cloth, made pots, and worked leather in order to build their churches and to pay the taxes demanded by their *encomendero*. Additional costs of the pueblo were defrayed partially by the crown and the *encomendero*. There were schools to teach the children Christian doctrine, Spanish literacy, arithmetic and music. Christian education for the community at large was usually provided in weekly group lessons. Emphasis was placed on the basics: prayers, the creed, the commandments, and the sacraments. At first, the friars were the teachers in the pueblo, but later educated Natives did the teaching.

The greatest boost to the growth of Catholicism in the new Spanish territories came as a result of the event that took place on December 9, 1531. On that day the Virgin Mary is said to have appeared to an elderly native man at Tepeyac, on a hill northwest of Mexico City. His name was **Juan Diego**. In the vision, he was instructed to tell the bishop to build a church on the site at Tepeyac. In a second appearance, three days later, the Virgin instructed Juan Diego to pick flowers and take them to the bishop. As he opened his cloak to present the flowers, a miraculous event took place. A type of Spanish rose not grown in Mexico fell out of his cloak, and on the cloak was imprinted a painted image of Mary, now known as **Our Lady of Guadalupe**. Because of this apparition, devotion to Mary became the central devotion of Spanish-American Catholicism. Even today, many people associate Spanish-American Catholic spirituality with the image of Our Lady of Guadalupe.

Perhaps the best known of the friars in the New World was **Bartolomé de Las Casas** (1474-1566). As a young cleric he moved to the West Indies (modern-day Haiti and the Dominican Republic). In 1502, he was the first to be ordained a priest in the New World. Once a land owner, now a Dominican friar, De Las Casas began to question the morality of the enslavement of the Native Americans. He recognized that the *encomienda* system was destroying the native peoples and determined that the system was immoral. He began to preach the cause of the Native Americans in the colony and traveled back and forth to Spain to have his voice heard before the council responsible for the governing of the Indies. In his enthusiasm, he suggested to the crown in 1516 that the colonies be permitted to import Africans as slaves, rather than forcing the indigenous peoples into slavery, a proposal he later regretted.

While de Las Casas was concerned about the morality of slavery, his was primarily an ecclesial concern: because they were Christians, Native Americans living in the pueblos should not be enslaved. He was not addressing the larger question of the morality of a state commercial enterprise that required the use of slaves. However, in defense of de Las Casas, it should be noted that he was not responsible for initiating the importing of Africans as slaves to the New World. Portugal already had begun an African slave trade in 1442. The Spanish crown had given permission for this practice only in 1511. Spain had been at war with the Muslims for years, and believed that the enslaving of prisoners of war was legitimate. Since sub-Saharan Africans also lived in Muslim territory (according to Spain's geography), the Spanish felt justified in making slaves of them as well.

According to canon or church law (in this case adapted from Aristotle and Roman law) one could legally enslave or have another person under captivity for various reasons. Captives of war could be enslaved, although later this law was modified so that only non-Christian captives could be made slaves. Likewise, criminals were often punished with slavery. In this case, slavery was seen as a substitute for capital punishment. Sometimes those who could not repay their debts were enslaved. Since failure to pay one's debts was also a criminal offense, the debt was "paid" with a period of servitude. In some cases children were sold by their (usually impoverished) parents into slavery. Likewise, adults sometimes sold themselves into slavery. Those who were destitute and hopeless could at least gain shelter and subsistence in this way. Finally, many people were slaves because they had been born to a slave mother. Slavery therefore became part of the caste system, a station in life that was passed from generation to generation.

Bartolomé de Las Casas challenged the morality of the laws governing the *encomienda* system and appealed to Rome on behalf of the Native Americans living in the pueblos. As a result, in 1537 Pope Paul III, in the bull "*Sublimis Deus,*" set forth the rights of the Native Americans and challenged their enslavement. However, the pope did not address the morality of slavery itself, but only the more technical legal aspects of "title" (right of ownership). Slavery, in this day, was understood to be a question of property rights and not human rights. Thus, although the pope supported de Las Casas, the core issue of the immorality of slavery remained unresolved. Nonetheless, de Las Casas continued to fight.

In 1544 Bartolomé de Las Casas became the bishop of Chiapas in southern Mexico. He quickly instructed his priests not to absolve the slaveholders of their sins until they promised to free their Native American slaves. By Easter of 1545 the Spaniards rioted because they could not fulfill their Easter duty (the requirement that every Catholic receive the Eucharist at least once a year during the Easter season). Threats became public and de Las Casas, faced with a violent uprising, returned to Spain and resigned his see in 1547. Still he did not cease fighting against illegitimate slavery. While he did not change the slave trade in the encomienda system, he was able to bring to public debate the issue of morality and challenge the attitudes of the explorers as they encountered peoples in different parts of the world. Perhaps Bartolomé de Las Casas' greatest contribution was his challenge to Aristotle's principles on slavery, thus helping to lay the foundation for today's understanding of "human rights."

By 1575 some 9,000 *encomienda* system campuses were to be found in Latin America. At its peak, the population of the pueblos was well into the millions. However, their numbers steadily declined after that, because the evangelizing effort in many regions still included slavery. Moreover, the kind of Christianity being offered was not catholic (universal). In fact, the Spanish themselves could not distinguish between the Christian message and their Spanish culture which was the bearer of the message, and their efforts to impose Spanish culture on the indigenous peoples resulted in disaster. Fortunately, the failure of the *encomienda* system would give rise to a new Spanish missionary effort known as "the mission," the fifth stage in Christian missionary expansion. Before this could happen, however, there were also lessons to be learned in missionary ventures in the Orient.

IV. The Mission to the Orient

The Roman Catholic Church had learned many lessons over the years concerning the ways in which missionary expansion ought to be conducted. Principal among these was that the system of Royal Patronage, which appeared to be so effective in the early decades of the 16th century, was no longer concerned with the missionary task of teaching the Christian message. Patronage had become, quite simply, an instrument of colonial and imperial policies. Gradually the church realized that relying on the new religious orders of the Catholic Reformation to spread Christianity would be more effective and less harmful to the local populations than relying on state governments like those of Portugal and Spain, which had been given all such rights as part of the system of Royal Patronage.

Foremost among the new religious orders of the Catholic Reformation were the Jesuits founded by St. Ignatius Loyola (1491-1556) and the Capuchins founded by Matthew de Bascio (d. 1552). Almost immediately after its creation, the Jesuit order became the backbone of the mission effort. One of the first Jesuit missionaries to the East was **St. Francis Xavier** (1506-1552), a companion of Ignatius Loyola. In 1542, Francis Xavier began his missionary preaching in Goa, the Portuguese seaport in India. Skilled at language and flexible in lifestyle, he attracted many of the lower-caste to the faith both in India and Ceylon, but he was not able to convert the upper classes. By 1545 the Jesuits had sent additional missionaries to Goa, so that Xavier himself was able to move on to Malacca on the Malay peninsula while sending Jesuits to other Portuguese seaports in the Orient. However, it was not until he reached Japan that he realized that something was wrong with his mission policy. Xavier noticed that, unlike his experience in India, "apostolic poverty" did not impress the Japanese. He changed his dress to a better quality of dress like the local leaders, and within two years he had over two thousand converts. Thus the practice of missionaries adapting to the cultural norms of the indigenous peoples gradually became a standard part of mission policy.

Due to the exceptional growth of the Catholic Church in the East, the Jesuits appointed Xavier to be the superior of the new Jesuit province of India in 1551. He had already established a mission center for learning the languages and customs of the many peoples of the East. However, Xavier's final interest was China. He studied the language and set out for the coast near Canton in 1552. While trying to finalize his plans to move to the interior, he fell sick with a fever. Francis Xavier died on the morning of December 3, 1552. Though he was originally buried in China, the Jesuits exhumed his body and returned it to Goa, where it is enshrined today. Despite the fact that he was never able to preach the Christian message in China, Xavier's dreams were not lost, since he had set the pattern for future missionary activity there, and others would soon follow.

An Italian Jesuit, **Matteo Ricci** (1552-1610) followed Xavier's missionary example with a special emphasis on conversion through learning. He sought to confront the learned people of China in their own language and following their customs, and to use his superior talent to impress them with Christianity. The annals of the missions of China mark as important the day of his arrival: September 10, 1582. Ricci adopted the garb of a Buddhist monk and by 1585 he and his companion had dedicated a church and residence in Chao-king. His vision of winning the Confucian masters, whom he believed the masses would then follow into the Christian faith, was in process. He robed himself in the square hat and silks of a scholar and gradually gained a reputation as the "Doctor for the Great West Ocean." Thus Christianity was granted the respect and privileges due to members of the Mandarin bureaucracy. Finally, in 1598, Ricci made his first move toward Beijing. Initially he was unsuccessful, but in 1601 he presented gifts to the throne and was granted residence and a subsidy for his reflections in mathematics and astronomy. Known throughout the realm as "Li Ma-ton," Matteo Ricci remains the most celebrated foreign figure in Chinese literature.

The Jesuits would continue to be successful in their missionary work in India and China, primarily because they had chosen to become a part of the culture in which they had come to live. They took the dress and lifestyle of the holy men of those cultures, and even participated in the native religious ceremonies—at least those that were not incompatible with Christianity. They learned the native languages and the traditions of the native peoples, and only gradually introduced elements of Christian doctrine and practice as the culture would allow. Of course, not everyone was happy with this blending of Christianity with native culture and religious practice. By the beginning of the 18th century, the Jesuits were experiencing a strong backlash of opposition from church leadership in Rome. However, before this would happen, the Catholic Church would move into its fifth stage of mission expansion.

V. The Congregation for the Propagation of the Faith

By the latter half of the 16th century a church commission was formed to serve the spiritual needs of the newly encountered non-Christian populations. Thus Pope Clement VIII established a congregation (an executive department of the curia responsible for the administration of some aspect of church life) for mission affairs in 1599, and laid the foundation for the fifth stage of missionary expansion. The church at Rome had already been moving to take the "mission apostolate" out of the hands of the colonizing countries, but Rome had an even greater concern for these mission communities as the Protestant Reformation grew. Finally, in 1622 Pope Gregory XV created a formal body to deal with missionary activity in non-Christian lands. It was given the official title the "Sacred Congregation for the Propagation of the Faith." Within five years (1627) Pope Urban VIII had provided this formal body with a central missionary training seminary, the Collegium Urbanum (Urban College), which became the first center for mission training in Europe.

Francesco Cardinal Ingoli (d. 1649), the first secretary of the Congregation for the Propagation of the Faith, set the framework for the "Catholic Missionary Movement." After an investigation into the state of the missions, Ingoli established the basic principles of the Catholic missionary process:

(1) Missionary work would be free of the authority of the colonial country (especially Spain and Portugal).

(2) Apostolic vicars (bishops) would be appointed, who had a clear relationship with Rome.

(3) More secular clergy would be employed in the mission effort to keep a balance with the religious orders.

(4) An indigenous clergy must be developed as rapidly as possible in every part of the world.

In 1659, ten years after the death of Cardinal Ignoli, the following instruction was issued to the bishops by the Congregation for the Propagation of the Faith:

> *Do not regard it as your task, and do not bring any pressure to bear on the peoples, to change their manners, customs, and uses, unless they are evidently contrary to religion and sound morals. What could be more absurd than to transport France, Spain, Italy, or some other European country to China? Do not introduce all that to them, but only the faith, which does not despise or destroy the manners and customs of any people, always supposing that they are not evil, but rather wishes to see them preserved unharmed. It is the nature of men to love and treasure above everything else their own country and that which belongs to it; in consequence there is not stronger cause for alienation and hate than an attack on local customs, especially when these go back to a venerable antiquity. This is more especially the case, when an attempt is made to introduce the customs of another people in the place of these which have been abolished. Do not draw invidious contrasts between the customs of the peoples and those of Europe; do your utmost to adapt yourselves to them.*

This respect for the newly encountered communities and the suggestion of a gradual movement toward Christian living by setting an example did not materialize immediately. In actuality, the imperial political powers (Spain and Portugal) maintained control of their colonies for a considerable time afterward. Much of the Roman plan for the Catholic missionary movement was not achieved until the 20th century, when the first group of indigenous bishops was ordained in 1939. Yet gradually the passage of time would bring new players and new attitudes into the colonizing effort.

VI. French Missions in the New World

The year 1588 marked a major change in European history and world colonization efforts. The Spanish Armada was defeated by the British, thus ending the growth of the Spanish empire. At the same time other powers in Europe were beginning to explore the New World. France was a major participant in this adventure. By 1630, France had become a leading colonial power, partly due to the political leadership of Cardinal Richelieu (1585-1642). He had entrusted the missionary efforts of France to his

Capuchin secretary and confessor, **Père Joseph Leclerc du Tremblay** (d. 1538). It was Fr. Joseph who sent the Capuchins to most of the colonies of France. Eventually, Fr. Joseph du Tremblay was made the first "prefect apostolic" (religious superior) of what is today called New England.

The Capuchin friars were the primary French missionaries in the New World. By 1633 they had established stations in the Antilles (St. Kitts) and La Heve and Port Royal (Maine). Within five years they had expanded to the islands of St. Vincent, Martinique, Dominica, Marie Galante and Guadeloupe in the Caribbean. Guadeloupe became the main station for their missionary activity. By 1647 the church in Rome had approved a proposal to establish a college on the island of Les Saints, much like the one in Goa, for the training of friars in the languages and customs of the people of the area. At the same time friars were being called to do missionary work in Africa. They were assigned to missions in the Ivory Coast (1634), the Congo (1645), and the Cameroons (1650). In the early 18th century they would turn their attention to North America as the center of French mission activity. Their mission policy was similar to what the Jesuits had done in the Orient: they became part of the culture they were coming to evangelize and they taught about Christianity by example. Because these missionary efforts were under the direct control of the church in Rome, they were able to prevent the newer colonizing countries (like France) from developing a social and economic system similar to the Royal Patronage system found in the Spanish and Portuguese colonies.

VII. Inculturation

Recently there has been a renewed awareness that the message of Christianity ought not be bound to any one cultural form, but that it should be able to reach all peoples within their own cultural context. This awareness is expressed by the term **inculturation**. It is an extension and adaptation of the sociological term **enculturation**. *Culture* is "a society's design for living" (Luzbetak, 156). Thus enculturation refers to the process by which an *individual* learns to live and act within a particular culture in such a way that the culture's particular pattern of actions and thought becomes second-nature. One normally enculturates to one's home society as one grows up. Inculturation refers to the process by which a *religion* "learns" to live and act within a culture different from the one in which it began in such a way that the religion acts naturally within that culture's pattern of actions and thought. The inculturated religion, like an enculturated individual, may challenge the culture, but it does so in terms the culture can understand.

The first Christian inculturation took place within the first few centuries of its existence, when a religious movement that began in a Palestinian Jewish culture "learned" to live and act within a Greco-Roman culture. It accomplished the task so well that today many people think of Christianity as a Western religion. If the church is to successfully inculturate itself into a new society, the two primary agents in mission are the Holy Spirit and the local church (local leaders and lay Christians who belong to the society where the mission is working). Missionaries and leaders of the world-wide church need to trust both. If the local leaders have truly experienced the deep reality at the core of the religion then they are the best people, under the guidance of the Holy Spirit, to express that reality and to shape appropriate ways to live it out in the language, art, music, architecture, and cultural patterns of their own society. Diversity of cultures allow the Christian message to be interpreted in new and more meaningful ways for all peoples. At the same time, the Christian message can bring enlightenment and growth to individual cultures. The result is an experience of mutual enrichment.

Key Terms:

sanctuary
indigenization
Marco Polo
Ibn Batuta
Henry the Navigator
Afonso the Good
Royal Patronage
Encomienda-Doctrina System
Juan Diego

Our Lady of Guadalupe
Bartolomé de Las Casas
Capuchins
Francis Xavier
Matteo Ricci
Père Joseph Henry Leclerc du Trembley
inculturation
enculturation

Questions for Reading:

1. Review the four "phases" of the missionary expansion of Christianity. When did each phase occur, and what areas were covered in it? Who led the missions, and how were conversions brought about?

2. Discuss the relationship between exploration and mission. What motives did the missionaries and the explorers have in common?

3. Review the main events of the Portuguese mission to Africa, and explain why this mission was largely a failure.

4. Explain how Spain and Portugal came to dominate the missions in the New World, and evaluate their performance in this area.

5. Who is Bartholomé de Las Casas? How and why did he try to reform the missions in the New World? What impact did his efforts have?

6. How were the missions conducted by the Jesuits and Capuchins *different* from those conducted under the direction of the Spanish and Portugese? Who were the main leaders of the missions conducted by the Jesuits and Capuchins? What were their major accomplishments?

Works Consulted/Recommended Reading:

Arias, David. *Spanish Roots of America*. Huntington, IN: Our Sunday Visitor Press, 1992.

Blaut, J. M. *1492: The Debate on Colonialism, Eurocentrism, and History*. Trenton, NJ: Africa World Press, 1992.

Davis, Kortright. "'Sunshine Christopher': Bearer of Christ in Caribbean History." *The Journal of Religious Thought 49* (1992-1993) 7-24.

De Las Casas, Bartolomé. *The Devastation of the Indies: A Brief Account*. Trans. Herma Briffault. Baltimore: Johns Hopkins University Press, 1992.

Holder, John. "The Issue of Race: A Search for a Biblical/Theological Perspective." *The Journal of Religious Thought* 49 (1992-1993) 44-59.

Hopkins, Dwight N. "Columbus, the Church, and Slave Religion." *The Journal of Religious Thought* 49 (1992-1993) 25-35.

Luzbetak, Louis J. *The Church and Cultures: New Perspectives in Missiological Anthropology*. Maryknoll, N.Y.: Orbis Books, 1988.

Neill, Stephen. *A History of Christian Missions*. New York: Penguin Books, 1984.

Riga, Peter J. "Columbus, the Church and the Indians: A Reflection." *The Journal of Religious Thought* 49 (1992-1993) 36-43.

Shorter, Aylward. *Toward a Theology of Inculturation*. Maryknoll, N.Y.: Orbis Books, 1988.

Williams, Eric. *From Columbus to Castro: The History of the Caribbean, 1942-1969*. New York: Vintage Books, 1970.

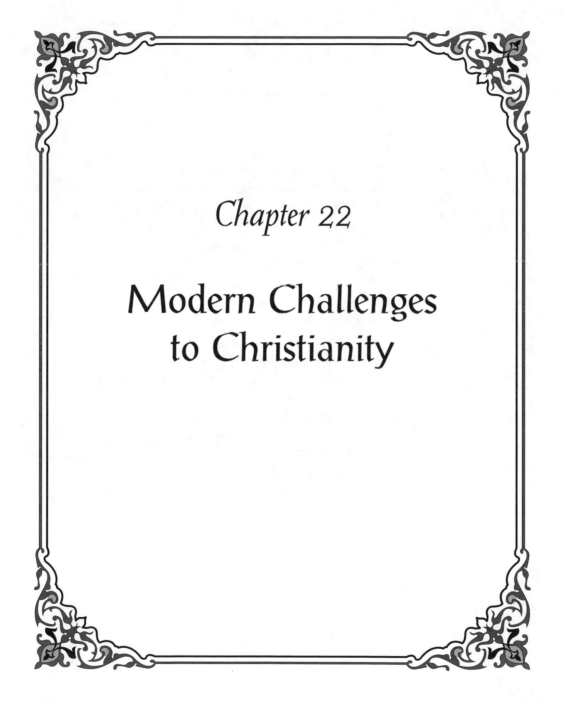

Chapter 22

Modern Challenges
to Christianity

Timeline

1543 AD	Nicholas Copernicus proposes his theory that the earth and other planets revolved around the sun.
1610	Galileo Galilei discovers evidence in support of Copernicus' theory.
c. 1624	The writings of Lord Herbert of Cherbury are published, later providing some of the foundational principles of Deism.
1687	Isaac Newton publishes his **Principia** in which he shows that the laws by which the planets move are the same laws that govern the motion of bodies on earth.
c. 1700	Beginning of the movement known as the Enlightenment.
1848	Karl Marx publishes the **Communist Manifesto**.
1859	Charles Darwin publishes **The Origin of Species** describing his theory of evolution, thereby raising significant questions about the authority of the Bible.
1864	Pope Pius IX condemns many of the ideas of liberalism, including the separation of church and state and religious freedom.
1871	Charles Darwin publishes **The Descent of Man**, which argues that humans descended from animal ancestors.
1927	Sigmund Freud publishes **The Future of an Illusion**, in which he argues that religion is a childish stage of human development.

Modern Challenges to Christianity

From the beginning of its existence, Christianity has always had to face the challenges and demands of the contemporary world. During the Reformation, the challenge that faced Western Christians was to decide what kind of Christian they wanted to become: Catholic or Protestant. As we move into the modern world, educated people are faced with a different and more radical kind of question: whether to be Christian at all. The modern world has seen developments in natural science, history, economics, philosophy, and psychology that have had enormous implications for religious belief. Some elements of the knowledge developed in these fields have served as attacks on the very heart of Christianity, forcing Christians to reexamine the foundations of their faith.

This chapter will deal with challenges to traditional Christianity from about 1600 to the present. The range of challenges to the church over four centuries is vast; here we will mention only a few of the most prominent challenges. We will begin with perhaps the strongest challenge to Christianity: the claim of the natural sciences to have developed a better and more reliable path to knowledge than that found in Christianity. In the modern world, science becomes so successful at explaining its subject matter—whether it is human beings or the world—that the scientific way of looking at the world has become deeply ingrained in the modern human consciousness. For many modern people, it is simply taken for granted that the only way of understanding reality properly is the scientific way. Thus the Christian worldview that was shared almost universally in the West in medieval times has been replaced by a scientific worldview, and Christianity has struggled to maintain its place in a world dominated by science.

I. The New Cosmology

Although there was occasional speculation in both antiquity and the middle ages that the sun was the center of the universe, it was the geocentric (earth-centered) universe of Aristotle and Claudius Ptolemy (Greek astronomer, c. 140 AD) which became the standard until the 17th century. Aristotle pictured the earth at the center of the universe, orbited by the moon, Mercury, Venus, the Sun, Mars, Jupiter, and Saturn, in that order.

This **cosmology** (picture of the cosmos or universe) was accepted by medieval Christian thinkers such as Aquinas and Dante. But beyond the sphere of the fixed stars Christian thinkers placed the empyrean heaven where God and the angels dwelt. Thus medieval Christians would have assumed that Jesus after his resurrection ascended into the empyrean, above the realm of the stars.

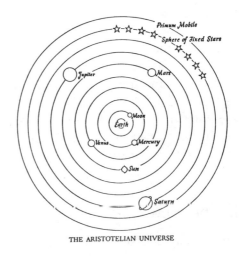

THE ARISTOTELIAN UNIVERSE

Figure 22.1 : The Aristotelian universe.

In 1543 a Polish astronomer, **Nicholas Copernicus**, published *On the Revolutions of the Heavenly Spheres*, which proposed that the earth and other planets revolved around the sun. This proposal did not immediately cause controversy; it was only an interesting hypothesis. But in 1610 **Galileo Galilei** focused his new telescope on Jupiter and discovered that the planet had four moons revolving around it. This showed that, contrary to Aristotelian theory, not all heavenly bodies revolved around the earth. Because of this discovery (and other related discoveries), Galileo championed Copernicus' theory (Langford, 39-41).

This new cosmology was a challenge to traditional Christianity partly because it appeared to contradict the Bible, which was thought to teach that the sun revolved around the earth, and that the earth was the center of the universe. For example, Joshua 10:12-13 states that Joshua prayed that the sun would stand still, and the sun did stand still. In addition, Psalm 93:1 states "He [God] has established the world firm; it shall never be moved." Galileo was told that he could teach Copernicus' theory as a hypothesis, but he insisted on teaching it as fact (though he did not actually have sufficient evidence to prove it to be fact). Eventually, in 1616, the Holy Office (a disciplinary arm of the church) condemned the Copernican theory as heresy, and forbade Galileo to teach it.

As Pope John Paul II has recently admitted, this was a disastrous mistake. It had long been held in Catholic tradition that the Bible is not meant to teach scientific fact. Rather, the Bible teaches those truths about God and humanity which are necessary for human salvation. As Cardinal Baronius said at the time of Galileo: "The Holy Ghost intended to teach us [in scripture] how to go to heaven, not how the heavens go." But the condemnation of Galileo permanently damaged the authority of the Catholic Church, especially among scientists, many of whom to this day see the church as opposed to science. The lesson to be learned from this is that various disciplines have to respect the boundaries proper to their own discipline and not intrude on the territory of other disciplines (John Paul II, 370-373). Theology cannot teach matters falling within the domain of science (such as whether the sun revolves around the earth). Conversely, science should not presume to teach in areas which cannot be investigated by its material and mathematical methods (such as whether God exists, whether humans have a soul, and whether there is life after death). Rather, the church teaches that science and theology, reason and revelation, are complementary: *both* are necessary for a complete understanding of reality, since reality is both material and spiritual.

The Copernican universe also proved to be a challenge to traditional Christianity because once people realized that the stars were immensely distant, and the universe itself possibly infinite in size, the earth and humanity seemed to be only specks in a ocean of emptiness. Moreover, it was hard to visualize where heaven might be. In the medieval cosmos, heaven was above the sphere of the stars. But where was it in the universe as modern people saw it? Christian theologians, of course, realized that God, being spiritual, was everywhere; but what about the resurrected body of Jesus, which is material? If Jesus "ascended to heaven" after his resurrection, where did he go? We can of course speak of a higher state of being or higher dimensions, but this is vague and hard to visualize for most people. Partly because of the difficulties just mentioned, many people today think of the ascension and resurrection as myth, and tend to think of heaven as an entirely spiritual state, whereas in traditional Christian belief, heaven is both a spiritual state *and* a state of the resurrected body.

II. The New Science

Modern physical science was inaugurated in the 17th century through the work of Galileo Galilei, Francis Bacon, Rene Descartes, Isaac Newton, and others. What the new science displaced was the older Aristotelian belief that nature functioned like a living organism, and that natural entities such as plants and animals were animated by "substantial forms"—approximately what we would call souls. Rather, the new science came to view nature as a vast machine, like a watch or clock, governed not by souls but by mechanical principles alone. Several steps were important in this process.

A. Empirical Method

Francis Bacon insisted that progress in science must depend on observation and experimentation with nature, not on abstract reasoning alone. Science since then has been strongly empirical; it restricts itself to physical evidence and observation. If a principle cannot be proven true or false by physical (usually experimental) evidence, it is not considered to be scientific. As Bacon realized and the 18th century philosopher David Hume later emphasized, this tends to drive a wedge between "facts" which can be "proven" by scientific method, and values, which cannot. The result has been that scientific "facts" are thought to be objectively true, and values merely subjective opinions. This distinction conflicts with traditional Christianity, which sees values as grounded in the will of God and hence as being objectively true.

B. Mathematical Method

Galileo argued that the laws of nature are mathematical laws, and modern scientists have agreed with him. An example is Galileo's formulation of the law of falling bodies. By measuring the time and speed with which balls rolled down inclined planes, he was able to derive a mathematical formula which shows that the speed of a falling body is proportional to the time which it has fallen, because its rate of acceleration is constant (32 feet per second). In Galileo's experiments with rolling balls we can see the essentials of modern scientific method: careful observation and experiment, mathematical measurement, and the expression of the findings in a mathematical law.

C. The Atomic Theory of Matter

The Aristotelian view had been that matter was made up of four basic elements: fire, air, earth, and water. Aristotle also taught that the stars were composed of a fifth, ethereal kind of matter more rarified than any found on earth. During the 17th century the notion developed that the world was composed of tiny unchanging corpuscles—atoms—which in various combinations make up all that exists. Everything from rocks to plants, animals, and human bodies was thought to be composed of these atoms. This opposed the Aristotelian view that the essence of any thing was its substantial form (an internal organizing principle which made a thing what it was), or, loosely speaking, its "soul." If everything could be explained as combinations of atoms, there was no need to speak of internal "forms" or "souls;" all that was needed was atoms, and forces to hold them together. The world was thus reduced to matter and force.

D. Mechanistic Philosophy

The culmination of the new science was expressed in the synthesis of **Isaac Newton**, published in Latin in 1687 under the title *Mathematical Principles of Natural Philosophy* (usually known as the *Principia*). Newton was able to show that the laws by which the planets moved were the same laws that governed the motion of bodies on earth. Matter was essentially passive: it remained either at rest or in motion unless moved by an external force. The motion of the planets was due to their inertial momentum (inertia being the the tendency of a body to remain at rest or in motion in the same straight line unless acted upon by another body) and the force of gravity. Thus the explanation of the cosmos according to mechanical principles—matter, external force, and inertia—was largely complete, and the way was open for viewing the universe as a vast machine.

The new understanding of the world as a machine was to have far-reaching implications. Effectively it removed God from the world. The world ran on its own—without God's help—like a perfectly designed clock or watch. The new mechanical philosophy, which in time came to influence the method of one science after another, eventually would lead to a worldview in which neither God, nor spirits, nor souls, had any real place in nature. Nature could be explained by the simple operation of mechanical laws, which made the existence of God and the human soul superfluous. This view came to prominence in the 18th century, in the writings of men such as Baron d'Holbach, who succeeded thereby in making atheism intellectually respectable. A similar mechanistic view continues to be argued today by some prominent scientists, who believe that the universe and life can be explained by the chance interactions of atoms, governed essentially by mechanistic laws.

III. The Challenge to Tradition

Modern science was founded in a spirit of skepticism and anti-traditionalism. Scientific method demanded that knowledge be verified by experiment, not simply accepted on faith from tradition. Indeed, much of Aristotle's physics, which had been accepted for centuries, proved to be incorrect. Thus 17th century scientists had good reason to be skeptical of tradition. This skepticism was embodied in the philosophy of **Rene Descartes**. Descartes began his philosophical method by doubting everything he had been taught—all tradition—and by believing only what could be shown by reason to be absolutely certain. Hence his famous line "*Cogito, ergo sum*"—"I think, therefore I am." Descartes could not doubt this statement, and he used his certainty about it as the foundation of his philosophy. Although Descartes himself lived and died a devout Catholic, his method of systematic doubt was extended by his philosophical successors to include most aspects of Christian revelation and tradition, and even the idea of tradition itself. Systematic doubt of what has been revealed by long dead religious teachers, like Moses and Jesus, and handed on in tradition, obviously poses a severe challenge to Christianity. Christianity, after all, rests largely on the teachings of Jesus, which were passed onto the apostles, handed on in tradition, and believed by subsequent generations on faith.

IV. Deism

The new mechanical philosophy, which understood the world as an exquisitely designed machine, produced a religious phenomenon called **Deism** (from Latin *Deus* meaning "God"). Deists believed in God, who designed the world-machine and started it going—as a clockmaker might make a watch and wind it up. But thereafter God did not intervene in the workings of the universe, which ran on its own like a watch. The idea that God had to intervene occasionally to adjust the motion of the planets was scornfully dismissed by the Deists, because it implied that God was an imperfect creator. A perfect creator would make a perfect creation: a world machine which needed no interventions to keep it going.

A rejection of the possibility of divine intervention entailed a rejection of much of Christian belief. Deists generally rejected prophecy, miracles, special providence, the incarnation, and the resurrection. They minimized special revelation, and argued instead that God had given people all the revelation they needed in nature itself. The magnificent design of nature pointed to a perfect creator. What Deists espoused, essentially, was a religion based on nature and reason alone. Thus, an early English Deist, Lord Herbert of Cherbury (1583-1648) maintained that there were only five religious truths: (1) God exists; (2) it is our duty to worship him; (3) virtue and piety are important parts of worship; (4) people ought to repent of their sins; (5) rewards or punishments will follow death. Notice that this creed says nothing about the divinity of Jesus, the Trinity, any providential action of God in history, miracles, or supernatural revelation. Typically, Deists argued that revelation was not necessary, and that it merely duplicated what could be known about God by reason.

Deism in England lasted about a century. But it did have important influences, particularly in France and America. Indeed, the most important idea of the Deists—that God created the world, but is extrinsic to it and does not intervene in it, so that the world runs by its own autonomous laws—is a very common idea today. Hindu children, when asked where God is, point to their hearts. Christian children, asked the same question, point to the sky: God is "outside" the world.

V. The Enlightenment

The developments of 17th century science, the emphasis on reason, and Deism all converged in the **Enlightenment**. The Enlightenment was an intellectual movement dating from about 1700-1789, which emphasized reason, science, the goodness and rights of humanity, religious toleration, progress, and human freedom.

The "apostles" of the Enlightenment were philosophers in England, France, Germany, and America, who through their writings permanently changed the intellectual landscape of the West. These philosophers include Thomas Jefferson and Benjamin Franklin in America; David Hume in England, Voltaire and Denis Diderot in France, and Immanuel Kant in Germany.

A. Enlightenment Rationalism

The Enlightenment has been called the Age of Reason. Its confidence in reason was derived in large part by the great successes of natural science—especially the work of Newton and of Descartes in the previous century. Newton's explanation of the laws of motion, which knit the earth and the heavens into a simple explanatory system, became the model for Enlightenment rationalism. **Rationalism** is the belief that reason alone can provide us with a knowledge of all reality. It is opposed to the belief that there are some dimensions of reality (e.g. God, the Trinity, the incarnation, afterlife) which are beyond reason, and which can only be known through revelation. Rationalism, then, sees no need to resort to supernatural revelation to understand nature or the world. Nature, it was thought, was governed by a few simple laws. Knowledge of these laws, and the laws of human society, would create a good life in this world. According to Ernst Cassirer,

> The basic idea underlying all the tendencies of the Enlightenment was the conviction that all human understanding is capable, by its own power and without any recourse to super-natural assistance, of comprehending the system of the world and that this new way of understanding the world will lead to a new way of mastering it (cited in the New Catholic Encyclopedia, 8:702).

What stood in the way of the progress envisioned by rationalists was superstition, ignorance, and feudal or clerical hierarchical authority. The enemy was tyranny and "priestcraft," as Enlightenment thinkers put it. For them, superstition, ignorance, and repressive authority were summed up in Christianity. Like the Deists, Enlightenment philosophers, if they were not atheists like Diderot and Hume, emphasized a religion which was simple, rational, virtuous, and non-supernatural, in which Jesus was a simple teacher of practical moral wisdom, but not the incarnate son of God. This view can be seen in the words of Thomas Jefferson:

> When we shall have done away with the incomprehensible jargon of the Trinitarian arith-metic, that three are one and one is three; when we shall have knocked down the artificial scaffolding, reared to mask from view the very simple structure of Jesus; when, in short, we shall have unlearned everything which has been taught since his day, and got back to the pure and sim-ple doctrines he inculcated, we shall then be truly and worthily his disciples (cited in McGrath, 186).

Similarly, the great German philosopher Immanuel Kant argued that where Jesus endorsed what is reasonable, he should be respected, but where he went against reason, his teaching should be rejected.

Many Enlightenment figures (e.g. Voltaire) were Deists. Voltaire believed in a Creator God, whose grandeur was expressed in nature, but rejected the Christian beliefs in the incarnation, resurrection, providence, miracles, and sacraments, as irrational. He was fiercely opposed to Christianity, and, especially in the last years of his life, poured scorn on supernatural revelation, the Trinity, the virgin birth of Jesus, the presence of Christ in the Eucharist, and religious authority gen-erally. His *Dictionnaire Philosophique* was burned by authorities in Geneva, the Netherlands, France, and Rome. The following passage, in which Voltaire mocks the Christian (and Jewish) idea that the scriptures were inspired by the Holy Spirit, captures his wit and irony:

> While the style of Kings and Chronicles [books of the Old Testament] is divine, still, the actions reported in these histories are perhaps not so divine. David assassinates Uriah, Ishbosheth and Mephibosheth are assassinated, Absalom assassinates Amnon, Joab assassinates Absalom, Solomon assassinates Adonijah…. I pass over in silence many other assassinations. It must be admitted that if the Holy Spirit wrote this history, he didn't choose a very edifying subject (cited in Gay, 394).

Generally, the French Enlightenment, led by Voltaire and Denis Diderot, was much more anti-Christian and anti-clerical than either the English, American, or German Enlightenment. Voltaire's attitude to Christianity (and to democracy) is summed up in his words to Frederick the Great, King of Prussia: "Your majesty will do the human race an eternal service in extirpating this infamous superstition [Christianity], I do not say among the rabble, who are not worthy of being enlightened and who are apt for every yoke; I say among the well-bred, among those who wish to think" (cited in Cragg, 241). Much of the Enlightenment's **anti-clericalism** (antagonism toward priests and clergy) survives in France to this day, especially among French intellectuals.

The Enlightenment's skepticism of anything supernatural was particularly evident in its cri-tique of miracles. The Scottish philosopher David Hume argued that the laws of nature are so firmly established by universal common experience, that any testimony of a violation of those laws (i.e. a miracle) would be unconvincing (Hume, Section x, Part I). Similarly, Diderot stated that even if the whole population of Paris assured him that a man had risen from the dead, he would not believe it. Such skepticism—much of which persists to this day—has made it more difficult for Christianity to defend the doctrine of Jesus' divinity on the basis of his miracles and his resurrection. Few thinkers before the Enlightenment had doubted that miracles occurred, or that Jesus had been a great miracle worker. Jesus' miracles and resurrection were among the "proofs" offered for Jesus' divinity, for who but God could perform miracles such as his? But after the rationalist critique of miracles (especially Hume's), many intellectuals assumed that miracles had been shown to be superstitions or absurdities. This led to skepticism about Jesus' divinity as well.

B. Human Nature and Progress

A major disagreement between traditional Christianity and the Enlightenment philosophers centered on the nature of humanity. Both Catholic and Protestant Christians, following Augustine, had taught that human beings were born with original sin. This did *not* mean that people were by nature evil—after all, everything created by God is good. But it did mean that human beings were born with a natural tendency towards selfishness and sin. Enlightenment thinkers denied this, asserting that humanity had no inherent propensity to sin, but was naturally inclined to good. The evils in human society were due to ignorance, superstition, and entrenched political and religious authority. These could be overcome with proper education and freedom from superstition, dogmatic religion, and political tyranny. The most radical assertions were made by Jean Jacques Rousseau, who argued that humans in a state of nature were naturally free and equal, and that the establishment of organized society itself, with its institution of private property, was responsible for the inequality between persons.

This belief in the inherent goodness of humanity, in the power of reason, and in the advances of natural science, led to an optimistic belief in progress. In Europe the greatest exponent of progress was the Marquis de Condorcet. He argued that the history of the past showed that the human race is moving to an ultimate perfection. The future would bring (1) equality among nations, (2) equality of freedom and rights among individuals, and (3) the indefinite perfectibility of human nature itself, intellectually, morally, and physically. Condorcet was hostile to all religion, to monarchy, and especially to Christianity. His optimism was based on his belief that the true system of the universe had been discovered by Newton, and the true understanding of human nature by John Locke. Such progress in understanding, Condorcet thought, would continue and be spread by public education so as to elevate the whole race of humanity.

Not all thinkers were as optimistic as Condorcet. Benjamin Franklin combined a faith in scientific progress with skepticism about moral progress:

> *The rapid progress true science now makes occasions my regretting sometimes that I was born too soon. It is impossible to imagine the height to which may be carried, in a thousand years, the power of man over matter. We may perhaps learn to deprive large masses of their gravity, and give them absolute levity, for the sake of easy transport. Agriculture may diminish its labor and double its produce; all diseases may by sure means be prevented or cured....O that moral science were in as fair a way of improvement, that men would cease to be wolves to one another, and that human beings would at length learn what they now improperly call humanity!"* (Franklin, 802).

C. Freedom and Religious Toleration

Enlightenment thinkers were passionate advocates of liberty, by which they meant freedom from political and religious authoritarianism. It must be remembered that France before the French Revolution (1789) was still governed by kings, and that freedom of religious belief was largely unknown. The medieval idea, going back to Constantine, had been that religious unity was essential to the unity of a people and a country. Before the Enlightenment, this was accepted by both Catholics and Protestants, with the exception of a few groups, notably the Anabaptists (literally "rebaptizers," part of the Radical Reformation), and the Quakers. In France, Louis XIV in 1685 revoked the Edict of Nantes, which had granted religious liberty to Protestants. Thereafter, Protestants, atheists, and dissenters from Catholicism, the official religion imposed by the French king, could be punished by civil law. Even in England, dissenters from the "established" or national church, the Church of England (Anglican), were subject to various penalties until well into the 19th century. For example, they could not hold civil office or go to the universities. Nor was religious liberty universal in the United States until after the American revolution and the signing of the U.S. constitution (which were themselves the products of Enlightenment thought).

Enlightenment notions of political liberty derived largely from the 17th century English thinker, John Locke, who had maintained that governments derived their legitimacy from the consent of the governed. Rousseau, in France, also argued this. Although the Enlightenment philosophers were generally not proponents of democracy (recall Voltaire's views of the masses, above), they did argue for republican forms of government, in which people govern themselves through elected representatives.

Ideas of religious freedom followed from the Enlightenment notion that the "natural religion" of humanity was a simple belief in God the creator, virtue, and the goodness and freedom of humanity. From this perspective wars over religious differences were scandalous and irrational, and were essentially the result of religious authorities trying to force assent upon everyone. Enlightenment philosophers looked back on the religious wars of past centuries (e.g. the French wars of religion, 1562-1598, the Thirty Years war in Germany, 1618-1648, the English civil war, 1640-1660) as abominations. They argued that the kind of coercion practiced by most religious authorities destroyed free choice, which was the essence of religious commitment. As Diderot wrote:

> The mind can only acquiesce in what it accepts as true. The heart can only love what seems good to it. Violence will turn a man into a hypocrite if he is weak, and into a martyr if he is strong…. Teaching, persuasion, and prayer, these are the only legitimate means of spreading the faith (cited in Bokenkotter, 270).

The Enlightenment quest for religious freedom was largely successful. In America, freedom of religion is written into the Bill of Rights. The First Amendment reads, in part, "Congress shall make no law respecting an establishment of religion, or prohibiting the free exercise thereof." Since the 18th century, freedom of religion has become generally accepted worldwide. The Second Vatican Council (1962-1965) issued a document declaring that all persons ought to enjoy freedom of religion.

VI. Criticism of the Enlightenment and its Aftermath

The aftermath of the Enlightenment in France was the French Revolution (1789-1815), in which the ideas of Voltaire, Rousseau, and others were carried to extremes by radicals. The radicals instituted a reign of terror to enforce their demands, executing the king and queen of France and thousands of others on the guillotine. They also attempted to displace Christianity with a "religion of reason," and went so far as to enthrone a goddess of reason (played by an actress) on the high altar of Notre Dame Cathedral in Paris. In light of the French Revolution, the confidence of the Enlightenment in the goodness of humanity, progress, and the power of reason came under criticism. In England, the conservative reaction was voiced by Edmund Burke, who argued that the rationalism and skepticism of the Enlightenment thinkers had led to the wholesale destruction of social tradition and values. Tradition, in Burke's analysis, was not just a result of political and religious repression; it was the repository of the wisdom of the race. Through tradition, what had worked well in the past was handed on to the future. This was particularly true of social values, which should not be lightly over-thrown for untested, idealized, and rationalist social schemes. The Catholic defense of tradition was similar. Religious tradition, while it might be deformed in some instances, is basically an accumulation of the insights and wisdom of the race in spiritual matters, and it ought to be received with respect, not rejected because it is "unscientific." The Romantic reaction, which dominated the 19th century, asserted that the excessive Enlightenment emphasis on reason had ignored the importance of mystery, wonder, beauty, and intuition in life. This reaction resulted in powerful Romantic movements in music, painting, and literature.

Again, the assumption of Enlightenment thinkers that reason alone could explain all of reality has been criticized as too exclusive. Are there not other types of knowledge, for example knowledge of another person, or mystical knowledge, or intuition of spiritual things, which go beyond reason, and know dimensions of reality that reason cannot explore? As the great French scientist and philosopher Blaise Pascal put it: "The heart has its reasons which reason cannot know." Moreover, in the light of the savage dictatorships and wars of the 20th century, many people have lost faith in the natural goodness of humanity and in the notion of unlimited progress.

Nonetheless, many of the Enlightenment ideas have become permanent fixtures of the modern world. Most persons today accept that religious choice ought not be coerced and that diversity of religions should be tolerated. Most parties accept the basic Enlightenment idea that governments ought to rest on the consent of the governed and that humans have certain inalienable human rights. Even the skepticism engendered towards myth, miracles, the resurrection, and the supernatural, has become a permanent part of modern life. The Enlightenment was also the first epoch in Western history when a large number of intellectuals became atheists, and when atheism became intellectually respectable. This legacy also is still with us.

The Enlightenment, then, marked the end of the centuries when the Christian church had uncontested moral and intellectual authority, and when the church, allied with the state, could ensure (often by force) uniformity of religious belief in a given region or country. After the Enlightenment, Christianity has had to survive in an atmosphere of denominational and religious diversity and in an atmosphere of increasing intellectual secularism and skepticism.

VII. The Nineteenth Century

In the vast and crowded canvas of the 19th century, we will focus on three significant movements: the challenge posed by liberalism, the problems created for Christianity by the theory of evolution, and the rise of scientific historical and biblical criticism.

A. Liberalism

Liberalism in the 19th century carried forward the Enlightenment ideas that humans were naturally good and free, and that the source of their corruption was decadent social institutions. Therefore, liberals thought, the best atmosphere for human development was freedom: political freedom from kings, tyrants, a ruling class, and a national church, and economic freedom from government restrictions such as tariffs, price controls, etc. Nineteenth century liberals, especially in Europe, tended to be anti-Christian and especially anti-clerical. Their goal was a complete separation of church and state, and the foundation of autonomous secular nation-states, governed by representative democracies. In Italy, this led to the movement to unite Italy as a secular state, which entailed the takeover of the papal states (a large region in central Italy governed directly by the pope). This movement was largely successful: the papal states were virtually dissolved in 1870. All that remains of them now is the Vatican City, a one square mile enclave in Rome governed by the pope and the curia (administrative officials of the Catholic Church appointed by the pope). Naturally 19th century popes resisted this, and in the process opposed all that liberalism stood for. This opposition was voiced forcefully by Pope Pius IX (reigned 1846-78), in his Syllabus of Errors (1864), which condemned many liberal ideas, such as the separation of church and state and religious freedom. This position of the Catholic Church was not substantially changed until the Second Vatican Council (1962-1965).

Economic liberalism, or the doctrine of *laissez faire* (a French phrase meaning roughly, "let people act alone"), was and is the doctrine that there should be no interference by the state in the free market.

> *Economic liberalism rested on the assumption that there are certain natural laws of economic production and distribution (precisely analogous to the physical laws which govern the universe) that, if not interfered with, will naturally produce wealth, reward the industrious, and punish the indolent* (Hallowell, 704).

The doctrine of economic liberalism was set out in Adam Smith's classic *Wealth of Nations*. There Smith argued that individuals, in pursuing their own self-interest, are led by the action of an "invisible hand" to also promote the public or common good.

In practice, pure *laissez-faire* capitalism led to horrendous injustices: child labor in factories and mines, sixteen hour workdays, dangerous working conditions, no provision for sickness, accidents, or retirement; in short, extreme exploitation of workers by owners. One response to this was the socialism developed by Karl Marx and others (see below). Another response, more common in the West, has been the development of laws which regulate child labor, demand worker compensation for job-related injuries, limit the length of workdays and workweeks, impose work safety standards, and limit environmental damage. The only examples of unregulated economies now are in Third World countries, where worker exploitation continues.

The Catholic Church opposed and continues to oppose unrestricted economic liberalism. Popes from Leo XIII (reigned 1878-1903) to John Paul II (1978-) have written extensively on this question. While the church insists on the right of individuals to own private property, so as to support families, it also insists on the limitation of the free market by provisions for the common good. As John Paul II puts it: there is a social mortgage on private property. The rights of property owners are not absolute, but are to be balanced by the rights of the larger community, including the rights of workers. The exact nature of this balance continues to be a matter of extensive debate.

B. The Theory of Evolution

Although many of the church fathers (e.g. Augustine) were open to a symbolic interpretation of the stories in Genesis 1-11, by early modern times it was held by both Catholics and Protestants that Genesis 1-11 was an historically accurate account of the creation of the world and humanity. Bishop James Ussher (an Irish Protestant), using only biblical data (such as the ages of Adam and his descendants) in the 17th century put the creation of the earth at 4004 B.C. Following Genesis, all species were thought to have been created directly by God in their present form, during the first six days of creation.

During the 18th and 19th centuries, however, the science of geology gradually developed. By the early 1800's geologists realized that the major features of the earth (mountains, valleys, etc.) had been shaped, not suddenly by catastrophes like Noah's flood, but by very gradual processes, such as creation of sedimentary rocks by deposit of sediment in ancient oceans, the uplifting of rocks to form mountains, and erosion. Since the rate of change brought about by these processes is extremely slow, geologists reasoned that the earth had to be much older than the Genesis account indicates.

In 1859 Charles Darwin published his epochal book *The Origin of Species by Means of Natural Selection*. Here Darwin brought together an enormous mass of evidence and offered a simple, plausible explanation for the emergence of species by natural processes alone, rather than by the miraculous creation of God. This explanation is known as the theory of **evolution**. All living species, he argued, are made up of members which have individual variations. Also, all species overpopulate, so that only some—those individuals whose physical traits are best adapted to the environment—survive. Since only the survivors leave progeny, the offspring will carry the physical traits of their parents, while the traits of those who do not survive will die out. Thus over many generations, traits which are advantageous in a particular environment will develop in the species, while disadvantageous traits will be eliminated from the population. Gradually, this transformation of the character of individuals in a species will lead to the development of new species. Thus, for example, in a population of horse-like animals, some individuals in each generation are born with longer than average necks: these individuals can eat leaves on trees which short-necked individuals cannot reach. Therefore they will tend to survive in the struggle for existence and leave more progeny. This process, repeated over thousands of generations, would lead to a long-necked species of horse—the giraffe, which eats leaves from acacia trees that shorter-necked animals cannot reach. It should be noted that animal breeders have practiced these same principles for centuries.

Darwin did not invent the notion of evolution; what he did was provide a simple explanation of its mechanism. There were three elements to this explanation: (1) random variation among individuals, (2) a struggle for existence, so that only some survive, and (3) **natural selection**, i.e. the principle that over generations, certain traits are "selected" for survival, while other traits perish (this has been called the "survival of the fittest"). In addition, he accumulated a huge amount of evidence in favor of the theory.

The Origin of Species made an immediate, powerful, and lasting impact: the first edition of 1250 copies sold out in one day. Although met with vigorous opposition from scientists as well as churchmen, Darwin's ideas eventually triumphed; the theory of the emergence of species by gradual evolution has become accepted as fact in almost all intellectual circles. Probably no single idea so decisively separates modern from pre-modern times as the idea of evolution.

In 1871 Darwin published *The Descent of Man*, in which he argued that human beings, like other animals, emerged from animal ancestors, and were not miraculously created by God. This was taken as attacking the Christian belief that humans are made in God's image, that they have a spiritual soul, intellect, and free will, and that humans are therefore different in *kind*, not just in *degree*, from the animals. Rather, one could argue from Darwin that humans are made in the image of their animal ancestor, and therefore differ from animals only in degree: humans are like apes, only with a larger brain and the ability to use language. Thus with Darwin the modern scientific attempt to explain all phenomena by natural causes alone was extended to the creation of humanity also. Darwin himself, once an Anglican Christian, lost his faith as a result of his own theory.

Darwin's ideas are incompatible with a literal reading of Genesis 1-3. Thus a battle emerged between those who defended Darwin, and those who argued that Genesis, being the revealed word of God, had to be right and Darwin had to be wrong. From about 1895 to 1920, evangelical Protestant churches (e.g. Baptists and Presbyterians) split between those who accepted evolution and those who rejected it. Those who rejected it—called Fundamentalists, because they thought of themselves as upholding the fundamentals of Christianity—in many cases separated from their parent denominations. Recently, for example, Missouri and Wisconsin Synod Lutherans, insisting that Genesis must be read literally, separated from the mainline Evangelical Lutheran Church of America. Many evangelical Christian denominations, such as the Southern Baptists, today reject the teaching of evolution. In some cases, evolution is not being taught in public schools because of pressure from anti-evolutionist groups. This pressure exists even to the present day.

Acceptance of evolution in Roman Catholicism came in 1950, when Pope Pius XII, in an encyclical, *Humani Generis*, said that Catholics could teach that the human body emerged from animal ancestors, though each individual human soul is created directly by God (thus making each person an image and a child of God). Catholic theologians agree that Genesis 1-11 contains spiritual and theological truth about God and humanity, but was not intended to be a scientific account of human origins.

Many apologists for modern evolutionary theory argue that evolutionary theory is sufficient to explain the whole process of creation by natural causes alone, and that no God or transcendent causes exist. This view is contrary to Catholic teaching about creation. Most Catholic theologians maintain that God creates the world and humanity *through* the process of evolution, an idea known as "theistic evolution." Whereas Genesis tells us *who* created the world, the theory of evolution tells us *how* it was created. It should be noted, however, that though the fact of emergence of living things and humans from simple life forms is almost indisputable, the *mechanism* by which the process of evolution operates is by no means certain, and remains in dispute among biologists.

C. Scientific History

Though a critical use of historical texts developed during the Renaissance, in the 19th century the notion of a truly scientific history emerged, whose aim was to be as objective as the natural sciences, on which it was modelled. Pre-modern historians told their historical stories with a view to teaching moral lessons. For example, the Roman historian, Sallust, describes the decline of the Roman Republic and the rise of the Roman Empire (in which the people were ruled by dictators) as due to a loss of public virtue and morality, and the rise of corruption due to the love of wealth and power. Ancient historians also depicted historical events as controlled by supernatural as well as natural causes. The biblical book of the Acts of the Apostles, for example, sees the expansion of the early Christian church as due to the power of the Holy Spirit, which inspires the apostles, works miracles through them, and converts their hearers. Finally, ancient historians tended to repeat the words of other historians without checking their veracity.

Scientific history, which emerged first in Germany, changed many of the practices of pre-modern history. First, scientific history sought to eliminate the biases and values judgments of the author from the telling of history. These modern historians wished to describe history "as it actually was." Second, it became axiomatic for them (as for all modern scientists) to assume that past events were controlled by the same forces which control present events, and that these forces were natural, not supernatural. Thus modern historians, even if Christian, would probably not describe the expansion of the early church as due to the Holy Spirit. Instead they would focus on "natural" causes, such as the state of society, economics, and the superiority of Christian morality and social welfare systems (Bokenkotter, 37-38). Finally, scientific historians did not accept the work of earlier historians uncritically (as the ancients often did); they sought to verify the data by returning to primary sources, such as archival records, contemporary accounts, and letters, and to inform the reader of these sources by footnote citations and bibliography.

This scientific view of history was modelled on the natural sciences, especially Darwin's theory of evolution, which explained the past in terms of natural causes only. This in turn has had an incalculable influence on our modern view of the world. In both scholarly and popular writing events are typically explained by social, economic, political, psychological, or other causes. There is usually no reference to God's action or providence, since the scientific view is skeptical of ascribing the cause of events to supernatural activity. The scientific view of history has therefore been a major shaper of the modern secular and anti-supernatural view of the world.

D. Scientific Biblical Criticism

The scientific view of history in turn led to a scientific **historical criticism** of the Bible. Biblical scholars of the 19th and 20th centuries increasingly treated the Bible like any other book, subjecting it to scientific scrutiny and asking if the events it records can be verified historically the same way that other historical facts are verified. In addition, the developing science of archaeology was unearthing the records of ancient cultures contemporary with biblical cultures, and these records affected the interpretation of biblical stories.

In the centuries since the death of Christ, both the Old and New Testaments had come to be understood as inspired by God. The primary author of the texts was thought to be the Holy Spirit. This view was and is shared by both Christians and Jews. However, the notion of how inspiration took place was somewhat naive: the Holy Spirit was thought to have dictated the words of scripture to the ancient author. If that were the case, the Bible should be factually accurate in all respects. This view came to be substantially modified by the new biblical criticism, as the following example suggests.

In the late 19th century, the developing science of archaeology began unearthing texts of great relevance to the Bible. The British excavations at the great library of Assurbanipal, in Nineveh, were particularly important. Discovered were cuneiform texts which told the Babylonian myth of creation—the *Enuma Elish*—which had apparently served as a model for the authors of Genesis, and an ancient flood story (the *Epic of Gilgamesh*) with a hero like Noah, which account again seemed to have been a model for the story of the Noachic flood. The fact that the creation and flood stories in Genesis seem to have been influenced by earlier Babylonian accounts conflicts with the idea that the only influence on the biblical authors was the voice of the Holy Spirit.

Other excavations in Palestine itself, in Egypt, and other Near Eastern lands, have greatly increased our knowledge of the cultures and peoples contemporary with the biblical authors. As a result, it is now possible to read the biblical stories with a knowledge of the contexts in which they were written, something not possible before recent times. This, along with the rise of modern natural science, has led to a different understanding of the ancient texts, and hence of the meaning of inspiration. Genesis 1-11, for example, is read as a mythical account of origins, similar to the creation myths of the Babylonians and Egyptians (Israel's neighbors), which are not scientifically or historically accurate, but which nevertheless convey permanent spiritual truths about God and humanity through symbolic stories, such as the stories of the creation, the "Fall," and the flood.

But this view of inspiration has been fiercely resisted by many groups of Christians. As mentioned above, fundamentalist Christians insist that the biblical accounts are *literally inerrant*. The fundamentalist view is that every part of the Bible is completely accurate, including the parts about the origin of the world and human beings. These groups reject evolution, but they also reject modern biblical criticism, because they believe that it undermines Christian revelation.

VIII. Karl Marx and Marxism

Karl Marx, the founder of Marxist Socialism, lived from 1818-1883, but the influence of Marxism has been felt mainly in the 20th century. Marx's core idea is the economic interpretation of history. Whereas historians before Marx had argued that history was shaped by great persons, ideas, or events, Marx argued that economic forces determined historical change. Every society, he thought, is based on a certain kind of economic and technological foundation; this foundation largely determines who the ruling class will be, and what the ruling *ideas* will be. For Marx, the ruling ideas (of a society or period) are always the ideas of the ruling class. For example, early medieval European society was based on a feudal, agrarian economy. The ruling class therefore consisted of the large landowners: barons, dukes, princes, or kings. These landowners depended on peasant labor; therefore they emphasized a social code of hierarchy, honor, and fidelity to one's lord. But for Marx, these ideas of the ruling class were not *true*, they were simply *rationalizations*, designed to keep the peasants from stealing and rebelling. Eventually the feudal economic system was replaced by a system based on trade and commerce, and the new ruling class became the capitalists, who displaced the landed aristocracy as rulers. For Marx, this process, while gradual, was necessarily at some point violent. No ruling class voluntarily gives up power; therefore power must be wrested from them by the new emerging ruling class. In the transition from feudalism to capitalism this happened in a series of revolutions: the English civil war and revolution of 1688, the French revolution, the American revolution. In each of these revolutions, the commercial, capitalist, bourgeois (Marx's term) class took over power (violently) from the older landed aristocracy. But what determined the historical change was at bottom the change in the economic and technological conditions, from agrarian/feudal to commercial/capitalist.

Marx foresaw a further economic change taking place in his lifetime and a new ruling class emerging. The shift would be from a capitalist mode of production to a socialist mode of production, and the new ruling class would be the urban workers or proletariat, who would wrest power from their capitalist overlords. Marx hoped this would happen in the revolutions of 1848, for which he penned his famous book, the *Communist Manifesto*, which ends with the words, "Workingmen of all countries, unite!"

Marx's ideas, which form the core of modern communism, have posed an enormous challenge to Christianity in our time. He assumed that history is governed by simple economic forces, in the same way that 19th century science thought matter was governed by simple forces like gravity. Marx did not think there was any divine or spiritual influence in history. He was an atheist, who thought of religion as the "opium of the people," that is, as a drug which keeps the lower classes passive and resigned in their economic oppression. When that oppression was removed, religion would wither away, since people would be fulfilled and would no longer need the numbing effects of religion.

Marx's economic thought has proved to be simplistic. It is not used much by modern economists, even by Marxists. The reason for this is that it contains certain fatal flaws, notably a naive notion that under communism, in which private property is abolished, people will continue to work hard for the benefit of the whole society. As Marx wrote: "The free development of each is the free development of all." But in practice, Marxist socialism has tended to dampen initiative and the motivation to work, and productivity in Marxist countries, especially in agriculture, has plummeted. (The Soviet Russians had a saying: "They pretend to pay us, and we pretend to work.") Marxism has, however, been moderately effective in levelling out the disparity of wealth between classes, a problem that plagues capitalist countries in the West. In the United States, about 1% of the people own 40% of the wealth, a greater disparity than any other Western country.

At the intellectual level, Marxist thought introduced a seductive and infective tendency to dismiss ideas simply because they represent the ideas of a dominant or suspect class. Marx saw the ideas of the dominant class as convenient fictions designed to keep that class in power. Thus, for example, Marxists tend to dismiss ideas of capitalists just because they come from capitalists. This tendency has been echoed by other groups as well: capitalists dismiss communist ideas just because they come from communists, without asking if there is any truth in the ideas.

On the other hand, certain Marxist analyses reveal some important information about social structures. Some Latin American theologians use Marxist categories with great effectiveness to analyze the power structures of their societies. Many times what passes for Christianity might really be a rationalization designed to benefit ruling groups. For centuries the Latin American church taught the poor to accept their lot in this life, not to rebel or steal, so that they would be rewarded in heaven, a strategy which effectively kept oppressive rulers in power. Another example is embodied in the saying "God helps those who help themselves." Many people think this saying is biblical, but is not from the Bible, nor does it represent the thought of Jesus, who taught that God helps those who humbly ask for his mercy, and favors those who help the poor (Matt 25:31-46). Rather this saying, which is partly true and partly false, comes from Ben Franklin, an early capitalist, and represents a good example of warping the Gospel to justify capitalist ideas.

Most (but not all) Marxist regimes have been aggressively atheistic, and have persecuted Christians severely, in the former Soviet Union, Eastern Europe, China, and elsewhere. In fact, persecution and martyrdom has been more widespread in the 20th century than in any century since the end of the Roman persecutions in the 4th century AD.

IX. Sigmund Freud and Psychology

Sigmund Freud (1856-1939), a Viennese physician, was one of the founders of psychoanalysis, and modern psychological theory. He is remembered because of his discovery of the "unconscious" part of the mind. Through his medical practice, Freud recognized that some of his patients were suffering from traumatic memories which had been suppressed and forgotten. In effect, these memories had been pushed into the unconscious mind, from which they continued to influence the patient's conscious behavior in a manner unknown to the patient. Freud also discovered techniques like dream analysis and free association to uncover and analyze these repressed complexes.

In Freud's model of the mind, the conscious mind is called the "ego" (Latin for "I"). The repressed unconscious is called the "id" (Latin for "it"), and the conscience—the values internalized from one's society and parents—is called the "superego." The id he saw as composed of self-centered, pleasure-seeking drives and instincts such as anger, sex, hunger, etc. as well as repressed memories and fantasies. Civilized persons could not express the id directly, or civilization would descend into anarchy and savagery. It was the task of the ego to balance the drives of the id with the moral demands of the superego, and to express the drives of the id in civilized ways, mainly in love and work.

Freud's ideas achieved wide popularity in the 1920's, and have changed the intellectual landscape of the 20th century. We no longer have the naive confidence in the power of reason that Enlightenment thinkers did. Rather, Freudian thinking suggests that the rational ego seems to be a thin veneer over the selfish impulses of the unconscious mind. When that veneer is broken—because of alcohol, for instance—the drives of the id become easily expressed, often in destructive ways. Many fights and most date rape takes place when people have been drinking.

Freud's ideas have posed a strong challenge to religion. Influenced by 19th century science, he thought of religion as essentially wish-fulfillment. Each human being has an image of his or her father embedded in the unconscious, and each person projects this image of an all-powerful father onto God. We imagine God fulfilling all of our wishes in heaven, just as a child might imagine a father caring for all its needs. In his book, *The Future of an Illusion* (1927), Freud argued that religion was a childish stage of human development, and hoped that the human race would be able to advance beyond such illusions into the sober light of science.

Later psychologists have challenged Freud's model of the psyche as materialistic, mechanistic, and reductionistic. Some psychologists (e.g. Carl Jung, Viktor Frankl) have argued that the unconscious is not just composed of egoistical drives and instincts, but that there is also a spiritual side to the unconscious, such that the divine realm can make contact with the human through the unconscious (e.g. in dreams) as well as through the conscious mind (e.g. in prayer or visions). Generally speaking, though, both Freudian and non-Freudian psychology has tended to reduce religion to mere wishes and images composed by the human mind, rather than seeing religion as a true understanding of a transcendent reality which is independent of humanity.

It is certainly true that our perception of God (or anything, for that matter) is colored by our personal psychology and viewpoint. This has been recognized for centuries: Aquinas frequently repeats the medieval adage that "the thing known is in the mind according to the mode of the knower." Psychology has therefore been invaluable in its clarification of the contents, conscious and unconscious, of the human mind. But the question of whether or not God or any transcendent spiritual reality exists is a question that cannot be settled by psychology: it is a **metaphysical** question (in the area of speculative philosophy), not a psychological question. Many psychologists may assume that religious beliefs are nothing but figments (fictions) of the imagination, but it should be recognized that this is an assumption which goes beyond their competence as psychologists.

X. Conclusion

The modern challenge to Christianity has largely been driven by modern science, whose methods have been adopted by one field after another. Moreover, the main assumption of modern scientific method—that all events can be explained by natural and physical causes—has become a principal assumption of the modern mentality.

Fundamental to Christianity (and all other religions) is the belief that reality is comprised of both material (physical) and spiritual dimensions. There need be no conflict between science and Christianity if it is recognized that scientific methods are valid for investigation of material reality, while revelation, faith, and theology are valid means of discovering truths about spiritual reality. Certainly there are many areas of overlap. An example is investigation of the human person, in whom there are physical aspects, explored by disciplines such as biochemistry, but also spiritual aspects (such as free will, the soul, and the Holy Spirit), explored by philosophy and theology. In such areas a full understanding can be had only by recourse to many disciplines, scientific, philosophical, and theological.

Problems arise when either theology (as in the Galileo case) or science oversteps their legitimate boundaries, and claims to have answers that pertain to another discipline. Some scientific writers today claim that the *only* valid method of knowing is science, and that what cannot be known by science does not exist. But this belief, called **scientism**, cannot itself be proven scientifically, for there is no way to show scientifically that spiritual reality does not exist, since scientific methods are only valid for the investigation of physical reality.

Fortunately, in recent decades an exciting and fruitful dialogue has developed between science and theology. Some scientists are even writing books on theology, and many theologians are incorporating science into their theology. In many ways, theology and science are closer now than at any time since Darwin. Like any challenge, the challenge of science to Christianity has been difficult, but also offers great opportunity.

Key Terms:

cosmology	Enlightenment
Nicholas Copernicus	liberalism
Galileo Galilei	Charles Darwin
Isaac Newton	natural selection
Rene Descartes	evolution
Deism	Karl Marx
rationalism	Sigmund Freud
anti-clericalism	scientism

Questions for Reading:

1. Why was the New Cosmology a challenge to traditional Christianity?

2. Explain the New Science, and why it was a challenge to traditional Christianity.

3. Explain what Deism is, and how it differs from Christianity.

4. What is meant by the Enlightenment? What is Enlightenment Rationalism? Why was it such a challenge to traditional Christianity?

5. Explain the disagreement between Enlightenment philosophers such as Condorcet and traditional Christianity on the subject of human nature and progress. Which side do you think was right? Why?

6. Why did Enlightenment thinkers insist so strongly on freedom of religion? What did they see as opposed to religious freedom?

7. Describe the aftermath of the Enlightenment. What criticisms have been levelled against Enlightenment thought? What facets of Enlightenment thought have become widely accepted?

8. Explain the beliefs of (a) liberalism, (b) economic liberalism. How does Pope John Paul II criticize economic liberalism?

9. Why was the theory of evolution seen as a challenge to traditional Christian belief? How do Catholic theologians deal with this challenge? Explain the idea of theistic evolution.

10. How does scientific history differ from older forms of history? In what way has it been a major shaper of a secular view of the world.

11. Explain scientific biblical criticism. How has it changed the Catholic and mainline Protestant view of Genesis 1-11?

12. Explain the basic ideas of Karl Marx. Why has Marxism been a challenge to Christianity?

13. Explain Freud's model of the psyche. Why has modern psychology been a challenge to Christianity?

Works Consulted/Recommended Reading:

Bokenkotter, Thomas. *A Concise History of the Catholic Church*. Rev. ed. New York: Doubleday, Image, 1979.

Cragg, Gerald. *The Church and the Age of Reason*. Rev. ed. Harmondsworth, England: Penguin Books, 1966, 1974.

Franklin, Benjamin. "Letter to Joseph Priestly, 1780." In *Encyclopedia Brittanica*, 1968 edition, 9:802.

Gaustad, Edwin S. *Faith of Our Fathers*. San Francisco: Harper & Row, 1987.

Gay, Peter. *The Enlightenment*. New York: Random House, Vintage, 1966.

Hallowell, J. H. "Liberalism." In *New Catholic Encyclopedia*, 8:704.

Hume, David. *An Enquiry Concerning Human Understanding*. 2nd ed. Chicago: Open Court Publishing, 1966.

John Paul II. "Lessons of the Galileo Case." *Origins*, Nov. 12, 370-373.

Langford, Jerome J. *Galileo, Science, and the Church*. Rev. ed. Ann Arbor: University of Michigan Press, 1971.

McGrath, Alister. *Christian Theology: An Introduction*. Oxford: Blackwell, 1994.

Rousseau, Jean Jacques. *Discours sur l'origine et les fondements de l'inequalite parmi les hommes*. New York: Oxford University Press, 1922.

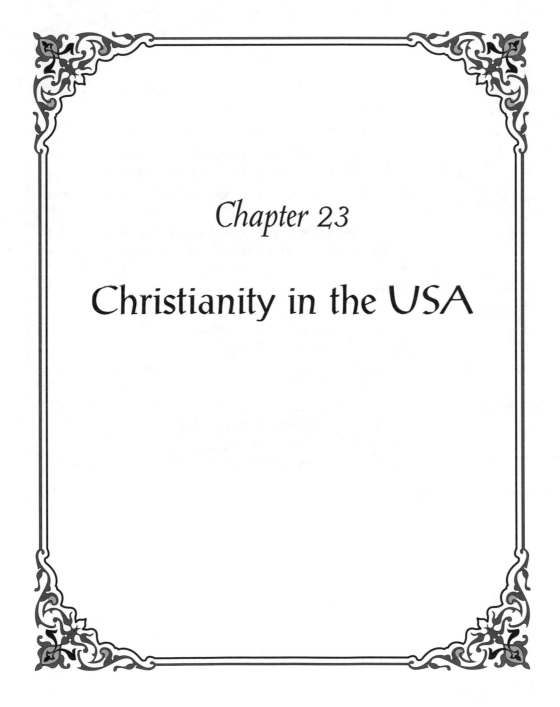

Chapter 23

Christianity in the USA

Timeline

1508-13 AD	Juan Ponce De León names Puerto Rico and Florida for the Spaniards.
1534	French explorers investigate the St. Lawrence Valley.
1540	Francisco Vásquez de Coronado and the Franciscan Juan de Padilla initiate an expedition into southwest United States.
1598	Juan de Oñate heads a colonization movement into the Rio Grande Valley.
1604	The French establish their first permanent settlement in the continental USA at Ste. Croix De Monts Island in Maine.
1607	The Jamestown settlement in the colony of Virginia is established.
1620	The Puritans, including both Presbyterians and Congregationalists, arrive on the Mayflower and establish a colony at Plymouth in Massachusetts.
c. 1650	Lutherans from Germany, Austria, and the Netherlands begin to migrate to America.
1682	William Penn founds the Pennsylvania colony as a haven for the "Religious Society of Friends," also known as the Quakers.
1718	The French Catholic settlement of New Orleans is established.

c. 1720	American Lutherans begin to organize into churches.
1737	John Wesley brings the Methodist pietist movement to the Americas.
c. 1740	The Great Awakening spreads throughout New England and the other British colonies. The beginning of the rise of denominationalism in the USA.
c. 1785	The first American Unitarian congregation is established at King's Chapel, Boston.
1792	The Baptist Missionary Society begins converting large numbers in the colonies to the Baptist tradition.
1830	Joseph Smith establishes the "Church of Jesus Christ of Latter-Day Saints," also known as the Mormons.
c. 1844	William Miller establishes the Seventh-Day Adventist church in the United States.
c. 1872	Charles Taze Russell establishes the International Bible Students Association, later known as the Jehovah's Witnesses.
1875	Mary Baker Eddy establishes the "Church of Christ, Scientist," also known as the Christian Scientists.
c. 1906	Pentecostal churches begin to emerge out of a variety of inter-denominational revivalist churches in America.
1914	The Assemblies of God Church is established in the United States.

Christianity in the USA

Christianity in the Americas did not begin with the signing of the Declaration of Independence, or even with the establishment of the British colonies on the Atlantic coast. In the land that is now known as the United States of America, indigenous peoples' experience of Christianity, at least for the first one hundred and twenty years, was Spanish and Catholic (1500-1620). Later there would be French missioners and finally the English settlements, but not until the early part of the 17th century.

This chapter will trace the history of the development of Christianity in the United States, beginning with the establishment of Spanish and French Catholicism in the century or so before the founding of the English colonies. It will also describe the three expressions of Christianity that would be found in the colonies of the upper Atlantic coast: traditional Christianity, the new theocracy, and the refuge of tolerance. Finally, it will give a brief description of the growth of denominationalism and the diversity of Christian churches that emerged in the late 18th and 19th centuries.

I. Spanish Christianity in the Americas

Juan Ponce De León was the primary Spanish explorer of the east coast of what would later be known as the United States of America. The island of Puerto Rico, in 1508, was the first territory to come under Spanish rule because of his colonizing efforts. Though it was named San Juan de Bautista by Columbus, Ponce De León called it the rich port (Puerto Rico). On Easter day in 1513 Ponce De León landed near the site of what is today St. Augustine, Florida. In keeping with the name of the feast day, he called the territory La Gran Pascua Florida (Grand Passover Full of Flowers). After a number of setbacks, the Spanish finally established a permanent colony and mission at St. Augustine in 1565. St. Augustine became the primary military outpost for the Spanish in Florida. It also became the first and oldest African-American settlement in the continental USA. Spanish colonization parties regularly included the Moors (Blacks) and others who spoke the languages of the trade routes. Therefore, blacks (free, military, and slave) were the mainstay of the garrison and part of the settlement population.

The Spanish established a dozen colonies in Florida by the end of the 17th century. By that time, St. Augustine was a thriving community of more than three thousand residents. The church was also flourishing, having already ordained seven of its own priests. The settlement of these colonies gave rise to a new people of great diversity in hue, who were Spanish in language and culture, and Catholic in faith. The Spanish who had been living among the Native Americans in their newly established colonies began to intermarry with both Native Americans and blacks after the first generation. These intermarriages gave rise to two mixed-race peoples: Mestizo (Spanish/Native American) and Mulatto (Spanish/Black).

Spanish explorations of new territories appeared to have two interests: "the exploiting of new lands for riches and the exploiting of new people for religion" (Bowden, 40). Both of these interests are demonstrated in the Spanish explorations of what would later be known as Mexico and southwest United States. For the first thirty years the Spanish never ventured northward outside of

Mexico. When they finally did, it was because they had heard tales of great riches in the cities to the north. In 1539 a mission was launched to map the area and determine the extent of the riches. **Esteban Azamor** and a friar, Marcos de Niza, were chosen to lead the party into Zuni territory. The Zuni Indian peoples killed Estaban, and Marcos ran for his life. This incident only heightened the Spanish belief that gold was to be found in the north. Therefore, in 1540 **Francisco Vásquez de Coronado** initiated the first major expedition into what later would be the USA. His friar counterpart was a Franciscan by the name of **Fr. Juan de Padilla**. For a year and a half they roamed from the Rio Grande to the Grand Canyon through central Kansas and the Texas panhandle. Fr. Padilla decided to remain in Kansas to begin a mission there. In the winter of 1542, Juan de Padilla became the first Christian martyr in the USA.

Since the Spanish explorers had found neither great wealth nor great urban civilizations to be plundered, the growth of the Spanish Christian influence in the southwest USA was a slow and gradual process. In 1598, **Juan de Oñate** was selected to head a definitive colonizing movement into the Rio Grande valley. The four hundred settlers who moved into the southwest were primarily farmers and traders who knew how to work for themselves. Because they stayed in their villages and learned to live off of the land, and did not take slaves or trespass on sacred land, they encountered few difficulties with the indigenous people. Oñate set about baptizing and instructing the Pueblo Indian people in the Christian way, sometimes by coercion, sometimes by threat of punishment. Such were the somewhat self-contradictory beginnings of indigenous American Christianity, which continues in the Southwest to the present.

II. French Missionary Activity in the Americas

A century of Spanish Catholicism had passed before the Native Americans of the North encountered European settlers and Christianity. The first Christians they met were French. Though the St. Lawrence Valley was initially explored in 1534, the first enduring French settlement in the continental USA was at Ste. Croix De Monts Island, in Maine in 1604. Quebec, the major inland settlement and outpost for the French, was founded in 1608. Because the French colonial explorers did not seek gold, but wanted to trade for furs, they sought not to conquer but to develop alliances with the indigenous communities. Thus the Huron, Algonquin, and Montagnais became their partners in a new trade system, which provided the French considerable wealth.

Although the first priests to serve the mission of New France were the Jesuits in 1611, they were removed only two years later due to some French political infighting. In their ten-year absence, a group of Franciscans was sent to develop the French mission to the indigenous peoples. Later when Cardinal de Richelieu took control of the missionary efforts of France in 1632, he selected both the Jesuits and the Capuchins to serve the people of New France. The Capuchins served Nova Scotia while the Jesuits developed the Christian community of the Huron. Some of the best known missionaries of New France were a part of this enterprise, including the North American martyrs Sts. Issac Jogues, John Brebeuf, Jean de Lalande (1646), St. Rene Goupil (1642) and a Mohawk maiden Blessed Kateri Tekakwitha (1680).

Yet the major French Christian influence in the Americas was not along the southern shore of the St. Lawrence Valley but in the Mississippi Valley and Louisiana Territory. Following the fur traders, the French missionary explorers moved through Wisconsin, Michigan, Illinois and Indiana. In 1670 a headquarters for the mission was established at St. Ignace on the Mackinac with Fr. **Jacques Marquette** (1637-1675) as the priest in charge. In 1673 Marquette and his companion **Louis**

Joliet (1641-1700) journeyed down the Mississippi to where it is joined by the Arkansas River. Franciscans joined Rene de LaSalle as he explored the Great Lakes in 1679-1680. Fr. **Louis Hennepin** (1640-1701), who provided the first written description of the Niagara Falls, led the friars on a mission effort into Minnesota in 1680. Two years later, Rene de LaSalle took friars on his journey to the mouth of the Mississippi. By 1720, the mission stations of the lower Mississippi Valley were officially recognized under the French colony of Louisiana, and all the northern territories under the Diocese of Quebec (1698).

The second prong of the French expansion into the Mississippi Valley came from the French settlements along the Gulf Coast. Biloxi (1699) was their first settlement, with both Capuchins and Jesuits serving as priests, though New Orleans (1718) became their best known settlement. These settlements were marked by two characteristics which distinguished them from earlier French colonies: the commingling of Native Americans and French settlers, and the development of slave labor for the plantation system. The French of the Mississippi Delta lived near and had regular interaction with the indigenous communities. However, the French nationals set a poor example for the native peoples, making the mission effort very difficult. In addition, the effect of the liquor trade and other abuses inflicted on Native Americans was evident here perhaps more than in any other colony. Some Natives had even been enslaved, though the majority of the slaves were Africans brought in from the Caribbean.

As the French settlements grew and became more prosperous, French trade in slaves also flourished. In an attempt to correct some of the abuses being inflicted on slaves, the French government introduced the **Code Noir** (Black Codes) in 1724. The Code regulated slave life and established guidelines for the owners in relationship to the slaves. While they did not allow miscegenation (interracial intimacy) of any kind, they also outlawed the public practice of any religion other than Catholicism. As a result, blacks were forced to become Catholics and Jews were expelled from all French territories.

In just over six years after the founding of the city of New Orleans much seemed to be out of hand. In order to bring some sense of civilization to the growing colonial world, the French initiated another level of church organization and presence into the budding society. In 1727 the **Ursuline Sisters** arrived and opened the first convent and private Catholic school for girls in the continental USA. The sisters not only provided education for young girls, but nursing for the sick, and hospitality for visitors in their guest house. With the establishment of the schools, French Louisiana now had all of the services of a Catholic community. In mind and heart they were a part of New France and they looked to the Diocese of Quebec for spiritual guidance. This fully functioning community was the second part of the foundation of Christianity in what would later be called the United States of America.

III. The English Colonies

Most discussions of American religious history tend to ignore the Spanish and French Catholic presence, while focusing on the Puritan English contributions to the development of the social and cultural history of the United States. Historians do this because the framing of the Constitution and much of the social life in the United States sprang from the joint effort of the Christian citizens of the colonies owned by England. However, by the time the Puritans established the Massachusetts

Bay colony in 1620, the residents of much of what is the United States today had already encountered either French or Spanish Catholicism.

In contrast with the predominantly Catholic influence of the Spanish and French colonies, the colonies of the upper Atlantic coast of North America (from New England through the Tidewater to Georgia) were settled by Protestants of various European countries. Jamestown of the colony of Virginia was the first Protestant settlement (1607). Its inhabitants were English and belonged to the Church of England. Several of the other colonies, however, represented the new English reformed churches and other European Protestant communities. As a result, the colonies of the upper Atlantic coast can be divided along the lines of the three expressions of Christianity that would be found in those areas: (1) traditional Christianity, (2) the new theocracy, and (3) the refuge of tolerance.

A. Traditional Christianity

Some of the English colonies, in particular the colonies of Virginia, North and South Carolina, and Georgia, were composed of settlers whose religious affiliation can be described as "traditional Christianity." These lands were royal colonies. The people who settled there maintained the traditions of the English crown. The Church of England (also known as the Anglican Church) nurtured their spiritual life and provided the religious structure for their society. They sought no reform or new religious freedom when they came to the New World. All saw themselves as remaining within the religious tradition of Britain, and considered themselves an extension of the British Empire.

B. The New Theocracy

The situation was somewhat different in the New England colonies (Plymouth and Massachusetts Bay, Connecticut, New Haven, and New Hampshire, in particular). The settlers of the New England colonies also were British, but they represented the new English reform churches which had been rejected by the English crown, most notably the Puritans. The **Puritans** originated in the 16th century as a reform movement within the Church of England. They sought to purify the Church of England of any evidence of its prior ties with the Roman Catholic Church: hence the name Puritan. Eventually the Puritan reformers divided into Congregationalists and Presbyterians, depending on the model of church organization they chose. **Congregationalists** opted for a form of church government in which each local congregation functioned independently, whereas the **Presbyterians** retained some of the hierarchical structure of the Church of England, while also placing greater importance on the local church. When they came to the New World, they wanted to create a new society built on scripture and cleansed of the doctrines and corruptions of some of the European reforms.

Some of the Puritans who fled persecution in England arrived on the Mayflower in 1620 and established what would later be known as the **Pilgrim** colony at Plymouth in Massachusetts. The name "pilgrim" is a reference to Heb 11:13-14, which describes Christians as strangers in search of their real heavenly home. The Pilgrims saw their venture into the New World as "starting up again under fresh initiative, in a divinely granted second chance for the human race, after the first chance had been so disastrously fumbled in the darkening Old World" (Lewis, 5). Therefore, they sought to establish a **theocracy** (meaning "rule by God") in their new colony. The term "theocracy" describes a society which has as its worldview a common set of beliefs about God and God's relationship with their community, and whose civil laws are governed by its religious agenda.

The Puritans who settled these new theocracies believed that they were called to this land by God. Theirs was a **Manifest Destiny**, because God was making a new covenant with them. They insured the stability of their communities by employing the principles of democracy in church government, a model which they believed reflected the style of the earliest form of Christianity. Authority rested in the independence of the local congregations. Moreover, only Puritans could be citizens in these new colonies. The congregational principle had within it a degree of intolerance, because of their belief that their colonizing effort was ordained by God. By the 1640s Massachusetts had a heresy law which required the death penalty for any person who denied that the Bible was the Word of God. The major exception in the New England colonies was Rhode Island. It was settled by exiles from Puritan colonies and, as a result, demonstrated considerable religious tolerance.

C. The Refuge of Tolerance

Whereas the New England colonies had very little tolerance for diversity, toleration became the hallmark of the mid-Atlantic colonies. The mid-Atlantic colonies consisted of New Amsterdam (later known as New York), West Jersey and East Jersey (later known as New Jersey), Pennsylvania, Delaware River and Maryland. New Amsterdam is a good example of the religious tolerance that characterized the mid-Atlantic colonies. It was a Dutch oasis, a royal Dutch colony, in the midst of a series of British holdings. The religion of these residents from Holland was **Dutch Reformed**— neither Anglican nor Puritan—but Calvinist in origin. Despite their Calvinist roots, they tended to have a more liberal theology, arguing for conditional predestination, giving more importance to human free will, and allowing for the possibility of unlimited atonement (Christ died to save all humanity, not just the elect).

New Amsterdam's religious tolerance is demonstrated in their sheltering of South America's Jewish refugees. Dutch territory was the only place in Europe or the colonies that Jews could live freely. In 1654 twenty-four Jewish immigrants arrived in New Amsterdam fleeing the inquisition-style persecution of the Portuguese in Brazil. Their arrival marked the beginning of the American Jewish community in New York.

Gradually, the Dutch colonists of New Amsterdam expanded across the river into New Jersey, where a variety of churches could later be found including English and Scottish Presbyterians, Dutch Reformed Christians, and the Society of Friends. The **Society of Friends**, also known as the Quakers, had their origin in the Anglican reform movements. They were opposed to traditional Calvinist doctrine, and like the Radical Reformers they refused to swear oaths or fight in war. They were persecuted in Europe and in many of the colonies. Even as late as the 1650s, Quakers arriving in Boston were arrested and deported. These rejected British subjects settled in New Jersey and by 1681 founded their own colony in Pennsylvania. Their religious tolerance is also evident in the fact that they opened their lands to more different groups of Christians than any other colony: German Lutherans, Mennonites, Moravians, Amish, Catholics, etc. In 1634, Maryland, also part of the refuge of toleration, was established as an English colony open to Catholics.

D. America's First Colleges

Within time, each colony founded institutions to educate its citizens both in the classics and in their Christian worldview. As might be expected, Pennsylvania, the colony/state with the most diverse Christian community had the most colleges. Six were established by 1800. Maryland was a close second with five. Thus Christianity was well institutionalized in the Atlantic colonies by the time the nation was established.

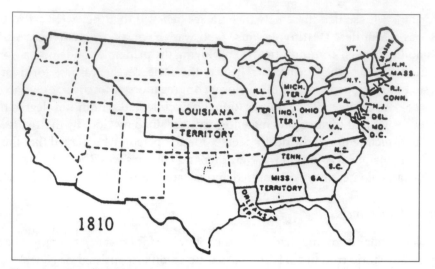

Figure 23.1: Map of U.S. Territories, 1810

America's First Colleges:

Connecticut: Yale (1701)
Delaware: University of Delaware (1743)
Georgia: University of Georgia (1785)
Massachusetts: Harvard (1636)
Maryland: Georgetown (1789)
                  Georgetown/Visitation (1799)
                  St. John's College (1696)
                  St. Mary's Seminary (1791)
                  Washington College (1706)
North Carolina: Louisburg (1787)
                  Salem (1772)
                  University of North Carolina (1789)
New Hampshire: Dartmouth (1769)
New Jersey: New Brunswick Theological Seminary (1784)
                  Rutgers (1766)
New York: Columbia (1754)
                  Hamilton (1793)
                  Union (1785)
Pennsylvania: Dickerson (1773)
                  Franklin & Marshall (1787)
                  Xenia Theological (1794)
                  University of Pennsylvania (1740)
                  University of Pittsburg (1787)
                  Washington & Jefferson (1780)
Rhode Island: Brown (1764)
South Caroliana: Charleston (1770)
Virginia: Hampden-Sydney (1776)
                  Washington & Lee (1749)
                  William & Mary (1693)

IV. The Great Awakening

As the preceding sections indicate, the founding of the English colonies was largely driven by a religious agenda. Yet, the central place given to Christianity especially in the New England colonies began to unravel in the middle part of the 17th century and into the 18th century. Enlightenment principles greatly influenced how American Christians viewed their religion. Most of the founding religious groups (Catholics, Anglicans, Congregationalists, Baptists, Presbyterians, Dutch Reformed and Lutherans) had colleges, and each adopted the principles of reason in order to observe and critique their Christian beliefs, scriptures and church policies and organizations. This new method of critical examination of theology forced individuals or groups within a particular church tradition to re-evaluate or refocus the theological positions that Christians had shared in the pre-Enlightenment period. More importantly, perhaps, the Puritan message about the absolute sovereignty of God and the utter depravity of humans had less and less appeal as people began to turn their attention to settling the new land and taking advantage of its opportunities for economic success. The Enlightenment offered a different view: a reasonable God and a message of religious tolerance.

Thus the 18th century saw a marked decline in people's interest and involvement in the religious agenda. In response to the moral and spiritual laxity or indifference they saw emerging in the colonies, several New England preachers initiated a movement known as the **Great Awakening**. This movement was designed to foster a spiritual "quickening," or awakening from religious laxity among Christians of the colonies. Itinerant preachers traveled the countryside preaching **revivals** (religious meetings designed to awaken in people an awareness of their sin and the need for forgiveness) and motivating the people to renew themselves in God. Stress was placed on visible signs of conversion—concrete behavior that indicated a commitment to God. Those who did not live in accord with the expectations of these preachers of "the Word" were openly denounced, a practice that has remained a part of the religious milieu of the USA even today.

Jonathan Edwards (1703-1758) and **George Whitefield** (1714-1770) were the two preachers who best represented this effort. Whitefield embodied the passion and energy of the revival movement, and made it an experience shared by all the colonies. Although he himself was a Methodist and companion of John Wesley's (a founder of the Methodist Church), he preached to anyone who would listen—regardless of their church affiliation. In 1740 when he began preaching in New England, he delivered 130 sermons and covered 800 miles in his first 73 days of travel. He made four similar trips, and in fact died at the beginning of the fifth. Edwards, on the other hand, provided the theological foundation for the revival movement. He was a Calvinist and an accomplished preacher, so he used his sermons as a way to argue theological positions about the moral and spiritual laxity of the Christians of his time. He was especially concerned about "Arminianism" (named after Jacob Arminius [1560-1609], the founder of the Dutch Reformed movement), a doctrine that allowed for the possibility that humans could do some good in the process of salvation. Edwards argued that they could not. He was very encouraged by the Great Awakening, seeing it as "the verification of Spirit at work in America proving it to be the site of God's final acts of redemption" (Hudson, 25-26).

While the traditional religious groups were uncomfortable with revivalism because they saw it as a threat to the good order of church and society, the preachers of the Great Awakening did bring a level of repentance and conversion into the country that was consistent with its self-understanding as the land of God's chosen. Thus, perhaps unknowingly, the revivals of the Great Awakening provided the spiritual fortitude for the American Revolution. In fact, the self-confidence and sense of election gained in this period of religious fervor may have contributed to the Revolution. The political issues of taxation and representation were fueled by fears that England might impose her religious will along with her political will on the colonies. Yet while the revivals were strongest in the theocracies of New England, none of the major framers of the Declaration of Independence or the Constitution (Madison, Hamilton, Jefferson) were residents of the theocratic communities. Rather, they were residents of the colonies of tolerance.

A second Great Awakening spread across the country toward the beginning of the 19th century, and with it came many questions about the fulfillment of the messianic mission in the new promised land. Some of its preachers believed that the revivals were part of God's plan to prepare for the millennium prophesied in the book of Revelation, the thousand year reign of peace and prosperity that would accompany Christ's second coming. Others believed that the revivals could actually bring about the millenium—provided that people responded positively and worked to restore the church to its original condition as it was in the early centuries of Christianity when it was guided by the apostles. This movement was called the Restoration movement. Led by Alexander Cambell and William Barton Stone, the Restoration movement tried to end denominationalism by restoring the church to an exclusively scriptural basis. The Christian Church/Disciples of Christ are its descendants.

Two American churches emerged out of this millenial expectation, namely the Seventh-Day Adventists and the Jehovah's Witnesses. The **Seventh-Day Adventists** originated with the prophecies of William Miller (1782-1849) concerning the end of the world. His prophecies were based on the books of Daniel and Revelation. He began to preach that Christ's coming would happen in 1843, and when Christ did not return in 1843, he predicted two other dates in 1844. By this time, somewhere between 50,000 and 1,000,000 people had left their congregations to wait for the end time. Once again they were disappointed. Seventh-Day Adventists no longer attempt to predict an exact day for the Second Coming. They observe Saturday as the proper day for worship and advocate a literal reading of the Bible as the only rule of faith. The **Jehovah's Witnesses** were founded by Charles Taze Russell (1852-1916). He prophesied that Christ would return secretly in 1874 and that the end time would come in 1914. His teachings were published in the pamphlet called *The Watchtower*. The Jehovah's Witnesses teach that the world is ruled by Satan, that all government, church, and business organizations are in league with Satan, and that only the elect of Jehovah (a version of God's name YHWH which was popular in the Renaissance period) will be admitted into the kingdom of God. They do not celebrate holidays like Christmas or Easter, nor do they salute the flag or perform military service. The Church of Jesus Christ of Latter Day Saints (whose members are called Mormons) is a product of this same movement.

V. Denominationalism

Although there were some who opposed the Great Awakening, its purpose was a sound one: to find a common ground for Christians to be renewed in their faith. Because the revivalist movements were experiential more than doctrinal—they sought conversion of the heart, not intellectual assent—religion became more of a personal and private affair. In fact, far from creating Christian unity, the revivalist movements greatly contributed to **denominationalism**. According to the principle of denominationalism, the fragmentation of the church into different Christian groups was not something to be lamented. The "true" Christian church, which consisted of all those who profess the basic tenets of Christianity, was understood as a unity, and this unity remained in spite of the differences among denominations. The individual churches with their peculiar forms of worship and organizational structures were to be regarded as *denominations* of the one true church which is Christianity. The revivalist movements, together with the religious toleration assured by the new Constitution of the United States, resulted in the proliferation of a wide variety of Christian denominations. These denominations can be grouped into families according to the particular concern they were seeking to address or the situation to which they were responding.

In the post-Enlightenment period, and after the signing of the U. S. Constitution which granted religious freedom to its citizens, American Christianity began to change quite drastically. As Christianity struggled to find its identity in this new reality, different Christian denominations began to emerge. People who had become accustomed to "freedom of choice" brought the principles of democracy into the churches. Therefore, in the spirit of congregational choice, **Liberal Protestants** (so named because of their more liberal interpretation of scripture) supported the people's right to believe as they wished, given what reason dictated. As a consequence, they moved away from the sectarian teachings of traditional churches to more universal views that they believed would cause less strain and debate in the community. **Unitarians** rejected the doctrine of the Trinity and denied the divinity of Christ in favor of the unity of God. **Universalists** proclaimed salvation for all, thus denying the doctrine of hell. They believed in the power of human reason to perfect the world. Of course, this high regard for humanity elicited a negative response and severe criticism from some of the more traditional churches.

Another factor in denominationalism was the European movement called Pietism. Inspired by a Bible-centered revivalism that fought against religious indifference by creating conversion in the heart, the Pietists shared and testified to the experience of God in their lives, but they were not hostile to the beliefs of traditional churches. They sought only to enhance their spiritual lives through the study of the Bible. European Lutheran churches were most affected by the Pietist movement, as were the Moravian Brethren and the English movement called Methodism. The **Methodists** began as a revival movement within the Anglican church. In 1737, John Wesley, the founder of the first Methodist prayer group, and his brother Charles came to Georgia as part of the Society for the Propagation of the Gospel. Although they had concluded that their American missionary trip was largely unsuccessful, they met some Moravian Christians in Georgia who encouraged them to launch another missionary venture—the Evangelical Revival. This revival movement consisted of a combination of sermons and hymn singing that took place wherever the opportunity arose—even in the market places. The Methodists finally established themselves as a denominational group separate from the Anglican church in 1784.

Some religious communities became impatient with human progress in responding to the call of the revivalist. They sought perfection in this world with an emphasis on sinlessness and love. These Christians believed that holiness was an attainable and necessary objective, and that Christians should be free of outward sin. This did not mean that people did not make mistakes, endure temptations, or suffer from sicknesses; perfection was always open to improvement. Thus the **Holiness churches** (Free Methodist Church, Church of God, Holiness Christian Church, and Church of the Nazarene) separated from the Methodist tradition to develop a lifestyle of personal holiness that reflected a more rigid code of behavior than that held by their parent churches. As a response to what they called the second grace of God (the conversion made available to the Christian through the revivals), they developed an asceticism that rejected worldliness. A person who responded positively to the personal call to conversion was said to be born again (hence the phrase "born again" Christian).

For other religious communities the simple asceticism of the holiness churches was not enough. They required a clearer verification of the presence of God in the believer's life. The **Pentecostal churches** (Assemblies of God, Church of God, Pentecostal Holiness Church, Apostolic Faith Church, Church of God in Christ, Full Gospel Fellowship, etc.) have their roots in the Baptist and Methodist traditions. They have had little doctrinal disagreement with their parent churches. However, they require believers to demonstrate their religious experience by **speaking in tongues** (*glossolalia*). This is the hallmark of the church whose members have sought and received the gifts of the Holy Spirit. Members are also seen to possess other gifts of the Spirit (healing, wisdom that discerns spirits, prophecy, and knowledge beyond the natural). However, these churches, sometimes known as "Holy Rollers," were not always well-received by traditional churches because of their loud, free, and spontaneous liturgical celebrations.

Other Christian denominations developed because their members sought an asceticism that created a community separate from the mainstream of secular society: the **Free churches** (Mennonites, Amish, Brethren, Quakers, and Free-Church Brethren). Rooted in the Radical Reformation movements, these communities of adult worshipers were non-liturgical. They could also be described as Biblical literalists. Their commitment to the gospel meant for them the refusal to swear oaths, strict opposition to war and violence (pacifism), aid to those in need, the refusal to hold public office, and an obligation to live the gospel in their daily lives. Though they did not believe in the notion of the elect, they called for a strong discipline for all who remained within the community. These non-state or free churches placed their emphasis on "free will." They preached a common priesthood of the believers and a doctrine of grace which has priority over works.

Perhaps the largest and most diversified Christian denomination in the USA is the **Baptist** tradition (Southern, American, National, etc.). While they live by many of the same tenets of freedom as the Free churches, the Baptists have their roots in the Puritan community of New England. However, theirs was a much more moderate Calvinist theology. In their formative years, they were influenced by the Dutch Mennonites. They were also influenced by millenialist movements who looked to the books of Daniel and Revelation, seeking "signs of the times" and a proper way of life for Christian believers. Unlike the Free churches, Baptists were fully involved in the community, not separate from it. They saw the structures of the world as part of God's creation, but they were not oriented toward establishing a theocracy. Salvation was possible for all, but true baptism had to be by immersion. This separated them from most other Christian faith communities.

Denominationalism in the United States was further advanced by the **fundamentalist movement**. Fundamentalism began as a defensive reaction to Liberal Protestantism and to the developments of modern science and the historical study of the Bible. It is called fundamentalism because of a series of pamphlets called "The Fundamentals" published in 1910-1915 by conservative Protestants, which stressed that there are certain "fundamental" beliefs of Christianity about which there could be no compromise. Arguments over fundamentalism resulted in the establishment of a variety of new churches including Plymouth Brethren, Bible Church, Grace Gospel Church, and Christian Liberty Church. Fundamentalism involved a completely new way of reading the Bible called **dispensationalism**. These churches saw the scriptures as a history of God's dealing with humanity, a history that could be divided into various stages called dispensations. The first five stages or dispensations were as follows: the time of Paradise, the time of Noah, the time of Abraham, the time of Israel, and the time of the Gentiles. Christians are now living in the sixth dispensation, the time of the Spirit. The Fundamentalists noted that each earlier stage had failed to realize the promise of God, but that they are now living at the edge of the seventh dispension, the fullness of time. Therefore, scripture ought to be read from this perspective in order to prepare for the final days. These apocalyptic themes continue to reoccur in the religious history of the United States.

Most American Christian denominations have some kind of connection to the Catholic and Protestant Reformations of the 16th century. There are two notable exceptions: the Mormons and the Christian Scientists. The **Mormons** or "the Church of Jesus Christ of Latter-Day Saints" was founded in New York in 1830 by Joseph Smith. Smith founded his new religion based upon a revelation which led to his discovery of the Golden Plates, on which the Book of Mormon was written. The Book of Mormon describes the history of the "lost tribes of Israel," from 600 BC to 421 BC, during which time these people migrated to America. Later, Christ is said to have appeared to them after the resurrection in order to establish the church. In Mormon belief, marriage is considered important for salvation and children are valued as the means by which souls are embodied as the first step to divinity. God was once a man who later achieved divinity, having successfully lived through the testing period of human life. The **Christian Scientists** or "the Church of Christ, Scientist" was founded by Mary Baker Eddy in 1875. Being a sickly person, she had consulted a mental healer for a cure. Based upon this experience and her own interpetation of the story of Jesus raising the daughter of Jairus (Mark 5:21-43), she developed a system of healing by spiritual influence. Eddy believed that people had within them the power of the mind to eliminate sickness and death. She also taught that God is spirit and all good, and humans, as a reflection of God, are also spiritual and good. The world of ideas is the only reality and matter does not exist.

VI. The Limits of Religious Tolerance

In their fervor to create a Christian land, those who considered themselves the elect, in particular, the New England colonists, kept at a distance those religious communities that they had not determined how to include. Native Americans, Africans (Negroes), Jews, and Catholics proved to be an on going challenge to this theocratic vision of the new world. In some cases, this lack of tolerance gave rise to more independent churches. The situation of African-American Christians is a good example. Various Protestant denominations worked to convert African-Americans to their churches, but then refused them the opportunity for full participation. As a result, African-Americans were forced to organize their own versions of these churches. In 1787, **Richard Allen** (1760-1831) led a protest of Negro Methodists in Philadelphia against practices that excluded African-Americans from full participation in the Methodist church. This protest community eventually became the AME (African Methodist-Episcopal) Church. African-Americans in New York had similar experiences and by 1796 had formed the AME-ZION church. These churches were established as an outgrowth of a revivalist denomination (Methodist) in states whose charter required tolerance. Yet, most churches at this time had not yet begun to determine how they would address the question of race.

Perhaps the most perplexing tolerance question for Protestant churches during the late 18th and early 19th centuries was the role and status of Catholics. The revolution against Britain could not have been won without the help of the French, who were strongly Catholic. After the French revolution, many Catholics were welcomed to these shores, both from France and from their islands in the Caribbean. As a result, the Catholic populations of Maryland and the Mississippi Delta grew considerably. The areas of the frontier had already been settled by Catholics of French or Spanish heritage. In addition, Catholics were immigrating from Ireland to the traditional colonies and the tolerance colonies. Together, immigration and incorporation provided the Americas with an extensive Catholic population. While there was limited tolerance for Catholics who stayed in their own territory, Protestants still considered Roman Catholics to be their enemies.

A contributing factor to Protestant discrimination against Roman Catholics was the creation of the Catholic school system. Prior to this time, most Christians accepted the public schools as the proper forum to train the young to be good Christian citizens. In establishing a separate Catholic school system, Catholics were responding to two concerns. On the one hand, they created Catholic schools to insure the proper instruction of their children in the Catholic faith. To guarantee this effort, ten new congregations of sisters were founded by the 1830s. On the other hand, Catholics tended to establish their parishes and schools along ethnic lines. The Catholic schools provided immigrants with a way to preserve their culture, language, and many other social structures along with their religious practice. However, many Protestant Christians resented this dual resistance to Americanization. Catholics were suspect for these reasons, as well as a host of others. As immigrants, Catholics were resented as a source of cheap labor and because of their apparent lack of social discipline. Because they immigrated from monarchies, Protestants feared that they would not become fit citizens in a democratic government. Finally, Catholics' allegiance to the pope was very problematic for American Protestants.

Another religious community that received only limited tolerance in the New World was the Jews. With the first immigrants arriving in 1654, Jewish communities learned rather quickly to what extent tolerance in the colonies was real and they adapted accordingly. The first Jews to arrive were known as the **Sephardim**, the term given to Spanish and Portuguese Jewish immigrants. By 1700 they had been joined by others from northern Europe, the **Ashkenazim**, a term given to German Jewish immigrants. Together, they created five major Jewish centers by 1800: New York; Newport, Rhode Island; Philadelphia; Savannah, Georgia; and Richmond, Virginia. The Jews, like the Catholics, sought acceptance in the society and a place to live in freedom.

VII. Volunteerism and Social Justice

Throughout the history of the United States, religious groups of all kinds have been influential in helping to clarify the country's identity in light of the Constitution. Who is a citizen? What does "life, liberty and the pursuit of happiness" mean? What are the limits of freedom? How do the concepts of "election" and "equality" work together in a civil society? The primary way in which this has taken place is through the principle of **volunteerism**. People participated in volunteer activities which they considered to be for the good of the community (religious or secular). The stimulus for these movements often came from individual churches or denominations, but they were not limited to the membership of those denominations. The issues that they addressed most often involved some concern about morality or social justice for the disadvantaged. Historically, these issues have caused considerable difficulty, perhaps because they force us to redefine how we see ourselves as citizens and members of religious groups. Slavery, women's rights, laborers' rights, civil rights, indeed basic acceptance of the differences of people have torn at the very fiber of the religious and civil structures of the United States.

A. Slavery

When French Catholics immigrated to these shores after the revolution in France, they brought with them a community of free negroes. Thus Baltimore received its first free black immigrants in 1793. These Christians experienced numerous problems almost immediately. Many of these free blacks were educated, skilled, and accepted as citizens among the French. The people of Baltimore needed and valued their skills and services, but Baltimore was a southern slave city. Quakers and some Methodists had prohibitions against slavery, but no one had addressed the discomfort which the French had made so visible. White citizens knew how to deal with their slave population, but they did not know how to relate to free blacks. In 1817 the American Society for the Return of the Negroes to Africa was founded. This group sent free blacks to Sierra Leone and later bought the land known today as Liberia. In the midst of these efforts, Christian groups began to join together to abolish slavery. Unfortunately, while they addressed the evils of the institution of slavery, few addressed the behavior or the attitudes required to live with the former slave. The questions of rights and citizenship were not acknowledged. Thus the cycle of racism began.

Slavery was a major contributing factor in the American Civil War. The arguments for and against slavery covered the areas of religion, biology, and economics. Churches were split, North and South, over the debate (e.g. Southern Methodist and Southern Baptist). Some volunteer groups began to provide slaves with access to the services otherwise available to citizens, including education, jobs, and housing. Finally, the 13th amendment to the Constitution abolished slavery. However, the ongoing struggles have taught Christians the lesson that laws do not change attitudes. The willingness to consider African Americans as human beings and to treat them with respect would not be addressed for another century, when the Civil Rights movement of 1950s and 60s would speak with a religious voice calling the United States to live up to its creed. **Martin Luther King, Jr.** (1929-1968) was the one who would lead the fight of those who found the Christian principles of human dignity and a call to justice in both the Bible and in the Constitution of the United States.

B. Women's Rights and Laborers' Rights

Parallel to the debate over the rights of African-Americans was the problem of the roles and rights of women and laborers. Women had long been the power behind the charitable activities of most communities, religious and secular. They became the frontline soldiers in many of the social debates of 19th-century society. Likewise, elementary education, Sunday schools, and home and foreign missions would have been ineffective without the extensive labor force of the women of the United States. Yet they were not considered to be citizens with the rights and privileges of men. On the issue of labor rights, citizens of the USA had grown intolerant of immigrants, especially those who were culturally and religiously different from the earlier settlers of these shores. Therefore, immigrants arriving at the end of the 19th century were being exploited as an economic opportunity, a cheap labor force, for the owners of industry during the industrial revolution. Even child labor was commonplace.

The industrial revolution of the 19th century resulted in prosperity for owners of industry, but it also created massive poverty among its workers. Out of English liberal Protestantism came two voices who sought to make social concern an issue for mainstream Christians: Frederick Maurice and William Booth. Maurice, a Christian Socialist, argued that poverty was not a curse (against those who would say that poverty was an indicator of those who not among God's elect), but the result of exploitation, and that the churches' proper role was to make the gospel relevant in such a way as to rid society of its social ills. Booth, the founder of the **Salvation Army**, focused on developing practical solutions to the problems of poverty brought on by the industrial revolution and awakening Christians' consciences to the human suffering which it created.

In the later 19th and early 20th century, the White Anglo-Saxon Protestant society (WASP) had begun to identify its solution to social problems in terms of the **Social Gospel**. Their solution was to establish a kind of theocracy whose worldview was inspired by the writings of Walter

Rauschenbush (1861-1918). Like Maurice, Rauschenbush argued that poverty was not a divine curse but a result of human exploitation. He believed that the church should be seen as the vehicle for spreading God's kingdom on earth, and therefore should be primarily concerned about social justice. Moreover, he believed that Christians had a *collective* responsibility for the poor—in contrast to what the American ideals of capitalism and individualism would suggest. Thus Rauschenbush's followers sought to enlist the churches in supporting a particular political program in order to change the social structure of the nation. They hoped that by changing social structures they could establish God's kingdom on earth, and thereby "Christianize" the United States (Weaver, 197). Unfortunately, the WASP culture created an environment in which racism and nationalism flourished, as opportunists played one group against another to their own economic and social benefit.

Immigrant and labor struggles continued to surface in the early 20th century, further heightening the ethnic, racial and religious tensions which had begun to surface in the 19th century. In sum, this land was not the "promised land" that immigrants expected. These labor battles were religious cries for rights, equality, and acceptance as citizens. Though women could now vote and unions had created better working conditions for laborers, the elect still struggled for status and dominance while working to create the "kingdom" on earth. The tension continues today as religious groups attempt to discern in their theology the will of God and to make it a reality in their ethical guidelines and their social justice programs.

Key Terms:

theocracy	Free Churches
Refuge of Tolerance	Baptists
Great Awakening	Fundamentalists
Revivals	Seventh-Day Adventists
Denominationalism	Jehovah's Witnesses
congregationalist	Mormons
Sephardim	Christian Scientists
Ashkenazim	Salvation Army
Liberal protestants	dispensationalism
Pietists	volunteerism
Holiness churches	Social Gospel
Pentecostals	

Questions for Reading:

1. Describe the character of Spanish Catholic missionary activity in the Americas. When and where did it begin? What were its goals? Who were some of its major figures?

2. Describe the character of French Catholic missionary activity in the Americas. When and where did it begin? What were its goals? Who were some of its major figures?

3. Describe the three expressions of Christianity that could be found in the colonies of the upper Atlantic coast:

(a) traditional Christianity

(b) the new theocracy

(c) the refuge of tolerance

Where were they located and how did they differ from one another?

4. What was the Great Awakening? Who were its major preachers and what did they hope to accomplish? How did the second Great Awakening differ from the first?

5. What is denominationalism?

6. What are the major families of Christian churches in the USA? How does each distinguish itself from the others?

7. What is the Social Gospel? What was its purpose? Why was it not successful in accomplishing its goals?

Works Cited/Recommended Reading:

Bowden, Henry Warner. *American Indians and Christian Missions: Studies in Cultural Conflict*. Chicago: University of Chicago Press, 1981.

Brown, Joseph E. *The Spiritual Legacy of the American Indian*. New York: Crossroad, 1993.

Davis, Cyprian. *A History of Black Catholics in the United States*. New York: Crossroad, 1990.

Frazier, E. Franklin and C. Eric Lincoln. *The Negro Church in America/ The Black Church Since Frazier*. New York: Schocken Books, 1974.

Glazer, Nathan. *American Judaism*. Chicago: University of Chicago Press, 1989.

Hennesey, James. *American Catholics: A History of the Roman Catholic Community in the United States*. New York: Oxford University Press, 1981.

Hudson, Winthrop and John Corrigan. *Religion in America: A Historical Account of the Development of American Religious Life*. New York: MacMillan Publishing Co., 1992.

Lewis, R. W. B. *The American Adam*. Chicago: University of Chicago Press, 1986.

Mead, Sidney. *The Lively Experiment: The Shaping of Christianity in America*. New York: Harper & Row, 1963.

Metzger, Bruce and Murphy, Roland, eds. *The New Oxford Annotated Bible with Apocrypha*, New Revised Standard Version. New York: Oxford University Press, 1991.

Weaver, Mary Jo. *Introduction to Christianity*. 2nd ed. Belmont, CA: Wadsworth Publishing Company, 1991.

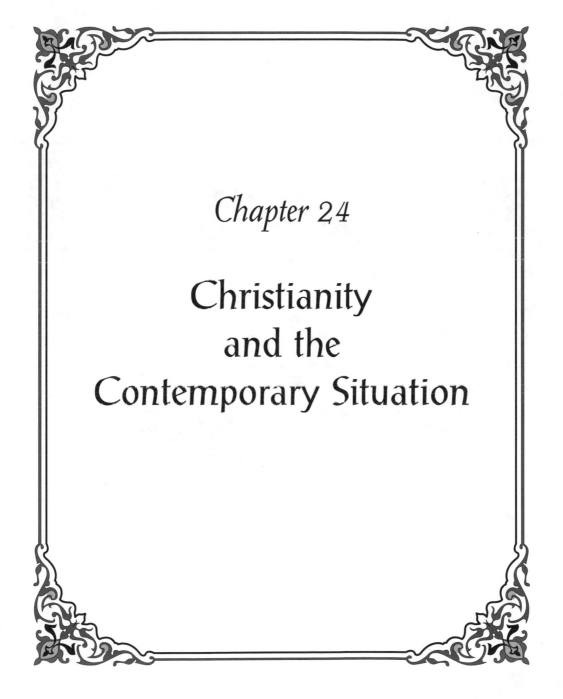

Chapter 24

Christianity
and the
Contemporary Situation

Christianity and the Contemporary Situation

I n every time period, Christianity has had to adjust to changing cultural realities. However, the radical changes of the Age of Enlightenment and its aftermath made Christianity's adjustment to the modern period especially difficult. In the Roman Catholic Church the need for renewal was heightened by the fact that the church had changed very little from the time of the Council of Trent (1547-1563). In fact, during the pontificate of Pius IX (1846-1878), the church had taken a defensive attitude toward modern developments. In his *Syllabus of Errors* (1864), Pius had rejected many modern movements and ideas. One proposition which was condemned as an error was this: "The Roman Pontiff can and ought to reconcile and harmonize himself with progress, with liberalism, and with modern civilization" (cited in Bokenkotter, 324).

This chapter will discuss the key developments of the Second Vatican Council, the council that brought the Roman Catholic Church into the age of modernity. It will also trace several movements that have emerged as forces for change in the modern period, as Christian churches have attempted to adapt themselves to diverse cultural experiences and rapidly changing circumstances.

I. Second Vatican Council

The **Second Vatican Council** was the name given to a gathering of Catholic bishops, abbots, and theological experts which took place between 1962 and 1965. It met to discuss major questions facing the Catholic Church as it sought to adapt itself to the modern world. Catholics called the Second Vatican Council an ecumenical (i.e. universal) council, since it was a council of all Catholic bishops. Protestant and non-Christian observers were present, though they could not vote; only Catholic bishops could vote. Thus from a Protestant and Eastern Orthodox point of view the council was not fully ecumenical, since it did not address the needs of *all* Christians. Nevertheless, Vatican II was one of the most important councils in the history of the Catholic Church.

During the 19th century and the early part of the 20th century, the Catholic Church was, for the most part, resistant to adapting to the scientific, cultural, and philosophical developments of the modern period. Pope Pius XII took a major step in 1943 when he issued an encyclical letter (i.e. a letter to all bishops) entitled *Divino Afflante Spiritu*. This encyclical encouraged Catholic scholars to use modern methods of biblical criticism in their study of the Bible, and urged Catholic laypersons to read the Bible. Yet, in most areas of Catholic life the church remained unchanged. The mass was still said in Latin, Protestants were still seen as heretics, and there was little dialogue with non-Christian religions or with modern science.

Finally, when Pope John XXIII (reigned 1958-1963) announced his intention of calling an ecumenical council things began to change quite radically. He attributed this idea to the inspiration of the Holy Spirit. Many assumed the council would simply reaffirm the teachings of the Councils of Trent (1547-1563) and Vatican I (1870). But when the council opened on Oct 11, 1962, in the Basilica of St. Peter's in Rome, John emphasized that while the church was committed to handing on the sacred doctrine of past councils, it was also important to present this doctrine in a way suitable to the present. "The substance of the ancient doctrine of the deposit of faith is one thing, and the way it is presented is another" he said (Abbott, 715). The spirit of the council came to be summarized in the Italian word **aggiornamento**, meaning roughly, "a bringing up to date."

Bearing in mind that the council saw itself as passing on ancient teachings, but also modernizing them, we may discern five major areas of development that flowed from the council: reform of the liturgy, an understanding of the church as "people of God," an interest in ecumenism, dialogue with the secular world, and a theology of revelation.

A. Reform of the Liturgy

Most obvious to the average Catholic were the changes in the liturgy. Before the council, all Catholic masses were said in Latin, and the priest celebrated the mass with his back to the people, except when he had finished reading the Epistle and Gospel in Latin and would turn toward the people to reread the two scripture readings in translation. The sanctuary where the priest celebrated was separated from the nave (body) of the church by a railing, and laity were not allowed in the sanctuary. The whole structure of the celebration emphasized a two-tier church: clergy were separated from laity both by the altar rail and by language (though many lay Catholics did learn enough Latin to follow the mass).

The first document issued by the council, the *Constitution on the Sacred Liturgy*, introduced sweeping reforms. The mass could now be celebrated in the vernacular (the language of the people) as well as in Latin. The altar was turned around, so that the priest faced the people. This made the mass more of a dialogue with the congregation rather than a monologue prayer said by the priest on behalf of the people. More popular and contemporary forms of music were allowed. Indeed, the Second Vatican Council resulted in an explosion of new Catholic hymns and music. Eventually, lay readers and lay ministers (to distribute the Eucharist) were allowed to take an active role in the mass. Private devotions during the mass (e.g. saying the rosary) were discouraged, since there was a renewed sense of the mass as a communal celebration.

Figure 24.1: Interior of the Liverpool Cathedral: aerial view. Note the circular seating arrangement and the central placement of the altar.

One of the consequences of these changes toward more active participation in the mass was a change in church architecture. From the time of Constantine until the Second Vatican Council, Catholic church buildings usually were built in the shape of a Latin cross, with the clergy and sanctuary separated from the laity. After Vatican II, new churches were often built in circular or semi-circular form so that the congregation surrounded the altar, and even older churches were rearranged inside so that the congregation sat on three sides of the altar. This new architecture emphasized the active participation of the whole congregation in the liturgy.

B. The Church as People of God

A second major area of development resulting from the council was a new understanding of the church. Prior to the Second Vatican Council, the phrase "the church" had often tended to mean the hierarchy, as in the phrase "The church teaches." This conception of the church could be diagrammed like a pyramid: the pope was the leader at the top, and he alone was called the "vicar [representative] of Christ." Under him were the bishops, seen as deputies of the pope, then the priests, then members of religious orders (monks and nuns), then the laity at the bottom. Authority and power flowed from the top down but not from the bottom up. Catholic laity tended to look to the clergy and pope for answers. By contrast, the council's *Constitution on the Church* uses a variety of images for the church, but the primary one is of the church as the "Holy People of God." Within this one church the hierarchy has the special function of administering the sacraments, preserving the teaching of the apostles, and maintaining church discipline. However, the laity are no less a part of the church than are the clergy. Likewise, bishops are not just deputies of the pope, but are called "vicars of Christ" along with the pope. The head of the church, according to Vatican II, is the pope *and* the bishops, acting together as a college, not the pope alone.

The notion of the church as the whole people of God was not a new one. The imagery comes from the Old Testament language about the covenant. Vatican II was returning to a more ancient conception of the church, and correcting a tendency which came about because of a misinterpretation of the First Vatican Council (1870)—that the Holy Spirit speaks to the church only through the pope, who then tells the rest of the church what to believe. In fact, the Holy Spirit speaks through all the members of the church. It is the task of the **magisterium** (the teaching office of the church, made up of the pope and the bishops) to discern the movement of the Spirit within the larger church, and to proclaim it officially. The best example of this is the Second Vatican Council itself. Its teachings were not simply the thoughts of the pope, accepted without question by the bishops. In fact, popes John XXIII and Paul VI intervened only rarely in the council's proceedings. The proclamations of Vatican II were the result of a long collective discernment process, in which theological experts spoke and bishops debated until consensus was reached. Thus they represent, to a great degree, the mind of the whole church, the people of God.

While the Second Vatican Council introduced a different way of thinking of the church, it still preserved the teaching of the First Vatican Council concerning papal infallibility. According to this doctrine, the pope can speak infallibly for the whole church in certain very rare instances. Even then, when the pope speaks infallibly, he expresses, not just his own belief, but the belief of the entire church. For example, when Pius IX declared in 1869 that Mary had been conceived without original sin (the doctrine of the immaculate conception), he first polled all the bishops of the church to find out if this was in fact the belief of the larger church. Pius XII did the same thing before his declaration, in 1950, that Mary had been assumed bodily into heaven after her death. An "infallible" or "irreformable" teaching, then, is one taught with the highest authority in the Catholic Church, but one in which the pope speaks the mind of the *whole* church. Such teachings have been very rare.

A practical result of the revised conception of the church as the whole "People of God" is the creation of parish councils. Previously, priests usually had the sole authority in a parish. After Vatican II, the priest and bishop still retained legal rights to make decisions for the local parish, but most parishes instituted parish councils, made up of laypersons, to advise and assist the priest in parish administration. Another result was the development of national conferences of bishops, such as the U.S. Conference of Catholic Bishops. The bishops of a given nation meet together periodically (usually once a year) to discuss issues facing their churches. Since the Second Vatican Council, the U.S. Conference of Catholic Bishops has issued notable teaching statements on war and peace, the U.S. economy, the environmental crisis, and other matters. Again, this reflects the Second Vatican Council's notion that the bishops are not just deputies of the pope but, as successors to the apostles, are teaching authorities in their own right. A third result of the council is the emergence of lay theologians. Prior to the council, religion in Catholic schools and colleges was taught by priests or nuns. After the council, Catholic university departments of theology opened their facilities to lay students of theology, so that laypersons could earn graduate degrees in theology and teach theology in colleges. Now most theology teachers in Catholic colleges are lay persons.

C. The Ecumenical Movement

A third major area of development flowing from the Second Vatican Council involves the relationship of Catholic Christians to non-Catholic Christians and non-Christian religions. Before Vatican II, Protestants were viewed as heretics or schismatics who were therefore not a part of the church (Pius XII, *Mystici Corporis*, 23; cited in Carlen, 41). In contrast, the documents of Vatican II address Protestants as "separated brethren," not as heretics. The *Decree on Ecumenism* states that a chief concern of the council was to restore unity among Christians. It further states that all baptized Christians are in real, though imperfect, communion with the Catholic Church.

A result of these discussions at the council is greatly improved relations between Catholic and non-Catholic Christians. It is now frequent to have marriages between Catholics and Protestants. Catholic theologians regularly use Protestant texts in their research, writing, and teaching. In Minnesota, the Lutheran and Catholic bishops have committed themselves to a covenant or agreement on major points of the Christian faith, the first time such a thing has happened anywhere in the world.

In addition to the *Decree on Ecumenism*, the Second Vatican council issued a document on non-Christian religions which affirms that the Catholic Church respects all that is true and holy in any religion. It notes that Jews, Muslims, and Christians all worship the same God, and it condemns any form of discrimination based on race or religion. The council continued to uphold the traditional teaching that the fullness of revelation is found only in Jesus the Christ, but it also said that other religions "often reflect a ray of that Truth which enlightens all men" (*Decree on Non-Christian Religions*, §2). Although the precise meaning of this statement is disputed, it suggests that some degree of revelation is also found in non-Christian religions. Since Vatican II, extensive dialogue between Catholics and Jews, Muslims, Buddhists, and Hindus has developed.

The Second Vatican Council also modified traditional teaching on the salvation of non-believers. Some biblical passages seem to state that only those believing in Christ will be saved (e.g. Acts 4:12). Others imply that non-Christians can also be saved (e.g. Acts 10:34-35). For centuries many in the Catholic Church had maintained that there was no salvation outside the church—implying that non-Christians could not be saved. Many fundamentalists still believe this. However, Vatican II stated that even non-believers could be saved:

> *Those also can attain to everlasting salvation who through no fault of their own do not know the gospel of Christ or His Church, yet sincerely seek God and, moved by his grace, strive by their deeds to do his will as it is known to them through the dictates of conscience* (Lumen Gentium, §16).

Decades ago it was normal for Christians to grow up and live in ethnically and religiously homogenous communities; German Catholics lived with German Catholics and went to German Catholic parishes, Polish, Irish, or Italian Catholics did likewise, as did German and Scandinavian Lutherans. Each group inhabited their own urban neighborhoods or towns, and attended ethnic parishes. All this has changed, so that now Christians grow up, work, and live next to Christians of differing denominations, as well as persons of different religions. This situation is called "**pluralism**," meaning that societies (all over the world) are increasingly made up of a plurality of races, nationalities, and religions.

The advent of worldwide pluralism means that Christianity, whether Catholic, Protestant, or Orthodox, can no longer impose itself simply because it is the religion of a particular state or region. In the future, Christianity will have to persuade persons on the basis of its intrinsic truth and the lifestyle of its members. People will no longer be Christian just because their parents were; they will be Christian because they have chosen it. Thus we have returned to a situation similar to that of the early Christian centuries, when Christianity was one religion among many in a vast, pluralistic civilization.

D. Dialogue with the Secular World

A fourth major development following the Second Vatican Council involved a renewed dialogue between Catholics and the secular world, and a call for Catholics to cooperate with all persons of good will in promoting human dignity. Whereas the 19th century church tended to cut itself off from the secular world, Vatican II encouraged dialogue and cooperation with secular thought and movements. Catholic theologians now routinely work in conjunction with various secular disciplines such as psychology, sociology, economics, political science, and the natural sciences. A major emphasis of the modern church (and of Pope John Paul II) is to present Catholic teachings before the whole world. This is in accordance with the Vatican II pronouncement that the church is to be a sign of salvation to the whole world. The imagery of the church as a sign of salvation is considerably different from earlier imagery of the church as an ark to which members can flee from the world to safety.

E. The Theology of Revelation

A fifth development resulting from the Second Vatican Council concerns the theology of revelation. Before Vatican II, the tendency was to regard divine revelation as a fixed body of doctrine (the "deposit of faith") handed down from Jesus to the apostles and from the apostles to the church without development or change. Such a view makes no allowance for the fact that the church's *understanding* of revelation (though not the revelation itself) develops through time. In fact, the history of Christianity contains many examples of how the church's understanding of revelation has developed over time (e.g., the doctrines of the Trinity and the incarnation of Christ). The Vatican II *Document on Divine Revelation* makes this point in an extremely important passage:

The tradition which comes from the apostles develops in the church with the help of the Holy Spirit. For there is a growth in the understanding of the realities and the words which have been handed down…For, as the centuries succeed one another, the Church constantly moves forward toward the fullness of divine truth until the words of God reach their complete fulfillment in her (Document on Divine Revelation, §8).

This teaching of Vatican II did not contradict the teachings of previous councils concerning revelation, but developed them in the light of modern insights and understanding. The Catholic belief is that the bishops and the pope are given a special charism by the Holy Spirit, so that when discerning and teaching on matters of faith and morals, their decisions will be guided by that same Spirit. Again, there is no better evidence for that belief than the Second Vatican Council itself. Its decisions and teachings, arrived at after extensive discussion and consultation with Catholic laity and non-Catholic Christians, have been almost unanimously accepted by the whole church, conservative and liberals alike. Thus the Spirit continues to guide the church towards the fullness of understanding and truth, which will be achieved only at the end of time.

II. Other Contemporary Movements

The Catholic Church's resolve at the Second Vatican Council to engage itself in the issues of the modern world set the stage for a variety of other movements that are in some ways unique to the modern world. Here we will mention the intersection of science and theology, the Catholic Church's social teaching, the impact of feminism on Christian theology and church organization, and the emergence of liberation theology, feminist theology, and black theology.

A. Science and Theology

In recent decades there has been greatly renewed interest in the relation between theology and science, both on the part of scientists, especially physicists, and on the part of theologians. The American Association for the Advancement of Science has recently inaugurated sessions on religion and science for the first time in its history. The John Templeton Foundation is sponsoring courses on religion and medicine in leading medical schools. In colleges and graduate schools interdisciplinary courses in theology and science are proliferating. Two spectacular developments in astronomical physics have contributed to this new trend: the "Big Bang" theory, and new evidence for design in the universe.

Up until the mid-20th century, most secular scientists believed that the universe had no beginning (i.e., it was eternal). However, modern discoveries have suggested that all the galaxies are moving apart from each other, leading to the theory that the universe began in a colossal explosion. According to the "Big Bang" theory of the origins of the universe, all the matter/energy in the universe exploded outward from a tiny point at the beginning of time. One cannot speak of either space or time "before" the Big Bang. Rather, time, space, and matter all apparently emerged in a single instant. This raises the obvious question, "What caused the Big Bang?" Some scientists hold that there was a succession of universes before this one, each created by a process of expansion, collapse, and re-expansion. However, the physical evidence currently available does not support this oscillating universe model. Others are content to say that the question has no answer. Many Christians would say that God created the universe from nothing. The Big Bang theory is consistent with that belief: if there was a creation from nothing, this is how it might look.

In the same way that the Big Bang theory forced people to re-examine the question of the source of creation both from a scientific and a theological perspective, so too new evidence for design in the universe raised a similar set of questions. Until modern times, the argument from design had appeared to be an irrefutable argument for the existence of God. How could the universe be so perfectly and beautifully designed, so the argument went, unless it had a designer? William Paley, an English theologian, had argued that if one found a watch in a barren desert, one would assume it had been designed and made by an artificer (a craftsperson), not that it had somehow had come into being by accidental processes. So it is with nature. The human eye, for instance, is so intricately designed and so perfectly adapted to its surroundings, that it could not have been created by chance, but must have been created by a designer-artificer, namely, God, who designed and created all of nature.

However, Charles Darwin's explanation about different species emerging due to evolutionary processes in which small variations were filtered by natural selection seemed to have destroyed arguments like the one advanced by Paley. A Darwinian would have argued that some primitive creatures by random mutation were born with light-sensitive cells which gave them a survival advantage in their environment. Consequently they left more progeny, some of which had more highly developed light-sensitive cells. They in turn left more progeny whose light-sensitive cells were beginning to develop into primitive eyes, and so on. As a consequence, since the introduction of Darwin's theory of the evolution of the species, theologians did not rely much on the argument from design to prove the existence of God.

Now more recent cosmology has shown an incredible degree of balance in the laws and physical constants of the universe. The strength of gravity, for example, has to exactly balance the initial rate of expansion of the universe in the first moments of the Big Bang. If the universe had expanded slightly faster (or if the gravitational force had been slightly less), the matter in the universe would have kept on expanding so fast that it would never have condensed into stars and galaxies, and life could never have appeared. On the other hand, if the rate of expansion had been slightly slower (or the gravitational attraction slightly stronger), matter would have condensed into stars too rapidly, and the heavy elements necessary for life could not have been created in the interior of the stars. The gravitational force, then, had to be exactly balanced by the rate at which the emerging universe expanded just after the initial explosion. Physicists have discovered a whole series of such amazing accidents.

John Polkinghorne, an English particle physicist, an ordained Anglican priest, and now president of Queens' College, Cambridge, has given what is probably the best explanation of the relation between theology and science. Science, he says, in its explorations of physical reality, eventually raises questions it cannot answer. For example, "Why are the physical laws so precisely balanced?" Theology does have an answer for these questions: God created the universe, therefore it shows traces of God's design. Science and theology, then, are complementary, not in conflict. Each supplements the other, and together they give a complete explanation for why the universe is the way it is. This is a modern restatement of the position of Thomas Aquinas in the 13th century, who argued that reason leads to and supports faith, and faith completes reason.

B. Catholic Social Teaching

Beginning with Pope Leo XIII's encyclical letter *Rerum Novarum* in 1891 there has been a steady stream of writings by popes, conferences of bishops, the Second Vatican Council, and individuals trying to deal with the new social issues raised by the developments of the modern period. These include the industrial revolution, capitalism, socialism, communism, the Great Depression of the 1930s, nuclear weapons and the "cold war." Here are some of the key themes that Catholic social teaching has emphasized in dealing with these issues, particularly as they relate to human dignity and the common good.

(1) Teaching about the *common good* emphasizes that politicians, church officials, and business leaders have a responsibility to manage government and the economy in a way that will benefit *all* people, not just a small elite. This theme flows out of the church's teaching concerning the *human dignity* of every person: all humans have worth independent of what they can do, all have an eternal destiny. Therefore all humans should recognize their common standing, and live in *solidarity* with each other.

(2) Ownership of *private property* is important for the common good because people care for property better when they own it. They have more incentive to work well, and they have the security of being able to pass something on to their children. However, there is a *social mortgage* on private property: the right to private property is secondary to the principle that God created the earth and its goods for the common good of all humans. No one has the right to own and manage large areas of productive land or a monopoly corporation, if as a result they become rich and other humans starve.

(3) Workers ought to be paid a *living wage*, earning enough to support themselves, a spouse, and a family in decent conditions, including nourishing food, adequate clothing, decent housing, education, and health care. No one has the right to pay laborers less, even if the "market" forces workers to accept less.

(4) The principle of *subsidiarity* states that power and control should not be centralized beyond necessity. Higher levels of political and economic organization should not take over responsibilities that lower levels can accomplish. However, higher levels should provide whatever aid the lower levels may need to carry out their responsibilities. For example, decisions about child care are best handled on the family and local level. They should not be taken over by state levels of government, except to insure the rights of children to quality care.

(5) All human activity is *labor*: both the assembly line welder and the chief executive officer "work." In contrast, *capital* is concerned with the things that people use to do their work (e.g., factories, machines, books, accumulated files of information). Furthermore, capital is the result of human work: humans have made the things workers (including managers) use to do their work. Therefore, labor always has priority over capital.

According to Catholic social teaching, humans ought to be able to accomplish three things in their work: they should be able express themselves in a creative way, to support their families, and to make a contribution to the larger society. If their work does not allow them to accomplish all three things, Catholic social teaching would indicate that there is something wrong with the way their work has been organized.

Catholic social teaching has also addressed issues of modern war, in particular, the possibility of nuclear war. The Second Vatican Council said:

> *Any act of war aimed indiscriminately at the destruction of entire cities or of extensive areas along with their population is a crime against God and man himself. It merits unequivocal and unhesitating condemnation* (Pastoral Constitution on the Church in the Modern World, §80).

The U.S. Conference of Catholic Bishops further specified that Christians must refuse to legitimate the idea of a nuclear war that kills people indiscriminately.

> *Under no circumstances may nuclear weapons or other instruments of mass slaughter be used for the purpose of destroying population centers or other predominantly civilian targets* (The Challenge of Peace, §147).

> *We do not perceive any situation in which the deliberate initiation of nuclear warfare, on however restricted a scale, can be morally justified* (The Challenge of Peace, §150).

As this brief review suggests, Catholic social teaching embraces a wide range of issues including a theology of work, the justice of capitalism, and the morality of war. Broadly understood, it also provides an umbrella for talking about several other movements that emerge within Christian churches of the modern period—namely, the impact of feminism on Christian theology, as well as the emergence of black theology and liberation theology. All three movements address in some fashion issues of human dignity, solidarity, and social justice.

III. Liberation Theology

Over the centuries since the first Spanish and Portuguese conquests, Catholic Church leaders in Latin America have usually supported political and economic leaders who oppressed their people. Theological arguments have often been used to support that oppression. For example, the poor were told that it was their obligation to be obedient to the authorities. They were told that they ought to be glad to suffer as Christ had suffered and that they would receive their reward in heaven if they accepted suffering on earth. As a result of Catholic social teaching and the Second Vatican Council, some church leaders in Latin America (clergy and laity) began to support the poor against their nations' leaders and to challenge those leaders to take responsibility for their nation's poverty. This shift in emphasis was called the **preferential option for the poor**. In reaction, some of the elite felt that the church, or at least certain elements in the church, had abandoned them.

Liberation theology, as a movement, began in 1971 in Latin America when Gustavo Gutierrez, a Peruvian theologian, published a book titled *A Theology of Liberation*. Liberation theologians argue that the dominant reality of our world is oppression, and that Christians who take the Bible and the message of Jesus seriously ought to have something to say to it. Christianity cannot preach the Kingdom of God as good news to people who are living desperate lives. Liberation theology often appeals to the biblical imagery of the Israelites in slavery in Egypt to explain God's activity on behalf of the poor. God *confronted* Pharaoh and *rescued* the Israelites from their human slavery. Finally, they argue that *oppressors* are harmed even more by their injustice than the oppressed are: oppressors lose their humanity, their relationship with God, and their eternal destiny in heaven. Thus liberation theology aims to liberate both oppressors and the oppressed.

A. Base Christian Communities

In the parishes of Latin America, where the poor and their needs had often been ignored, because there are few priests and much poverty, small groups formed called **base Christian communities**. These communities provide a place for discussion, mutual support, and common action. More traditional clergy were sometimes alarmed by this development, both because they feared a transfer of power from clergy to laity and because these small local groups often raised embarrassing political questions, even about the church itself, and engaged in activities that threatened the status quo from which the elites were benefiting.

Laity, empowered by small-scale local action, began to form larger associations and networks and to hold regional and national meetings. In Brazil, the bishops quickly approved of the base Christian communities, providing yearly discussion guides and protecting them from hostile political pressures. Some of the church leadership in other countries have been less encouraging or positively hostile to the base communities. The integrated discussion and action of these base Christian communities came to be called **praxis**. Praxis is activity that is reflected upon and consciously chosen to produce a particular effect, a transformation of society. The activity and the reflection go together and influence each other.

B. Structural Violence

A key insight of liberation theology is the concept of *structural violence*. If the laws and the way they are carried out result in half of the children in a country dying before age five, as is true in many Latin countries, then those people who develop, support, defend, or fail to confront those laws and practices are guilty of violence against the poor. One can share guilt for the death of children by sup

Figure 24.2: Nossa Senhora Aparecida, one of two thousand *favelas* (slums) in Sao Paolo, Brazil, which all together house approximately two million people. This *favela* has piped water and sewers, but the sewers are so clogged that most sewage runs on the surface in open ditches. A base Christian community was organized here in about 1968. Photo by David Smith, 1988.

porting laws and practices that prevent adequate nutrition, even if one never physically attacks the children directly. The Base Christian Community movement and liberation theology have come under attack in some circles because of the criticism that they accept violent revolution as a valid response to injustice. Some are accused of being communists. The Vatican Congregation for the Teaching of the Faith has published two documents on liberation theology endorsing its "preferential option for the poor," but also expressing cautions about its use of Marxist methods of analysis. A passage from the first document illustrates that, despite its concerns about liberation theology, the Congregation does not intend to support oppression by unjust governments:

> In certain parts of Latin America, the seizure of the vast majority of the wealth by an oligarchy of owners bereft of social consciousness, the practical absence or the shortcomings of a rule of law, military dictators making a mockery of elementary human rights, the corruption of certain powerful officials, the savage practices of some foreign capital interests constitute factors which nourish a passion for revolt among those who thus consider themselves the powerless victims of a new colonialism in the technological, financial, monetary or economic order. The recognition of injustice is accompanied by a pathos which borrows its language from Marxism, wrongly presented as though it were scientific language (Instruction on Certain Aspects of the "Theology of Liberation", VII,12).

From its beginnings in the Latin American situation, liberation theology has inspired or encouraged those in situations of oppression or marginalization to make sociological analyses of their situation and to use theological reflection to come to a just and meaningful response. Some examples of related movements are feminist theology which analyzes the oppression of women, black theology which analyzes the effects of slavery and segregation, and Oriental liberation theologies which analyze interfaith relations with non-Christian religions and the injustices caused by Western colonialism. We will examine in greater detail two of these related movements, namely, feminist theology and black theology.

IV. Feminism and the Christian Churches

Modern feminism is a movement which has striven for equality between women and men and for recognition of women's role in history. Its impact on Christianity has had both a practical dimension and a theological dimension. On a practical level, feminism has challenged people to ask how women can achieve equality in the Christian churches. On a theological level, feminist theologians have sought to reconstruct women's place in the history of religious traditions and to introduce women's perspectives into questions about the nature of God and humanity's relationship to God.

A. Equality of Women in the Churches

In Western Christianity, women make up the majority of persons who attend church services and participate in the churches' ministries of service to others. This seems especially true in the Latin American and Mediterranean Catholic countries. In contrast, throughout most of Christian history the leaders of the churches have been exclusively male. This pattern has gradually started to change in the 20th century, as women have gained more equal status with men in other areas of secular culture. Many mainline Protestant denominations (e.g. ELCA Lutheran, Presbyterian, Methodist, Episcopal, United Church of Christ) now ordain women pastors. At the same time, there are other denominations that do not (e.g., Southern Baptist, and Wisconsin/Missouri Synod Lutherans).

Likewise, in non-Protestant traditions, Eastern Orthodox Christians and Roman Catholics do not ordain women. At the heart of the problem of the equality of women in the churches is the issue of ordination. A number of arguments have been advanced both for and against women's ordination.

Those who argue against women's ordination do so on the basis of tradition. In ancient Israel, there were female prophets and judges (e.g, Miriam and Deborah), but the priests who offered sacrifices to God for the people were male. Among Jesus' followers there were women, but the prominent apostles, those who assumed leadership in the early church, were male. Since Jesus did not commission women to be apostles, modern churches which claim to follow Jesus' teachings and practices say that they do not have the authority to ordain women. Another argument heard mainly in Roman Catholic circles is that the priest represents Christ before the congregation, and therefore should bear a natural (i.e., physical) resemblance to Christ.

Against these arguments, other Christians argue that the Bible, as well as Christian doctrine and practices within the church, have been reinterpreted over time to adapt to the needs of people and to account for cultural changes. The New Testament indicates that Jesus did not prohibit slavery, and that Paul tacitly accepted it, but modern churches do not condone slavery on that account. Likewise, modern churches ought not prohibit women's ordination, simply because the patriarchal culture in which Jesus lived would have made it unlikely that women be included among his twelve apostles. Nonetheless, Paul seems to indicate the presence of women apostles in the early church (see Rom 16:7). Another argument advanced by supporters of women's ordination is the possibility that the early church *did* ordain women, but that the records have been expurgated by the male writers who handed on the tradition. Some feminist biblical scholars (e.g. Elisabeth Schüssler Fiorenza) argue this. A third argument involves the notion that the priest represents Christ. Supporters of women's ordination argue that a woman can represent Christ in the celebration of the liturgy in the same way that a man does. If the priest should bear a natural (i.e., physical) resemblance to Christ, why should gender be the deciding factor? Should we not also demand that the priest be Jewish, as Jesus was? It is the spiritual similarity to Jesus (i.e. similarity in love) that really matters.

The question of women's ordination remains a deeply divisive issue among Christians and one that will not be easily resolved. The case for or against women's ordination is made even more difficult by the lack of historical information concerning the organization and structure of the early church. Perhaps part of the difficulty lies in the fact that, although the issue is most often argued on theological grounds, it is also an issue of appropriate definitions of women's roles in society and human resistance to change.

B. Feminist Theology

Feminist theology examines many of the traditional themes of theology (e.g., God, Jesus, creation, the nature of the human person, and the role of the church), but it does so from the point of view of women's experience. Typically, the feminine perspective emphasizes wholeness, ecological interconnectedness, and human relatedness. Some would argue that it differs from a male perspective which emphasizes distinctness, domination, and power. In fact, feminist theology cannot be easily compartmentalized or stereotyped because women's experiences are so diverse. Some feminist theologians argue that, since almost the entire Christian tradition, even the scriptures, has been written from a male point of view, it largely ignores the distinctive experiences and perspective of women. Thus, one of the tasks of feminist theologians is to recover women's history and spirituality within the churches, and create a theology that resonates with women's experience.

Feminist theology also concerns itself with how we image God. Sally McFague, for example, argues that, although feminine images of God as mother, lover, and friend can be found both in the Bible and in Christian tradition, the images of God as father, king, and judge have dominated our language about God. She reminds her readers that all our images of God are metaphorical or analogical, and argues that feminine or non-dominative images are actually more appropriate for God than images which connote dominance. Similarly, she argues that images which stress the immanence (nearness) of God should be used to balance images which stress God's transcendence (otherness). An exclusively male tradition has resulted in reinforcing patriarchal images of God (God as warrior, king, father, etc.). Feminist theology is a way in which we might revise our images and concepts of God.

Feminist theologians generally stress relationships of mutuality and partnership over relationships of hierarchy and dominance. Some radical Catholic feminists argue that the whole hierarchical structure of the church is a result of male domination, and should be replaced altogether with a more egalitarian ecclesial structure. Other more moderate feminist theologians suggest that more wholistic and relationally oriented models of church can exist in tandem with more hierarchical models for the well-being and healing of the whole church community.

Since women have been excluded from leadership in most religions, one finds feminist theology in a variety of religious traditions (Judaism, Islam, Buddhism, etc.). Overall, feminist theologians are very concerned with justice for women and other marginalized groups. Consequently, they focus on theological questions of human dignity and solidarity. Feminist theologians have also been concerned about ecological issues. Authors such as McFague and Rosemary Radford Reuther argue that Western attitudes that condone the exploitation of nature have led to much environmental destruction. These attitudes stem from a patriarchal point of view which values dominance over interrelatedness. Thus, eco-feminist theologies focus on creation and humanity's relatedness to the earth.

V. Black Theology

Christianity has had an ambiguous relationship with the institution of slavery in the United States. On the one hand, slaveholders were quick to point to the many biblical texts that seem to accept slavery. On the other hand, abolitionists argued that the whole message of Christianity was primarily one of human dignity and liberation from oppression. Similarly, for the slaves themselves, Christianity was a "knife that cuts both ways." They were often forced to convert to Christianity and to attend church services; many slaveholders seemed to think that this would create a more docile slave population.

Yet, because of the liberating message of Christianity, many slaves heard the Gospel as a call for their release. So, for example, in one of the most important musical traditions of the slaves—the spirituals—a Christian story was often used as a coded message of escape and liberation. No slaveholder could reprimand a slave for singing about one of the most memorable stories in the Bible:

> *Go down, Moses,*
> *Way down to Egypt land.*
> *Tell old Pharaoh,*
> *"Let my people go!"*

But of course this song also applied to the slaves' own situation. Many slaves understood it as a plea for *their* release from captivity—just as the Israelites had been freed from Egypt.

The ambiguous relationship between Christianity and slavery came to the fore once again in the 1960s civil-rights movement. Black leaders argued among themselves about the appropriateness of Christianity for blacks. After all, it was the religion of the oppressor that was forced on the black slaves and used for centuries to justify slavery. On the other side of the argument, black leaders would say that Jesus himself proclaimed "release to the captives," and worked "to let the oppressed go free" (Luke 4:18). They would also appeal to the writings of Paul, saying that he prepared the way for the abolitionists by claiming that in Christ "there is no longer …slave or free" (Gal. 3:28). Perhaps the best-known advocates of the two sides of this argument were Martin Luther King, Jr. and Malcolm X. King was a Baptist minister, and he believed that Christianity was essentially about freedom; he saw it as fundamentally supportive of civil rights for African-Americans. When he wrote one of his most eloquent pleas, his "Letter from the Birmingham Jail," he modeled it, in part, on the letters of St. Paul. Malcolm X, on the other hand, believed that Christianity had been corrupted by racist assumptions, which could be observed over a century of post-Civil-War American history. During this era, so-called "Christians" advocated and carried out segregation, Jim Crow laws, and lynchings. Malcolm X eventually put his views into practice by converting to Islam—a faith that he considered much more appropriate for peoples of African descent.

The debate between "Martin and Malcolm" was not only about religious faith. It was also about the strategies for changing racial attitudes. Both sides agreed on the need to rethink and redefine all sorts of societal structures, including economic opportunity, education, criminal justice, and politics. However, they differed about how to achieve those goals. Some leaders, such as King, argued for slow, measured change, in close collaboration with white leaders (who held most of the power). Others, such as Malcolm X, argued that blacks should take charge of their own liberation, and should seek to throw off the burden of racial oppression by whatever means necessary. This approach eventually became known as the "Black Power" movement. Would Christianity always be attached to King's vision of slow, collaborative change? Or was it equally compatible with "Black Power"?

In 1969, a recent Ph.D. graduate published his doctoral dissertation, which argued for a radical interpretation of Christianity—one which allied it very firmly with the Black Power movement. The author was James H. Cone, and his book was entitled *Black Theology and Black Power*. One year later, Cone wrote a somewhat more scholarly treatment of the same issues, published as *A Black Theology of Liberation*. Together, these two books have been enormously influential in shaping the movement known as Black theology. Black theology argues that racism should be understood through the theological category of *sin*. Racism can be seen in individual racist acts (just as sin can be seen in individual sinful acts); but more importantly, racism can be structural. It can be "built in" to particular systems, just as sin seems to be "built in" to the human race. God's act of redemption through Jesus Christ not only frees us from sin in the ordinary sense; it also frees us from our racist behavior and sets us on a path toward ending racism. Black theology makes considerable use of the Bible, pointing to God's tendency to side with the underdog—the slaves (such as Israel in Egypt), the powerless (such as the poor, the widow, and the orphan), and all those who are marginalized by their society (for example, Jesus' ministry to the blind, the sick, prostitutes, tax collectors, and other "undesirables" of his own culture).

Black theology claims that, in American culture today, the most marginalized people are African-Americans. Brought to this country against their will, completely cut off from the structures of power for centuries (and only recently attaining some small measure of equality), they are the modern-day "underdogs" who receive God's favor. For Christianity to operate in racially-polarized America, it must become aware of God's special care for African-Americans, and must fight the sin of racism with the same kind of energy that it gives to fighting other moral ills.

Black theology is closely related to both feminist theology and liberation theology. In fact, it is sometimes combined with these approaches in an attempt to recognize the special circumstances of those who are marginalized by society in more than one way—by being black and female, for example, or being black and poor. Since the days of Cone's pioneering work, black theology has expanded and developed in highly sophisticated ways. Its advocates include James Evans, who has written a systematic theology from an African-American perspective; Cornel West, who has provided considerable philosophical support (and pure inspiration) to the movement; Katie Geneva Cannon, who has developed a distinctive African-American feminist perspective (sometimes called "Womanist" theology), and Cain Hope Felder, who has examined how racial assumptions affect biblical interpretation. The movement has also been inspired by the development of theological themes in the work of African-American novelists, such as Alice Walker and Toni Morrison.

VI. Concluding Reflections

As the history of Christianity has demonstrated, every historical situation and cultural context presents new challenges and opportunities for the revelation of God's Word in the world. In each time and place, Christianity has had to redefine itself and adapt to changing circumstances. Church organization has changed radically since the rather charismatic and informal time of house churches and missionary preachers in the 1st and 2nd centuries. In the American Christian churches, denominationalism has resulted in an intricate arrangement of churches which differ significantly in both doctrine and organization, but still call themselves Christian. Likewise, Christian churches experience a wide diversity in worship styles and lifestyle expectations—both deriving from the churches' attempts to further refine their doctrine and practice for a changing world.

None of these changes happen in isolation from the wider culture in which Christianity exists. The challenges and opportunities which Christian churches face today are further heightened by rapid advances in technology, by the widening gap between those who have sufficient resources to live a life of dignity and those who do not, and by the pluralism of modern society which provides the opportunity for peoples of different religions, cultures, and worldviews to work together in shared ventures. The gospel message of Jesus continues to be relevant as the inspired Word of God even in this time. However, as in any other time, the Word must be reinterpreted and appropriated in new ways. Thus Christian communities continue to draw upon their tradition and look for the guidance of the Holy Spirit in discerning how they might fulfill their mission of Christ's presence in the world.

Key Terms:

Second Vatican Council	pluralism
aggiornamento	preferential option for the poor
magisterium	base Christian communities
ecumenism	praxis

Questions for Reading:

1. When the Second Vatican Council was called, what was its purpose? Why did some persons consider it to be an ecumenical council, while others did not?

2. Describe the major contributions of the Second Vatican Council in the following areas:

   a. reform of the liturgy

   b. church as "People of God"

   c. the ecumenical movement

   d. dialogue with the secular world

   e. the theology of revelation

3. Why is there a renewed interest in the interchange of theology and science today? What can they do together that they cannot do separately?

4. What are the central concerns of modern Catholic social teaching?

5. What is liberation theology? In what way is it concerned with a preferential option for the poor? Why?

6. What are some of the contributions of feminist theology? In what ways does it challenge traditional religious understandings about God and the world?

7. What are some of the contributions of black theology? In what ways does it challenge traditional religious understandings about God and the world?

Works Consulted/Recommended Reading:

Abbott, Walter M., S.J., ed. *The Documents of Vatican II*. New York: Herder and Herder/ Association Press, 1966.

Berryman, Phillip. *Liberation Theology: Essential Facts About the Revolutionary Movement in Latin America— and Beyond*. Philadelphia: Temple University Press, 1987.

Bokenkotter, Thomas. *A Concise History of the Catholic Church*. Rev. ed. New York: Doubleday, 1979.

Carlen, Claudia, ed. *The Papal Encyclicals. 1939-1958*. Wilmington, NC: McGrath Publishing Co. 1981.

Cone, James H. *Black Theology and Black Power*. New York: Seabury, 1969.

_____. *A Black Theology of Liberation*. Maryknoll, NY: Orbis, 1986.

Flannery, Austin P., ed. *Vatican Council II: The Conciliar and Post Conciliar Documents*. Collegeville MN: Liturgical Press, 1975.

Gremillion, Joseph, ed. *The Gospel of Peace and Justice: Catholic Social Teaching since Pope John*. Maryknoll NY: Orbis Books, 1976.

Gutierrez, Gustavo. *A Theology of Liberation*. Maryknoll NY: Orbis Books, 1973.

McFague, Sally. *Models of God: Theology for an Ecological, Nuclear Age*. Philadelphia: Fortress, 1987.

National Conference of Catholic Bishops. *The Challenge of Peace: God's Promise and Our Response*. Washington DC: National Conference of Catholic Bishops, 1983.

National Conference of Catholic Bishops. *Economic Justice for All: Pastoral Letter on Catholic Social Teaching and the U.S. Economy.* Washington DC: National Conference of Catholic Bishops, 1986.

Ross, Susan, and Hilkert, Mary Catherine, O.P., "Feminist Theology: A Review of Literature," *Theological Studies* 56 (1995) 327-352.

Sullivan, Francis, S. J. *Salvation Outside the Church? Tracing the History of the Catholic Response.* Mahwah, NJ: Paulist, 1992.

Glossary

abbot ∽ the spiritual leader who governs an organized community of monks.

Abelard, Peter (1079-1142 AD) ∽ the most celebrated of the 12th century university masters, who wrote numerous books and used the newly publicized logic of Aristotle to detect and resolve contradictions within traditional theological authorities such as the Bible and the church fathers. His career came to a sudden halt when he had an affair with a young woman named Heloise, whom he had been hired to tutor. Her family castrated him and he became a monk.

Abraham ∽ first patriarch of the Israelite people (lived 18th century BCE), with whom God formed an everlasting covenant; claimed as an ancestor by Jews, Christians, and Muslims.

absolution ∽ forgiveness for the guilt associated with sin.

Afonso the Good (1482-1543 AD) ∽ Catholic king of the Congo who tried unsuccessfully to oversee the conversion of his people to Catholicism while holding back the greed of the Portuguese colonists who were enslaving them.

aggiornamento ∽ meaning "a bringing up to date." This term describes the spirit of the Second Vatican Council as it attempted to reinterpret the church's doctrine and reform its practice in a way that was suitable to the present.

agnostic ∽ someone who is unsure about the existence of God or gods.

Ali ∽ Muhammad's cousin and son-in-law, the fourth caliph of the Islamic people assassinated in 661 AD. The Shi`ites (meaning "partisans of Ali") take their name from his.

alienation of property ∽ during the early medieval period, the practice of deeding church goods as the private inheritance of bishops' or priests' children.

Allah ∽ the Muslim name for God; the one and only God.

allegorical ∽ term used to describe a method of interpreting scripture; it involves looking for a hidden spiritual meaning beneath the bare literal meaning of the text.

Amos ∽ 8th-century BCE prophet who condemned the social injustice of the northern kingdom of Israel and foresaw its destruction by the Assyrians.

anchorite/anchoress ∽ a hermit who pledges his or her life to prayer and contemplation. During the middle ages, they lived in small enclosed rooms attached to a church, where they could be spiritual counselors for the people of the area.

animism ∽ worship of the forces of nature.

Anselm of Canterbury (1033-1109 AD) ∽ Benedictine monk and archbishop of Canterbury, Anselm is known for his "debt satisfaction" theory of atonement and for his ontological argument for the existence of God.

anthropocentric ∽ human-centered.

anthropology ∽ the study of human beings, or a particular view about the nature of human beings. Christian anthropology is primarily concerned with theological explanations concerning humanity's relationship to God, the human condition, and the promise or potential of a renewed humanity.

anti-clericalism ∽ antagonism toward priests and clergy.

Antony of Egypt (251-356 AD) ∽ the father of Christian monasticism. Antony felt that Christ's teachings called him to sell all of his possessions and devote himself completely to following the gospel through a life of prayer in isolation from the world. Many Christians—early, medieval, and modern—have been inspired to follow his example.

apocalyptic ∽ term describing a person, group, or text expressing the beliefs that the present world is evil and corrupt and that God will soon bring an end to it, destroying the evildoers and rescuing the righteous.

Apocrypha ∽ name given to the seven books that are included in the Old Testament by Catholics and Orthodox Christians, but excluded from the scriptures by Protestants and Jews.

Apollinaris of Laodicaea ∽ Christian theologian (circa 4th century AD) who solved the problem of the dual nature of Christ (human and divine) by saying that Christ had a human body but not a human soul. His views came to be regarded as heretical.

apologist ∽ meaning "defender." The apologists of the early church attempted to respond to pagan criticisms of Christianity by explaining what Christians believed and how they lived their lives.

apostasy ∽ falling away from the faith.

apostle ∽ from the Greek word "apostello" which means "to send out." It is used by Christians to refer to "one who is sent out by Jesus to preach the word about him."

Aquinas, Thomas (1224/5-1274 AD) ∽ Catholic theologian and saint; author of the *Summa Theologiae*, a comprehensive overview of Christian theology; best known for his integration of the philosophy of Aristotle into Christian faith, his view of the compatibility of reason and revelation, and his "proofs" for God's existence.

Aristotle ∽ Greek philosopher and scientist of the 4th century BCE; his ideas were seen as a challenge to religions like Christianity because—without any access to divine revelation—he developed an account of reality that seemed more complete, more sophisticated, and more coherent than that of Christianity.

Arius ∽ a 4th-century priest who taught that only God the Father was God in the true sense; the Son (Jesus Christ) was less than God. His teaching was rejected at the Council of Nicaea (325 AD) and the Council of Constantinople (381 AD) and came to be regarded as heretical.

Ark of the Covenant ∽ (1) a container for sacred objects of the Israelites, including the tablets of the Ten Commandments; (2) the "throne" on which Yahweh sat invisibly.

article ᖰ the basic unit of many medieval theological works such as the *Summa Theologiae* of Thomas Aquinas. Each article considered one question. An article began by reviewing the arguments for and against the proposition, proceeded to give the author's own view, and finally replied to the arguments with which the author ultimately disagreed.

asceticism ᖰ the training or discipline of the passions and the appetites. In the case of hermits and monks, the practice was designed to foster spiritual development.

Ashkenazim ᖰ the term given to Jewish immigrants to the Americas from northern Europe.

atheist ᖰ someone who denies that God or gods exist.

Augsburg Confession ᖰ a statement of faith drafted by Philip Melanchthon, representing the Lutheran position at the Diet of Augsburg (1530 AD). The diet which was called to resolve differences between Protestants and Catholics failed, but Lutherans signed Melanchthon's statement, making it one of the most important documents of Lutheran doctrine even today.

Augustine of Hippo (354-430 AD) ᖰ theologian and bishop of Hippo; his conversion from a great sinner to a great saint is described in the autobiographical work *Confessions*; best known for his opposition to Donatism and Pelagianism, his theological doctrines of grace, original sin, and predestination, and his solution to the problem of evil.

Averroes (1126-1198 AD) ᖰ medieval Muslim scholar, known for his learned commentaries on the works of Aristotle.

Avicenna (980-1037 AD) ᖰ medieval Muslim scholar, noted for medical commentaries on the classical Greek physician-scholars Galen and Hippocrates, mathematical commentaries on the classical Greek mathematician Euclid, and philosophical commentaries on Aristotle.

Avignon Papacy ᖰ the period in the late middle ages when the pope moved his court to Avignon, France. Before the papacy would return to Rome, the church leadership would be involved in an even greater struggle for power called the "Great Schism."

Baptism ᖰ the Christian rite of initiation, which brings about the forgiveness of sins, makes the person a member of the Christian community, and confers the Holy Spirit on the person.

baptistery ᖰ in the early church, a Christian building used for Baptism; later, a place in the church set aside for Baptism. The baptisteries of the early church had a centered design, and the focus was on the baptismal font into which the candidate stepped.

Baroque ᖰ an ornate style of art and architecture that was especially popular in Roman Catholic churches and among Roman Catholic artists during the Catholic Reformation. The Baroque style was designed to dramatically illustrate the truths of Catholic orthodoxy, but also to involve the viewer in the experience of faith by appealing to their emotions and overwhelming them with a sense of awe.

Bartolomé de Las Casas (1474-1566 AD) ᖰ the Spanish Catholic bishop in the territories of the New World who argued that the enslavement of the native peoples was immoral and should be stopped.

basilica ᖰ a style of Christian church architecture, distinguished from other churches by its adaptation of the standard rectangular layout of royal audience halls and public buildings in Roman cities. The Christian version of a basilica was conceived as an audience hall for Christ, the heavenly king.

Batuta, Ibn (1304-1368 AD) 〜 an Arab scholar and traveler who was partly responsible for the European colonization and missionary efforts in Africa, since he revealed the presence of gold in that region.

believer's baptism 〜 the idea, popularized by the churches of the "Radical Reformation," that since baptism involves entering into a covenant with God, it requires an act of conscious, active belief on the part of the person being baptized. Since only adults are old enough to formulate such belief and make such a decision, infant baptism is ruled out.

Benedict of Nursia (480-547 AD) 〜 founder of the Benedictine monastery at Monte Cassino and author of the Rule for Monasteries which eventually became the primary style of monasticism in the West.

benevolence 〜 goodness.

Bible, Polyglot 〜 a single Bible in which the text was presented in several languages. Polyglot Bibles were especially popular in the 16th and 17th centuries AD.

biblical theology 〜 a study of the written documents found in the Bible, how these documents were formed, how they were selected to be part of the Bible, what they meant to the original "authors" and "audience," and what they might mean for contemporary belief and practice.

bishop 〜 meaning "overseer." In early Christianity, bishops were overseers of local churches, chiefly responsible for teaching but also for presiding at Eucharist. Later, bishops are overseers of groups of churches known as a diocese.

breviary 〜 a prayer book containing the Liturgy of the Hours, the official prayer of priests and monks, composed of psalms and readings from the Bible and other religious literature.

Caesaro-papism 〜 term applied by some Western writers to the Byzantine political theory, meaning that the civil ruler ("Caesar") also served as head of the church ("pope").

Caliph 〜 one of the successors of Muhammad chosen to govern the Islamic people after his death; one who rules a Muslim nation.

Calvin, John (1509-1564 AD) 〜 the French reformer and theologian who led the Swiss city of Geneva through the Reformation. Calvin is known especially for the doctrines of election and double predestination, and for grappling with the problem of authority after the Protestant rejection of the authority of Rome. His teachings are most influential in the Christian Reformed Church and the Presbyterian Church.

canon 〜 (1) the collection of authoritative writings of a particular religious group; (2) the "rule" or norm of religious truth in the Christian tradition.

Cappadocian Fathers 〜 a group of Christian priests, including Basil of Caesarea (330-79 AD), his brother Gregory of Nyssa (331/40-c.395), and Basil's friend Gregory of Nazianzus (c.329-90), whose theological advances and appropriation of Greek philosophical thought are reflected in the clarifications of the Nicene Creed adopted at the Council of Constantinople (381 AD).

Capuchins ⟿ A reform branch of the Franciscan movement, this religious order was official recognized in 1528, during the Catholic Reformation. They get their name from the unique four-pointed hood which they wore with their brown habit.

Carmelites, Discalced ⟿ a reform branch of the Carmelite order founded by Teresa of Avila and John of the Cross in 1581. The term "discalced" means "unshod," referring to the spiritual practice of going barefoot in order to fulfill Jesus' mandate to provide themselves with nothing for the journey, not even sandals for their feet (Matt 10:9-10).

catechism ⟿ from a Greek word meaning "to instruct." A catechism is a manual of Christian doctrine used to instruct believers in the Christian faith. They were especially popular in the 16th century among both Protestant and Catholic reformers, because of the emphasis on religious instruction for ministers as well as laity.

catechumen ⟿ a candidate for baptism who is undergoing instruction in the Christian religion.

cathedral ⟿ a bishop's church.

Catherine of Siena (c. 1347-1380 AD) ⟿ a mystic of the late medieval period, she was a Dominican tertiary and influential in bringing an end to the Avignon papacy, only to see it fall into the situation of the Great Schism. Catherine's prayer life had led her into a vision of mystical marriage to Christ. Her visions often were of the nourishing and cleansing blood of the sacrifice of Christ on the cross.

catholic ⟿ meaning "universal." The term is also used in a restrictive sense to refer to a tradition within Christianity, namely, the Roman Catholic Church, or to describe those churches that claim a continuity of leadership that goes back to the early Christian churches (e.g., Eastern Orthodox Christians, Anglicans, and Episcopalians).

cenobitic monasticism ⟿ the form of monasticism in which monks live together in a community, rather than as hermits.

Chalcedon, Council of ⟿ an ecumenical council held in 451 AD which considered the question of Christ's human and divine nature, and taught that the incarnate Jesus Christ possessed a complete human nature and a complete divine nature united in one person.

Christ ⟿ from a Greek word meaning "anointed one." Christians use it to refer to Jesus as God's anointed, the fulfillment of the prophecy made to David concerning an heir who would be an eternal king (2 Sam 7).

christology ⟿ meaning "words or teaching about the Christ." A study concerned with who Jesus is and what his role is in God's relationship with humanity.

Church of Jesus Christ of Latter-Day Saints ⟿ also known as the Mormons, this American church was founded in 1830 by Joseph Smith, based upon a vision he had concerning the appearance of the risen Christ in the Americas. In Mormon belief, marriage is considered important for salvation and children are valued as the means by which souls are embodied as the first step to divinity.

Church of Christ, Scientist ⟿ also known as the "Christian Scientists," this American church was founded by Mary Baker Eddy in 1875. Eddy believed that people had within them the power of the mind to eliminate sickness and death. She also taught that God is spirit and all good, and humans, as a reflection of God, are also spiritual and good.

churches, Baptist ⤳ this family of Christian churches is similar to the Free churches in their emphasis on "free will." However, their roots are in the Puritan community of New England. They were also influenced by the Dutch Mennonites and millenialist movements who looked to the books of Daniel and Revelation, seeking "signs of the times" and a proper way of life for Christian believers.

churches, free ⤳ a family of Christian churches rooted in the radical Reformation movements. They developed because their members sought an asceticism that created a community separate from the mainstream of secular society. These free or non-state churches place their emphasis on "free will" and preach a common priesthood of the believers. The family includes Mennonites, the Amish, the Brethren, Quakers, and Free-Church Brethren.

churches, holiness ⤳ a family of Protestant churches who seek perfection in the world by developing a lifestyle of personal holiness and following a rigid code of behavior. It includes the Free Methodist Church, the Church of God, the Holiness Christian Church, and the Church of the Nazarene.

churches, independent fundamentalist ⤳ this family of Protestant churches holds a dispensationalist perspective with regard to scripture. They believe that scripture tells the history of God's dealing with humanity, a history that can be divided into various stages called dispensations. Christians are living on the edge of the seventh dispension, the fullness of time, and therefore they ought to read the scriptures from this perspective in order to prepare for the final days.

churches, Pentecostal ⤳ a family of Protestant churches whose members demonstrate their Christian faith through the gifts of the Holy Spirit, in particular, healing, wisdom to discern spirits, prophecy, and speaking in tongues (glossolalia). It includes the Assemblies of God, the Church of God, the Pentecostal Holiness Church, the Apostolic Faith Church, the Church of God in Christ, and the Full Gospel Fellowship.

conciliarism ⤳ a theory of church authority advanced by the bishops of the Roman Catholic Church during the Great Schism. According to this theory, the bishops, when they were gathered together in an official council, had the right to make binding decisions independent of the pope in time of crisis.

concubinage ⤳ during the early medieval period, the practice among some clergy of maintaining concubines in a relationship something like marriage.

confessors ⤳ in early Christianity, those who were arrested during persecution and stood firm in their faith but who were not put to death. Confessors enjoyed great prestige in the churches, and some claimed the right to forgive sins.

congregationalist ⤳ a model of church organization based upon the style of the earliest Christian communities. Its leaders are part of the local community and their authority comes from within the local community.

Consistory ⤳ the governing council of the Calvinist Geneva, consisting of members from the city government, the church leadership, and the laity.

Constantine (reigned 306-337 AD) ⤳ the first Christian emperor of Rome. He ended the persecution of Christians and paved the way for the establishment of Christianity as the sole legal religion in the Roman Empire. He established the practice of calling ecumenical councils to resolve urgent issues affecting the whole church, and his reign marked the beginning of a huge expansion in the Christian church.

Constantinople, Council of ∽ an ecumenical council held in 381 AD which affirmed the Nicene Creed and added clauses about the divinity of the Holy Spirit.

Constantinople (also called Istanbul or Byzantium) ∽ a major city in what is modern-day Turkey, and a center of Christianity; formerly the capital of the Eastern Roman Empire (or Byzantine Empire); seat of one of the five patriarchs (along with the bishops of Rome, Alexandria, Antioch, and Jerusalem) who together governed Christianity in its early centuries; seat of the foremost of the four patriarchs (along with the bishops of Alexandria, Antioch, and Jerusalem) who govern the Eastern Orthodox Christian Church to this day.

contrition ∽ sorrow for sin.

Copernicus, Nicholas ∽ 16th century Polish astronomer who proposed that the earth and other planets revolved around the sun.

cosmology ∽ the study of the nature and structure of the universe, or a particular view ("picture") of the nature and structure of the universe.

Counter-Reformation ∽ a term given to the efforts of those who, during the Protestant Reformation, were loyal to the pope and supportive of the customary practices of the Roman Catholic Church in order to counter (go against) the teachings and practices of the Protestant reformers.

covenant ∽ a sacred or formal agreement between two parties.

Cranmer, Thomas ∽ archbishop of Canterbury for most of the early years (1533-1553) of the English Reformation, he wrote the *Thirty-Nine Articles*, which sets out the specific similarities and differences between the Church of England and the Roman Catholic Church, and the *Book of Common Prayer*, a hugely popular and influential liturgical document.

creed ∽ a short summary of belief.

crusades ∽ a series of military campaigns from Christian Europe, between 1095 and 1291 AD, aimed at recapturing the Holy Land (Palestine and Syria) and protecting the Eastern Byzantine Empire from Turkish Muslim encroachment.

Darwin, Charles ∽ 19th century scientist who developed the theory of evolution and the principle of natural selection.

David ∽ the greatest of the kings of Israel (reigned 1000-961 BCE), known for his military genius, musical abilities, love of Yahweh, and his occasional moral failures.

Deism ∽ the view (popular during the Enlightenment) that God created the world but does not thereafter intervene in its operation. In this view, the world is like a watch or clock, which runs on its own without the help of the watchmaker, God.

denomination ∽ a particular church tradition, having a common doctrine and organizational structure, within the Christian faith.

denominationalism ❧ according to this principle, the individual Christian churches, with their particular forms of worship and their unique organizational structures, are understood to be denominations of the one true church which is Christianity, and not separate churches.

Descartes, Rene ❧ 17th century French philosopher, known for his skepticism about the value of tradition. He began his philosophical method by doubting everything he had been taught—all tradition—and by believing only what could be shown by reason to be absolutely certain.

Deuteronomistic Historian ❧ author(s) of a series of books of the Old Testament/Hebrew Bible, whose agenda was to show how Israel's fortunes were correlated to her obedience to the terms of the covenant with God.

Deuteronomistic History ❧ name given to a series of books of the Old Testament written by the Deuteronomistic Historian, books which emphasized the necessity of Israel adhering strictly to its covenant with God.

Diaspora ❧ those Jews who were "dispersed" outside the traditional Jewish homeland in Palestine.

diet ❧ a formal assembly or meeting.

disciple ❧ a learner or a follower. Christians used the term to refer to those who followed Jesus.

dispensationalism ❧ a Christian perspective on history which says that scripture tells the history of God's dealings with humanity, a history that can be divided into various stages called dispensations. Christians are living in the sixth stage, the age of the Spirit, and are about to enter the seventh dispensation, the fullness of time. Therefore they ought to read the scriptures from this perspective in order to prepare for the final days.

docetism ❧ from a Greek word meaning "to seem" or "to appear to be." The belief of some early Christians that Jesus Christ did not really become flesh but only seemed to have a body. In reality he was a spiritual being who could not suffer or die.

Doctor of the Church ❧ an honor reserved for those whose teaching and scholarship have reflected Catholic Christian beliefs and been important in the lives and faith of others.

doctrine ❧ the official teachings or principles of a religion.

Documentary Hypothesis ❧ the theory that the Pentateuch was produced by combining four strands of tradition (the Yahwist, the Elohist, the Deuteronomist, and the Priestly Writer) over a long period of time (9th- 5th centuries BCE).

dogma ❧ doctrines or teachings that have been proclaimed authoritatively by a given religion or church.

Dominicans ❧ an order of "beggar" friars founded by St. Dominic, also called the "Order of Preachers." Known for their radical understanding of the vow of poverty, their primary vocation was to preach and hear confessions.

Donatists ❧ a group of Christians (primarily in North Africa) which split from the main body of the church in the 4th century AD in a dispute over whether priests or bishops who collaborated with Roman persecutors of Christianity could retain their offices or administer the sacraments; Donatists maintained that clergy needed to be free from any serious sin to administer the sacraments validly, but were vigorously opposed by Augustine.

double predestination ᗌ the Calvinist idea that God has already chosen some people for salvation and others for damnation, a result of emphasizing God's sovereignty and knowledge over human free will.

dualism ᗌ (1) in gnosticism, a way of looking at reality as divided between two hostile divine powers, one representing good and the other evil; (2) a way of looking at reality in terms of polar opposites (belief/unbelief; darkness/light; truth/falsehood).

ecumenical council (or general council) ᗌ a universal (or "worldwide") gathering of Christian bishops called to resolve urgent issues affecting the whole church.

ecumenical ᗌ meaning "worldwide;" (1) term applied to a general council or synod of church leaders supposedly attended by representatives of Christians throughout the world; (2) term applied to efforts designed to bring unity and cooperation between divided Christian churches or between Christians and non-Christians.

Edict of Worms (1521 AD) ᗌ the statement issued by the emperor of the Holy Roman Empire of the German nation to declare Martin Luther an outlaw and a heretic.

Edwards, Jonathan (1703-1758 AD) ᗌ a Calvinist minister who was one of the more famous revival preachers of the Great Awakening, an 18th-century spiritual renewal movement in the English colonies.

election ᗌ the idea, emphasized most strongly by John Calvin, that God mysteriously chooses to enter into special relationship with some persons and groups, but not with others.

Encomienda-Doctrina system ᗌ a cooperative effort between the *encomendero* (conquistador or his descendant) and the *doctrinero* (usually a mendicant friar)to build a sound economic and spiritual base in the Spanish territories of the New World.

enculturation ᗌ a term used to describe the process by which an individual learns to live and act within a particular culture in such a way that the culture's particular pattern of actions and thought becomes second-nature to the person.

Enlightenment, the ᗌ an intellectual movement dating from about 1700-1789, which emphasized reason, science, the goodness and rights of humanity, religious toleration, progress, and human freedom.

episcopacy ᗌ government by bishops. The adjectival form of the word is episcopal (e.g., "episcopal authority" is the authority of the bishop).

Episcopal Church ᗌ the American branch of the Anglican communion, which consists of all churches which trace their roots to the Church of England.

Erasmus, Desiderus (c. 1466-1536 AD) ᗌ a scholar of the Renaissance period, learned in the writings of both the Latin and Greek early church writers. His reconstruction of the New Testament text became the basis for many subsequent translations into the vernacular (language of the people).

Essenes ᗌ a Jewish group of the 1st century CE, who withdrew into the desert to await the end of the world.

Eucharist ᗌ meaning "to give thanks;" the Christian ritual reenactment of Jesus' last supper with his disciples.

evolution 〜 the theory advocated by Charles Darwin about the development of species. The theory of evolution claims that species emerge by natural processes alone (e.g., natural selection) rather than by the miraculous creation of God.

Exile 〜 the period during the 6th century BCE when the Judeans were held captive in Babylon by the Babylonians.

Exodus 〜 literally, "road out;" (1) the second book of the Hebrew Bible/Old Testament; (2) the mass departure of the Israelites from slavery in Egypt through the saving action of God.

expiation 〜 a sacrificial offering to God for the removal of sin.

Ezekiel 〜 6th-century BCE prophet who counseled the Judeans in exile in Babylon that with renewed faithfulness to the covenant God would allow them to return to their land.

"Fall, the" 〜 the theological doctrine which holds that human beings were originally created in a state of perfection, but lost that state when they sinned against God.

faith 〜 (1) a relationship of trust in God; (2) personal insight or knowledge-in-action about God; (3) belief in a set of propositions about God, humanity, and the created order which carry a claim to be true.

feudal system 〜 an economic and political system which characterized the early medieval period in the Western Roman Empire. Wealthy landlords deeded large tracts of land to vassals who, in return, agreed to provide certain services like military assistance for the landlords. The vassals, in turn, required serfs or peasants to work the land.

Former Prophets 〜 a group of books of the Old Testament consisting of the historical books of Joshua, Judges, I & II Samuel, and I & II Kings, which include the stories of several early prophets like Samuel, Nathan, Elijah, and Elisha; also called the Deuteronomistic History.

Freud, Sigmund 〜 19th-20th century founder of psychoanalysis, a branch of psychology, known especially for his investigations into the unconscious aspects of the human mind. Freud was a critic of religion, believing that religious ideas (like God) were fictitious projections of child-like wishes.

Galilei, Galileo 〜 17th century astronomer and scientist who attempted to prove the Copernican theory that the earth revolves around the sun. He was disciplined by the church for advocating views that were contrary to the Bible and church teaching.

glossolalia 〜 a Greek term meaning "speaking in tongues," one of the gifts of the Holy Spirit.

gnosticism 〜 from the Greek word gnosis, meaning "knowledge." Gnostics claimed to have access to a special kind of knowledge known to them alone and by which they could be saved. They believed that there were two gods: one being the supreme godhead of the divine realm (representing good) and the other the creator of the physical universe (representing evil). Gnostics believed that human beings belonged to the divine realm and their goal was to return there unharmed by this physical world.

gospel 〜 meaning "good message" or "good news;" (1) a written account of the life of Jesus Christ; (2) a version of the Christian message.

grace 〜 unmerited assistance given to human beings by God for their salvation.

Great Awakening ⟿ a spiritual renewal that took place in the English colonies of the 18th century. It was designed to foster a spiritual "quickening," or awakening among Christians who had become lax in their faith.

Great Schism ⟿ the period in the late middle ages when the Roman Catholic church had two and, for a brief period, three reigning popes at the same time. Civil leaders joined forces behind the one whom they considered to be the true pope, producing a schism (split) in the church.

Gregorian chant ⟿ A repertoire of music consisting of chants used in the city of Rome together with the native chants of the Frankish churches, mandated by Charlemagne to be used as church music throughout the empire.

Gregory I (c. 540-604 AD) ⟿ also known as "Gregory the Great." Statesman, theologian, and prodigious writer, he was a fierce supporter of the reforms advocated by the monastery at Cluny, speaking out against the practices of simony, alienation of property, and lay investiture.

hadith ⟿ reports concerning the sayings and deeds of Muhammad, six major collections of which were compiled during the first 300 years of Islamic history. Their status and authority is second only to the Qur'an.

Hagia Sophia ⟿ the great "Church of Holy Wisdom" in Constantinople, where the patriarch of Constantinople held services and the Byzantine emperors were crowned, until 1453, when the city of Constantinople was conquered by the Muslims and the church became a mosque.

Hanukkah ⟿ the Jewish holiday celebrating the consecration of the Temple following the victory over the Greeks in the Maccabean revolt.

Hellenization ⟿ the attempt, initiated by Alexander the Great, to impose Greek culture on the peoples conquered by the Greeks.

Henry VIII ⟿ king of England (reigned 1509-1547), who led his country through the Reformation. At first a supporter of Catholicism against the reformers, Henry eventually broke with the pope and the Catholic church and established the Church of England with himself at its head, at least in part in a dispute with Rome over Henry's desire to divorce his wife.

Henry the Navigator (1394-1460 AD) ⟿ Portuguese prince who explored and colonized Africa, spreading Christianity along the way.

heresy ⟿ false teaching, or teaching that goes against orthodoxy (correct teaching, in the eyes of the church).

Hesychia ⟿ "inner stillness" or "silence of the heart;" a spiritual state sought by some Eastern Orthodox Christians, especially monks.

hijra ⟿ an Arabic term meaning "migration." The migration of Muhammad and his followers from Mecca to Medina in 622 AD marks the beginning of the Muslim calendar, since it corresponds with the establishment of the first Muslim community.

historical criticism ⟿ (1) a development of the Renaissance movement; the use of historical knowledge to evaluate ancient writings, as well as existing traditions and institutions; (2) a modern approach to the study of the Bible, whereby the Bible is subjected to scientific scrutiny and the critic attempts to discover if the events it records can be verified historically the same way that other historical facts are verified.

historical theology ⏝ a study of the development of the Christian faith in the various periods of history after the biblical era.

Holy of Holies ⏝ the innermost part of the Temple in Jerusalem, where God's presence is believed to have dwelled. Entrance was restricted to once per year by the high priest.

Hosea ⏝ 8th-century BCE prophet of Israel who used the imagery of marital infidelity to characterize Israel's relationship with Yahweh.

humanism ⏝ Renaissance humanism was a literary and historical movement to recover the Latin and Greek classics, and with them, a more secular and individualistic view of humanity. Modern humanism is a philosophy which focuses on and exalts humanity.

Hus, Jan (1372-1415 AD) ⏝ a reformer of the late medieval period. Like his contemporary, John Wycliffe, he preached against abuses in the church and challenged some of the churches doctrines. He was eventually executed as a heretic.

icon ⏝ a visual representation of Christ, his mother, angels or saints. This religious art form is usually associated with Eastern Christianity.

iconoclasm ⏝ meaning "image breaking." During the Reformation, some reformers forcibly entered churches and removed or destroyed statues, stained glass, and paintings containing images.

iconoclast ⏝ one who is opposed to the veneration of icons.

iconodule ⏝ one who supports the veneration of icons.

Ignatius of Loyola (1491 or 1495-1556 AD) ⏝ founder of the Society of Jesus, also known as the Jesuits. A Spaniard, Ignatius was trained as a knight, but he took up his life dedicated to the church after reading devotional books, including a life of Christ and lives of the saints, during a long convalescence.

imperial cult ⏝ in the Roman world, a partly political and partly religious ceremony in honor of the emperor who was recognized as a superhuman or divine figure.

incarnation ⏝ meaning "enfleshment;" the Christian doctrine which asserts that God became human, specifically, that the divinity called "the Word" (or Logos or the Son) became human, or took on flesh, in the person of Jesus of Nazareth.

inculturation ⏝ a term used to describe the process by which a religion "learns" to live and act within a culture different from the one in which it began, so that the religion gradually comes to act naturally within that culture's pattern of actions and thought.

indigenization ⏝ the church policy that the native people of a country in which missionary work is being done should eventually take charge of the church in that country.

inerrancy, biblical ⏝ the belief that the Bible is completely accurate in all respects and contains no mistakes whatsoever.

inquisition 〜 a legal body set up to investigate and punish heretics. Although the inquisition itself was usually under the jurisdiction of church officials, civil leaders were often called upon to execute whatever punishments were assigned.

inspiration 〜 in Christian theology, a term that describes the belief that the Bible was written under the influence of the Holy Spirit and that it contains the Word of God. Christian churches have differing understandings about how inspiration took place.

inspiration, verbal 〜 the theory that God (or the Holy Spirit) told the biblical authors what to write word-for-word.

Isaac 〜 son of Abraham (by his wife Sarah) and patriarch of the Israelite people, with whom the covenant with the Israelites is continued and through whom the promises to Abraham are fulfilled.

Isaiah 〜 8th-century BCE prophet. Among his many prophecies was a reassurance to the people of Judah that possession of the Temple and a Davidic king would protect them from harm.

Ishmael 〜 son of Abraham by his wife's maid Hagar, who is sent away into the desert but rescued by God; claimed by the Muslims as the son of Abraham through whom they are descended.

Islam 〜 meaning "submission" to the one God. One of the three major religions that trace their roots back to Abraham. A person who practices Islam is called a Muslim, that is, one who has submitted to God.

Israel 〜 (1) the Israelite people, so named after their common ancestor Jacob, who is re-named Israel by God; (2) the country in which the Israelites dwelled; (3) the name of the northern kingdom of the Israelites, from 922 BCE until it was conquered by the Assyrians in 721 BCE.

Jacob 〜 son of Isaac and patriarch of the Israelite people, re-named "Israel" by God. Jacob migrated from Canaan to Egypt with his twelve sons.

Jehovah's Witnesses 〜 an American church that emerged out of the millenial expectation that accompanied the second Great Awakening, a spiritual renewal that spread across the United States and its territories toward the beginning of the 19th century. They teach that the world is ruled by Satan, that all government, church, and business organizations are in league with Satan, and that only the elect of Jehovah (a version of God's name YHWH) will be admitted into the kingdom of God.

Jeremiah 〜 6th-century BCE prophet who warned the people of Judah of their coming destruction by the Babylonians and counseled them to rely on faith and justice rather than on their possession of the Temple and a Davidic king.

Jerusalem Conference 〜 a meeting of Christian leaders held in Jerusalem in 48 or 49 CE. It was attended by Paul and Barnabas and the leaders of the Jerusalem church, and its purpose was to determine whether Gentile converts to Christianity needed to follow all of the requirements of Judaism.

Jerusalem 〜 the capital city of Israel, and later Judah; site of the Temple.

jihad 〜 considered by some Muslims to be a sixth pillar of the faith; inner striving to purify oneself of the forces of evil and to follow the way of Allah. A *jihad* might consist of corporate attempts to purify the Islamic community of anti-Islamic features or warfare to defend Islamic land or spread Islamic territorial jurisdiction.

John Cassian (360-435 AD) ⌒ known as the "father of Western monasticism," he sought to establish a standardized form of monasticism for the Western Roman Empire based upon the ideals of Eastern monasticism.

John of the Cross (1542-1591 AD) ⌒ a follower of Teresa of Avila, the co-founder of the Discalced Carmelites, a reform branch of the Carmelite order, and a Spanish mystic. His writings include the *Ascent of Mount Carmel* and the *Dark Night of the Soul*.

Joseph ⌒ favorite son of Jacob and founder of one of the twelve tribes of Israel, he was sold into slavery in Egypt but eventually ascended to become a high government official.

Joshua ⌒ the successor to Moses, who led the Israelites into the promised land of Canaan and conquered the peoples who dwelled there.

Judah ⌒ the name of the southern kingdom of the Israelites, from 922 BCE until it was conquered by the Babylonians in 597 BCE.

Judge (Hebrew *shofet*) ⌒ in ancient Israel, a military and political leader who was chosen by God to rescue the Israelites from oppression brought about by their sin.

Julian of Norwich (c. 1342-after 1413 AD) ⌒ an English mystic of the late middle ages. She is the author of *Showings*, in which she describes a series of visions she received during a brief illness and offers her theological reflections on that mystical experience. She also reflects on the motherhood of Christ, the meaning of sin, and the question of why God allows sin and evil to exist.

justification by works ⌒ the theory that one can achieve a right relationship with God by avoiding sin and atoning for any transgressions with good deeds.

justification by faith ⌒ the theory that one cannot achieve a right relationship with God through good works, but can be given salvation as a free gift that one accepts through faith.

justification ⌒ (1) generally, making straight that which is crooked or ragged; (2) in theology, being in a right relationship with God.

Justinian ⌒ Byzantine emperor from 527-565 AD, best known for compiling the "Codex Juris Civilis" (Code of Civil Law) and for rebuilding the great "Church of Holy Wisdom" (or Hagia Sophia) in Constantinople.

**Ka`ba** ⌒ a pilgrimage site located at Mecca consisting of a cube-shaped building in the courtyard of the Grand Mosque in Mecca. If health and finances permit, Muslims are encouraged to make a pilgrimage or *hajj* to the *Ka`ba* once during their lifetime to commemorate the key events from the founding era of Islam and from the time of Abraham.

Kingdom of God ⌒ the reign of God on earth, which is manifested in the coming of Jesus Christ, in the Spirit's continued presence in the world, and in the conviction that God will triumph over the forces of evil.

kosher ⌒ in Judaism, the special dietary restrictions required by the Torah, whereby certain foods are prohibited (e.g. pork) and other foods must be prepared according to certain guidelines.

Latter Prophets ⟜ a group of books of the Old Testament attributed to Israelite prophets of the 8th-5th centuries BCE and containing their prophecies and/or accounts of their lives.

Law, the ⟜ the first major group of books of the Hebrew Bible or Old Testament, along with the Prophets and the Writings; consists of the first five books; also known as the Pentateuch or Torah.

lay investiture ⟜ during the early medieval period, the emperor and secular leaders took upon themselves the right to appoint bishops, abbots and other church officials.

Logos ⟜ a Greek word meaning "word" or "reason." John's gospel uses this term to describe Jesus as the revelation of God.

Lollards ⟜ a group of reformers in the late middle ages (1300-1500) who attempted to put into practice the ideals of John Wycliffe. They were active in several social uprisings, and as a result many were put to death for their heretical ideas and their radical political actions.

Maccabees ⟜ the family who led the revolt by the Jews against the Greeks in the 2nd century BCE.

magisterium ⟜ the teaching office of the Roman Catholic Church, made up of the pope and the bishops.

Maimonides, Moses (1135-1204 AD) ⟜ medieval Jewish scholar; author of the *Guide of the Perplexed*, in which he synthesized rabbinic Judaism and the Muslim form of Aristotelian philosophy. He also wrote very influential works on medicine and Jewish law.

Manichees ⟜ a quasi-Christian cult deriving its name from Mani, a 3rd century AD prophet, which believed in a dualism of evil matter and good spirit. They taught that people could liberate spirit from matter through the strict practice of asceticism.

Manifest Destiny ⟜ a term used to describe the Pilgrims' belief that their call to come to the New World was a divinely granted second chance for the human race, and that God was making a new covenant with them.

Marburg Colloquy ⟜ the debate between Martin Luther and Ulrich Zwingli held in 1529. Zwingli and Luther found that they could not resolve their differences but Zwingli did force Luther to see that reconciliation with the Catholic church was not really possible.

martyr ⟜ from the Greek term meaning "witness." A martyr is someone who, under persecution, dies rather than give up his or her faith.

Marx, Karl ⟜ 19th century philosopher and economist, who advocated the socialist economic system, and on whose ideas communism is built. Marx was an outspoken critic of religion, calling it the "opium of the people," since he believed that it was like a drug which kept the lower classes passive and resigned in their economic oppression.

Mecca ⟜ the most holy city in Islam. It is the location of the *Ka`ba* or pilgrimage site where Muslims go to commemorate the key events from the founding era of Islam and from the time of Abraham. It is also revered as the birthplace of Muhammad and, according to Muslim tradition, the site of Ishmael's rescue.

Medina ⟜ the city in which Muhammad founded the first Islamic community in 622 CE.

memoria ∽ a type of church building built to honor the tomb of a saint or martyr, or a holy site. Memoriae had a centered design, focusing attention on the place of honor.

messiah ∽ meaning "anointed one;" a Jewish and Christian term for a person sent by God to rescue or save people.

Methodist Church ∽ an independent Protestant church, founded by John Wesley, that began as a reform movement within the Church of England. It differed from the Church of England in its greater emphasis on personal spirituality, Bible study, evangelistic preaching, and lively services.

monasticism ∽ from the Greek word *monos,* meaning "one," "unique," "solitary," or "alone." A rule and way of life for Christian men or women dedicated to holiness.

monk ∽ from the Greek word *monachos,* meaning a single or a solitary person, the word monk was coined in the 4th century as a name for the many men and women who had begun to withdraw to secluded desert regions to lead lives of prayer and spiritual discipline. Later it would come to refer to any person who abandoned life in the everyday world to devote themselves completely to their religion.

monophysite ∽ from the Greek words for "of one nature;" one who holds that Jesus did not have two natures—one human and one divine—but only one. Eutyches, for example, believed that the humanity of Christ had been absorbed into his single divine nature.

monotheism ∽ belief in only one god.

moral theology ∽ a study of the values arising from Christian beliefs and the behaviors that are congruent or incongruent with these values.

Moses ∽ greatest prophet of Israel, who led the Israelites out of slavery in Egypt and into the promised land of Canaan, and who received from God on Mount Sinai the Law on which the Israelite covenant with God is based.

mosque ∽ Arabic term meaning "place of prostration" or "place of prayer." Ordinarily, mosques have an open space where the daily prayer is performed. On one wall is a niche that indicates the direction of Mecca. It also contains a pulpit with a staircase from which the *imam* (the leader of prayer) presents the sermon at Friday noon prayers.

Muhammad (570-632 AD) ∽ first leader and greatest prophet of Islam. According to Muslim tradition, the one god Allah sent the angel Gabriel to deliver messages to Muhammad to be recited aloud as guidance to the followers. The revelations were later collected and recorded in the Islamic scriptures known as the Qur'an.

Muslims ∽ followers of the Islamic faith.

mystery religions ∽ in the Greek and Roman religious world, secret cults that conducted ritual initiations into the mysteries of a particular god or goddess. Their celebrations usually involved purification rituals and sacred meals.

mysticism ∽ a spiritual phenomenon that expresses itself in direct, intense experiences of union and oneness with God. Generally, the mystical journey consists of three phases: purgation (cleansing from sin), illumination (an attraction to all the things of God), and union (the state of oneness with God).

myth ∽ a story that articulates a people's most profound sense of themselves and their world.

Nathan ∽ an Israelite prophet during the reign of King David, known for prophesying about the everlasting dynasty of David and for exposing the sin of David with Bathsheba.

natural selection ∽ a principle of the theory of evolution, which holds that individuals in a species who have characteristics that are advantageous for survival in their environment will survive, while individuals without these characteristics will perish. Gradually, this transformation of the character of individuals in a species will lead to the development of new species.

nepotism ∽ the practice of allowing dispensations from church law for the advancement of one's relatives.

Nestorian ∽ one who accepts the christology promoted by Nestorius, who held that Jesus had two separate natures (one the perfect man without sin who is son of Mary in the flesh, the other the divine word of God or Logos settled within him); a term sometimes applied to the ancient Assyrian Church of the East.

Nestorius ∽ a 5th-century AD patriarch of Constantinople, who taught that it was inappropriate to call Mary the Mother of God, on the grounds that God could not be said to have been born; at best she was only the Mother of Christ, the man. His views were condemned at the Council of Ephesus in 431.

Newton, Isaac ∽ 17th century mathematician and scientist who was able to explain the motion of the planets by means of natural laws (e.g., the law of gravity) rather than the will of God, and hence was a major contributor in the development of the "mechanistic" view of the universe.

Nicaea, Council of ∽ an ecumenical council held in 325 AD which maintained the true divinity of the Son (Jesus Christ) against the teaching of Arius.

nominalism ∽ a philosophical movement that addresses issues of human knowledge. It argues that knowledge can be derived only from the experience of individual things. Universals such as "humanity" or "truth" do not really exist.

Ockham's Razor ∽ A philosophical principal advanced by William of Ockham (c. 1285-1347 AD) concerning knowledge: cut away useless ideas and explanations and accept the simplest hypothesis that can explain the data.

omnipotent ∽ all-powerful.

omniscient ∽ all-knowing.

original sin ∽ the idea that human beings are born with a predisposition or inclination to sin, as a result of the sin of Adam and Eve.

orthodoxy ∽ meaning "right teaching" or "right opinion." The term is often used to describe doctrine or teaching that is declared by the church (or any religious authority) to be correct and binding for believers, and is contrasted with heresy.

Our Lady of Guadalupe ∽ (1) title given to Mary, the mother of Jesus, based on her miraculous appearance to Juan Diego at Tepeyac, Mexico in 1531; (2) a painted image of the appearance of Mary to Juan Diego.

pagan ⤲ a term used (especially in Roman times) to describe those persons who are neither Christians nor Jews.

papal bull ⤲ a formal document issued by the pope.

parousia ⤲ meaning "coming" or "presence." Used by early Christians to describe the anticipated return of Jesus Christ at the end time to judge humankind.

Passover ⤲ the Jewish holiday that celebrates the event when God rescued the Israelites from captivity in Egypt by killing the firstborn sons of the Egyptians but "passing over" the houses of the Israelites (c. 1250 BCE).

patriarch ⤲ (1) an early father of a people or (male) founder of a group, like Abraham, Isaac, and Jacob; (2) bishop of one of the "leading seats" of early Christianity: Rome, Alexandria, Antioch, Constantinople, and Jerusalem.

patriarchal sees ⤲ the "head or leading seats" of early Christianity, that is, the five cities which were the most important Christian centers: Rome, Jerusalem, Alexandria, Antioch, and Constantinople.

patristic ⤲ an adjective describing a period in Christian history, roughly the 2nd century to the 5th century. The period is so named because the major writers of the time are known as the "fathers" ("patres" in Latin) of the church.

Pelagius ⤲ a Christian monk (4th-5th centuries AD) who introduced the "Pelagian" notions that original sin did not seriously damage the human capacity to do good, that human nature remained essentially good, and that human beings could lead holy lives if they exerted sufficient effort; these notions were opposed by Augustine and eventually condemned as heretical by the Catholic Church.

penance ⤲ a penalty for sin; the sacrament of forgiveness of sin. Common forms of penance include praying, fasting, giving alms, making a pilgrimage, or being denied communion.

penitent ⤲ a person who is denied communion because of serious sin such as murder, adultery, or apostasy, and who is doing penance (a penalty) for that sin.

Pentateuch ⤲ the first five books of the Hebrew Bible or Old Testament, also known as the Torah or the Law.

"People of the Land" ⤲ in ancient Judaism, the poor and uneducated peasant farmers who comprised the majority of the Jewish population.

Pharisees ⤲ a Jewish group of the 1st century CE, consisting of scholars who emphasized the study of the Torah and the necessity of observing the laws strictly in one's daily life.

Philistines ⤲ enemies of ancient Israel, who used their monopoly on iron weapons to defeat the Israelites prior to the reign of King David.

Pietists ⤲ a family of Protestant churches that were established out of a Bible-centered revivalism and a desire to fight against religious indifference by focusing on sharing the experience of God in their lives. It includes the Methodists, Scandinavian evangelical churches, and Moravian Christians.

Pilgrims ⤲ the English Puritan settlers who arrived on the "Mayflower" in 1620 to establish the Massachusetts Bay colony. The name "pilgrim," a reference to Heb 11:13-14, was given to these founders a decade later, and was formally adopted in 1798.

pluralism ∿ a term used to describe the situation of the modern world in which societies are increasingly made up of a variety of races, nationalities, and religions.

Polo, Marco (1254-1324 AD) ∿ an Italian traveller who visited the lands of the Far East and returned to Europe to spread the news, sparking the European interest in exploration for commercial gain and missionary expansion.

polytheism ∿ belief in many gods.

predestination ∿ the idea that God has foreordained that some people will be saved and others damned.

Priestly Tradition (Priestly Writer) ∿ according to the Documentary Hypothesis, the latest of the four sources that were combined to form the Pentateuch, written around the 5th century BCE or later.

Priests ∿ (1) in ancient Judaism, people who were specialists in conducting sacrifices; (2) in Christianity, ordained clergy.

prophet ∿ a spokesperson for God, chosen by God to reveal his will to people.

Prophets, the ∿ the second major group of books of the Old Testament, along with the Law and the Writings, consisting of historical narratives (the Former Prophets) and books bearing the names of actual prophets (the Latter Prophets).

Protestant ∿ a term used to describe members of the churches that trace their ultimate origin to the Reformation of the 16th century; it derives from an incident in the early period of the reformation in which six German princes protested a declaration of the Second Diet of Speyer (1529) designed to suppress Lutheranism.

Protestants, liberal ∿ a family of Protestant churches so named because of their more liberal interpretation of scripture. It includes the Unitarian and Universalist churches, both of whom down-play individual differences in Christian doctrine so that people can come together as a united church.

Pseudo-Dionysius the Areopagite ∿ the pseudonym of an anonymous Syrian monk of the early 6th century who authored several important and influential theological works. He is perhaps most famous for his so-called "via negativa" ("negative approach") in which all affirmations concerning God must be denied since the divine reality so far supersedes any word that can be said about it.

pseudonymity ∿ the practice of writing a document with a false name attached to it. Pseudonymous writings were quite common in the ancient world, in part as a way of honoring famous people in a particular culture or religious tradition and in part as a way of increasing the authority of the document.

purgatory ∿ a place or state following death in which sinners destined for heaven undergo the punishment still remaining for forgiven sins and thereby are "purged" or made ready for heaven.

Q ∿ representing the German word "Quelle," meaning "source." A (hypothetical) written document or documents, mostly containing parables and sayings of Jesus, used as a source for the gospels of Matthew and Luke.

Qur'an ∿ the sacred writings of Islam. The Qur'an consists of the revelations which the angel Gabriel delivered to Muhammad from the one god Allah for the guidance of the followers.

Rabbi ∿ (1) in ancient Judaism, a teacher (especially of the Torah); (2) in modern Judaism, an ordained clergyman.

rationalism ∿ the belief that reason alone can provide us with a knowledge of all reality. It is opposed to the belief that there are some dimensions of reality (e.g. God) which are beyond reason, and which can only be known through revelation.

recapitulation ∿ a doctrine about redemption taught by Irenaeus, a 2nd-century bishop. Irenaeus said that the redemption effected by Jesus Christ was a "doing over again" of all that had gone wrong in human history.

redaction ∿ (1) an act or instance of editing something; (2) the part of a document that has been added by a later editor.

redemption ∿ a theological term used to describe the idea that we have been bought back or ransomed from our sinfulness for God.

Reformation, Catholic ∿ a term given to the efforts of those Roman Catholics who wanted to bring about the internal rebirth of Catholic sensibility—in theology, spirituality, religious piety, and morality—in the 16th century, during the time of the Protestant Reformation.

Refuge of Tolerance ∿ a term used to describe the mid-Atlantic English colonies whose leaders had considerable tolerance for religious diversity, in comparison to some of their neighbors, thereby providing a refuge for Jews, Quakers, Mennonites, Moravians, Amish, and Catholics.

relics ∿ the bodily remains of martyrs or other saints.

religion ∿ a worldview that involves belief in some god or power beyond human existence, together with actions or teaching that support that belief (ritual, stories, doctrine, organizational structure, and ethical conduct).

Renaissance ∿ meaning "rebirth;" a cultural movement that began in Italy approximately 1350 CE and spread to other European countries by the time it came to a close in 1600. It involved a renewed interest in the Latin and Greek classics, a focus on the individual person and the natural world, and a more scientific approach to history and literature. It was accompanied by a burst of creative activity in art and architecture.

restorationism ∿ the idea that the way to reform and renew Christianity was to "restore" the church to the original structures, beliefs, and practices that prevailed during the time of Jesus and the apostles.

revelation ∿ (1) God's act of disclosing Godself to believers; (2) that which has been revealed by God through nature and human conscience, but also through the Bible, mystical experience, and worship.

revival ∿ a religious meeting designed to awaken in people an awareness of their sin and their need for forgiveness. Revival meetings were part of the Great Awakening, an 18th-century spiritual renewal movement in the English colonies.

Ricci, Matteo (1552-1610) ∿ an Italian Jesuit known for his successful missionary work in China.

righteousness, passive or alien ᔟ term used by Martin Luther (1483-1546) to explain that God is the one who justifies people. Salvation does not depend on a person's own goodness or righteousness, but on God's righteousness.

Roman Rite ᔟ a primary form of liturgy for the Roman Catholic Church. In an attempt to unify his empire, Charlemagne ordered that the Christian worship practices of the city of Rome should become the norm throughout his territories. A collection of these prayers was popularly believed to have been composed by Pope Gregory I.

Romanesque architecture ᔟ the style of buildings developed during the Carolingian and Ottonian dynasties of early medieval Europe. The structures featured stone vaulted ceilings, heavy walls and piers, and small openings for light, creating a fortress-like impression.

sacrament ᔟ a symbolic ritual consisting of words and visible gestures or material substances (bread, wine, water, oil, etc.) which, when properly performed for a recipient disposed to its action, becomes the means of transmitting the grace of God. All Christians agree on two sacraments—Eucharist and Baptism—while Catholics would add five others: Penance, Confirmation, Matrimony, Holy Orders, and Extreme Unction (now called "Anointing of the Sick").

sacramentals ᔟ a term used to describe certain religious practices and objects that are similar to sacraments in the fact that they have tangible qualities (water, oil, rosary, etc.) but they are different from sacraments in the fact that they are not publicly celebrated and are not considered to be instituted or inspired by Christ.

sacramentary ᔟ a book containing the prayers needed by a priest to celebrate the Eucharist and (sometimes) other sacraments.

sacrifical atonement ᔟ making up for one's sins with a sacrifical offering; specifically in Christianity, the idea that our sins are forgiven through the death of Jesus Christ on the cross.

Sadducees ᔟ a Jewish group of the 1st century CE, consisting especially of the priests who ran the Jerusalem Temple.

salvation ᔟ a theological term referring to the state of being saved or rescued from harm.

Salvation Army ᔟ founded by William Booth in 1865, its initial concern was to create practical solutions to the problems of poverty brought on by the industrial revolution and to awakening Christians' consciences to the human suffering which it created. It continues to play an important role in serving the needs of the economically disadvantaged in the spirit of the Christian message.

sanctification ᔟ a theological term used to describe the idea of someone or something being made holy for God.

sanctuary ᔟ the principle that all who take refuge from civil authority in a church or on church land must not be removed without the permission of the abbot or bishop.

Saul ᔟ the first king of Israel (reigned 1020-1000 BCE), who was replaced by David when God found him unworthy to be king.

scholasticism ᔟ name given to the theology which was written and studied in the medieval schools and universities. In general, scholastic theology, the theology of the "Schoolmen," tried to harmonize faith with reason. Scholasticism tried to take the undeniable truths uncovered by philosophers like Aristotle and show how they were compatible with Christianity.

scientism ∾ the claim that the only valid method of knowing is science, and that what cannot be known by science does not exist.

scribes ∾ (1) in ancient Judaism, the class of people who could read and write and who made their living from these skills. They are portrayed in the gospels as enemies of Jesus and associates of the Pharisees. (2) In the ancient and medieval world, people whose occupation involved the copying of manuscripts.

scriptures ∾ sacred writings or texts.

Second Isaiah ∾ a 6th-century BCE prophet and the author of chapters 40-55 of the book of Isaiah, who foretold the Jews' return from exile.

Second Temple ∾ the Temple in Jerusalem that was built following the destruction of Solomon's Temple by the Babylonians; destroyed by the Romans in 66 CE.

seminary ∾ school of theology especially designed for the training of priests. The Council of Trent (1545-1563) ordered that every Roman Catholic diocese establish a seminary for the training of its priest candidates. Many dioceses still retain their own seminaries today.

Sephardim ∾ the term given to Spanish and Portuguese Jewish immigrants to the Americas.

Septuagint ∾ the Greek translation of the Hebrew scriptures.

Seventh-Day Adventists ∾ an American church that emerged out of the millenial expectation that accompanied the second Great Awakening, a spiritual renewal that spread across the United States and its territories toward the beginning of the 19th century. They observe Saturday as the proper day for worship and view a literal reading of the Bible as the only rule of faith.

Shari`a ∾ the Islamic law code which is based upon the Qur'an and the *sunna*, or way of the prophet, together with human reason and community consensus.

Shi`ites ∾ meaning "partisans of Ali," Muhammad's cousin and son-in-law. This Muslim group arose soon after the death of Muhammad, as a consequence of a dispute over how the position of caliph (Muslim ruler) ought to be filled. Today, it continues to be a minority group within the Islamic faith.

shofet ∾ the Hebrew term for a judge, a military and political leader who was chosen by God to rescue the Israelites from oppression brought about by their sin.

simony ∾ the buying and selling of spiritual things, including church leadership positions.

Social Gospel ∾ a term used to describe the solution of the White Anglo-Saxon Protestant society (WASP) to social problems of the late 19th and early 20th century. Inspired by the writings of Walter Rauschenbush (1861-1918),the Social Gospel movement said that the church should be seen as the vehicle for spreading God's kingdom on earth, and therefore should be primarily concerned about social justice. They hoped to "Christianize" the United States by changing the social structure of the nation.

Society of Jesus ∿ also known as the Jesuits, this religious order was founded by Ignatius of Loyola in 1534. Dedicated to the service of the pope, they played an important role in the Catholic Reformation both as missionaries and teachers.

Solomon ∿ successor to his father David as king of Israel (reigned 961-922 BCE), known for his wisdom, excessive wealth, and the building of the Temple in Jerusalem.

soteriology ∿ the study of salvation. Christian soteriology is primarily concerned with the saving work of Jesus Christ.

Spiritual Exercises ∿ developed by Ignatius of Loyola, this month-long spiritual examination allows the individual to participate in the drama of sin and salvation, leading to a turning over of everything, especially the will, to obedience to one's religious superior, to the teachings of the church and its traditions, for the spread of the faith.

studia humanitatis ∿ meaning "humane studies" or liberal arts, including Latin and Greek literature, history, and ethics. In studying Latin, students learned to read, write, reason, and speak well—skills that were especially necessary for civic leaders and scholars.

suffering servant ∿ a figure in the book of Isaiah who suffers on behalf of the whole people and wins forgiveness for their sins.

sunna ∿ the "way of the prophet"; sayings of the prophet Muhammad and reports of his deeds, as recorded in the *hadith*.

Sunnis ∿ meaning "those who followed the example or custom of Muhammad." In the dispute concerning who was qualified to assume the position of leader of the Muslim community, this group argued that it should be someone who best exemplified Muhammad's thought and way of life, rather than someone who was related to Muhammad by blood. Today, it is the main body of the Islamic faith, comprising approximately 85% of Muslims worldwide.

Symeon the New Theologian (942-1022 CE) ∿ an Eastern Christian mystic and theologian representative of the spirituality and theology of the early medieval period.

synagogue ∿ a Jewish place of worship, where the Torah is read and interpreted.

synoptic problem ∿ the question concerning the literary relationship between the gospels of Matthew, Mark, and Luke, which are so similar that it is almost universally believed that one or more of their authors used another gospel as a source.

synoptic gospels ∿ the gospels of Matthew, Mark, and Luke, which tell the same general story of the life and teaching of Jesus in the same way.

systematic theology ∿ a study of the basic formulations of Christian belief (called "dogmas" or "doctrines") and their relationship to one another.

Tanakh ∿ an acronym for Torah (Law), Nevi'im (Prophets), and Khetubim (Writings); a term used to refer to the the Jewish scriptures.

Temple ∿ (1) any building dedicated to the worship of a god or gods, at which sacrifices are usually performed; (2) the building in Jerusalem in which Israelites performed sacrifices and in which they believed God dwelled; first built by Solomon in the 10th century BCE, destroyed by the

Babylonians in 587 BCE, rebuilt later in the 6th century BCE after the return from the Exile, refurbished by King Herod in the 1st century BCE, and destroyed by the Romans in 70 CE.

Teresa of Avila (1515-1582 AD) ∿ founder of the Discalced Carmelites, a reform branch of the Carmelite order, and a Spanish mystic. Her writings include the *Life*, an autobiographical account of her life, and the Interior Castle, a description of her method of prayer.

tertiary ∿ a layperson who follows an adapted rule of a founder of a monastery or a friar movement and the ideals or charisms of that group, but does so outside of the convent or monastery. Examples include the third order Dominicans and the third order Franciscans.

testament ∿ a synonym for "covenant," this term is applied by Christians to the two major collections of books of the Bible.

theocentric ∿ God-centered.

theocracy ∿ literally "the rule of God," a system of government which has as its worldview a common set of beliefs about God and God's relationship with their community, and whose civil laws are governed by its religious agenda.

Theodosius I (reigned 379-385 CE) ∿ emperor of Rome who established Christianity as the sole legal religion in the Roman Empire and who affirmed the Nicene Creed as the benchmark of orthodox Christian faith.

theology ∿ an intellectual discipline that explores (religious) reality from a particular perspective, namely God as ultimate ground and goal of all reality; in the words of Anselm, it is "faith seeking understanding."

Torah ∿ (1) the Hebrew scriptures as a whole; (2) the first five books of the Hebrew Bible or Old Testament, also known as the Pentateuch or the Law; (3) the Jewish Law, or system of laws, believed to have been revealed by God to Moses and set down in writing in the first five books of the Old Testament.

transubstantiation ∿ a teaching about how the Eucharist is the body and blood of Jesus Christ. The accidents (physical appearance) remain as bread and wine, but the substance changes and becomes the body and blood of Jesus Christ.

treasury of merit ∿ in the late medieval period, a treasury of surplus good works of the saints and of Christ. The pope could draw from this treasury and transfer excess merits to a repentant sinner in the form of an indulgence.

Trent, Council of ∿ declared by Roman Catholics to be an ecumenical council, this church council met over a period of 18 years (1545-1563) to address doctrinal and practical issues of reform, both within the Catholic Church and in response to the Protestant Reformation.

tribal confederacy ∿ the form of government practiced by the Hebrews after the conquest of Canaan but before the establishment of the monarchy, whereby each tribe lived separately and governed itself, coming together as a nation only in times of crisis.

Two-Source Hypothesis ∿ a theory which explains the literary relationship among the synoptic gospels by suggesting that the writers of the gospels of Matthew and Luke used the gospel of Mark and a hypothetical source Q (a written document or documents mostly containing parables and say-ings of Jesus) as sources for their gospels.

umma ∽ an Arabic term meaning "community."

university ∽ originally the "guild" or association of teachers and students united in the "craft" of teaching and learning. Universities developed into institutions of higher learning with permanent faculties and offered basic degrees in the "arts" and more advanced degrees in various fields of specialization.

Vatican Council II (1962-1965) ∽ a gathering of Catholic bishops, abbots, and theological experts called by Pope John XXIII to renew the religious life of the church and to bring it into the modern world.

vernacular ∽ language of the common people.

voluntarist principle ∽ the idea, popularized by the churches of the "Radical Reformation," that becoming a a Christian (and a member of a Church) always requires an active decision. It never occurs simply because of where people live or because of their parents' beliefs.

Vulgate ∽ a Latin translation of the Bible, containing also the books of the Apocrypha, widely used in the West at least from the 6th century CE and declared by the Council of Trent to be the only authoritative translation of the Bible.

Wesley, John ∽ an 18th century English theologian and reformer. Wesley was originally a member of the Church of England, but when he tried to reform the Church of England, he met with resistence and he and his followers eventually broke away to form the Methodist Church.

works of satisfaction ∽ prayers, fasting, pilgrimages, or works of piety assigned to a person in the sacrament of penance to remove the penalties or consequences of sin.

Whitefield, George (1714-1770) ∽ a Medodist minister who was one of the more famous revival preachers of the Great Awakening, an 18th-century spiritual renewal movement in the English colonies.

Wycliffe, John (1330-1384) ∽ a reformer of the late medieval period. He preached against abuses in the church and challenged some of the church's doctrines. He also advocated the translation of the Bible into English, the language of the people.

Xavier, Francis (1506-1552) ∽ a companion of Ignatius of Loyola, the founder of the Jesuit order, and the leader of the Catholic mission to India, Japan, and China.

Yahwist ∽ according to the Documentary Hypothesis, the earliest of the four sources that were eventually combined to form the Pentateuch, written around the 9th century BCE.

YHWH (Yahweh) ∽ the name for God most commonly used in the Hebrew Bible/Old Testament.

Yom Kippur ∽ the "Day of Atonement;" a Jewish holiday in which people reflect upon their sins. In ancient Judaism, this was the only day in which the high priest would enter the Holy of Holies to offer a sacrifice.

Zealots ∽ a Jewish group of the 1st century CE, who advocated the violent overthrow of the Romans and led the disastrous revolt of 66-70 CE.

Zwingli, Ulrich (1484-1531) ⮂ Swiss reformer and theologian, known especially for his emphasis on justification by grace alone, his "spiritual" understanding of the Eucharist, his exclusive reliance on the Bible rather than church traditions and proclamations, and his opposition to priestly celibacy and the use of images in worship. Zwingli was killed defending the city of Zurich, the city he led through the Reformation, against attack by Catholics.

Index